The Guide to Cooking Schools

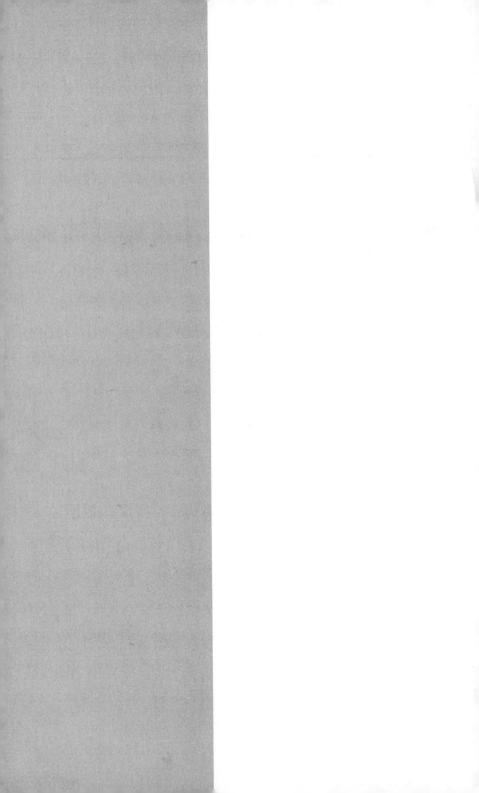

2004

The Guide to Cooking Schools

Sixteenth Edition

Inquiries concerning this book should be addressed to: Editor, ShawGuides, P.O. Box 231295, New York, New York 10023, Phone: (212) 799-6464, Fax: (212) 724-9287, E-mail: info@shawguides.com, URL: www.shawguides.com.

Library of Congress Catalog Card Number 88-92516
ISSN 1040-2616
ISBN 0-945834-31-4

Printed in the United States of America by
R. R. Donnelley & Sons Company

Introduction

First published, in 1989, The Guide to Cooking Schools is the only comprehensive resource to career and recreational culinary and wine education programs worldwide. This 16th annual edition contains descriptions of 499 career and 665 recreational cooking and wine programs worldwide, The number of programs and students has increased every year as has the interest in food, cooking, and wine education. The opportunities for employment as a cook or chef in the foodservice industry continue to exceed the supply of qualified individuals. Experienced chefs in top restaurants can become celebrities, star in reality television shows, and earn an income commensurate with their status.

If you love to cook and are eager to learn new techniques, replicate the dishes you've enjoyed in fine dining establishments, try new foods and equipment, and meet interesting people, a local cooking course or a cooking vacation will expand your knowledge and widen your circle of friends. Cooking is a chance to be creative, to experiment, to share a special and memorable meal with the people you care for.

Looking for the right gift for a friend or relative who enjoys cooking, good food, and fine wine? ShawGuides Cooking and Wine School Gift Certificates make it easy for you to give a thoughtful, useful gift of lasting value. Perfect for any occasion, a ShawGuides Gift Certificate eliminates guesswork and transfers decision-making to the recipient, who can use your gift to purchase a cooking or wine class, course, vacation, or product at any one of dozens of cooking and wine schools worldwide. Certificates are available in any amount with a $50 minimum. They are mailed and/or e-mailed worldwide at no additional cost. For more information or to purchase a certificate, call 212-799-6464, e-mail info@shawguides.com or visit our website at www.shawguides.com/gc.

CHOOSING A CAREER SCHOOL

1. How long is the program? Career programs range from a few weeks to four years or more. Curricula for programs of a year or less consist primarily of culinary courses that prepare you for an entry level position. College degree programs include general education courses and electives that provide a more well-rounded education. The 3-year apprenticeship program sponsored by the American Culinary Federation (ACF) offers paid on-the-job training in a foodservice establishment and the opportunity to earn a college degree.

2. Is it affordable? Tuition ranges from a few hundred dollars at community colleges to over $10,000 per program or year at trade schools that offer a specialized curriculum. If cost is an obstacle, inquire about scholarships or loans, which are offered by many schools and some culinary organizations.

3. What are the scheduling options? If you're unable to attend classes full-time, consider programs that permit you to enroll part-time or offer flexible schedules.

4. How qualified is the faculty? Instructor credentials should include certification by the American Culinary Federation, college degree, and/or industry experience.

5. Is the school accredited? A school in operation for five years or more should be accredited. Colleges are accredited by one of six regional associations, private and trade schools by three organizations.

6. Is real-world experience part of the program? Some schools have student-staffed foodservice facilities on-campus where students are required to work as part of the program. Others offer intern- or externships in an off-campus setting.

7. What courses, textbooks, and course materials are provided? Has the school's curriculum adapted to today's healthier lifestyles with emphasis on fresh ingredients, nutrition, and a variety of international cuisines. Do they offer specialized courses in the subjects that interest you?

8. What kind of job offers can you expect? Will the school's placement office be able to find you a position in the setting you desire? Obtain the names of graduates and contact them to determine whether the school met their expectations for training and placement.

CHOOSING A COOKING VACATION

1. What can you expect to learn? Are the dishes appealing and suited to your expertise? Will you be learning the how's and why's of cooking, rather than just following recipes?

2. Will classes be demonstration or hands-on? Hands-on classes are necessary for learning techniques. Demonstrations are appropriate for experienced cooks and those who prefer observing to participating. Most vacation programs combine both.

3. What are the cooking and lodging facilities like? For hands-on classes will you have your own work station and utensils? Are appliances modern and in good working condition? Is the space large enough for everyone to move about comfortably? For demonstrations, is there an overhead mirror and is seating close enough that you'll be able to see clearly? Is lodging part of a chain or rated by a recognized travel guide? Do the rooms have private baths?

4. What are the qualifications of the instructor? If the teacher has written a cookbook, obtain a copy to determine whether the recipes appeal to you. If the teacher is a chef, will the recipes be adapted to a home kitchen? Request copies of some of the recipes that will be prepared and speak with the instructor to get a sense of his or her teaching style and communication skills.

5. What is scheduled during non-cooking time? Some vacation programs emphasize cooking over other activities, some offer a few classes with more time devoted to sightseeing, visiting food-related sites, shopping, dining out, or at leisure. Obtain a detailed itinerary so you'll know what to expect.

6. What is covered by the cost? The cost always covers classes and the meals prepared, usually covers sightseeing, most other meals, and ground transportation, and sometimes covers lodging and airfare. Find out what your payment covers and how much you should budget for the rest.

7. Request the names of recent participants and contact them. Did the program meet their expectations, does it offer the features you desire, would they would recommend it?

Although we strive to make each listing accurate, changes do occur. For updates and new listings, check our web site – http://www.shawguides.com – which contains the unabridged contents of this directory, updated daily and accessible at no charge.

May you find pleasure and success in all your culinary endeavors.

ShawGuides

ACCREDITING AGENCIES

ACCET Accrediting Council for Continued Education and Training
ACCSCT Accrediting Commission of Career Schools/Colleges of Technology
ACF American Culinary Federation
ACICS Accrediting Council for Independent Colleges and Schools
COE Council on Occupational Education
MSA Middle States Association of Colleges and Schools
NASC Northwest Association of Schools and Colleges
NCA North Central Association of Colleges and Schools
NEASC New England Association of Schools and Colleges
SACS Southern Association of Colleges and Schools
WASC Western Association of Schools and Colleges

Contents

1

Career and Professional Programs

ALABAMA

ACF BIRMINGHAM CHAPTER
Birmingham

Sponsor: American Culinary Federation chapter. Program: 3-yr apprenticeship, degree program through Jefferson State Community College. Curriculum: culinary, core. Total enrollment: 25.

Costs: $3,500 in-state, $5,000 out-of-state. Beginning salary $5/hr, $0.40 increases every 6 mos. Housing costs are $350-$500/mo.

Contact: Doug Allen, CEC, Acting Coordinator, ACF Birmingham Chapter, 750 Lakeshore Parkway, Birmingham, AL 35211; 205-328-ROUX, doug_allen@saksinc.com, www.acfbirmingham.org.

BISHOP STATE COMMUNITY COLLEGE
Mobile/Year-round

Sponsor: 2-yr college. Program: 6-quarter, 90 cr-hr certificate/114 cr-hr (or 2-sem+summer term/74 cr-hr) AAS degree in Commercial Food Service. Established: 1963. Accredited by ACF, SACS. Calendar: semester. Curriculum: culinary, core. Admit dates: Aug, Jan. Total enrollment: 25. 100% of applicants accepted. 75% receive financial aid. 25% enrolled part-time. S:T ratio 10:1. 100% of graduates obtain jobs within 6 mos. Facilities: Fully equipped kitchen.

Courses: Nutrition, commercial food service, purchasing, menu planning, dairy, meats, sauces, poultry, seafood, baking, garde manger, F& B mgmt, cake decorating.

Faculty: 2 certified chefs.

Costs: $50/cr-hr in-state, $100/cr-hr out-of-state. Admission requirements: HS diploma or GED.

Contact: Levi Ezell, Director, Commercial Food Service, Bishop State Community College, 414 Stanton St., Mobile, AL 36617; 334-473-8692, Fax 334-473-7915, cfs@bscc.cc.al.us, www.bscc.cc.al.us.

CULINARD – THE CULINARY INSTITUTE OF VIRGINIA COLLEGE
Birmingham/Year-round *(See also page 203) (See display ad page 13)*

Sponsor: Virginia College, a private, proprietary institution of higher education. Program: 24-mo (106 cr-hr) AOS degree in Culinary Arts; 27-mo (118 cr-hr) AOS degree in Pastry, Baking & Confectionery Arts; 18-mo (40 cr-hr) weekend diploma program in Culinary Arts. Established: 2000. Accredited by ACICS, Culinary Arts AOS program ACF accredited. Calendar: quarter. Curriculum: core. Admit dates: Oct, Jan, Apr, July. 96 each admission period. S:T ratio 16:1. Facilities: 7 instructional kitchens, full-service restaurant, full-service bakery, 10 classroom lecture facility, conferencespace.

Courses: Food Production, Patisserie, Garde Manger, Computer Fundamentals, Marketing & Menu Planning, Mixology & Viniculture, Purchasing, Dining Room Service, Human Relations, Nutrition, Confiserie & Center Pieces. Continuing ed courses for practicing professionals.

Faculty: Faculty is selected for academic qualifications & business experience. Credentials include advanced degrees & industry certifications.

Costs: $325/credit-hour. Total cost for Culinary Arts is $34,450+$995 tools/uniform fee. Total cost for Pastry, Baking & Confectionery Arts is $38,350+$1,125 tools/uniform fee. Admission requirements: HS diploma or equivalent, admissions interview, assessment exam, letters of recommendation, personal statement, deposit. Scholarships: yes. Loans: yes.

Contact: Bibbi McLaughlin, Vice President of Admissions, CULINARD The Culinary Institute of Virginia College, 65 Bagby Drive, Suite 100, Birmingham, AL 35209; 205-802-1200, 877-429-CHEF (2433), Fax 205-802-7045, admissions@culinard.com, www.culinard.com.

FAULKNER STATE COMMUNITY COLLEGE
Gulf Shores/Year-round

Sponsor: 2-year college. Program: 1-yr/26 sem-hr certificate & 2-yr/75-76 sem-hr AAS degree in Culinary Arts. Established: 1994. Accredited by SACS, ACF,CHRIE. Calendar: semester.

Curriculum: culinary, core. Admit dates: Aug, Jan, May. Total enrollment: 90. 25 each admission period. 90% of applicants accepted. 80% receive financial aid. 10% enrolled part-time. S:T ratio 15:1. 100% of graduates obtain jobs within 6 mos. Facilities: New 18,000-sq-ft building.

COURSES: Food safety & production, baking & pastry, food styling. Externship: 2,250 hrs. Continuing education: sanitation, nutrition, personnel management.

FACULTY: Gerhard Brill, CEC, pastry chef Jim Hurtubise, Ron Koetter, CEC, CCE, CMB, AAC, Program Coordinator.

COSTS: $68/sem-hr, in-state; $136/sem-hr, out-of-state. Admission requirements: HS diploma or GED & entrance exam. Scholarships: yes. Loans: yes.

CONTACT: Ron Koetter, Program Coordinator, Faulkner State Community College, 3301 Gulf Shores Pkwy, Gulf Shores, AL 36542; 251-968-3108, Fax 251-968-3120, rkoetter@faulknerstate.edu, www.faulknerstate.edu.

JEFFERSON STATE COMMUNITY COLLEGE

Birmingham/Year-round

Sponsor: 2-year college. Program: 34-hour Culinary Apprentice Option leading to an AAS degree (requires 6,000-hour on-the-job internship), 28-hour Food Service Management option. Established: 1988. Accredited by ACF. Calendar: semester. Curriculum: culinary, core. S:T ratio 10:1. 100% of graduates obtain jobs within 6 mos.

COURSES: Food preparation, meal management, baking, garde manger, beverage management. ACF 6,000-hr apprenticeship.

COSTS: $59/cr-hr. Admission requirements: HS diploma or GED, essay, references. Scholarships: yes. Loans: yes.

CONTACT: George White, Program Coordinator, Jefferson State Community College, 2601 Carson Rd., Birmingham, AL 35215-3098; 205-853-1200, Fax 205-815-8499, gwhite@jscc.cc.al.us, www.jscc.cc.al.us.

LAWSON STATE COMMUNITY COLLEGE

Birmingham/September-May

Sponsor: College. Program: 21-month certificate in Culinary Arts. Established: 1949. Accredited by SACS. Admit dates: Quarterly. S:T ratio 23:1. 50% of graduates obtain jobs within 6 mos.

FACULTY: 2 full-time.

COSTS: Tuition $39/credit-hour in-state, $78/credit-hour out-of-state. Admission requirements: HS diploma or equivalent and admission test.

CONTACT: Deborah Harris, Lawson State Community College, Commercial Food Preparation, 3060 Wilson Rd., SW, Birmingham, AL 35221-1717; 205-925-2515, dharris@cougar.ls.cc.al.us, www.ls.cc.al.us.

TRENHOLM STATE TECHNICAL COLLEGE

Montgomery/Year-round

Sponsor: Public post-secondary occupational education institution. Program: 42-cr-hr (12-mo) certificate in Culinary Arts, 64-cr-hr (24-mo) associate degree in Culinary Arts Applied Technology, 6,000-hr Chef Apprenticeship-Mgmt option, 74-cr-hr Hospitality Mgmt associate degree option. Established: 1980. Accredited by COE, ACF. Calendar: semester. Curriculum: culinary, core. Admit dates: Jan, May, Aug. Total enrollment: 101. 65+ each admission period. 90% of applicants accepted. 50% receive financial aid. 10% enrolled part-time. S:T ratio 8:1. 95% of graduates obtain jobs within 6 mos. Facilities: Free-standing Culinary Arts Ctr, classrooms, dining rooms, conference room, computer lab, culinary library.

COURSES: Food production, catering, garde manger, nutrition, menu design, table service, hospitality mgmt. Apprenticeship & training at approved sites.

FACULTY: ACF-certified chef instructors, members of the American Academy of Chefs.

COSTS: $67/sem-cr-hr, ~$300/sem for uniforms, books, insurance. Admission requirements: 17 yrs

of age, HS diploma or GED. Scholarships: yes. Loans: yes.

CONTACT: Mary Ann Campbell, CEC, CCE, AAC, Director of Culinary Arts, Trenholm State Technical College, Culinary Arts, Hospitality Mgmt, 1225 Air Base Blvd., Montgomery, AL 36108; 334-420-4495, Fax 334-420-4491, mcampbell@trenholmtech.cc.al.us, www.Trenholmtech.cc.al.us.

WALLACE STATE COMMUNITY COLLEGE

Hanceville/Year-round

Sponsor: 2-yr college. Program: 18-month diploma in Commercial Food Technology, 24-month degree in Commercial Foods. Established: 1979. Accredited by SACS. Calendar: semester. Curriculum: culinary, core. Admit dates: Aug, Jan, June. Total enrollment: 18. 100% of applicants accepted. 80-90% receive financial aid. 5% enrolled part-time. S:T ratio 15:1. 98% of graduates obtain jobs within 6 mos. Facilities: Classroom & lab.

FACULTY: 2 full-time.

COSTS: Tuition is $1,100-$1,300 in-state. Admission requirements: HS diploma or equivalent.

CONTACT: Donna Jackson, Dept. Chair, Wallace State Community College, Commercial Foods & Nutrition, Box 2000, Hanceville, AL 35077; 256-352-8227, Fax 256-352-8228, www.wallace.edu.

ALASKA

ALASKA VOCATIONAL TECHNICAL CENTER (AVTEC)

Seward/Year-round

Sponsor: Trade-technical school. Program: Professional Cooking and Baking program consisting of 4 certificates (1,470 hrs): Food Service Worker, Culinary Baker, Cooks Helper/Prep Cook, Cook/Culinarian. Established: 1972. Accredited by ACF, COE. Curriculum: culinary. Admit dates: Aug, Oct. Total enrollment: 30. 16 each admission period. S:T ratio 10:1. 80% of graduates obtain jobs within 6 mos. Facilities: 3rd Street Café open-to-the-public restaurant, full service volume kitchen,full service bakery, two dining rooms,classrooms.

COURSES: Nutrition, A la Carte Cooking, Culinary Baking, Dining Room Service, Buffet Catering, Purchasing & Inventory, Beverage Management, Resume Writing, Volume Foods, Pastry Arts, International Foods. 200-hr externship for Cook/Culinarian & Culinary Baker certificates. Professional upgrades available.

FACULTY: Dept. Head Robert E. Wilson, CEC, CCE; Elizabeth K. Fackler, CEPC, CCE; Kevin M. Lane, CCC.

CONTACT: Robert E. Wilson, Dept. Head, Alaska Vocational Technical Center (AVTEC), Culinary Arts, P.O. Box 889, 809 2nd Ave., Seward, AK 99664; 800-478-5389, 907-224-4152, Fax 907-224-4143, robert_wilson@labor.state.ak.us, www.avtec.alaska.edu/Culinary.htm.

UNIVERSITY OF ALASKA – ANCHORAGE

Anchorage/Year-round

Sponsor: University. Program: 2-year AAS degree in Culinary Arts, BA degree in Hospitality & Restaurant Management. Curriculum: core.

COURSES: Food preparation, baking skills, cost control, operations, and management.

CONTACT: Nancy Overpeck, University of Alaska-Anchorage, 3211 Providence Dr. - Cuddy 126, Anchorage, AK 99508; 907-786-1487, Fax 907-786-1402, afnlo@uaa.alaska.edu, www.uaa.alaska.edu.

UNIVERSITY OF ALASKA-FAIRBANKS

Fairbanks/August-April

Sponsor: University. Program: 2-year certificate & 2-year AAS degree in Culinary Arts. Established: 1879. Accredited by NASC, ACCSCT. Calendar: semester. Curriculum: culinary, core. Admit dates: Fall, spring. Total enrollment: 30-45. 85% of applicants accepted. S:T ratio 8-10:1. 95% of graduates obtain jobs within 6 mos.

FACULTY: 3 full-time, 7 part-time.

COSTS: Annual tuition in-state $77/credit hour, out-of-state $241/credit hour. Admission requirements: HS diploma or equivalent. Scholarships: yes.

CONTACT: Program Coordinator, University of Alaska - Tanana Valley Campus, Culinary Arts, PO Box 758080, Fairbanks, AK 99775; 907-474-5240, fycah@uaf.edu, www.tvc.uaf.edu/programs/cah-info.html#Facilities.

ARIZONA

ARIZONA CULINARY INSTITUTE

Scottsdale/Year-round

(See display ad page 17)

Sponsor: Private school for career culinay education. Program: Professional 9-mo diploma program in Culinary Arts, Baking & Restaurant Management. Established: 2001. Accredited by Arizona State Board for Private Postsecondary Education. Curriculum: culinary. Admit dates: Every 6 weeks. Total enrollment: ~240. ~18-36 each admission period. 75% of applicants accepted. ~70% receive financial aid. S:T ratio 7:1. 98% of graduates obtain jobs within 6 mos. Facilities: New 18,000-ft facility with 5 kitchens, 2 classrooms & a student-run du Jour restaurant.

COURSES: Basic Culinary Arts I & II, Saucier & Meat Fabrication, Baking, Restaurant Mgmt, Wines & Spirits, Advanced Baking, Pastry & Showpieces, Restaurant Operations, Intl Cuisine/du Jour Restaurant, Internship. Students complete the program with a 3-mo paid internship. Opportunities available locally & nationally.

FACULTY: 11 full-time faculty with formal culinary education, ~6 years teaching experience plus industry work experience.

COSTS: $15,045 tuition, $1,140 fee (knives, uniforms, books), $25 application fee. Admission requirements: HS diploma, GED, essay, 3 personal references. Scholarships: yes. Loans: yes.

LOCATION: Central Scottsdale, Phoenix metropolitan area.

CONTACT: Keith Herron, Admissions Director, Arizona Culinary Institute, 10585 N. 114th St., #401, Scottsdale, AZ 85259; 480-603-1066, 866-294-CHEF (2433) toll free, Fax 480-603-1067, info@azculinary.com, www.azculinary.com. Darren Leite, President & Co-Founder.

ARIZONA WESTERN COLLEGE

Yuma/August-June

Sponsor: State-supported community college. Program: One-year (1-semester, 24-credit) program. Established: 1996. Accredited by NCA. Calendar: semester. Curriculum: culinary. Admit dates: Aug, Jan. Total enrollment: 30. 15 each admission period. 100% of applicants accepted. 50% receive financial aid. 20% enrolled part-time. S:T ratio 15:1. 50% of graduates obtain jobs within 6 mos. Facilities: Fully-equipped kitchen/lab and dining room.

COURSES: Classic European-style preparation. Interns do voluntary placement under contract with local country club.

FACULTY: One full-time registered dietitian with master's degree, 1 part-time AAS prepared chef instructor with 20 yrs experience, including operating his own restaurant.

COSTS: $1,750 for the year. Admission requirements: Open enrollment. Placement tests in reading & math, application, personal essay. Scholarships: yes. Loans: yes.

CONTACT: Nancy Meister, Coordinator, Arizona Western College, Culinary Arts Program, Box 929, Yuma, AZ 85366; 928-344-7779, Fax 928-317-6119, Nancy.Meister@azwestern.edu, www.awc.cc.az.us.

THE ART INSTITUTE OF PHOENIX – CULINARY ARTS

Phoenix/Year-round

(See display ad page 135)

Sponsor: Private school specializing in the creative & applied arts. Program: 18-mo AAS degree in Culinary Arts (24-mo in the evening), certification in Sanitation & Safety & Nutrition, 2- to 9-mo diploma programs in The Art of Cooking & Baking & Pastry. Established: 1996. Accredited by ACICS. Calendar: quarter. Curriculum: core. Admit dates: Oct, Jan, Apr, July. Total enrollment: 200+. 40 each admission period. 90% of applicants accepted. 70% receive financial aid. 7% enrolled part-time. S:T ratio 18:1. 100% of graduates obtain jobs within 6 mos. Facilities: 3 production kitchens, dining lab, 3 computer labs, learning resource center, student lounge & restaurant.

Courses: Include culinary skills, food production, regional cuisine, nutrition, baking & pastry, catering, a la carte cooking, hospitality, facilities & design, purchasing & cost control, general ed.

Faculty: Director Bill Sy, MBA, CEC, Walter Leible, CMC, Eric Watson, Jim Diamond, Robert Nicklin, Steven Durham, JoAnn Ayers, CWPC, Mark Gerding, Stephanie Green, RD, Jennifer Sedig.

Costs: $305/cr-hr, $4,880/qtr. Application fee $150, supply kit $650, lab fee $250/qtr, (program total $31,580). Admission requirements: HS diploma or equivalent, 150-word essay, interview. Scholarships: yes. Loans: yes.

Contact: Valerie Chaparro, Director of Admissions, Art Institute of Phoenix-Culinary Arts Program, 2233 W. Dunlap Ave., Phoenix, AZ 85021; 800-474-2479, Fax 602-216-0439, chaparrv@aii.edu, www.aipx.edu.

CENTRAL ARIZONA COLLEGE

Coolidge/Year-round

Sponsor: 2-year college. Program: AAS degrees in Culinary Apprenticeship and Hotel/Restaurant Management, 18-credit Cook's Certificate, 17-credit certificate in Restaurant Management. Accredited by NCACS, ACF. Calendar: semester. Curriculum: culinary. Total enrollment: 800. 60 each admission period. S:T ratio 10:1.

Courses: Include Food Service Management, Advanced Food Preparation, Basic Baking & Garde Manger, Culinary Practicum, Dining & Beverage Service, ServSafe.

Faculty: 2 full-time faculty.

Costs: In-state $40/credit, $48/special lab credit; non-resident $80/credit, internship fee $43/credit.

Contact: Glenna McCollum, Dietetic Education Program Director, Central Arizona College, 8470 N. Overfield Rd., Coolidge, AZ 85228; 800-465-1016 X4497/520-426-4497, Fax 520-426-4476, nutrition@python.cac.cc.az.us, www.cac.cc.az.us/dep.

MARICOPA SKILL CENTER

Phoenix/Year-round

Sponsor: Community college division. Program: 14- to 27-week certificates in Cook's Apprentice, Kitchen Helper, Baker's Helper, Pantry Goods Maker. Established: 1962. Accredited by NCA. Curriculum: culinary. Admit dates: Any Monday. Total enrollment: 25. open each admission period. 100% of applicants accepted. 80% receive financial aid. 10% enrolled part-time. S:T ratio 7:1. 80% of graduates obtain jobs within 6 mos. Facilities: Commercial kitchen.

Courses: Entry level job preparation. On-site student cafeteria.

Faculty: 3 full-time: Dan Bochicchio, CWC, and 2 assistants.

Costs: ~$2,835 (oe/oe), $225 lab fee. Admission requirements: At least 16 years old. Scholarships: yes.

Contact: Richard Sandoval, Instructor, Maricopa Skill Center, 1245 E. Buckeye Rd., Phoenix, AZ 85034-4101; 602-238-4378, Fax 602-238-4307, sandisandoval@aol.com, www.gwc.maricopa.edu/msc/clusters/fp.html.

PHOENIX COLLEGE

Phoenix/August-May

Sponsor: 2-yr college. Program: AAS degree & 16-wk certificate of completion programs in Culinary Studies & Foodservice Administration. Established: 1972. Accredited by NCA. Calendar: semester. Curriculum: culinary, core. Admit dates: Aug & Jan. Total enrollment: 38. 40 each admission period. 98% of applicants accepted. 20% receive financial aid. 60% enrolled part-time. S:T ratio 18:1. 95% of graduates obtain jobs within 6 mos. Facilities: 5,000-sq-ft of teaching facilities, the latest equipment, on-site 40-seat restaurant.

Courses: Nutrition, menu planning, commercial baking, garde manger, professional cooking, French, American regional, & intl cuisines, food purchasing & mgmt, customer service, sanitation, safety. Banquet food & beverage service externship. Cont. ed. courses available.

Faculty: Chefs Scott Robinson, Steve Slansky, Michael Whelan, Guentar Haub, Ray Vicencio.

Costs: ~$3,200. Admission requirements: GED. Scholarships: yes. Loans: yes.

Contact: Scott Robinson, Program Director, Phoenix College, 1202 W. Thomas Rd., Phoenix, AZ 85013; 602-285-7901/7765, Fax 602-285-7705, scott.robinson@pcmail.maricopa.edu, www.pc.maricopa.edu/departments/aahs/culinary/index.html.

PIMA COMMUNITY COLLEGE

Tucson/September-May

Sponsor: State-supported college. Program: 2-semester certificate & 2-year AAS degree in Culinary Arts. Established: 1972. Accredited by NCA. Admit dates: Jan, May, Aug. Total enrollment: 50. 22 each admission period. 100% of applicants accepted. 92% enrolled part-time. S:T ratio 18:1. 90% of graduates obtain jobs within 6 mos. Facilities: 1 kitchen, 2 classrooms.

Courses: Hot Foods, Garde Manger, Bakery, Nutrition, Stewarding, Dining Room Operations, Menu Planning. 4-year degree continuation at Northern Arizona University.

Faculty: 11 full-time and part-time.

Costs: $1,200 for certificate, ~$500 for fees & supplies. Admission requirements: HS diploma and 1 year food service experience.

Contact: Simone Gers, Dept. Chair, Pima Community College, Hospitality, 1255 N. Stone Ave., Tucson, AZ 85703; 800-860-7462, 520-206-5091, Simone.Gers@pima.edu, http://dv.pima.edu/~culinary.

SCOTTSDALE COMMUNITY COLLEGE

Scottsdale/August-May

Sponsor: State-supported college. Program: 9-month certificate, 2-year AAS degree in Culinary Arts. Established: 1985. Accredited by NCA. Calendar: semester. Curriculum: culinary, core. Admit dates: Aug, Jan. Total enrollment: 72. 36 each admission period. 60% of applicants accepted. 80% receive financial aid. S:T ratio 12:1. 100% of graduates obtain jobs within 6 mos. Facilities: 10,000-sq-ft kitchen, 2 classrooms, 2 student-run dining rooms.

Courses: Hospitality management, culinary principles, menu planning, hot foods, bakery/pastry, garde manger, nutrition, applied math, sanitation; student-operated restaurant.

Faculty: 4 full-time, 6 part-time.

Costs: Annual tuition in-state $1,800, out-of-state $5,600, includes course fee of $350/semester. Admission requirements: HS diploma and application/interview. Scholarships: yes. Loans: yes.

Contact: Karen Chalmers, Director, Scottsdale Community College, Culinary Arts Program, 9000 E. Chaparral Rd., Scottsdale, AZ 85256; 480-423-6241, Fax 480-423-6091, karen.chalmers@scc-mail.maricopa.edu, www.sc.maricopa.edu.

SCOTTSDALE CULINARY INSTITUTE, LE CORDON BLEU

Scottsdale/Year-round *(See display ad page 19)*

Sponsor: Culinary & Baking Arts College. Program: 15-mo AOS degree in Le Cordon Bleu Culinary Arts, 9-mo certificate in Le Cordon Bleu Patisserie & Baking. Established: 1986. Accredited by ACCSCT, ACF. Curriculum: culinary. Admit dates: Jan, Feb, Apr, May, July, Aug, Oct, Nov. Total enrollment: 1,000+. 80-140 each admission period. 70% of applicants accepted. 70% receive financial aid. S:T ratio 16:1. 98% of graduates obtain jobs within 6 mos. Facilities: 45,000-sq-ft main campus facility: 7 kitchens, bakery, meat fabrication shop, student-run restaurant, classrooms, resource center, library; 53,000-sq-ft Sky Bridge campus facility: teaching & demo kitchens, classrooms, student-run restaurant.

Courses: Degree program: Classic French techniques, international cuisine, traditional & contemporary trends, nutrition, restaurant management. Certificate program: Artisan Bread Production, Sugar & Chocolate Work, European Pastries, Wedding Cakes. Final 8-12 wks are a national paid externship program.

Faculty: 60+ full-time American & European-trained professionals.

Costs: $34,000 for degree program, $16,000 for certificate program. Additional $2,200 fee for text-

books & supplies & $95 application fee for each program. Admission requirements: HS diploma or GED & application. Scholarships: yes. Loans: yes.

CONTACT: Director of Admissions, Scottsdale Culinary Institute, Le Cordon Bleu, 8100 E. Camelback Rd., Suite 1001, Scottsdale, AZ 85251; 800-848-CHEF (2433), Fax 480-990-0351, admissions@scichefs.com, www.chefs.com.

ARKANSAS

ACF CENTRAL ARKANSAS CULINARY SCHOOL OF APPRENTICESHIP

Little Rock/Year-round

Sponsor: ACF Central Arkansas Chapter. Program: 3-yr apprenticeship program with 198 classroom hrs yearly & 2,000 hrs of paid on-the-job training under supervision of an ACF-Certified Chef. Established: 1993. Accredited by ACF. Calendar: semester. Curriculum: culinary. Admit dates: Aug. Total enrollment: 35. 20 each admission period. 90% of applicants accepted. 75% receive financial aid. S:T ratio 15:1. 100% of graduates obtain jobs within 6 mos. Facilities: Classroom training at Technology Center in Quality Foods Headquarters Bldg. Courses: Sanitation & Safety, Hospitality, Business Math, Nutrition, Menu Planning & Design, Food & Beverage Svc, Purchasing & Receiving, Supervisory Mgmt, Basic Baking, Garde Manger, Advanced Food Prep. 6,000-hrs paid training under supervision of an ACF-Certifiable Executive Chef. Courses taught for ACF renewal in Nutrition, ServSafe, Supervision.

FACULTY: 1 full-time & 8 adjunct faculty with certification in coursework &/or masters degree.

COSTS: $2,000/yr + books, uniform, knife kit. Beginning salary $6.50/hr min. Admission requirements: HS diploma or equivalent, 18 yrs oldmin, writing skills & math proficiency exam, interview with Board of Directors. Scholarships: yes. Loans: yes.

CONTACT: Will Hutchison C.S.C., Executive Director, ACF Central Arkansas Culinary School of Apprenticeship, Box 3275, Little Rock, AR 72203; 501-831-CHEF, Fax 501-255-2108, arkansaschef@aristotle.net, http://arkansaschefs.com.

OZARKA COLLEGE CULINARY ARTS PROGRAM

Melbourne/August-May

Sponsor: Public 2-year college. Program: 9-mo technical certificate program, 2-yr AAS General Technology degree option. Established: 1975. Accredited by Higher Learning Commission. Calendar: semester. Curriculum: culinary, core. Admit dates: Aug, Jan. Total enrollment: 15. 6 each admission period. 60% of applicants accepted. 80% receive financial aid. 10% enrolled part-time. S:T ratio 15:1. 80% of graduates obtain jobs within 6 mos. Facilities: Culinary lab with adjoining classroom.

COURSES: Food safety, basic principles & techniques of food preparation, dining room service & catering, baking, advanced topics. Student-managed catering service.

FACULTY: 1 instructor.

COSTS: Tuition $1,500/yr, fees $250/yr. Admission requirements: HS graduate or GED. Scholarships: yes. Loans: yes.

CONTACT: Richard Tankersley, Chef, Ozarka College Culinary Arts Program, PO Box 10, 218 College Dr., Melbourne, AR 72556; 870-368-7371/800-821-4335, Fax 870-368-4733, rtankersley@ozarka.edu, www.ozarka.edu/d_cularts.cfm.

CALIFORNIA

AMERICAN RIVER COLLEGE

Sacramento/Year-round

Sponsor: 2-yr college. Program: 1-yr/39 unit certificate & 2-yr AA degree in Culinary Arts/Restaurant Mgmt. Established: 1976. Accredited by NRA. Calendar: semester. Curriculum: culinary, core. Admit dates: Jan, June, Aug. Total enrollment: 200. 100% of applicants accepted. S:T ratio 15:1. Facilities: Lab classrooms & commercial kitchen.

COURSES: Food theory & prep, professional cooking, restaurant mgmt & production, baking & pastry, cost control, purchasing, advertising & sales, beverage operations. On-campus fine dining restaurant internship (required), 360-hr off-campus (optional).

FACULTY: 2 full-time, 4 part-time.

COSTS: $12/unit in-state, $138/unit out-of-state. Admission requirements: College level reading & writing. Scholarships: yes. Loans: yes.

CONTACT: Brian Knirk, Program Coordinator, American River College, 4700 College Oak Dr., Sacramento, CA 95841; 916-484-8656, Fax 916-484-8880, KnirkB@arc.losrios.edu, www.arc.losrios.edu/~chef.

THE ART INSTITUTE OF CALIFORNIA – LOS ANGELES

Santa Monica/Year-round *(See display ad page 135)*

Sponsor: Private college. Program: 77-wk (2-yr) AS degree in Culinary Arts, 132-wk (3-yr) BS degree in Culinary Management. Established: 1997. Accredited by ACICS. Calendar: quarter. Curriculum: core. Admit dates: July, Oct, Jan, Apr. Total enrollment: 340. 40-120 each admission period. 90% of applicants accepted. 75% receive financial aid. 32% enrolled part-time. S:T ratio 20:1. 90% of graduates obtain jobs within 6 mos. Facilities: 4 kitchens, classrooms, dining lab room.

COURSES: Sanitation, Nutrition, Knife Skills, Cooking Techniques, Meat Fabrication, Garde Manger, Buffet, a la Carte, Baking, Patisserie, Soups, Sauces, Restaurant & Menu Design, Food History.

FACULTY: Includes Joe Zoellin CEC, CCE, Kurt Struwe CEC, CCE, Dan Drumlake CCE, CEC, Mial Parker CCE, CEC, Sean Ryan, Dominique Fournier, Silvain Rivet, Haley Nguyen.

COSTS: $5,680/quarter. Fees $150, supply kit $655, lab fees $300/quarter. Admission requirements: Interview, proof of HS graduation, final transcripts or GED. Scholarships: yes. Loans: yes.

CONTACT: Joe Zoellin, Culinary Arts Director, The Art Institute of Los Angeles, 2900-31st St., Santa Monica, CA 90405; 888-646-4610, 310-752-4700, Fax 310-752-4708, zoellinj@aii.edu, www.aicala.artinstitutes.edu.

THE ART INSTITUTE OF CALIFORNIA – ORANGE COUNTY

Santa Ana/Year-round *(See display ad page 135)*

Sponsor: Visual & practical arts school. Program: AS degree (112 qtr credits) in Culinary Arts. Established: 2001. Accredited by ACCST. Calendar: quarter. Curriculum: culinary, core. Admit dates: Rolling. Total enrollment: 103. Varies each admission period. S:T ratio 24:1. Facilities: 55,000 sq-ft facility.

COURSES: Culinary arts with focus on practical & business aspects.

FACULTY: 7 culinary instructors.

COSTS: $39,172. Admission requirements: Personal interview, essay. Scholarships: yes. Loans: yes.

CONTACT: Ken Post, Director of Admissions, The Art Institute of California-Orange County, 3601 W. Sunflower Ave., Santa Ana, CA 92704-9888; 888-549-3055, 714-830-0200, Fax 714-556-1923, postk@aii.edu, www.aicaoc.aii.edu.

THE ART INSTITUTE OF CALIFORNIA – SAN DIEGO

San Diego/Year-round *(See display ad page 135)*

Sponsor: Private college. Program: AS degree program in Culinary Arts consisting of seven 11-wk quarters, 112 credits, 1,969 hours. Established: 2002. Accredited by ACCSCT. Calendar: quarter. Curriculum: culinary. Admit dates: July, Oct, Jan, Apr. Total enrollment: 80. Facilities: New 76,000-sq-ft building with 3 kitchens, classrooms, labs.

COURSES: Intro to the theory & practice of hospitality, baking & pastry, catering, a la carte kitchen, regional cuisine, purchasing, cost control. Externship required.

COSTS: $5,680/qtr, application fee $50, enrollment fee $100, starting kit $860, lab fee $300/qtr. Admission requirements: Interview, HS graduate, GED accepted. Scholarships: yes. Loans: yes.

CONTACT: Sandy Park, Director of Admissions, The Art Institute of California-San Diego, 7650 Mission Valley Rd., San Diego, CA 92108; 858-598-1399, 800-591-2422, Fax 858-457-0903, parks@aii.edu, www.aicasd.artinstitutes.edu.

CABRILLO COLLEGE

Aptos/Year-round

Sponsor: Community college. Program: 30-unit certificate & 60 unit AS degree in Culinary Arts & Hospitality Management. AS degree in Baking. Established: 1972. Calendar: semester. Curriculum: core. Admit dates: Aug, Jan. Total enrollment: 200+. 150-200 each admission period. 100% of applicants accepted. 70% enrolled part-time. 100% of graduates obtain jobs within 6 mos. Facilities: Restaurant kitchen, quantity foods kitchen, bake shop, lecture/demonstration room, student-run restaurant.

COURSES: Include culinary arts, baking and pastry arts, cake decorating, garde manger, culinary specialties, chocolate. Both internships & externships offered.

FACULTY: 3 full-time 5 part-time.

COSTS: Annual tuition for full-time students $464 in-state, $4,820 out-of-state. Off-campus housing available. Admission requirements: HS diploma or equivalent. Scholarships: yes. Loans: yes.

CONTACT: Katherine Niven, Director of Culinary Arts, Cabrillo College, Culinary Arts & Hospitality Mgmt., 6500 Soquel Dr., Aptos, CA 95003; 831-479-5749, kaniven@cabrillo.cc.ca.us, www.cabrillo.cc.ca.us/divisions/has/cahm/index.html. Admissions: 831-479-6213.

CALIFORNIA CULINARY ACADEMY

San Francisco/Year-round *(See also page 208) (See display ad page 23)*

Sponsor: Culinary & hospitality career academy. Program: 15-mo AOS degree program in Le Cordon Bleu Culinary Arts; 30-wk certificate program in Baking & Pastry Arts; 45-wk AOS degree program in Le Cordon Bleu Hospitality & Restaurant Management. Established: 1977. Accredited by ACF, ACCSCT. Curriculum: culinary, core. Total enrollment: 1,200. 95% of applicants accepted. 85% receive financial aid. S:T ratio 16:1. 98% of graduates obtain jobs within 6 mos. Facilities: 75,000+ sq-ft historic building with professional production & garde manger kitchens, baking & pastry kitchens, butchery, confiseries, lecture classrooms & labs, retail shop, student-staffed restaurant.

COURSES: Sequential learning curriculum includes nutrition, food prep & presentation, wine studies, baking & pastry, butchery, purchasing, restaurant & hotel mgmt/operations, mixology/beverage, externship. Externship opportunities in variety of restaurants, resorts, bakeries, hotels worldwide. Weekend consumer education classes for the home chef.

FACULTY: 75+ chef instructors including Master Chefs, Executive Chefs; qualified & experienced in global cuisine, baking & pastry, hospitality; guest professionals.

COSTS: Admission requirements: Proof of HS graduation, GED, or equivalency, & personal interview. Scholarships: yes. Loans: yes.

CONTACT: Nancy Seyfert, V.P. of Admissions, California Culinary Academy, Admissions Dept., 625 Polk St., San Francisco, CA 94102; 800-229-CHEF (2433), 415-771-3500, Fax 415-771-2194, admissions@baychef.com, www.baychef.com.

CALIFORNIA SCHOOL OF CULINARY ARTS

Pasadena/Year-round *(See display ad page 25)*

Sponsor: Private career school. Program: 15-mo AOS degree program in Le Cordon Bleu Culinary Arts; 12-mo diploma program in Le Cordon Bleu Hospitality & Restaurant Management; 30-wk diploma program in Le Cordon Bleu Patisserie & Baking. Established: 1994. Accredited by ACICS. Calendar: quarter. Curriculum: culinary, core. Admit dates: Jan, Feb, Apr, May, July, Aug, Oct, Nov. Total enrollment: 1,100. 235 each admission period. 75% of applicants accepted. 80% receive financial aid. S:T ratio 16:1. Facilities: 80,000-sq-ft space includes fine dining restaurant, 30 kitchen labs, learning resource center.

COURSES: Include Food History, Sanitation, Purchasing, Nutrition, Wine & Beverage, Supervision. Externship/placements in area hotels, restaurants, catering, personal chefs, airlines & cruise ships.

FACULTY: 100.

COSTS: $39,500 for degree program, fees $100, uniform deposit $390, off-campus lodging ~$600-$800/mo; $24,000 for Hospitality & Restaurant Mgmt diploma program; $22,500 for Patisserie &

Baking diploma Program. Admission requirements: Interview, HS diploma or equivalent, entrance test for Hospitality & Restaurant Mgmt Program. Scholarships: yes. Loans: yes.

Location: The Arts district, opposite Pasadena Playhouse, 12 min by freeway from downtown Los Angeles & near Old Town Pasadena.

Contact: Admissions Office Manager, California School of Culinary Arts, 521 E. Green St., Pasadena, CA 91101; 888-900-2433, 626-403-8490, Fax 626-403-4835, info@scsca.com, www.calchef.com.

CALIFORNIA SUSHI ACADEMY

Venice/Year-round

Sponsor: Private school devoted to teaching sushi preparation. Program: 126-hr (3-mo) Basic Course meets 3 hrs daily MWF; 144-hr (3-mo) Professional Course meets 4 hrs on Tue, Thu, Sat. AM, PM, & evening sessions. 1- & 2-week custom intensives for experienced chefs. Calendar: quarter. Curriculum: culinary. Total enrollment: 36. 60 each admission period. 100% enrolled part-time. S:T ratio 10/class.

Courses: Japanese restaurant dishes, sushi history & artistry, utensil use, sauces, seasonal & special occasion dishes, basic fish knowledge & management skills. 18 (36) hrs on-the-job training for Basic (Professional) Course.

Costs: $1,925 + $75 registration fee/course. Admission requirements: No experience required.

Contact: Phil Yi, Director, California Sushi Academy, 1611 Pacific Ave. (School), Venice, CA 90291; 310-581-0213, Fax 310-306-2605, email@sushi-academy.com, www.sushi-academy.com.

CHAFFEY COLLEGE

Alta Loma/Year-round

Sponsor: Public 2-year community college. Program: 1-year certificate in Culinary Arts, 2-year associate degree in Culinary Arts & Foodservice Management. Established: 1986. Accredited by WASC. Calendar: semester. Curriculum: culinary. Admit dates: Jan, June, Aug. Total enrollment: 52. 20+ each admission period. 100% of applicants accepted. 85% receive financial aid. 80% enrolled part-time. S:T ratio 18:1. 98% of graduates obtain jobs within 6 mos.

Courses: Management. Internship required prior to certificate.

Faculty: 2 full- & 17 part-time.

Costs: $12/unit, books $150/semester. Admission requirements: HS diploma preferred. Scholarships: yes. Loans: yes.

Contact: D. Suzanne Johnson, Dept. Chair, Chaffey College-Hotel & Foodservice Management, 5885 Haven Ave., Alta Loma, CA 91737-3002; 909-941-2711, Fax 909-466-2831, sjohnson@chaffey.cc.ca.us, www.chaffey.cc.ca.us.

CITY COLLEGE OF SAN FRANCISCO

San Francisco/August-May

Sponsor: College. Program: 4-semester AS degree in Hotel and Restaurant Operations, Award of Achievement & ACF certificate. Established: 1935. Accredited by WASC, ACF. Calendar: semester. Curriculum: culinary, core. Admit dates: Aug, Jan. Total enrollment: 200. 86 each admission period. 90% of applicants accepted. S:T ratio 20:1. 95% of graduates obtain jobs within 6 mos. Facilities: 4 kitchens and 3 classrooms, student-run restaurant, cafeteria and quick service cafe.

Courses: Includes elementary and advanced foods, bake shop, advanced pastry, meat analysis, garde manger, operations, purchasing, accounting, marketing, sanitation, nutrition, and general education. 240-hour externship.

Faculty: 11 full-time and 6 part-time.

Costs: Annual tuition in-state $390, out-of-state $3,720. Admission requirements: Age 18, or HS diploma. Scholarships: yes. Loans: yes.

Contact: Lynda Hirose, Advisor/Placement Counselor, City College of San Francisco, Hotel & Restaurant, 50 Phelan Ave., San Francisco, CA 94112; 415-239-3152, Fax 415-239-3913, lhirose@ccsf.edu, www.ccsf.edu/hotelandrestaurant. Additional contact: Edward Hamilton, Dept. Chair.

COLLEGE OF THE DESERT

Palm Desert/Year-round

Sponsor: 2-year college. Program: 20-unit certificate in Basic Culinary Arts, 62-unit AA degree in Culinary Management. Calendar: semester. Curriculum: culinary, core.

Courses: Principles of cooking, baking, pantry, operations management.

Costs: $13/unit in-state, $140.25/unit out-of-state.

Contact: Steve Beno, Professor of Culinary Arts, College of the Desert, 43500 Monterey Ave., Palm Desert, CA 92260; 760-776-7384, SBeno@collegeofthedesert.edu, www.desert.cc.ca.us.

COLLEGE OF THE SEQUOIAS

Visalia/August-May

Sponsor: 2-year college. Program: 11- to 13-unit certificate in Food Service, 28-unit certificate in Food Service Management, 20-unit certificate in Dietetic Service Supervisor, AS degree in Food Service. Established: 1993. Calendar: semester. Curriculum: culinary. Admit dates: Aug, Jan. Total enrollment: 100. 50 each admission period. 100% of applicants accepted. 40% receive financial aid. 60% enrolled part-time. S:T ratio 20:1. Facilities: Commercial food lab.

Courses: Commercial food, food service management, nutrition.

Faculty: 3 full- and 4 part-time instructors (R.D.s and chef).

Costs: Enrollment fee $12/unit for all students, non-resident tuition $118/unit. Loans: yes.

Contact: Barbara Reynolds, Consumer/Family Instructor, College of the Sequoias, 915 S. Mooney Blvd., Visalia, CA 93277; 559-730-3717, Fax 559-737-4810, barbarar@cos.edu, www.sequoias.cc.ca.us.

COLUMBIA COLLEGE

Sonora/August-May

Sponsor: California community college. Program: 2-year AS degree in Culinary Arts/Hospitality Management; 10 culinary certificates. Established: 1977. Accredited by WASC, ACF. Calendar: semester. Curriculum: culinary. Admit dates: Aug, Jan. Total enrollment: 125. 30 each admission period. 99% of applicants accepted. 40% receive financial aid. 40% enrolled part-time. S:T ratio 10-15:1. 90% of graduates obtain jobs within 6 mos. Facilities: 2 kitchens, 4 classrooms, 3-star restaurant.

Courses: Cooking, baking, pastry, restaurant desserts, wines, bartending, garde manger, service, restaurant management. 38 hrs of culinary courses required for graduation.

Faculty: 2 full-time, 7 part-time. Qualifications: full-time: lifetime teaching credential and industry experience; part-time: A.S. degree + 6 yrs industry experience.

Costs: Annual tuition in-state $312, out-of-state $3,144. Health & student fees $30/semester. Average on-campus housing (180 spaces) $300/mo. Average off-campus housing $500/mo. Admission requirements: Admission test. Scholarships: yes. Loans: yes.

Contact: Gene Womble, Hosp. Mgmt. Program Coordinator, Columbia College, Hospitality Mgmt., 11600 Columbia College Dr., Sonora, CA 95370; 209-588-5135, Fax 209-588-5316, wombleg@yosemite.cc.ca.us, http://columbia.yosemite.cc.ca.us/hospmgmt.html.

CONTRA COSTA COLLEGE

San Pablo/September-May

Sponsor: College. Program: 2-year certificate. Established: 1962. Calendar: semester. Curriculum: culinary. Admit dates: Aug, Jan. Total enrollment: 75-100. 90% of applicants accepted. S:T ratio 20-25:1. 90% of graduates obtain jobs within 6 mos.

Faculty: 2 full-time, 2 part-time.

Costs: $11/unit enrollment fee in-state, non-resident tuition; $155/unit tuition + $11/unit enrollment fee out-of-state. Admission requirements: Admission test. Loans: yes.

Contact: David Rosenthal, Instructor, Contra Costa College, Culinary Arts, 2600 Mission Bell Dr., San Pablo, CA 94806; 510-235-7800 x4320, drosenthal@contracosta.cc.ca.us, www.contracosta.cc.ca.us.

THE CULINARY INSTITUTE OF AMERICA AT GREYSTONE

Napa Valley/Year-round *(See also page 107. 209, 253) (See display ad page 108)*

Sponsor: The CIA's Greystone campus, a continuing education center for food & wine professionals. Program: Fundamental to advanced 2- to 5-day courses for foodservice professionals; 30-week Baking & Pastry Arts Certificate Program. Established: 1995. Accredited by MSA, ACCSCT. Curriculum: culinary. Admit dates: On-going. Total enrollment: 3,500/yr. 18/class session each admission period. S:T ratio 18:1. Facilities: 15,000-sq-ft open teaching kitchens that include Bonnet Cooking Suites & Bongard Hearth ovens, 125-seat Ecolab Theatre, on-campus vineyards & gardens.

COURSES: Culinary skill development, world cuisines, garde manger, advanced culinary programs, professional baking & pastry, baking & pastry arts certificate program, wine programs, executive chef seminars. Other than certificate program, exclusively devoted to continuing education.

FACULTY: 11 full- & part-time instructors, visiting instructors include chef/owners of fine restaurants, also drawn from the 140 instructors at the Hyde Park, NY, campus.

COSTS: From $850 for 30 hrs of instruction to $18,000 for the Baking & Pastry Arts Certificate Program. Lodging available at the on-campus Guest House. Admission requirements: For cooking production classes, a min of 6 mos experience in a professional kitchen. Scholarships: yes. Loans: yes.

LOCATION: 90 min north of San Francisco, in the Napa Valley.

CONTACT: Susan Cussen, Director of Marketing, CE, The Culinary Institute of America, 2555 Main St., St. Helena, CA 94574; 800-888-7850, ciaprochef@culinary.edu, www.ciaprochef.com.

CYPRESS COLLEGE

Cypress/Year-round

Sponsor: College. Program: 1-yr certificate, 2-yr AS degree in Food Service Management, Hotel Operations, & Culinary Arts. Established: 1975. Accredited by WASC. Calendar: semester. Curriculum: culinary, core. Admit dates: Aug, Jan. Total enrollment: 100. 30 each admission period. 90% of applicants accepted. 45% receive financial aid. 70% enrolled part-time. S:T ratio 16:1. 85% of graduates obtain jobs within 6 mos. Facilities: 1 kitchen, 4 classrooms, student-run dining room.

COURSES: Basic food production, advanced cooking techniques, quantity food production, intl gourmet foods, dining room service, costing, kitchen mgmt, menu planning, kitchen design, baking & pastry, pantry skills. 225-hr salaried externship.

FACULTY: 2 full-time, 12 part-time.

COSTS: In-state $12/unit, out-of-state $114/unit. $5/lab fee. Off-campus housing ~$250-$750/mo. Admission requirements: HS diploma or equivalent. Scholarships: yes. Loans: yes.

CONTACT: Michael Bird, Dept. Chair, Cypress College, Hospitality Mgmt./Culinary Arts, 9200 Valley View, Cypress, CA 90630; 714-826-2220 #208, Fax 714-527-8238, mbird@cypress.cc.ca.us, http://cypresscollege.org.

DIABLO VALLEY COLLEGE

Pleasant Hill/Year-round

Sponsor: College. Program: Program in Culinary Arts, Baking & Patisserie, Restaurant Management & Hotel Administration. Established: 1971. Accredited by ACF, WASC. Calendar: semester. Curriculum: core. Admit dates: Aug, Jan. Total enrollment: 750. 50 each admission period. 100% enrolled part-time. S:T ratio 24:1. 100% of graduates obtain jobs within 6 mos. Facilities: Include a fully-equipped food production kitchen, demonstration laboratory, 130-seat open-to-the-public restaurant.

COURSES: Advanced food preparation, catering, garde manger, menu planning, costing, nutrition cuisine and baking, restaurant operations. One semester externship at local hotels & restaurants.

FACULTY: 5 full-time, 14 part-time. Qualifications: BA degrees and 7 years industry experience. Includes Jack Hendrickson, Chris Draa, Nader Sharkes, Robert Eustes, Paul Bernhardt.

COSTS: In-state tuition for first semester is $225. Fees & deposits: $11/unit for residents, $127/unit for non-residents, $135/unit for international students. Average off-campus housing cost is $500/mo. Admission requirements: HS diploma or equivalent. Scholarships: yes. Loans: yes.

CONTACT: Nader Sharkes, Department Chair, Diablo Valley College, Hotel & Restaurant Management Dept., 321 Golf Club Rd., Pleasant Hill, CA 94523; 925-685-1230 x2252, Fax 925-825-8412, NSharkes@dvc.edu, www.dvc.edu.

EPICUREAN SCHOOL OF CULINARY ARTS

Los Angeles/Year-round

Sponsor: Private school. Program: 9-month Professional Chef certificate program (Pro Chef I & Pro Chef II). Established: 1985. Calendar: semester. Curriculum: culinary. Admit dates: Year-round. Total enrollment: 15. 50 each admission period. 100% of applicants accepted. 100% enrolled part-time. S:T ratio 15:1. Facilities: Teaching kitchen with 5 work stations.

COURSES: Classic French and contemporary cuisines, breads and pastries, food costing, accounting.

FACULTY: 4 part-time instructors are CIA & CCA graduates. Includes Karen Umland, Carol Cotner.

COSTS: $2,800 for Pro Chef I & II. Admission requirements: None.

CONTACT: Diana Tracy, Epicurean School of Culinary Arts, 8759 Melrose Ave., Los Angeles, CA 90069; 310-659-5990, Fax 310-659-0302, epicurean5@aol.com, www.epicureanschool.com.

GLENDALE COMMUNITY COLLEGE

Glendale/August-May

Sponsor: College. Program: 2-year certificates in Culinary Arts, Restaurant Management, Hotel Management, & Dietary Services. Established: 1974. Accredited by State. Calendar: semester. Curriculum: culinary. Admit dates: Aug. Total enrollment: 338. 95% of applicants accepted. 50% enrolled part-time. S:T ratio 35:1. 80-85% of graduates obtain jobs within 6 mos.

COURSES: Restaurant & cost control mgmt, quantity foods & purchasing. Other required courses: wine & beverages, catering, baking, dining room service, intl cooking, nutrition. Externships.

FACULTY: 1 full-time, 5 part-time. Qualifications: BS or MS degree, at least 6 years experience.

COSTS: Annual tuition in-state $13/unit, out-of-state $130/unit. Admission requirements: HS diploma or equivalent.

CONTACT: Yeimei Wang, Prof. of Food & Nutrition and Coordinator, Glendale Community College, Culinary Arts Dept., 1500 N. Verdugo Rd., Glendale, CA 91208; 818-240-1000 x5597, Fax 818-549-9436, ywang@glendale.edu, www.glendale.cc.ca.us.

GROSSMONT COLLEGE

El Cajon/Year-round

Sponsor: 2-year college regional occupational program. Program: 1-year certificate in Culinary Arts, 2-year associate degree in Culinary Arts. Established: 1988. Calendar: semester. Curriculum: culinary, core. Admit dates: Aug, Jan, June. Total enrollment: 350. 150 each admission period. 100% of applicants accepted. 35% receive financial aid. 40% enrolled part-time. S:T ratio 25:1. 95% of graduates obtain jobs within 6 mos. Facilities: Classroom, lab, cafeteria, internships in fine restaurants.

COURSES: Basic, intermediate and advanced culinary skills and knowledge, baking and pastry arts,health/nutrition, culinary competition, professional demeanor and abilities. 2-semester intern/externship with certificate and associate degree.

FACULTY: 11 instructors: 3 executive chefs (2 Culinary Olympic Gold Medal Winners/team members).

COSTS: $12/unit in-state ($180/sem), $121/unit out-of-state ($1,815/sem). Loans: yes.

CONTACT: Joseph Orate, Professor, Coordinator of Culinary Arts Program, Grossmont College, 8800 Grossmont College Dr., El Cajon, CA 92020; 619-644-7469/7550, Fax 619-644-7190, joe.orate@gcccd.net, http://grossmont.gcccd.cc.ca.us/culinaryarts.

HIGH SIERRA CHEFS ASSOCIATION

South Lake Tahoe/Year-round

Sponsor: American Culinary Federation chapter. Program: 3-yr apprenticeship; degree program through Lake Tahoe & Truckee Meadows Community Colleges. Established: 1978. Curriculum: culinary, core. Admit dates: Ongoing. Total enrollment: 12. S:T ratio 12:1. 100% of graduates obtain jobs within 6 mos. Facilities: Community college classrooms, labs & sponsoring property kitchens.

FACULTY: 3 full-time, ACF certified.

COSTS: $185 dues, $500-$1,000 over 3 yrs. Beginning salary is ~$7/hr with increases annually. Housing is $300-$500/mo. Scholarships and employer educational reimbursements offset tuition costs. Admission requirements: HS diploma or equilavent, essay. Scholarships: yes.

CONTACT: Steve Fernald, Culinary Arts Instructor/Apprenticeship Coord., High Sierra Chefs Association, One College Drive, South Lake Tahoe, CA 96150; 530-541-4660 x334, Fax 530-541-7852, fernald@ltcc.cc.ca.us.

IET NATURAL CHEF TRAINING

Cotati & Santa Cruz/Year-round

Sponsor: Private vocational school. Program: 5-mo (450-hr) weekday course or 10-mo (450-hr) weekend course leading to certification in natural foods cooking. Emphasis on nutritional & therapeutic cooking, personal chef training, & mastery of kitchen skills. Established: 1984. Accredited by California Bureau for Private Postsecondary & Vocational Ed. Calendar: semester. Curriculum: culinary. Admit dates: March & September (weekday course), Jan (weekend course). Total enrollment: 36. 99% of applicants accepted. S:T ratio 12:2. 95% of graduates obtain jobs within 6 mos. Facilities: Classrooms with professional kitchens.

COURSES: Hands-on classes in the use of herbs & spices, seasonal, local & organically grown vegetables, fruits, seeds, edible flowers, whole grains, legumes, sea vegetables, chicken, fish, protein alternatives. Seminars, culinary labs & extented ed courses at Calif State Universities.

FACULTY: IET director Edward Bauman, M.Ed., Ph.D; Trish Jacobs, DC; Catherine McConkie, NC; Marcy Roth, NC; Bonnie Tempesta, CNC.

COSTS: $5,600. Admission requirements: HS diploma or equivalent.

CONTACT: IET, 7981 Old Redwood Highway, Suite F, Cotati, CA 94931; 800-987-7530, 707-794-8781, Fax 707-795-3375, iet@sonic.net, www.iet.org.

INSTITUTE OF TECHNOLOGY

Roseville/Year-round

Sponsor: Private school founded in 1994 by Jim & Laura Hines. Program: 8-mo diploma in Culinary Arts. Established: 2002. Accredited by California Private Post Secondary, ACCSCT. Curriculum: culinary, core. Admit dates: Every 5 wks. Total enrollment: 130. 15 each admission period. 95% of applicants accepted. 90% receive financial aid. S:T ratio 15:1. 100% of graduates obtain jobs within 6 mos.

COURSES: Safety & Sanitation, Culinary Accounting, Purchasing, Garde Manger, Buffet Catering, Classical French, Nutrition & Supervision, Baking & Pastry. 180-hr internship, Sacramento-area hotels, country clubs & restaurants.

FACULTY: 4 part-time instructors, 1 full-time director.

COSTS: $9,800. Loans: yes.

CONTACT: Kelly Jean Galvin, Andmissions, Institute of Technology, 333 Sunrise Ave., #400, Roseville, CA 95661; 916-797-6337, Fax 916-797-6338, davalos@it-email.com, www.it-colleges.com. Chef David Avalos, CCE, Director of Culinary Arts, 916-797-6337.

LAGUNA CULINARY ARTS PROFESSIONAL CHEF PROGRAMS

Laguna Beach/Year-round

Sponsor: Private school. Program: 6-mo full-time Professional Chef Program; 20-wk part-time Professional Baking & Pastry Program. Established: 2002. Calendar: quinmester. Curriculum: culinary. Admit dates: Jan, Mar, July, September. 8 each admission period. 75% of applicants accepted. S:T ratio 8:1. 90% of graduates obtain jobs within 6 mos. Facilities: Industry-current kitchen, full-service working bakery.

COURSES: Chef: Intl Cuisines, Baking, Restaurant Mgmt. Baking & Pastry: Breads, Pastries, Desserts, Specialty Cakes, Chocolate, Sugar Work, Candies. Non-paid externships are guaranteed.

Faculty: Chef Program Director Sevan Abdessian, formerly chief chef instructor at the California School of Culinary Arts; Baking & Pastry Program Director Karen Oliphint, a graduate of the CIA-Greystone & pastry chef for 4-star resorts.

Costs: Chef Program $17,500, Baking & Pastry Program $10,750. Includes uniforms, tools, supplies. Admission requirements: HS diploma or equivalent.

Contact: Laguna Culinary Arts, 550 South Coast Hwy., #7, Laguna Beach, CA 92651; 949-494-0745, 888-288-0745, Fax 949-494-0136, nancy@lagunaculinaryarts.com, www.lagunaculinaryarts.com/pages/ProfChefProg.html.

LAKE TAHOE COMMUNITY COLLEGE

South Lake Tahoe/Year-round

Sponsor: Part of California Community College System. Program: 33-wk certificate in Culinary Arts, advanced certificate in Culinary Arts, AA degree in Culinary Arts. Established: 1999. Accredited by WASC. Calendar: quarter. Curriculum: culinary, core. Admit dates: Sept, Jan, Apr. Total enrollment: 60. 24 each admission period. 100% of applicants accepted. 50% enrolled part-time. S:T ratio 12:1. 50% of graduates obtain jobs within 6 mos. Facilities: Newly-equipped culinary arts facilities constructed in 2002.

Courses: Integrated curriculum emphasizing hands-on, business, & human relations skills. Classical cuisine supplemented with a global orientation. Summer externships.

Faculty: One full-time, Certified Chef de Cuisine, former ACF Director of Education. Part-time pastry chefs, winemakers, chefs, business owners.

Costs: ~$300/yr tuition & fees, ~$300/yr for books, uniforms, tools, $300-$500/mo housing expense. Admission requirements: HS diploma or equivalent. Scholarships: yes.

Contact: Stephen C. Fernald, CCC, Instructor, Lake Tahoe Community College, One College Dr., South Lake Tahoe, CA 96150; 530-541-4660 x334, Fax 530-541-7852, fernald@ltcc.cc.ca.us, www.ltcc.cc.ca.us/depts/culinary%5Farts.htm.

LANEY COLLEGE

Oakland/Year-round

Sponsor: Community college. Program: 2-year AA degree in Culinary Arts, 2-year certificate in Retail Baking. Established: 1948. Accredited by WASC. Admit dates: Aug, Jan. Total enrollment: 200. 60 each admission period. 80% of applicants accepted. 70% receive financial aid. 10% enrolled part-time. S:T ratio 12:1. 100% of graduates obtain jobs within 6 mos. Facilities: Include 7 kitchens and classrooms, a student-run restaurant, retail bakery.

Faculty: 5 full-time, 4 part-time.

Costs: Tuition in-state $12/unit, out-of-state $138/unit.

Contact: Wayne Stoker, Culinary Arts Co-Dept. Chair, Laney College, Culinary Arts Dept., 900 Fallon St., Oakland, CA 94607; 510-464-3407, Fax 510-464-3240, wstoker@peralta.cc.ca.us, http://laney.peralta.cc.ca.us. Additional contact: Cleo Ross cross@peralta.cc.ca.us.

LONG BEACH CITY COLLEGE

Long Beach/Year-round

Sponsor: 2-yr college. Program: 18 mo certificate & 2-yr AS degree in culinary arts and commercial baking & pastry. Certificate programs in hotel, restaurant institutional cooking, commercial cake decorating, food prep, professional gourmet cooking. Established: 1949. Accredited by WASC. Total enrollment: ~480. 75% enrolled part-time. S:T ratio 1:30. Facilities: Include 4 demo labs, 4 food production kitchens, gourmet dining room, bake shops.

Courses: Include food prep, nutrition, sanitation, baking & pastry, food services work experience.

Faculty: 5 full-time, 16 part-time.

Costs: $11/cr in-state, $129/cr out-of-state. Scholarships: yes.

Contact: Frank Madrigal, Chef, Long Beach City College, 4901 E. Carson St., Long Beach, CA 90808; 562-938-4471, www.lbcc.cc.ca.us/cg/pdf/culinaryarts.pdf.

LOS ANGELES MISSION COLLEGE

Sylmar/Year-round

Sponsor: 2-year college. Program: 2-year/60-64 unit AAS degree in Culinary Arts. Calendar: semester. Curriculum: core.

Costs: $13/unit in-state, $128/unit out-of-state.

Contact: Sandra Lampert, Los Angeles Mission College, Culinary Arts, Instructional Building, Sylmar, CA 91342; 818-364-7696, Fax 818-364-7755, sandilampert@sbcglobal.net, www.lamission.edu/culinary.

LOS ANGELES TRADE-TECHNICAL COLLEGE

Los Angeles/September-May

Sponsor: College. Program: 2-year (48-unit) certificates and AA degrees in Culinary Arts and Professional Baking. Established: 1927. Accredited by WASC, ACF. Calendar: semester. Curriculum: culinary, core. Admit dates: July/August, December/January. Total enrollment: 280. 90 each admission period. 95% of applicants accepted. 70% receive financial aid. S:T ratio 26:1. 95% of graduates obtain jobs within 6 mos. Facilities: Include 3 kitchens, 6 classrooms.

Courses: Culinary Arts, Professional Baking. Enology, culinary competition, artisan breads, vegetarian cookery, food retailing.

Faculty: 11 full- & 6 part-time. Qualifications: AA degree, ACF certification, industry experience.

Costs: Annual tuition in-state $300+, out-of-state $500+. $600 for tools, uniforms, books. Total expense for 4 semesters is ~$1,500 minimum. Admission requirements: HS graduate or 18 years of age. Scholarships: yes. Loans: yes.

Contact: Carole K. Lung, Associate Dean, Los Angeles Trade-Technical College, Culinary Arts Dept., 400 W. Washington Blvd., Los Angeles, CA 90015; 213-763-7331, culinary@lattc.edu, www.lattc.cc.ca.us.

MODESTO JUNIOR COLLEGE

Modesto/August-May

Sponsor: Public 2-year college. Program: 1-year certificate & 2-year AS degree in Culinary Arts. Established: 1998. Accredited by WASC. Calendar: semester. Curriculum: culinary. Admit dates: Aug. Total enrollment: 30. 30 each admission period. 20% of applicants accepted. S:T ratio 15:1. Facilities: Food production kitchen, bake shop, classroom, lecture room.

Courses: Food purchasing & preparation, intro to food service, international cuisine, menu & facilities design, nutrition, baking & pastry, culinary French, kitchen management, cost control.

Faculty: 1 full-time, 2 part-time.

Costs: $12/unit, 14 units,semester. $125 lab fee. Scholarships: yes. Loans: yes.

Contact: Bob Glatt, CCE, CEC, Chef Instructor, Modesto Junior College – Culinary Arts, 435 College Ave., Modesto, CA 95350; 209-575-6975, Fax 209-575-6989, glattb@yosemite.cc.ca.us, http://mjc.yosemite.cc.ca.us.

NAPA VALLEY COOKING SCHOOL

St. Helena/Year-round *(See also page 215) (See display ad page 32)*

Sponsor: Napa Valley College. Program: 14-mo certificate (Professional Training for Fine Restaurants) that consists of 9 mo's of school & 5 mo's of externship. Established: 1996. Curriculum: culinary. Admit dates: Aug. Total enrollment: 18. 18 each admission period. 75% of applicants accepted. 50% receive financial aid. S:T ratio 9:1. 100% of graduates obtain jobs within 6 mos. Facilities: Modern teaching kitchen.

Courses: Basic to advanced techniques, food & wine education. Special emphasis on skills for entry & advancement in fine restaurants. Externships in Europe, Asia, & the US.

Faculty: Northern California chef-instructors. Guest lecturers include area chefs, growers, specialty food producers, viticulturists, & winemakers. Includes Executive Chef Barbara Alexander & Chef Christopher Mazzanti.

Costs: ~$13,000. Off-campus housing ~$600/mo. Admission requirements: HS diploma or equivalent & industry experience recommended. Scholarships: yes. Loans: yes.

Contact: Barbara Alexander, Executive Chef, Napa Valley Cooking School, 1088 College Ave., St. Helena, CA 94574; 707-967-2930, Fax 707-967-2909, BAlexander@campus.nvc.cc.ca.us, www.napacommunityed.org/cookingschool.

NATIONAL CULINARY & BAKERY SCHOOL

San Diego/Year-round

Sponsor: Private school specializing in training for culinary & baking arts. Program: Accelerated certificate programs in Culinary & Baking Arts. Established: 1994. Curriculum: culinary. Admit dates: Open enrollment all year. 10 max each admission period. 95% of applicants accepted. 5% receive financial aid. S:T ratio 10:1. 100% of graduates obtain jobs within 6 mos. Facilities: 2 commercial culinary kitches, 1 bakery kitchen, classroom, restaurant & banquet facilities.

Courses: Basic to advanced. Hands-on & lecture courses. 50-hour externship offered throughout San Diego. Job placement assistance available. Culinary & Bakery Arts to keep up with industry standards, individual training for practicing professionals.

Faculty: Professional Certified Executive Chefs by the ACF, Professional Chef Assn. & Les Toques Blanch Intl. 30+ years of professional experience.

Contact: National Culinary & Hospitality School, 8400 Center Dr., San Diego, CA 92108; 888-321-CHEF, 619-283-0200, natlschools@nationalschools.com, www.nationalschools.com.

THE NEW SCHOOL OF COOKING

Los Angeles/Year-round

Sponsor: Private school. Program: 20- & 30-wk part-time professional chef's training, 10-wk part-time professional pastry training, recreational classes, kid's camp. Established: 2000. Curriculum:

culinary. Admit dates: Year-round. 12/class each admission period. 100% of applicants accepted. 100% enrolled part-time. S:T ratio 12:1. Facilities: 1,400-sq-ft professional kitchen classroom with instructor demo area & hands-on student work area.

Courses: Professional chef & pastry training focuses on classic culinary technique.

Faculty: Professional chef & CCA graduate Karen Umland Hillenburg & Carol Cotner Thompson. Cindy Mushet, Tante Marie graduate.

Costs: $2,400 Pro 1, $1,200 Pro 2, $1,200 Pro Baking.

Contact: Anne Smith, Director, The New School of Cooking, 8690 Washington Blvd., Culver City, CA 90232; 310-842-9702, annesmith@newschoolofcooking.com, www.newschoolofcooking.com.

ORANGE COAST COLLEGE

Costa Mesa/August-May

Sponsor: College. Program: 1-year certificate, 2-year AA degree. Established: 1964. Accredited by WASC, ACF. Calendar: semester. Curriculum: culinary. Admit dates: Jan, Aug. Total enrollment: 350. 100-125 each admission period. 100% of applicants accepted. 40% enrolled part-time. S:T ratio 15:1. 100% of graduates obtain jobs within 6 mos. Facilities: Full-service cafeteria (seats 300), 80-seat restaurant, full-service bakery.

Courses: Culinary and cook apprenticeship program. 180 hours of work experience required.

Faculty: 15 full-time.

Costs: Tuition in-state $120/yr, out-of-state $102/unit. Admission requirements: HS diploma or equivalent. Scholarships: yes. Loans: yes.

Contact: Bill Barber, Program Coordinator for Culinary Arts, Orange Coast College, Hospitality Dept., 2701 Fairview Blvd., Box 5005, Costa Mesa, CA 92628-5005; 714-432-5835 x2, Fax 714-432-5609, wbarber@mail.occ.cccd.edu, www.occ.cccd.edu.

ORANGE COAST COMMUNITY COLLEGE

Costa Mesa/Year-round

Sponsor: Community College affiliated withAmerican Culinary Federation chapter. Program: 3-yr ACF Apprenticeship Certificate,2-yr Advanced Culinary Certificate, 1-yr Basic Culinary Certificate,AA Degree in Culinary Arts. Established: 1964. Accredited by ACF, WACS. Calendar: semester. Curriculum: culinary, core. Admit dates: Aug,January,June. Total enrollment: 200. 75 each admission period. 100% of applicants accepted. 45% receive financial aid. 65% enrolled part-time. S:T ratio 16 to 1. 95% of graduates obtain jobs within 6 mos. Facilities: Full-service cafeteria seats 300.80-seat restaurant open to the public.

Courses: Basic cooking methods, presentation. Apprentice Program 6,000 hours.Culinary Certificates Internship 160 hours.

Faculty: 6 full-time6 part-time.

Costs: Culinary Certificates - $11/unit + books, uniforms, knives. Apprenticeship - $110 ACF fee, $55/yr + above costs. Beginning salary & increases negotiable. Housing cost is $600-$1,000/mo. Scholarships: yes. Loans: yes.

Contact: Bill Barber, Program Coordinator, Orange Empire Chefs Association, Orange Coast Community College, 2701 Fairview Rd., P.O. Box 5005, Costa Mesa, CA 92628-5005; 714-432-5835 x2, wbarber@mail.occ.cccd.edu, www.orangecoastcollege.com.

OXNARD COLLEGE

Oxnard/August-May

Sponsor: College. Program: 2-year certificate, 2-year degree. Established: 1985. Accredited by WASC. Calendar: semester. Curriculum: culinary, core. Admit dates: Aug, Jan. Total enrollment: 75-125. 30 each admission period. 100% of applicants accepted. 20% receive financial aid. 40% enrolled part-time. S:T ratio 12:1. 95% of graduates obtain jobs within 6 mos. Facilities: Training kitchen with dining room.

Courses: Management of foodservice facilities.

Faculty: 1 full-time, 5 part-time.

Costs: Tuition in-state $11/unit, out-of-state $130/unit. Admission requirements: HS diploma or equivalent. Scholarships: yes. Loans: yes.

Contact: Frank Haywood, Instructor, Oxnard College, Hotel & Restaurant Mgmt., 4000 S. Rose Ave., Oxnard, CA 93033; 805-986-5869, Fax 805-986-5865, fhaywood@vcccd.net, www.oxnardcollege.edu.

QUALITY COLLEGE CULINARY ARTS

Fresno/Year-round

Sponsor: Private career school. Program: 18-wk Culinary Arts program, 12-wk Advanced Baking & Pastry Arts program, 40-wk Food and Beverage Manager certificate program. Established: 1994. Curriculum: culinary, core. Admit dates: Every Monday. Total enrollment: ~40. 82% of applicants accepted. 100% receive financial aid. 10% enrolled part-time. S:T ratio 10:1. 99% of graduates obtain jobs within 6 mos. Facilities: 8,000-sq-ft building with 3 classrooms, 3 labs, fullservice restaurant.

Courses: Stocks & Sauces, Nutrition, Menu Planning, Principals of Cooking, Dairy, Meat Identification & Merchandising, Seafood Identification, Culinary Bakeshop, Dining Room, Garde Manger. Lab/externship. Offered.

Faculty: 5 instructors, three CEC, one CEC & CCE, one Certified Baker.

Costs: $5,000. 100% financing if qualified. Student housing available if outside 150 miles. Admission requirements: 17+ yrs of age. Scholarships: yes. Loans: yes.

Contact: Lon Edwards, Director, Quality College of Culinary Arts, 1570 N. Wishon, Fresno, CA 93728; 559-497-5050, Fax 559-264-4454, director@qualityschool.com, www.qualityschool.com.

SAN DIEGO CULINARY INSTITUTE, INC.

La Mesa/Year-round

Sponsor: Private postsecondary vocational school. Program: 352-hr certificate in Basic Professional Culinary Skills (full- or part-time).1150-hr (30-wk) certificate in Baking & Pastry Arts. Established: 2000. Accredited by State of California. Curriculum: culinary. Admit dates: Rolling. Total enrollment: 120/yr. 50-60 each admission period. 80-90% of applicants accepted. 100% enrolled part-time. S:T ratio 1:16 max. 98% of graduates obtain jobs within 6 mos. Facilities: 5000-sq-ft facility with 2 fully-equipped kitchen class rooms, central kitchen, library, lecture room.

Courses: Culinary program focuses on cooking methods & skills (not recipes). Baking & Pastry program emphasizes classical methods & skills plus production/costs/new products. Baking & Pastry Arts program includes 100-hr paid externship.

Faculty: Must have 5 yrs minimum executive chef experience & teaching skills. Includes founder Harold Meyberg; Exec Chefs Kurt Waefler & Bo Friberg CMPC, Exec Pastry Chef Sara Polczynksi; instructor Ralph Randau. All certified by BPPVE.

Costs: Basic Professional Culinary Skills tuition, books, uniforms, knife kit: $10,130. Baking & Pastry Arts tuition, books, uniforms, tool kit: $18,000. Admission requirements: HS diploma or GED. Scholarships: yes. Loans: yes.

Contact: Harold Meyberg, Founder/President, San Diego Culinary Institute, Inc., 8024 La Mesa Blvd., La Mesa, CA 91941; 619-644-2100, Fax 619-644-2106, info@sdci-inc.com, www.sdci-inc.com. hmeyberg@sdci-inc.com or contact Lili Meyberg: lmeyberg@sdci-inc.com.

SAN FRANCISCO BAKING INSTITUTE

San Francisco/Year-round

Sponsor: Private school. Program: 2-day to 2-week seminars on subjects that includes artisan and holiday breads. Established: 1991. 12-15 max each admission period. 100% of applicants accepted. Facilities: Bakery/classroom with the latest bakery production equipment.

Courses: Include Artisan Breads, Rustic Pastry for the Artisan Baker, Viennoiserie, Holiday Breads. All courses are appropriate for continuing education purposes.

Faculty: Guest instructors include David Norman and Richard Bourdon.

Costs: From $480 for 2-3 day seminars to $750 for week-long seminars.

CONTACT: Didier Rosada, Head Instructor, San Francisco Baking Institute, 390 Swift Ave., #13, South San Francisco, CA 94080; 650-589-5784, Fax 650-589-5729, contact@sfbi.com, www.sfbi.com.

SAN FRANCISCO CULINARY/PASTRY PROGRAM

San Francisco/Year-round

Sponsor: Hotel & Restaurant Employees Local 2 Union/Union Properties. Program: State of California Div of Apprenticeship Standards: Certification as Journeyman Cook. Established: 1976. Curriculum: culinary.

COSTS: Beginning salary is 55% of journeyman wage with 5% increases every 6 mos. Admission requirements: Age 16, HS diploma or GED.

CONTACT: Joan Ortega, Director, San Francisco Culinary/Pastry Program, 760 Market St., #1066, San Francisco, CA 94102; 415-989-8726, Fax 415-989-2920, joanlortega@aol.com.

SAN JOAQUIN DELTA COLLEGE

Stockton/August-May

Sponsor: 2-yr college. Program: 1-sem certificate in Basic Culinary Arts, 3-sem certificate in Advanced Culinary Arts, 4-sem AS degree in Culinary Arts, 2-sem certificate in Dietetic Services Supervisor. Established: 1979. Accredited by ACF, WASC. Calendar: semester. Curriculum: core. Admit dates: Rolling. Total enrollment: 80. 20-30 each admission period. 100% of applicants accepted. 40% receive financial aid. 40% enrolled part-time. S:T ratio 15:1. 90% of graduates obtain jobs within 6 mos. Facilities: 2 kitchens, 2 classrooms, student-run restaurant.

COURSES: Culinary arts, baking, restaurant operations, nutrition, menu planning, purchasing, sanitation/safety, cost technology, garde manger, beverage mgmt. Work experience available.

FACULTY: 2 full-time, 1 part-time. Qualifications: Master's degree. Includes Char Britto, RD, FADA, & John Britto, CEC, CCE.

COSTS: In-state $12/unit, out-of-state $125/unit. Housing is $400/mo. Admission requirements: HS graduate or age 18. Scholarships: yes.

CONTACT: John Britto, Program Coordinator, San Joaquin Delta College, Culinary Arts Dept., 5151 Pacific Ave., Stockton, CA 95207; 209-954-5582, Fax 209-954-5600, jbritto@deltacollege.edu, www.deltacollege.org/div/fchs/cularts.html.

SANTA BARBARA CITY COLLEGE

Santa Barbara/August-May

Sponsor: College. Program: 2-year certificate, 2-year AS degree in Culinary Arts & Restaurant-Hotel Management. Established: 1970. Accredited by WASC, ACF. Calendar: semester. Curriculum: culinary. Admit dates: Fall, spring. Total enrollment: 120. 50 each admission period. 80% of applicants accepted. 60% receive financial aid. S:T ratio 10-15:1. 100% of graduates obtain jobs within 6 mos. Facilities: Include 6 kitchens and classrooms, a gourmet dining room, coffee shop, bake shop, lecture/lab room, cafeteria, and snack shop.

COURSES: International cuisine, wines, bar management, production service, nutrition, meat analysis, garde manger, baking, and restaurant ownership. Paid internships.

FACULTY: 3 full-time, 6 part-time, and 11 lab teaching assistants.

COSTS: Annual tuition in-state $500, out-of-state $3,360. Average off-campus housing cost $350/mo. Admission requirements: HS diploma or equivalent. Scholarships: yes. Loans: yes.

CONTACT: Randy Bublitz, Chairperson, Santa Barbara City College, Hotel/Restaurant & Culinary Dept., 721 Cliff Dr., Santa Barbara, CA 93109-2394; 805-965-0581 #2457, Fax 805-963-7222, bublitz@sbcc.edu, www.sbcc.net.

SANTA ROSA JUNIOR COLLEGE

Santa Rosa/Year-round

Sponsor: College. Program: 1-year certificate. Accredited by WASC. Total enrollment: 25-40. S:T ratio 100. 100% of graduates obtain jobs within 6 mos.

Faculty: 3 full-time, 10 part-time.

Costs: Tuition in-state $12/unit, out-of-state $121/unit + $12/unit enrollment fee.

Contact: Harriett Lewis, Santa Rosa Jr. College, Consumer & Family Studies Dept., 1501 Mendocino Ave., Santa Rosa, CA 95401; 707-527-4395, msalinge@floyd.santarosa.edu, www.santarosa.edu.

SHASTA COLLEGE

Redding/Year-round

Sponsor: 2-year college. Program: 1-year certificate, 2-year AA program. Established: 1966. Calendar: semester. Curriculum: culinary, core. Admit dates: June, Dec, Aug. Total enrollment: 35. 35 each admission period. 100% of applicants accepted. 50% receive financial aid. 50% enrolled part-time. S:T ratio 35:1. 100% of graduates obtain jobs within 6 mos.

Faculty: 1 instructor, Mike Piccinino, a member of the California Chefs Association, Certified Executive Chef, and Certified Culinary Educator.

Costs: $11/sem-cr in-state, $116/sem-cr non-resident. Admission requirements: HS diploma or GED.

Contact: Michael Piccinino, Culinary Arts Instructor, Shasta College, 11555 N. Old Oregon Trail, Redding, CA 96003; 530-225-4829, Fax 530-225-4829, mpiccinino@shastacollege.edu, www.shastacollege.edu. rgerard@shastacollege.edu.

SUSHI CHEF INSTITUTE

Los Angeles; Tokyo/Year-round

Sponsor: Japanese cooking school. Program: 4-wk basic, professional & advanced sushi chef certificate programs; 1-wk intensive & 1-day weekend classes; 4-hr private class. Established: 2002. 15 max each admission period.

Courses: Basic: Japanese culture, traditional cuisine, ingredients, utensils. Professional: rice, fish & roll-sushi preps, decoration & garnish. Advanced: Nigiri sushi & special rolls, fusion dish sauces & decoration, food cost & restaurant operation.

Faculty: Chef Andy Matsuda was head sushi chef at a restaurant in Kobe for 4 years.

Costs: 4-wk courses $2,900 + $100 fee; 1-wk intensive $1,500; 1-day class $80; private class $400. Admission requirements: Basic class completion required for professional class. Professional class completion & 1+ yrs experience as a chef required for advanced class.

Contact: Sushi Chef Institute, 927 Deep Valley Dr., #299, Rolling Hills Estate, CA 90274; 310-544-0863, Fax 310-541-3087, jangle@sushischool.net, www.sushischool.net. Japan school: http://academy.sushi.ne.jp.

TANTE MARIE'S COOKING SCHOOL

San Francisco/Year-round

Sponsor: Small private school. Program: 6-month certificate programs in culinary arts (full-time) & pastry (part-time), nonvocational evening & weekend courses, cooking vacations, cooking parties. Established: 1979. Curriculum: culinary. Admit dates: Apr, Oct. Total enrollment: 24-28. 14 each admission period. 95% of applicants accepted. 5% receive financial aid. 50% enrolled part-time. S:T ratio 14:1. 95% of graduates obtain jobs within 6 mos. Facilities: Tile floors, wooden counters, 6 ovens, 20 burners.

Courses: Culinary courses cover basic French techniques, breads and pastries, desserts, ethnic cuisines, food purchasing and handling, menu planning, and taste development. 4-week externship in a local quality restaurant, bakery, or hotel.

Faculty: Founder Mary Risley studied at Le Cordon Bleu and La Varenne. Guest instructors.

Costs: Tuition is $15,000 for the 6-month culinary certificate course, $6,000 for the 6-month part-time pastry course. Local apartments are available. Admission requirements: HS diploma. Scholarships: yes. Loans: yes.

Location: On San Francisco's Telegraph Hill, near Fisherman's Wharf and public transportation.

Contact: Peggy Lynch, Administrative Director, Tante Marie's Cooking School, 271 Francisco St., San Francisco, CA 94133; 415-788-6699, Fax 415-788-8924, peggy@tantemarie.com, www.tantemarie.com.

WESTLAKE CULINARY INSTITUTE
Westlake Village/Year-round

Sponsor: Private school. Program: 24-session professional series, 5-session baking series, 3-session catering series, certificate granted upon completion. Established: 1988. Curriculum: culinary. Admit dates: Variable. Total enrollment: 36. 12 each admission period. 80% of applicants accepted. 5% receive financial aid. 100% enrolled part-time. S:T ratio 12:1. 90% of graduates obtain jobs within 6 mos. Facilities: 1,500-sq-ft demo/participation facilities with 2 kitchens, cookware store.

COURSES: Include classical food preparation, skills, methods, techniques and presentation, international cuisines, menu costing and planning.

FACULTY: Cecilia DeCastro, CCP, and guest instructors.

COSTS: $2,750 for the professional series, $595 for the baking series, $295 for the catering series. Admission requirements: Commitment, written application, basic skills, attitude.

CONTACT: Phyllis Vaccarelli, Owner/Director, Let's Get Cookin', 4643 Lakeview Canyon Rd., Westlake Village, CA 91361; 818-991-3940, Fax 805-495-2554, lgcookin@aol.com, www.letsgetcookin.com.

COLORADO

ACF CULINARIANS OF COLORADO
11 cities/Year-round

Sponsor: ACF Chapter. Program: 3-yr apprenticeship; degree program through any Colorado community college with 42 semester credit hrs earned. Established: 1970's. Curriculum: culinary. Admit dates: January through May. Total enrollment: 39. 30 each admission period. 100% of applicants accepted. 75% receive financial aid. 100% of graduates obtain jobs within 6 mos. Facilities: Warren Tech Center in Lakewood, Colorado. Courses: Apprentices attend class one night/wk & are required to attend classes in Nutrition, Management & Sanitation.

COSTS: $2,100/three years. Apprentices must maintain a Junior Membership with the ACF for $75/yr. Admission requirements: HS diploma or equivalent, age 17 or older. Scholarships: yes.

CONTACT: Tiffany Brewster, Director of Apprenticeship, ACF Culinarians of Colorado Apprenticeship Program, 1937 Market Street, Denver, CO 80202; 303-308-1611, Fax 303-308-9400, cochefs@prodigy.net, www.acfchefs.org/chapter/co013.html.

THE ART INSTITUTE OF COLORADO – CULINARY ARTS
Denver/Year-round *(See display ad page 135)*

Sponsor: Private school. Program: 12-mo Diploma program in The Art of Cooking, 21-mo AAS degree in Culinary Arts, 39-mo BA degree in Culinary Management. Established: 1994. Accredited by ACICS, ACF. Calendar: quarter. Curriculum: culinary, core. Admit dates: Jan, Apr, July, Oct. Total enrollment: 450. 100 each admission period. 98% of applicants accepted. 75% receive financial aid. 15% enrolled part-time. S:T ratio 20:1. 97% of graduates obtain jobs within 6 mos. Facilities: Include 5 kitchens, classrooms, full dining facility, computer lab.

COURSES: Basic skills, baking & pastry, food production, garde manger, a la carte, dining room, sanitation, nutrition, mgmt, cost control, wines & spirits, facilities design, general ed courses. 1 quarter internship required. Study-abroad program to France offered twice a year for course credit. 11 wk Certificate program, Baking & Pastry.12 mo Diploma program, The Art of Cooking.

FACULTY: 16 full-time, 14 part-time. Qualifications: professional certification, BA degree, 20 yrs experience.

COSTS: $5,472 ($342/cr-hr) quarterly. Application fee $50, enrollment fee $100, $300/quarter lab fee, $925 supply kit. Admission requirements: HS diploma or equivalent & essay. Scholarships: yes. Loans: yes.

CONTACT: Barbara Browning, V.P., Director of Admissions, Art Institute of Colorado-Culinary Arts, 1200 Lincoln Street, Denver, CO 80203; 800-275-2420, Fax 303-860-8520, aicinfo@aii.edu, www.aic.artinstitutes.edu.

COLORADO MOUNTAIN CULINARY INSTITUTE

Keystone & Vail/Year-round *(See also page 219)(See display ad above)*

Sponsor: Colorado Mountain College with Keystone Resort & foodservice operations in Vail. Program: 3-yr (68 semester credit) program: AAS in Culinary Arts & ACF Certificate of Apprenticeship. Established: 1993. Accredited by NCA. Curriculum: culinary, core. Admit dates: June (Keystone), September (Vail). Total enrollment: 70 in 3-yr program. 15-20 each admission period. 40% of applicants accepted. 50% receive financial aid. S:T ratio 6-15:1. 100% of graduates obtain jobs within 6 mos. Facilities: Keystone: Preferred Hotel & Resort with 20+ restaurants. Vail: Sonnenalp Resort, Game Creek Club, Lodge at Vail, & Vail Cascade Hotel, Cascade Resort, Grouse Mountain Grille, LaTour, Larkspur, Ritz-Carlton.

COURSES: 6,000 hrs of structured work experience + 850 hrs of classroom lecture required for graduation. 6,000-hr ACF apprenticeship.

FACULTY: Keystone: Director is Chef Kevin Clarke,CEC; Vail: Director is Todd Rymer,CEC. Each program has 6-10 part-time instructors, all with industry experience.

COSTS: Annual tuition in-district $41/credit, in-state $69/credit, out-of-state $220/credit. $850 initial program fee. Housing $350-$450/mo. Admission requirements: Admission packet, 6 mos work experience, interview, essay, hs/college transcripts. Scholarships: yes. Loans: yes.

CONTACT: Chef Kevin Clarke or Chef Todd Rymer, Directors of Culinary Education, Colorado Mountain Culinary Institute, Admissions, PO Box 10001SG, Glenwood Springs, CO 81602; 800-621-8559, Fax 970-947-8324, JoinUs@coloradomtn.edu, www.coloradomtn.edu.

COOK STREET SCHOOL OF FINE COOKING

Denver/Year-round *(See display ad page 39)*

Sponsor: Private culinary school. Program: 3 mo full-time day & 6 mo part-time evening Food & Wine Career Program in Denver followed by optional 3 wks of travel & culinary education in France & Italy. Short courses & specialty classes also offered. Established: 1999. Licensed by the Colorado Private Occupational School Board. Calendar: trimester. Curriculum: culinary. Admit dates: Day program: Jan, May, Aug. Night program: July. Total enrollment: 24. 24 each admission period. 85% of applicants accepted. 85% receive financial aid. S:T ratio 8:1. 90% of graduates obtain jobs within 6 mos. Facilities: 5,000-sq-ft facility includes 3,000-sq-ft teaching kitchen with commercial-grade equipment & custom-built wood-fired bread oven.

COURSES: Menu-based curriculum explores the principles & techniques of classical European cuisine, including bread & pastry work. Externships available for graduates.

FACULTY: Experienced staff of professional chef-instructors.

COSTS: Tuition $11,850, application fee $150; European tour $5,900. Admission requirements: HS diploma or GED, application, essay, interview. Scholarships: yes. Loans: yes.

CONTACT: Admissions, Cook Street School of Fine Cooking, 1937 Market St., Denver, CO 80202; 303-308-9300, Fax 303-308-9400, info@cookstreet.com, www.cookstreet.com.

COOKING SCHOOL OF THE ROCKIES

Boulder; Provence - Avignon/Year-round

Sponsor: Private school. Program: Full-time 6-mo Professional Culinary Arts diploma program: 5 mos training in Boulder, the 6th month in France. Part-time, 24-wk Chef Track program includes a 6-wk paid externship. 4-wk Professional Pastry Arts program. Established: 1996. Accredited by ACCET; Dept. of Higher Education of the State of Colorado. Calendar: semester. Curriculum: culinary. Admit dates: All. Total enrollment: 16. 16 each admission period. 50% receive financial aid. S:T ratio 8:1. 90% of graduates obtain jobs within 6 mos. Facilities: Modern, fully-equipped professional kitchen.

COURSES: Emphasis on classic & regional French cuisine. Prepare meals/cook daily. Tasting/palate development, including wine knowledge. Exploration of culinary career. Pastry emphasis on classic French patissiere & country-style desserts. Externships may be available for qualified students in local restaurants & catering establishments.

FACULTY: Andrew Floyd, formerly of Occidental Grill; Gallit Sammon, formerly with The Greenbrier Resort; Jason Aili, honors graduate of the California Culinary Academy.

COSTS: $19,500 tuition for full-time culinary program (includes airfare, room & board in France); $3,450 for month-long Pastry Program; $6,850 for 24-wk, part-time Chef Track program (includes 6-wk paid externship). Admission requirements: HS diploma, personal essay, interview. Loans: yes.

CONTACT: Abi Finelli, Director of Admissions & Placement, Cooking School of the Rockies, Professional Culinary Arts Program, 637 S. Broadway, Ste. H, Boulder, CO 80305; 303-494-7988, 877-249-0305, Fax 303-494-7999, abigail@cookingschoolrockies.com, www.cookingschoolrockies.com.

CULINARY INSTITUTE OF COLORADO SPRINGS

Colorado Springs/Year-round

Sponsor: Division of Pikes Peak Community College. Program: 2-yr AAS degree in Culinary Arts, 1-yr certificate in Culinary Arts, 1-yr certificate in Baking. Established: 1986. Accredited by The Higher Learning Commission. Calendar: semester. Curriculum: culinary, core. Admit dates: Aug, Jan, June. Total enrollment: Culinary 170, baking 30. 120 each admission period. 100% of applicants accepted. 75% receive financial aid. 50% enrolled part-time. S:T ratio 15:1. 70% of graduates obtain jobs within 6 mos. Facilities: Includes industrial kitchen & classrooms.

COURSES: Food prod & cooking, catering, buffets, tableside cooking, wine & spirits, soups, sauces, advanced cuisine & garde manger, cake & pastry prep, purchasing, restaurant mgmt, menu planning. Internships with local & state employers. Language classes.

FACULTY: 1 full-time, 5 part-time. Qualifications: ACF certification. Includes George J. Bissonnette, CCE, CEC; Robert Hudson, CSC, Dept. Chair; Michael Paradiso, Heidi Block, Mary Piche, Ken King.

COSTS: In-state $2,500/yr, out-of-state $10,000/yr. Off-campus housing $400+. Admission requirements: Admission test. Scholarships: yes. Loans: yes.

CONTACT: Rob Hudson, Dept. Chair, Culinary Institute of Colorado Springs, BSBS Div., PPCC, 5675 S. Academy Blvd., Colorado Springs, CO 80906; 719-540-7371, Fax 719-540-7453, rob.hudson@ppcc.edu, www.ppcc.edu.

FOOD4THOUGHT FOOD & BEVERAGE STYLING SCHOOL

Denver/Year-round

Sponsor: Food Stylist Jaqueline Buckner. Program: 3-day food styling seminars & private instruction. Certificate/diploma. Established: 1995. Admit dates: Year-round. 6 max each admission period. 75% of applicants accepted. S:T ratio 3:1 max. 90% of graduates obtain jobs within 6 mos. Facilities: Fully-equipped commercial food photography studio with modern kitchen.

Courses: Include working on a professional set, hands-on food prep for the camera, special fx, hot & cold beverages, ice cream, pizza, grill marking, food styling techniques, marketing.

Faculty: Food Stylist Jaqueline Buckner, 20+ yrs styling food for TV & print,

Costs: $3,200/3-day seminar includes meals,supplies, finished 4x5 format film.

Contact: Jacqueline Buckner, Food4Thought Food & Beverage Styling School, 7670 Berwick Ct., Boulder, CO 80301; 303-530-3416, Fax 303-604-2666, Jackie@food4film.com, www.food4film.com.

JOHNSON & WALES UNIVERSITY AT DENVER

Denver/Year-round *(See display ad page 145)*

Sponsor: Private nonprofit career institution (branch campus). Program: 1-year accelerated AAS degree in Culinary Arts for those with a bachelor's degree or higher, 2-year AAS degree in Culinary Arts, 4-year BS degree in Food Service Management. Established: 2000. Accredited by NEASC, ACICS-CCA. Calendar: quarter. Curriculum: culinary. Admit dates: Sept, Dec, Mar. Total enrollment: 539 full time, 14 part time. Facilities: 17,000-sq-ft of kitchen and restaurant space, 4 hot kitchens, bake shop, beverage lab, dining room, computer center, classroom.

Courses: Lab courses, professional development, menu planning, nutrition, sanitation, cost control, garde manger, advanced patisserie/dessert, advanced dining room procedures, international, classical French, & American regional cuisines, stocks & sauces. Co-op & internships offered, 11-week rotation at major U.S. foodservice employers.

Faculty: Includes Christine Stamm, MS, CWE, & James Griffin, MS, CEC, CEC.

Costs: Tuition $18,444, general fee $750. Admission requirements: HS diploma or equivalent. Scholarships: yes. Loans: yes.

Contact: Dave McKlveen, Director of Admissions, Johnson & Wales University at Denver, 7150 Montview Blvd., Denver, CO 80220; 303-256-9300, Fax 303-256-9333, admissions@jwu.edu, www.jwu.edu/denver/index.htm.

MESA STATE COLLEGE

Grand Junction/Year-round

Program: 2-year AAS degree and 1-year certificate of Occupational Proficiency in Culinary Arts. Established: 1998. Calendar: semester. Admit dates: Fall & spring. Total enrollment: 47. 20% enrolled part-time. S:T ratio 8:1. Facilities: Modern kitchen & bakery labs, full-service instructional restaurant.

Courses: Scratch cooking & baking, dining room mgmt, menu planning, food service supervision, cost controls, purchasing, marketing & computer applications for food service. Internships available.

Faculty: 3 full-time, 4 part-time.

Costs: Tuition in-state $812/sem, out-of-state $3,132/sem; program fees $275.

Contact: Daniel Kirby, Dept. Chair, Colorado Culinary Academy, Mesa State College, 2508 Blichmann Ave., Grand Junction, CO 81505; 970-255-2632, Fax 970-255-2650, dkirby@mesastate.edu, www.mesastate.edu/schools/utec/cul.htm.

PUEBLO COMMUNITY COLLEGE

Durango & Pueblo/Year-round

Sponsor: 2-yr college. Program: 5 certificates (15-16 cr) & 69.5 cr-hr AAS degree programs in Culinary Arts & Hospitality Studies. Degree students choose from mgmt, production or hospitality tracks. Established: 1984. Calendar: semester. Curriculum: core. Admit dates: All. Total enrollment: 70. Open each admission period. 100% of applicants accepted. 85% receive financial aid. 30% enrolled part-time. S:T ratio 10:1. 95% of graduates obtain jobs within 6 mos. Facilities:

College's kitchen, dining areas, classrooms; computers in Library Learning Ctr.

COURSES: Food prep, cost controls, purchasing, customer service, merchandising, production, nutrition, sanitation (including HACCP). 270-hr internship, 30-hr work exploration course.

FACULTY: Dept. Chair Carol Himes, M.Ed., FMP, CHE; Chuck Becker, FMP; Lorna Starr-Marsico, AA, Food Svc. Admin; Gwen Speaks, M.Ed., BS.

COSTS: $85/cr-hr in-state, $364/cr-hr out-of-state. Admission requirements: HS diploma or GED. Scholarships: yes. Loans: yes.

CONTACT: Carol Himes, M.Ed., Dept. Chair, Pueblo Community College, 900 W. Orman Ave., Pueblo, CO 81004-1499; 719-549-3071, Fax 719-543-7566, carol.himes@pueblocc.edu, www.pueblocc.edu.

SCHOOL OF NATURAL COOKERY
Boulder

Sponsor: Private trade school specializing in wholefoods, vegetarian cuisine. Program: Personal Chef Training: 4 months.Teacher training: 3 months cooking + practice teaching & observation. Students may set own pace. Established: 1991. Calendar: semester. Curriculum: culinary. Total enrollment: 32/yr. 8 each admission period. 95% of applicants accepted. 10% receive financial aid. 25% enrolled part-time. S:T ratio 4-8:1. 98% of graduates obtain jobs within 6 mos. Facilities: Modern, residential-style kitchen, clients' homes.

COURSES: Technique & theory of cooking without recipes, grains, vegetable protein, meal composition; practice teaching; marketing & self- management, family & gourmet presentation. Restaurant & foodservice externship for qualifying graduates, some animal food cooking. Continuing education: 2-week Vegan Gastronomy for experienced students.

FACULTY: 4 instructors, certified chef, cookbook authors.

COSTS: Foundation Course $8,000 plus $2,300 each for Personal Chef & Teacher Training (discount for both). Admission requirements: HS grad or equivalent or written essay & interview. Scholarships: yes. Loans: yes.

CONTACT: Joanne Saltzman, Director, School of Natural Cookery, P.O. Box 19466, Boulder, CO 80308; 303-444-8068, Fax On request, info@naturalcookery.com, www.naturalcookery.com.

WARREN OCCUPATIONAL TECHNICAL CENTER
Golden/August-May

Sponsor: Public institution. Program: 1-semester (options for 2nd & 3rd semesters) certificate in Restaurant Arts. Established: 1974. Accredited by State, NCA. Calendar: semester. Curriculum: culinary. Admit dates: Aug, Jan. Total enrollment: 60. 45 each admission period. 98% of applicants accepted. 2% receive financial aid. 25% enrolled part-time. S:T ratio 20:1. 95% of graduates obtain jobs within 6 mos. Facilities: Kitchen, 60-student classroom, 2 dining rooms and a restaurant.

COURSES: Production, nutrition, baking, safety & sanitation. Externship provided.

FACULTY: 3 full-time with master's degree in vocational education.

COSTS: Tuition in-state $1,600/semester, out-of-state $2,464/semester. Parking fee $50, materials $10. Off-campus housing cost is $350/mo. Admission requirements: Diploma or GED. Scholarships: yes. Loans: yes.

CONTACT: David Bochmann, Warren Occupational Technical Center, 13300 W. 2nd Place, Lakewood, CO 80228-1256; 303-982-8600, Fax 303-982-8547, dbochman@jeffco.k12.co.us, http://jeffco.k12.co.us.

CONNECTICUT

CENTER FOR CULINARY ARTS
Cromwell/Year-round

Sponsor: Private professional culinary arts school offering ACF-accredited culinary arts programs. Program: 15-mo diploma program in Culinary Arts, 6-mo certificate program in Baking & Pastry Arts. Established: 1997. Accredited by ACCSCT. Calendar: trimester. Curriculum: culinary. Admit dates: Sept, Jan, April for Culinary Arts. October & January for Baking & Pastry Arts. Total enrollment: 110. 36 each admission period. 75% of applicants accepted. 85% receive financial aid. 50% enrolled part-time. S:T ratio 9:1. 95% of graduates obtain jobs within 6 mos. Facilities: Kitchens with the latest professional equipment & cookware, dining room, classrooms.

Courses: Culinary Arts courses follow 3 tracks: Cooking, Baking & Kitchen Management. Courses range from breakfast cookery to classic French, butchery to bakery, preparation to presentation, international cuisine to computers in the kitchen. 2 internship assignments for each culinary arts student. 125+ foodservice establishments participate in the internship program.

Faculty: 5 full-time & 12 adjunct faculty members.

Costs: $14,300-$16,400 for Culinary Arts, $3,800 for Baking & Pastry Arts. Textbooks, knife kit, uniforms & shoes additional. Admission requirements: Interview, passion for cooking. Scholarships: yes. Loans: yes.

Contact: Mike Frechette, Admissions Rep, Center for Culinary Arts, 106 Sebethe Dr., Cromwell, CT 06416; 860-613-3350, Fax 860-613-3353, mfrechette@centerforculinaryarts.com, www.centerforculinaryarts.com.

CONNECTICUT CULINARY INSTITUTE

Farmington & Suffield/Year-round *(See display ad above)*

Sponsor: Private culinary school. Program: Advanced Culinary Arts program (15 mos full-time/22 mos part-time), Professional Pastry & Baking program (8 mos full-time/11 mos part-time). Part-time & eves also available. Established: 1988. Accredited by ACCSCT, State Dept. of Higher Education. Calendar: semester. Curriculum: core. Admit dates: Continuous enrollment. Total enrollment: 200+. 12 each admission period. 88% of applicants accepted. 65% receive financial aid. 38% enrolled part-time. S:T ratio 15:1. 98% of graduates obtain jobs within 6 mos. Facilities: Multiple kitchens, live ChefCam, restaurant labs open-to-the-public, 2,500-volume culinary library, placement office.

Courses: Hands-on, small class size. Students practice techniques in classroom kitchens, school-run restaurants & in paid externship. Advanced Culinary Arts Program includes a 660-hr paid externship. Continuing ed courses include sanitary food handling, nutrition, business, low-cholesterol cooking.

Faculty: Includes 24 full-time chefs, 5 adjunct. Industry experience ~10+ yrs with awards & honors.

Costs: Tuition: Advanced Culinary Arts Program $18,900, Professional Pastry & Baking Program $11,125. Registrationfee $50, materials/supplies $1,125. Admission requirements: HS diploma or equivalent, personal interviews. Scholarships: yes. Loans: yes.

Location: Farmington is between Boston & NYC, near Hartford. Suffield is near Springfield.

Contact: Mike Phelps, Admissions Director, Connecticut Culinary Institute, Talcott Plaza, 230 Farmington Ave., Farmington, CT 06032; 860-677-7869, 800-762-4337, Fax 860-676-0679, ct.culinary.inst@snet.net, www.ctculinary.com. Branch Campus, 1760 Mapleton Ave., Suffield, CT 06078.

DEPT. OF FOOD STUDIES & GASTRONOMY, UNIV. OF NEW HAVEN

West Haven/Year-round *(See display ad above)*

Sponsor: University of New Haven, School of Hospitality & Tourism, Dept. of Food Studies & Gastronomy. Program: BS in Food studies & Gastronomy (121 credits), AS degree in Food Studies & Gastronomy (64 credits), certificate in Gastronomy & Culinary Arts (4 courses, 12 credits, National Sanitation Certificate). Established: 1997. Accredited by NEASC & State. Calendar: semester. Curriculum: culinary, core. Admit dates: Jan, May, Sep. Total enrollment: 40. 20 each admission period. 98% of applicants accepted. 60% receive financial aid. 60% enrolled part-time. S:T ratio ~10:1. 100% of graduates obtain jobs within 6 mos. Facilities: Cooking labs, dining room, computer room, library, university settings.

Courses: Classical cooking techniques with emphasis on health & sanitation principles, gastronomy. 600 hrs practicum & 400 hrs internship required. Weekly seminars with guest chefs.

Faculty: Patrick Boisjot, chair, 25 yrs experience as chef/educator, former head chef/director of French Culinary Institute, NY. 4 full-time faculty.

Costs: $309/credit + lab fees, knife set, jackets & books. Admission requirements: HS diploma & interview. Scholarships: yes. Loans: yes.

Location: Southeast Connecticut shore, accessible from Interstate 95.

Contact: Patrick Boisjot, Director, Dept of Food Studies & Gastronomy, University of New Haven, 300 Orange Ave., West Haven, CT 06516; 203-932-7362/7353, Fax 203-932-7083, maries@newhaven.edu, www.newhaven.edu. Admissions 800-DIALUNH.

GATEWAY COMMUNITY COLLEGE

New Haven/Year-round

Sponsor: College. Program: 1-year certificate in Culinary Arts, 2-year degree in Food Service Management. Established: 1987. Accredited by State, NEASC. Calendar: semester. Curriculum: culinary. Admit dates: Sept, Jan. Total enrollment: 80. 20-30 each admission period. 100% of applicants accepted. 40% receive financial aid. 60% enrolled part-time. S:T ratio 15:1. 100% of graduates obtain jobs within 6 mos. Facilities: Include 1 lab, many classrooms, restaurant.

FACULTY: 2 full-time, 4 part-time.

COSTS: Annual tuition in-state $1,980, out-of-state $5,900. Average off-campus housing $500/mo. Admission requirements: HS diploma or equivalent. Loans: yes.

CONTACT: Stephen Fries, Director, Gateway Community College, Hospitality Mgmt., 60 Sargent Dr., New Haven, CT 06511; 203-285-2175, sfries@gwcc.commnet.edu, www.gwctc.commnet.edu/culinary.html.

MANCHESTER COMMUNITY COLLEGE

Manchester/September-May

Sponsor: 2-yr college. Program: 1-yr certificate in Culinary Arts, AS degree in Foodservice Mgmt, 12-cr Professional Bakers certificate. Established: 1977. Accredited by ACF, NEASC. Calendar: semester. Curriculum: culinary. Admit dates: Sept, Jan. Total enrollment: 200. 200 each admission period. 100% of applicants accepted. 75% receive financial aid. 80% enrolled part-time. S:T ratio 15:1. 100% of graduates obtain jobs within 6 mos. Facilities: 2 commercial kitchens, classrooms, 100-seat dining room.

COURSES: Principles of Cooking, Quantity Food Prod & Purchasing, Intl Foods, Catering Mgmt, Baking & Pastry, Decorative Work, Sanitation & Safety, Applied Nutrition. Externship provided.

FACULTY: 6 full-time with master's degree or equivalents.

COSTS: Tuition in-state $1,155/sem (full time, 12 credits), $3,194 for Culinary Arts certificate 1-yr program. Application fee $20. Admission requirements: HS diploma or equivalent. Scholarships: yes. Loans: yes.

CONTACT: Jayne Pearson, Hospitality Program Chairperson, Manchester Community College, Div of Hospitality Mgmt, Great Path, M.S.#4, Box 1046, Manchester, CT 06040-1046; 860-512-2785, Fax 860-512-2621, jpearson@mcc.commnet.edu, www.mcc.commnet.edu/dept/hospitality.

NAUGATUCK VALLEY COMMUNITY COLLEGE

Waterbury/September-May

Sponsor: 2-yr college. Program: AS degree (4 sem full-time) in Foodservice Mgmt & Hotel Mgmt. Established: 1982. Accredited by NEASC. Calendar: semester. Curriculum: culinary, core. Admit dates: Sept, Jan. Total enrollment: 100. 100% of applicants accepted. 30% receive financial aid. 40% enrolled part-time. S:T ratio 12:1. 100% of graduates obtain jobs within 6 mos. Facilities: Commercial kitchen lab, formal dining room, modern computer labs & classrooms; wine & viticulture lab.

COURSES: Professional food prep & service, mgmt & supervision of foodservice operations, wine study, hotel operations, travel & tourism, hospitality law.

FACULTY: 7 full- & part-time faculty with advanced degrees & industry experience.

COSTS: $1,155/sem in-state full-time (12 cr or more). $309/3-cr course. Admission requirements: Open. Scholarships: yes. Loans: yes.

CONTACT: Todd Jones, Program Coordinator, Naugatuck Valley Community-Technical College, E-519B, 750 Chase Pkwy., Waterbury, CT 06708; 860-575-8175, tjones@nvcc.commnet.edu, http://155.43.16.5/hospman.

NORWALK COMMUNITY COLLEGE

Norwalk/August-May

Sponsor: 2-yr community college. Program: 6-mo & 1-yr 30-credit certificate programs in Culinary Arts, associate degree in Restaurant/Foodservice Management. Established: 1992. Accredited by NEASC. Calendar: semester. Curriculum: culinary, core. Admit dates: Aug, Sept, Jan. Total enrollment: 190. 95 each admission period. 100% of applicants accepted. 50% receive financial aid. 75% enrolled part-time. S:T ratio 16:1. 100% of graduates obtain jobs within 6 mos. Facilities: High-tech fully-equipped kitchen.

COURSES: 2 baking courses, 4 food prep courses, 1 sanitation, 1 safety & maintenance course, 1 nutrition course. 400-hr paid co-op work experience.

FACULTY: 2 full- & 9 part-time instructors.

COSTS: $1,1980/yr tuition & fees, $600 other expenses. Admission requirements: HS diploma &

placement test. Scholarships: yes. Loans: yes.

Contact: Tom Connolly, Coordinator, Hosp. Mgmt. & Culinary Arts, Norwalk Community College, 188 Richards Ave., Norwalk, CT 06854-1655; 203-857-7355, Fax 203-857-3327, nk_connolly@commnet.edu, www.ncc.commnet.edu.

DELAWARE

DELAWARE TECHNICAL & COMMUNITY COLLEGE

Newark/September-May

Sponsor: College. Program: 2-year AAS degree in Culinary Arts, 2-year AAS degree in Foodservice Management. Established: 1994. Accredited by MSA. Calendar: semester. Curriculum: culinary. Admit dates: Aug. Total enrollment: 45. 24 each admission period. 80% of applicants accepted. 50% receive financial aid. 80% enrolled part-time. S:T ratio 12:1. 100% of graduates obtain jobs within 6 mos. Facilities: One training kitchen and dining room.

Faculty: 3 full-time (2 are CEC), 4 part-time (1 is FMP).

Contact: David Nolker, CEC, Dept. Chair, Delaware Technical & Community College, 400 Stanton-Christiana Rd., Newark, DE 19713; 302-453-3757, Fax 302-368-6620, dnolker@hopi.dtcc.edu, www.dtcc.edu.

FLORIDA

ACF CENTRAL FLORIDA CHAPTER – APPRENTICESHIP

Orlando/Year-round

Sponsor: ACF chapter. Program: 3-yr ACF Apprenticeship graduates earn Certified Culinarian from ACF. Accredited by ACF, SACS, COE. Calendar: quinmester. Curriculum: culinary. Admit dates: Aug, Oct, Jan, Mar. Total enrollment: 35. 100% of applicants accepted. S:T ratio 15:1. 100% of graduates obtain jobs within 6 mos. Facilities: Kitchen facility with up-to-date equipment, separate bakery & garde manger areas, classroom/dining room.

Courses: Intro to Foodservice Industry, Sanitation, Food Prep, Food & Beverage Service, Nutrition, Menu Planning, Garde Manger, Purchasing, Baking, Supervisory Mgmt. 6,000 hrs of on-the-job training over the 3 yrs.

Faculty: David W. Weir, CEC, CCE, Apprenticeship Coordinator, full time instructor.

Costs: $300. Beginning salary is $6.50/hr with 25 cent increases annually. Admission requirements: HS diploma or GED, age 17 min.

Contact: David Weir, CEC, CCE, Culinary Apprenitceship Coordinator, ACF Central Florida Chapter, Mid Florida Tech, Culinary Arts, 2900 W. Oak Ridge Rd., Orlando, FL 32809; 407-855-5880 #2286, Fax 407-251-6197, weird@ocps.k12.fl.us, http://mft.ocps.k12.fl.us.

ACF GULF TO LAKES CHEFS CHAPTER

Eustis/Year-round

Sponsor: American Culinary Federation chapter. Program: 3-yr apprenticeship; degree program through Lake County Vocational Tech Center. Curriculum: culinary. Total enrollment: 16.

Costs: Costs are paid by school. Beginning salary is subject to local wage scale with 25 cent increases every 6 mos.

Contact: James Aro, CEC, Chef Instructor, ACF Gulf to Lakes Chefs Chapter, 2001 Kurt St., Eustis, FL 32726-0616; 352-589-2250 x152, chefrotz@earthlink.net, www.gulftolakeschefs.com.

ACF PALM BEACH COUNTY CHEFS

Palm Beach Gardens/Year-round

Sponsor: ACF chapter. Program: 3-yr apprenticeship; degree program through Palm Beach Community College is completed by 80%. Curriculum: culinary. Total enrollment: 28.

Costs: $300/yr. Beginning salary is $6/hr with 50 cent increases every 6 mos. Housing is $400/mo.

CONTACT: Dominick Laudia, CEC, ACF Palm Beach County Chefs, PO Box 970206, Boca Raton, FL 33497-0206; 561-712-3426, Chefnooch@aol.com, www.acfpalmbeach.com.

ACF TREASURE COAST CHAPTER

Stuart/Year-round

Sponsor: ACF chapter. Program: 3-yr apprenticeship. Curriculum: culinary. Total enrollment: 30.

COSTS: $160+texts & materials. Beginning salary is $5-$6/yr with increases every 3 mos.

CONTACT: E. Scott Sibley, President, ACF Treasure Coast Chapter, 321 Shady Lane, Port Saint Lucie, FL 34952; 772-340-0339, tcchefs@hotmail.com.

ART INSTITUTE OF FT. LAUDERDALE – SCHOOL OF CULINARY ARTS

Ft. Lauderdale/Year-round *(See display ad page 135)*

Sponsor: Proprietary school. Program: 12-month diploma in The Art of Cooking, 18-month AS degree program in Culinary Arts, 36-month program in Culinary Management. Established: 1991. Accredited by ACCSCT, ACF. Calendar: quarter. Curriculum: culinary, core. Admit dates: Jan, Apr, July, Oct. Total enrollment: 350. 60-100 each admission period. 90% of applicants accepted. 80% receive financial aid. S:T ratio 19:1. 98% of graduates obtain jobs within 6 mos. Facilities: 4 kitchens & classrooms, student-run restaurant.

COURSES: Includes basic cooking, product identification, baking & pastry, knife skills, nutrition, garde manger, international cuisine, menu planning, wine appreciation, restaurant service.

FACULTY: 10 full-time ACF-certified instructors.

COSTS: Tuition $350/cr. Application fee $50. On-campus housing $1,395/quarter. Off-campus housing ~$600/mo. Admission requirements: HS diploma or equivalent. Scholarships: yes. Loans: yes.

CONTACT: Klaus Friedenreich, Master Chef, Art Institute of Ft. Lauderdale-School of Culinary Arts, 1799 S.E. 17th St., Ft. Lauderdale, FL 33316; 954-463-3000 x708/800-275-7603 x708, Fax 954-728-8637, friedenk@aii.edu, www.aifl.artinstitutes.edu. Eileen Northrop 954-463-3000 X 420.

ATLANTIC TECHNICAL CENTER OF GREATER FT. LAUDERDALE

Coconut Creek/Year-round

Sponsor: Public institution. Program: 1,050-hour certificate in Culinary Arts. Established: 1976. Accredited by COE, ACF. Calendar: quarter. Curriculum: core. Admit dates: Open. Total enrollment: 80. 65 each admission period. 90% of applicants accepted. 35% receive financial aid. 35% enrolled part-time. S:T ratio 12:1. 95% of graduates obtain jobs within 6 mos. Facilities: Student-run restaurant, private function room, cafeteria, 3 kitchens, computer lab, 2 classrooms, media center.

COURSES: Hot & cold foods, bakery, nutrition, sanitation, supervision, dining room mgmt, purchasing, wine & beverage, catering. Industry Cooperative Education.

FACULTY: 6 full-time, 1 CEC & CCE, 1 CMB.

COSTS: Program tuition $2,052; books, uniforms $145. Admission requirements: Admission test & basic academic skills. Scholarships: yes. Loans: yes.

CONTACT: Martin Wilcox, CEC. CCE., Department Head, Atlantic Technical Center, Culinary Arts, 4700 N.W. Coconut Creek Pkwy., Coconut Creek, FL 33066; 954-977-2066, Fax 954-977-2019, wilcox_m@firn.edu, www.atlantictechcenter.com. Susan Tretakis, Program Counselor, 954-977-2087.

CAPITAL CULINARY INSTITUTE OF KEISER COLLEGE

Tallahassee/Year-round

Sponsor: 4-year private college with 8 locations in Florida. Program: 2-year AS degree in Culinary Arts. Continuing education courses. Established: 1977. Accredited by SACS, ACF. Calendar: trimester. Curriculum: culinary, core. Admit dates: Rolling admissions every 4 weeks. 18 each admission period. 80% of applicants accepted. 90% receive financial aid. S:T ratio 13:1. 90% of graduates obtain jobs within 6 mos. Facilities: 4 full kitchens, 115-seat banquet room.

COURSES: Include: Baking & Pastry, French Cuisine, International Cuisine, American Regional Cuisine, Food Service, Dining Service, Stocks & Sauces. 12 cr-hr culinary arts externship required.

FACULTY: 4 full & 3 part-time faculty, 1 full-time Dean.

COSTS: $5,060 for day students, $4,220 for night students. Admission requirements: HS completion or GED, entrance exam & interview. Scholarships: yes. Loans: yes.

CONTACT: Jim Wallis, Director of Admissions, Capital Culinary Institute of Keiser College, 1700 Halstead Blvd., Tallahassee, FL 32308; 850-906-9494, 877-CHEF-123, Fax 850-906-9497, admissions-tal@keisercollege.edu, www.capitalculinaryinstitute.com.

CHARLOTTE TECHNICAL CENTER

Port Charlotte/August-June

Sponsor: Technical post-secondary school. Program: Certificate of completion (1,500 hrs, 5 quarters) in Commercial Foods & Culinary Arts. Established: 1980. Accredited by COE. Calendar: quarter. Curriculum: culinary. Admit dates: July, Oct, Jan, Mar. Total enrollment: 30. 99% of applicants accepted. 75% receive financial aid. S:T ratio 10:1. 100% of graduates obtain jobs within 6 mos. Facilities: Fully equipped kitchen, lab, classroom.

COURSES: Cooks Assistant, Commercial Cook, Specialty Cook. Cooperative jobs available. Part-time specialty courses in Breakfast/Baking/Buffet & Salads/Commercial Cook.

FACULTY: 3 full-time faculty, 1 part-time aide.

COSTS: ~$600/quarter. Admission requirements: T.A.B.E. assessment. Scholarships: yes.

CONTACT: Dick Santello, Admissions Counselor, Charlotte Technical Center, 18300 Toledo Blade Blvd., Port Charlotte, FL 33948-3399; 941-255-7500, Fax 941-255-7509, Richard_Santello@ccps.k12.fl.us, http://CharlotteTechCenter.ccps.k12.fl.us.

DAYTONA BEACH COMMUNITY COLLEGE

Daytona Beach/Year-round

Sponsor: 2-year college. Program: AAS degree in Culinary Management, 18- to 24-month program. Established: 1997. Accredited by SACS. Calendar: semester. Curriculum: culinary, core. Admit dates: August (Fall) and January (Spring). Total enrollment: 80. 20-30 each admission period. 99% of applicants accepted. 80% receive financial aid. 25% enrolled part-time. S:T ratio 12:1. 85% of graduates obtain jobs within 6 mos. Facilities: Production, baking and lab kitchen.

COURSES: Food Production I and II, Baking, Garde Manger, American and International Cuisine, Sanitation, Food and Beverage Cost Control. Internship: one-semester (6 credit hours).

FACULTY: 3 full-time & 5 part-time faculty. All are credentialed & have years of industry experience.

COSTS: $50.36 per credit hour for Florida residents, $187.32 per credit hour for non-resident. (64 credit hours total) Uniform/tools $400, lab fees $50 per food production class. Admission requirements: HS diploma or equivalent. Scholarships: yes. Loans: yes.

CONTACT: Jeff Conklin, CEC, Program Manager, Daytona Beach Community College, P.O. Box 2811; Bldg #39, Room #149, Daytona Beach, FL 32120-2811; 904-255-8131 #3735, Fax 904-254-3063, conklij@dbcc.cc.fl.us, www.dbcc.cc.fl.us.

FLORIDA CULINARY INSTITUTE

West Palm Beach/Year-round

Sponsor: Proprietary institution, a division of New England Institute of Technology at Palm Beach. Program: 18-mo AS degree programs in Culinary Arts, International Baking & Pastry, and Food & Beverage Management. Established: 1987. Accredited by ACF, COE. Calendar: quarter. Curriculum: culinary, core. Admit dates: Jan, Apr, July, Oct. Total enrollment: 600. 200 each admission period. 95% of applicants accepted. 75% receive financial aid. S:T ratio 18:1. 100% of graduates obtain jobs within 6 mos. Facilities: Include 8 kitchens & 9 classrooms, Cafe Protege gourmet restaurant.

COURSES: 6 quarters including food preparation, facilities planning, nutrition, purchasing, baking, classical American & international cuisine, management. Day, afternoon, & evening classes meet 5 hrs daily, Mon-Thur. Continuing education courses & seminars available.

FACULTY: 20 full-time. Includes Dean of Culinary Education David Pantone, CEPC, CCE, AAC Chairman of Culinary Education John Carlino CEC, CCE, Michael Barber, CCE, Dan Birney,

CCE, August Carreiro, CEC, CCE, Manfred Schmidtke, CMB, Jeffrey Baron, CEC, CCE.

COSTS: $16,000/academic yr. Off-campus housing ~$350-$500/mo. Admission requirements: HS diploma or equivalent. Advanced credit awarded through a testing program. Scholarships: yes. Loans: yes.

CONTACT: David Conway, Associate Director of Culinary Admissions, Florida Culinary Institute, 2400 Metrocentre Blvd., West Palm Beach, FL 33407-9985; 800-TOP-CHEF (867-2433), 561-842-8324, Fax 561-842-9503, dconway@floridaculinary.com, www.floridaculinary.com.

GULF COAST COMMUNITY COLLEGE

Panama City/Year-round

Sponsor: 2-yr college. Program: 2-yr AS degree in Culinary Mgmt. Established: 1988. Accredited by SACS, ACF. Calendar: semester. Curriculum: core. Admit dates: Fall, spring. Total enrollment: 70. 20 each admission period. 100% of applicants accepted. S:T ratio 16:1. Facilities: student-run restaurant.

FACULTY: 2 full-time, 1 part-time. John Holley, CCE; Jon Bullard, CCE; Jimmy Walsh, CCC.

COSTS: Tuition in-state $49/credit, out-of-state $183/credit. Lab fees $8-$9. Admission requirements: HS diploma or equivalent. Scholarships: yes. Loans: yes.

CONTACT: Richard Stewart, Chair/Coordinator, Business/Culinary, Gulf Coast Community College, Culinary Mgmt., 5230 W. U.S. Hwy 98, Panama City, FL 32401; 850-872-3850, Fax 850-913-3319, rstewart@ccmail.gc.cc.fl.us, www.gc.cc.fl.us.

HILLSBOROUGH COMMUNITY COLLEGE

Tampa/Year-round

Sponsor: Community college. Program: 2-yr (64-cr-hr) AS degree in Culinary Arts. Established: 1984. Accredited by ACF, SACS. Calendar: semester. Curriculum: core. Admit dates: Aug, Jan, May, July. Total enrollment: 51. Varies each admission period. 98% of applicants accepted. 60% receive financial aid. 85% enrolled part-time. S:T ratio 12:1. 100% of graduates obtain jobs within 6 mos.

FACULTY: 1 full-time, 3 part-time.

COSTS: $48.50/cr-hr. Admission requirements: HS diploma or equivalent. Scholarships: yes. Loans: yes.

CONTACT: George Pastor, Ed.D., CEC, CCE, Dept. Chair, Hillsborough Community College, 4001 Tampa Bay Blvd., Tampa, FL 33614; 813-253-7316, GPastor@hcc.cc.fl.us, www.hcc.cc.fl.us.

INSTITUTE OF THE SOUTH FOR HOSPITALITY & CULINARY ARTS

Jacksonville/Year-round

Sponsor: 2-yr college. Program: 2-yr AS degree. Established: 1990. Accredited by SACS, ACF, CHRIE. Calendar: semester. Curriculum: culinary, core. Admit dates: Aug, Jan. Total enrollment: 130. 40 each admission period. 98% of applicants accepted. 30% receive financial aid. 80% enrolled part-time. S:T ratio 15:1. 98% of graduates obtain jobs within 6 mos. Facilities: 3 kitchens, 4 classrooms, 2 restaurants.

COURSES: Culinary courses. 2 externships at 300 hrs, throughout the community at major properties.

FACULTY: 4 full-time, 6 part-time. Includes Chefs Ron Wolf, Rick Grigsby, Joe Harrold & Brad Duffell. Qualifications: ACF certified. Professor Margaret Wolson.

COSTS: Annual tuition in-state $832, out-of-state $3,328. Admission requirements: HS diploma or equivalent. Scholarships: yes. Loans: yes.

CONTACT: Richard Donnelly, Instructional Program Manager, Florida Community College at Jacksonville, Inst. of the South for Hospitality & Culinary Arts, 4501 Capper Rd., Jacksonville, FL 32218; 904-766-5572, Fax 904-713-4858, bwright@fccj.org, www.fccj.org.

JOHNSON & WALES UNIVERSITY AT NORTH MIAMI

North Miami/Year-round *(See display ad page 145)*

Sponsor: Private nonprofit career institution (branch campus). Program: 2-year AS in Culinary Arts and Baking & Pastry Arts, 4-year BS program in Culinary Arts. Established: 1992. Accredited by NEASC. Calendar: quarter. Curriculum: culinary, core. Admit dates: Rolling. Total enrollment: 870 full time; 62 part time. ~80% of applicants accepted. ~80% receive financial aid. 5% enrolled part-time. S:T ratio 20:1. 98% of graduates obtain jobs within 6 mos. Facilities: Laboratory kitchens, academic classrooms, library, computer laboratory, conference center.

COURSES: Culinary fundamentals, advanced culinary technologies, culinary principles, professional studies & academic courses. Term-long internships scheduled for all Baking & Pastry, Culinary, Hotel-Restaurant majors. Continuing education: The Culinary Arts Weekend program.

FACULTY: 27 full-time, 5 part-time.

COSTS: College of Culinary Arts annual tuition $18,444. Other costs: $750 general fee, $200 orientation fee, on-campus housing $6,777. Admission requirements: HS diploma or equivalent. Scholarships: yes. Loans: yes.

CONTACT: Jeffrey Greenip, Director of Admissions, Johnson & Wales University at North Miami, Admissions Office, 1701 N.E. 127th St., North Miami, FL 33181; 800-232-2433, Fax 305-892-7020, admissions@jwu.edu, www.jwu.edu/florida.

MARCHMAN TECHNICAL EDUCATION CENTER

New Port Richey/September-June

Sponsor: Private trade-technical school. Program: 1-year (6 hours/day) and 2-year (3 hours/day) certificate programs in Commercial Foods. Established: 1984. Calendar: semester. Curriculum: culinary, core. Admit dates: Aug, Jan. Total enrollment: 60. 60 each admission period. 90% of applicants accepted. 10% receive financial aid. S:T ratio 30:2. 90% of graduates obtain jobs within 6 mos. Facilities: Full commercial kitchen and classroom, 300-seat dining facility.

COURSES: Encompasses all facets of food business: cooking and managerial. Articulation with Johnson and Wales in Miami, Florida for HS students.

FACULTY: 1 instructor with 20+ years restaurant experience.

CONTACT: Peter Kern, Commercial Foods Instructor, Marchman Technical Education Center, 7825 Campus Dr., New Port Richey, FL 34653; 727-774-1700, Fax 727-774-1791, jwhitake@pasco.k12.fl.us, http://mtec.pasco.k12.fl.us.

MCFATTER SCHOOL OF CULINARY ARTS

Davie/Year-round *(See display ad above)*

Sponsor: Public, post-secondary occupational educational facility. Program: 1-year certificate. Established: 1996. Accredited by COE. Calendar: quarter. Curriculum: culinary, core. Admit dates: Each 9-week term. Total enrollment: 50. 10-20 each admission period. 100% of applicants accepted. 50-75% receive financial aid. 10% enrolled part-time. S:T ratio 20:1. 100% of graduates obtain jobs within 6 mos. Facilities: Cafeteria, cafe, dining room.

COURSES: Baking & pastries, food production, garde manger, service. Other required courses: 30 hours each of sanitation, nutrition, supervisory management.

FACULTY: 2 full-time, 2 part-time. Includes Program Coordinator/Dept. Head V. Paul Citrullo, Jr., CEC, Chef Kay Bolm, Chef Rolf Stahli CEPC, Chef Bruce Utieri.

COSTS: Tuition is $501/9-wk term (270 hrs) full time. Other costs include books, uniforms, supplies. Admission requirements: Basic skills testing. Scholarships: yes.

LOCATION: 5 miles from Ft. Lauderdale.

CONTACT: V. Paul Citrullo, Jr., CEC, Exec. Chef/Director of Culinary Arts, McFatter Vocational Tech Center, 6500 Nova Dr., Davie, FL 33317; 954-382-6543, Fax 954-370-1647, chefpaul2@yahoo.com, www.mcfattertech.com/culinary.htm.

MIAMI LAKES EDUCATIONAL CENTER

Miami Lakes/Year-round

Sponsor: Trade-technical HS & adult voc center. Program: 13- to 14-mo (1,500-hr) diploma program in Culinary Arts, including Cooking (750 hrs) & Baking (750 hrs). Transfers to other area institutions receive 1-yr credit. Established: 1978. Accredited by COE, SAACS. Calendar: trimester. Curriculum: culinary. Admit dates: Jan, Apr, July, Oct. Total enrollment: 40. 8-10 each admission period. 80% of applicants accepted. 40% receive financial aid. S:T ratio 16:1. 80-85% of graduates obtain jobs within 6 mos. Facilities: Full kitchen & bake shop. Classrooms with modern equipment.

COURSES: Hands-on culinary arts. Food safety manager class. On-the-job training & industrial coop education available.

FACULTY: 2 certified instructors, 1 for baking & 1 for cooking.

COSTS: ~$600/trimester. Admission requirements: 2-wk orientation class. Scholarships: yes. Loans: yes.

CONTACT: Manny Delgado, CCE, CEC, CFE, Chef Instructor, Miami Lakes Technical Education Center, 5780 N.W. 158th St., Miami Lakes, FL 33014; 305-557-1100 Ext. 2264, Fax 305-557-7391, mannyd@gate.net, http://mlec.dadeschools.net/culinary_arts.html. Additional e-mail: delgadoM@mlec.dadeschools.net.

MID-FLORIDA TECHNICAL INSTITUTE

Orlando/Year-round

Sponsor: Institution. Program: 1,500-hour certificate. Established: 1970. Accredited by SACS, COE. Admit dates: Open. Total enrollment: 50. 50 each admission period. 100% of applicants accepted. 25% receive financial aid. 15% enrolled part-time. S:T ratio 15-20:1. 100% of graduates obtain jobs within 6 mos. Facilities: Full kitchen for hands-on lab.

COURSES: Job entry level. Available for HS students. Apprenticeship.

FACULTY: 2 full-time instructors.

COSTS: $630/semester full time, $315/semester part time. Scholarships: yes. Loans: yes.

CONTACT: Gerald Krotky, Chef Instructor, Mid-Florida Technical Institute, Commercial Cooking-Culinary Arts, 2900 W. Oakridge Rd., Orlando, FL 32809; 407-855-5880 x2285, Fax 407-251-6197, krotkyg@ocps.k12.fl.us, http://mft.ocps.k12.fl.us.

ORLANDO CULINARY ACADEMY – LE CORDON BLEU

Orlando/Year-round *(See display ad page 115)*

Sponsor: Career culinary academy. Program: 15-mo AOS degree in Le Cordon Bleu Culinary Arts. Established: 2002. Accredited by ACICS. Curriculum: culinary, core. 95% of applicants accepted. 95% receive financial aid. S:T ratio 16:1. Facilities: 4 demo/interactive kitchens with computer monitors, 5 prod kitchens, 175-seat student-operated fine dining restaurant, on/off-site catering, computer lab, retail store.

COURSES: French classical culinary program with progressive learning year. Block system of instruction including: basics through Principles of European & Asian Cuisine to Advanced Garde Manger, Baking & Pastry. Externships available in resorts, hotels & upscale restaurants under supervision of a professional chef or mgr.

COSTS: $31,800. Application fee $100, graduation fee $200, books, uniforms & equipment ~$1,500. Admission requirements: HS transcript or GED, personal interview with application & essay. Scholarships: yes. Loans: yes.

CONTACT: Leigh Hughes, Director of Admissions, Orlando Culinary Academy, 8511 Commodity Circle, Orlando, FL 32819; 866-OCA-CHEF, 407-888-4000, Fax 407-888-4019, lhughes@orlando-culinary.com, www.orlandoculinary.com.

PENSACOLA JR. COLLEGE CULINARY MANAGEMENT PROGRAM
Pensacola/Year-round

Sponsor: College. Program: 2-yr (64-cr-hrs) AAS degree. Established: 1995. Accredited by SACS, ACF. Calendar: semester. Curriculum: culinary, core. Admit dates: Fall, spring, summer. Total enrollment: 75. S:T ratio 14:1. Facilities: Enlarged, updated culinary & baking labs, student-run restaurant.

Courses: Culinary Skills, Basic & Advanced Baking, Intll Cuisines, Classical Production & Service. Competition opportunities. 1 cr-hr.

Faculty: Chef Travis Herr CEC,CCE, Coordinator/Instructor; Chef Bill Hamilton CEC,CCE.

Contact: Travis Herr CEC,CCE, Pensacola Jr. College, Culinary Management, 1000 College Blvd., Pensacola, FL 32504; 850-484-2506, therr@pjc.edu, www.pjc.edu.

PINELLAS TECHNICAL EDUCATIONAL CENTER
N. Clearwater/Year-round

Sponsor: Technical center. Program: 13-month diploma in Culinary Arts. Established: 1965. Accredited by ACF, COE. Calendar: trimester. Curriculum: culinary. Admit dates: Monthly. Total enrollment: 50. 6-10 each admission period. 100% of applicants accepted. 75% receive financial aid. S:T ratio 15:1. 100% of graduates obtain jobs within 6 mos. Facilities: Include 2 kitchens, 2 classrooms and a student-run restaurant.

Faculty: 4 full-time.

Costs: Tuition in-state $1.25/student contact hour, ~$375/trimester. Average off-campus housing cost $350/mo. Admission requirements: Admission test. Scholarships: yes. Loans: yes.

Contact: Vincent Calandra CCE, Dept. Chair, Pinellas Technical Educational Center, Culinary Arts Dept., 6100 154th Ave., N. Clearwater, FL 33760; 813-538-7167 x1140, Fax 813-538-7203, vcalandra@ptecclw.pinellas.k12.fl.us, www.ptecclw.pinellas.k12.fl.us.

PINELLAS TECHNICAL EDUCATIONAL CENTER
St. Petersburg/Year-round

Sponsor: Trade school. Program: 1,800-hour diploma in Culinary Arts. Accredited by SACS. Admit dates: Open. Total enrollment: 52. 10 each admission period. 100% of applicants accepted. 60% receive financial aid. S:T ratio 17:1. 95% of graduates obtain jobs within 6 mos. Facilities: Include kitchen, baking lab and classroom.

Faculty: 2 full-time, 1 part-time. Includes Dr. Warren Laux, Dr. Tom Maas, Alvin Miller, Fred Lemiesz.

Costs: Annual tuition $495 resident. Books $42. Admission requirements: Admission test.

Contact: Victoria Butler, Pinellas Technical Educational Center, Culinary Arts Dept., 901 34th St. South, St. Petersburg, FL 33711; 727-538-7167 x1020, VButler@ptec.pinellas.k12.fl.us, www.ptecclw.pinellas.k12.fl.us.

ROBERT MORGAN VOC TECH INSTITUTE
Miami/Year-round

Sponsor: Dade County Public School. Program: Two 15-wk trimester courses in Commercial Cooking (800 hrs) & Commercial Baking (700 hrs), 212-hr course in Cake Decoration. Established: 1979. Accredited by SACS, COE. Calendar: trimester. Curriculum: culinary. Admit dates: Open. Total enrollment: 220-250. 50 each admission period. 100% of applicants accepted. 30% receive financial aid. 30% enrolled part-time. S:T ratio 15:1. 95% of graduates obtain jobs within 6 mos.

Courses: Food preparation & presentation, safety, sanitation, use of leftovers, storage, customer relations, employability, personal hygiene, menu planning, principles of entrepreneurship.

Faculty: 3 full- and 2 part-time Florida certified instructors.

Costs: $1.20/hr in-state, $3.25/hr out-of-state, $5.25/hr part-time. Admission requirements: 10th grade. Scholarships: yes. Loans: yes.

Contact: Giorgio Moro, Food Services Coordinator, Robert Morgan Vocational Technical Institute, Culinary Arts Program-18180 SW 122nd Ave., Miami, FL 33177; 305-253-9920 x197, Fax 305-253-3023, gmoro@dadeschools.net, www.dade.k12.fl.us/8911.

SARASOTA COUNTY TECHNICAL INSTITUTE

Sarasota

Sponsor: Institution. Program: 2 yr/1,485-hour certificate. Established: 1967. Accredited by SACS. Admit dates: Open. 90% of applicants accepted. 100% of graduates obtain jobs within 6 mos.

Faculty: 1 full-time.

Costs: $2,055/yr in-state, $10,080/yr out-of-state.

Contact: Dee Zulauf, Sarasota County Technical Institute, Culinary Arts, 4748 Beneva Rd., Sarasota, FL 34233; 941-924-1365 x312, dee_zulauf@sarasota.k12.fl.us, www.sarasotatech.org.

SHERIDAN VOC-TECH CENTER

Hollywood/Year-round

Program: 1,500-hr Commercial Foods & Culinary Arts program. Established: 1968. Total enrollment: 100. 60% enrolled part-time. S:T ratio 15:1. Facilities: Demo lab, food production kitchen, teaching kitchen, dining room, computer labs.

Courses: Include food prep & serving, baking, commercial food service equipment, food purchasing & costing.

Faculty: 4 full-time, 2 part-time.

Costs: $917/semester.

Contact: Guidance Office, Sheridan Voc-Tech Center, Culinary Arts Program, 5400 Sheridan St., Hollywood, FL 33021; 954-985-3245/3262, Fax 954-985-3229, sheridan@sheridantechnical.com, www.sheridantechnical.com.

SOUTH FLORIDA COMMUNITY COLLEGE

Avon Park/August-June

Sponsor: College. Program: Vocational certificate in Food Management, Production, & Services. AS degree in Hospitality Management. Established: 1965. Accredited by SACS. Calendar: semester. Curriculum: culinary. Admit dates: Aug, December. Total enrollment: 15-30. Varies each admission period. 75-80% of applicants accepted. 50% enrolled part-time. S:T ratio 12:1. 80-90% of graduates obtain jobs within 6 mos. Facilities: College-owned historic Hotel Jacaranda, in downtown Avon Park.

Courses: Food production, general hospitality and education.

Faculty: 1 full- and 2 part-time.

Contact: Professor of Hospitality Management, South Florida Community College, 600 W. College Dr., Avon Park, FL 33825; 941-453-6661 x337, Fax 941-453-8023, info@sfcc.cc, www.sfcc.cc.fl.us.

THE SOUTHEAST INSTITUTE OF CULINARY ARTS

St. Augustine/Year-round

Sponsor: A division of the First Coast Technical Institute. Program: 18-mo (1,500-hr) certificate & diploma program. Established: 1970. Accredited by ACF, COE, SACS. Calendar: quinmester. Curriculum: culinary, core. Admit dates: Every 9 wks. Total enrollment: 600+. 15-20 each admission period. 95% of applicants accepted. 40% receive financial aid. 20% enrolled part-time. S:T ratio 15-20:1. 99% of graduates obtain jobs within 6 mos. Facilities: Modern commercial kitchens, demo theater, labs & classrooms.

Courses: include epicurean service, garde manger, advanced bakeshop, buffet catering, purchasing & receiving, a la carte. Specialized certificates awarded for portions of course. Hospitality mgmt programs at area colleges offer credit toward AS degree. International program in Czech Republic.

Faculty: 15 instructors, all ACF-certified or pending, 5 part-time instructors; all state certified with min 6 yrs experience.

Costs: $5,000 in-state, $15 registration fee, $415/quinmester fee, $600 for supplies. Off-campus lodging $400/mo. Admission requirements: 16 yrs or older, HS diploma or equivalent. Scholarships: yes.

CONTACT: Chef David S. Bearl, CCC, CCE, Program Coordinator/Division Head, The Southeast Institute of Culinary Arts, 2980 Collins Ave., St. Augustine, FL 32094-9970; 904-829-1060, 904-829-1061, Fax 904-824-6750, bearld@fcti.org.

WALT DISNEY WORLD AT VALENCIA COMMUNITY COLLEGE

Orlando/Year-round

Sponsor: Valencia Community College. Program: 2-yr (64 cr-hr) AS degree in Culinary Mangement, three separate 2-yr degrees in Hospitality Management, 2-year degree in Restaurant Management. Established: 1997. Accredited by SACS. Calendar: semester. Curriculum: culinary. Admit dates: Jan, May, Aug. Total enrollment: 330. 5 each admission period. 100% of applicants accepted. 30% receive financial aid. 77% enrolled part-time. S:T ratio 18:1. 85% of graduates obtain jobs within 6 mos. Facilities: Audio-visually equipped demo studio kitchen, baking & pastry kitchen, modern restaurant kitchen, computer lab with 30 computers & POS simulation, front desk, modern classrooms.

COURSES: Basic to advanced techniques ranging from intro to food & beverage cost control to quantity food production, baking & pastries, classic & international cuisine courses.

FACULTY: Swiss-trained Certified Executive Chef (CEC) is program manager; several area chefs are adjunct faculty & guest chefs.

COSTS: $5.000 in-state, $13.000 out-of-state for 64 credit-hours (~2 years). Lab fees, internship fees, books, housing are extra. No on-campus housing; off campus housing required. Admission requirements: HS diploma or equivalent. Scholarships: yes. Loans: yes.

CONTACT: Pierre Pilloud, CEC, Program Director, Walt Disney World Center for Hospitality & Culinary Art, Valencia Community College, W. Campus, 1800 S. Kerkman Rd., Orlando, FL 32811; 407-582-1880, Fax 407-273-9754, ppilloud@valencia.cc.fl.usTAB, http://valencia.cc.fl.us.

GEORGIA

THE ART INSTITUTE OF ATLANTA – CULINARY ARTS

Atlanta/Year-round *(See also page 228)(See display ad above)*

Sponsor: Private college of creative professional studies, member of The Art Institutes, with 23 locations in the U.S. Program: 7-quarter AA degree in Culinary Arts, 8-quarter AA degree in Culinary Arts with a concentration in baking and pastry. Established: 1991. Accredited by ACF, SACS. Calendar: quarter. Curriculum: culinary, core. Admit dates: Jan, Apr, July, Oct. Total enrollment: 430. 50-100 each admission period. 95% of applicants accepted. 85% receive financial aid. 16% enrolled part-time. S:T ratio 18:1. 95.5% of graduates obtain jobs within 6 mos. Facilities: 15,000-sq-ft facility with 5 teaching kitchens, purchasing lab, sanitation lab, classrooms, full-service teaching dining room, library, student lounge.

COURSES: Food production, baking & pastry, garde manger, kitchen procedures, sanitation, nutrition, menu planning, presentation, restaurant operation, kitchen management, purchasing, classical, international & nouvelle cuisines. Core general ed curriculum. 7th quarter intern/externships at an Atlanta restaurant or in the food service industry. Community ed programs. 1-day hands-on workshops on a variety of culinary techniques, 6-week certificate program in baking & pastry.

Faculty: 18 full-time & adjunct chef instructors many of whom are also working chefs.

Costs: $5,088/qtr, application fee $50, lab fee $275/qtr. College-sponsored housing $2,013/qtr. Culinary kit $740 (1st qtr. only). Admission requirements: HS diploma or equivalent, application with essay, SAT/ACT or COMPASS test scores. Requirements vary for transfer students, applicants with a college degree, & intl students. Scholarships: yes. Loans: yes.

Location: The 2,400-student campus is in Atlanta's Dunwoody area.

Contact: Admissions Office, Art Institute of Atlanta-Culinary Arts, 6600 Peachtree Dunwoody Rd., 100 Embassy Row, Atlanta, GA 30328; 800-275-4242, 770-394-8300, Fax 770-394-0008, aiaadm@aii.edu, www.aia.artinstitutes.edu.

ATLANTA AREA TECHNICAL SCHOOL

Atlanta

Sponsor: Career institution. Program: 18-month diploma. Established: 1967. Accredited by SACS. Admit dates: Quarterly. S:T ratio 12:1. 92% of graduates obtain jobs within 6 mos.

Faculty: 6+ full-time.

Costs: Tuition $296/quarter full-time, $23/credit part-time. Admission requirements: HS diploma or equivalent and admission test.

Contact: Andrew G. Phillips, Director, Atlanta Area Technical School, Culinary Arts Program, 1560 Stewart Ave. S.W., Atlanta, GA 30310; 404-756-3715, Fax 404-756-0932, aphillip@admin1.atlanta.tec.ga.us, www.atlantatech.org/Programs_Credit/human_serv.htm.

AUGUSTA TECHNICAL INSTITUTE

Augusta/Year-round

Sponsor: State technical school. Program: 4-quarter certificate program in Food Service, 6-quarter diploma in Culinary Arts. Established: 1985. Accredited by SACS. Calendar: quarter. Curriculum: culinary. Admit dates: Sept, Mar. Total enrollment: 36. 15 each admission period. 90% of applicants accepted. 100% receive financial aid. 3% enrolled part-time. S:T ratio 18:1. 100% of graduates obtain jobs within 6 mos. Facilities: Include 1 kitchen, 2 classrooms, and local restaurants.

Courses: Basic food preparation, introduction to baking, garde manger, nutrition and menu management, safety and sanitation, and consumer education. Other required courses: office accounting, computer literacy. 150-hr salaried internship. Diploma from Educational Foundation of the NRA on completion of 6 qtrs. Continuing education: catering, cake decoration, sanitation.

Faculty: 2 full-time.

Costs: Quarterly tuition $274 in-state, $548 out-of-state. Application fee $15. Average off-campus housing cost $500/mo. Admission requirements: HS diploma or GED. Scholarships: yes.

Contact: Augusta Technical Institute, Culinary Arts, 3116 Deans Bridge Rd., Augusta, GA 30906; 706-771-4028, Fax 706-771-4034, bcrobert@augusta.tec.ga.us, www.augusta.tec.ga.us.

CHATTAHOOCHEE TECHNICAL COLLEGE

Decatur/Year-round

Sponsor: Technical college. Program: AAT degree (109 credits) in Culinary Arts, diploma (92 credits) in Culinary Arts, certificate programs (16-17 credits) in Culinary Skills & Culinary-Stewarding. Accredited by SACS, ACF. Calendar: quarter. Admit dates: Spring, Summer, Fall, Winter.

Courses: Include principles of Cooking, American Regional Cuisine, Food Service Purchasing & Control, Baking Principles, Banquet Prep & Presentation, Pantry, Hors d'oeuvres and Canapes, Garde Manager, Nutrition & Menu Development, Contemporary Cuisine.

Costs: In-state: $312/qtr full-time (12 or more credits), $26/credit part-time (less than 12 credits); Out-of-state: $624/qtr full-time, $52/credit part-time.

Contact: Michael Bologna, Chattahoochee Technical College, 980 South Cobb Dr., Marietta, GA 30060; 770 -528-4545, Fax 770-528-4465, mbolonga@chattcollege.com, www.chat-tec.com.

LE CORDON BLEU COLLEGE OF CULINARY ARTS ATLANTA

Tucker/Year-round

(See display ad above)

Sponsor: Private school. Program: 15-month diploma in Culinary Arts. Established: 2003. Curriculum: culinary. Admit dates: Every 6 weeks. 70-80 each admission period. S:T ratio 32:1. Facilities: 60,000-sq-ft facility with up–to-date well- equipped kitchens & classrooms, computer labs, library, bookstore.

Courses: Le Cordon Bleu skill set, culinary fundamentals, purchasing & cost control, nutrition, baking, pastry, wines, restaurant management. 12-wk industry-related externship required.

Costs: $33,800 includes tuition & fees. Admission requirements: HS diploma or equivalent. Scholarships: yes. Loans: yes.

Location: Northeast Atlanta.

Contact: Janice Davidson, Director of Admissions, Le Cordon Bleu College of Culinary Arts Atlanta, 1927 Lakeside Parkway, Tucker, GA 30084; 770-938 4711, 866-315-2433, Fax 770-938-4571, info@atlantaculinary.com, www.atlantaculinary.com.

SAVANNAH TECHNICAL COLLEGE

Savannah/Year-round

Sponsor: Public institution. Program: 6-quarter diploma & 2-yr AAA degree in Culinary Arts. Established: 1981. Accredited by SACS, ACF. Calendar: quarter. Curriculum: culinary, core. Admit dates: Spring & fall. Total enrollment: 75. 24 each admission period. 100% of applicants accepted. 85% receive financial aid. 75% enrolled part-time. S:T ratio 20:1. 100% of graduates obtain jobs within 6 mos. Facilities: Include kitchen, classroom, student-run restaurant.

Courses: Sanitation, food prep, purchasing & cost control, baking, garde manger, nutrition. English, math, intro to computers, employability skills also required. 300-hr internship, restaurant.

Faculty: 1 full-time, 1 part-time. Includes Marvis T. Hinson, CFBE, CCE, M.Ed, CCWA.

Costs: In-state $312/quarter, out-of-state $624/quarter. Fees ~$79, uniforms, knives & tools $400, books ~$150/quarter. Admission requirements: HS diploma or equivalent & placement test or SAT. Scholarships: yes.

Contact: Marvis Hinson, Dept. Head, Savannah Technical College, Culinary Arts, 5717 White Bluff Rd., Savannah, GA 31405-5594; 912-303-1833, Fax 912-303-1760, mhinson@savtec.org, www.savtec.org.

THE WINE SCHOOL

Atlanta; Internet/August-June

Sponsor: Wine professional. Program: Three 6-week Diploma courses/yr, advanced classes, weekend courses at client venues, online courses. Established: 1978.

Faculty: Anita Louise LaRaia, member SWE, author of Wine FAQs, former online wine expert CNN.com.

Costs: $350 for Diploma Course.

Contact: Anita Louise LaRaia, Director, The Wine School, P.O. Box 52723, Atlanta, GA 30355; 770-901-9433, Fax 770-901-9969, anitalaraia@msn.com, www.anitalaraia.com.

HAWAII

CULINARY INSTITUTE OF THE PACIFIC

Pearl City/Year-round

Sponsor: 2-year college. Program: 2-year AAS degree in Food Service, 1.5-year certificate in Food Service, 1-semester certificate in Food Preparation, 2-semester certificates in Baking & Dining Room. Established: 1974. Accredited by WASC, ACF. Calendar: semester. Curriculum: core. Admit dates: Aug, Jan. Total enrollment: 80-100. 25-30 each admission period. 100% of applicants accepted. 40% receive financial aid. 20% enrolled part-time. S:T ratio 15-20:1. 90% of graduates obtain jobs within 6 mos. Facilities: 3 kitchens, 5 classrooms, 1 restaurant, 2 cafe/dining rooms.

Courses: Provides students with technical knowledge and basic skills training for a professional food service career. Minimum 75 hrs in a commercial kitchen required second semester.

Faculty: 5 full-time with 15-20 years industry experience, 3 part-time.

Costs: Semester tuition in-state $468, out-of-state $2,856. Admission requirements: Age 18 or 17 with HS diploma. Scholarships: yes. Loans: yes.

Location: 6,000-student, 49-acre campus on the peninsula between Pearl City & Waipahu.

Contact: Tommylynn Benavente, Program Coordinator, Leeward Community College, Food Service, 96-045 Ala Ike, Pearl City, HI 96782; 808-455-0298/808-455-0300, Fax 808-455-0471, tlbenave@hawaii.edu, http://alaike.lcc.hawaii.edu/FoodService/default.htm.

KAPI'OLANI COMMUNITY COLLEGE

Honolulu/Year-round

Sponsor: 2-year college, a campus of the University of Hawaii. Program: 2-yr AS degrees in Culinary Arts & Patisserie, 18-mo certificate program in Culinary Arts, 1-yr certificate program in Culinary Arts & Patisserie. Established: 1947. Accredited by ACF, CAHM, WASC. Calendar: semester. Curriculum: culinary, core. Admit dates: Fall, spring, summer. Total enrollment: 500. 100% of applicants accepted. 25% receive financial aid. 50% enrolled part-time. S:T ratio 20:1. 98% of graduates obtain jobs within 6 mos. Facilities: 9 kitchens, 7 classrooms, 1 demo auditorium, 5 restaurants.

Courses: Asian/Pacific & International Cuisine, Fundamental Baking, Garde Manger, Patisserie, Confiserie, Food & Beverage Cost Control & Management. Walt Disney World Orlando College Program, seasonal jobs at resorts on Lanai, summer culinary tours to Asia. Programs offered in various cuisines to train the novice culinary enthusiast & the industry chef.

Faculty: 14 full-time, 6 part-time, all with industry experience.

Costs: Annual tuition in-state $45/cr, out-of-state $242/cr. $30 fee/sem. Off-campus housing ~$500/mo. Admission requirements: Age 18, or 17 with HS diploma or GED. Scholarships: yes. Loans: yes.

LOCATION: On the slopes of Diamond Head Crater, 2 mi from Waikiki.

CONTACT: Lori Maehara, Assistant Professor/Counselor, Kapiolani Community College, Food Service & Hospitality Education, 4303 Diamond Head Rd., Honolulu, HI 96816; 808-734-9466, Fax 808-734-9212, lmaehara@hawaii.edu, www.kcc.hawaii.edu.

KAUAI COMMUNITY COLLEGE
Lihue/August-May

Sponsor: 2-year college. Program: 1-year certificate and 2-year AAS degree in Culinary Arts. Calendar: semester. Curriculum: core.

COSTS: $41.50/credit in-state, $240.50/credit out-of-state.

CONTACT: Clarence Nishi, Chief, Kauai Community College, 3-1901 Kaumualii Hwy., Lihue, HI 96766; 808-245-8311 x265, Fax 808-245-8297, cnishi@mail.kauaicc.hawaii.edu, www.kauaicc.hawaii.edu.

MAUI CHEFS ASSOCIATION
Kahului/Year-round

Sponsor: American Culinary Federation chapter. Program: 3-yr apprenticeship; degree program through Maui Community College is completed by 50%. Established: 1975. Accredited by ACF. Calendar: semester. Curriculum: culinary, core. Admit dates: Open. Total enrollment: 6. 35 each admission period. 80% of applicants accepted. 50% receive financial aid. 20% enrolled part-time. S:T ratio 15:1. 100% of graduates obtain jobs within 6 mos. Facilities: New facility to open in 2003.

FACULTY: 5 full-time instructors.

COSTS: $525 in-state, $2,913 out-of-state/semester. Beginning salary is $10-$11.50/hr with increases every 6 mos. Housing cost is $600-$800/mo. Scholarships: yes. Loans: yes.

LOCATION: 3 locations include resort & restaurant. Contact: Christopher Speere, Culinary Educator, Maui Chefs Association, Maui Community College, 310 Kaahumanu Ave., Box 1284, Kahului, HI 96732; 808-984-3479, Fax 808-984-3314, speere@hawaii.edu, www.mauicc.hawaii.edu.

MAUI COMMUNITY COLLEGE/CULINARY ARTS PROGRAM
Kahului/August-May

Sponsor: 2-year college. Program: 1-year certificate, 2-year AAS degree-Culinary, 2-year AAS degree-Baking. Established: 1969. Accredited by ACF. Calendar: semester. Curriculum: culinary, core. Admit dates: Aug, Jan. Total enrollment: 100. 45 each admission period. 100% of applicants accepted. 25% receive financial aid. 30% enrolled part-time. S:T ratio 15:1. 98% of graduates obtain jobs within 6 mos. Facilities: Include 2 kitchens, 2 classrooms, 1 restaurant, 1 cafe/dining room.

COURSES: Culinary Arts or Baking Specialties. Internships & externships available.

FACULTY: 8 full-time, 5 part-time.

COSTS: Annual tuition in-state $47.50/cr, out-of-state $246.50/cr. 2-bedroom $997/semester. Admission requirements: Minimum 18 yrs, HS graduate or transfer from another institution. Scholarships: yes. Loans: yes.

CONTACT: Robert Santos, Program Coordinator, Maui Community College, Culinary Arts, 310 Kaahumanu Avenue, Kahului, HI 96732; 808-984-3225, Fax 808-984-3314, santosro@hawaii.edu, http://mauicc.hawaii.edu/about_mcc/info.htmlx#top.

IDAHO

BOISE STATE UNIVERSITY
Boise/August-May

Sponsor: University. Program: 6-mo, 1-yr, & 18-mo certificates; 2-yr AAS degree. Established: 1969. Accredited by ACF, NCA. Calendar: semester. Curriculum: culinary. Admit dates: Aug, Jan. Total enrollment: 35-50. 25/semester each admission period. 5% enrolled part-time. S:T ratio ~10:1. 97% of graduates obtain jobs within 6 mos.

FACULTY: 3 full-time & 4 adjunct chefs.

Costs: In-state $1,995/semester, out-of-state $3,360/semester + $1,995 fee. Admission requirements: HS diploma or equivalent & admission assessment. Scholarships: yes. Loans: yes.

Contact: Vern Hickman, CCC, CCE, Chef Instructor, Boise State University, Culinary Arts, 1910 University Dr., Boise, ID 83725; 208-426-4199, Fax 208-426-1948, vhickman@boisestate.edu, http://selland.boisestate.edu/academic_programs/CCA.htm.

COLLEGE OF SOUTHERN IDAHO

Twin Falls/September-May

Sponsor: Community college. Program: 2-year AAS, 1-year technical certificate. Established: 1986. Calendar: semester. Curriculum: core. Admit dates: Open. Total enrollment: 20. 12 each admission period. 32% of applicants accepted. 90% receive financial aid. S:T ratio 10:1. 90% of graduates obtain jobs within 6 mos.

Courses: Culinary arts, Food production. Internships provided in summer. Cooperative education during school year.

Faculty: 2 full-time, 6 part-time.

Costs: Tuition in-state $615/semester, out-of-state $1,615/semester. On-campus room & board is $1,625; average off-campus housing cost is $350/mo. Admission requirements: HS diploma or equivalent. Scholarships: yes.

Contact: Pamela Namer, Program Coordinator, College of Southern Idaho, Hotel-Restaurant Mgmt., P.O. Box 1238, 315 Falls Ave., Twin Falls, ID 83303-1238; 208-733-9554 x2380, 800-680-0274 x2380, Fax 208-736-2136, pnamer@csi.edu, www.csi.edu/l4.cfm?chef.

IDAHO STATE UNIVERSITY SCHOOL OF APPLIED TECHNOLOGY

Pocatello/Year-round

Sponsor: University. Program: 2.5-semester certificate program in Culinary Arts Technology, AAS degree in Culinary Arts Technology. Calendar: semester. Curriculum: core. Admit dates: Aug, Jan, May. Total enrollment: 20. 15 each admission period. 100% of applicants accepted. S:T ratio 14:01. 100% of graduates obtain jobs within 6 mos.

Courses: Food preparation & service, nutrition, purchasing, human relations, job search. 4-credit internship last semester of degree program.

Costs: $992/semester (resident). Supplies $556.

Contact: David K. Hanson, Dept. Chair, Idaho State University School of Applied Technology, Campus Box 8380, Pocatello, ID 83209-8380; 208-236-3327, Fax 208-236-4641, hansdavi@isu.edu, www.isu.edu.

NORTH IDAHO COLLEGE

Coeur d'Alene/Year-round

Sponsor: College. Program: 36.5 credit-hour certificate in Culinary Arts. Calendar: semester. Curriculum: culinary.

Courses: Breakfast cooking & catering, pantry, stock, soup, sauce prep, line & grill cooking, baking.

Costs: Annual tuition is $1,128-$1,687/credit in-state, $3,884-$4,443/credit out-of-state. Room and board $3,510/yr. Books & supplies $225-$2,300/yr.

Contact: Richard Schultz, North Idaho College, 1000 W. Garden Ave., Coeur d'Alene, ID 83814; 208-769-3458, rick_schultz@nidc.edu, www.nidc.edu.

ILLINOIS

THE ART OF STYLING FOOD

Elmwood Park

Sponsor: Food stylist Donna Lafferty. Program: 7-day certificate courses in styling food for still & motion photography. Established: 1993. Admit dates: May, Oct. 7 max each admission period. S:T ratio 1:1. Facilities: 250-sq-ft professional kitchen with work stations & overhead mirror.

Courses: 7-day, 64-hr course includes shopping trip to specialty shops. Students also work with a food photographer for their own set-up & photo.

FACULTY: Donna Lafferty has 22 yrs experience styling for still & motion advertising. Clients include Edy's Grand Ice Cream, Kraft Foods, The Oprah Winfrey Show.

COSTS: $2,500 for out of state/country students; $5,250 for Illinois residents. Admission requirements: Students must know how to cook.

CONTACT: Donna Lafferty, Food Art Studio, 2733 N. 75th Ct., Elmwood Park, IL 60707-1433; 708-456-8415, dlafferty@ameritech.net, www.ameritech.net/users/dlafferty/1FoodStylist.html.

BELLEVILLE AREA COLLEGE
Granite City/Year-round

Sponsor: College. Program: 1-yr certificate programs in Culinary Arts (15 cr-hrs), Foodservice (16 cr-hrs), & Hospitality Food Service (31 cr-hrs); 2-yr AAS degree in Hospitality Food Service Management (71 cr-hrs). Accredited by ACF. Calendar: semester.

COSTS: $44/cr-hr in-district, $107/cr-hr out-of-district, $150 for uniforms & supplies.

CONTACT: Steven Nigg, Program Coordinator, Belleville Area College, 4950 Maryville Rd., Granite City, IL 62040-2699; 618-235-2700 x5436, steve.nigg@swic.edu, www.southwestern.cc.il.us/instruction/hfsm/index.jsp.

COLLEGE OF DUPAGE
Glen Ellyn/Year-round

Sponsor: College. Program: 1-year certificate & 2-year AAS degree in Food Service Administration & Culinary Arts, 1-year certificate in Pastry Arts. Established: 1966. Accredited by NCA, RBA, NRA, ACF. Calendar: quarter. Curriculum: culinary, core. Admit dates: Sept, Jan, Mar, June. Total enrollment: 200. 50-125 each admission period. 100% of applicants accepted. 25% receive financial aid. 30% enrolled part-time. S:T ratio 15:1. 100% of graduates obtain jobs within 6 mos. Facilities: Include kitchen, pastry shop, classrooms, restaurant, dining room.

COURSES: Food preparation, classical cuisine, baking & pastry, merchandising, cake decorating, garde manger, wines & international cuisine. Externship provided.

FACULTY: 4 full-time, 12 part-time. Includes George C. Macht, CHA, CFE, FMP, Chris Thieman, CEC, CCE, Rolfe Sick, CMP, Jim Zielinski, FMP.

COSTS: In-district $35/credit hour. Admission fee $10. Texts, uniforms, tools & fees vary. Off-campus ~$500/mo. Admission requirements: HS diploma or equivalent. Scholarships: yes. Loans: yes.

CONTACT: George Macht, Coordinator/Professor, College of DuPage, Culinary Arts/Pastry Arts, 425 Fawell Blvd., Glen Ellyn, IL 60137; 630-942-3663, Fax 630-858-9399, machtg@cdnet.cod.edu, www.cod.edu/Catalog/F/FoodServ.htm.

COLLEGE OF LAKE COUNTY
Grayslake, Vernon Hills & Waukegan/Year-round

Sponsor: 2-year community college. Program: 1-yr certificate in Culinary Arts, Food Service Management or Professional Cooking; AAS in Food Service Management. Established: 1987. Accredited by NCA. Calendar: semester. Curriculum: culinary, core. Admit dates: Aug, Jan, June. Total enrollment: 50. 20 each admission period. 95% of applicants accepted. 10% receive financial aid. 50% enrolled part-time. S:T ratio 10:1. 98% of graduates obtain jobs within 6 mos. Facilities: Include 2 kitchens & 3 classrooms.

COURSES: Cooking, baking, nutrition, menu planning. Externship: 8- or 16-week part-time. CVOC 5 IDPH Food Service Refresher Course. FSM 299 courses are elective, advanced or special interest topics.

FACULTY: 1 full-time, 7 part-time. Qualifications: minimum 2-yr culinary school &/or master's degree.

COSTS: Tuition $56/cr-hr. Other fees: lab, equipment, uniforms. Admission requirements: Math & language proficiency exam or GED, ACT, Military. Scholarships: yes. Loans: yes.

CONTACT: Mr. Cliff Wener, Instructor, College of Lake County, Food Service Program, 19351 W. Washington St., Grayslake, IL 60030-1198; 847-543-2823, Fax 847-543-3823, crwener-fsm@clcillinois.edu, www.clcillinois.edu.

THE COOKING AND HOSPITALITY INSTITUTE OF CHICAGO

Chicago/Year-round *(See display ad above)*

Sponsor: Private institution. Program: 16-mo/4-sem (65-cr-hr) AAS degree in the Le Cordon Bleu Culinary Program, and in the Le Cordon Bleu Patisserie & Baking Program. Established: 1983. Accredited by ACCSCT, ACF. Calendar: semester. Curriculum: core. Admit dates: 6 times/yr. Total enrollment: 900. 90% of applicants accepted. 70% receive financial aid. S:T ratio 16:1. 95% of graduates obtain jobs within 6 mos. Facilities: 8 fully-equipped instructional kitchens, on-site restaurant.

Courses: Combines classical French techniques & American technology. Courses cover qualitative & quantitative cooking, menu planning, recipe development. Baking/pastry courses cover production techniques, food as art form, yeast breads, decoration. Students gain fine dining experience working in the on-site restaurant, The CHIC Cafe.

Faculty: Instructors are ACF certified & accomplished in their fields of expertise.

Costs: $8,750/sem. Registration fee $150. Books & supplies ~$3,200 (entire program). Admission requirements: HS diploma or equivalent. Scholarships: yes. Loans: yes.

Contact: Catherine Brokenshire, Director of Admissions, The Cooking and Hospitality Institute of Chicago, 361 W. Chestnut, Chicago, IL 60610; 312-944-2725, 877-828-7772 (toll-free), Fax 312-944-8557, cbrokenshire@chicnet.org, www.chicnet.org.

ELGIN COMMUNITY COLLEGE

Elgin/Year-round

Sponsor: College. Program: 2-yr associate degree in Culinary Arts, Restaurant Management, and Baking & Pastry. Established: 1972. Accredited by Illinois Community College Board, ACF. Calendar: semester. Curriculum: culinary, core. Admit dates: Aug, Jan. Total enrollment: 225. 30-40 each admission period. 80% of applicants accepted. 30% enrolled part-time. S:T ratio 15-30:1. 100% of graduates obtain jobs within 6 mos. Facilities: 4 kitchens, 3 classrooms, culinary training center.

Faculty: 3 full-time, 8 part-time. Qualifications: ACF-certification.

Costs: $44/cr-hr in-district, $260/cr-hr out-of-district. Books & uniforms ~$200. Off-campus housing ~$400-$600/mo. Admission requirements: HS diploma or equivalent. Scholarships: yes. Loans: yes.

Contact: Michael Zema, Director, Elgin Community College, Hospitality Dept., 1700 Spartan Dr., Elgin, IL 60123; 847-214-7461, Fax 847-888-7995, admissions@mail.elgin.cc.il.us, www.elgin.cc.il.us.

FRENCH PASTRY SCHOOL, INC. AT CITY COLLEGES OF CHICAGO

Chicago/Year-round

Sponsor: Pastry school founded by World Pastry Cup chefs Sebastien Canonne & Jacquy Pfeiffer. Program: 24-wk certificate in Pastry Arts focusing on classic French methods, contemporary aesthetics & production techniques. Established: 1996. Calendar: semester. Curriculum: culinary. Admit dates: January & July. S:T ratio 16:1. 90% of graduates obtain jobs within 6 mos. Facilities: Purpose built pastry kitchens with the latest equipment.

Courses: Confectionery, ice cream & sorbets, sugar decoration, breakfast pastries, plated desserts, petit fours, wedding cakes, French cakes & tarts, competition skills.

Faculty: Chef Jacquy Pfeiffer co-founder/instructor, 25+ yrs experience, named one of the Top Ten Pastry Chefs in the US by Pastry Art and Design. Instructor John Kraus was named 2002 Patisfrance Pastry Chef of the Year & 2002 National Dessert Champion.

Costs: $14,900 includes books, uniforms, supplies.

Contact: Rowena Frith, French Pastry School, 226 W. Jackson Blvd., Chicago, IL 60606; 312-726-2419, Fax 312-726-2446, FrenchPastrys@aol.com, www.frenchpastryschool.com.

THE ILLINOIS INSTITUTE OF ART CHICAGO – CULINARY ARTS

Chicago/Year-round *(See display ad page 62)*

Sponsor: 2-yr college. Program: 18-mo AAS degree. Established: 2000. Accredited by ACCSCT. Calendar: quarter. Curriculum: core. Total enrollment: 220. 95% of applicants accepted. 98% receive financial aid. 30% enrolled part-time. S:T ratio 17:1. 100% of graduates obtain jobs within 6 mos. Facilities: 18,000-sq-ft new facility with 4 complete kitchens & restaurant & 2 more kitchens planned.

Courses: Baking & Pastry; Garde Manger; Nutrition;Menu Management; Dining Room Operations; Wine & Beverage Management; Nutrition; Safety & Sanitation; Regional Cuisine.

Faculty: 7 full-time, 7 part-time, all with industry experience.

Costs: $310/cr-hr, $4,960/quarter. Admission requirements: HS diploma or GED. Personal or phone interview. Scholarships: yes. Loans: yes.

Contact: Janis Anton, Director of Admissions, The Illinois Institute of Art Chicago-Culinary Arts, 180 N. Wabash, Chicago, IL 60601; 800-351-3450, 312-280-3500, Fax 312-364-9451, antonj@aii.edu, www.ilic.artinstitutes.edu.

THE INSTITUTE OF CULINARY ARTS AT ROBERT MORRIS COLLEGE

Aurora/Year-round

Sponsor: Private college specializing in applied education. Program: AAS degree in Culinary Arts, BBA degree in Hospitality Mgmt. Established: 2003. Accredited by NCA. Calendar: quarter. Curriculum: culinary, core. Admit dates: July, Sept, Feb. Total enrollment: 60. 60 each admission period. 90% of applicants accepted. 90% receive financial aid. S:T ratio 18:1. Facilities: Newly constructed.

Courses: Include Taste of the World, Cooking for Health, Garde Manger, A la Minute Cookery. Mandatory internships at leading Chicago-area restaurants & food service industries.

Faculty: 2 full- & 4 part-time faculty, AAS in Culinary, Bachelors in related field.

Costs: $4,550/quarter. Admission requirements: 2.0 HS GPA or GED. Scholarships: yes. Loans: yes.

Contact: Nancy Rotunno, Director, The Institute of Culinary Arts at Robert Morris College, DuPage Campus, 905 Meridian Lake Dr., Aurora, IL 60504; 877-Cook RMC (877-266-5762), Fax 312-935-6819, nrotunno@robertmorris.edu, www.robertmorris.edu/culinary.

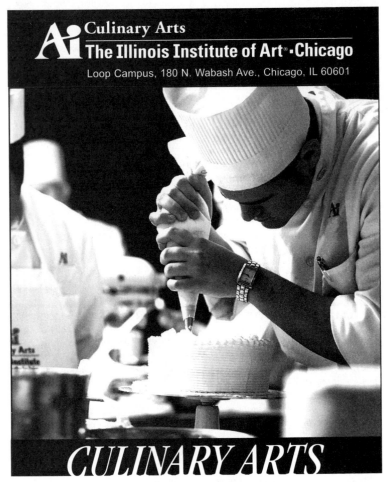

JOLIET JUNIOR COLLEGE
Joliet/Year-round

Sponsor: College. Program: 2-yr certificate/AAS degree in Culinary Arts and Baking & Pastry Certificate Program. Established: 1970. Accredited by NCA, ACF. Calendar: semester. Curriculum: culinary. Admit dates: Aug, Jan, May, June. Total enrollment: 200. 100 each admission period. 98% of applicants accepted. 40% receive financial aid. 10% enrolled part-time. S:T ratio 16:1. 95% of graduates obtain jobs within 6 mos. Facilities: Include 3 kitchens, demo kitchen, 3 classrooms, pastry shop.

Costs: $50/cr-hr in-state. Admission requirements: HS diploma or equivalent & admission test.

Contact: Michael McGreal, Dept. Chair, Joliet Junior College, Culinary Arts/Hotel-Restaurant Mgmt., 1215 Houbolt Ave., Joliet, IL 60431-8938; 815-280-2255, mmcgreal@jjc.edu, www.jjc.edu.

KENDALL COLLEGE, THE SCHOOL OF CULINARY ARTS
Evanston/Year-round *(See display ad above)*

Sponsor: Private college. Program: 2-yr AAS degree in Culinary Arts, 4-yr BA degree in Hospitality Management, certificate programs in Professional Cookery or Baking and Pastry Arts. Established: 1985. Accredited by ACF, NCA. Calendar: quarter. Curriculum: culinary, core. Admit dates: Rolling admissions. Total enrollment: ~300. 48-60 each admission period. 85% of applicants accepted. 87% receive financial aid. 30% enrolled part-time. S:T ratio 17:1. 99% of graduates obtain jobs within 6 mos. Facilities: 7 professional kitchens including 2 pastry & 1 demo, a fine dining restaurant & cafeteria.

Courses: Include fundamental & advanced culinary skills. Business management courses include Menu & Facilities Planning, Dining Room Service, Professional Ethics. Beginning students work in cafeteria, bakery; advanced students work in restaurant. 10-wk internship required. Culinary fundamental series in cooking.

Faculty: 18 full-time: M. Artlip, B. Bansberg, D. Bush, F. Chlumsky, J. Draz, R. Epskamp, W.

Freund, S. GrandPre, C. Koetke, F. Leroux, A. Meyer, M. Maloiseau, J. McGrath, E. Sikorski, K. Temkkit, K. Tenbergen, P. Tinaglia, C. Tual.

Costs: Culinary Arts $5,395/term, $21,580/yr (4 quarters). Admission requirements: 2.0 GPA or above, 18 ACT or above. Scholarships: yes. Loans: yes.

Location: The first suburb north of Chicago, 2 blocks from public transport & Lake Michigan.

Contact: Carl Goodmonson, Director of Admissions, Kendall College, The School of Culinary Arts, 2408 Orrington Ave., Evanston, IL 60201; 847-448-2304, 877-588-8860, Fax 847-448-2120, admissions@kendall.edu, www.kendall.edu.

LEXINGTON COLLEGE

Chicago/September-May

Sponsor: Independent institution. Program: 66 cr-hr AAS degree in Hospitality Management. Established: 1977. Accredited by The Higher Learning Commission. Calendar: semester. Curriculum: culinary, core. Admit dates: Sept, Jan. Total enrollment: 52. 20 each admission period. 90% of applicants accepted. 90% receive financial aid. 10% enrolled part-time. S:T ratio 8:1. 95% of graduates obtain jobs within 6 mos. Facilities: Include culinary & demo labs, 3 classrooms, library, computer lab, bookstore, student commons.

Courses: Professional food production, baking & pastries, food & beverage sales, garde manger, purchasing, quantity food production, sanitation, nutrition, general ed. Internship required. Evening & weekend programs.

Faculty: 2 full-time, 10 part-time.

Costs: $6,300/sem; books, student fees, equipment $875/sem; culinary lab fees $200/sem. Admission requirements: HS diploma or equivalent, ACT or SAT test scores, letter of recommendation. Scholarships: yes. Loans: yes.

Contact: Megan Warmouth, Director of Admissions, Lexington College, 310 S. Peoria St., Chicago, IL 60607; 312-226-6294, Fax 312-226-6405, admissio@lexingtoncollege.edu, www.lexingtoncollege.edu.

LINCOLN LAND COMMUNITY COLLEGE

Springfield/Year-round

Sponsor: Community college. Program: 2-yr diploma, 1-yr certificate, specialty classes. Established: 1994. Calendar: semester. Curriculum: culinary, core. Admit dates: Year-round. Total enrollment: 50. 50 each admission period. 100% of applicants accepted. 35% receive financial aid. 50% enrolled part-time. S:T ratio 15:1. 100% of graduates obtain jobs within 6 mos. Facilities: Training kitchen.

Courses: Culinary Arts, Pastry, Food Production, Baking, Purchasing, Garde Manger, Nutrition. Students work in area hotels & restaurants & receive credit & paid positions. Special topics classes.

Faculty: 12 instructors, 6 certified by the ACF, 1 instructor MSRD.

Costs: $52/cr-hr. Scholarships: yes. Loans: yes.

Contact: Jay Kitterman, Director, Hospitality Management, Lincoln Land Community College, Hospitality Management, 5250 Shepherd Rd., Springfield, IL 62794; 217-786-2772, Fax 217-786-2495, jay.kitterman@llcc.cc.il.us, www.llcc.cc.il.us.

MORAINE VALLEY COMMUNITY COLLEGE

Palos Hills/Year-round

Sponsor: Community college. Program: Certificate programs in Culinary Arts Management, Baking/Pastry Arts, Beverage Management, and Restaurant/Hotel Management. AAS degree programs in Culinary Arts Management and Restaurant/Hotel Management. Established: 1967. Calendar: semester. Curriculum: culinary, core.

Costs: In-district (out-of-district, out-of-state) $44 ($179, $204)/cr-hr. Scholarships: yes. Loans: yes.

Contact: Anne Jachim, Moraine Valley Community College, 10900 S. 88th Ave., Palos Hills, IL 60465; 708-974-5320, Fax 708-974-1184, jachim@morainevalley.edu, www.morainevalley.edu/hospitality.

REND LAKE COLLEGE

Ina/Year-round

Sponsor: College. Program: One-year/32 credit-hour occupational certificate in Culinary Arts Management. Calendar: semester. Curriculum: culinary.

COURSES: Quantity food preparation, nutrition, menu planning, cost management, job strategy.

COSTS: Tuition in-district $36/cr-hr, out-of-district $124/cr-hr, out-of-state $160/cr-hr.

CONTACT: Eddie Billinglsey, Dept. Chair / AAA, Rend Lake College, 468 N. Ken Gray Pkwy., Ina, IL 62846; 618-437-5321 x 260/800-369-5321 x260, Fax 618-437-5677, billingsley@rlc.cc.il.us, www.rlc.cc.il.us.

TRITON COLLEGE

River Grove/Year-round

Sponsor: College. Program: 2-year AAS degree in Culinary Management, AAS degree in Hotel Management. Established: 1970. Accredited by NCA. Calendar: semester. Curriculum: culinary, core. Admit dates: Aug, Jan. Total enrollment: 150. 30 each admission period. 90% of applicants accepted. 20% receive financial aid. 30% enrolled part-time. S:T ratio 12:1. 97% of graduates obtain jobs within 6 mos. Facilities: 2 kitchens and classrooms, demonstration kitchen, ice carving facility, and student-run restaurant.

COURSES: Garde manger, international cooking, ice carving, food production, food theory, menu planning, purchasing, cost control, nutrition, service, and baking. Externship provided. Continuing education: international cooking, sanitation, and nutrition.

FACULTY: 3 full-time, 10 part-time.

COSTS: $43/credit hour in-district, $128.25/credit-hour out-of-district. Application fee $25. Other fees approximately $100/semester. Average off-campus housing cost $300/mo. Admission requirements: HS diploma or equivalent. Scholarships: yes. Loans: yes.

CONTACT: Jerome J. Drosos, Coordinator, Triton College, Hospitality Industry Administration, 2000 Fifth Ave., River Grove, IL 60171; 708-456-0300 #3624, Fax 708-583-3108, jdrosos@triton.cc.il.us, www.triton.cc.il.us.

WASHBURNE CULINARY INSTITUTE

Chicago/Year-round

Sponsor: City colleges of Chicago. Program: 80-week certificate in Chef Training. Established: 1937. Curriculum: culinary. Admit dates: Sept, Jan, May. Total enrollment: 150. 25 each admission period. 100% of applicants accepted. 75% receive financial aid. S:T ratio 21:1. 98% of graduates obtain jobs within 6 mos. Facilities: 6 kitchens, 6 classrooms.

COURSES: 85% hands-on training, 5 days/wk. Continuing education: ice carving.

FACULTY: 7 full-time.

COSTS: Annual tuition of $4,600 includes cutlery, books, & uniforms. Application fee $200 if cash-paying student; none if financial aid. Admission requirements: HS diploma or equivalent and admission test. Scholarships: yes.

CONTACT: Dean Jaramillo, Department Program Director, Washburne Culinary Institute, Chef Training Program, 6800 S. Wentworth Ave., Chicago, IL 60621; 773-602-5487, Fax 773-602-5452, www.ccc.edu/washburne.

WILLIAM RAINEY HARPER COLLEGE

Palatine/August-May

Sponsor: Community college. Program: 1-yr certificates in Culinary Arts, Baking, Hotel Mgmt, & Restaurant Mgmt. 2-yr AAS degree in Hospitality Mgmt. Established: 1970. Accredited by NCA. Calendar: semester. Curriculum: culinary, core. Admit dates: Aug, Jan, June. Total enrollment: 180. 60 each admission period. 95% of applicants accepted. 60% receive financial aid. 65% enrolled part-time. S:T ratio 15:1. 100% of graduates obtain jobs within 6 mos. Facilities: 3 kitchens including a production bakery & kitchen, demo lab, classrooms.

COURSES: Garde manger, classical cuisine, cake decorating, basic & advanced culinary, basic & advanced baking, sanitation.

FACULTY: 2 full-time, 10 part-time. Certified chefs & bakers, most with a master's degree.

COSTS: $67/cr in-district (+ $5.25/hr), $280/cr out-of-district; application fee $25, lab fee $50/lab class, books $60/class, $10 reg fee & $30 student activity fee/sem. Off-campus housing ~$500-$800/mo. Admission requirements: Open admissions, assesment testing. Scholarships: yes. Loans: yes.

CONTACT: Michael Held, Director of Admissions, William Rainey Harper College, 1200 W. Algonquin Rd., Palatine, IL 60067-7398; 847-925-6506, Fax 847-925-6044, pbeach@harpercollege.edu, www.harpercollege.edu/catalog/2000/career/hosp/index.htm.

WILTON SCHOOL OF CAKE DECORATING

Woodridge/Year-round

Sponsor: Private school. Program: Career-oriented 1- to 10-day cake decoration & candy making diploma courses. Established: 1929. Admit dates: Open. Total enrollment: 350. 20/class max each admission period. 100% of applicants accepted. S:T ratio 15:1. Facilities: The 2,200-sq-ft school includes a classroom, teaching kitchen, student lounge, & retail store.

COURSES: 10-day (67-hr) Master Course covers basic cake decorating & design; 5-day courses cover chocolate, Lambeth method, Australian techniques, catering; 3- & 4-day courses cover gum paste & pulled sugar; 1-day courses cover a variety of topics.

FACULTY: 2 full-time, 10 part-time instructors with 2-23 yrs teaching experience. Backgrounds include art instructor, cake stylist, author, bakery, culinary, foodservice.

COSTS: From $80 for 1 day to $775 for a 10-day course.

CONTACT: School Coordinator, Wilton School of Cake Decorating and Confectionery Art, 2240 W. 75th St., Woodridge, IL 60517; 630-810-2211, Fax 630-810-2710, cweeditz@wilton.com, www.wilton.com.

INDIANA

ACF SOUTH BEND CHEFS & COOKS ASSOCIATION

Notre Dame/Year-round

Sponsor: ACF chapter. Program: 3-yr apprenticeship; degree program through Ivy Tech State College. Established: 1992. Calendar: semester. Curriculum: culinary, core. Admit dates: January through December. Total enrollment: 12. 24 each admission period. 90% of applicants accepted. S:T ratio 1:12. 100% of graduates obtain jobs within 6 mos. Facilities: Full service kitchens.

COURSES: On-the-job training with 12 lecture & kitchen lab classes over 3 years. 6 extra summer classes can be taken to earn AOS degree & ACF Culinary Certification.

COSTS: $4,446/3 yrs (6,000 hrs). Beginning salary is $8.50/hr with 8% increases every 1,000 hrs. Additional $1,780 for AOS degree. Admission requirements: College placement test, references, hand written essay, interview. Scholarships: yes. Loans: yes.

CONTACT: Denis F. Ellis, CEC, AAC, ACF South Bend Chapter, 1043 University of Notre Dame, 213 South Dining Hall, Notre Dame, IN 46556-1043; 219-631-5416, Fax 219-631-7994, denis.f.ellis.1@nd.edu.

BALL STATE UNIVERSITY

Muncie/Year-round

Sponsor: University. Program: 2- and 4-year degree programs in Food Management. Established: 1975. Curriculum: core. Admit dates: Aug, Jan, May. Total enrollment: 35. S:T ratio 17:1. 100% of graduates obtain jobs within 6 mos. Facilities: Classrooms, computer lab, 3 kitchen production labs with the latest equipment.

COURSES: Food management with some hands-on instruction.

FACULTY: All instructors have advanced college degrees and industry experience.

COSTS: Annual tuition $3,316 in-state, $8,872 out-of-state. Room & board $4,120. Admission requirements: Min score of 920 on SAT or 19 ACT with class rank in top 50%. Scholarships: yes.

CONTACT: Lois Altman, Ed.D., Associate Professor, Ball State University, 2000 University Ave., Muncie, IN 47306; 765-285-5931, Fax 765-285-2314, 00laaltman@bsu.edu, www.bsu.edu.

IVY TECH STATE COLLEGE

East Chicago, Gary, Valparaiso City/Year-round

Sponsor: Public State 2-Year College. Program: 2-yr AAS degree & 1-yr technical certificate in Hospitality Administration. Established: 1981. Accredited by NCA, ACF. Calendar: semester. Curriculum: culinary, core. Admit dates: Open Rolling. Total enrollment: 100. 15 each admission period. 90% of applicants accepted. 50% receive financial aid. 30% enrolled part-time. S:T ratio 12:1. 100% of graduates obtain jobs within 6 mos. Facilities: Include full kitchen at 3 locations, catering facilities, restaurant, bakeshop.

COURSES: Include portfolio program: wine, culinary/hotel specialty, catering, baking. Externship: 16 wks, 144 hrs. French studies with Premier Sommelier & Chef of France, special interest courses.

FACULTY: 2 full-time, 7 part-time. Program director Muhammad Siddiqui.

COSTS: $73.80/cr-hr in-state, $148.75/cr-hr out-of-state. Admission requirements: HS diploma or equivalent. Scholarships: yes. Loans: yes.

CONTACT: Bob Forster, Ivy Tech State College, Hotel & Restaurant Mgmt./Culinary Arts, 1440 E. 35th Ave., Gary, IN 46409; 219-981-1111, Fax 219-981-4415, rforster@ivytech.edu, www.gary.ivytech.edu.

IVY TECH STATE COLLEGE

Fort Wayne/Year-round

Sponsor: College. Program: 2-yr AAS degree in Hospitality Administration with Culinary Arts or Pastry Arts Specialty. Established: 1981. Accredited by NCA, ACF. Calendar: semester. Curriculum: culinary. Admit dates: Year-round. Total enrollment: 140. 75 each admission period. 100% of applicants accepted. 75% receive financial aid. 42% enrolled part-time. S:T ratio 10-12:1. 100% of graduates obtain jobs within 6 mos. Facilities: Include 5 kitchens & classrooms, pastry arts lab, large full service kitchen.

COURSES: Basic foods, soups, stocks, sauces, nutrition, meat cutting, special & classical cuisines, fish & seafood, pantry & breakfast, garde manger, catering, breads, pastries, cake decoration, chocolates. Externship: 144-hr, salaried, in an ACF approved site.

FACULTY: 2 full-time, 12 part-time. Includes Program Chair Alan Eyler, CCE, CFBE, & Chef Instructor Jerry Wilson with 35 yrs industry experience.

COSTS: Annual tuition $1,835 in-state, $3,335 out-of-state. Admission requirements: HS diploma or equivalent & admission test. Scholarships: yes. Loans: yes.

CONTACT: Alan Eyler, CCE, CFBE, Program Chair, Ivy Tech State College, Hospitality Administration, 3800 N. Anthony Blvd., Fort Wayne, IN 46805; 219-480-4240, Fax 219-480-4171, aeyler@ivy.tec.in.us, www.ivytech.edu/catalog/hospitality.pdf.

IVY TECH STATE COLLEGE

Indianapolis/Year-round

Sponsor: College. Program: 2-year AAS degree in Culinary Arts, Baking & Pastry Arts, & Hotel Restaurant Management, Certification Dietary Management. Established: 1986. Accredited by NCA, ACF, CAHM, DMA, RBA. Calendar: semester. Admit dates: Aug, Jan, May. Total enrollment: 225. 60 each admission period. 100% of applicants accepted. 75% receive financial aid. 50% enrolled part-time. S:T ratio 10:1. 100% of graduates obtain jobs within 6 mos. Facilities: 2 kitchens, classrooms, cafeteria.

COURSES: Include basic food theory & skills, sanitation, classical French techniques. Externship: 5 mos. Continuing education: 2+2 programs set up with more than 28 4-yr colleges & universities.

FACULTY: 3 full-time, 15 part-time. Qualifications: Associate degree, 5 years experience, certifiable.

COSTS: Annual tuition $3,000 in-state, $4,650 out-of-state. Off-campus housing ~$300/mo. Admission requirements: HS diploma or equivalent & admission test. Scholarships: yes. Loans: yes.

CONTACT: Chef Vincent Kinkade, Chair, Ivy Tech State College, Hospitality Administration, One W. 26th St., Indianapolis, IN 46208; 317-921-4619, Fax 317-921-4753, vkinkade@ivy.tec.in.us, www.ivytech.edu.

VINCENNES UNIVERSITY
Vincennes/August-May

Sponsor: Public institution. Program: 2-year AS degree in Culinary Arts. Established: 1983. Accredited by NCA. Calendar: semester. Curriculum: culinary, core. Admit dates: Open. Total enrollment: 60. 30+ each admission period. 100% of applicants accepted. 90% receive financial aid. 5% enrolled part-time. S:T ratio 12:1. 100% of graduates obtain jobs within 6 mos. Facilities: Include kitchen, 3 classrooms, hands-on lab and restaurant.

COURSES: Quantity foods, pastry and bake shop, haute cuisine, food facility design, hospitality, sanitation, purchasing, supervision, and general education. Other required courses: core curriculum 22 to 23 hrs. Externship provided. Continuing education: ACF regional chefs conduct hands-on classes.

FACULTY: 2 full-time, 1 part-time. Qualifications: combined 58 yrs in industry with AS & BA degrees.

COSTS: Annual tuition $2,000 in-state, $5,200 out-of-state. Application fee $20. Student activities fee $18. On-campus housing: 3,000 spaces. Admission requirements: HS diploma or equivalent. Scholarships: yes. Loans: yes.

CONTACT: Phyllis Richardson, Vincennes University, Culinary Arts, Hoosier Hospitality Center, Vincennes, IN 47591; 812-888-5741, Fax 812-888-4586, prichardson@indian.vinu.edu, www.vinu.edu/factsheets.asp?ctid=188.

IOWA

CHEF DE CUISINE/QUAD CITIES
Bettendorf/Year-round

Sponsor: ACF chapter. Program: 3-yr apprenticeship; degree program through Scott Community College. Curriculum: culinary. Total enrollment: 25.

COSTS: $4,500 for 3 yrs. Beginning salary is $5/hr with 25 cent increases every 6 mos.

CONTACT: Jennifer Cook-DeRosa, Culinary Arts/Apprenticeship Facilitator, ACF Chef de Cuisine/Quad Cities, Scott Community College, 500 Belmont Rd., Bettendorf, IA 52722; 319-359-7531 #278.

DES MOINES AREA COMMUNITY COLLEGE
Ankeny/Year-round

Sponsor: College. Program: 2-yr AAS degree in Culinary Arts. Established: 1975. Accredited by NCA, ACF. Calendar: semester. Curriculum: culinary, core. Admit dates: Fall, spring. Total enrollment: 100. 50 each admission period. 100% of applicants accepted. 60% receive financial aid. 25% enrolled part-time. S:T ratio 15:1. 90% of graduates obtain jobs within 6 mos. Facilities: Include 2 kitchens, demo lab, classrooms, restaurant.

COURSES: French restaurant exchange. Externship provided.

FACULTY: 3 full-time, ACF-certified.

COSTS: $59.40/cr-hr in-state, $112.40/cr-hr out-of-state. Application fee $10. Average off-campus housing $300/mo. Admission requirements: HS diploma or equivalent & admission test.

CONTACT: Robert Anderson, Program Chair, Des Moines Area Community College, Culinary Arts, 2006 S. Ankeny Blvd., #7, Ankeny, IA 50021; 515-964-6532, Fax 515-965-7129, RLAnderson@dmacc.cc.ia.us, www.dmacc.cc.ia.us.

INDIAN HILLS COMMUNITY COLLEGE
Ottumwa/Year-round

Sponsor: 2-year college. Program: 18-month AAS degree in Culinary Arts, 9-month diploma in Culinary/Baking Assistant. Established: 1969. Accredited by NCA. Calendar: semester. Curriculum: culinary. Admit dates: Fall, spring. Total enrollment: 35. 15-20 each admission period. 100% of applicants accepted. 85% receive financial aid. S:T ratio 12:1. 97% of graduates obtain jobs within 6 mos. Facilities: Include 2 kitchens, fully equiped bakery lab, 3 classrooms, student-run dining room.

Faculty: 2 full-time. Mary Kivlahan, program director & instructor; Mark Fisher, bakery instructor.

Costs: $57/credit-hour in-state, $82/credit-hour out-of-state. On-campus housing: 472 spaces. Average off-campus housing cost is $350/mo. Admission requirements: HS diploma or equivalent and admission test. Scholarships: yes.

Contact: Mary Kivlahan, Program Director, Indian Hills Community College, Culinary Arts Dept, 525 Grandview, Bldg. #7, Ottumwa, IA 52501; 515-683-5196, Fax 515-683-5184, jsapp@ihcc.cc.ia.us, www.ihcc.cc.ia.us.

IOWA LAKES COMMUNITY COLLEGE

Emmetsburg/Year-round

Sponsor: College. Program: 2-year AAS degree in Culinary Arts and/or Hotel, Motel, Restaurant Management program. Established: 1974. Accredited by NCA, NRA, AHMA, DMA. Calendar: semester. Curriculum: core. Admit dates: Sept, Jan. Total enrollment: 30-40. 95% of applicants accepted. 70% receive financial aid. S:T ratio 10-12:1. 95% of graduates obtain jobs within 6 mos. Facilities: 2 kitchens, 2 classrooms, 1 restaurant, 1 banquet facility.

Costs: Annual tuition $2,500 in-state, $3,000 out-of-state. Dormitory spaces available on campus. Admission requirements: HS diploma or equivalent & admission test. Scholarships: yes. Loans: yes.

Contact: Robert Halverson, Professor/Coordinator, Iowa Lakes Community College, So. Attendance Ctr., Culinary Arts, 3200 College Dr., Emmetsburg, IA 50536; 712-852-5256, Fax 712-852-2152, rhalverson@iowalakes.edu, www.ilcc.cc.ia.us/programs_study/business/hotel_restaurant.htm.

IOWA WESTERN COMMUNITY COLLEGE

Council Bluffs/August-May

Sponsor: College. Program: 2-year AAS degree in Culinary Arts. Established: 1974. Accredited by NCA, ACF. Admit dates: Fall, spring. Total enrollment: 30-40. 10-20 each admission period. 95% of applicants accepted. 80% receive financial aid. 1% enrolled part-time. S:T ratio 10-12:1. 95% of graduates obtain jobs within 6 mos. Facilities: Include kitchen and 2 classrooms.

Faculty: 2 full-time, 3 part-time. Includes P. Swope, B. Gauke, B. Leeder, CCE, N. Johnson, L. Harrill.

Costs: Tuition in-state $58/cr-hr, out-of-state $81/cr-hr. Room & board $1,500-$2,000/semester. Admission requirements: HS diploma or equivalent & admission test. Scholarships: yes.

Contact: Robert Graunke, Professor, Iowa Western Community College, Food Service Mgmt./Culinary Arts, 2700 College Rd., Box 4-C, Council Bluffs, IA 51502; 712-325-3238/712-325-3398, Fax 712-325-3335, bgraunke@iwcc.edu, http://iwcc.cc.ia.us.

KIRKWOOD COMMUNITY COLLEGE

Cedar Rapids/August-April

Sponsor: 2-yr community college. Program: 1-yr Bakery certificate, 2-yr AAS degrees in Culinary Arts & Restaurant Management, 1-yr Food Service Training Diploma. Established: 1972. Accredited by NCA, ACF. Calendar: semester. Curriculum: culinary, core. Admit dates: Fall, spring. Bakery admission fall only. Total enrollment: 190. 64/fall, 32/spring. 100% of applicants accepted. 60-70% receive financial aid. 25% enrolled part-time. S:T ratio 16:1. 95% of graduates obtain jobs within 6 mos. Facilities: Includes 1 kitchen with 2 food labs & a bakery lab, 4 classrooms, restaurant.

Courses: Includes food production, culinary arts, garde manger, bakery, wines & spirits, purchasing, menu planning, nutrition, personnel mgmt, service techniques, restaurant law.

Faculty: 5 full-time, 2 part-time. Qualifications: college degrees & industry experience. Includes Mary Jane German, MS, RD; Mary Rhiner, MA, RD; David Dettman, AAS; Amy Wyss, AAS.

Costs: In-state $78/cr-hr, out-of-state $156/cr-hr. Off-campus housing ~$325-$425/mo. Admission requirements: HS diploma or equivalent, placement test. Scholarships: yes. Loans: yes.

Contact: Mary Jane German, Asst. Professor/Coordinator, Kirkwood Community College, 6301 Kirkwood Blvd. S.W., PO Box 2068, Cedar Rapids, IA 52406; 319-398-4981, Fax 319-398-5667, mgerman@kirkwood.cc.ia.us, www.kirkwood.edu/businessdept/programs/culinar.htm.

SCOTT COMMUNITY COLLEGE
Bettendorf/Year-round

Sponsor: College. Program: 3-year AAS degree & 6,000-hour apprenticeship in sanitation & cook certification from ACF. Established: 1991. Admit dates: Fall. Total enrollment: 30. 10-15 each admission period. 60% of applicants accepted. 75% receive financial aid. 5% enrolled part-time. S:T ratio 10:1. 100% of graduates obtain jobs within 6 mos.

COURSES: Nutrition, sanitation, menu planning, mgmt, beverages, garde manger, hot food, baking, purchasing, general ed courses. Externship: 6,000-hour, salaried, in restaurant or hotel setting.

FACULTY: 1 full-time, 8 part-time. Qualifications: chef instructors certified by ACF, lecture instructors 4-year degrees, all have industry experience and ACF membership.

COSTS: $58.50/cr-hr in-state. Application fee $25, books, uniform, knives, ACFEI registration $650 (one-time). Off-campus housing ~$300-$400/mo. Admission requirements: Admission test.

CONTACT: Bradley Scott, Scott Community College, Culinary Arts, 500 Belmont Rd., Bettendorf, IA 52722-6804; 563-441-4246, Fax 563-344-0384, bscott@eicc.edu, www.eicc.edu.

KANSAS

AMERICAN INSTITUTE OF BAKING
Manhattan/Year-round

Sponsor: Nonprofit educational & research institution. Program: 20-wk Baking Science & Technology course, 10-wk Bakery Maintenance Engineering program. Established: 1919. Accredited by NCA. Calendar: semester. Curriculum: culinary. Admit dates: July & Feb. ~55-60 each admission period. 90% of applicants accepted. 25% receive financial aid. S:T ratio 15:1. 95% of graduates obtain jobs within 6 mos. Facilities: Bread shop with 1,500 loaves/hr capacity oven, cake shop with carbon dioxide freezer, in-store bakery, cookie & cracker pilot plant.

COURSES: Baking Science courses include cake & sweet goods and bread & roll production, food product safety. Maintenance Engineering courses include refrigeration, basic electricity, motor controls. Continuing ed and correspondence courses include the 50-lesson Science of Baking.

FACULTY: 7 full-time.

COSTS: 20-wk program is $5,000+. Registration fee is $45. Admission requirements: HS diploma or equivalent & min 2 yrs bakery experience (or completion of Science of Bakingcorrespondence course). Scholarships: yes. Loans: yes.

CONTACT: Ken Embers, Registrar, American Institute of Baking, 1213 Bakers Way, Manhattan, KS 66505-399; 800-633-5137/785-537-4750, Fax 913-537-1493, info@aibonline.org, www.aibonline.org.

JOHNSON COUNTY COMMUNITY COLLEGE
Overland Park/Year-round

Sponsor: College. Program: 2- to 3-yr AOS degree. Established: 1975. Accredited by NCA, ACF. Calendar: semester. Admit dates: July, Nov. Total enrollment: 500. 140 each admission period. 80% of applicants accepted. 100% enrolled part-time. S:T ratio 20:1. 100% of graduates obtain jobs within 6 mos.

COSTS: Annual tuition $1,700 in-state, $5,100 out-of-state. Off-campus housing ~$500/mo. Admission requirements: HS diploma or equivalent, admission test. Scholarships: yes. Loans: yes.

CONTACT: Lindy Robinson, Academic Director, Johnson County Community College, 12345 College Blvd, Overland Park, KS 66210-1299; 913-469-8500, Fax 913-469-2560, lrobinsn@jccc.net, www.jccc.net/cat/courses/hmgt.htm.

KANSAS CITY KANSAS AREA VOCATIONAL TECHNICAL SCHOOL
Kansas City/August-May

Sponsor: Public institution. Program: 720-hour certificate in Professional Cooking, certificate in Cooking & Baking. Established: 1975. Accredited by State. Calendar: quarter. Curriculum: culinary. Admit dates: Open. Total enrollment: 20. 99% of applicants accepted. 60% receive financial aid. 50% enrolled part-time. S:T ratio 5:1. 88% of graduates obtain jobs within 6 mos. Facilities:

Include working kitchen, classroom, cafeteria, child care center, banquet facilities.

COURSES: Food preparation, cooking and presentation; safety and sanitation, baking, serving. Externship provided.

FACULTY: 4 full-time. Includes Sharyn Gassmann, BS, MS, M. Mollentine, L. Benson, S. Cole.

COSTS: Annual tuition $780. Application fee $25. Other fees: $50. Admission requirements: Admission test.

CONTACT: Matt Miller, Program Director, Kansas City Kansas Area Vocational Technical School, 2220 W. 59th St., Kansas City, KS 66104; 913-627-4149, Fax 913-627-4109, mamille@gw.kckps.k12.ks.us, www.kckats.com.

NORTHEAST KANSAS AREA VOCATIONAL TECHNICAL SCHOOL

Atchison/August-May

Sponsor: Trade & technical college. Program: 2-yr (67 credit) diploma & AAS degree (83-85 credits) in Food and Beverage Management. Established: 1969. Accredited by State. Admit dates: Open. Total enrollment: 12. 90% receive financial aid. 30% enrolled part-time. S:T ratio 15:1. 100% of graduates obtain jobs within 6 mos. Facilities: Include student-run kitchen facility, off site catering.

COURSES: Professional cooking, baking, purchasing, sanitation. Externship provided.

FACULTY: 1 full-time.

COSTS: ~$945/semester.

CONTACT: Marianne Estes, Northeast Kansas Area Vocational Technical School, 1501 West Riley, Atchison, KS 66002; 913-367-6204, Fax 913-367-3107, mestes@nekatech.net, www.nektc.net/op_fabm.html.

WICHITA AREA TECHNICAL COLLEGE

Wichita/August-May

Sponsor: Technical college. Program: 2-yr AAS, 1-yr diploma. Established: 1975. Accredited by State. Calendar: semester. Curriculum: culinary, core. Admit dates: Aug, Jan. Total enrollment: 21. 95% of applicants accepted. 80% receive financial aid. S:T ratio 6:1. 95% of graduates obtain jobs within 6 mos.

COURSES: Culinary knowledge & skills.

FACULTY: 3 full-time, 2 certified culinary educators on staff.

COSTS: $60/cr-hr + books, supplies, parking, uniforms. Admission requirements: HS diploma or equivalent & admission test.

CONTACT: Colette Baptista, CEC, CCE, Program Specialist, Wichita Area Technical College, Food Service, 324 N. Emporia, Wichita, KS 67202; 316-677-1370, cbaptista@wichitatech.com, www.wichitatech.com.

KENTUCKY

BOWLING GREEN TECHNICAL COLLEGE

Bowling Green/Year-round

Sponsor: Career institution. Program: 2-yr AAT degree in Culinary Arts. Certificate in Catering & diplomas in Professional Baking & Kitchen Management. Established: 1998. Accredited by COE. Calendar: semester. Curriculum: culinary, core. Admit dates: Jan, May, Aug. Total enrollment: 15. 5 each admission period. 100% of applicants accepted. 80% receive financial aid. 4% enrolled part-time. S:T ratio 7:1. Facilities: Include commercial kitchen, banquet facilities, dining room, classroom.

COURSES: Include culinary and general education courses. 120 hours of co-op or practicum. Wilton Cake decorating, Dietary Aide Training. Guest Chef seminars.

FACULTY: 2 full-time, Lisa Hunt, MS; Executive Chef Michael Riggs, MA in Education.

COSTS: $760 per semester. Admission requirements: 18 ACT, HS diploma or equivalent. 16 ACT, HS diploma or equivalent for certificate and diploma programs. Scholarships: yes. Loans: yes..

CONTACT: Lisa Hunt or Mike Riggs, Senior Instructors, Bowling Green Technical College, 1845 Loop Drive, Bowling Green, KY 42101; 270-746-7461, lisaa.hunt@kctcs.net, www.bgtc.net.

ELIZABETHTOWN TECHNICAL COLLEGE

Elizabethtown/August-May

Sponsor: Public institution (formerly Kentucky Tech Elizabethtown). Program: 1-year Restaurant Cook diploma, 18-month Kitchen Supervisor & Food Service Healthcare diploma,2-year AAS degree. Established: 1966. Accredited by COE. Calendar: semester. Curriculum: culinary, core. Admit dates: Aug, Jan, June. Total enrollment: 18. 18 each admission period. 95% of applicants accepted. 60% receive financial aid. S:T ratio 10:1. 95% of graduates obtain jobs within 6 mos. Facilities: Kitchen, classroom and restaurant.

Courses: Quantity food production, bakery & pastry arts. Externship: 5 months (120 hours). Continuing education courses available.

Faculty: 1 full-time (Brenda Harrington, CCE), 2 part-time.

Costs: Semester tuition $725 in-state, $2,175out-of-state plus books & uniforms. Off-campus housing cost ~$2,500. Admission requirements: HS diploma or equivalent and admission test. Scholarships: yes.

Contact: Brenda Harrington, Instructor, Elizabethtown Technical College, Culinary Arts, 505 University Dr., Elizabethtown, KY 42701; 270-766-5133 x3128, Fax 270-766-5224, brenda.harrington@kctcs.net.

JEFFERSON COMMUNITY COLLEGE

Louisville/August-May

Sponsor: 2-yr college. Program: 2-yr AAS degree. Certificate option (no general ed requirements). Established: 1974. Accredited by ACF, SACS. Calendar: semester. Curriculum: culinary, core. Admit dates: Apr, May, Aug, Dec, Jan. Total enrollment: 86. 22 each admission period. 90% of applicants accepted. 80% receive financial aid. 40% enrolled part-time. S:T ratio 11:1. 96% of graduates obtain jobs within 6 mos. Facilities: Commercial kitchen with new equipment installed 2000. Teaching lab, kitchen, executive dining room, library, computer labs, research learning center, classrooms.

Courses: Labs: Elementary Food Prep, American & European Pastries, Garde Manger & Menu Planning, Catering. Lecture courses: Nutrition, Sanitation, Food Cost & Portion control.

Faculty: 2 full-time, 2 part-time.

Costs: Annual tuition $1,450 in-state, $4,350 out-of-state. Admission requirements: HS diploma or equivalent and admission test. Scholarships: yes. Loans: yes.

Contact: Gail Crawford, Program Coordinator, Jefferson Community College, Downtown Campus, 109 E. Broadway, Louisville, KY 40202;, gail.crawford@kctcs.net.

KENTUCKY TECH-DAVIESS COUNTY CAMPUS

Owensboro/August-June

Sponsor: Independent institution. Program: 4- to 5-semester certificate/diploma in Culinary Arts. Established: 1971. Accredited by SACS. Calendar: semester. Curriculum: culinary. Admit dates: Aug. Total enrollment: 24. 2-6 each admission period. 100% of applicants accepted. 90% receive financial aid. 50% enrolled part-time. S:T ratio 18:1. 85% of graduates obtain jobs within 6 mos. Facilities: Include kitchen and classroom.

Courses: Include culinary and general education courses. 150 hours of co-op and occupational training. Continuing education: cake decorating.

Faculty: One full-time, Dudley Mitchell. Qualifications: BS in Home Economics/Occupational Foodservice, meets state requirements.

Costs: $175/quarter. Application fee $25. Admission requirements: TABE test, HS diploma or equivalent. Scholarships: yes. Loans: yes.

Contact: Kaye Evans, Counselor, Kentucky Tech-Daviess County Campus, Student Services, 15th and Frederica St., Owensboro, KY 42301; 502-687-7260, Fax 502-687-7208, kay.evans@kctcs.net.

SULLIVAN UNIVERSITY'S NATIONAL CENTER FOR HOSPITALITY STUDIES

Louisville/Year-round *(See display ad page 73)*

Sponsor: Division of Sullivan University. Program: 18-mo AS degree programs in Culinary Arts, Baking & Pastry Arts, Hotel/Restaurant Management, &Professional Catering; 36-mo BS/BA in Hospitality Studies; 9-12 mo diplomas in Professional Cooking & Professional Baking. Established: 1987. Accredited by SACS, ACF. Calendar: quarter. Curriculum: culinary, core. Admit dates: Jan, Mar, June, September. Total enrollment: 700. 100-150 each admission period. 85% of applicants accepted. 93% receive financial aid. 18% enrolled part-time. S:T ratio 18:1. 100% of graduates obtain jobs within 6 mos. Facilities: A la carte cafe, 5 bakery labs, international, 2 garde manger, 2 basic skills labs, catering, computer labs, retail bakery, fine dining restaurant, catering company.

Courses: Include theory & skills, regional & intl cuisine & pastry, business mgmt, sanitation, nutrition & meal planning, menu design. Students in each program also participate in a related practicum. Culinary Arts program students work in on- & off-campus restaurants, Winston's & Kentucky Cove. Externship provided.

Faculty: 45-member resident faculty & 65-member adjunct faculty. Includes Director of the National Center for Hospitality Studies, Certified Master Pastry Chef Walter Rhea.

Costs: Tuition $24,480. Comprehensive supplies fee $990/lab. Nearby apartments $345/mo. Admission requirements: HS diploma or equivalent plus satisfactory scores on a basic test. Scholarships: yes. Loans: yes.

Location: Watterson Expressway & Bardstown Road in suburban Louisville.

Contact: Greg Cawthon, Director of Admissions, Sullivan University's National Center for Hospitality Studies, 3101 Bardstown Rd., Louisville, KY 40205; 800-844-1354, 502-456-6505, Fax 502-456-0040, admissions@sullivan.edu, www.sullivan.edu.

WEST KENTUCKY TECHNICAL COLLEGE

Paducah/Year-round

Sponsor: Career institution. Program: 18-mo diploma/AAS degree in Culinary Arts; degrees in Food & Beverage Mgmt and Catering; certificates in Culinary Arts, Fundamentals, Catering, Advanced Catering, Beverage Mgmt, Advanced Culinary Arts. Established: 1979. Accredited by SACS. Calendar: semester. Curriculum: culinary, core. Admit dates: Jan, May, Aug. Total enrollment: 36. S:T ratio 20:1. 80% of graduates obtain jobs within 6 mos.

Costs: In-state $1,185/sem, out-of-state $3,555. Admission requirements: HS diploma or equivalent & admission test. Scholarships: yes. Loans: yes.

Contact: Vicki Koehler, Culinary Arts Director, West Kentucky Technical College, Culinary Arts, 5200 Blandville Rd., Box 7408, Paducah, KY 42002-7408; 502-554-4991 ext 232, Fax 502-554-9754 x221, vicki.koehler@kctcs.net, www.westkentucky.kctcs.edu.

LOUISIANA

ACF NEW ORLEANS CHAPTER

New Orleans/Year-round

Sponsor: ACF chapter. Program: 3-yr apprenticeship; degree program through Delgado Community College completed by 90%. Curriculum: culinary. Total enrollment: 190.

Costs: $3,600. Housing cost is $350-$550/mo.

Contact: Dr. M. Bartholomew, ACF New Orleans Chapter, Delgado Community College, 615 City Park Ave., Bldg. 11, New Orleans, LA 70119-4399; 504-483-4208, Fax 504-483-4893, mbarth@dcc.edu.

BOSSIER PARISH COMMUNITY COLLEGE

Bossier City

Sponsor: College. Program: 9-month certificate. Established: 1986. Accredited by ACF. Admit dates: Aug. Total enrollment: 25. 98% of applicants accepted. S:T ratio 13:1. 100% of graduates obtain jobs within 6 mos.

Faculty: 2 full-time, 4 part-time.

Costs: $3,100/yr. Admission requirements: HS diploma or equivalent & admission test. Scholarships: yes. Loans: yes.

Contact: Elizabeth Dickson, Chef/Coordinator, Bossier Parish Community College, Culinary Arts, 2719 Airline Drive North, Bossier City, LA 71111; 318-747-4567, Fax 318-742-8664, edickson@bpcc.cc.la.us, www.bpcc.cc.la.us.

CHEF JOHN FOLSE CULINARY INSTITUTE

Thibodaux/Year-round

Sponsor: Regional university. Program: 2-yr AS degree in Culinary Arts, 4-yr BS degree in Culinary Arts. Established: 1994. Accredited by SACS. Calendar: semester. Curriculum: culinary, core. Admit dates: Rolling. Total enrollment: 200. 40-50 each admission period. 90% of applicants accepted. 44% receive financial aid. 14% enrolled part-time. S:T ratio 15:1. 100% of graduates obtain jobs within 6 mos. Facilities: 2 newly-equipped teaching kitchens, 2 demo classrooms.

Courses: Classic culinary knowledge & regional American cuisine, culinary operations, product development, nutrition. Sophomore & senior externship, each 360 hrs paid work experience. Externships throughout U.S & abroad. Continuing ed courses year-round.

Faculty: 5 full- & 1 part-time faculty members. Robert Harrington, Ph.D., CEC; Carol Gunter, MBA, CEC; George Kaslow, MS; Kenneth Perry, MS, CEC; Randolph Cheramie, BA; John Folse, CEC, AAC.

Costs: $1,184/sem in-state, $3,752/sem out-of-state. Non-resident fee waiver available. Additional fees & equipment $650 + $250/lab course. Admission requirements: HS GPA 2.5+ or ACT score of 19 or top 50% of HS class. Scholarships: yes. Loans: yes.

Contact: Dr. Robert Harrington, Dean, Chef John Folse Culinary Institute, Nicholls State University, P.O. Box 2099, Thibodaux, LA 70310; 985-449-7100, 877-NICHOLLS, Fax 985-449-7089, jfci-info@nicholls.edu, www.nicholls.edu/jfolse.

CULINARY INSTITUTE OF NEW ORLEANS

New Orleans/Year-round

Sponsor: Private school. Program: 900-hr (7-mo) certificate & 1,800-hr (14-mo) diploma/AOS degree in Culinary Arts; 180-hr (6-wk) certificate in Professional Baking. Established: 1984. Accredited by COE. Curriculum: culinary. Admit dates: Continuous. Total enrollment: 250/yr. 18/mo each admission period. 90% of applicants accepted. 82% receive financial aid. S:T ratio 18:1. 100% of graduates obtain jobs within 6 mos. Facilities: 3 bake shops, 2 cafeterias, 3 catering services, 3 demo labs, 3 food prodkitchens, 8 classrooms, 3 gourmet dining rooms, 2 public restaurants.

Courses: Product Knowledge, Cooking Theory, Food Sci, Culinary Arts, Sanitation, Baking, Wine, Nutrition, Dining Room & Banquet Mgmt, Nutrition. 195- & 405-hr paid externships.

Faculty: 8 full-time.

Costs: Certificate (diploma/degree) programs: tuition $9,000 ($18,000), textbooks/clothing/equipment $730 ($1,114), fees $1,550 ($3,025). Scholarships: yes. Loans: yes.

Contact: Bob Koehl, Director, Culinary Institute of New Orleans, 2100 St. Charles Ave., #1, New Orleans, LA 70140; 504-525-2433, Fax 504-525-2466, cino2100@aol.com, www.ci-no.com.

DELGADO COMMUNITY COLLEGE

New Orleans/Year-round

Sponsor: 2-yr college. Program: 2-yr/6,000-hr Culinary Arts Apprenticeship AAS degree & Pastry Arts certificate. Established: 1926. Accredited by ACF. Calendar: semester. Curriculum: core. Admit dates: Aug. Total enrollment: 200. 75 each admission period. 90% of applicants accepted. 50% receive financial aid. S:T ratio 15:1. 100% of graduates obtain jobs within 6 mos. Facilities: 2 labs, 9 lecture rooms.

Courses: Include pastry & management. Apprenticeship.

Faculty: 4 full-time, all ACF-certified; 2 part-time.

Costs: $800/sem in-state, $2,000 out-of-state. Admission requirements: GED or HS diploma, 2 reference letters. Scholarships: yes. Loans: yes.

CONTACT: Dr. Mary P. Bartholomew, Culinary Arts Director, Delgado Community College-Culinary Arts Dept., 615 City Park Ave., New Orleans, LA 70119; 504-483-4208, Fax 504-483-4893, mbarth@dcc.edu, www.dcc.edu.

LOUISIANA TECHNICAL COLLEGE – BATON ROUGE CAMPUS

Baton Rouge/Year-round

Sponsor: Public institution. Program: 1-year diploma/certificate in Culinary Arts. Established: 1974. Calendar: quarter. Curriculum: culinary. Admit dates: Year-round. Total enrollment: 15-Oct. 6 each admission period. 95% of applicants accepted. 45% receive financial aid. 20% enrolled part-time. S:T ratio 12:1. 95% of graduates obtain jobs within 6 mos. Facilities: Include 2 kitchens.

COURSES: Sanitation, nutrition, food and beverage management, professional cooking.

FACULTY: 1 full-time. Michael Travasos. Qualifications: bachelor's degree, industry experience.

COSTS: Annual tuition $420. Application fee $9.50. Books, uniforms, equipment $215. Average off-campus housing cost is $300/mo.

CONTACT: Michael Travasos, Louisiana Technical College-Baton Rouge Campus, Admissions, 3250 N. Acadian Throughway, Baton Rouge, LA 70805; 225-359-9202, Fax 225-359-9296, mtravasos@brti.tec.la.us, www.brti.tec.la.us.

LOUISIANA TECHNICAL COLLEGE – LAFAYETTE CAMPUS

Lafayette

Sponsor: Technical college. Program: 18-mo (1800-clock-hr) diploma program in Culinary Arts & Occupations. Established: 1979. Accredited by ACF, COE. Calendar: quarter. Curriculum: culinary. Admit dates: Aug, Nov, Feb-Mar, May. Total enrollment: 45. 20 each admission period. 100% of applicants accepted. 25% receive financial aid. S:T ratio 15:01. 100% of graduates obtain jobs within 6 mos.

FACULTY: 3 instructors.

COSTS: $105/quarter. Admission requirements: 16 yrs. of age, interest in culinary field, HS diploma or GED by date of completion of program.

CONTACT: Chef Earline Thomas, Louisiana Technical College, Lafayette Campus, 1101 Bertrand Dr., Lafayette, LA 70506-4909; 318-262-5962, Fax 318-262-5122, earlinet@lafayette.tec.la.us, http://ltcl.lafayette.tec.la.us/diploma/personal/culinary1.html.

LOUISIANA TECHNICAL COLLEGE – SIDNEY N. COLLIER CAMPUS

New Orleans/Year-round

Sponsor: Career institution. Program: 18-month certificate. Established: 1957. Accredited by SACS. Admit dates: Open. Total enrollment: 20. 100% of applicants accepted. S:T ratio 20:1. 80% of graduates obtain jobs within 6 mos.

FACULTY: 30 full-time, 1 part-time.

COSTS: $105/qtr, $630 for program (6 qtrs/18 mos).

CONTACT: Edward James, Instructor, Louisiana Technical College - Sidney N. Collier Campus, Culinary Arts, 3727 Louisa St., New Orleans, LA 70126; 504-942-8333 x147, Fax 504-942-8337, ejames@theltc.net, www.angelfire.com/la2/collier.

NUNEZ COMMUNITY COLLEGE

Chalmette/Year-round

Sponsor: 2-year college. Program: 1-year/33-credit-hour certificate and 2-year/68-credit-hour AAS degree in Culinary Arts and Occupations. Calendar: semester. Curriculum: culinary, core.

COURSES: Basic food preparation, baking, meat, poultry, seafood, soups, stocks, sauces, garde manger, patisserie, food & beverage purchasing, cost control.

COSTS: For 12+ credit-hours: in-state $488, out-of-state $1,523 plus technology fee.

CONTACT: Donna Clark, Nunez Community College-Culinary Arts, 3700 LaFontaine St., Chalmette, LA 70043; 504-680-2457, dclark@nunez.cc.la.us, www.nunez.cc.la.us.

SCLAFANI'S COOKING SCHOOL, INC.

Metairie/Year-round

(See display ad above)

Sponsor: Post-secondary proprietary school. Program: 4-wk (120-hr) certificate of completion program in commercial cooking/baking. Established: 1987. Licensed by Louisiana State Board of Regents Post-Secondary Career & Occupational Skill Training. Calendar: quarter. Curriculum: culinary. Admit dates: Monthly. Total enrollment: 120. 10-15 each admission period. 90% of applicants accepted. 60% receive financial aid. S:T ratio 10:1. 98% of graduates obtain jobs within 6 mos. Facilities: Classroom/dining room, commercial kitchen prep room, storage area.

COURSES: Culinary arts, baking, food cost math, ServSafe Certification course (sanitation & safety), supervisory skills, principles of cooking & production. 16 points towards ACF re-newal certification or 16 points towards initial ACF certification are achievable.

FACULTY: 4 full-time. Includes Administrative Instructor Frank P. Sclafani, Sr., CEC, FMP; chef/instructor Chef Angelique Connors; Administrative Asst. Dianne F. Sclafani & Juanita Dowell.

COSTS: $2,995 includes $150 reg fee, text books, chef jacket. Off-campus housing cost ~$50+/day. Admission requirements: Age 18 or older; must pass 7th grade level reading & math.

LOCATION: 3 miles from New Orleans.

CONTACT: Frank P. Sclafani, Sr., CEC, FMP, President, Sclafani's Cooking School, Inc., Culinary Arts, 107 Gennaro Pl., Metairie, LA 70001-5209; 504-833-7861, 800-583-1282, Fax 504-833-7872, info@sclafanicookingschool.com, www.sclafanicookingschool.com.

MAINE

EASTERN MAINE TECHNICAL COLLEGE

Bangor/Year-round

Sponsor: 2-year college. Program: 66-hr AAS degree in Culinary Arts, 33-hr Food Service Specialist certificate. Calendar: semester. Curriculum: culinary. Total enrollment: 55. 20% enrolled part-time. S:T ratio 10:1. Facilities: Include food production kitchen, bakeries & bake shop, dining room, computer labs.

COURSES: Include Culinary Skills Development, Professional Cooking & Service, Sanitation.

FACULTY: 2 full-time, 4 part-time.

COSTS: Tuition $1,122/sem in-state, $3,283/sem out-of-state. Scholarships: yes.

CONTACT: Elizabeth Russell, Director of Admissions, Eastern Maine Technical College, Culinary Arts Dept., 354 Hogan Rd., Bangor, ME 04401; 207-941-4680, Fax 207-941-4683, erussell@emtc.org, www.emtc.org/Technologies/culinary_arts.

SOUTHERN MAINE COMMUNITY COLLEGE

South Portland/September-May

Sponsor: State-owned institution. Program: 2-yr associate degree in Culinary Arts. Established: 1958. Accredited by NEASC. Calendar: semester. Curriculum: culinary, core. Admit dates: Rolling.

Total enrollment: 70. 80 each admission period. 75% of applicants accepted. 65% receive financial aid. 10% enrolled part-time. S:T ratio 16:1. 90% of graduates obtain jobs within 6 mos. Facilities: Include 8 kitchens & classrooms, restaurant.

Courses: Baking, food development, buffet, classical cuisine, dining room mgmt, general ed courses. Bartending & cake decorating.

Faculty: 6 full-time with college degrees &/or ACF certification.

Costs: In-state $3,100/yr, out-of-state $5,800/yr. On-campus housing: 140 spaces; room & board $4,800. Admission requirements: HS diploma or equivalent & admission test. Scholarships: yes. Loans: yes.

Contact: Robert Weimont, Director of Admissions, Southern Maine Community College, 2 Fort Rd., South Portland, ME 04106; 207-767-9520, Fax 207-767-9671, bweimont@smtc.edu, www.smtc.edu.

YORK COUNTY COMMUNITY COLLEGE

Wells/Year-round

Sponsor: 2-yr college. Program: 68-cr AAS degree in Culinary Arts, 1-yr Food Service Specialist certificate. Established: 1995. Accredited by NEASC. Calendar: semester. Curriculum: core. Admit dates: Sept, Jan, May. Total enrollment: 52. 99% of applicants accepted. 80% receive financial aid. 50% enrolled part-time. S:T ratio 12:1. Facilities: Demo lab, food prod & teaching kitchens, computer lab.

Courses: Culinary skills, garde-manger, food purchasing & prep, baking, sanitation. Students participate in internship.

Faculty: 1 full-time, 7 part-time.

Costs: Tuition $2,312/yr in-state, $5,066/yr out-of-state. Program fees $350. Admission requirements: HS or GED completion. Scholarships: yes.

Contact: Leisa Grass, Director of Admissions, York County Technical College, 112 College Dr., Wells, ME 04090; 207-646-9282, Fax 207-641-0837, admissions@yctc.net, www.yctc.net/student_services/courses/culinary.htm.

MARYLAND

ALLEGANY COLLEGE OF MARYLAND

Cumberland/Year-round

Sponsor: 2-year college. Program: 2-year AS degree in Culinary Arts. Established: 1998. Curriculum: culinary. Admit dates: Jan, Aug. Total enrollment: 26. 48% enrolled part-time. S:T ratio 10:1. Facilities: Food production kitchen, teaching kitchen, computer lab.

Courses: Include culinary skills, kitchen management. 2 paid internships.

Faculty: 2 full-time, 5 part-time.

Costs: $3,060/yr in-state, $5,984/yr out-of-state. Scholarships: yes.

Contact: David Sanford II, Allegany College of Maryland, Culinary Arts, 12401 Willowbrook Rd., SE, Cumberland, MD 21502; 301-784-5308, dsanford@ac.cc.md.us, www.ac.cc.md.us/careers/hospitality/chef.

ANNE ARUNDEL COMMUNITY COLLEGE

Arnold/Year-round

Sponsor: 2-year public community college. Program: AAS degree in Chef Apprentice, Pastry Apprentice, Hospitality Mgmt., Culinary; Certificate programs in Hospitality Mgmt., Culinary, Baking & Pastry, Catering. Established: 1988. Accredited by MSA. Calendar: semester. Curriculum: culinary, core. Admit dates: Sept, Jan, May. Total enrollment: 150. 60 each admission period. 100% of applicants accepted. 45% enrolled part-time. S:T ratio 16:1. 90% of graduates obtain jobs within 6 mos. Facilities: Modern training facilities & 5 dedicated smart classrooms; 2 campuses.

Courses: Industry-current curriculum based upon skill standards. Apprentice Program, sponsored by the ACF, requires 6,000 apprentice-hrs. Other degree options require 1 semester practicum. Continuing professional education, contract training.

Faculty: 4 full-time, 15 part-time.

Costs: $62/cr-hr. Admission requirements: Open enrollment. Apprentice students must submit application, 2 letters of reference, essay, & transcripts. Scholarships: yes. Loans: yes.

Contact: Scott Strong, Director, Anne Arundel Community College, 101 College Pkwy., Arnold, MD 21012; 410-777-2398, Fax 410-777-1143, wsstrong@aacc.edu, www.aacc.edu.

BALTIMORE INTERNATIONAL COLLEGE

Baltimore; County Cavan/Year-round *(See display ad page 80)*

Sponsor: Independent college offering specialized degree and certificate programs through its School of Culinary Arts, School of Business & Management, and Division of Evening & Weekend Studies. Program: 3 baccalaureate degrees: Culinary Mgmnt; Hospitality Mgmnt; Hospitality Mgmnt w/concentration in Marketing. 4 associate degrees: Prof. Cooking; Prof. Baking & Pastry; Prof. Cooking & Baking; Food & Beverage Mgmnt; Certificate: Culinary Arts. Established: 1972. Accredited by MSA. Calendar: semester. Curriculum: culinary, core. Admit dates: Jan, May, September. Total enrollment: 850. 100-270 each admission period. 95% of applicants accepted. 90% receive financial aid. S:T ratio 13:1. 98% of graduates obtain jobs within 6 mos. Facilities: 2 campuses: Baltimore Campus includes 19 buildings; Virginia Park Campus is an historic, 100-acre campus in County Cavan, Ireland.

Courses: Each program builds from a foundation of theories & techniques to advanced techniques & special projects. Core courses include math, science, English, nutrition, history, & psychology. Degree programs include an Honors Program featuring 5 wks of study in Ireland with the possibility of internship abroad on college's campus or externship in degree major field.

Faculty: 45-member faculty. Academic faculty hold degrees through doctorate level. European-trained chefs at the Virginia Park campus in Ireland hold credentials from the City & Guilds of London.

Costs: $6,371/semester (15 wks) for baccalaureate & associate's degree students, $4,194/semester for certificate students. Student activity fee/semester $92. Comprehensive fees $150-$2,361/semester. Admission requirements: HS diploma or equivalent & satisfactory SAT, ACT, or college admissions test score required. Scholarships: yes. Loans: yes.

Location: The Baltimore campus is in Baltimore, MD; the Virginia Park campus is 50 mi northwest of Dublin, Ireland.

Contact: Lori L. Makowski, Director of Admissions, Baltimore International College, 17 Commerce St., Baltimore, MD 21202; 800-624-9926, 410-752-4710, Fax 410-752-3730, admissions@bic.edu, www.bic.edu.

INTERNATIONAL SCHOOL OF CONFECTIONERY ARTS, INC.

Gaithersburg/Year-round

Sponsor: Proprietary school. Program: 2-day to 1-wk certificate courses in confectionery arts. Established: 1982. Admit dates: Weekly. Total enrollment: 400/yr. 12-16 each admission period. 100% of applicants accepted. 3% receive financial aid. S:T ratio 4:1. 100% of graduates obtain jobs within 6 mos. Facilities: 2,400-sq-ft area with 16 work stations, overhead mirrors, marble tables, decorating & candy-making equipment.

Courses: Sugar pulling, blowing, & casting, chocolate & cake decoration, Swiss candy making, gum paste, pastillage, plated desserts.

Faculty: Ewald Notter has won gold medals in intl competitions; taught in Europe & the Far East; judges competitions; authored The Text Book of Sugar Pulling & Blowing; & created a chocolate & sugar video series for The CIA.

Costs: $275-$950 includes breakfast & lunch. Nearby lodging ~$64/night. Admission requirements: Courses are for professionals & culinary students only.

Contact: Petr Nepozitek, Admissions, International School of Confectionery Arts, Inc., 9209 Gaither Rd., Gaithersburg, MD 20877; 301-963-9077, Fax 301-869-7669, ESNotter@aol.com, www.notterschool.com.

L'ACADEMIE DE CUISINE
Gaithersburg/Year-round

Sponsor: Proprietary vocational school. Program: 48-wk full-time Culinary Career Training program, 34-wk part-time Pastry Arts program, part-time certificate courses, continuing ed & nonprofessional courses, culinary & cultural program in France. Established: 1976. Accredited by ACCET & approved by the Maryland Higher Education Commission. Calendar: semester. Curriculum: culinary. Admit dates: Jan, Mar, July, September. Total enrollment: 60 culinary, 60 pastry. 30 culinary, 15 pastry each admission period. 85% of applicants accepted. 61% receive financial aid. S:T ratio 15:1. 100% of graduates obtain jobs within 6 mos. Facilities: 35-station practice & pastry kitchen & 35-seat demo classroom.

COURSES: Curriculum is based on classic French technique & covers food prep & presentation, pastries & desserts, wine selection, catering, menu planning. Placement in fine dining restaurants/hotels/pastry shops in metropolitan D.C. Advanced/continuing ed courses: wedding cakes, sugar, chocolate, catering, sanitation.

FACULTY: 5 full-, 3 part-time. School President Francois Dionot, graduate of L'Ecole Hoteliere de la Societe Suisse des Hoteliers, IACP founder; Peter K. Moore; graduates Somchet Chumpapo, Mark Ramsdell, Theresa Souther.

COSTS: Full-time Culinary Career program $19,420 + $885 fees. Pastry Arts program $12,000 + $600 fees. Certificate course $1,400-$2,645. Continuing ed $1,400-$2,550. Admission requirements: HS diploma or equivalent & 18 yrs of age. Completed application, 2 letters of reference & an interview. Scholarships: yes. Loans: yes.

CONTACT: Barbara Cullen, Admissions, L'Academie de Cuisine, 16006 Industrial Dr., Gaithersburg, MD 20877-1414; 301-670-8670, 800-664-CHEF, Fax 301-670-0450, info@lacademie.com, www.lacademie.com. Additional contact: Patrice Dionot.

MASSACHUSETTS

BERKSHIRE COMMUNITY COLLEGE
Pittsfield

Sponsor: College. Program: 1-yr certificate, 2-yr AAS degree. Established: 1977. Accredited by NEASC. Calendar: semester. Curriculum: culinary, core. Admit dates: Fall, spring. Total enrollment: 15/sem. Facilities: Full kitchen lab, use of local hotel kitchen/dining room for quantity food dinners.

COURSES: Includes baking, garde manger, quantity foods production, sanitation, purchasing & food service management. Externship provided.

FACULTY: 2 full-time, 2 part-time.

COSTS: $88/credit-hour in-state, $105/credit-hour out-of-state. Admission requirements: HS diploma or equivalent and learning skills assessment. Loans: yes.

CONTACT: Nancy Simonds-Ruderman, Professor of Hotel & Restaurant Management, Berkshire Community College, Culinary Arts, 1350 West St., Pittsfield, MA 01201-5786; 413-499-4660 #229, Fax 413-447-7840, nruder@cc.berkshire.org, http://cc.berkshire.org.

BOSTON UNIVERSITY CULINARY ARTS
Boston/Year-round

Sponsor: Boston University. Program: 4-month certificate in the Culinary Arts Related programs include: Master of Liberal Arts with concentration in Gastronomy, Certificates in Wine Studies and Cheese Studies, Personal Chef Certification. Established: 1986. Calendar: semester. Curriculum: culinary. Admit dates: Rolling. Total enrollment: 24. 12 each admission period. S:T ratio 6:1. 100% of graduates obtain jobs within 6 mos. Facilities: Demonstration room with overhead mirror, classroom, 8 restaurant stations in the laboratory kitchen.

COURSES: Classic & modern techniques & theory, ethnic/regional cuisine, food history, dining room theory/practice, purchasing. Masters program includes food history & anthropology, food writing, nutrition, archaeology. Wine programs include WSET certificate. Short & long term non-credit seminars in the arts and culinary arts.

FACULTY: 1 full-time, 30 part-time. Includes Jacques Pepin, Jasper White, Chris Kimball, Jody Adams, Ihsan Gurdal, Jim Dodge, Mary Ann Esposito.

COSTS: Culinary certificate tuition $8,500, application fee $50. Admission requirements: Some foodservice experience preferred. Loans: yes.

CONTACT: Rebecca Alssid, Director of Special Programs, Boston University Culinary Arts, 808 Commonwealth Ave., Boston, MA 02215; 617-353-9852, Fax 617-353-4130, ralssid@bu.edu, www.bu.edu/lifelong.

BRISTOL COMMUNITY COLLEGE

Fall River/September-May

Sponsor: College. Program: 2-year AAS degree. Established: 1985. Accredited by NEASC. Calendar: semester. Curriculum: culinary. Admit dates: September. Total enrollment: 22-24. 22-24 each admission period. 80% of applicants accepted. 70% receive financial aid. 20% enrolled part-time. S:T ratio 6:1. 75% of graduates obtain jobs within 6 mos.

COURSES: Courses are designed to enhance the cook's skill & knowledge for restaurant work.

FACULTY: 1 full-time, 3 part-time.

COSTS: Tuition in-state & R.I. $6,000, out-of-state $18,255. Scholarships available for 2nd year students. Scholarships: yes. Loans: yes.

CONTACT: John Caressimo, CCE, Culinary Director, Bristol Community College, 777 Elsbree St., Fall River, MA 02720; 508-678-2811 #2111, Fax 508-730-3290, jcaressi@bristol.mass.edu, www.bristol.mass.edu.

BUNKER HILL COMMUNITY COLLEGE

Boston/Year-round

Sponsor: 2-year college. Program: 1-year/29-credit certificate and 2-year/64-credit AS degree in Culinary Arts. Calendar: semester. Curriculum: culinary, core. Admit dates: Sept, Jan. Total enrollment: 180. 80-90 each admission period. 95% of applicants accepted. 40% receive financial aid. 10% enrolled part-time. S:T ratio 10-12:1. 99% of graduates obtain jobs within 6 mos.

COURSES: Food & beverage management, purchasing, baking, facilities planning, banquet, classical, buffet catering, accounting. 660 hours of employment required.

FACULTY: 4 full- and 2 part-time.

COSTS: $78/credit in-state, $248/credit out-of-state. Admission requirements: HS diploma. Scholarships: yes. Loans: yes.

CONTACT: Cheryl Senato, Professor, Bunker Hill Community College, 250 New Rutherford Ave., Boston, MA 02129-2991; 617-228-2336, Fax 617-228-2082, csenato@bhcc.mass.edu, www.bhcc.mass.edu/degreeandcetprog/hospitality.htm. Marybeth Barton: mbarton@bhcc.mass.edu.

THE CAMBRIDGE SCHOOL OF CULINARY ARTS

Cambridge/Year-round *(See also page 239)(See display ad page 83)*

Sponsor: Proprietary school. Program: 37-wk Professional Chef diploma program, 15 wk certificate program, continuing ed classes, culinary tours to Europe. Established: 1974. Accredited by ACCSCT, licensed by the Commonwealth of Mass. Dept. of Education. Calendar: quarter. Curriculum: culinary. Admit dates: Sept, Jan, May. Total enrollment: 339. 113 each admission period. 90% of applicants accepted. S:T ratio 12-15:1. 90% of graduates obtain jobs within 6 mos. Facilities: 3 lecture spaces & adjacent practice kitchens professionally equipped with commercial grade equipment, culinary library.

COURSES: Emphasis on classical culinary principles & techniques, food science. Curriculum includes: food basics, baking, regional Italian & French cuisine, classical French, haute & nouvelle cuisine, garde manger. Flexible day/evening scheduling. Continuing ed classes for novices & professionals include basic skills, advanced baking, specialty subjects such as cheese, chocolate, wines, international cuisines.

FACULTY: 6 full- & 5 part-time instructors approved by the Commonwealth of Mass. Dept. of Education. President, founder, & instructor Roberta Avallone Dowling, CCP, holds diplomas from Julie Dannenbaum, Marcella Hazan, Madeleine Kamman, & Richard Olney.

COSTS: Professional 37-wk program $18,300, 15-week certificate program $8,500, $45 application fee for each program, $300-$1,100 for equipment, books, & fees. Admission requirements: Min. age 18 & have a HS diploma or equivalent. Loans: yes.

LOCATION: 5 miles from downtown Boston, 1 mile from Harvard Square.

CONTACT: Gwenn Legters, Director of Admissions, The Cambridge School of Culinary Arts, 2020 Massachusetts Ave., Cambridge, MA 02140-2104; 617-354-2020, Fax 617-576-1963, info@cambridgeculinary.com, www.cambridgeculinary.com.

DELPHIN'S GOURMANDISE SCHOOL OF PASTRY

Marblehead/August-June

Sponsor: Private school. Program: 240-hr (6-month) part-time Certificate Pastry Program that emphasizes the basics. 1- to 3-day workshops & evening classes. Established: 2000. Licensed by state. Calendar: trimester. Curriculum: culinary. Admit dates: Jan-June, Aug-Dec. Total enrollment: 24. 6 each admission period. 90% of applicants accepted. 100% enrolled part-time. S:T ratio 6:1. 95% of graduates obtain jobs within 6 mos. Facilities: Kitchen/class room.

COURSES: Doughs, fillings, cakes, mousses, decorating, chocolate molding, pulled sugar. Technique, chemistry & history of French pastry covered in each unit. Available internally.

FACULTY: Master Pastry Chef Delphin Gomes, co-owner of Delphin's Gourmandise Fine French Patisserie, received the Best of Boston award from Boston Magazine.

COSTS: $6,000/certificate program, $295-$840/workshop, $85/class. Admission requirements: HS diploma.

CONTACT: Tone Gomes, Program Director, Delphin's Gourmandise School of Pastry, 258 Washington St., Marblehead, MA 01945; 781-639-2311, Fax 781-631-2311, DGschoolofpastry@aol.com, www.delphins.com.

EPICUREAN CLUB OF BOSTON

Boston/Year-round

Sponsor: ACF chapter. Program: 3-yr apprenticeship; degree program through Bunker Hill Community College is completed by 60%. Curriculum: culinary. Total enrollment: 5.

COSTS: Housing cost is $700+.

CONTACT: Americo DiFronzo, CEC, Epicurean Club of Boston, 29 Johnson Street, Saugus, MA 01906-1745; 781-231-1115, DiFronzoA@aol.com, www.theEpicureanClubofBoston.com.

ESSEX AGRICULTURAL AND TECHNICAL INSTITUTE

Hathorne/September-May

Sponsor: Career institution. Program: 2-year AAS degree in Culinary Arts & Food Service. Established: 1968. Accredited by NEASC. Calendar: semester. Curriculum: culinary. Admit dates: Sept, Jan. Total enrollment: 65. 40 each admission period. 50% of applicants accepted. 20% receive financial aid. 12% enrolled part-time. S:T ratio 15:1. 60% of graduates obtain jobs within 6 mos. Facilities: Include 6 kitchens and classrooms, bakery and restaurant.

COURSES: Restaurant operation, baking, garde manger, international cuisine, buffet, specialty food production, cakes and pastries, American regional cuisine, and nutrition. Externship provided.

FACULTY: 4 full-time. Includes Division Chair C. Naffah, P. Kelly, L. Bassett, J. Cristello.

COSTS: Annual tuition $2,400. Acceptance fee $30. Other fees approximately $1,830. Admission requirements: HS diploma or equivalent. Scholarships: yes. Loans: yes.

CONTACT: Admissions Coordinator, Essex Agricultural and Technical Institute, Admissions, 562 Maple St., Box 362, Hathorne, MA 01937-0362; 978-774-0050 #210, Fax 978-774-6530, admin@agtech.org, www.agtech.org.

HOLYOKE COMMUNITY COLLEGE

Holyoke/September-May

Sponsor: 2-year Community College. Program: 10-month certificate in Culinary Arts, AS degree in Hospitality Management. Established: 1991. Accredited by NEASC. Calendar: semester. Curriculum: culinary, core. Admit dates: Sept, Jan. Total enrollment: 50. 50 each admission period. 100% of applicants accepted. 50% receive financial aid. 20% enrolled part-time. S:T ratio 12:1 lab. 90% of graduates obtain jobs within 6 mos. Facilities: Include 2 kitchens, bakeshop, dining room.

COURSES: Include professional cooking skills, a la carte & banquet, costing & purchasing, food production, dining room service, baking & pastry, nutrition, sanitation. External work hours required. Evening courses in various culinary topics, sanitation, nutrition.

FACULTY: 4 full-time, 4 part-time.

COSTS: In-state $2,605/yr, out-of-state $6,275/yr. Fees ~$40. Admission requirements: HS diploma or equivalent, math competency test. Scholarships: yes. Loans: yes.

CONTACT: Kristine Ricker Choleva, Department Chair, Holyoke Community College, Hospitality Management & Culinary Arts, 303 Homestead Ave., Holyoke, MA 01040; 413-552-2408, Fax 413-534-8975, kcholeva@hcc.mass.edu, www.hcc.mass.edu. Admissions Department 413-552-2580.

INTERNATIONAL INSTITUTE OF CULINARY ARTS

Fall River/September-June *(See display ad page 85)*

Sponsor: Private 2-yr culinary institute. Program: 2-yr Grande Diploma in Culinary Arts/Restaurant Hospitality; 1-yr Culinary Certificate program; 1-yr Diploma in Baking/Pastry Arts. Established: 1997. Calendar: semester. Curriculum: culinary, core. Admit dates: Open. Total enrollment: 50. Open each admission period. 61% of applicants accepted. S:T ratio 8:1. 100% of graduates obtain jobs within 6 mos. Facilities: Bake shop, 2 catering services,classrooms, lecture rooms, food prod kitchen, 4 gourmet dining rooms, library, 6 public restaurants, 6 teaching kitchens.

COURSES: Incl Baking & Pastry, Beverage Mgmt, Buffet Catering, Confectionery, Cost Control, Culinary Skills, Food Prep, Garde Manger, Intl Cuisine, Meal & Hospitality Planning, Meat Cutting, Menu Design, Nutrition. In-house internship positions.

FACULTY: 6 full-time instructors: 3 industry professionals & 1 Master Chef.

COSTS: $19,000/ per yr for 2-yr Culinary program; $19,000/1-year Culinary certificate program; $19,000/1-yr Baking/Pastry Arts.Each student receives $5,000 scholarship upon entering the IICA (for each year); certain standards must be met & maintained. Admission requirements: HS diploma or GED with 2.0 GPA. Scholarships: yes. Loans: yes.

LOCATION: 20 miles east of Providence, 60 miles south of Boston.

CONTACT: Theodore Karousos, Director of Admissions, International Institute of Culinary Arts, 100 Rock St., Fall River, MA 02720; 508-675-9305, 888-383-2665, Fax 508-678-5214, info@iicaculinary.com, www.iicaculinary.com.

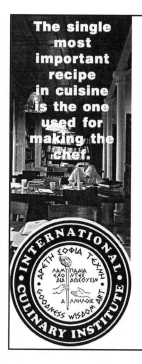

MASSASOIT COMMUNITY COLLEGE
Brockton

Sponsor: College. Program: 2-year degree. Established: 1982. Accredited by State. Admit dates: September. Total enrollment: 60. S:T ratio 20-35:1. 93.5% of graduates obtain jobs within 6 mos.

FACULTY: 3 full-time, 2 part-time.

COSTS: Tuition in-state $72/credit, out-of-state $204/credit. Admission requirements: HS diploma.

CONTACT: David Portesi, Department Chair, Massasoit Community College, Culinary Arts, 1 Massasoit Blvd., Brockton, MA 02402; 508-588-9100 x1697, dportesi@massasoit.mass.edu, www.massasoit.mass.edu/acad_depts/human/culinary/culinary_home.htm.

MINUTEMAN REGIONAL VOCATIONAL TECHNICAL SCHOOL
Lexington/Year-round

Sponsor: Independent trade school. Program: 3-yr diploma, 2-yr post-graduate course, 90-day retraining courses in Culinary, Baking, Hotel & Rest. Mgmt. Established: 1973. Calendar: quarter. Curriculum: culinary, core. Total enrollment: 150. 25 each admission period. 95% of applicants accepted. S:T ratio 10:1. 99% of graduates obtain jobs within 6 mos. Facilities: 6 kitchens & classrooms.

COURSES: Sanitation, nutrition, management, purchasing, computer skills, applied math, and applied science. Externship: 20 weeks, hotel/restaurant.

FACULTY: 10 certified full-time vocational educators.

COSTS: Annual tuition in-state $6,200. Uniform fee: $100. Admission requirements: Admission test. Scholarships: yes.

CONTACT: John Fitzpatrick, Director, Minuteman Tech, Foodservice, 758 Marrett Rd., Lexington, MA 02173; 781-861-6500 #200, Fax 781-863-1254, jfitzpatrick@minuteman.org, www.minuteman.org.

NEWBURY COLLEGE

Brookline/September-May

Sponsor: 4-yr & 2-yr independent college. Program: BS in Hotel, Restaurant & Service Mgmt, AS in Culinary Arts, Travel & Convention Mgmt., Food Service Mgmt., Hotel & Restaurant Administration. Established: 1981. Accredited by NEASC. Calendar: semester. Curriculum: culinary, core. Admit dates: Sept, Jan. Total enrollment: 240. 140 each admission period. 85% of applicants accepted. 80% receive financial aid. 10% enrolled part-time. S:T ratio 15:1. 99% of graduates obtain jobs within 6 mos. Facilities: Include 7 production kitchens & the Weltman Dining Room.

COURSES: Include international & regional cuisines, equipment, sanitation, nutrition, menu planning, general ed. A 12- to 18-week salaried externship is provided.

FACULTY: 10 full- & 6 part-time faculty members are active industry professionals.

COSTS: Annual tuition is $13,540 & culinary program fee is $1,170. On-campus room & board are provided for 400 students at $7,280. Admission requirements: HS diploma or GED & 2.0 GPA. Scholarships: yes. Loans: yes.

CONTACT: Francois Nivaud, Dean of School of Hotel & Restaurant Mgt., Newbury College, Office of Admission, 129 Fisher Ave., Brookline, MA 02445; 617-730-7007, 800-NEWBURY, Fax 617-731-9618, fnivaud@newbury.edu, www.newbury.edu.

NORTH SHORE COMMUNITY COLLEGE

Danvers/Year-round

Sponsor: 2-year college. Program: 2-year associate degree in Culinary Arts & Food Service. Established: 1965. Admit dates: Jan, September. Total enrollment: 52. 25% enrolled part-time. S:T ratio 14:1. Facilities: Include 3 demo labs, food production kitchen, teaching kitchen, bake shop.

COURSES: Include knife-handling, nutrition & food sciences, management, facilities planning, personnel administration, food history & culture.

FACULTY: 4 full-time, 2 part-time.

COSTS: Tuition $2,190/yr in-state, $8,610/yr out-of-state; program fees $250. Scholarships: yes.

CONTACT: George Anbinder, Dept. Chair, North Shore Community College, Hathorne Campus Berry Hall, Room 103, Danvers, MA 01923; 781-762-4000, ext. 1537, Fax 978-762-4021, ganbinde@northshore.edu, www.northshore.edu.

MICHIGAN

ACF MICHIGAN CHEFS DE CUISINE ASSOCIATION

Farmington Hills/September-July

Sponsor: ACF chapter/Michigan Chefs. Program: 3-yr apprenticeship; degree program through Oakland Community College. Established: 1978. Accredited by ACF. Calendar: semester. Curriculum: culinary. Total enrollment: 65. 20 each admission period. Facilities: 3 floors including labs & production kitchen.

COURSES: Baking/pastry apprenticeship.

FACULTY: 8 chefs. Certified Executive Pastry Chefs, Certified Executive Chefs.

COSTS: $1,500/yr. Beginning salary is $7/hr with increases every 6 mos. Admission requirements: Interview. Scholarships: yes. Loans: yes.

CONTACT: John McCormack, CEC, CCE, AAC, ACF Michigan Chefs de Cuisine Association, 1240 Muirwood Court, Rochester Hills, MI 48306; 248-377-9032, john@gatewayfood.com.

ACF OF NORTHWESTERN MICHIGAN

Bellair/Year-round

Sponsor: ACF chapter. Program: 3-yr apprenticeship; degree program Lake Michigan College. Curriculum: culinary. Total enrollment: 36.

COSTS: $2,800 for 3 yrs. Beginning salary is $6/hr with increases every 6 mos. Housing is $280/mo.

CONTACT: Lucille House, CCC, ACF of Northwestern Michigan, 6285 Swamp Road, Frankfort, MI 49635; 231-995-7196, Fax 231-995-1134, lhouse@nmc.edu.

BAKER COLLEGE CULINARY ARTS

Muskegon/Year-round

Sponsor: Private 2- & 4-yr college. Program: 2-yr AB in Culinary Arts; 2-yr AB & 4-yr BBA in Food & Beverage Mgmt. Certificate in Baking & Pastry Arts. Established: 1997. Calendar: quarter. Curriculum: culinary, core. Admit dates: Sept, Jan, Apr, June. Total enrollment: 200. ~25 each admission period. 99% of applicants accepted. 70% receive financial aid. 100% enrolled part-time. S:T ratio 12:1. 100% of graduates obtain jobs within 6 mos. Facilities: Main culinary arts kitchen, new industry-current baking & pastry kitchen, student-run fine-dining restaurant, student center grill, classrooms, library, auditorium, recreation facilities.

COURSES: Culinary & baking, garde manger, menu planning, nutrition, mgmt, finance, software applications. 240-hr internship/co-op. Placements in Michigan & surrounding areas.

FACULTY: 2 full-time, 4 part-time. Program director & full-time faculty are ACF-accredited.

COSTS: Annual tuition $7,560. Application fee $20. Uniforms, books, cutlery $1,200. On-campus housing available. Admission requirements: HS diploma or GED. Scholarships: yes. Loans: yes.

CONTACT: Kathy Jacobson, Director of Admissions, Baker College Culinary Arts, 1903 Marquette Ave., Muskegon, MI 49442; 231-777-5200, Fax 231-777-5201, jacobs_k@muskegon.baker.edu, www.baker.edu.

CULINARY STUDIES INSTITUTE/OAKLAND COMMUNITY COLLEGE

Farmington Hills/September-June

Sponsor: 2-yr college. Program: 2-yr AAS program in Culinary Arts, Food Service Management, Hotel Management, Chef Apprentice, Pastry Arts Certficate. Established: 1978. Accredited by ACF. Calendar: semester. Curriculum: culinary, core. Admit dates: Sept, Jan, May. Total enrollment: 260. 98% of applicants accepted. 35% receive financial aid. 25% enrolled part-time. S:T ratio 12:1. 90% of graduates obtain jobs within 6 mos. Facilities: 3 floors of kitchens, labs & classrooms & 2 student-run restaurants.

COURSES: Cookery, breads & pastries, garde manger, ice carving, intl cuisine, culinary competition, Serve Safe certification, wine & spirits, fronthouse mgmt, legal issues. Host the 3 -yr Southwest Michigan A.C.F Apprenticeship program that leads to chef certification.

FACULTY: 8 full-time, 6 part-time. Includes Chairperson Susan Baier FMP; Kevin Enright CEC, CCE AAC, Roger Holden CPC, CCE; Doug Ganhs CEC,Dan Rowlson, CCE; DarleneLevinson FMP, Chris Galli CPC.

COSTS: In-county $51/cr-hr, out-of-county $83/cr-hr. Lab fee ~$50/course. Admission requirements: Open. Students must successfully complete Intro to Culinary Arts to enter program. Scholarships: yes. Loans: yes.

CONTACT: Susan Baier, Dept. Chair, Oakland Community College, Hospitality/Culinary Arts, 27055 Orchard Lake Rd., Farmington Hills, MI 48334; 248-522-3701, Fax 248-522-3706, smbaier@occ.cc.mi.us, www.oaklandcc.edu.

GRAND RAPIDS COMMUNITY COLLEGE

Grand Rapids/August-May *(See display ad page 88)*

Sponsor: 2-yr college. Program: 2-yr AAAS degree in Culinary Arts & Culinary Management, certificate in Baking & Pastry Arts. Established: 1980. Accredited by ACF, NCA. Calendar: semester. Curriculum: culinary, core. Admit dates: Jan, Aug. Total enrollment: 400. 80 each admission period. 95% of applicants accepted. 60% receive financial aid. 30% enrolled part-time. S:T ratio 18:1. 99% of graduates obtain jobs within 6 mos. Facilities: Include 8 kitchens, 6+ classrooms, beverage lab, 3 bakeries, bistro, banquet rooms, food/beverage library, auditorium, 2 storerooms; student-run restaurant & deli-bakery, open to the public.

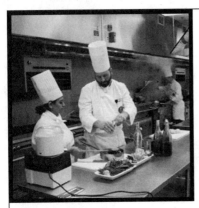

Courses: Basic & advanced culinary & baking skills, ice carving, banquets & catering, garde manger, restaurant operations, international studies. Externship: 240-hr, summer semester, throughout US & abroad. ~50 non-credit seminars/yr, clubs, international study tours.

Faculty: 12 full-time, 7 part-time. Qualifications: equivalent of a bachelor's degree & min 6 yrs industry experience in mgmt. Most have master's degrees or are master chefs.

Costs: Culinary Arts: $8,775 resident, $13,500 non-resident, $17,550 out-of-state. Culinary Management: slightly less. Baking & Pastry Arts: ~50%. Application fee $20. Books, uniforms, cutlery kit: $1,450. Admission requirements: HS diploma or equivalent & admission test. Scholarships: yes. Loans: yes.

Contact: Marcia Arp, Grand Rapids Community College, Hospitality Education, 151 Fountain, N.E., Grand Rapids, MI 49503-3263; 616-234-3690, Fax 616-234-3698, marp@grcc.edu, www.grcc.edu.

GREAT LAKES CULINARY INSTITUTE

Traverse City/Year-round

Sponsor: College. Program: 2-year AAS degree in Culinary Arts. Established: 1978. Accredited by ACF. Calendar: semester. Curriculum: culinary, core. Admit dates: Open. Total enrollment: 90. 75 each admission period. 100% of applicants accepted. 65% receive financial aid. 45% enrolled part-time. S:T ratio 15:1. 98% of graduates obtain jobs within 6 mos. Facilities: Include 6 kitchens, restaurant, classrooms, bake shop, computer labs.

Costs: In-county $65/cr-hr, out-of-county $110/cr-hr, application fee $15. On-campus housing:120 spaces, ~$2,200 with meal plan. Admission requirements: HS diploma or equivalent. Scholarships: yes. Loans: yes.

Contact: Fred Laughlin, Dept. Chair, Northwestern Michigan College, Culinary Arts, 1701 E. Front St., Traverse City, MI 49686; 231-995-1197, Fax 231-995-1134, Flaughlin@nmc.edu, www.nmc.edu/culinary.

HENRY FORD COMMUNITY COLLEGE
Dearborn/Year-round

Sponsor: 2-yr college. Program: AA degree. Established: 1972. Accredited by ACF. Calendar: semester. Curriculum: culinary. Admit dates: Throughout the year. Total enrollment: 200. 40 each admission period. 100% of applicants accepted. 80% receive financial aid. 60% enrolled part-time. S:T ratio 16:1. 90% of graduates obtain jobs within 6 mos. Facilities: 2 kitchens, student-run dining room.

FACULTY: 4 full-time, 6 part-time.

CONTACT: Dennis Konarski, CFE, CCE, Culinary Director, Henry Ford Community College, Culinary Arts, 5101 Evergreen Rd., Dearborn, MI 48128; 313-845-9651, Fax 313-845-9784, dennis@hfcc.net, www.henryford.cc.mi.us.

MACOMB COMMUNITY COLLEGE
Clinton Township/September-May

Sponsor: 2-yr college. Program: 2-yr AAS degree in Culinary Arts, ACF-Certified Culinarian, NRA diploma, 1-yr certificate in Supervision, 1-yr certificate in Production, ACF Apprenticeship program. Established: 1972. Accredited by ACF. Calendar: semester. Curriculum: culinary. Admit dates: Fall, spring, summer. Total enrollment: 223. 100% of applicants accepted. 35% enrolled part-time. S:T ratio 16:1. 99% of graduates obtain jobs within 6 mos. Facilities: 3 full-service kitchen labs, student/faculty restaurant.

COURSES: ACF apprenticeship program. Ice carving.

FACULTY: 3 full-time, 5 part-time.

COSTS: Tuition in-county $57/cr-hr, out-of-county $85/cr-hr. Admission requirements: U.S. citizen or permanent resident whose HS class has graduated or is at least age 18. Scholarships: yes. Loans: yes.

CONTACT: David Schneider, CEC, CCE, Dept. Coordinator, Macomb Community College, Culinary Arts, 44575 Garfield Rd., Clinton Township, MI 48038; 586-286-2088, Fax 586-286-2250, schneiderd@macomb.edu, www.macomb.edu.

MONROE COUNTY COMMUNITY COLLEGE
Monroe/September-May

Sponsor: Independent 2-yr college. Program: 2-yr AOC degree/certificate in Culinary Skills & Mgmt. Established: 1981. Accredited by NCA, ACF. Calendar: semester. Curriculum: core. Admit dates: September. Total enrollment: 36. 20 each admission period. 80% of applicants accepted. 25% receive financial aid. 25% enrolled part-time. S:T ratio 18:1. 87% of graduates obtain jobs within 6 mos. Facilities: Include 2 kitchens, classroom, restaurant.

COURSES: Restaurant production, baking, buffet, institutional food, mgmt, sanitation, nutrition, garde manger, ice carving, menu planning, a la carte, dining room procedure, general ed. Externship provided. Articulation agreement with Sienna Heights College.

FACULTY: 2 full-time. Includes K. Thomas, CCE, CEC & 1 technician, V. LaValle.

COSTS: $47/cr-hr in-county, $75/cr-hr out-of-county, $83/cr-hr out-of-state. Technology fee $3/cr-hr, application fee $21. Off-campus housing cost is ~$400/mo. Admission requirements: HS diploma or equivalent & admission test. Scholarships: yes. Loans: yes.

CONTACT: Kevin Thomas, Instructor, Monroe County Community College, Culinary Arts, 1555 S. Raisinville Rd., Monroe, MI 48161; 734-384-4150, kthomas@monroeccc.edu, www.monroeccc.edu.

MOTT COMMUNITY COLLEGE
Flint/Year-round

Sponsor: 2-year college. Program: 66 credit-hour/83 contact-hour AAS degree in Culinary Arts, 65 credit-hour/80 contact-hour AAS degree in Food Service Management.

COSTS: Tuition is $56/contact-hr in-state, $82/contact-hr out-of-district, $109/contact-hr out-of-state.

CONTACT: Grace Alexander, Instructor/coordinator, Mott Community College, 1401 E. Court St., Flint, MI 48503; 810-232-7845, galexand@mcc.edu, www.mcc.edu.

NORTHERN MICHIGAN UNIVERSITY

Marquette/August-April

Sponsor: University. Program: 1-year certificate, 2-year AAS degree, 4-year BS degree, program in Culinary Arts, Restaurant & Institutional Management. Established: 1970. Accredited by NCA. Calendar: semester. Admit dates: Sept, Jan. Total enrollment: 74. 36 each admission period. 100% of applicants accepted. 80% receive financial aid. 25% enrolled part-time. S:T ratio 18:1. 100% of graduates obtain jobs within 6 mos. Facilities: Include 1 kitchen and 4 classrooms, computer lab, restaurant and meat-cutting room.

COURSES: Cooking, baking, garde manger, sanitation, purchasing, and general education.

FACULTY: 4 full-time. Qualifications: bachelor's or master's degrees.

COSTS: Tuition in state $1,493/sem full-time, out-of-state $2,633/sem full-time. Application fee $50. On-campus housing: 2,000 spaces at $2,300 per year. Average off-campus housing cost: $2,000/yr. Admission requirements: HS diploma or equivalent. Scholarships: yes. Loans: yes.

CONTACT: Kathy Solka, Northern Michigan University, College of Technology & Applied Sciences, D.J. Jacobetti Center, Room 123, Marquette, MI 49855; 906-227-2135, Fax 906-227-2156, ksolka@nmu.edu, www.nmu.edu/technology.

SCHOOLCRAFT COLLEGE

Livonia/August-April

Sponsor: Two-year college. Program: 2-year certificate/AAS degree in Culinary Arts & Culinary Management. Established: 1966. Accredited by NCA. Calendar: semester. Admit dates: Jan, Aug. Total enrollment: 232. 12-78 each admission period. 100% of applicants accepted. 40% enrolled part-time. S:T ratio 14:1. 100% of graduates obtain jobs within 6 mos. Facilities: Include 8 kitchens & classrooms, pastry kitchen, butcher shop, bakery, restaurant.

COURSES: Baking, pastries, a la carte, intl cuisine, butchery. Externship: 16-wk, salaried, restaurants.

FACULTY: 5 full-time, 6 part-time. Qualifications: ACF certification.

COSTS: Tuition $54/cr-hr resident, $80/cr-hr non-resident. Lab fees $35-$105. Admission requirements: HS diploma or equivalent & admission test. Scholarships: yes. Loans: yes.

CONTACT: Bruce Konowalow, Director of Culinary Arts, Schoolcraft College, Culinary Arts, 18600 Haggerty Rd., Livonia, MI 48152-2696; 734-462-4423, Fax 734-462-4581, bkonowal@schoolcraft.cc.mi.us, www.schoolcraft.cc.mi.us.

WASHTENAW COMMUNITY COLLEGE

Ann Arbor/September-June

Sponsor: 2-yr college. Program: 1-year certificate in Food Service Production Specialist and a 2-year AAS degree in Culinary Arts and Hotel & Restaurant Management. Established: 1975. Accredited by NCA, ACF. Calendar: semester. Curriculum: culinary. Total enrollment: 80-120. 50 each admission period. 90% of applicants accepted. 10% receive financial aid. 60% enrolled part-time. S:T ratio 16-25:1. 95% of graduates obtain jobs within 6 mos. Facilities: Include kitchen, bake shop, and student-run dining room.

COURSES: 50% culinary courses, 25% business courses, 25% general studies. Externship: 300-hour, salaried. Continuing education year-round.

FACULTY: 4 full-time. Qualifications: bachelor's or master's degree and ACF certification.

COSTS: $52/cr-hr in-district, $77/cr-hr out-of-district, $98/cr-hr out-of-state. $23 registration fee/semester. Off-campus housing cost $400-$600/mo. Admission requirements: HS diploma or equivalent and admission test. Scholarships: yes.

CONTACT: Don Garrett, Dept. Chair, Washtenaw Community College, Culinary Arts & Hospitality Mgmt., 4800 E. Huron River Dr., Ann Arbor, MI 48106-0978; 734-973-3601, Fax 734-677-5414, dgarrett@wccnet.org, www.washtenaw.cc.mi.us.

MINNESOTA

THE ART INSTITUTES INTERNATIONAL MINNESOTA

Minneapolis/Year-round *(See display ad page 135)*

Sponsor: Private school. Program: 7-qtr AAS & 4-qtr certificate program in Culinary Arts. Established: 1998. Accredited by ACICS, ACF. Calendar: quarter. Curriculum: culinary, core. Admit dates: Year-round. Total enrollment: 180. 94% receive financial aid. S:T ratio 20:1. 100% of graduates obtain jobs within 6 mos. Facilities: Specialized educational kitchens, dining lab.

COURSES: Basic skills & techniques, purchasing & cost control, human relations, kitchen mgmt, intl cuisine, nutrition, dining room procedures, garde manger, baking & pastries, a la carte kitchen. 3-mo externship with a quality food service operation in the greater Minneapolis area.

FACULTY: 12 instructors.

CONTACT: Director of Admissions, The Art Institutes International Minnesota, 15 S. 9th St., Minneapolis, MN 55402; 612-332-3361, Fax 612-332-3934, aimadm@aii.edu, www.aim.artinstitutes.edu.

HENNEPIN TECHNICAL COLLEGE

Brooklyn Pk, Eden Prairie/August-May

Sponsor: Career college. Program: 64-cr AAS degree in Culinary Arts, 50-cr diploma/certificate in Culinary Arts. Established: 1972. Accredited by NCA, ACF. Calendar: semester. Curriculum: culinary. Admit dates: Fall, spring. Total enrollment: 60. 24 each admission period. 100% of applicants accepted. 40% receive financial aid. 10% enrolled part-time. S:T ratio 15:1. 98% of graduates obtain jobs within 6 mos. Facilities: Include 3 kitchens, 3 classrooms & restaurant.

FACULTY: 4 full-, 3 part-time; ACF certified or certifiable.

COSTS: Annual tuition $2,228 in-state, $4,456 out-of-state. ~$550 for supplies. $20 application fee. Admission requirements: Placement test & application. Scholarships: yes. Loans: yes.

CONTACT: Carlo Castagneri, Lead Instructor, Hennepin Technical College-Brooklyn Park Campus, Culinary Arts, 9000 Brooklyn Blvd., Brooklyn Park, MN 55445; 612-425-3800 x2116, Fax 612-550-2119, Carlo.Castagneri@htc.mnscu.edu, www.htc.mnscu.edu.

HIBBING COMMUNITY COLLEGE

Hibbing/Year-round

Sponsor: 2-year college. Program: 103-credit diploma and 113-credit AAS degree programs in Food Service Management. Calendar: semester. Curriculum: culinary.

COSTS: Tuition is $66/credit in-state, $132/credit out-of-state plus fees.

CONTACT: Dan Lidholm, Department Head, Hibbing Community College, 2900 E. Beltline, Central Campus, Hibbing, MN 55746; 800-224-4422 #7228, Fax 218-262-7222, dan.l@ins.hcc.mnscu.edu, www.hibbing.tec.mn.us.

LE CORDON BLEU CULINARY PROGRAM AT BROWN COLLEGE

Mendota Heights/Year-round *(See display ad page 93)*

Sponsor: Private culinary college. Program: Le Cordon Bleu Culinary Program60-wk/90-credit AAS degree program ending in a 6-wk internship. The core of the curriculum is hands-on teaching of cooking and baking skills and providing training for cooks and apprentice chefs. Established: 1999. Accredited by ACCSCT. Calendar: quarter. Curriculum: culinary. Admit dates: Continuous admissions. Total enrollment: 627. 96/6 wks each admission period. 95% of applicants accepted. 85% receive financial aid. S:T ratio ~16:1. Facilities: Includes 6 instructional kitchens, restaurant, deli.

COURSES: Include: Intro to Culinary Arts, Purchasing & Cost Control, Hotel & Restaurant Butchery, Basic Soups, Garde Manger, A La Carte Kitchen, Dietetics, Sanitation, Baking & Pastry, Intl Cuisine. 6-wk internship that provides progressive training experience structured to fit student's background & career goals. Overseas internships available to students meeting a GPA of 3.5 or higher.

FACULTY: 20 faculty members with a combined 400 yrs experience in the culinary arts field.

COSTS: Tuition $36,322. Admission requirements: HS diploma or GED. Scholarships: yes. Loans: yes.

LOCATION: Near the Mall of America & Minneapolis/St. Paul Intl Airport.

CONTACT: Heather McBree, Director of Admissions, Le Cordon Bleu Culinary Program at Brown College, 1440 Northland Dr., Mendota Heights, MN 55120; 800-528-4575, Fax 651-675-4700, chef-info@browncollege.edu, www.chef-bc.com.

NORTHWEST TECHNICAL COLLEGE

Moorhead/September-May

Sponsor: Career college. Program: 2-year diploma in Chef Training. Established: 1966. Accredited by State, NCA. Calendar: semester. Curriculum: core. Total enrollment: 40-50. 25 each admission period. 80% receive financial aid. 10% enrolled part-time. S:T ratio 20-25:1. 89% of graduates obtain jobs within 6 mos. Facilities: 2 kitchens, 1 classroom, 2 restaurants.

COURSES: Quantity food preparation, food purchasing and cost controls, menu planning.

FACULTY: 2 full-time. Includes Kim E. Brewster, CEC, CCE, Colleen Kraft.

COSTS: Annual tuition in-state $1,996, out-of-state $3,840. Other fees: $150/semester meal fee, $105/semester uniform fee, $20 admission application fee. Off-campus housing cost is $250/mo. Admission requirements: HS diploma or equivalent. Loans: yes.

CONTACT: Kim Brewster, Dept. Chairperson, Northwest Technical College, Chef Training, 1900 28th Ave. S., Moorhead, MN 56560; 800-426-5603 x572, Fax 218-236-0342, kim.brewster@ntcmn.edu, www.ntcmn.edu.

ST. CLOUD TECHNICAL COLLEGE CULINARY ARTS

St. Cloud/August-May

Sponsor: College. Program: 32-week diploma. Established: 1972. Accredited by NCA. Calendar: semester. Curriculum: culinary, core. Admit dates: Open. Total enrollment: 20. 24 each admission period. 100% of applicants accepted. 90% receive financial aid. S:T ratio 24:1. 80% of graduates obtain jobs within 6 mos. Facilities: 2 kitchens.

FACULTY: 1 full-time: Jay Thomas.

COSTS: $2,695 plus $390 for books and supplies. Admission requirements: HS diploma or GED. Scholarships: yes. Loans: yes.

CONTACT: Diane Wysoski, Assistant to the President, St. Cloud Technical College, Culinary Arts, 1540 Northway Dr., St. Cloud, MN 56303-1240; 320-654-5000, Fax 320-654-5981, dmw@cloud.tec.mn.us, http://sctconline.com.

ST. PAUL TECHNICAL COLLEGE

St. Paul/Year-round

Sponsor: Career college. Program: 3-semester (55 credits) diploma program, 2-year (72 credits) AAS degree, short order cooking certificate (25 credits). Established: 1967. Accredited by NCA, ACF. Curriculum: culinary. Admit dates: Aug, Jan. Total enrollment: 40-50. 25 each admission period. S:T ratio 16:1. 95% of graduates obtain jobs within 6 mos.

FACULTY: 3-1/2 full-time.

COSTS: Tuition in-state $76.57/credit hour, out-of-state $145/credit hour. Admission requirements: HS diploma or equivalent and admission test. Scholarships: yes. Loans: yes.

CONTACT: Manfred Krug, Culinary Director, St. Paul Technical College, Culinary Arts, 235 Marshall Ave., St. Paul, MN 55102; 612-221-1300/1398, Fax 612-221-1416, Manfred.Krug@sptc.mnscu.edu, www.sptc.mnscu.edu.

SOUTH CENTRAL TECHNICAL COLLEGE

North Mankato/September-July

Sponsor: Career college. Program: 15-mo, 52-cr diploma & 2-yr, 72-cr AAS degree in Hotel, Restaurant & Institutional Cooking. Established: 1968. Accredited by NCA. Calendar: semester.

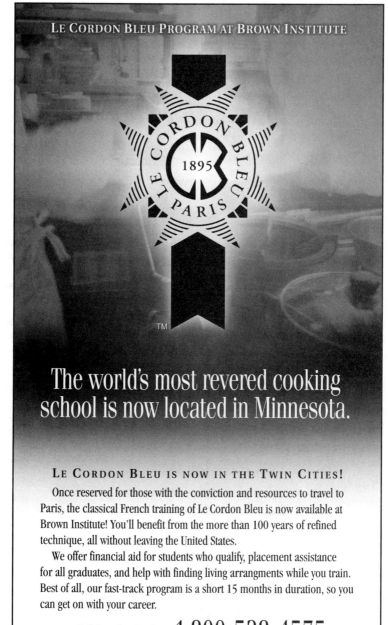

Curriculum: culinary. Admit dates: Aug, Jan, May. Total enrollment: 25. 7-8 each admission period. 100% of applicants accepted. 90% receive financial aid. 10% enrolled part-time. S:T ratio 17:1. 95% of graduates obtain jobs within 6 mos. Facilities: Include 2 kitchens, bakery & classroom.

COURSES: Include food prep, inventory control, cost control, mgmt, menu design, problem solving, microcomputers, employment search skills.

FACULTY: 1 full-time.

COSTS: In-state $74/sem-cr, out-of-state $148/sem-cr. Books & uniforms $520. Off-campus housing $300/mo. Admission requirements: HS diploma or equivalent. Scholarships: yes. Loans: yes.

CONTACT: Jim Hanson, Instructor, South Central Technical College, Culinary Arts, 1920 Lee Blvd., P.O. Box 1920, North Mankato, MN 56003; 507-389-7229, Fax 507-388-9951, JimH@tc-mankato.scm.tec.mn.us, www.sctc.mnscu.edu.

MISSISSIPPI

HINDS COMMUNITY COLLEGE

Jackson/August-May

Sponsor: 2-yr college. Program: 1-yr certificate & 2-yr AAS degree program in Culinary Arts. Accredited by SACS. Calendar: semester. Curriculum: culinary, core. Admit dates: Jan, Aug. Total enrollment: 50. 20 each admission period. 100% of applicants accepted. 80% receive financial aid. 15% enrolled part-time. S:T ratio 16:1. 100% of graduates obtain jobs within 6 mos. Facilities: Full-scale commercial kitchen with all major equipment.

COURSES: Fundamentals of culinary arts, French techniques, international & American cuisine, baking, garde manger. 6-mo paid internship at approved dining facility, at least 20 hrs/wk.

FACULTY: 3 faculty: BS in Hospitality Management, certified chef/instructor with BBA, MS in Hospitality Management.

COSTS: $515 for full-time students (12-19 hrs), $25 registration fee. Deferred payment plan. Admission requirements: HS diploma or GED. Scholarships: yes. Loans: yes.

CONTACT: Kathleen Bruno, Chef/Instructor, Hinds Community College, Culinary Arts Program, 3925 Sunset Dr., Jackson, MS 39213; 601-987-8130, Fax 601-982-5804, Gata1967@aol.com, www.hinds.cc.ms.us.

MISSISSIPPI UNIVERSITY FOR WOMEN CULINARY ARTS INSTITUTE

Columbus/Year-round *(See display ad page 95)*

Sponsor: Public university. Program: 4-year BS (52 sem hrs): required minor (18-21 sem hrs) in Entrepreneurship/Small Business Development, Food Journalism, Food Art, Nutrition/Wellness; minor (22 sem hrs) in Culinary Arts. Established: 1997. Accredited by SACS. Calendar: semester. Curriculum: core. Admit dates: Aug, Jan. Total enrollment: 65. Open each admission period. S:T ratio 12:1. 100% of graduates obtain jobs within 6 mos. Facilities: 5 kitchens, classrooms in renovated building listed in National Register of Historic Places.

COURSES: Classic cooking techniques, small quantity food preparation. Correlate minor required, culinary entrepreneurship studies. 6 sem-hour internship required; international internship optional. Community education & professional development classes.

FACULTY: 3 full-time; 3 part-time. Chef/Director, nutritionist/RD, chef-instructors.

COSTS: $1,527 ($3,687.50) fees/sem in-state (out-of-state), Academic Common Market available; $1,515 living expenses, $100 for food preparation classes. Admission requirements: College prep curriculum with 2.0 GPA/850 SAT, 2.5 GPA/760 SAT, or 3.2 SAT. Scholarships: yes. Loans: yes.

LOCATION: Small town in NE Mississippi, ~5 hrs from Atlanta, New Orleans & Gulf Coast beaches.

CONTACT: Sarah Labensky, CCP, Director, Mississippi University for Women, Box W-1639, Columbus, MS 39701; 877-GO-2-THE-W x7472, 662-241-7472, Fax 662-241-7627, cularts@muw.edu, www.muw.edu/interdisc.

MISSOURI

ACF CHEFS & COOKS OF SPRINGFIELD/OZARK

Springfield/Year-round

Sponsor: ACF chapter. Program: 3-yr apprenticeship. Curriculum: culinary. Total enrollment: 19.

COSTS: Beginning salary is minimum wage with increases every 6 mos.

CONTACT: John E. Blansit, CEC, VP, ACF Chefs & Cooks of Springfield/Ozark, MO ; 417-890-0906, porchef@aol.com, Marcel Bonetti, CEC AAC; 308 Fairway St., Nixa MO 65714. 417-725-2392.

ST. LOUIS COMMUNITY COLLEGE-FOREST PARK

St. Louis/August-May

Sponsor: 2-yr college. Program: 2-year AAS degree, apprenticeship leading to ACF certification. Established: 1976. Accredited by NCA. Calendar: semester. Curriculum: culinary. Admit dates: Aug, Jan. Total enrollment: 150. 50 each admission period. 100% of applicants accepted. 40% enrolled part-time. S:T ratio 20:1. 98% of graduates obtain jobs within 6 mos. Facilities: 30,000-sq-ft facility: 4 kitchens, student-operated restaurant, classrooms.

COURSES: Meat analysis, garde manger, pastry, baking, nutrition, food specialties, catering, general education, involvement with Junior Chef Organization. Other required courses: 20 hours. Externship: 150-hour, salaried, each semester.

FACULTY: 4 full-time, 25 part-time. Qualifications: masters degree and industry experience. Includes Dept. Chair Kathy Schiffman, Scott Vratarich, Reed Miller, Mike Downey, CCE, CCC.

COSTS: Annual tuition: $1,200 in-state, $1,700 out-of-state. Off-campus housing $450/mo. Admission requirements: HS diploma or equivalent & admission test. Scholarships: yes. Loans: yes.

CONTACT: Kathy Schiffman, Dept. Chair, St. Louis Community College-Forest Park, Culinary Mgmt., 5600 Oakland Ave., St. Louis, MO 63110; 314-644-9747, Fax 314-644-9992, kschiffman@stlcc.edu, www.stlcc.cc.mo.us/fp/hospitality/hospitality.html.

MONTANA

UNIVERSITY OF MONTANA – COLLEGE OF TECHNOLOGY

Missoula/Year-round

Sponsor: Public career institution. Program: 1-year certificate & 2-year AAS degree in Food Service Management. Established: 1973. Accredited by ACF, NASC. Calendar: trimester. Curriculum: culinary, core. Admit dates: Aug, Jan. Total enrollment: 62. 25 each admission period. 90% of applicants accepted. 30% receive financial aid. 5% enrolled part-time. S:T ratio 15:1. 90% of graduates obtain jobs within 6 mos. Facilities: 1 kitchen, classrooms, 1 restaurant.

COURSES: Comprehensive program includes culinary skills and foodservice management. A summer baking program is also available.

Faculty: Includes F. Sonnenberg, CEC, R. Lodahl, M.M. Barton, CPC, S. Bartos, CC.

Costs: Annual tuition $2,400 resident, $5,000 non-resident. Application fee $30. Other fees $400. Off-campus housing cost $300/mo. Admission requirements: HS or equivalent and admission test. Scholarships: yes. Loans: yes.

Contact: Ross Lodahl, Interim Program Director, University of Montana-College of Technology, Culinary Arts, 909 S. Avenue West, Missoula, MT 59801-7910; 406-243-7816, Ross.Lodahl@mso.umt.edu, www.cte.umt.edu.

NEBRASKA

ACF PROFESSIONAL CHEFS OF OMAHA

Omaha/Year-round

Sponsor: ACF chapter. Program: 3-yr apprenticeship; degree program through Metro Community College is completed by 80%. Curriculum: culinary. Total enrollment: 20.

Costs: $3,300. Beginning salary is $7/hr with variable increases annually.

Contact: Chris Zeeb, CEC, ACF Professional Chefs of Omaha, Metropolitan Community College, Bldg. 10, Box 3777, 30th & Fort Sts., Omaha, NE 68103-0777; 402-449-3397, cmzeeb@msn.com, www.acfchefs.org/presidents_portal/ACFChapter.cfm?ChapterChoice=NE032.

CENTRAL COMMUNITY COLLEGE

Hastings/September-June

Sponsor: 2-yr college. Program: 2-year certificate/AAS degree in Culinary Arts. Established: 1971. Accredited by NCA. Calendar: semester. Curriculum: core. Admit dates: Open. Total enrollment: 40. 10 each admission period. 100% of applicants accepted. 80% receive financial aid. S:T ratio 8:1. 95% of graduates obtain jobs within 6 mos. Facilities: 1 kitchen, 4 classrooms, restaurant.

Courses: Bake shop, pantry, entrees, intl cuisine, advanced sauces, pastries, garde manger.

Costs: Annual tuition in-state $1,440, out-of-state $1,920. Uniform & supplies $50. On-campus dorms available. Admission requirements: HS diploma or equivalent. Scholarships: yes. Loans: yes.

Contact: Jaye Kieselhorst, Program Supervisor, Central Community College, Hotel, Motel, Restaurant Mgmt., P.O. Box 1024, Hastings, NE 68902; 402-461-2572, Fax 402-461-2454, jkieselhorst@cccneb.edu, www.cccneb.edu.

METROPOLITAN COMMUNITY COLLEGE

Omaha/Year-round

Sponsor: 2-yr college. Program: 1- to 2-year AAS degree programs in Culinary Arts, Foodservice Management, Chef Apprentice, Culinology (TM), Bakery Arts, Culinary Management. Established: 1976. Accredited by ACF, CAHM. Curriculum: culinary, core. Admit dates: Sept, Dec, Mar, June. Total enrollment: 450. 75 each admission period. 95% of applicants accepted. 68% receive financial aid. 48% enrolled part-time. S:T ratio 18:1. 76% of graduates obtain jobs within 6 mos. Facilities: Kitchens, classrooms, restaurant.

Faculty: 3 full-time, 18 part-time.

Costs: Tuition in-state ~$35/cr-hr, out-of-state ~$50/cr-hr. Other fees cover uniforms, tools. Admission requirements: HS diploma or equivalent. Scholarships: yes. Loans: yes.

Contact: Jim Trebbien, Division Representative, Metropolitan Community College, Food Arts & Management, Box 3777, Omaha, NE 68103-0777; 402-457-2510, Fax 402-457-2515, jtrebbien@metropo.mccneb.edu, www.mccneb.edu.

SOUTHEAST COMMUNITY COLLEGE

Lincoln/Year-round

Sponsor: 2-yr college. Program: 18-mo AS degree in Culinary Arts. Established: 1988. Accredited by NCA, ACF. Calendar: quarter. Curriculum: core. Admit dates: Sept, Mar. Total enrollment: 100. 25 each admission period. 100% of applicants accepted. 30% enrolled part-time. S:T ratio 15:1.

95-100% of graduates obtain jobs within 6 mos. Facilities: Include kitchen & 2 classrooms.

Courses: Advanced food, buffet decorating & catering, professional baking, advanced pastry, culinary nutrition. Externship: 220-hr, salaried.

Faculty: 2 full-time, 2 part-time. Qualifications: associate degree. Includes Gerrine Schreck Kirby, CCE, CWC; Jo Taylor, MA, RD; Lois Cockerham, BS; Erin Coudill, MS, RD.

Costs: Annual tuition in-state $31.50/cr-hr, out-of-state $36.50/cr-hr. Fees $37. Admission requirements: HS diploma or equivalent. Scholarships: yes. Loans: yes.

Contact: Jo Taylor, Program Chair, Southeast Community College, Food Service, 8800 'O' St., Lincoln, NE 68520-9989; 402-437-2465, Fax 402-437-2404, jtaylor@southeast.edu, www.southeast.edu/Programs/Curriculum/FOOD.htm.

NEVADA

AMERICAN CULINARY ALLIANCE

Las Vegas/Year-round

Sponsor: Professional job bank, mentoring service, provider of customized foodservice training. Program: Community College of Las Vegas & University of Nevada-Las Vegas 2- & 4-yr degrees in Hotel/Restaurant Management & Cook Certification with the ACF. Established: 1993. Calendar: semester. Curriculum: culinary, core. Admit dates: Open. Total enrollment: 30-45. 5-10/yr each admission period. 10% of applicants accepted. 25% receive financial aid. 15% enrolled part-time. S:T ratio 1:1. 100% of graduates obtain jobs within 6 mos. Facilities: All o.j.t./apprenticeship training accrues within the apprentice's place of employment & local post-secondary schools.

Faculty: Advisory committee includes National Program Director Robert Shell, CCC, CCE, West Coast Director Steve Fernald, CCC, CCE, East Coast Director Tim Murray, CC.

Costs: Total cost is $2,000-$3,000. Admission requirements: Age 18, HS diploma or equivalent, pass pre-apprenticeship courses. Scholarships: yes. Loans: yes.

Contact: Robert B. Shell, CCC, CCE, Program Director, American Culinary Alliance, 764 E. Twain Ave., #14G, Las Vegas, NV 89109; 702-866-2809, Fax 702-458-4977, aca4chefs@aol.com.

THE ART INSTITUTE OF LAS VEGAS

Las Vegas/Year-round *(See display ad page 135)*

Sponsor: Private career school. Program: 21-month (112 cr-hr, 7 qtr) AS degree program in Culinary Arts. Established: 2002. Accredited by ACCSCT. Calendar: quarter.

Courses: Skills & Techniques, Business Essentials, General Education.

Faculty: Includes one Certified Master Chef.

Costs: $316/cr-hr, application & enrollment fee $150.

Contact: Suzanne Noel, Director of Admissions, The Art Institute of Las Vegas, 2350 Corporate Circle, Las Vegas, NV 89074; 800-833-2678, noels@aii.edu, www.ailv.artinstitutes.edu.

COMMUNITY COLLEGE OF SOUTHERN NEVADA – CHEYENNE CAMPUS

North Las Vegas/Year-round

Sponsor: 2-year college. Program: 1-year certificate and 2-year AAS degree in Hotel, Restaurant, and Casino Management with Culinary Arts emphasis. Established: 1990. Accredited by NASC, ACF. Calendar: semester. Curriculum: culinary, core. Admit dates: Open. Total enrollment: 400. 100% of applicants accepted. S:T ratio 15:1. 100% of graduates obtain jobs within 6 mos.

Faculty: 4 full-time, 18 part-time.

Costs: Tuition is $42.50/credit in-state. Out-of-state tuition is $63.50/credit for 1-6 credits and $42.50/credit plus $2,075/semester for 7 credits or more.

Contact: Jill Mora, Culinary Director, Community College of Southern Nevada, Culinary Arts, 3200 E. Cheyenne Ave., Z1A, North Las Vegas, NV 89030; 702-651-4656, Fax 702-651-4116, jill_mora@ccsn.nevada.edu, www.ccsn.nevada.edu.

FRATERNITY OF EXECUTIVE CHEFS OF LAS VEGAS

N. Las Vegas/Year-round

Sponsor: ACF chapter. Program: 3-yr apprenticeship; degree program through University of Las Vegas. Curriculum: culinary. Total enrollment: 11.

Costs: $165. Beginning salary is 80% of cook's helper's wages with increases annually. Housing cost is $350-$500.

Contact: Robert O'Brien, Fraternity of Executive Chefs of Las Vegas, PO Box 93933, Las Vegas, NV 89193; 702-734-0410, bobrien@mrgmail.com, www.acfchefs.org/chapter/nv013.html.

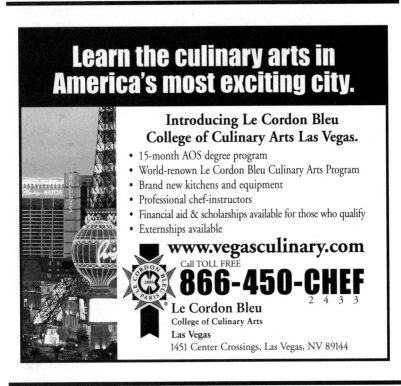

LE CORDON BLEU CULINARY ARTS LAS VEGAS

Las Vegas/Year-round *(See display ad above)*

Sponsor: Private school. Program: 15-month diploma in Culinary Arts. Established: 2003. Accredited by ACCSCT. Curriculum: culinary. Admit dates: Every 6 weeks. Total enrollment: 80. 80 each admission period. S:T ratio 16-40:1. Facilities: New 60,000-sq-ft facility includes 6 production kitchens, 4 demo kitchens, computer classroom, library, bookstore, student-staffed fine dining restaurant.

Courses: Curriculum based on the principles of Escoffier with emphasis on modern techniques & trends. Courses include culinary fundamentals and purchasing & cost control. 3 month externship.

Faculty: Chef and associate chef instructor for each production & demo class.

Costs: $34,600 includes supplies & fees. Admission requirements: Personal interview & essay. Scholarships: yes. Loans: yes.

Location: Near the Las Vegas Strip and the 215 & 95 freeways, in the Red Rock Canyons region.

Contact: Renee Brattin, Director of Admissions, Le Cordon Bleu Culinary Arts Las Vegas, 1451 Center Crossing Rd., Las Vegas, NV 89144; 702-365-7690, 866-450-2433, rbrattin@vegasculinary.com, www.vegasculinary.com.

TRUCKEE MEADOWS COMMUNITY COLLEGE

Reno/September-May

Sponsor: 2-yr college. Program: 2-yr AAS degree in Culinary Arts, 1-yr certificate in Culinary Arts or Baking & Pastry. Established: 1980. Accredited by State, NCA, ACF. Calendar: semester. Curriculum: culinary, core. Admit dates: Aug, Jan. Total enrollment: 130. 75 each admission period. 95% of applicants accepted. 30% receive financial aid. 70% enrolled part-time. S:T ratio 16:1. 75% of graduates obtain jobs within 6 mos. Facilities: Include 8 kitchens & classrooms, student-run restaurant.

COURSES: Cooking, baking, pastry, garde manger, sauces, business chef, nutrition, sanitation, general education. Available. Summer workshops for secondary school teachers; sanitation.

FACULTY: 1 full-time, 10 part-time.

COSTS: In-state $49/credit hour, out-of-state $1,995 + $61/credit hour unless eligible for good neighbor tuition. Application fee $15. Off-campus housing $500-600/mo. Admission requirements: HS diploma or equivalent. Scholarships: yes. Loans: yes.

CONTACT: Karen Cannan, Culinary Arts Instructor, Program Coordinator, Truckee Meadows Community College, Culinary Arts, 7000 Dandini Blvd., RDMT-207-L, Reno, NV 89512-3999; 775-674-7917, Fax 775-674-7980, info@tmcc.edu, www.tmcc.edu.

UNIVERSITY OF NEVADA LAS VEGAS CULINARY ARTS MANAGEMENT

Las Vegas/Year-round

Sponsor: 4-yr college. Program: 4-yr BS degree in Culinary Arts Mgmt designed for community college transfers; freshmen are accepted. Established: 1998. Accredited by NACS. Calendar: semester. Curriculum: culinary, core. Admit dates: Aug, Jan. Total enrollment: 187. 16-20 each admission period. S:T ratio 25:1. Facilities: Lab, demo & production kitchens, dining room, full bar.

COURSES: 63-credit core courses include Dining Room Service, Baking, Basic Cooking, Saucier, Basic Garde Manger, & 20+ electives. Externships at restaurants & hotels locally & worldwide.

FACULTY: 10 full-time, 4 part-time. Includes Chef Claude Lambertz, Program Director; Nicolas Horcasitas, Director of Purchasing & Special Events; Professor John Stefanelli; Dr. Donald Bell; Chef Jean Hertzman.

COSTS: Resident $72/cr-hr; nonresident $150/cr-hr for 1-6 credits or $72/cr-hr + $3,174 for 7+ credits. Admission requirements: SAT, 2.5 GPA for upperclassmen. Scholarships: yes. Loans: yes.

CONTACT: Claude Lambertz, Program Director, University of Nevada Las Vegas Culinary Arts Management, 4505 Maryland Pkwy., Las Vegas, NV 89154-6022; 702-895-4466, Fax 702-895-4871, clambertz@ccmail.nevada.edu, www.unlv.edu/Tourism/culinary.html. Sherri Theriault, Office of Student Affairs: 702-895-1739, stheriault@ccmail.nevada.edu.

NEW HAMPSHIRE

ATLANTIC CULINARY ACADEMY – LE CORDON BLEU

Dover/Year-round *(See display ad page 100)*

Sponsor: Two-year private college. Program: 12-month program leading to an associate degree in Culinary Arts and Le Cordon Bleu diploma. Established: 1996. Accredited by NEASC. Calendar: semester. Curriculum: culinary, core. Admit dates: Monthly. Total enrollment: 100+. 16 each admission period. 86% of applicants accepted. 85% receive financial aid. S:T ratio 16:1. 94% of graduates obtain jobs within 6 mos. Facilities: Newly renovated 20,000-sq-ft facility featuring 4 modern kitchens, 1 restaurant, pastry shop and coffee shop.

COURSES: Le Cordon Bleu curriculum covers such areas as: A la Carte Fine Dining, Baking & Pastry, Flavors of the World, and Business Management. Six-week internship required at end of training. Continuing ed available.

FACULTY: Full-time instructors and local area chefs who are on staff as part time instructors.

COSTS: ~$27,000 includes books, supplies, uniforms and tuition for both degree and diploma programs. Admission requirements: HS diploma, interview, letters of recommendation, application with fee. Scholarships: yes. Loans: yes.

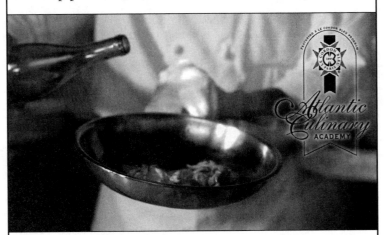

LOCATION: 10 minutes from the coast, or a short drive to the White Mountains.

CONTACT: Bill Bayliss, Director of Admissions, Le Cordon Bleu @ Atlantic Culinary Academy, 23 Cataract Ave., Dover, NH 03820; 877-628-1222, Fax 603-749-0837, bbayliss@mcintoshcollege.com, www.atlanticculinary.com.

THE BALSAMS CULINARY APPRENTICESHIP SCHOOL

Dixville Notch/Year-round

Sponsor: Cooking school in a privately owned, 4-star resort hotel. Program: 3-1/2 yr program granting certification with the ACF & AOS degree. Calendar: quarter. Curriculum: culinary, core. Admit dates: June. Total enrollment: 20. 10 each admission period. 50% of applicants accepted. 80% receive financial aid. S:T ratio 1.5:1. 100% of graduates obtain jobs within 6 mos. Facilities: The Balsams hotel kitchens, garde manger & full bakery. Hotel also has a butcher shop, 3 outlets & main dining room. Apprenticeship center with lodging, demo kitchen & banquet area.

COURSES: Sanitation, Nutrition, Knife Skills, Cooking Techniques, Meat Fabrication, Garde Manger, Buffet, Breakfast Cookery, Baking, Patisserie, Restaurant & Menu Design, Purchasing & Receiving, Food History, general ed courses. Six 8-wk externships required.

FACULTY: 13 chef-supervisors, 5-7 instructors from New Hampshire Technical College.

COSTS: ~$3,000/yr + equipment & textbooks. Tuition for classes through New Hampshire Technical College. Admission requirements: HS diploma or equivalent, min 1 yr experience in the cooking industry or participation in a culinary arts program. Scholarships: yes. Loans: yes.

CONTACT: Steven Learned, Executive Chef, The Balsams Culinary Apprenticeship School, Rt. 26, Dixville Notch, NH 03576; 603-255-3861, 603-255-2661, Fax 603-255-4670, plearned@ncia.net, www.thebalsams.com.

NEW HAMPSHIRE COMMUNITY TECHNICAL COLLEGE

Berlin/Year-round

Sponsor: Career college. Program: 2-yr AAS degree & 1-yr diploma in Culinary Arts, 24-cr certificate in Food Service Production. Established: 1966. Accredited by NEASC. Calendar: semester. Curriculum: core. Admit dates: Open. Total enrollment: 30. 20 each admission period. 76% of applicants accepted. 89% receive financial aid. 10% enrolled part-time. S:T ratio 15:1. 100% of graduates obtain jobs within 6 mos. Facilities: 3 kitchens, classrooms.

COURSES: Soups & sauces, food prod, meat fabrication, sanitation, baking, patisserie, classical desserts, garde manger, charcuterie, buffet, food sculpture & design, menu analysis, restaurant design, marketing. Externship provided.

FACULTY: 2 full-time. Includes K. Hohmeister & S. Griffiths.

COSTS: Annual tuition $3,500 in-state, $$4,950 New England regional, $7,590 out-of-state. Summer externship $110/cr in-state, $165/cr New England, out-of-state $253/cr. Other fees: $90. Admission requirements: HS diploma or equivalent. Scholarships: yes. Loans: yes.

CONTACT: Kurt Hohmeister, Department Chair, New Hampshire Community Technical College, Culinary Arts, 2020 Riverside Dr., Berlin, NH 03570; 800-445-455, 603-752-1113, Fax 603-752-6335, khohmeister@tec.nh.us, http://comet.berl.tec.nh.us/courses/cook.html.

SOUTHERN NEW HAMPSHIRE UNIVERSITY CULINARY PROGRAM

Manchester/September-May *(See display ad page 102)*

Sponsor: University. Program: 2-yr AAS degree in Culinary Arts; can be transferred into a 4-yr BS degree in a hospitality management program. Established: 1983. Accredited by ACFEI. Calendar: semester. Curriculum: culinary. Admit dates: Rolling. Total enrollment: 120. 75 each admission period. 75% of applicants accepted. 90% receive financial aid. 10% enrolled part-time. S:T ratio 15:1. 100% of graduates obtain jobs within 6 mos. Facilities: New facility with the latest equipment: 2 bakeshop labs, 2 production labs, 75-seat restaurant open to the public, demo classroom, computer center, 5 classrooms.

COURSES: Include culinary skills, bakeshop, food production, garde manger, nutrition, general ed courses. Other required courses: menu & facilities planning, cost control, dining room mgmt, classical, regional, intl cuisine. Externship: 3 month, salaried, with travel opportunities. 2+2 program toward BS in Hospitality Management.

FACULTY: 5 full-time, 6 part-time, all with industry experience & teaching credentials.

COSTS: Annual tuition $18,264. Knife set $250, books $500, uniforms $120. On-campus room & board $7,648/yr. Admission requirements: HS diploma (or equivalent), SAT scores, essay, letters of recommendation. Scholarships: yes. Loans: yes.

CONTACT: Sean Woolford, Asst. Director of Admission, Southern New Hampshire University Culinary Program, Manchester, NH 03106; 800-642-4968, Fax 603-645-9693, admission@snhu.edu, www.snhu.edu.

NEW JERSEY

ACADEMY OF CULINARY ARTS – ATLANTIC CAPE COMM. COLLEGE

Mays Landing/August-May *(See also page 246)(See display ad page 103)*

Sponsor: 2-yr college. Program: 2-year AAS degree in Culinary Arts & Food Service Management, certificate in Baking & Pastry Arts, intensive six-month program. Established: 1981. Accredited by MSA. Calendar: semester. Curriculum: culinary. Admit dates: Sept, Jan. Total enrollment: 300. 160 each admission period. 100% of applicants accepted. 60% receive financial aid. 15% enrolled part-time. S:T ratio 18:1. 100% of graduates obtain jobs within 6 mos. Facilities: Include 8 kitchens with the latest equipment, 4 classrooms, computer lab, bake shop, retail store, 100-seat gourmet restaurant with new garden terrace.

COURSES: Food Purchasing, Essentials of Catering, Nutrition, Baking, Classical Pastry, Int'l Food Preparation, Garde Manger, Menu & Facility Design, Hot Food Prep, Applied Dining Room Ops, Intro to Wines, Diversified Cuisines, Restaurant Production. Travel & learn opportunities available in USA & Europe. Also offers non-credit classes in entry level skills.

FACULTY: 15 full-time international faculty with professional designations.

COSTS: ~$4,000/semester, in-state. Housing lists available. Admission requirements: HS diploma or equivalent. Scholarships: yes. Loans: yes.

LOCATION: On ACCC's 536-acre campus 20 minutes from Atlantic City's boardwalk, 45 minutes from Philadelphia, 2 hours from New York City.

CONTACT: Regina Skinner, Director of Admissions & College Recruitment, Academy of Culinary Arts - Atlantic Cape Community College, Admissions, 5100 Black Horse Pike, Mays Landing, NJ 08330-2699; 609-343-5000, 800-645-CHEF, Fax 609-343-4921, accadmit@atlantic.edu, www.atlantic.edu/aca.

BERGEN COMMUNITY COLLEGE

Paramus/August-May

Sponsor: College. Program: 1-yr (18-30 cr) certificate in Culinary Arts, 2-yr (64-cr) degree in Hotel/Restaurant/Hospitality. Established: 1974. Accredited by MSA. Calendar: semester. Curriculum: culinary, core. Admit dates: Sept, Jan. Total enrollment: 125. 40-50 each admission period. 25% of applicants accepted. 10% receive financial aid. 20% enrolled part-time. S:T ratio 25:1. 100% of graduates obtain jobs within 6 mos. Facilities: 2 cooking labs, 2 dining rooms, 1 computer lab.

COURSES: Hands-on training integrated with management. Co-op training required.

FACULTY: 4 full-time. All master's level & industry trained.

CONTACT: Prof. David Cohen, Prof. Don Delnero, Bergen Community College-Hotel/Restaurant/Hospitality, 400 Paramus Rd., Paramus, NJ 07652; 201-447-7192, Fax 201-612-5240, dcohen@bergen.cc.nj.us, www.bergen.edu/ecatalog/subcrslist.asp?type.cbn=27.

CULINARY EDUCATION CENTER OF MONMOUTH COUNTY

Lincroft/Year-round

Sponsor: Brookdale Community College and Monmouth County Vocational School District. Program: 1-year (34.5-credit) certificate and 2-year (69.5-credit) AAS degree programs in Culinary Arts, 2-year AAS degree in Food Service Management. Established: 1998. Accredited by MSA. Calendar: semester. Curriculum: culinary, core. Admit dates: Sept, Jan. Total enrollment: 320. 50-85 each admission period. 100% of applicants accepted. 30% enrolled part-time. S:T ratio 16:1. Facilities: Include 3 kitchens, 2 baking kitchens, 2 dining rooms, computer lab, classrooms.

COURSES: Recipe interpretation, cooking techniques, nutrition, garde manger, baking, patisserie, regional cuisine, service & management. 350-400 hours of externship.

FACULTY: 10 full- and part-time faculty with advanced degrees and certifications, as well as professional culinary work experience.

COSTS: ~$3,500/ semester in-county. Total 2-year program cost ~$14,000 (includes tuition, fees, books, knife kit, uniforms). Admission requirements: HS diploma or equivalent, successful completeing of college placement test. Scholarships: yes. Loans: yes.

CONTACT: Shirley Sesler, Enrollment Specialist, Brookdale Community College, 765 Newman Springs Rd., Lincroft, NJ 07738-1597; 732-224-2371, Fax 732-842-0203, cberg@brookdale.cc.nj.us, www.brookdale.cc.nj.us.

HUDSON COUNTY COMMUNITY COLLEGE

Jersey City/September-May

Sponsor: 2-yr public college. Program: 2-yr AAS degrees & 1-yr certificates in Culinary Arts & Hospitality Mgmt. Specialized proficiency certificates in Hot Foods, Baking, & Garde Manger. Established: 1983. Accredited by MSA, State Commission on Higher Education, ACF. Calendar: semester. Curriculum: core. Admit dates: Aug, Jan. Total enrollment: 325. 125 each admission period. 90% of applicants accepted. 60% receive financial aid. 20% enrolled part-time. S:T ratio 15:1. 99% of graduates obtain jobs within 6 mos. Facilities: 4 instructional kitchens, 3 classrooms, instructional bar/lounge, formal dining room.

COURSES: 240 hrs. instruction in hot foods, garde manger, baking & dining room service; mgmt. 600-hr externship required for AAS degrees. Overseas student exchange/externships available.

FACULTY: 9 full-time, 24 part-time.

COSTS: AAS degree $12,344 in-county, $17,384 out-of-county, $22,424 out-of-state, includes fees, supplies, uniforms, books, insurance. Admission requirements: Open. HS diploma, GED, or 18+ yrs of age. Scholarships: yes. Loans: yes.

CONTACT: Dennis Baumeyer, Executive Director, Hudson County Community College-Culinary Arts Institute, 161 Newkirk St., Jersey City, NJ 07306; 201-714-2193, Fax 201-656-1522, dbaumeyer@hccc.edu, www.hccc.edu. Janine Nunez, 201-714-7193, jnunez@hccc.edu.

MIDDLESEX COUNTY COLLEGE

Edison/Year-round

Sponsor: College. Program: Certificate in Culinary Arts; and 2-year AAS in Hotel Restaurant, & Institution Management with Culinary Arts Management Option. Established: 1987. Accredited by MSA. Calendar: semester. Curriculum: culinary, core. Admit dates: Jan, May, September. Total enrollment: 70. 10 (summer) 30 (spring, fall) each admission period. 100% of applicants accepted. 85% receive financial aid. 40% enrolled part-time. S:T ratio 16:1. 100% of graduates obtain jobs within 6 mos. Facilities: Includes 1 kitchen, 3 classrooms.

COURSES: Food selection & preparation, baking, garde manger, food & beverage cost controls & purchasing, sanitation, beverage management, culinary techniques, externiship, & general education. Externship: 180 hours.

FACULTY: 6 full-time, 3 part-time.

COSTS: Annual tuition in-state $2,750, out-of-state $5,440. Application fee $25. Admission requirements: HS diploma or equivalent. Scholarships: yes. Loans: yes.

CONTACT: Marilyn Laskowski-Sachnoff, Dept. Chair, Middlesex County College, Hotel Restaurant & Institution Mgmt., 2600 Woodbridge Ave., P.O. Box 3050, Edison, NJ 08818-3050; 732-906-2538, Fax 732-906-7745, M_Laskowski_Sachnoff@middlesexcc.edu, www.middlesexcc.edu.

MORRIS COUNTY SCHOOL OF TECHNOLOGY

Denville/September-June

Sponsor: Trade-technical school. Program: 1- or 2-yr sequential program in Culinary Arts offering certificates in Hospitality Mgmt, Food Prep/Production, & ServSafe Sanitation. Established: 1977. Accredited by Dept. of Vocational Ed. Curriculum: culinary, core. Admit dates: Sept. Total enrollment: 90. 45-50 each admission period. 100% of applicants accepted. 10% receive financial aid. 90% enrolled part-time. S:T ratio 15:1. 95% of graduates obtain jobs within 6 mos. Facilities: 2 high-tech commercial kitchens, including a bakeshop in one.

COURSES: Food ID, Pantry, Cost Control, Soups, Stocks, Sauces, Purchasing, Baking, Menu

Development, Garde Manger, Meat, Poultry, Seafood, American Regional Cuisine. Guest speakers, field trips, job shadowing, internships, coop work, mentorships, apprenticeships. Cook-Apprentice 3-yr (9-course) certificate program for FMP & ACF certification credits.

FACULTY: 3 instructors with culinary degrees, teaching degrees, & industry experience.

COSTS: $1,050/yr part-time, $2,100/yr full-time. Admission requirements: Jr/sr level in HS, HS graduate. Scholarships: yes. Loans: yes.

CONTACT: MaryAnne Regan, Curriculum Supervisor, Morris County School of Technology, 400 E. Main St., Denville, NJ 07834; 973-627-4600 x224, Fax 973-627-6979, reganm@mcvts.org, www.mcvts.org.

PASSAIC COUNTY TECHNICAL INSTITUTE

Wayne/September-June

Sponsor: Vocational high school. Program: HS diploma in Culinary Arts. Established: 1970. Accredited by NJ State Dept. of Education. Calendar: semester. Curriculum: core. Admit dates: September. Total enrollment: 90+. 90+ each admission period. S:T ratio 10:1. Facilities: 3 kitchens, 3 student cafeterias faculty cafeteria, full service restaurant, bakeshop.

COURSES: Baking, cafeteria, production, pantry, table service. Students prepare 2,300 meals/day.

FACULTY: 9 culinary arts teachers: Michael Adams, Enrico Cannataro, JoAnn Demarest, Rose Marie Halas, Mearlyn Majette, John Nuzzo, Matt Vanaria, Lawrence Walden, Celeste Zaleski.

CONTACT: Michael W. Adams, Passaic County Technical Institute, 45 Reinhardt Rd., Wayne, NJ 07470; 973-389-4296, madams@pcti.tec.nj.us, www.pcti.tec.nj.us.

SALEM COUNTY VOCATIONAL TECHNICAL SCHOOLS

Woodstown

Sponsor: Career institution. Program: 2-year certificate in Culinary Arts. Established: 1976. Accredited by MSA. Admit dates: Sept, Jan. Total enrollment: 30. 75% of applicants accepted. S:T ratio 15:1. 85% of graduates obtain jobs within 6 mos.

FACULTY: 20 full-time.

COSTS: Annual tuition $3,000.

CONTACT: Eva Hoffman, Instructor, Salem County Vocational Technical Schools, Culinary Arts, Box 350, Woodstown, NJ 08098; 856-769-0101, Fax 856-769-4214, Info@scvts.org, www.scvts.org.

NEW MEXICO

ALBUQUERQUE TECHNICAL VOCATIONAL INSTITUTE

Albuquerque/Year-round

Sponsor: Community college/career institution. Program: Baking certificate, Professional Cooking certificate, Food Service Mgmt certificate, AAS in Culinary Arts. Established: 1965. Accredited by ACF. Calendar: trimester. Curriculum: culinary, core. Admit dates: Year-round. Total enrollment: 150. 130 each admission period. 100% of applicants accepted. 65% receive financial aid. 33% enrolled part-time. S:T ratio 16:1. 100% of graduates obtain jobs within 6 mos. Facilities: 1 baking lab & retail bakery, 2 kitchens, student-operated buffet, catering, bistro, fine dining restaurant, computer labs.

COURSES: Baking, Professional Cooking, Food Service Mgmt, Arts & Science. Co-op education. Cooking, baking, & catering classes, customized curriculum for the food service industry.

FACULTY: 10 full- & part-time. Includes Carmine Russo, CCC, CCE, Joyce Woodard, Michael Williams, CHE, CC, Elizabeth McGeehan, Joseph Chapa, Kerry Knoop, CPC.

COSTS: $1,097/term for full-time students. $30 reg fee + equipment & uniforms. Tuition for Occupational classes is free for residents & $123/cr-hr for non-residents. Admission requirements: Age 18+, HS diploma, GED or concurrent HS. Scholarships: yes. Loans: yes.

CONTACT: Carmine J. Russo, CCC, CCE, Program Chair, Albuquerque Technical Vocational Institute-TVI Community College, Culinary Arts, 525 Buena Vista SE, Albuquerque, NM 87106; 505-224-3755, Fax 505-224-3781, crusso@tvi.cc.nm.us, www.tvi.edu.

SANTA FE COMMUNITY COLLEGE

Santa Fe/Year-round

Sponsor: 2-yr college. Program: 2-yr certificate/AAS degree in Culinary Arts, 1-yr certificate. Established: 1985. Accredited by NCA. Calendar: quarter. Curriculum: culinary, core. Admit dates: August 20, Jan 10, June 1. Total enrollment: 190. 30 each admission period. 100% of applicants accepted. 20% receive financial aid. 20% enrolled part-time. S:T ratio 14:1. 100% of graduates obtain jobs within 6 mos. Facilities: Include 2 kitchens & classrooms, culinary lab, banquet facilities, restaurant.

Courses: Culinary courses, apprenticeship program, specialty topics, & Southwestern cuisine. Other required courses: nutrition, sanitation, food and beverage management, general studies. Externship provided, 2 credit-hours or 200 working-hours. Continuing education: 12 courses/semesterCourses range from Southwest to Asian & include baking classes.

Faculty: 1 full-time, 8 part-time. Qualifications: working executive chef.

Costs: Annual tuition in-county $20/cr-hr, out-of-county $25/cr-hr, out-of-state $45/cr-hr plus lab fees. Admission requirements: HS diploma or equivalent. Scholarships: yes. Loans: yes.

Contact: Director of Culinary Arts, Santa Fe Community College, Culinary Arts/Hospitality, 6401 Richards Ave., Santa Fe, NM 87502; 505-428-1600, Fax 505-428-1237, www.santa-fe.cc.nm.us.

UNITED STATES PERSONAL CHEF INSTITUTE

Rio Rancho/Year-round

Sponsor: Private school specializing in the teaching & development of Personal Chefs. Program: 5-day (50-hr) Mentorship Course that covers the USPCI's 3 core courses: Culinary Review, Personal Chef Basics, Advanced Personal Cheffing. Established: 1996. Curriculum: culinary. Admit dates: Ongoing. 100% of applicants accepted. S:T ratio 4:1.

Courses: Also includes Administration & Marketing and Culinary Theory & Techniques for the Personal Chef. USPCA summer conferences, seminars & workshops, taught by industry experts.

Faculty: Working Certified Professional Chefs.

Costs: $2,995. Loans: yes.

Location: Mentorship Course offered at the USPCI's Regional Offices in Phoenix, AZ, Cherry Hill, NJ & Atlanta, GA.

Contact: United States Personal Chef Institute, 481 Rio Rancho Blvd., Ste. B, Rio Rancho, NM 87124; 800-995-2138, 505-896-3522, Fax 505-994-6399, dentry@uspca.com, www.uspci.com.

NEW YORK

ACF OF GREATER BUFFALO

Lewiston/Year-round

Sponsor: ACF chapter. Program: 3-yr apprenticeship; degree program through Niagara County Community College or Erie Community College is completed by 100%. Curriculum: culinary. Total enrollment: 3.

Contact: Cornelia Walmsley, CCE, AAC, ACF of Greater Buffalo, PO Box 61, Buffalo, NY 14207; 716-688-5646, walmsley@pcom.net.

ADIRONDACK COMMUNITY COLLEGE

Queensbury/September-May

Sponsor: Proprietary college. Program: 1-year certificate & 2-year AAS degree in Food Service. Established: 1969. Accredited by MSA. Admit dates: Fall, spring. Total enrollment: 25. 70-80% receive financial aid. 75% enrolled part-time. S:T ratio 10:1. 90% of graduates obtain jobs within 6 mos. Facilities: Include 3 kitchens, classroom and restaurant.

Courses: 1 year of food preparation, 1/2 year of spa cuisine, 1/2 year of American regional cuisine. Externship: 1,000-1,200 hours. Continuing education: baking, wines and other topics.

Faculty: 1 full-time, 3 part-time.

COSTS: Tuition $1,075/semester in-state, $2,150/semester out-of-state plus activity fees. Admission requirements: HS diploma or equivalent.

CONTACT: William Steele, Program Coordinator, Adirondack Community College, Commercial Cooking, Bay Rd., Queensbury, NY 12804; 518-743-2200 x374, Fax 518-743-2317, info@acc.suny-acc.edu, www.suny.edu.

ALFRED STATE COLLEGE – CULINARY ARTS

Wellsville/August-May

Sponsor: 2-year college. Program: 2-year AOS degree program. Established: 1966. Accredited by MSA. Calendar: semester. Curriculum: culinary. Admit dates: Jan, Aug. Total enrollment: 60. 65/71 each admission period. 75% of applicants accepted. 87% receive financial aid. S:T ratio 8:1. 95% of graduates obtain jobs within 6 mos. Facilities: Comparative with the food industry.

COSTS: Tuition $3,200 in-state, $5,000 out-of-state; books, uniforms, tools ~$300/semester.

CONTACT: Director of Admissions, Alfred State College, Upper College Dr., Alfred, NY 14802; 800-4AL-FRED, Fax 607-587-4299, admissions@alfredstate.edu, www.alfredstate.edu.

THE ART INSTITUTE OF NEW YORK CITY

New York/Year-round *(See display ad page 135)*

Sponsor: Private college, formerly the New York Restaurant School. Program: 6-qtr/8-qtr full-time/part-time AOS degree in Culinary Arts & Restaurant Management, 4-qtr/6-qtr certificate in Culinary Arts, 3-qtr/4-qtr certificates in Pastry Arts & Restaurant Managment. Established: 1980. Accredited by ACICS. Calendar: quarter. Curriculum: culinary. Admit dates: Jan, Apr, July, Oct. Total enrollment: 1300. 400 each admission period. 80% of applicants accepted. 85% receive financial aid. 35% enrolled part-time. 90.6% of graduates obtain jobs within 6 mos. Facilities: 42,000-sq-ft recently renovated facility, 9 newly-equipped kitchens.

COURSES: Culinary Arts & Restaurant Mgmt: culinary theory & practice, basic cooking, food production, baking & pastry, sanitation & safety, accounting. AOS programs culminate in an externship.

FACULTY: 47 full- & 15 part-time faculty, all with a minimum 5 yr's experience.

COSTS: $21,351 for Culinary Arts, $16,378 for Pastry Arts, $14,787 for Restaurant Management, $38,987 for AOS degree program. $50 application fee, $100 registration fee required.

CONTACT: Shamika Boyd, Admissions, The Art Institute of New York City, 75 Varick St., New York, NY 10013; 212-226-5500/800-654-CHEF, Fax 212-226-5664, boyds@aii.edu, www.ainyc.aii.edu.

THE CULINARY INSTITUTE OF AMERICA

Hyde Park/Year-round *(See also page 27, 209, 253)(See display ad page 108)*

Sponsor: Independent, not-for-profit educational institution. Program: 38-mo bachelor's degree programs in Culinary Arts Management and Baking & Pastry Arts Management, 21-mo associate degree programs in Culinary Arts and Baking & Pastry Arts, continuing ed & nonvocational courses. Established: 1946. Accredited by MSA, ACCSCT, curricula registered with NY State Education Dept. Curriculum: culinary. Admit dates: 4 enrollment seasons with 16 entry dates/yr. Total enrollment: 2,300. ~90 each admission period. 70% of applicants accepted. 90% receive financial aid. S:T ratio 18:1. 98% of graduates obtain jobs within 6 mos. Facilities: 41 kitchens & bakeshops, 67,000-volume library, 4,000 instructional videos, learning resource & nutrition centers, bookstore, 5 student-staffed restaurants, student recreation center.

COURSES: Associate & Bachelor's degree programs give students comprehensive, hands-on experience in the theory & techniques of foodservice. Bachelor's degree programs provide additional managerial & conceptual skills. All degree programs include 18-wk paid externships off campus. Continuing Ed. Dept. offers 1- to 30-wk courses in cooking, baking, & management.

FACULTY: 140+ chefs & instructors from more than 13 countries.

COSTS: $17,640/yr for freshman/sophomore, $12,888/yr for junior/senior. Admission requirements: HS diploma or equivalent & min 6 mos foodservice experience, including work in a professional kitchen. Scholarships: yes. Loans: yes.

LOCATION: The 150-acre residential campus overlooks the Hudson River, ~1.5-2 hrs north of NYC.

CONTACT: Drusilla Blackman, Dean of Enrollment Management, The Culinary Institute of America, 1946 Campus Dr., Hyde Park, NY 12538; 800-CULINARY (800-285-4627), Fax (845) 451-1068, Admissions@culinary.edu, www.ciachef.edu.

ERIE COMMUNITY COLLEGE, CITY CAMPUS

Buffalo/September-May

Sponsor: 2-yr community college sponsored by Erie County. Program: 2-year AOS degree in Hotel Technology/Culinary Arts & 1 year certificate in baking. Established: 1985. Accredited by MSA. Calendar: semester. Curriculum: culinary. Admit dates: Fall & Jan./spring. Total enrollment: 80. 60% of applicants accepted. 70% receive financial aid. 10% enrolled part-time. S:T ratio 20:1. 75% of graduates obtain jobs within 6 mos. Facilities: 5 kitchens, classrooms, computer lab, student run restaurant.

FACULTY: 6 full-time,7 part-time.

COSTS: Annual tuition: in-state $1,980, out-of-state $3,960. Other fees $100. Admission requirements: HS diploma or equivalent and placement test. Scholarships: yes. Loans: yes.

CONTACT: Paul J. Cannamela, Asst. Professor, Erie Community College, Culinary Arts, 121 Ellicott St., Buffalo, NY 14203-2698; 716-851-1034, Fax 716-851-1129, cannamela@ecc.edu, www.ecc.edu.

THE FRENCH CULINARY INSTITUTE

New York/Year-round *(See also page 253)(See display ad page 110)*

Sponsor: Proprietary institution founded by Dorothy Cann Hamilton. Program: 600-hr 6-mo full-time & 9-mo part-time Grande Diplôme programs in Classic Culinary or Pastry Arts; 6-wk Diplôme du Boulanger program in the Art of International Bread Baking; Culinary Business courses in catering, restaurateuring, wine merchandising. Established: 1984. Accredited by ACCSCT. Curriculum: culinary. Admit dates: Rolling. Total enrollment: 850. 24 each admission period. 90% of applicants accepted. 75% receive financial aid. 60% enrolled part-time. S:T ratio 12:1. 98% of graduates obtain jobs within 6 mos. Facilities: 30,000-sq-ft facility with newly equipped culinary, pastry and bread kitchens, demonstration amphitheater, L'Ecole restaurant (open to the public; all food prepared by students).

COURSES: Classic Culinary Arts emphasizing French Techniques. Classic French pastry technique, traditional dessert composition. Classic artisanal breads, restaurant breads. Fundamentals of Catering, Fundamentals of Wine, Essentials of Restaurant Management. Culinary program features hands-on cooking experience in 5 stations (meat, fish, poultry, garde manger, pastry) at Restaurant L'Ecole. Ongoing placement assistance for work/externship provided after completion of Level I & continues after graduation. Seminars & workshops; Culinary Business Courses in catering, restaurateuring, wine merchandising.

FACULTY: 41 teachers & staff, including Dean of Studies Alain Sailhac, Dean of Special Programs Jacques Pépin, Master Chef André Soltner, Dean of Pastry Arts Jacques Torres, Dean of Wine Studies Andrea Immer, Visiting Dean Alice Waters, Marcella Hazen.

COSTS: $27,750/$25,750 for Classic Culinary Arts full-time /part-time, $25,750 for Classic Pastry Arts, $5,600 for International Bread Baking, $1,875 for Fundamentals of Catering, $895 for Fundamentals of Wine, $5,850 for Essentials of Restaurant Management. Admission requirements: HS diploma or equivalent, 150-word essay, personal interview. Scholarships: yes. Loans: yes.

LOCATION: New York City's historic SoHo district, adjacent to Chinatown.

CONTACT: David Waggoner, Dean of Enrollment, The French Culinary Institute, 462 Broadway, New York, NY 10013-2618; 888-FCI-CHEF/212-219-8890, Fax 212-431-3054, admission@frenchculinary.com, www.frenchculinary.com/shaw.

FULTON-MONTGOMERY COMMUNITY COLLEGE

Johnstown/Year-round

Sponsor: Public 2-year college. Program: 1-year certificate in Quantity Food, 2-year associate degree in Food Service Administration. Established: 1964. Accredited by MSA. Calendar: semester.

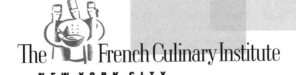

Curriculum: culinary. Admit dates: Jan, Sept. Total enrollment: 15. 75% of applicants accepted. 25% enrolled part-time. S:T ratio 7:1. Facilities: Food prod kitchen, dining room, lecture room.

COURSES: Baking, beverage mgmt., culinary skills, food prep & purchasing, nutrition.

FACULTY: 1 full-time, 3 part-time. Includes Anita N. Hanaburgh, Cynthia Fratianni, John Manzar.

COSTS: $1,115/sem full-time, $93/cr-hr part-time. Application fee $40. Scholarships: yes.

CONTACT: Alexandra Henderson, Professor, Food Service Administration, Fulton-Montgomery Community College, Route 67, Johnstown, NY 12095; 518-762-4651 x6104, Fax 518-762-4334, ahenders@fmcc.suny.edu, http://fmcc.suny.edu.

THE INSTITUTE OF CULINARY EDUCATION

New York/Year-round *(See also page 255)(See display ad above & pages 112, 113, 255)*

Sponsor: Private institute, formerly known as Peter Kump's New York Cooking School. Program: 26- to 39-week diploma programs in Culinary Arts, Pastry & Baking Arts, & Culinary Management. Flexible schedules. Continuing education & business courses, programs for professionals & non-professionals. Established: 1975. Accredited by ACCSCT, licensed by NY State Dept. of Education. Curriculum: culinary. Admit dates: Monthly. Total enrollment: 750. 75% of applicants accepted. 70% receive financial aid. S:T ratio 13:1. 96% of graduates obtain jobs within 6 mos. Facilities: 27,000-sq-ft facility includes 9 kitchens, wine studies center, confectionery lab, reference library.

COURSES: In addition to theory & hands-on training in the preparation & presentation of classic cuisines, culinary arts courses cover Italian & Asian cuisine, kitchen management, garde manger, pastry & baking, wine. 6-week apprenticeship at a restaurant/pastry shop, local & international. 1,200+ non-credit classes offered year-round. 3-day professional development classes in opening a restaurant, specialty food shop, catering business, or an inn. Food writing courses.

FACULTY: 45 chef-instructors. Founder Peter Kump was founding president of The James Beard

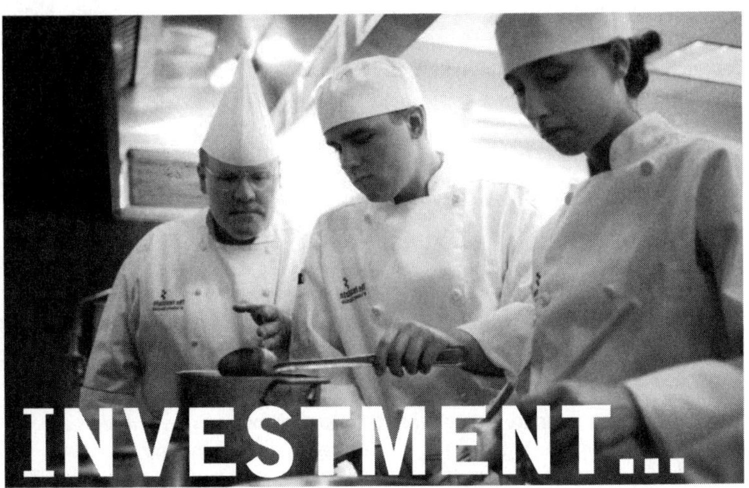

Starting seven years ago, we invested substantial time, money, and resources to give our students the best possible culinary education. We lengthened and redesigned our career programs to include cuisines and techniques from America, Asia, Italy and France, in order to meet the evolving tastes of today's diners. We also added a unique culinary-management program for those with entrepreneurial ambitions.

We built nine professionally equipped kitchens and, to make sure students got the most out of them, limited class size to 16. We created the most flexible course schedule around, with morning, afternoon, evening, and weekend classes. And, we continued to offer a rigorous 210-hour externship program in which students perfect their craft at some of the nation's most highly regarded restaurants. And the tuition investment? Still less than any culinary school in New York City.

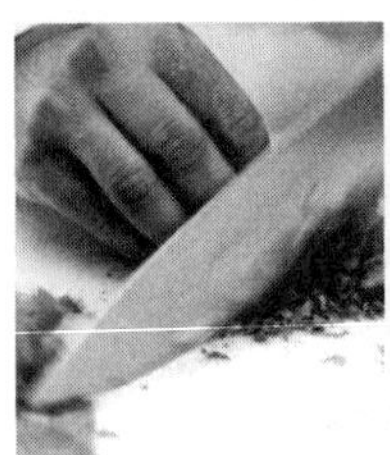

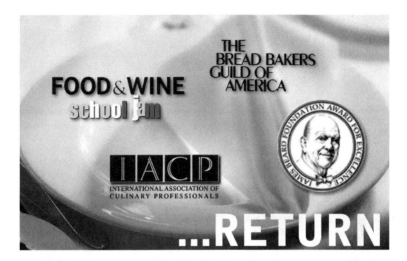

Foundation. Dir. of Pastry & Baking Nick Malgieri is one of Pastry Art & Design's Top 10 Pastry Chefs. Advisory board includes chefs Daniel Boulud & Lidia Bastianich.

COSTS: Culinary Arts program $19,300, Pastry & Baking Arts program $18,750, Culinary Management $11,000. Admission requirements: HS diploma or GED plus proof of 1 yr college or 1 yr professional work experience (any profession). Scholarships: yes. Loans: yes.

CONTACT: Stephen Tave, Director/Vice President, The Institute of Culinary Education, 50 W. 23rd St., New York, NY 10010; 800-522-4610, 212-847-0770, Fax 212-847-0726, stave@iceculinary.com, www.iceculinary.com.

INTERNATIONAL SOMMELIER GUILD

Grand Island/Year-round

Sponsor: Wine organization. Program: 23-wk Sommelier Diploma Program, 24-hr Wine Fundamentals Certificate Level 1 & 45- or 48-hr Certificate Level 2. Established: 1984. Calendar: semester. Total enrollment: 24 max. 24 each admission period. 75-80% of applicants accepted. 100% enrolled part-time. S:T ratio 24:1. 95+% of graduates obtain jobs within 6 mos.

FACULTY: 25 instructors with 10+ yrs hospitality & adult ed experience, Sommelier certification .

COSTS: $1,500-$3,100. Admission requirements: Legal drinking age, HS diploma or GED.

CONTACT: Daria Rozik, Administrator, International Sommelier Guild, 363 Lang Blvd., Grand Island, NY 14072; 866-412-0464, 302-622-3811, 905-858-1217, 416-699-3666, Fax 905-858-3440, info@internationalsommelier.com, www.internationalsommelier.com.

INTERNATIONAL WINE CENTER

New York/Year-round

Sponsor: Private wine school. Program: 8-session Intermediate Certificate Course, 15-session Advanced Certificate Course, 2-yr Diploma Course. Home study. Established: 1982. Admit dates: Year-round. 30-50 each admission period.

COURSES: Student earn official WSET credentials.

FACULTY: Master of Wine Mary Ewing Mulligan; all instructors with WSET diploma.

COSTS: $448-$1,875.

CONTACT: Linda Lawry, International Wine Center, 1133 Broadway, Ste. 520, New York, NY 10010; 212-627-7170, Fax 212-627-7116, IWCNY@aol.com, www.internationalwinecenter.com.

ITALIAN CULINARY INSTITUTE

New York/Year-round

Sponsor: Private culinary school. Program: Master class certificate courses (16 sessions) on Italian cooking for professionals. Established: 1999. Curriculum: culinary. Admit dates: Continuous. Total enrollment: 64. 16 each admission period. 80% of applicants accepted. 20% receive financial aid. S:T ratio 16:1. Facilities: Instructional demo kitchen equipped with a mix of professional & high end home equipment, 5 cooking stations for hands-on classes.

COURSES: Italian cooking with focus on regional specialties. Internship in Italian restaurants in NYC.

FACULTY: 8 Italian chefs & instructors.

COSTS: $1,600/8-wk program, includes textbook. Admission requirements: Culinary school graduate. Scholarships: yes. Loans: yes..

CONTACT: Silva Staffieri, Executive Assistant, Italian Culinary Institute's Master Class in Italian Cooking, 230 Fifth Ave., #1100, New York, NY 10001; 212-725-8764 x15, Fax 212-889-3907, pva@italiancookingandliving.com, www.italiancookingandliving.com.

JEFFERSON COMMUNITY COLLEGE

Watertown

Sponsor: 2-yr college. Program: 2-yr certificate/AAS degree. Established: 1975. Accredited by MSA. Admit dates: Aug, Jan. Total enrollment: 120. 100% of applicants accepted. S:T ratio 25:1. 95% of graduates obtain jobs within 6 mos.

FACULTY: 4 full-time.

COSTS: Annual tuition in-state $1,250 full-time, $84/cr part-time; out-of-state $2,318/sem, $168/cr. Admission requirements: HS diploma or equivalent.

CONTACT: Deborah McGloine, Assistant Professor, Jefferson Community College, Hospitality & Tourism, Outer Coffeen St., Watertown, NY 13601; 315-786-2333, dmcgloine@sunyjefferson.edu, www.sunyjefferson.edu. Anthony Louise, Assistant Professor, alouise@sunyjefferson.edu.

L'ECOLE DES CHEFS RELAIS GOURMANDS

Locations worldwide/Year-round *(See also page 307) (See display ad page 307)*

Sponsor: Relais & Chateaux Relais Gourmands. Program: 2- & 5-day internship programs with Michelin & Mobil-starred chefs. Program is offered to amateur cooks & culinary students only. Certificate upon completion. Established: 1999. Curriculum: culinary. Admit dates: Year-round. Total enrollment: 1 per chef/restaurant. Based upon chef availability each admission period. 80% of applicants accepted. S:T ratio 1:1. Facilities: On-site in the kitchens of noted restaurants in 17 countries.

COURSES: One-on-one instruction. Immersion in the restaurant kitchen with executive chef, garde-manger, saucier, sauté cook, pastry chef. Participation in staff meals, meetings.

FACULTY: Master chefs worldwide with 156 Michelin & 58 Mobil-starred chefs, including Daniel Boulud, Eric Ripert, Thomas Keller, Jean-Georges Vongerichten, Michel Troisgros, Guy Savoy, Alain Passard, Michel Rostang.

COSTS: 2-day (5-day) programs $1,100-$1,400 ($1,900-$2,950). Does not include travel or lodging. Must submit application form ($25 fee) & resume. ~80% of applicants accepted. Admission requirements: Resume & application.

LOCATION: France, USA, Canada, Argentina, Belgium, Denmark, Germany, Great Britain, Italy, Luxembourg, Netherlands, Norway, Spain, Sweden and Switzerland.

CONTACT: Jennifer L. Iannolo, Manager, L'Ecole des Chefs Relais Gourmands, 11 E. 44th St., #707, New York, NY 10017; 877-334-6464, Fax 212-856-0193, info@ecoledeschefs.com, www.ecoledeschefs.com.

MOHAWK VALLEY COMMUNITY COLLEGE

Rome/August-May

Sponsor: 2-year community college. Program: AOS degree in Culinary Arts Mgmt, Baking & Pastry emphasis, AAS degree Restaurant Management, Chef Training certificate. Established: 1946. Accredited by MSA. Calendar: semester. Curriculum: culinary, core. Admit dates: Aug, Jan. Total enrollment: 110. 45-55 FT, 20 PT, 18+ on-line each admission period. 94% of applicants accepted. 90% receive financial aid. 40% enrolled part-time. S:T ratio 14:1. 99% of graduates obtain jobs within 6 mos. Facilities: Cuisine & baking labs, 7 classrooms, demo kitchen, conference room, 110-seat dining room, computer lab, culinary library.

COURSES: Food Prep, Banquet & Catering, Computer, Safety/Sanitation, Baking, Cake Decorating, Pastry, Cost Controls, Purchasing, Nutrition, Food Merchandising. 15-wk corporate environment.

FACULTY: 3 full-time, 6 adjunct. Includes Director Mark Waldrop, MS.

COSTS: $1,250/sem full-time, $100/cr-hr part-time. Admission requirements: HS diploma or GED. Scholarships: yes. Loans: yes.

CONTACT: Mark Waldrop, Director of Hospitality, Mohawk Valley Community College, Hospitality Programs, 1101 Floyd Ave., Rome, NY 13440; 315-334-7710, Fax 315-334-7762, mwaldrop@mvcc.edu, www.mvcc.edu/catalog/hospitality. Admissions Dept: 315-792-5354, dkennelty@mvcc.edu.

MONROE COMMUNITY COLLEGE

Rochester/September-May

Sponsor: 2-yr college. Program: 2-yr certificate/AAS degree. Established: 1967. Accredited by MSA. Calendar: semester. Curriculum: core. Admit dates: Fall, spring. Total enrollment: 175. 60 each admission period. 80% of applicants accepted. 60% receive financial aid. 20% enrolled part-time. S:T ratio 18:1. 96% of graduates obtain jobs within 6 mos. Facilities: 4 kitchens, computer lab, dining room.

Faculty: 8-10 full- and part-time. Includes Chair E.F. Callens, CEC, CCE, CFE.

Costs: Tuition $1,205/semester in-state full-time, $105/credit-hour part-time. Out-of-state tuition is double. Admission requirements: HS diploma or equivalent.

Contact: Eddy Callens, Chairperson, Monroe Community College, Food Mgmt., Bldg. 3, Rm. 155, Rochester, NY 14623; 585-292-2542/2586, ecallens@monroecc.edu, www.monroecc.edu.

THE NATURAL GOURMET COOKERY SCHOOL

New York/Year-round *(See also page 257)(See display ad above)*

Sponsor: Proprietary school devoted to health supportive, natural foods cooking & theory. Program: 600+-hr, 4-mo full-time/10-mo part-time Culinary Arts Program, individual nonvocational courses for the public. Established: 1977. Accredited by ACCET. Curriculum: culinary. Admit dates: CTP begins 9 times/yr. 16 each admission period. 33% enrolled part-time. S:T ratio 16:1. 80% of graduates obtain jobs within 6 mos. Facilities: Include 2 newly renovated kitchens, classroom, & bookstore.

Courses: Vegetarian focus, emphasis on natural foods, health supportive cooking, contemporary presentation, preparation, techniques, knife skills, limited poultry & fish, baking & desserts, career opportunities, theoretical approaches to diet & health. A 95-hr internship in an outside food establishment is required. 30 classes, open to the public.

Faculty: 15 full/part-time faculty, incl founder Annemarie Colbin, MA, Certified Health Education Specialist, author of Food and Healing, The Book of Whole Meals, The Natural Gourmet; President Jenny Matthau, a graduate of the school.

Costs: $15,850 tuition includes books. $100 application fee. Nearby lodging begins at $500/mo. Admission requirements: HS diploma or equivalent. Scholarships: yes. Loans: yes.

Contact: Merle Brown, Director of Admissions, The Natural Gourmet Cookery School, 48 W. 21st St., 2nd Floor, New York, NY 10010; 212-645-5170, 212-627-COOK, Fax 212-989-1493, admissions@naturalgourmetschool.com, www.naturalgourmetschool.com.

NEW SCHOOL CULINARY ARTS

New York/Year-round

Sponsor: New School University. Program: Master class certificate courses in Cooking (25 sessions), Baking (15), Professional Catering (10), Italian Cooking (10), Restaurant Management (12); other programs for professionals & nonprofessionals. Established: 1919. Calendar: trimester. Curriculum: culinary. Total enrollment: 12 maximum in each Master class. 100% enrolled part-time. S:T ratio 12:1. Facilities: Bed & breakfast new instructional kitchen equipped with a mix of professional and high-end home equipment.

Courses: Master Class: basic skills, cuisine & pastry preparation, presentation, recipe development; Baking: pastries, breads & doughs, cake decoration, chocolate; Catering: food preparation, business aspects. Graduates are eligible for apprenticeships. Include restaurant management, cake decorating, opening a coffee bar, creating & selling a new food.

Faculty: 50+ faculty headed by Gary Goldberg, co-founder Martin Johner, incl Bruce Beck,

Miriam Brickman, James Chew, Richard Glavin, Arlyn Hackett, Micheal Krondl, Harriet Lembeck, Lisa Montenegro, Robert Posch, Dan Rosati, Stephen Schmidt, Carole Walter.

COSTS: Master Class $2,510 (+$475 materials fee) for Cooking, $1,505 (+$215) for Baking, $995 (+$205) for Catering. Most other professional management courses & Saturday workshops $70/session (+$15). Tuition-free kitchen assistantship.

CONTACT: Gary A. Goldberg, Executive Director, New School Culinary Arts, 131 West 23rd St., New York, NY 10011; 212-255-4141/800-544-1978, Fax 646-336-6317, NSCulArts@aol.com, www.nsu.newschool.edu/culinary.

NEW YORK CITY TECHNICAL COLLEGE

Brooklyn/September-May

Sponsor: Career college. Program: 2-year AAS degree & 4-year BS degree in Hospitality Management. Established: 1947. Accredited by MSA, state, ACPHA. Calendar: semester. Curriculum: core. Admit dates: Sept, Feb. Total enrollment: 600. 125 each admission period. 50% receive financial aid. 50% enrolled part-time. S:T ratio 15:1. 90% of graduates obtain jobs within 6 mos. Facilities: Include 5 kitchens, dining room, 3 classrooms, restaurant.

COURSES: Food and beverage cost control, culinary arts, baking and pastry arts, wines, beverage management. Externship: 8 weeks, in Italy, France, Germany, if qualified. Continuing education: garde manger, cake decorating, other subjects.

FACULTY: 13 full-time, 20-40 part-time. Includes Patricia S. Bartholomew, Chair.

COSTS: Annual tuition in-state $3,200, out-of-state $6,400. CUNY fee is $35. Textbooks $1,000, materials fee $10, uniforms $120. Average off-campus housing cost is $800/mo. Admission requirements: HS diploma or equivalent and admission test. Scholarships: yes. Loans: yes.

CONTACT: Francisco Betancourt, Chair, New York City Technical College, Hospitality Mgmt., 300 Jay St., #N220, Brooklyn, NY 11201; 718-260-5630, Fax 718-260-5997, fbetancourt@citytech.cuny.edu, www.nyctc.cuny.edu.

NEW YORK FOOD AND HOTEL MANAGEMENT SCHOOL

New York/Year-round

Sponsor: Proprietary institution. Program: 9-month certificate in Commercial Cooking & Catering. Established: 1935. Accredited by ACCST. Curriculum: culinary. Admit dates: Every 4 to 6 weeks. Total enrollment: 90. 20 each admission period. 80% of applicants accepted. S:T ratio 16:1. 89% of graduates obtain jobs within 6 mos. Facilities: Include 4 kitchens, 5 classrooms & restaurant.

COURSES: Skills development, quantity food production, food preparation, catering, restaurant operation, food purchasing, sanitation, baking & pastry production. Externship: 3 months.

FACULTY: 10 full-time & part-time.

COSTS: Annual tuition $7,515. Registration fee $100. Books $235, food lab fee $1,490, kits & uniforms $155. Admission requirements: HS diploma or equivalent or admission test.

CONTACT: Harold Kaplan, Vice-President, New York Food and Hotel Management School, Admissions, 154 W. 14th Street, New York, NY 10011; 212-675-6655, Fax 212-463-9194, nyfood@hotmail.com, www.nyfoodandhotelschool.com.

NEW YORK INSTITUTE OF TECHNOLOGY – CULINARY ARTS CENTER

Central Islip & Old Westbury/Year-round

Sponsor: Independent institution. Program: 19-month AOS degree in Culinary Arts. Certificate in Culinary Arts & certificate in Pastry & Baking. Established: 1984. Accredited by MSA, ACF. Calendar: semester. Curriculum: culinary, core. Admit dates: Fall, spring. Total enrollment: 140. 80/20 each admission period. 90% of applicants accepted. 85% receive financial aid. 15% enrolled part-time. S:T ratio 15:1. 99% of graduates obtain jobs within 6 mos. Facilities: Include 6 kitchens, bakery, 2-10 classrooms, computer software, 2 restaurants, ISDN lab.

COURSES: Classically-based, hands-on. Chocolate & Sugar, Ice Carving, Culinary Software. Externship: 3-mo, in restaurants & food service establishments. Extended ed courses during summer months.

FACULTY: 9 full-time, 3 part-time.

COSTS: Annual tuition $16,000. On-campus housing: 150 spaces, average cost $2,500/semester. Admission requirements: HS diploma or equivalent. SAT preferred. Scholarships: yes. Loans: yes.

CONTACT: New York Institute of Technology-Culinary Arts Center, Culinary Arts, 300 Carleton Ave., #66-118, PO Box 9029, Central Islip, NY 11722-9029; 631-348-3290, Fax 631-348-3247, admissions@nyit.edu, http://iris.nyit.edu/culinary. exted@nyit.edu.

NEW YORK UNIVERSITY

New York/September-July *(See also page 258)(See display ad above)*

Sponsor: Dept. of Nutrition, Food Studies and Public Health, The Steinhardt School of Education. Program: Bachelor's, master's, & doctoral degree programs in Food Studies, Food & Restaurant Management, Nutrition, and Community Public Health. Established: 1986. Accredited by MSA. Curriculum: core. Admit dates: Sept, Jan, Summer. Total enrollment: 60 in food program, many part-time. S:T ratio 10-15:1. 100% of graduates obtain jobs within 6 mos. Facilities: New teaching kitchen & library, computer, academic resources.

COURSES: Over 50 in food science & management, food culture & history, food writing, nutrition. Internship required for all students.

FACULTY: 9 full-time academic, 45 part-time academic & professional.

COSTS: $13,323 flat rate/semester for full-time undergraduates, including fees. $900/credit for graduate students + registration fees. Some housing available. Scholarships: yes. Loans: yes.

LOCATION: Washington Square, Greenwich Village.

CONTACT: Dr. Amy Bentley, Program Director, NYU Dept. of Nutrition, Food Studies and Public Health, 35 W. Fourth St.,, New York, NY 10012-1172; 212-998-5580, 800-771-4NYU, Fax 212-995-4194, nutrition@nyu.edu, www.education.nyu.edu/foodshaw.

NIAGARA COUNTY COMMUNITY COLLEGE

Sanborn/Year-round

Sponsor: 2-year college. Program: 2-year/66 credit-hour AOS degree in Food Service with Professional Chef emphasis. Calendar: semester. Curriculum: core.

Costs: $88/credit-hour in-state.

Contact: Sam Sheusi, Coordinator/Instructor, Niagara County Community College, 3111 Saunders Settlement Rd., Sanborn, NY 14132; 716-731-3271 #248, Fax 716-731-4053, sheusi@niagaracc.suny.edu, www.sunyniagara.cc.ny.us.

PAUL SMITH'S COLLEGE

Paul Smiths/Year-round *(See display ad above)*

Sponsor: College. Program: 2-year AAS degree in Culinary Arts, 1-year Baking certificate, 4-year BPS degree in Culinary Arts & Service Management. Established: 1946. Accredited by MSA, ACF. Calendar: semester. Curriculum: culinary, core. Admit dates: Sept, Jan. Total enrollment: 229 Sept. 116 each admission period. 85% of applicants accepted. 90% receive financial aid. 10% enrolled part-time. S:T ratio 14:1. 99% of graduates obtain jobs within 6 mos. Facilities: Include 6 campus Foods Laboratories, an a la carte kitchen, & a 60-seat dining room in addition to a fine dining restaurant in the college-owned Hotel Saranac.

Courses: Baking certificate curriculum covers journeyman skills, including advertising, merchandising, & management. Students produce goods for an on-campus bakery. During year two, 1 semester is spent in the College's Hotel Saranac, the other is an externship. Optional internship in France.

Faculty: 66 full-time, 12 part-time. Includes Robert Brown, CM, & Paul Sorgule, CCE, 1988 Culinary Olympics gold medalist.

Costs: Annual tuition $14,050. Culinary Arts program comprehensive fee is $545/semester. $30 application fee. Housing averages $3,000/yr; board is $3,000/yr. Admission requirements: HS completion or GED. SAT or ACT. Scholarships: yes. Loans: yes.

LOCATION: On the shore of the Lower St. Regis Lake, surrounded by 14,200 acres of college-owned forests & lakes in the Adirondack Mountains.

CONTACT: Melissa LaValley, Director of Admission, Paul Smith's College, Admissions, P.O. Box 265, Paul Smiths, NY 12970; 800-421-2605, 518-327-6227, Fax 518-327-6016, lavallm@paulsmiths.edu, www.paulsmiths.edu.

PROJECT RENEWAL
New York

Sponsor: Non-profit job training program in the culinary arts with placement & supportive services. Offered to people who are currently or formerly homeless, with emphasis on those in the recovery process. Program: 3-mo classroom training & 3-mo externship in Culinary Arts or Baking & Pastry. Established: 1992. Calendar: quarter. Curriculum: culinary. Admit dates: 4 cycles/yr. Total enrollment: 250/yr. 40 culinary/40 baking each admission period. 100% of applicants accepted. 100% receive financial aid. S:T ratio 20:1. 89% of graduates obtain jobs within 6 mos. Facilities: Modern training kitchen with 4 gas ranges, industrial equipment & utensils.

COURSES: Include stocks, sauces, meat, fish, poultry, skills needed for entry level food or baking positions. Placement in one of 30 affiliated corporate/restaurant kitchens.

FACULTY: 1 full-time culinary instructor. 2 part-time pastry/baking instructors.

COSTS: Preference for those sponsored by NYS Dept. of Education, VESID, which pays for training. Those not qualifying for VESID funding are paid for by HUD. Scholarships: yes.

CONTACT: Project Renewal, 200 Varick St., New York, NY 10014; 212-620-0340, Fax 212-243-4868, BarbaraH@projectrenewal.org, www.projectrenewal.org.

SCHENECTADY COUNTY COMMUNITY COLLEGE
Schenectady/Year-round

Sponsor: 2-yr college. Program: 2-yr degree, 1-yr certificate. Established: 1980. Accredited by MSA, ACF. Calendar: semester. Curriculum: culinary. Admit dates: Sept, Jan, June. Total enrollment: 340. 100 each admission period. 86% of applicants accepted. 22% enrolled part-time. S:T ratio 20:1. 88% of graduates obtain jobs within 6 mos. Facilities: 7 kitchens, restaurant, 2 dining rooms, banquet room.

COURSES: Other required courses: 600 hrs work experience. Externship available (Walt Disney World college program, Levy Restaurant at Kentucky Derby; Belmont Stakes & Saratoga.

FACULTY: 13 full-time, 22 part-time. Includes David Brough CEC,CCE, Paul Hiatt CEC, CCE, Susan Hatalsky CCE, CEC, Jim Rhodes, CEC, American Academy of Chefs, Toby Strianese, CCE, ACF Accrediting Team.

COSTS: $2,500 in-state, $5,000 out-of-state. Admission requirements: HS diploma or equivalent & placement testing. Scholarships: yes. Loans: yes.

CONTACT: Toby Strianese, Chair and Professor, Schenectady County Community College, Hotel, Culinary Arts, 78 Washington Ave., Schenectady, NY 12305; 518-381-1391, Fax 518-346-0379, strianaj@gw.sunysccc.edu, www.sunysccc.edu/academic/cularts/index.html.

SULLIVAN COUNTY COMMUNITY COLLEGE
Loch Sheldrake/September-May

Sponsor: 2-yr college. Program: 2-year AAS degree in Professional Chef & Hotel Technology. Established: 1965. Accredited by MSA, ACF. Calendar: semester. Curriculum: culinary. Admit dates: Sept, Jan. Total enrollment: 126. 75 each admission period. 95% of applicants accepted. 90% receive financial aid. 22% enrolled part-time. S:T ratio 14:1. 100% of graduates obtain jobs within 6 mos. Facilities: Include 7 kitchens and classrooms, restaurant.

FACULTY: 8 full-time. Qualifications: bachelor's or master's degree.

COSTS: ~$2,500 in-state, ~$4,500 out-of-state. Application fee $25. On-campus housing: 300 spaces. Average off-campus housing cost: $4,600. Admission requirements: HS diploma or equivalent and admission test. Scholarships: yes. Loans: yes.

CONTACT: Mark Sanok, Chairperson, Sullivan County Community College, Hospitality, 1000 LeRoy Rd., Box 4002, Loch Sheldrake, NY 12759-4002; 914-434-5750, Fax 914-434-4806, msanok@sullivan.suny.edu, www.sullivan.suny.edu.

SUNY COLLEGE OF AGRICULTURE & TECHNOLOGY

Cobleskill/August-May

Sponsor: 2- & 4-year College of Technology. Program: 2-year AOS degree in Culinary Arts, AAS degrees in Restaurant Management & Institutional Foods, Certificate in Commercial Cooking. Established: 1971. Accredited by MSA, ACF. Calendar: semester. Curriculum: culinary, core. Admit dates: August & January. Total enrollment: 120. 60 each admission period. 85% of applicants accepted. 80% receive financial aid. 5% enrolled part-time. S:T ratio 15:1. 99% of graduates obtain jobs within 6 mos. Facilities: Includes 5 kitchens, on-campus restaurant, catering facilities, USDA-certified meat cutting lab.

COURSES: Chinese, Asian, American, & International Cuisines, Baking & Pastry, Selecting & Cutting Meat for Restaurant Use. Externship provided. Fellowship available.

FACULTY: 10 full-time.

COSTS: $3,200/yr in-state, $5,000/yr out-of-state. Admission requirements: HS diploma or equivalent, good preparation in English, math, & lab science. Scholarships: yes. Loans: yes.

CONTACT: Clayton Smith, Director of Admissions, SUNY College of Agriculture & Technology at Cobleskill, Knapp Hall, Route 7, Cobleskill, NY 12043; 518-255-5525 or 800-295-8988, Fax 518-255-6769, admissions@cobleskill.edu, www.cobleskill.edu.

SUNY DELHI

Delhi/August-May

Sponsor: 2-yr & 4-yr public college. Program: AAS & BBA degrees in Culinary Arts. Established: 1994. Accredited by MSA. Calendar: semester. Curriculum: culinary, core. Admit dates: September & January. Total enrollment: 60. 40 each admission period. S:T ratio 10:1. Facilities: Hospitality center with catering & restaurant kitchens, catering facility, beverage lounge, on-site restaurant.

COURSES: Specialty courses in competition, meat cutting, advanced pastries and confections. ACF Competitions held on-campus. Summer externship required.

FACULTY: 2 certified executive chefs, bachelor's degree.

COSTS: $3,200/yr in-state, $5,000/yr out-of-state. Admission requirements: HS graduate with 1 yr general biology. Scholarships: yes. Loans: yes.

CONTACT: Rosalie Higgins, Dean, Business and Hospitality, SUNY Delhi College of Technology, 2 Main St., Delhi, NY 13753; 607-746-4550, Fax 607-746-4104, elwellja@delhi.edu, www.delhi.edu.

WESTCHESTER COMMUNITY COLLEGE

Valhalla/September-May

Sponsor: 2-yr college. Program: 2-year AAS degree in Food Service Administration. Established: 1946. Accredited by MSA. Calendar: semester. Curriculum: culinary. Admit dates: All year. Total enrollment: 100. 50 each admission period. 20% receive financial aid. 25% enrolled part-time. S:T ratio 15:1. 100% of graduates obtain jobs within 6 mos. Facilities: Include lab/demo kitchen, baking kitchen, production kitchen, bar/beverage management lab, instructional dining room.

COURSES: Food preparation, quantity food production, buffet catering, advanced foods, garde manger, bar/beverage management, and menu planning. Provided.

FACULTY: 4 full-time. Qualifications: MS. Includes Curriculum Chair D. Nosek, J. Snyder, T. Cousins.

COSTS: Annual tuition in-state $1,075/semester. Lab fees $15. Admission requirements: HS diploma or equivalent. Scholarships: yes.

CONTACT: Daryl Nosek, FMP, Curriculum Chair, Westchester Community College, Restaurant Mgmt., 75 Grasslands Rd., Valhalla, NY 10595-1698; 914-785-6765, Fax 914-785-6423, info@suny-wcc.edu, www.wcc.co.westchester.ny.us.

WILSON TECHNOLOGICAL CENTER
Dix Hills/Year-round

Accredited by IACET. Admit dates: Sept, Feb. Total enrollment: 169. 30% enrolled part-time. S:T ratio 15:1. Facilities: 3 food production kitchens, demo lab, dining room.

Courses: Culinary I & II, garde-manger, baking.

Faculty: 4 full-time.

Costs: $10,370/certificate.

Contact: Debra Tenenbaum, Administrator, Career & Tech Education, Wilson Technological Center, 17 Westminster Ave., Dix Hills, NY 11746; 631-667-6000, ext. 320, Fax 631-667-1519, dtenenba@wsboces.org, www.wilsontech.org.

NORTH CAROLINA

ALAMANCE COMMUNITY COLLEGE
Graham/Year-round

Sponsor: Public 2-year college. Program: 6-mo certificate in Culinary Specialist, 12-mo diploma in Culinary Professional, 24-mo associate degree in Culinary Technology. Established: 1959. Accredited by SACS. Calendar: semester. Curriculum: culinary, core. Admit dates: Jan, May, Aug. Total enrollment: 70. 30 each admission period. 100% of applicants accepted. 50% receive financial aid. 40% enrolled part-time. S:T ratio 15:1. 99% of graduates obtain jobs within 6 mos. Facilities: Bake shop, catering service, classroom, food production kitchen, gourmet dining room, computer & food labs.

Courses: Food prep & purchasing, garde manger, intl cuisine, menu design, baking, beverage mgmt, catering, confectionery, nutrition on Internet. 320-hr co-op experience required. Available in central area of NC. Nutrition, Supervision & Sanitation on Internet for ACF.

Faculty: 2 full-time, 1 part-time. Includes Doris Schomberg, CCE, Marvin Kimber, CEPC, Brian Bailey, CCC.

Costs: In-state: $496/sem full-time, $31/cr part-time. Out-of-state: $2,716/sem full-time, $169.75/cr part-time. $150 for uniforms & knives. Admission requirements: Open door policy. Scholarships: yes. Loans: yes.

Contact: Doris Schomberg, Dept. Head, Culinary Technology, Alamance Community College, PO Box 8000, Graham, NC 27253-8000; 336-506-4241, Fax 336-578-1987, schombed@alamance.cc.nc.us, www.alamance.cc.nc.us.

THE ART INSTITUTE OF CHARLOTTE – CULINARY ARTS
Charlotte/Year-round *(See display ad page 135)*

Sponsor: Private college of creative professional studies, member of The Art Institutes. Program: 21-month (7-quarter, 108-credit) AAS degree in Culinary Arts. Established: 2002. Accredited by ACICS. Calendar: quarter. Facilities: Industry-standard kitchens.

Courses: Food production skills, business of culinary arts, general studies.

Costs: $315/credit ($300/credit before 11/02). $50 application fee, $100 enrollment fee.

Contact: David Laughry, Director of Admissions, The Art Institute of Charlotte-Culinary Arts, Three LakePointe Plaza, 2110 Water Ridge Pkwy., Charlotte, NC 28217; 704-357-8020, Fax 704-357-1133, laughryd@aii.edu, www.aich.artinstitutes.edu.

ASHEVILLE-BUNCOMBE TECHNICAL COMMUNITY COLLEGE
Asheville/Year-round

Sponsor: 2-yr career college. Program: 2-yr AAS degree in Culinary Technology, 1-yr certificate in Baking & Pastry. Established: 1968. Accredited by SACS. Calendar: semester. Curriculum: culinary. Admit dates: Begins Sept. of year previous to official enrollment. Total enrollment: 70. 35 each admission period. 100% of applicants accepted. 25% receive financial aid. 55% enrolled part-time.

S:T ratio 11:1. 100% of graduates obtain jobs within 6 mos. Facilities: Include 2 kitchens, 4 classrooms, restaurant 1 day/wk, 2 dining rooms.

Courses: Food prep, baking, garde manger, classical cuisine, plate development, butchering, wine appreciation, dining room personnel, sanitation, intl & American regional cuisine, food science. Internship provided.

Faculty: 4 full-time, 5 part-time. Includes Sheila Tillman, BS, MA, Vincent Donatelli, Mark Moritz, Andrew Pratt, Charles deVries, CEPC, John Hofland, CEC, Jodee Sellers, Karen Spradley.

Costs: $1,130 in-state, $6,295 out-of-state. Activity fee $8-$10. Off-campus housing $300/mo. Admission requirements: HS diploma or equivalent & admission test. Scholarships: yes. Loans: yes.

Contact: Sheila Tillman, Chairperson, Asheville-Buncombe Technical Community College, Dept. of Hospitality Education, 340 Victoria Rd., Asheville, NC 28801; 828-254-1921 x232, Fax 828-251-6355, stillman@abtech.edu, www.abtech.edu.

CAPE FEAR COMMUNITY COLLEGE

Wilmington/Year-round

Sponsor: Public 2-year college. Program: 1-semester diploma, 1-year certificate, and 2-year associate degree in Culinary Technology. Established: 1959. Accredited by SACS. Calendar: semester. Curriculum: culinary. Admit dates: Jan, Aug. S:T ratio 15:1. Facilities: Food production & teaching kitchens, gourmet dining room & public restaurant, bake shop, classroom.

Courses: Food prep & purchasing, baking, nutrition, cost control, baking, beverage mgmt.

Faculty: 2 full-time, 5 part-time. Includes Valerie Mason, Diane Sinkinson.

Costs: In-state: $280/semester full-time, $20/credit-hour part-time. Out-of-state: $2,282/semester full-time, $163/credit-hour part-time. Scholarships: yes.

Contact: Valerie Mason, Lead Instructor, Culinary Arts, Cape Fear Community College, 411 N. Front St., Wilmington, NC 28401; 910-251-5960, vmason@capefear.cc.nc.us, http://cfcc.net.

CENTRAL PIEDMONT COMMUNITY COLLEGE

Charlotte/Year-round

Sponsor: 2-yr college. Program: 2-year AAS degree in Culinary Arts. Certificate programs in baking, culinary, garde manger, hot foods. Established: 1974. Accredited by SACS. Calendar: semester. Curriculum: culinary, core. Admit dates: Fall, winter, spring, summer. Total enrollment: 500. 100-150 each admission period. 75% of applicants accepted. 10% receive financial aid. 25% enrolled part-time. S:T ratio 15:1. 98% of graduates obtain jobs within 6 mos. Facilities: Include 4 kitchens, 3 classrooms, baking lab, small quantities lab, computer lab, restaurant.

Courses: Short-term (8 wk.) courses. Co-op education/work experiences available.

Faculty: 3 full-time C.I.A. graduates, 5 part-time.

Costs: Annual tuition in-state $800, out-of-state $4,800. Off-campus housing cost $400-$500/mo. Admission requirements: HS diploma or equivalent and admission test.

Contact: Robert G. Boll, FMP, CFE, Dept Head, Central Piedmont Community College, Culinary Arts, P.O. Box 35009, Charlotte, NC 28235; 704-330-6721, Fax 704-330-6581, bob_boll@cpcc.cc.nc.us, www.cpcc.cc.nc.us.

GUILFORD TECHNICAL COMMUNITY COLLEGE

Jamestown/Year-round

Sponsor: 2-yr community college. Program: 1-year & 2-year program in Culinary Technology, Hotel/Restaurant Management. Established: 1989. Accredited by ACF. Calendar: semester. Curriculum: culinary, core. Admit dates: Year-round. Total enrollment: 130. 45 each admission period. 90% of applicants accepted. 50% receive financial aid. 50% enrolled part-time. S:T ratio 15:1. 98% of graduates obtain jobs within 6 mos. Facilities: New facility with latest technology.

Courses: Garde manger, baking & pastry, dining room management, nutritional cuisine, customer service, classical cuisine, international & American regional. Co-op training.

Faculty: 4 full-time, 5 part-time. Qualifications: ACF-certified & minimum 5 yrs experience.

Includes Keith Gardiner, CEC,CCE,CFE; Norm Ruhe Jr, CEC; Joyce Hill Ms.Ed, CFE; Kelly Burton.

Costs: Tuition in-state $26.75/credit-hour, out-of-state $69.75/credit-hour. Admission requirements: Placement exam. Scholarships: yes.

Contact: Keith Gardiner CEC, CFE, Department Chair, Guilford Technical Community College, Culinary Technology, Box 309, Jamestown, NC 27282; 336-334-4822 #2347, Fax 336-841-4350, gardinerk@gtcc.cc.nc.us, http://technet.gtcc.cc.nc.us.

SANDHILLS COMMUNITY COLLEGE

Pinehurst/Year-round

Sponsor: 2-year college. Program: 2-year/70 semester-hour degree in Culinary Technology. Calendar: semester. Curriculum: core. Total enrollment: 75. S:T ratio 10:1. 95% of graduates obtain jobs within 6 mos.

Courses: Basic & advanced culinary skills, food science, baking, garde manger, international & American regional cuisine, pastry & confections, purchasing, food & beverage service.

Costs: Full-time students $280/semester in-state, $2,282/semester out-of-state. Scholarships: yes.

Contact: Ted Oelfke, Sandhills Community College, 2200 Airport Rd., Pinehurst, NC 28374; 910-695-3756, Fax 910-695-1823, oelfket@email.sandhills.cc.nc.us, www.sandhills.cc.nc.us.

SOUTHWESTERN COMMUNITY COLLEGE

Sylva/Year-round

Sponsor: Two-year college. Program: Two-year AAS degree in Culinary Technology, 16 credit-hour NCCCS certificate. Facilities: Classroom & teaching kitchen.

Courses: Basic & Advanced Culinary Skills, Menu Design, Nutrition, Food & Beverage Service, International & American Regional Cuisine.

Faculty: Program Coordinator Ceretta Davis.

Costs: In-state $440/semester full time, $27.50/credit-hour.

Contact: Ceretta Davis, Program Coordinator, Southwestern Community College, 447 College Dr., Sylva, NC 28779; 800-447-4091 x 256, 828-586-4091, x 256, Fax 828-586-3129, ceretta@southwest.cc.nc.us, www.southwest.cc.nc.us/cul/index.htm.

WAKE TECHNICAL COMMUNITY COLLEGE

Raleigh/Year-round

Sponsor: 2-yr community college. Program: 2-year associate degree in Culinary Arts. Established: 1985. Accredited by SACS. Calendar: semester. Curriculum: culinary, core. Admit dates: Year-round. Total enrollment: 105. 60 each admission period. 75% of applicants accepted. 10% receive financial aid. 15% enrolled part-time. S:T ratio 10:1. 98% of graduates obtain jobs within 6 mos. Facilities: Include kitchen and restaurant.

Courses: Foods, nutrition, sanitation, cost control, wine, inventory control, general education. Externship provided.

Faculty: 6 full-time, 1 part-time. Qualifications: BS, HRM, certified chefs. Includes Richard Roberts, Fredi Morf, Carolyn House, Jane Broden, James Hallett and John Berardi.

Costs: Annual tuition in-state $2,300. Off-campus housing cost is $500+/mo. Admission requirements: HS diploma or equivalent. Scholarships: yes. Loans: yes.

Contact: Alice Downum, Administrative Assistant, Wake Technical Community College, Culinary Technology, 9101 Fayetteville Rd., Raleigh, NC 27603; 919-662-3537, Fax 919-779-3360, agdownum@gwmail.wake.tec.nc.us, www.wake.tec.nc.us/catalog/associates/culinary.html. Richard Roberts, Dept. Head, 919-6623417.

WILKES COMMUNITY COLLEGE

Wilkesboro/Year-round

Sponsor: 2-year college. Program: 2-year degree in Culinary Technology. Accredited by SACS.

Courses: Culinary Skills, Baking, Garde Manger, Food & Beverage Service, Menu Design.

CONTACT: Jeanne Griffin, Dept. Chair, Wilkes Community College, PO Box 120, Wilkesboro, NC 28697; 336-838-6164, Fax 336-838-6547, griffinj@wilkes.cc.nc.us, www.wilkes.cc.nc.us.

NORTH DAKOTA

NORTH DAKOTA STATE COLLEGE OF SCIENCE

Wahpeton/August-May

Sponsor: 2-year post-secondary institution. Program: Three 18-month programs: associate degree in Chef Training & Management Technology, diploma in Chef Training & Management Technology, associate degree in Restaurant Management. Established: 1903. Accredited by NCACS. Calendar: semester. Curriculum: culinary, core. Admit dates: Aug, Jan. Total enrollment: 30-35. 18 each admission period. 95% of applicants accepted. 88% receive financial aid. 5% enrolled part-time. S:T ratio 18:1. 100% of graduates obtain jobs within 6 mos. Facilities: Modern, on-campus kitchen facilities & classrooms.

COURSES: 51 sem-hrs include Food Prep, Baking & Pastry, Catering, Gourmet Foods, Restaurant Mgmt, Short Order Cooking, Nutrition, Menu Planning. Must complete paid co-op training.

FACULTY: 2 full-time, each with formal training & practical industry experience.

COSTS: Annual tuition $1,768.50 in-state, $4,467.50 out-of-state. On-campus housing ~$1,000, 1,700 spaces. Admission requirements: HS diploma or equivalent. Scholarships: yes. Loans: yes.

CONTACT: Neil Rittenour, Program Director, North Dakota State College of Science, Culinary Arts, 800 N. 6th St., Wahpeton, ND 58076; 800-342-4325, Fax 701-671-2774, Neil.Rittenour@ndscs.nodak.edu, www.ndscs.nodak.edu/instruct/cul_arts.

OHIO

CINCINNATI STATE TECHNICAL & COMMUNITY COLLEGE

Cincinnati/Year-round

Sponsor: 2-yr career college. Program: 2-year AAB degree in Chef Technology, Restaurant Management, Hotel Management, 36-hour Culinary Arts Certificate program. Established: 1980. Accredited by ACF, NRA. Calendar: quinmester. Curriculum: core. Admit dates: Open. Total enrollment: 180. 60 each admission period. 100% of applicants accepted. 50% receive financial aid. 30% enrolled part-time. S:T ratio 15:1. 100% of graduates obtain jobs within 6 mos. Facilities: Include commercial kitchen.

COURSES: 7 culinary courses. Other required courses: 23 other courses. Co-op externship provided.

FACULTY: 4 full-time.

COSTS: Annual tuition $3,350 in-state, $6,000 out-of-state. Off-campus housing cost $350/mo. Admission requirements: HS diploma or equivalent and admission test. Scholarships: yes.

CONTACT: Jeff Sheldon, Dept. Chair, Cincinnati State Technical & Community College, Business Division, 3520 Central Pkwy., Cincinnati, OH 45223; 513-569-1637, Fax 513-569-1467, sheldonj@cinstate.cc.oh.us, www.cinstate.cc.oh.us/btd%2Dhm.htm.

COLUMBUS STATE COMMUNITY COLLEGE

Columbus/Year-round

Sponsor: 2-yr college. Program: 3-yr AAS degree in Chef Apprenticeship (Journeyman Chef), 2-yr AAS degree in Foodservice/Restaurant Management. Established: 1978. Accredited by NCA & ACF. Calendar: quarter. Admit dates: Sept, Mar. Total enrollment: 200. ~60 each admission period. 80% enrolled part-time. S:T ratio 15:1. 100% of graduates obtain jobs within 6 mos. Facilities: Classrooms, food labs, computer labs, off-site industry training sites.

COURSES: General studies, business, foodservice management, culinary courses, cooperative industry work experiences. 40 hours/wk on apprenticeship (6,000 hours total). Columbus State Culinary Academy offers 3-hr cooking classes for general public.

FACULTY: 4 full-time: Chair C. Kizer, CCE, M. Steiskal, CCE, D. Cobler, CEC, J. Taylor, CEC. 3-5 part-time industry professionals.

COSTS: $65/cr-hr in-state, $143/cr-hr out-of-state. Lab fees additional. Admission requirements: HS diploma, 2 letters of reference, essay, interview. Scholarships: yes. Loans: yes.

CONTACT: Carol Kizer, CCE, FMP, RD, Chairperson, Columbus State Community College, Hospitality Mgmt., 550 E. Spring St., Columbus, OH 43215; 614-287-5126, Fax 614-287-5973, hospitality@cscc.edu, www.cscc.edu.

CUYAHOGA COMMUNITY COLLEGE

Cleveland/Year-round

Sponsor: 2-yr community college. Program: 2-yr AAB degree in Culinary Arts & Restaurant Food Service Management. Pro mgmt courses & certification, ACF Apprentice Program (220 hrs for degree). 1-yr Baking Certificate. Established: 1969. Accredited by NCA. Calendar: semester. Curriculum: culinary, core. Admit dates: Aug, Jan. Total enrollment: 175. 60-80 each admission period. 95% of applicants accepted. 60% receive financial aid. 60% enrolled part-time. S:T ratio 10:1. 95% of graduates obtain jobs within 6 mos. Facilities: Include 3 kitchens, 2 classrooms, computer lab, restaurant.

COURSES: Mgmt/food prep, haute cuisine, garde manger, purchasing, accounting, menu planning. Internships in local restaurants, country clubs, hotels, & some tourist locations. Safety & sanitation, nutrition, food prep, wines.

FACULTY: 6 full-time, 9 part-time. Qualifications: degree & industry experience, CEC, CCE.

COSTS: Annual tuition in-state (out-of-county, out-of-state) $58.40 ($77.55, $159.90)/sem-hr. Lab fees $300. Off-campus housing $500/mo. Admission requirements: Testing in English/math. Scholarships: yes. Loans: yes.

CONTACT: Jan DeLucia, Program Manager, Cuyahoga Community College, Hospitality Mgmt., 2900 Community College Ave., Cleveland, OH 44115; 216-987-4081, Fax 216-987-4086, julia.patterson@tri-c.edu, www.tri-c.cc.oh.us. Julia Patterson.

HOCKING COLLEGE

Nelsonville/Year-round

Sponsor: Career college. Program: 2-year certificate/AAS degree. Established: 1979. Accredited by NCA, ACF. Calendar: quarter. Curriculum: culinary. Admit dates: Sept, Jan, Mar, June. Total enrollment: 198. 100% of applicants accepted. 65% receive financial aid. S:T ratio 15:1. 98% of graduates obtain jobs within 6 mos.

COURSES: Training in for-profit Ramada Inn. Internship available.

FACULTY: 6 full-time, includes Tom Landusky CEC.

COSTS: Annual tuition in-state $2,151, out-of-state $4,302. Admission requirements: HS graduate, GED, or ability to benefit. Scholarships: yes. Loans: yes.

CONTACT: Tom Lambrecht, Exec. Director, Hocking College, 3301 Hocking Pkwy., Nelsonville, OH 45764; 740-753-3531, 800-282-4163, Fax 740-753-5286 Attn: Lisa, admissions@hocking.edu, www.hocking.edu.

INTERNATIONAL CULINARY ARTS & SCIENCES INSTITUTE

Chesterland/Year-round

Sponsor: Proprietary culinary school. Program: Certificate & diploma programs in Culinary Arts & Pastry Arts. Established: 1989. Calendar: quarter. Curriculum: culinary. Admit dates: Jan, Apr, September. Total enrollment: 100. 90% of applicants accepted. 50% enrolled part-time. S:T ratio 12:1. 80% of graduates obtain jobs within 6 mos. Facilities: 2 fully-equipped 600-sq-ft professional kitchens, library, dining room, culinary garden.

COURSES: Classical European with emphasis on technique & hands-on training. Opportunities to apprentice at local restaurant & assist in recreational classes. Continuing education available.

FACULTY: 14 full- & part-time, all graduates of professional programs. Owner/director Loretta Paganini, born & schooled in Italy, culinary consultant to area restaurants, food writer, cookbook author & guest chef on local TV.

COSTS: Certificate $6,000, diploma $13,000. Admission requirements: HS Diploma or GED, entrance exam. Loans: yes.

CONTACT: Ruthann Kostadinov, Student Services Director, Loretta Paganini School of Cooking, 8623 Mayfield Rd., Chesterland, OH 44026; 440-729-7340, Fax 440-729-4546, icasi@lpscinc.com, www.icasi.net.

OWENS COMMUNITY COLLEGE

Toledo/Year-round

Sponsor: 2-yr college. Program: 2-yr AAB degree in Food Service Mgmt. Established: 1968. Accredited by NCA. Calendar: semester. Curriculum: core. Admit dates: Aug, Jan, June. Total enrollment: 75. 100% of applicants accepted. 75% receive financial aid. 45% enrolled part-time. S:T ratio 18:1. 95% of graduates obtain jobs within 6 mos. Facilities: Production kitchen & dining room.

COURSES: Food service management. 300 hours of cooperative work experience in summer.

FACULTY: 1 full-time, 4 part-time.

COSTS: $75/cr-hr in-state, $140/cr-hr out-of-state. Admission requirements: Assessment of reading, writing, and math skills. Scholarships: yes. Loans: yes.

CONTACT: Tekla Madaras, Dept. Chair, Owens Community College, HRI, P.O. Box 10,000 - Oregon Rd., Toledo, OH 43699-1947; 419-661-7214, Fax 419-661-7251, tmadaras@owens.cc.oh.us, www.owens.cc.oh.us.

SINCLAIR COMMUNITY COLLEGE

Dayton/Year-round

Sponsor: 2-yr college. Program: 2-year Associate Degree in Hospitality Management/Culinary Arts Option. Established: 1993. Accredited by ACF. Calendar: quarter. Curriculum: culinary, core. Admit dates: Year-round. Total enrollment: 200. 100% of applicants accepted. 30% receive financial aid. 40% enrolled part-time. S:T ratio 15:1. 100% of graduates obtain jobs within 6 mos. Facilities: 3 kitchens, 150-seat dining room, classrooms.

COURSES: Food preparation, garde manger, butchery & fish management, pastry & confectionery, classical foods, baking, foodservice mgmt. 3 quarters required, minimum 20 hours/wk part-time.

FACULTY: 3 full-time, 8 part-time. Qualifications: certified by ACF, NRA, AM&HA. Steven Cornelius, CCE, FMP, Assoc. Professor; Frank Leibold, CEC, CWPC, Asst. Professor, Derek Allen, CHE, Instructor.

COSTS: Tuition in-county $29.50, in-state $49, uniforms & knife kit $300, lab fees $50-$100. Admission requirements: HS diploma or GED. Scholarships: yes. Loans: yes.

CONTACT: Steven Cornelius, Dept. Chair, Sinclair Community College, Hospitality Mgmt., 444 W. Third St., Dayton, OH 45402-1460; 937-512-5197, Fax 937-512-5396, scorneli@sinclair.edu, www.sinclair.edu.

UNIVERSITY OF AKRON

Akron/September-April

Sponsor: University. Program: 1-yr certificate & 2-yr AAS degree in Culinary Arts. Established: 1968. Calendar: semester. Curriculum: culinary, core. Admit dates: Fall, spring. Total enrollment: 130. 30+ each admission period. 100% of applicants accepted. 50% receive financial aid. 50% enrolled part-time. S:T ratio 15:1. 95% of graduates obtain jobs within 6 mos. Facilities: Working restaurant & kitchen.

COURSES: Hospitality management courses in addition to culinary arts. Externship provided.

FACULTY: 4 full-time.

COSTS: Tuition $140 ($338)/credit-hour in-state (out-of-state). Admission requirements: HS diploma or equivalent. Scholarships: yes. Loans: yes.

CONTACT: Larry Gilpatric, Assoc. Prof., University of Akron, Hospitality Mgmt., Gallucci Hall #102, Akron, OH 44325-7907; 330-972-5370, 800-221-8308, Fax 330-972-8876, gilpatric@uakron.edu, www.uakron.edu.

OKLAHOMA

ACF CULINARY ARTS OF OKLAHOMA

Oklahoma City/Year-round

Sponsor: ACF chapter. Program: 3-yr apprenticeship; degree program through Oklahoma State University. Curriculum: culinary. Total enrollment: 12.

COSTS: Beginning salary is minimum wage.

CONTACT: Geni Thomas, CEPC, CEC, ACF Culinary Arts of Oklahoma, 4337 Dahoon Dr., Okalhoma City, OK 73120; 405-340-1010, Fax 405-340-1267, www.acfchefs.org/presidents_portal/ACFChapter.cfm?ChapterChoice=OK032.

MERIDIAN TECHNOLOGY CENTER

Stillwater/August-May

Sponsor: Career institution. Program: 1,050-hr certificate. Established: 1975. Accredited by State. Calendar: semester. Curriculum: core. Admit dates: August & January. Total enrollment: 36. S:T ratio 18:1. 85% of graduates obtain jobs within 6 mos. Facilities: 1 kitchen, 1 classroom, 2 restaurants.

FACULTY: 3 full-time.

COSTS: Annual tuition in-district $1,500, out-of-district $3,000. Admission requirements: Assessment, interview.

CONTACT: Meridian Technology Center, 1312 So. Sangre Rd., Stillwater, OK 74074; 405-377-3333, Fax 405-377-9604, info@meridian-technology.com, www.meridian-technology.com/full_time/culinary_arts.asp.

OKLAHOMA STATE UNIVERSITY

Okmulgee/Year-round

Sponsor: University. Program: 24-month AAS degree in Food Service Management, Culinary Arts. Established: 1946. Accredited by NCA. Calendar: trimester. Curriculum: culinary, core. Admit dates: Aug, Jan, Apr. Total enrollment: 170. 50 each admission period. 90% of applicants accepted. 80% receive financial aid. 10% enrolled part-time. S:T ratio 12:1. 90% of graduates obtain jobs within 6 mos. Facilities: Include 4 kitchens and 8 classrooms.

COURSES: Pastry production, food preparation, garde manger, hot food production, meat identification, dining room management, nutrition, & general education courses. Externship provided.

FACULTY: 7 full-time each with 10-35 years experience, college level culinary arts, ACF certification.

COSTS: Tuition in-state $70/cr-hr, out-of-state $150/cr-hr. On-campus housing: 1,000 spaces, cost ~$1,300-$1,600/semester. Admission requirements: Admission test. Scholarships: yes. Loans: yes.

CONTACT: Judy Achemire, Sr. Adm. Asst., Oklahoma State University, Hospitality Services Technology, 1801 E. 4th St., Okmulgee, OK 74447; 918-293-5030, Fax 918-293-4618, judyach@osu-okmulgee.edu, www.osu-okmulgee.edu/hosp.

PIONEER TECHNICAL CENTER

Ponca City

Sponsor: Career institution. Program: 1-year certificate. Established: 1972. Accredited by NCA. Total enrollment: 36. S:T ratio 6:1. 100% of graduates obtain jobs within 6 mos.

FACULTY: 3 full-time.

COSTS: Annual tuition $962 for residents, $1,924 for non-residents. Admission requirements: HS diploma or equivalent.

CONTACT: Dee Price, Instructor, Pioneer Technical Center, Commercial Foods, 2101 N. Ash, Ponca City, OK 74601; 580-762-8336 x242, Fax 580-765-5101, deep@pioneertech.org, www.pioneertech.org.

OREGON

CASCADE CULINARY INSTITUTE

Bend/September-June

Sponsor: Central Oregon Community College. Program: Certificate of completion in Culinary Arts. Established: 1993. Calendar: quarter. Curriculum: culinary. Admit dates: Dec, Mar, September. Total enrollment: 24. 24 each admission period. 100% of applicants accepted. 90% receive financial aid. S:T ratio 16:1. 100% of graduates obtain jobs within 6 mos. Facilities: Kitchen, dining room, deli operation.

COURSES: Hot Food Prod, Baking, Garde Manger, Dining Room Service, Sanitation, Nutrition.

FACULTY: 2 full- and 2 part-time CEC, CCE.

COSTS: $3,316 in district, $9,455 out of state, $500 knife kit. Dorm & meals $5,286/yr. Admission requirements: HS diploma or GED. Scholarships: yes. Loans: yes.

CONTACT: Timothy H. Hill, Cascade Culinary Institute, 2600 NW College Way, Bend, OR 97701; 541-383-7713, Fax 541-383-7508, thill@cocc.edu, www.cocc.edu/culinary.

INTERNATIONAL SCHOOL OF BAKING

Bend/Year-round *(See display ad above)*

Sponsor: Private school. Program: 1- to 20-day customized courses that focus on European breads & pastries. Established: 1986. Curriculum: culinary. Total enrollment: 1 or 2/course. S:T ratio 1: 2. Facilities: Modern baking facility.

COURSES: Ingredient function, bakery start-up, troubleshooting, European artisan breads and pastries. Students can select their own curriculum. Schedule: 8-hour daily hands-on sessions.

FACULTY: Director Marda Stoliar has taught European bread making since 1965, owned a French bakery, and is a baking consultant in China, Hong Kong, and Macau for U.S. Wheat Associates.

COSTS: From $450/day/student includes ingredients. List of nearby lodging is provided on request.

LOCATION: In Oregon's Cascade Mountains, a 3-min drive from downtown Bend.

CONTACT: Marda Stoliar, Director, International School of Baking, 1971 NW Juniper Ave., Bend, OR 97701; 541-389-8553, Fax 541-389-3736, marda@schoolofbaking.com, www.schoolofbaking.com.

LANE COMMUNITY COLLEGE

Eugene/September-June

Sponsor: Independent college. Program: Certificate program & 2-yr AAS degree in Culinary Arts & Culinary option. Established: 1976. Curriculum: core. Admit dates: Open. Total enrollment: 85-105. 25-50 each admission period. 100% of applicants accepted. 60-70% receive financial aid. 3% enrolled part-time. S:T ratio 18:1. 95% of graduates obtain jobs within 6 mos. Facilities: Include 2 kitchens, 1 dining room, deli/bake shop, & 4-6 classrooms.

COURSES: Intro to foods, restaurant lab, buffet, baking, sanitation, safety, menu planning, general ed courses. Externship: 325-450-hr, in commercial, institutional, or single proprietor settings.

FACULTY: 3 full-time, 3 part-time. Qualifications: ACF certifications with BS, AAS degrees, & training from European cooking schoolsl.

COSTS: Annual tuition $36/cr-hr in-state, $116/cr-hr out-of-state. Lab & student fees. Off-campus housing ~$350-$800/mo. Admission requirements: Limited enrollment. Scholarships: yes. Loans: yes.

CONTACT: Duane Partain, Coordinator, Lane Community College, Culinary Food Service, 4000 E. 30th Ave., Eugene, OR 97405-0640; 541-747-4501 x 2531, Fax 541-988-4738, partaind@lanecc.edu, www.lanecc.edu/instadv/catalog/bis/programs/food.htm.

LINN-BENTON COMMUNITY COLLEGE

Albany/September-June

Sponsor: 2-yr college. Program: 2-yr AAS degree in Culinary Arts/Hospitality Services with Chef Training Option; 2-yr AAS degree in Wine & Food Dynamics (must be 21 yrs old). Established: 1973. Accredited by NASC. Calendar: quarter. Curriculum: core. Admit dates: Sept, Jan, Mar. Total enrollment: 30. 15 each admission period. 100% of applicants accepted. 50% receive financial aid. 5% enrolled part-time. S:T ratio 5:1. 100% of graduates obtain jobs within 6 mos.

FACULTY: 6 full-time. Includes S. Anselm, J. JarschkeG. Snyder.

COSTS: $43/cr in-state, $130/cr out-of-state. Application fee $20, tools & uniforms ~$300.

CONTACT: Scott Anselm, Linn-Benton Community College, Culinary Arts, 6500 SW Pacific Blvd., Albany, OR 97321; 541-917-4388, Fax 541-917-4395, anselms@linnbenton.edu, www.linnbenton.edu/programs/cheftraining.html.

OREGON COAST CULINARY INSTITUTE

Coos Bay/Year-round

Sponsor: Southwestern Oregon Community College. Program: 1-yr Chef Training certificate, 2-yr Culinary Arts Management Training associates degree. Established: 2001. Accredited by NASC. Calendar: quarter. Curriculum: culinary. Admit dates: September. Total enrollment: 20. 90% receive financial aid. S:T ratio 16:1. Facilities: Food production & teaching kitchens, classroom.

COURSES: Basic Food Prep, Pastry & Baking, Intro to Vineyards & Beverages, Menu Planning & Design, Garde Manger, Regional & Intl Cuisines, A La Carte Cooking, Nutrition, Restaurant Mgmt, Inventory Control & Purchasing. 36-hr internship in a supervised setting.

FACULTY: 2 full-time. Director Robert Gregson CEC has 35+ yrs experience in Europe & the U.S. & previously taught at the Florida Culinary institute.

COSTS: Degree $12,000/yr full-time, Certificate$6,600/yr full time. Degree application fee $250. Textbooks, knife set, uniforms included. Admission requirements: HS diploma or GED.

CONTACT: Robert Gregson CEC, Director, Oregon Coast Culinary Institute, 1988 Newmark, Coos Bay, OR 97420; 877-895-CHEF, 541-888-7195, Fax 541-888-7194, rgregson@occi.net, www.occi.net.

WESTERN CULINARY INSTITUTE – LE CORDON BLEU PROGRAMS

Portland/Year-round *(See also page 264)(See display ad page 132)*

Sponsor: Private school. Program: 15-mo Le Cordon Bleu AOS degree in Culinary Arts. 14-mo Le Cordon Bleu AOS degree in Hospitality & Restaurant Management. Established: 1983. Accredited by ACF, ACCSCT. Curriculum: culinary. Admit dates: Every 6 weeks. Total enrollment: 900. 100 each admission period. 90% of applicants accepted. 80% receive financial aid. S:T ratio 16-35:1. 98% of graduates obtain jobs within 6 mos. Facilities: Include up-to-date, well-equipped kitchens, classrooms, & 4 open-to-the-public restaurants.

COURSES: Curriculum is based on the principles of Escoffier with emphasis on modern techniques & trends. Courses include culinary fundamentals, purchasing & cost control, intl. cuisines, nutrition, baking, pastry, wines, restaurant management. 6-wk externship in an approved foodservice operation for culinary arts.9-wk externship for hospitality & restaurant management.6-wk externship for patisserie & baking certificate program.

FACULTY: The 28-member faculty is made up of individuals with international experience & training, many of whom have won culinary awards.

COSTS: Culinary tuition & fees: $36,398. Hospitality & Restaurant Management tuition & fees: $27,120. Patisserie & Baking tuition & fees: $19,951. Student Coordinator assists in finding suitable lodging. Admission requirements: HS diploma or equivalent. Scholarships: yes. Loans: yes.

CONTACT: Ryon Koapuiki, Director of Admissions, Western Culinary Institute, 1316 S.W. 13th Ave., Portland, OR 97205; 800-666-0312, 503-223-2245, Fax 503-223-5554, info@westernculinary.com, www.westernculinary.com. LCB Hospitality & Restaurant Management Program, 1717 S.W Madison St., 888-848-3202, www.restaurantmanagement.com.

PENNSYLVANIA

ACF LAUREL HIGHLANDS CHAPTER – CHEF APPRENTICESHIP

Youngwood/Year-round

Sponsor: ACF Chapter (Laurel Highlands Chapter/Westmoreland County CC). Program: 3-yr chef apprenticeship; degree program through Westmoreland County CC. Established: 1981. Accredited by ACF, MSA. Calendar: semester. Curriculum: culinary, core. Admit dates: Aug, Jan. Total enrollment: 48. 48 each admission period. 100% of applicants accepted. 37% receive financial aid. 78% enrolled part-time. S:T ratio 17:1. 100% of graduates obtain jobs within 6 mos. Facilities: Industry-standard kitchens feature 6 individual test kitchens; specialty pastry & confection area; quantity foods prod area; mixology area & retail sales outlet.

COURSES: Paid apprenticeship, culinary competitions, 10-day culinary study tour of Italy. Paid internships in restaurants, resorts, clubs, hotels & institutions.

FACULTY: 4 full-time, 18 part-time. Qualifications: ACF certification, experience in field, academic requirements. Includes Mary B. Zappone, CCE, MS; Cheryl Shipley, RD; Carl Dunkel, CWC, CCE; Cindy Komarinski, MBA.

COSTS: In-county resident tuition $52/cr. Fees: $2/cr, lab fee $20/culinary course. Out-of-county & non-Pennsylvania residents are charged double & triple tuition respectively. Beginning salary is minimum. Admission requirements: HS diploma or equivalent & admission test. Scholarships: yes.

CONTACT: Mary Zappone, CCE, ACF Laurel Highlands Chapter, Westmoreland County Community College, Culinary Arts, Armbrust Rd., Youngwood, PA 15697-1895; 724-925-4016, Fax 724-925-4293, zapponm@astro.westmoreland.cc.pa.us, www.wccc-pa.edu.

ACF PITTSBURGH CHAPTER

Whitacre/Year-round

Sponsor: ACF chapter. Program: 3-yr apprenticeship; degree program through Community College of Allegheny County completed by 80%. Curriculum: culinary. Total enrollment: 60.

COSTS: $4,000. Beginning salary is negotiable with 25 cent increases every 6 mos.

LOCATION: Most desirable settings are hotels, clubs, restaurants.

CONTACT: Jeffrey P. Ward, CEC, CCE, Secretary, ACF Pittsburgh Chapter, Pittsburgh, PA ; 412-566-2593 x4801, jward49921@aol.com.

THE ART INSTITUTE OF PHILADELPHIA – CULINARY ARTS

Philadelphia/Year-round *(See display ad page 135)*

Sponsor: Proprietary school. Program: 6-quarter/18-month AST degree program in Culinary Arts. Established: 1997. Accredited by ACCSCT. Calendar: quarter. Curriculum: culinary. Admit dates: Oct, Jan, Apr, July. Total enrollment: 150. 50 each admission period. Facilities: New 33,000-sq-ft facility. Three kitchens: baking & pastry, a la carte, skills.

COURSES: Hands-on instruction in culinary techniques, baking & pastry. Day & evening options.

FACULTY: Chef director is Joseph Shilling, BS in HRIM from Penn State, AOS degree from CIA.

COSTS: $4,425/quarter. Admission requirements: HS diploma or GED, interview.

CONTACT: Tim Howard, Director of Admissions, The Art Institute of Philadelphia-Culinary Arts, 1622 Chestnut St., Philadelphia, PA 19103; 800-275-2474, 215-567-7080, Fax 215-246-3358, howardt@aii.edu, www.aiph.artinstitutes.edu.

THE ART INSTITUTE OF PITTSBURGH – CULINARY ARTS

Pittsburgh/Year-round *(See display ad page 135)*

Sponsor: Private college of creative professional studies, member of The Art Institutes. Program: 12-month (39-credit) diploma in The Art of Cooking, 21-month (116-credit) AS degree in Culinary Arts, 36-month (179-credit) BS degree in Culinary Management. Established: 2002. Accredited by ACICS. Facilities: Three newly equipped kitchens (skills, a la carte, baking, pastry, garde manger) covering 10,000 square feet.

FACULTY: Includes one Certified Executive Chef.

COSTS: $326/credit, $50 application fee, $100 enrollment fee.

CONTACT: Elaine Cook-Bartolie, Director of Admissions, The Art Institute of Pittsburgh-Culinary Arts, 420 Boulevard of The Allies, Pittsburgh, PA 15219; 800-275-2470, bartolie@aii.edu, www.aip.artinstitutes.edu.

BUCKS COUNTY COMMUNITY COLLEGE

Newtown/Year-round

Sponsor: 2-yr college, 3 year registered Apprenticeship Program. Program: 3-yr degree/apprenticeship/culinary program. Established: 1968. Accredited by MSA. Calendar: semester. Curriculum: culinary, core. Admit dates: Year-round. 40 each admission period. 80% enrolled part-time. S:T ratio 15-18:1. 95% of graduates obtain jobs within 6 mos. Facilities: Include 2 kitchens, dining room, lab, computer labs.

COURSES: Chef Apprenticeship, Catering Management. 6,000 hrs paid OJT.

FACULTY: 3 full-time, 4 part-time. Qualifications: ACF-certif & AA, AAS or AOS degree required for part-time. ACF-certif with BSc/BA or masters degree for full-time.

COSTS: Tuition $78/cr-hr in-county, $156/cr-hr out-of-county. No on-campus housing or food lab fees for credit courses. Admission requirements: HS diploma or equivalent, college placement tests, essay/interview. Scholarships: yes. Loans: yes.

CONTACT: Earl R. Arrowood, Jr., Professor, Chef Apprenticeship & Culin. Coordin., Bucks County Community College, Business Dept., 275 Swamp Rd., Newtown, PA 18940; 215-968-8241, Fax 215-504-8509, arrowood@bucks.edu, www.bucks.edu. Martin Goldman, Tourism & Hospitality Coordinator, 215-968-8249, goldman@bucks.edu. College Admissions B.C.C.C.,215-968-8119.

COMMONWEALTH TECHNICAL INSTITUTE

Johnstown/Year-round

Sponsor: Proprietary school. Program: 8-mo diploma in Kitchen Helper, & 16-mo AST degree in Culinary Arts. Established: 1975. Accredited by ACCSCT. Calendar: trimester. Curriculum: core.

Ai
Culinary Arts
The Art Institutes℠

Admit dates: Every 4 mos. Total enrollment: 45. 12-15 each admission period. 40% receive financial aid. S:T ratio 15:1. Facilities: Include 3 kitchens & classrooms & a part-time restaurant.

Courses: Baking, sanitation, nutrition, food preparation, cooking methods & techniques, menu writing, table service. Externship: 2 mos.

Costs: $16,836. On-campus housing: 400 spaces. Admission requirements: HS diploma or equivalent.

Contact: Adele Sternberg, Commonwealth Technical Institute, Culinary Arts, 727 Goucher St., Johnstown, PA 15905-3092; 814-255-8233, Fax 814-255-3406, asternberg@dli.state.pa.us.

COMMUNITY COLLEGE OF ALLEGHENY COUNTY

Monroeville

Sponsor: 2-yr college. Program: 2-yr certificate/AAS degree. Established: 1967. Accredited by MSA. Admit dates: Open. Total enrollment: 175. S:T ratio 15:1. 100% of graduates obtain jobs within 6 mos.

Costs: Annual tuition in-state $68/credit, out-of-county $136/credit, out-of-state $204/credit.

Contact: Timothy Sullivan, Professor, Community College of Allegheny County, Hospitality Mgmt., 595 Beatty Rd., Monroeville, PA 15146; 724-325-6736, tsullivan@ccac.edu, www.ccac.edu.

COMMUNITY COLLEGE OF ALLEGHENY COUNTY

Pittsburgh

Sponsor: 2-yr college. Program: 2-year AAS degree in Culinary Arts. Established: 1974. Accredited by MSA. Admit dates: Fall, spring. Total enrollment: 60. 20-15 each admission period. 25% of applicants accepted. 50% receive financial aid. 50% enrolled part-time. S:T ratio 2:1.

Courses: Include basic foods, culinary artistry, nutrition, baking, costing. Externship: 240 hours.

Costs: Tuition is $68/credit in-state, $136/credit out-of-county, $204/credit out-of-state.

Contact: Community College of Allegheny County, Culinary Arts, 808 Ridge Ave., Jones Hall, Rm. 012, Pittsburgh, PA 15212; 412-237-2698, Fax 412-237-4678, www.ccac.edu.

COMMUNITY COLLEGE OF BEAVER COUNTY

Monaca/Year-round

Sponsor: 2-year college. Program: 2-semester/34 credit-hour certificate in Culinary Arts, 3-semester/34 credit-hour certificate in Mastery of Culinary Arts, 2 year/64 credit-hour AAS degree in Culinary Arts. Calendar: semester. Curriculum: culinary, core.

Courses: Commercial foods, moist & dry heat preparation principles, stocks/soups/sauces/starches/eggs, line cooking/advanced buffet, management, food preparation & services.

Costs: $1,728/yr.

Contact: Community College of Beaver County, 1 Campus Dr., Monaca, PA 15061-2588; 800-335-0222, 724-775-8561, admissions@ccbc.cc.pa.us, www.ccbc.cc.pa.us.

COMMUNITY COLLEGE OF PHILADELPHIA

Philadelphia/Year-round

Sponsor: 2-year college. Program: 63 credit-hour AAS degree in Culinary Arts-Chef, ACF-approved chef-apprenticeship program. Calendar: semester. Curriculum: core.

Costs: Tuition is $75/credit-hour in-state, $225/credit-hour out-of-state.

Contact: Mark Kushner, Community College of Philadelphia, 1700 Spring Garden St., Philadelphia, PA 19130; 215-751-8000/8797, mkushner@ccp.cc.pa.us, www.ccp.cc.pa.us.

DREXEL UNIVERSITY

Philadelphia/Year-round

Sponsor: Private 4-year university. Program: 4-yr BS degree in Culinary Arts & 4-yr BS degree in Hospitality Management. Established: 1894. Accredited by MSA. Curriculum: culinary, core. Admit dates: Rolling. Total enrollment: 170. 65% of applicants accepted. 80% receive financial aid. 20% enrolled part-time. S:T ratio 10:1. Facilities: 10,000 sq-ft includes 4 kitchens & a restaurant.

Faculty: 7 full-time, 20 part-time.

COSTS: $18,842/yr + fees. Admission requirements: SAT score req'd. Scholarships: yes. Loans: yes.

CONTACT: Francis McFadden, Program Director, Drexel University-Hospitality Management Department, Academic Building, 33rd & Arch Streets, # 110, Philadelphia, PA 19104; 215-895-4919, Fax 215-895-2426, chef-fran@drexel.edu, www.drexel.edu/hospitality. Main Dept. 215-895-2411, Hospitality.Mgt@Drexel.edu.

HARRISBURG AREA COMMUNITY COLLEGE

Harrisburg/Year-round

Sponsor: 2-yr college. Program: 2-year certificate/AA program in Culinary Arts. Established: 1965. Accredited by MSA, ACBSP. Calendar: semester. Curriculum: culinary, core. Admit dates: Aug, Jan, May. Total enrollment: 200. 48 each admission period. 76% of applicants accepted. 50% receive financial aid. 50% enrolled part-time. S:T ratio 15-20:1. 100% of graduates obtain jobs within 6 mos. Facilities: Include production kitchen, demonstration kitchen, culinary classroom, weekly luncheons.

COURSES: Culinary arts, quantity foods, and 20 other courses. Externship: 3-month, salaried.

FACULTY: 3 full- & 3 part-time. Qualifications: bachelor's degree, master's preferred, certifiable by ACF.

COSTS: Annual tuition in-state $150/credit hour, out-of-state $222.50/credit hour. $30 to enroll.

CONTACT: Marcia W. Shore, M.S.Ed., CCE, AssociateProfessor, Coordinator Culinary Arts Prog, Harrisburg Area Community College, One HACC Dr., Harrisburg, PA 17110-2999; 717-780-2674, Fax 717-231-7670, mwshore@hacc.edu, www.hacc.edu.

INDIANA UNIVERSITY OF PENNSYLVANIA – CULINARY ARTS

Punxsutawney/Year-round

(See display ad above)

Sponsor: University. Program: 16-month certificate in Culinary Arts, guaranteed transfer to IUP BS degree in Hospitality Management or Food and Nutrition with up to 42 credits of advanced standing. Established: 1989. Accredited by MSA, ACF. Calendar: semester. Curriculum: culinary. Admit dates: September. Total enrollment: 100. 100 each admission period. 75% of applicants accepted. 90% receive financial aid. S:T ratio 14:1. 99% of graduates obtain jobs within 6 mos. Facilities: Include 5 production and 2 lecture/demonstration classrooms and computer lab.

COURSES: Include cuisine and pastry preparation, purchasing, nutrition, wine appreciation, international cuisine, and menu and facility design. A 450-hour salaried externship is required.

FACULTY: 8 full-time.

COSTS: Tuition $5,521/semester. Application fee is $30. A $119 activity fee is required each semester. On-campus lodging is $1,100 ($1,682)/semester for a double (single) room. Admission requirements: HS diploma or equivalent. Scholarships: yes. Loans: yes.

LOCATION: 25 miles north of Indiana in rural Punxsutawney.

CONTACT: Enid Maggiore, Director of Administrative Services, IUP Academy of Culinary Arts, Office of Admissions, Punxsutawney, PA 15767; 800-438-6424, Fax 814-938-1159, culinary-arts@iup.edu, www.iup.edu/culinary.

JNA INSTITUTE OF CULINARY ARTS

Philadelphia/Year-round

(See display ad above)

Sponsor: Private culinary institute. Program: 60-wk associate degree in Culinary Arts/Restaurant Mgmt; 30-wk diploma in Food Service Training (Professional Cooking);20-wk diploma in Specialized Food Service Mgmt. Established: 1988. Accredited by ACCSCT. Curriculum: culinary. Admit dates: Rolling. Total enrollment: 60. 15 each admission period. 70% of applicants accepted. 90% receive financial aid. 10% enrolled part-time. S:T ratio 10:1. 98% of graduates obtain jobs within 6 mos. Facilities: 2 commercial kitchens, 1 demo kitchen, 1 demo area, classrooms.

Courses: Courses are a combination of hands-on labs, demos, & projects. Lectures are a part of training. Externship, most paid. NRAEF Diploma Partners, ProMgmt Program, FMP Certification, Applied Food Service Certification.

Faculty: 6 full- & 4 part-time, all with formal training &/or experience.

Costs: $4,500-$14,000. $75 registration fee, no application fee. Admission requirements: HS diploma or equivalent. Scholarships: yes. Loans: yes.

Contact: Robert Fox, Director of Admissions, JNA Institute of Culinary Arts, 1212 S. Broad St., Philadelphia, PA 19146; 215-468-8800, Fax 215-468-8838, admissions@culinaryarts.com, www.culinaryarts.com.

KEYSTONE COLLEGE

La Plume/September-May

Sponsor: Private college. Program: 2-yr AAS degree in Culinary Arts, dual major with Hotel/Restaurant Mgmt. Established: 1996. Accredited by MSA. Calendar: semester. Curriculum: culinary, core. Admit dates: Aug. Total enrollment: 35. 35 each admission period. 100% of applicants accepted. 90% receive financial aid. 20% enrolled part-time. S:T ratio 6-12:01.

Costs: Tuition is $13,180/yr, room & board $6,800/yr. Admission requirements: HS diploma or GED, SAT/ACT, 1 letter of recommendation. Scholarships: yes. Loans: yes.

Contact: Sarah Keating, Director of Admissions, Keystone College, One College Green, La Plume, PA 18440-1099; 570-945-6953, Fax 570-945-7916, admissns@keystone.edu, www.keystone.edu.

LEHIGH COUNTY VOCATIONAL-TECHNICAL SCHOOL

Schnecksville/August-May

Sponsor: Continuing Ed Department of Lehigh County Voc-Tech School. Program: 20-wk certificate program offering both front & back of house training. Established: 1979. Calendar: semester. Curriculum: culinary. Admit dates: August & January. Total enrollment: 12 students. 12 students each admission period. 90% of applicants accepted. 50% receive financial aid. S:T ratio 6:1. 95% of graduates obtain jobs within 6 mos. Facilities: 80-seat restaurant with professional kitchen.

Faculty: 1 Certified Executive Chef, 2 state certified educators/consultants.

Costs: $2,510. Admission requirements: Interview, basic math skills, 18 years or over.

Contact: Gary Fedorcha, Lehigh County Voc-Tech School, 4500 Education Park Dr., Chef Training, Schnecksville, PA 18078; 610-799-1318, Fax 610-799-1314, FedorchaG@cliu.org, www.lcti.org/home.htm.

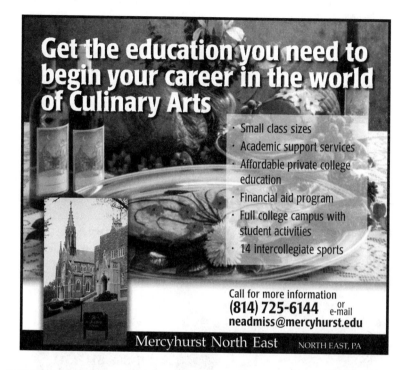

MERCYHURST NORTH EAST – THE CULINARY AND WINE INSTITUTE

North East/September-May *(See display ad above)*

Sponsor: Private 2-yr college. Program: 2-yr AS degree in Hotel, Restaurant & Institutional Management with a concentration in Culinary Art;1-yr Culinary Art Certificate. Established: 1995. Accredited by MSA. Calendar: trimester. Curriculum: culinary, core. Admit dates: Sept, Nov, Mar. Total enrollment: 70. 40 each admission period. 97% of applicants accepted. 100% receive financial aid. 18% enrolled part-time. S:T ratio 15:1. 100% of graduates obtain jobs within 6 mos. Facilities: 3 professional kitchens, bake shop, 30-seat dining room, receiving & storage area.

Courses: Specialized courses in wines & wine-making; traditional culinary courses emphasizing management & thinking skills. 420-hour paid externship after 3 terms in quality dining facility.

Faculty: 3 full-time, 5 part-time, with industry experience & educational background.

Costs: Tuition $8,820/yr. Fees $2,559/yr, books ~$600. On-campus dorms $5,598/yr including board. Admission requirements: HS graduate or equivalent, math & English placement test. Scholarships: yes. Loans: yes.

Contact: Director of Admissions, Mercyhurst College-North East, The Culinary & Wine Institute, North East, PA 16428; 800-825-1926, 814-725-6144, Fax 814-725-6251, neadmiss@mercyhurst.edu, http://northeast.mercyhurst.edu.

NORTHAMPTON COMMUNITY COLLEGE

Bethlehem/Year-round

Sponsor: 2-yr college. Program: 45-wk specialized diploma in Culinary Arts, AAS degree in Culinary Arts. Established: 1993. Accredited by MSA. Calendar: trimester. Curriculum: culinary, core. Admit dates: Mar, September. Total enrollment: 52. 26 each admission period. 100% of applicants accepted. 30% receive financial aid. S:T ratio 26:1.Facilities: 4,000-sq-ft modern kitchen & bakery.

Courses: Sanitation, Product Identification Baking, Meat Cutting,Pantry, Skill Development, Garde Manger, & 23 weeks of Restaurant Operations.

Faculty: 4 full-time. Qualifications: culinary degree & 20+ years of professional experience. Includes Duncan Howden & Scott Kalamar.

Contact: D. Howden, Northampton Comm. College, Culinary Arts, 3835 Green Pond Rd., Bethlehem, PA 18017; 610-861-5593, Fax 610-861-5093, dhowden@northampton.edu, www.northampton.edu.

ORLEANS TECHNICAL INSTITUTE

Philadelphia

Sponsor: Career institution. Program: 30-week specialized diploma in Food Preparation. Established: 1978. Admit dates: Open. 85% of graduates obtain jobs within 6 mos.

Faculty: 1 to 2 full-time.

Costs: Tuition is $2,550 (Food Service) for the 480-hr class. Admission requirements: Admission test.

Contact: Shirley Randall, Orleans Technical Institute, Culinary Arts, 1330 Rhawn St., Philadelphia, PA 19111; 215-728-4175, srandall1017@yahoo.com, www.jevs.org/schools_jobs.asp.

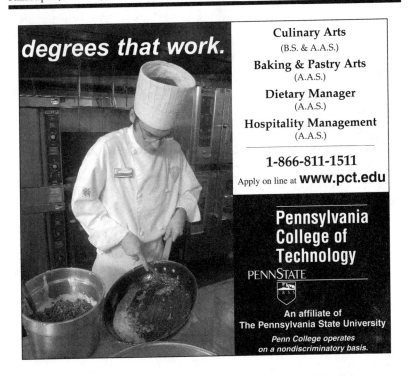

PENNSYLVANIA COLLEGE OF TECHNOLOGY

Williamsport/Year-round *(See display ad above)*

Sponsor: 2/4-year college. Program: 2-year AAS degree in Hospitality Management, Baking/Pastry Arts, Culinary Arts, Dietary Manager Technology, BS degree in Culinary Arts. Established: 1981 Accredited by MSA, ACF, CAHM, DMA. Calendar: semester. Curriculum: culinary, core. Admit dates: Fall, spring. Total enrollment: 120. 72 each admission period. 95% of applicants accepted. 86% receive financial aid. 15% enrolled part-time. S:T ratio 12:1. 100% of graduates obtain jobs within 6 mos. Facilities: Include 10 kitchens & classrooms, retail restaurant, catering & meeting facilities, theatre lounge, bed & breakfast, conference center, retreat center.

COURSES: Cooking, baking, service, sanitation, supervision, management skills, & nutrition. Emphasis on problem-solving, communications, math applications, teamwork, leadership skills. Summer semester internships required.

FACULTY: 9 full-time, 12 part-time. Qualifications: college degree & ACF certification. 70% ACF certified, 100% certifiable.

COSTS: Annual tuition in-state $233/credit hour, out-of-state $303/credit hour. Application fee $20, other fees $47. Off-campus housing cost $250-$450/mo. Admission requirements: HS diploma or equivalent and admission test. Scholarships: yes. Loans: yes.

LOCATION: 97-acre, 4,300-student campus 200 miles from Pittsburgh & Philadelphia.

CONTACT: Chet Schuman, Director of Admissions, Pennsylvania College of Technology, School of Hospitality, One College Ave., Williamsport, PA 17701-5799; 570-326-3761 x4761, 800-367-9222, Fax 570-320-5260, cschuman@pct.edu, www.pct.edu.

PENNSYLVANIA CULINARY INSTITUTE

Pittsburgh/Year-round *(See display ad above)*

Sponsor: Private career training institution. Program: 16-mo AST degree programs in Le Cordon Bleu Culinary Arts & Le Cordon Bleu Pastry Arts. 16-mo ASB degree program in Hotel & Restaurant Mgmt. Established: 1986. Accredited by ACCSCT, ACFEI. Calendar: semester. Curriculum: culinary. Admit dates: Rolling. Total enrollment: 1,400. 90% receive financial aid. S:T ratio 24:1. 99% of graduates obtain jobs within 6 mos. Facilities: Include 10 kitchens, 18 classrooms, full-service dining room lab & mixology lab, library resource center & computer lab.

COURSES: Include food prep & skill development, advanced classical & intl cuisine, garde manger, nutrition, wines & spirits, menu planning, dining room mgmt. 4-mo (540-hr) paid off-site externship.

FACULTY: 33 chef instructors, ACF-certified as Culinary Educators & Certified Chefs; 17 mgmt faculty.

COSTS: Tuition $8,500/sem (programs typically 4 sem's), enrollment fee $100, books & supplies ~$4,070. Admission requirements: Enrollment fee, application, interview, HS diploma or GED. Scholarships: yes. Loans: yes.

CONTACT: Jason Bennett, Director of Admissions, Pennsylvania Culinary Institute, 717 Liberty Ave., Pittsburgh, PA 15222; 800-432-2433 or 412-566-2433, Fax 412-566-2434, info@paculinary.com, www.paculinary.com.

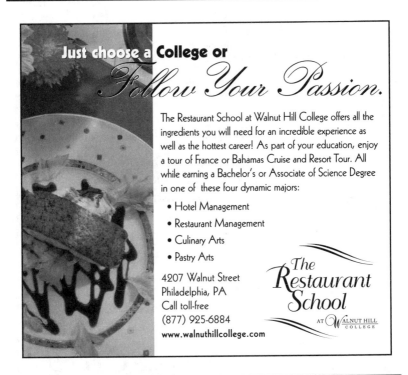

THE RESTAURANT SCHOOL AT WALNUT HILL COLLEGE

Philadelphia/Year-round *(See also page 268)(See display ad above)*

Sponsor: 4-year private college. Program: 2-yr AS & 4-yr BS degree programs in Culinary Arts, Pastry Arts, Restaurant Management. Established: 1974. Accredited by ACCSCT. Curriculum: culinary, core. Admit dates: Sept, Nov, Jan, May. Total enrollment: ~500. 200 each admission period. 87% of applicants accepted. 85% receive financial aid. 20% enrolled part-time. S:T ratio 18:1. 98% of graduates obtain jobs within 6 mos. Facilities: Include 5 classroom kitchens, two 85-seat demo kitchens, 3 classrooms, pastry shop, 4 student-run restaurants, computer lab, wine lab, library.

COURSES: Culinary Arts combines classroom instruction with apprenticeship; includes business mgmt, dining room svc, wines, 7 certification courses. Pastry Arts covers culinary & baking skills, baking science, chocolate, candies, 6 certification courses. Internships in area restaurants, hotels, & abroad. Both programs include an 8-day tour of France. Management programs include 7-day cruise & resort tour. Yes.

FACULTY: The 18-member professional faculty have a minimum of 12 yrs experience in the restaurant, foodservice, & hotel industry. 5 ACF-certified chefs, 1 master pastry chef.

COSTS: The $20,975 cost of each program includes trip to France. Other fees $1,000. On-campus dorm & apartments are available. Admission requirements: HS diploma or equivalent, reference letters, basic achievement test. Scholarships: yes. Loans: yes.

LOCATION: Restored mansion in University City, Philadelphia.

CONTACT: Karl D. Becker, Director of Admissions, The Restaurant School at Walnut Hill College, 4207 Walnut St., Philadelphia, PA 19104; 877-925-6884, 215-222-4200, Fax 215-222-4219, info@walnuthillcollege.com, www.walnuthillcollege.com.

WESTMORELAND COUNTY COMMUNITY COLLEGE

Youngwood/Year-round

Sponsor: 2-yr college. Program: 2- & 3-yr AAS degree in Culinary Arts and 2- & 3-yr Baking & Pastry degree, both with apprenticeship option; 16-mo Culinary Arts degree; 1-sem Culinary Arts certificate and 1-sem Baking/Pastry certificate. Established: 1981. Accredited by ACF, MSA. Calendar: semester. Curriculum: culinary, core. Admit dates: Aug, Jan. Total enrollment: 207. 207 each admission period. 100% of applicants accepted. 37% receive financial aid. 71% enrolled part-time. S:T ratio 17:1. 100% of graduates obtain jobs within 6 mos. Facilities: Industry-standard kitchens feature 6 individual test kitchens; specialty pastry & confection area; quantity foods production area; mixology area & retail sales outlet.

COURSES: Garde manger, quantity foods, purchasing & storage, baking, food specialties, hospitality marketing, classroom projects simulate student-run restaurant, 1-sem externships & 3-yr apprenticeships.

FACULTY: 4 full-time, 18 part-time. Qualifications: ACF certification, experience, academic requirements. Includes Mary B. Zappone, CCE, MS; Cheryl Shipley, RD; Carl Dunkel, CWC, CCE.

COSTS: In-county tuition $52/credit. Fees: $2/credit, lab fee $20/culinary course. Out-of-county & non-PA residents are charged double & triple tuition respectively. Admission requirements: HS diploma or equivalent & admission test. Scholarships: yes.

CONTACT: Mary Zappone, Professor, Westmoreland County Community College, Hospitality Dept., Armbrust Rd., Youngwood, PA 15697; 724-925-4016, Fax 724-925-4293, zapponm@astro.westmoreland.cc.pa.us, www.wccc-pa.edu. Additional contact: Chef Carl Dunkel.

THE WINE SCHOOL OF PHILADELPHIA

Philadelphia & Manayunk/Year-round

Sponsor: Private wine school. Program: Certificate of Wine Knowledge, Advanced Wine Degree, Master of Vinology Degree; weekly wine classes. Established: 2002. Calendar: semester. Admit dates: Year-round. Total enrollment: 500. 95% of applicants accepted. 100% enrolled part-time. S:T ratio 18-1. 100% of graduates obtain jobs within 6 mos.

FACULTY: President & CEO Keith Wallace, a wine industry veteran.

COSTS: $350-$1,000.

CONTACT: Keith Wallace, President, The Wine School of Philadelphia, 4417 Main St., Philadelphia, PA 19127; 267-295-1023, wineclass@winelust.com, http://winelust.com.

WINNER INSTITUTE OF ARTS & SCIENCES

Transfer/Year-round

Sponsor: Private school affiliated with Youngstown State University. Program: 50-wk diploma program in Culinary Arts. Students can take credit classes at Youngstown towards an associates degree. Established: 1997. Calendar: trimester. Curriculum: culinary. Admit dates: Jan, Mar, July, September. Total enrollment: 36. Up to 30 each admission period. 98% of applicants accepted. 90% receive financial aid. S:T ratio 7-16:1. 100% of graduates obtain jobs within 6 mos. Facilities: Kitchen with the latest equipment, banquet room, 4 classrooms, fully-equipped computer lab & library.

COURSES: Culinary Skills, Soups/Sauces/Starches, Meet & Poultry, Fish & Shellfish, Garde Manger, Baking & Patisserie, IntlCuisine, Purchasing & Receiving, Business/Math, Menu Planning. 300-hr paid externship. Faculty: 3 full-time chef instructors.

COSTS: Tuition $12,180, fees $1,650. Admission requirements: HS diploma or GED, entrance exam. Loans: yes.

CONTACT: Director, Winner Institute of Arts & Sciences, One Winner Place, Transfer, PA 16154; 888-414-CHEF, 724-646-2433, Fax 724-646-0218, info@winner-institute.com, www.winner-institute.com.

YORK TECHNICAL INSTITUTE

York & Mt.Joy/Year-round

Sponsor: Private proprietary 2-year institution. Program: Culinary Arts/Restaurant Management (21 mos), Pastry Arts (12 mos), Associate Degree in Specialized Business. Established: 1998. Accredited by ACCST. Calendar: quarter. Curriculum: culinary, core. Admit dates: Jan, July, Oct. Total enrollment: 175. 48/18 each admission period. 80% of applicants accepted. 90% receive financial aid. S:T ratio 20:1. 100% of graduates obtain jobs within 6 mos.

FACULTY: 6.

CONTACT: York Technical Institute, 1405 Williams Road, York, PA 17402; 717-757-1100, 800-227-9675, morrd@yti.edu, http://chefs.yti.edu.

YORKTOWNE BUSINESS INSTITUTE SCHOOL OF CULINARY ARTS

York/Year-round

Sponsor: 2-year private school. Program: ~16-month Associate in Specialized Technology degree in Culinary Arts (includes externship), ~8-month diploma in Professional Baking & Pastry, ~16-month Specialized Associate degree in Hotel, Convention & Hospitality Management. Established: 1998. Accredited by ACICS. Calendar: trimester. Curriculum: culinary, core. Admit dates: Every 4 months. Total enrollment: 100+. 50-60 each admission period. 90-100% of applicants accepted. 95% receive financial aid. 25% enrolled part-time. S:T ratio 10-20:1. 98-100% of graduates obtain jobs within 6 mos. Facilities: 5,000-sq-ft culinary arts center includes commercial teaching kitchens, presentation/staging area, classroom, dining area. Student-run restaurant. New baking & special events kitchen. Main building includes 12 classrooms, 5 computer labs, library.

COURSES: Food preparation, Baking, Foodservice, Sanitation Certification, Menu Design, Food Costing, Computer Training, Basic Accounting, Math, Business Restaurant Management Communications. 6-wk culinary arts externship, 4-wk baking & pastry externship, 6-wk hotel, convention & hospitality management externship.

FACULTY: 3-4 full-time, 2 part-time. Chef David Haynes CEC, Program Director.

COSTS: Culinary courses $272/credit hour,business/management courses $165/credit hour. Admission requirements: Qualification interview and tour required. Scholarships: yes. Loans: yes.

CONTACT: Bonnie Gillespie, Admissions Director, Yorktowne Business Institute, Inc., The School of Culinary Arts, West 7th Ave., York, PA 17404; 800-840-1004, 717-846-5000, Fax 717-848-4584, chef@ybi.edu, www.yorkchef.com.

RHODE ISLAND

JOHNSON & WALES UNIVERSITY/COLLEGE OF CULINARY ARTS

Providence/Year-round *(See display ad page 145)*

Sponsor: Private nonprofit career institution. Program: 2-yr AAS & 4-yr BS degree programs in Culinary Arts and Baking & Pastry Arts. 4-yr BS in Culinary Nutrition. Other degrees offered at different campuses. Established: 1973. Accredited by NEASC. Calendar: quarter. Curriculum: culinary, core. Admit dates: Sept, Dec, Mar. Total enrollment: 2,362 full-, 219 part-time. ~80% of applicants accepted. ~80% receive financial aid. 9% enrolled part-time. S:T ratio 18:1. 98% of graduates obtain jobs within 6 mos. Facilities: Modern teaching facilities, including 5 student-run restaurants.

COURSES: Culinary arts includes basic cooking & baking, classic & intl cuisines, food prep, nutrition, communication, menu design. Baking & Pastry includes ingredients, production techniques, pastries, desserts, chocolate & sugar artistry. Sophomore year internship at Radisson Airport Hotel & the University's foodservice training facilities or opportunity to participate in co-op in US or abroad (based on GPA & selection). Continuing ed programs. Fast program for HS students. 1 calendar-yr associate degree program for those with a BA in any field, or for industry professionals.

Faculty: 79 full-time.

Costs: $18,444/yr, general fee $750, orientation fee $200, room & board $6,777/yr + $825 for optional weekend meal plan. Admission requirements: HS diploma or equivalent. Scholarships: yes. Loans: yes.

Location: Near Providence's cultural & recreational facilities. Other campuses in Florida & Colorado.

Contact: Amy O'Connell, Asst. Director of Culinary Admissions, Johnson & Wales University, College of Culinary Arts, 8 Abbott Park Place, Providence, RI 2903; 800-342-5598, Fax 401-598-4787, ShawGuides@jwu.edu, www.jwu.edu.

SOUTH CAROLINA

GREENVILLE TECHNICAL COLLEGE

Greenville/Year-round

Sponsor: Career college. Program: 2-yr degree in Food Service Management, and 1-yr certificates in Baking & Pastry, Catering, Culinary Education, Dietary Manager, & Hotel/Restaurant Mgmt. Established: 1977. Accredited by ACF, SACS, ACBSP. Calendar: semester. Curriculum: culinary, core. Admit dates: Semesters (3). Total enrollment: 175. 45 each admission period. 75% of applicants accepted. 100% receive financial aid. 5.5% enrolled part-time. S:T ratio 15:1. 100% of graduates obtain jobs within 6 mos. Facilities: Include kitchen & 3 classrooms.

Courses: A la carte, Competition, Buffet, Nutrition, Food production, Dining Room Operations.

Faculty: 3 full-time, 5 part-time.

Costs: $996/semester in-county resident,$1,080/semester out-of-county, $25 application fee. Admission requirements: HS diploma or equivalent & admission test. Scholarships: yes.

CONTACT: Denise Bishop, Greenville Technical College, Info Center Dept., P.O. Box 5616, Station B, Greenville, SC 29606-5616; 864-250-8272, Fax 864-250-8689, bishop@gvltec.edu, www.greenvilletech.com.

HORRY-GEORGETOWN TECHNICAL COLLEGE

Conway/Year-round

Sponsor: Career college. Program: 2-yr degree in Culinary Arts Technology, certificate in Food Service, certificate inPastry Arts, personal ACF certification. Established: 1985. Accredited by SACS, ACF. Calendar: semester. Curriculum: core. Admit dates: Aug, Jan, May. Total enrollment: 105. 40 each admission period. 100% of applicants accepted. 60% receive financial aid. 10% enrolled part-time. S:T ratio 10:1. 100% of graduates obtain jobs within 6 mos. Facilities: Include 4 kitchens, 3 dining rooms, 3 restaurants.

COURSES: Food production, sanitation, nutrition, a la carte, buffet, menu planning. Externship provided. Continuing education courses available.

FACULTY: 12 full- & part-time. Includes Dept. Head C. Catino, K. Gerba, C. LaMarre, S. DePalma.

COSTS: In-state $600/sem, out-of-state $1,431/sem. Application fee $15. Off-campus housing cost ~$250-$350/mo. Admission requirements: HS diploma or equivalent & admission test. Scholarships: yes. Loans: yes.

CONTACT: Carmen Catino, Dept. Head, Horry-Georgetown Technical College, Culinary Arts, P.O. Box 1966, 2050 Hwy. 501 East, Conway, SC 29526; 803-347-3186, Fax 803-347-4207, catino@hor.tec.sc.us, www.hor.tec.sc.us.

TRIDENT TECHNICAL COLLEGE

Charleston/Year-round

Sponsor: Career college. Program: 2-semester certificate & 4-semester diploma programs & associate degree in Culinary Arts. Established: 1986. Accredited by SACS, ACF. Calendar: semester. Curriculum: culinary. Admit dates: Open. Total enrollment: 85. 75-85 each admission period. 93% of applicants accepted. 40% receive financial aid. 5% enrolled part-time. S:T ratio 15:1. 100% of graduates obtain jobs within 6 mos. Facilities: Includes 10 kitchens & classrooms, student-run restaurant.

FACULTY: 4 full- & 4 part-time.

COSTS: Annual tuition $1,572 in-county, $1,836 out-of-county, $3,266 out-of-state. Application fee $20. Off-campus housing $400/mo. Admission requirements: HS diploma or equivalent & admission test. Scholarships: yes. Loans: yes.

CONTACT: Frankie Miller, Dean, Trident Technical College, Division of Hospitality & Tourism, P.O. Box 118067, HT-P, Charleston, SC 29423-8067; 843-722-5542, Fax 843-720-5614, frankie.miller@tridenttech.edu, www.tridenttech.edu.

SOUTH DAKOTA

MITCHELL TECHNICAL INSTITUTE

Mitchell/Year-round

Sponsor: Career school. Program: 13-mo diploma in Culinary Arts. Established: 1968. Accredited by NCA. Calendar: semester. Curriculum: culinary. Admit dates: Program begins ~July; open admission dates. Total enrollment: 24. 24 each admission period. 95% of applicants accepted. 85% receive financial aid. S:T ratio 8:1. 100% of graduates obtain jobs within 6 mos. Facilities: Include 3 kitchens, 3 classrooms, 54-seat restaurant, library, computer labs.

COURSES: Comprehensive culinary program focusing on quantity & restaurant production. National certifications in nutrition, supervision, sanitation. Capstone course is 12-wk apprenticeship.

FACULTY: 3 full-time.

COSTS: Tuition $60/cr-hr in-state & out-of-state. Annual fees excluding tuition ~$2,400. Annual cost of living ~$4,200. Admission requirements: HS diploma or equivalent & admission test. ACT recommended. Scholarships: yes. Loans: yes.

CONTACT: Randy Doescher, Department Head, Mitchell Technical Institute, 821 N Capital, Mitchell, SD 57301; 605-995-3030, Fax 605-996-3299, questions@mti.tec.sd.us, http://mti.tec.sd.us. Admissions Office, Tim Edwards: 800-952-0042; Janet Greenway 800-952-0042.

TENNESSEE

MEMPHIS CULINARY ACADEMY

Memphis/Year-round

Sponsor: Private trade school. Program: 10-week certificate program offered 4 times/yr. Established: 1984. Accredited by TN Higher Education Commission. Calendar: quarter. Curriculum: culinary. Admit dates: Jan, Apr, June, September. Total enrollment: 40. 10 each admission period. S:T ratio 6:1. 95% of graduates obtain jobs within 6 mos.

COURSES: Include culinary skills, baking, nutrition, and kitchen rotation.

COSTS: $3,750. Admission requirements: HS diploma. Scholarships: yes.

CONTACT: Elaine Wallace, Memphis Culinary Academy, 1252 Peabody Avenue, Memphis, TN 38104; 901-722-8892, ewallacechef@hotmail.com.

NASHVILLE STATE TECHNICAL INSTITUTE

Nashville/Year-round

Sponsor: 2-yr college. Program: 2-yr associate degree in Culinary Science. Accredited by SACS.

COURSES: Baking Skills, Culinary I, II & III, Nutrition & Menu Planning, Purchasing & Cost Control, Baking & Pastry, Garde Manger & Catering. Two 300-hr cooperative work assignments.

COSTS: $710/semester, $56/credit-hour.

CONTACT: Ken Morlino, Asst. Prof., Nashville State Technical Institute, 120 White Bridge Rd., Nashville, TN 37209; 615-353-3783, morlino_k@nsti.tec.tn.us, www.nscc.edu/catalog/dcul.html.

WALTERS STATE COMMUNITY COLLEGE CULINARY ARTS SCHOOL

Sevierville & Morristown/Year-round

Sponsor: 2-yr community college. Program: 2-yr AAS degree & 1-yr certificate program in Culinary Arts. 1-yr Personal Chef certificate program. 2-yr AAS degree in Hotel & Restaurant Mgmt. Established: 1997. Accredited by SACS, ACF. Calendar: semester. Curriculum: culinary, core. Admit dates: Aug, Jan, May. Total enrollment: 125. 12-15/class each admission period. 100% of applicants accepted. 50-100% receive financial aid. 43% enrolled part-time. S:T ratio 12-15:1. 90-100% of graduates obtain jobs within 6 mos. Facilities: Open-to-the-public instructional dining room. Full campus services for the core courses.

COURSES: Sanitation & Safety, Nutrition & Menu Planning, Tableservice & Beverage Mgmt, Culinary Arts, Bakery & Pastry Skills, Purchasing & Cost Control, Garde Manger & Catering, Int'l Cuisine & Buffet.

FACULTY: 1 full-time, 4 adjunct. All are culinary school graduates or 15+ yrs on-the-job experience.

COSTS: ~$1,600/yr in-state + books, uniforms, knives. Admission requirements: 2-yr program requires HS diploma or GED, 1-yr program does not. Scholarships: yes. Loans: yes.

CONTACT: Sheila Morris, Enrollment Development Department, Walters State Community College, 500 S. Davy Crockett Parkway, Morristown, TN 37813-6899; 423-585-2664, Fax 423-585-6786, Sheila.Morris@ws.edu, www.ws.edu/businessdiv/culinary%20arts/default.asp.

TEXAS

THE ART INSTITUTE OF DALLAS – CULINARY ARTS

Dallas/Year-round *(See display ad page 135)*

Sponsor: 2-year private college. Program: Professional 18-month curriculum leading to an AAS degree in Culinary Arts & AAS degree in Restaurant and Catering Management. Established: 1999. Accredited by SACS. Calendar: quarter. Curriculum: culinary, core. Admit dates: Every 11 weeks.

Total enrollment: ~230. 25-80 each admission period. 50% of applicants accepted. 70% receive financial aid. S:T ratio 20:1. 100% of graduates obtain jobs within 6 mos. Facilities: 2 kitchens, 1 bake shop, 1 restaurant with kitchen.

COURSES: Culinary skills, American Regional, Bakeshop, International, Garde Manger, Nutritional & Health-Related Cooking. Externship required for graduation, site approval required.

FACULTY: Full-time 5, part-time 4.

COSTS: $37,000. Admission requirements: Assessment test and essay. Scholarships: yes. Loans: yes.

CONTACT: Keith Petrovello, Director of Admissions, The Art Institute of Dallas-Culinary Arts, 8080 Park Lane, Dallas, TX 75291; 800-275-4243, 214-692-8080, Fax 214-750-9460, petrovek@aii.edu, www.aid.artinstitutes.edu.

THE ART INSTITUTE OF HOUSTON – CULINARY ARTS

Houston/Year-round *(See display ad page 135)*

Sponsor: Proprietary school. Program: 21-mo AAS degree in Culinary Arts, 18-mo AAS degree in Restaurant & Catering Mgmt, diploma program in Culinary Arts. Established: 1992. Accredited by ACF, SACS. Calendar: quarter. Curriculum: culinary, core. Admit dates: Jan, Apr, July, September. Total enrollment: ~450. 40-80 each admission period. 75% receive financial aid. 10% enrolled part-time. S:T ratio 24:1. 90% of graduates obtain jobs within 6 mos. Facilities: Include 5 teaching kitchens, bakery, deli, open-to-the-public restaurant.

COURSES: Basic cooking, food production, garde manger, a la carte, baking, nutrition, sanitation, purchasing & cost controls, dining room mgmt, mgmt by menu. 24 hrs of general ed required. 2 internships/externships required, in 5th & 6th quarters.

FACULTY: 12 full- & part-time. Includes Michael F. Nenes, CEC, CCE; Larry Matson, CWC; Peter Lehr, CEC.

COSTS: Tuition $4,875/qtr or $325/cr-hr. Application fee $50, lab fee $300/qtr, supply kit $800. Off-campus housing $1,360/qtr. Admission requirements: HS diploma or equivalent & interview, ASSET test. Scholarships: yes. Loans: yes.

LOCATION: 70,000-sq-ft facility in the Galleria.

CONTACT: Director of Admissions, Art Institute of Houston-Culinary Arts, 1900 Yorktown, Houston, TX 77056; 800-275-4244, 713-623-2040, Fax 713-966-2797, aihadm@aii.edu, www.aih.artinstitutes.edu.

AUSTIN COMMUNITY COLLEGE

Austin/Year-round

Sponsor: Public 2-year college. Program: 2-yr AAS degree in Culinary Arts, 22-credit Culinarian certificate, 34-credit certificate in Culinary Arts. Accredited by ACF.

COURSES: Include food preparation, American regional & international cuisine, baking & pastry, nutrition, viticulture, sanitation & safety.

FACULTY: Brian Hay, MS, ACF, Chef Brian McCormick, Chef Reuel Smith, CCE, CEPC.

CONTACT: Brian Hay, Associate Professor, Austin Community College-Eastview Campus, 3401 Webberville Rd., Rm 3159, Austin, TX 78702; 512-223-5173, Fax 512-223-5191, bhay@austincc.edu, www.austincc.edu/hospmgmt.

CULINARY ACADEMY OF AUSTIN

Austin/Year-round

Sponsor: Private career school. Program: 1-yr Professional Culinary Arts program, 3-mo Intro to Culinary Arts program, 3-mo Pastry Arts program. Established: 1998. Accredited by Texas Workforce Commission, COE. Calendar: quarter. Curriculum: culinary. Admit dates: Jan, Apr, July, Oct. Total enrollment: 35. 10-12 each admission period. 70% of applicants accepted. 50-75% receive financial aid. 20% enrolled part-time. S:T ratio 8:1. 100% of graduates obtain jobs within 6 mos. Facilities: Well-equipped commercial kitchen, bakeshop, catering operation, 2 classrooms, dining room, demo area, resource room/computer room.

Courses: Sequential curriculu.. Food production, bakeshop, regional & intl cuisine, culinary culture & history, nutrition, sanitation, menu planning, brigade system, business. Externships required. Internships with restaurants & bakeries. Recreational classes, workshops for culinary professionals.

Faculty: 2 full-time CECs, 1 part-time. Culinary professionals are guest lecturers.

Costs: $4,845-$17,944 includes uniforms, chef tool kit, textbooks, lab fees. Admission requirements: Application, HS diploma or equivalent. Scholarships: yes. Loans: yes.

Contact: Elizabeth Falto-Mannion, Office Administrator, Culinary Academy of Austin, Inc., 2823 Hancock Dr., Austin, TX 78731; 512-451-5743, Fax 512-467-9120, emannion@culinaryacademyofaustin.com, www.culinaryacademyofaustin.com.

CULINARY INSTITUTE ALAIN & MARIE LENÔTRE

Houston/Year-round *(See also page 273)(See display ad above)*

Sponsor: Proprietary institution. Program: 20-wk day or 40-wk eve (748-hr) Sous-Chef Cooking/Catering or Baking/Pastry diploma. 30-wk day or 60-wk eve (1122-hr) Culinary Arts diploma, five 5-wk (50-hr) wine programs. Established: 1998. Accredited by ACCSCT Workforce Commission. Calendar: quinmester. Curriculum: culinary. Admit dates: Year-round. Total enrollment: 296. 37 each admission period. 90% of applicants accepted. 25% receive financial aid. 30% enrolled part-time. S:T ratio 10:1. 95% of graduates obtain jobs within 6 mos. Facilities: 14,000-sq-ft newly-equipped baking, pastry, bread, chocolate, sugar, ice-cream, cuisine, catering labs, lounge, cafeteria, conference room, amphitheater.

Courses: Restaurant cooking, catering, professional baking/pastry, breads, ice cream, chocolate, sugar, decor, international topics, guest chefs. Internships in USA & France.

Faculty: Technical Director Alain LeNotre, 4 full-time (day courses) & 4 part-time (even courses) French and European chefs rotating every 3 yrs, 1 sommelier conseil, 1 oenologue.

Costs: Program A or B: $17,450 plus tools, uniforms & fees. Program C: $20,975 plus tools, uniforms & fees. Enrollment by the week available. Admission requirements: HS diploma or GED. Scholarships: yes. Loans: yes.

Location: Central Houston, 30 min from NASA Space Center, 1 hr from Galveston Island on the Gulf of Mexico.

Contact: Alain LeNotre, CEO, Culinary Institute Alain & Marie LeNôtre, 7070 Allensby St., Houston, TX 77022; 888-LeNotre/713-692-0077, Fax 713-692-7399, lenotre@wt.net, www.lenotre-alain-marie.com.

DEL MAR COLLEGE

Corpus Christi/Year-round

Sponsor: State-supported institution. Program: 1-yr certificate, 2-yr AAS degree in Culinary Arts (ACF-accredited), Hotel/Motel Mgmt, Restaurant Mgmt. 4-yr BS degree in Restaurant Mgmt (2 yrs Del Mar College + 2 yrs Texas A&M-Kingsville). Established: 1963. Accredited by SACS. Calendar: semester. Curriculum: culinary, core. Admit dates: June, Aug, Jan. Total enrollment: 175. 60 each admission period. 100% of applicants accepted. 40% receive financial aid. 30% enrolled part-time. S:T ratio 15:1. 90% of graduates obtain jobs within 6 mos. Facilities: Restaurant, 4 classrooms, 2 labs, herb garden.

Courses: Saucier, Garde Manger, Intl Cuisine, Baking, Pastry, Cake Decorating, Culinary Competition, Buffet, A La Carte Cooking, American Regional Cuisine. 2- or 3-sem paid internships.

Faculty: 4 full-time, 11 part-time.

Costs: In-state $2,500/yr. Out-of-state/intl student $3,600/yr. Off-campus housing ~$600-$800. Admission requirements: HS diploma or equivalent, admission test. Scholarships: yes. Loans: yes.

Contact: Bob Ard, Professor & Chair, Del Mar College, Dept. of Hospitality Mgmt., 101 Baldwin, Corpus Christi, TX 78404-3897; 361-698-1734, Fax 361-698-1829, bard@delmar.edu, www.delmar.edu.

EL CENTRO COLLEGE

Dallas/Year-round

Sponsor: College. Program: A.A.S. and certificate programs in Food & Hospitality Services, Baking/Pastry, and Culinary Arts. Established: 1971. Accredited by SACS. Calendar: semester. Curriculum: culinary, core. Admit dates: Jan, Aug, May-June. Total enrollment: 400. 350-400 each admission period. 100% of applicants accepted. 40% receive financial aid. 65% enrolled part-time. S:T ratio 20-35:1. 98% of graduates obtain jobs within 6 mos. Facilities: Include 3 kitchens, 4 classrooms, pastry/bakery labs, computer lab.

Courses: Hands-on classes in food preparation & baking. Food service management courses and certification in sanitation and safety also offered. Apprenticeship-ACF available.

Faculty: 4 full-time, 12 part-time.

Costs: Annual tuition in-county $500, out-of-county $900. Admission requirements: HS diploma or equivalent and admission test. Scholarships: yes. Loans: yes.

Contact: Beth Sonnier, Director Food & Hospitality Institute, El Centro College, Main and Lamar, Dallas, TX 75202; 214-860-2368, bbs5531@dcccd.edu, www.dcccd.edu/cat0001/programs/culi.htm.

EL PASO COMMUNITY COLLEGE

El Paso/Year-round

Sponsor: Two-year public college. Program: 1-yr certificate, 2-yr AAS degree in Food Service, Culinary Arts. Established: 1992. Accredited by SACS. Calendar: semester. Curriculum: culinary, core. Admit dates: July/Aug, Dec/Jan, Apr/May. Total enrollment: 40. 15 each admission period. 90% of applicants accepted. 70% receive financial aid. 50% enrolled part-time. S:T ratio 18:1. 100% of graduates obtain jobs within 6 mos. Facilities: Full kitchen.

Courses: Cooking, service, mgmt. Co-op working experiences. Concurrent continuing ed courses.

Faculty: 1 full-time (AAS), 1 part-time instructor (master's degree, registered dietitian).

Costs: $75 ($200-$250)/1 credit hr + $24 ($50) ea additional + $29 fees + $9 ($29+$9) ea additional hr after 6 credit hrs for residents (nonresidents) of Texas & some New Mexico counties. Admission requirements: HS diploma, GED, TASP exam. Scholarships: yes. Loans: yes.

Contact: El Paso Community College, 919 Hunter Dr., El Paso, TX 79915; 915-831-5148, Restaurant 915-831-5061, Fax 915-831-5146, ClaudiaG@epcc.edu, www.epcc.edu.

GALVESTON COLLEGE – CULINARY ARTS ACADEMY

Galveston/Year-round

Sponsor: 2-year community college. Program: 1-yr certificates in Culinary Arts & Culinary/Hospitality Management, 2-yr AAS degree in Culinary Arts/Hospitality Management. Established: 1987. Accredited by SACS. Calendar: semester. Curriculum: culinary, core. Admit dates: Jan, June, July, Aug. Total enrollment: 50-60. 30-40 each admission period. 95% of applicants accepted. 100% receive financial aid. 10% enrolled part-time. S:T ratio 20:1. 97% of graduates obtain jobs within 6 mos. Facilities: Include kitchen, bakeshop & classroom.

Faculty: Leslie Bartosh, CCC, FMP; Cheryl Lewis.

Costs: Annual tuition $400 in-state, $600 out-of-state. Admission requirements: HS diploma or equivalent & admission test. Scholarships: yes. Loans: yes.

CONTACT: Leslie Bartosh, CCC, FMP, Director of Culinary Arts, Galveston College, 4015 Ave. Q, Galveston, TX 77550; 409-763-6551 #304, Fax 409-765-5353, chef@gc.edu, www.gc.edu/chef.

HOUSTON COMMUNITY COLLEGE SYSTEM

Houston/Year-round

Sponsor: College. Program: Certificate in Culinary Arts, certificate in Pastry & Baking. Established: 1972. Accredited by SACS. Calendar: semester. Curriculum: culinary. Total enrollment: 200. 25 each admission period. 60% receive financial aid. 25% enrolled part-time. S:T ratio 15-20:1. 95% of graduates obtain jobs within 6 mos.

COURSES: Culinary Arts and/or Baking & Pastry.

FACULTY: 3 full-time, 2 part-time.

COSTS: Annual tuition $1,176/in-district, $1,974 out-of-district, $4,284 out-of-state, includes fees. Admission requirements: HS/GRE. Scholarships: yes. Loans: yes.

CONTACT: Eddy VanDamme, Dept. Chair, Houston Community College System, Culinary Services, Houston, TX 77002; 713-718-6046, Fax 713-718-6044, eddy.vandamme@hccs.edu, www.hccs.cc.tx.us.

ODESSA COLLEGE

Odessa/Year-round

Sponsor: College. Program: 2-yr certificate/AAS. Established: 1990. Accredited by SACS. Calendar: semester. Curriculum: culinary, core. Admit dates: Open. Total enrollment: 35-50. 35-50 each admission period. 75% of applicants accepted. 65% receive financial aid. 10-15% enrolled part-time. S:T ratio 10-15:1. Facilities: Training kitchen/lab, dining room.

FACULTY: 2 full-time.

COSTS: Tuition $207 for first three credit-hours, $19 for each additional credit-hour. Admission requirements: HS diploma or equivalent and admission test. Scholarships: yes.

CONTACT: Peter Lewis, Dept. Chair, Odessa College, Culinary Arts, 201 W. University, Odessa, TX 79764; 915-335-6320, Fax 915-335-6860, plewis@odessa.edu, www.odessa.edu/dept/culin.

ST. PHILIP'S COLLEGE

San Antonio/Year-round

Sponsor: College. Program: 2-year AAS degree. Established: 1979. Accredited by SACS, ACF. Calendar: semester. Curriculum: culinary. Admit dates: Aug, Jan, June. Total enrollment: 335. 335 each admission period. 80% receive financial aid. 50% enrolled part-time. S:T ratio 15:1 lab. 90% of graduates obtain jobs within 6 mos. Facilities: Include 3 kitchens, classrooms, computer lab, restaurant.

COURSES: Garde manger, intl food preparation, baking principles. 16-week externship available.

FACULTY: 5 full-time.

COSTS: Annual tuition in-district $504, out-of-district $966, out-of-state $1,932. Admission requirements: HS diploma or equivalent & admission test. Scholarships: yes. Loans: yes.

CONTACT: William Thornton, Associate Professor FMP,CCE, St. Philip's College, Tourism, Hospitality & Culinary Arts 1801 ML KING Dr., San Antonio, TX 78203; 210-531-3315, Fax 210-531-3351, wthornton@accd.edu, www.accd.edu.

SAN JACINTO COLLEGE CENTRAL

Pasadena/Year-round

Sponsor: Public 2-year college. Program: 18-month certificate in Culinary Arts, 2-year associate degree in Culinary Arts. Established: 1961. Accredited by SACS. Calendar: semester. Curriculum: culinary. Admit dates: Jan, June, September. Total enrollment: 90. 55% enrolled part-time. S:T ratio 15:1. Facilities: Food production kitchen, 4 classrooms, library, cafeteria.

COURSES: Food prep & purchasing, international cuisine, meat cutting & fabrication, nutrition, baking & pastry, confectionery. Paid internships.

FACULTY: 2 full-time, 6 part-time. Includes Leonard Pringle DTR, Cynthia Lundberg.

COSTS: In-state: $16/cr-hr. Out-of-district: $30/cr-hr. Out-of-state: $60/cr-hr. Fees ~$200.

CONTACT: Leonard Pringle, Dept. Chair, Culinary Arts, San Jacinto College-Central Campus, 8060 Spencer Hwy., Pasadena, TX 77501-2007; 281-542-2099, Fax 281-478-2790, lpring@central.sjcd.cc.tx.us, www.sjcd.cc.tx.us.

SAN JACINTO COLLEGE NORTH – CULINARY ARTS

Houston/September-July

Sponsor: College. Program: 2-year & 3-year AAS degree. Established: 1986. Accredited by SACS. Calendar: semester. Curriculum: culinary. Admit dates: Sept, Jan. Total enrollment: 20-30. 25 each admission period. 90% of applicants accepted. 50% receive financial aid. S:T ratio 12:1. 70% of graduates obtain jobs within 6 mos.

FACULTY: 3 full-time. 2 ACF chefs, CEC/CCE.

COSTS: Tuition $262/semester in-district, $430/semester out-of-district. Admission requirements: H.S. diploma-GED. Scholarships: yes. Loans: yes.

CONTACT: George J. Messinger, CEC, CCE, Dept. Chairman/Executive Chef, San Jacinto College North, Culinary Arts, 5800 Uvalde, Houston, TX 77049; 281-459-7150, Fax 281-459-7132, gmessi@sjcd.cc.tx.us, www.sjcd.cc.tx.us. Additional contact: Francois Lefebvre, CEC 281-459 7110.

TEXAS CHEFS ASSOCIATION

Dallas or Houston/Year-round

Sponsor: ACF chapter with 14 sub-chapters in Texas. Program: 3-yr apprenticeship in Dallas or Houston. Associate's degree. Established: 1968. Curriculum: culinary. Admit dates: Aug/Sept or Dec/Jan. Total enrollment: 120. Facilities: San Jacinto College in Houston, El Centro Comm. College in Dallas.

COSTS: College tuition plus Texas Chefs Assn. membership dues. Scholarships: yes. Loans: yes.

CONTACT: Chris LaLonde CEC, Apprenticeship Chair, Texas Chefs Association, El Centro College, Dallas, TX 75202; 214-860-2209, Fax 214-860-2049, crl5531@dcccd.edu. George Messinger CEC, CCE, Houston Apprenticeship Chair, 19826 Atascocita Dr., Humble, TX 77346; 281-459-7150.

TEXAS CULINARY ACADEMY

Austin/Year-round *(See display ad page 115)*

Sponsor: Independent nonprofit institution, formerly Le Chef College of Hospitality Careers. Program: 17-month diploma program in Culinary Arts, 2-year AAS degree program in Culinary Arts and Food & Beverage Management. Established: 1981. Accredited by COE. Calendar: trimester. Curriculum: culinary, core. Admit dates: Continuous. Total enrollment: 130. 95% of applicants accepted. 90% receive financial aid. S:T ratio 12:1. 96% of graduates obtain jobs within 6 mos. Facilities: 36-station culinary lab, 6 lecture rooms, learning center, computer lab, conference room.

COURSES: Diploma & degree programs cover cuisine & pastry preparation, pantry production & garde manger, production, control, planning & presentation. Degree program also includes food & beverage management & general ed courses. diploma program includes 720-hour paid externship.

FACULTY: President Harvey M. Giblin, M.Ed., Andre Touboulle, CMC; Christian Echterbille, CMC; Walter Irmschler, CEC; Gary Ackerman; Michael Carter; 5-member general ed faculty.

COSTS: $16,840 for Culinary Arts diploma, $27,360 for AAS degree. Admission requirements: HS diploma or GED. Scholarships: yes. Loans: yes.

CONTACT: Texas Culinary Academy, 11400 Burnet Rd., #2100, Austin, TX 78758; 888-5LeChef, 512-323-2511, Fax 512-323-2126, LeChef@onr.com, www.txca.com.

TEXAS STATE TECHNICAL COLLEGE

Waco/Year-round

Sponsor: 2-yr technical-vocational college. Program: 1-yr certificate & 2-yr AAS degree programs in Food Service/Culinary Arts. Established: 1965. Accredited by SACS. Curriculum: culinary, core. Admit dates: Sept, Jan. Total enrollment: 75. 25 each admission period. 100% of applicants accepted. 75% receive financial aid. 10% enrolled part-time. S:T ratio 12-15:1. 100% of graduates obtain jobs within 6 mos. Facilities: Former Air Force base Officers' Club.

Courses: Job entry training & skills. Sanitation & Safety, Basic Food Prep, Nutrition, Food Prod & Planning, Quantity Procedures, Dining Room Service, Menu Mgmt, Purchasing. 3-mo co-op, not mandatory. DMA certificate training.

Faculty: 5 full-time.

Costs: $47.50/cr-hr in-state. Admission requirements: CPT. Scholarships: yes. Loans: yes.

Contact: Dr. Debby DeFee, Dept. Chair, Texas State Technical College, Food Service/Culinary Arts, 3801 Campus Dr., Waco, TX 76705-1696; 800-792-8784, 254-867-4868, Fax 254-867-3663, webmaster@tstc.edu, http://culinaryartcollege.com. ddefee@tstc.edu.

UTAH

BRIDGERLAND APPLIED TECHNOLOGY CENTER

Logan/Year-round

Sponsor: State applied technology center. Program: 1100-hr program consisting of basic food preparation courses (food production, sanitation, garde manger, baking, catering). Established: 1989. Calendar: quarter. Curriculum: culinary. Admit dates: Open admission. 100% of applicants accepted. 80% receive financial aid. 90% enrolled part-time. S:T ratio 7-10:1. 100% of graduates obtain jobs within 6 mos. Facilities: 2 classrooms, large production lab, on-site cafeteria.

Faculty: 2 full time.

Costs: $330/quarter. Loans: yes.

Contact: Anne Parish, Bridgerland Applied Technology Center, 1301 N. 600 West, Logan, UT 84321; 435-750-3021, Fax 435-752-2016, aparish@m.batc.tec.ut.us, www.batc.tec.ut.us.

SALT LAKE COMMUNITY COLLEGE

Salt Lake City/Year-round

Sponsor: 2-yr college. Program: 2-year full-time & 3-year part-time Apprentice Chef program. Established: 1984. Accredited by NASC, ACF. Curriculum: culinary, core. Admit dates: Rolling. Total enrollment: 50. 40-50 each admission period. 90% of applicants accepted. 40-50% enrolled part-time. S:T ratio 12:1. 100% of graduates obtain jobs within 6 mos. Facilities: Include kitchen, 8 classrooms, video and reference library.

Courses: Food prep, sanitation, baking, menu design, nutrition. AAS degree requires 24 cr in general ed. 50% must be scratch cooking. Continuing ed: classes & workshops for culinary professionals.

Faculty: 2 full-time and 8 part-time.

Costs: Full-time tuition $771/quarter in-state, $2,427/quarter out-of-state. $20 application fee. Average off-campus housing cost is $300/mo. Admission requirements: HS diploma or equivalent and admission test. Loans: yes.

Contact: Joe Mulvey, Apprenticeship Director, Salt Lake Community College, P.O. Box 30808, Salt Lake City, UT 84130-0808; 801-957-4066, Fax 801-957-4612, mulveyjo@slcc.edu, www.slcc.edu.

UTAH STATE UNIVERSITY

Logan/Year-round

Sponsor: University. Program: 4-year BS degree in Culinary Arts & Foodservice Management, major in culinary arts and minor in a business discipline. Established: 1994. Accredited by NASC. Calendar: semester. Curriculum: culinary, core. Admit dates: Ongoing. Total enrollment: 40. 100% of applicants accepted. 50% receive financial aid. S:T ratio 12:1. 100% of graduates obtain jobs within 6 mos. Facilities: On campus facilties include classrooms, labs, campus foodservice outlets.

Courses: General culinary and food service management.

Faculty: 2 full-time, one with masters, one with PhD, one is Certified Executive Chef; several part-time faculty. Jeffrey P. Miller, CEC, CCE; Von Mendenhall, PhD; John McDonald, Chef.

Costs: Plateau (12-18 credits) tuition is $1,122.62 in-state, $3,400.88 out-of-state. Admission requirements: HS diploma or equivalent. Scholarships: yes. Loans: yes.

CONTACT: Jeffrey Miller, CEC, CCE, Co-Director, CA/FSM Program, Utah State University, 8700 Old Main Hill, Logan, UT 84322-8700; 435-797-0897, Fax 435-797-2379, chefjeff@cc.usu.edu, www.usu.edu/~famlife/nfs/culinaryarts.

UTAH VALLEY STATE COLLEGE
Orem/August-April

Sponsor: College. Program: 2-yr AAS degree in Culinary Arts. Established: 1992. Accredited by NASC. Admit dates: Open. Total enrollment: 35. 15 each admission period. 90% of applicants accepted. 80% receive financial aid. 10% enrolled part-time. S:T ratio 12:1. 100% of graduates obtain jobs within 6 mos. Facilities: Include 3 kitchens, 3 classrooms, restaurant & food service operation.

COURSES: Food prod, nutrition, sanitation, garde manger, buffet. Externship: 5-week, salaried.

FACULTY: 3 full-time. Qualifications: certified chef, work experience.

COSTS: Tuition in-state $760/semester, out-of-state $2,387/semester. Other fees: $100 class fee, $300 supplies fee. Average off-campus housing cost $200/mo. Admission requirements: HS diploma.

CONTACT: Julie Slocum, CA Academic Advisor, Utah Valley State College, Business Dept., 800 W. 1200 South, Orem, UT 84058; 801-863-8914, Fax 801-863-7112, slocumju@uvsc.edu, www.uvsc.edu/ca.

VERMONT

NEW ENGLAND CULINARY INSTITUTE
Montpelier and Essex/Year-round *(See display ad page 155)*

Sponsor: Private career institution. Program: 2-yr AOS degree programs in Culinary Arts and Food & Beverage Management, upper level 1-1/2-yr Bachelors degree in Food & Beverage Management, 10-mo certificate program in Basic Cooking. Established: 1979. Accredited by State of Vermont, ACCSCT. Calendar: semester. Curriculum: culinary. Admit dates: Sept, Dec, Mar, June. Total enrollment: 700. 168 each admission period. 90% of applicants accepted. 80% receive financial aid. S:T ratio 7:1. 98% of graduates obtain jobs within 6 mos. Facilities: 12 kitchens, 14 classrooms. Each campus offers a variety of restaurants, bakery, catering operation & banquet dept.

COURSES: Integration into real restaurant operation. In culinary arts program 75% of class time is spent preparing food for the public. Remaining classes cover cooking theory, food & wine history, wine & beverage mgmt, tableservice, purchasing. AOS programs & BA program each offer 700-hr paid internships.

FACULTY: 63-member faculty, 19-member administrative staff, 3 advisory boards.

COSTS: AOS in Culinary Arts: $25,975/yr includes room, board, knives, uniforms. BA: $41,210/2 academic yrs includes room, board, uniforms. Admission requirements: HS diploma or equivalent, reference letters, essay, interview. Advanced placement students must pass a written exam & practical. Scholarships: yes. Loans: yes.

LOCATION: Montpelier campus is 3 hrs from Boston, Essex Junction campus is in a Bulington suburb.

CONTACT: Dawn Hayward, Director of Admissions, New England Culinary Institute, Admissions Dept., 250 Main St., Montpelier, VT 05602; 877-223-6324, Fax 802-225-3280, info@neci.edu, www.neci.edu.

VIRGINIA

THE ART INSTITUTE OF WASHINGTON
Arlington/Year-round *(See display ad page 135)*

Sponsor: Private college, member of The Art Institutes, with 29 locations in the U.S. & Canada. Program: 7-quarter AA degree program in Culinary Arts. Established: 2000. Accredited by ACF, SACS. Calendar: quarter. Curriculum: culinary, core. Admit dates: July, Oct, Jan, Apr. Facilities: 14,000-sq-ft facility with 4 teaching kitchens, classrooms, & full-service teaching dining room.

COURSES: Basic culinary skills, food production, baking & pastry, garde manger, kitchen procedures, sanitation & safety, nutrition, restaurant operation, purchasing, menu planning, kitchen

mgmt, classical, intl & nouvelle cuisines. Internship/externship required in the 6th quarter.

CONTACT: Ann Marie Drucker, Director of Admissions, The Art Institute of Washington, 1820 N Fort Myer Dr., Ground Floor, Arlington, VA 22209; 703-358-9550, 877-303-3771, Fax 703-358-9759, druckera@aii.edu, www.aiw.artinstitute.edu.

J. SARGEANT REYNOLDS COMMUNITY COLLEGE

Richmond/Year-round

Sponsor: Community college. Program: 68 cr-hr AAS degree in Culinary Arts. Established: 1973. Accredited by SACS. Calendar: semester. Curriculum: culinary, core. Admit dates: Ongoing. Total enrollment: 140. 40 each admission period. 100% of applicants accepted. 40% receive financial aid. 80% enrolled part-time. S:T ratio 18:1. Facilities: Classrooms, labs, commercial production kitchen, food service & conference space, computer technology labs.

COURSES: Competency-based technical & managerial education & training. ACF recertification courses, advanced theory & technique for professionals & managers.

FACULTY: 12 instructors including Certified Hotel Administrator, Registered Dietitian, & Ph.D.

COSTS: Full degree program $4,054 in-state, $10,771 out-of-state.

CONTACT: David Barrish, CHA, Director, J. Sargeant Reynolds Community College, P.O. Box 85622, Richmond, VA 23285-5622; 804-786-2069, Fax 804-786-5465, dbarrish@jsr.vccs.edu, www.jsr.vccs.edu/hospitality.

NORTHERN VIRGINIA COMMUNITY COLLEGE

Annandale/Year-round

Sponsor: 2-yr college. Program: 1-yr certificate in Culinary Arts. Established: 1997. Accredited by SACS. Calendar: semester. Curriculum: culinary. Admit dates: Fall, spring semesters. Total enrollment: 40. 40 each admission period. 100% of applicants accepted. 30% receive financial aid. 80% enrolled part-time. S:T ratio 20:1. Facilities: 2 classrooms, computer lab, commercial kitchen, dining room.

COURSES: Skills for culinary positions. Apprenticeship program available.

FACULTY: 6 full-time, 1 part-time.

COSTS: $56.54/cr-hr in-state, $202.47/cr-hr out-of-state.

CONTACT: Benita Wong, CCC, CCE, Culinary Arts Instructor, Northern Virginia Community College, 8333 Little River Tpk., Annandale, VA 22003-3796; 703-323-3457, Fax 703-323-3509, bwong@nvcc.edu, www.nvcc.edu.

STRATFORD UNIVERSITY – SCHOOL OF CULINARY ARTS

Falls Church/Year-round

Sponsor: Private university. Program: 30-mo BA degree in Hospitality Mgmt.,15-mo AAS degree in Culinary Arts, 12-mo diploma program in Culinary Arts. Established: 1990. Accredited by ACICS, ACF, SCHEV. Calendar: quarter. Curriculum: core. Admit dates: Every 5 wks. Total enrollment: 350. 40 each admission period. 85% of applicants accepted. 80% receive financial aid. 1% enrolled part-time. S:T ratio 15:1. 95% of graduates obtain jobs within 6 mos. Facilities: 4 kitchens with latest equipment, 5 classrooms, 2 dining rooms, cafe.

COURSES: Culinary theory, nutrition, sanitation, sauces & entrees, baking, intl cuisine, a la carte production, chocolate & sugar arts, wines, presentation, garde manger, hospitality mgmt, purchasing & receiving, dining room service, accounting. 3-12 wk optional externship. Individual courses.

FACULTY: 15 full-time & 4 part-time ACF-certified chefs. Guest chefs are frequent lecturers. Chef Daniel Traster, Director, is a Yale University & CIA graduate.

COSTS: Tuition $250/cr-hr; books & supplies additional. Nonrefundable application fee $100. Off-campus housing & food costs ~$1,000/mo. Admission requirements: HS diploma or GED. Entrance exam. Scholarships: yes. Loans: yes.

CONTACT: Admissions, Stratford University, School of Culinary Arts, Falls Church, VA 22043-2403; 800-444-0804, 703-821-8570, Fax 703-556-9892, culinary@stratford.edu, www.stratford.edu.

TIDEWATER COMMUNITY COLLEGE CULINARY ARTS
Norfolk/Year-round

Sponsor: 2-yr community college. Program: AAS degree in Culinary Arts. Established: 1997. Accredited by SACS. Calendar: semester. Curriculum: culinary, core. Admit dates: May, Aug, December. Total enrollment: 45. 100% of applicants accepted. 70% receive financial aid. 60% enrolled part-time. S:T ratio 20:1. 100% of graduates obtain jobs within 6 mos.

COURSES: 43 culinary program credits: Nutrition, Food Prep, Commercial Food Presentation, Intro to Meat, Principles of Baking, Garde Manger, Intro to Culinary Arts, Sanitation & Safety, Inventory & Cost Control, Coordinated Internship. General ed. Internship.

CONTACT: Chef John Cappellucci, Tidewater Community College Culinary Arts, 300 Granby St., Norfolk, VA 23510-9956; 757-822-1350, 757-822-1111, jcappellucci@tcc.edu, www.tc.cc.va.us/culinary/index.htm.

VIRGINIA INTERMONT COLLEGE – CULINARY ARTS
Bristol/Year-round *(See display ad above)*

Sponsor: 4-yr private college affiliated with the Baptist General Assn of Virginia. Program: 2-yr AS degree in Culinary Arts. Established: 2002. Accredited by SACS. Calendar: semester. Curriculum: culinary. Admit dates: Rolling. S:T ratio 14:1.

COURSES: Sanitation & Safety, Culinary Arts, Baking & Pastry, Intl Cuisine. 1-sem paid internship.

FACULTY: Richard K. Erskine, CEC, CPC, 23 yrs industry experience & 7 yrs teaching, was awarded Chef of the Year honors & the ACF Presidential Medal. Instructors are industry chefs.

COSTS: $18,690/yr residential, $13,220/yr off-campus. Scholarships: yes. Loans: yes.

CONTACT: Richard Erskine, Director of Culinary Arts, Virginia Intermont College - Culinary Arts, 1013 Moore St., Bristol, VA 24201; 423-989-0088, Fax 423-989-3750, richarderskine@vic.edu, www.vic.edu.

WASHINGTON

THE ART INSTITUTE OF SEATTLE
Seattle/Year-round *(See display ad page 135)*

Sponsor: 2-yr college. Program: 7-quarter AAA degree in Culinary Arts, 4-quarter diploma in Baking & Pastry, 4-quarter diploma in The Art of Cooking. Established: 1996. Accredited by NASC, ACF. Calendar: quarter. Curriculum: core. Admit dates: Rolling. Total enrollment: 300. 60 each admission period. 65% of applicants accepted. 75% receive financial aid. 13% enrolled part-time. S:T ratio 19:1. 95% of graduates obtain jobs within 6 mos. Facilities: Kitchens & classroom space, dining room overlooking Puget Sound.

COURSES: Basic skills, baking & pastry, desserts, American regional, classical, intl & Mediterranean, health-related cooking, charcuterie, cost mgmt, menu & facility planning, dining room operations.

FACULTY: 18 culinary instructors with industry experience.

COSTS: $13,680/academic yr for AAA degree programs, $8,208/academic yr for Diploma programs. Admission requirements: HS diploma & admissions interview. Scholarships: yes. Loans: yes.

CONTACT: Lori Murray, Associate Director of Admissions, Art Institute of Seattle, Admissions Dept., 2323 Elliott Ave., Seattle, WA 98121; 800-275-2471, 206-448-6600, Fax 206-448-2501, aisadm@aii.edu, www.ais.artinstitutes.edu.

BATES TECHNICAL COLLEGE

Tacoma/Year-round

Sponsor: Two-year college. Program: 22-month AST degree in Culinary Arts. Accredited by ACCSCT. Calendar: quarter.

COURSES: Preparing and Cooking Breakfast Items, Preparing Sandwiches, Cooking Fruits, Vegetables, Starches, Preparing and Cooking Entrees.

FACULTY: Roger Knapp, Ricardo Saenz.

COSTS: $720/quarter.

CONTACT: Ricardo Saenz, Bates Technical College, 1101 S. Yakima Ave., Tacoma, WA 98405; 253-680-7247, Fax 253-680-7211, rsaenz@bates.ctc.edu, www.bates.ctc.edu.

BELLINGHAM TECHNICAL COLLEGE

Bellingham/September-July

Sponsor: 2-yr technical college. Program: Certificates of completion & AAS degrees in Culinary Arts & Baking, Pastry, & Confections. Established: 1957. Accredited by ACF, NACS. Calendar: quarter. Curriculum: culinary, core. Admit dates: Quarterly & others times with instructor's permission. Total enrollment: 40. 40 each admission period. 90% of applicants accepted. 30% receive financial aid. 20% enrolled part-time. S:T ratio 20:1. 94% of graduates obtain jobs within 6 mos. Facilities: Instructional space, industrial kitchen/bakeshop, fine dining restaurant, deli/baking, demo kitchen.

COURSES: Culinary students operate an on-campus full-service restaurant. Baking students operate an on-campus bakeshop & prepare desserts for the restaurant. Various courses to upgrade food management & culinary skills.

FACULTY: Michael S.Baldwin, CEC, & William Pifer, Master Baker, CMB.

COSTS: Quarterly tuition & fees are $769 for Culinary Arts, $769 for Baking, Pastry & Confections. No on-campus housing. Admission requirements: 16 yrs or older, HS graduate, basic skills. Scholarships: yes. Loans: yes.

CONTACT: Michael Baldwin, Culinary Arts instructor, Bellingham Technical College, Culinary Arts, 3028 Lindbergh Ave., Bellingham, WA 98225; 360-715-8350 #400, Fax 360-676-2798, mbaldwin@belltc.ctc.edu, www.beltc.ctc.edu/index.html. Additional contact: bpifer@belltc.ctc.edu.

CLARK COLLEGE CULINARY ARTS PROGRAM

Vancouver/Year-round

Sponsor: Community college. Program: 1- & 2-yr certificate or AAS degrees in cooking, baking, & bakery/restaurant mgmt. Established: 1958. Accredited by NWACC. Calendar: quarter. Curriculum: culinary, core. Admit dates: Jan, Mar, June, Sept. Total enrollment: 80. 15 (cooking), 10 (baking) each admission period. 80% applicants accepted. 50% receive financial aid. S:T ratio 5:1. 95% of graduates obtain jobs within 6 mos. Facilities: Modernized facility operates like a hotel kitchen. Students make all foods sold on-campus. Baking students operate the campus' retail bakery.

COURSES: Cooking includes food prep, advanced meat cutting, ice carving, wine appreciation, cake decoration & pastillage. Baking includes fundamentals the 1st year & specialized courses the 2nd year; theory, merchandising, bake shop mgmt. 5-wk internships available.

FACULTY: 12-member faculty. Includes cooking instructors Larry Mains, CEC, CCE, AAC, George Akau, CCE, AAC, Glenn Lakin, & baking instructors Per Zeeberg & Jean Williams.

COSTS: 1-yr program is $3,000 in-state, $3,500 out-of-state. 2-yr program is $6,000 in-state, $7,000 out-of-state. Program can be 9 or 18 mos. Nearby off-campus housing. Admission requirements: HS diploma or equivalent. Scholarships: yes. Loans: yes.

CONTACT: Larry Mains, Director, Culinary Arts, Clark College, 1800 E. McLoughlin Blvd., Vancouver, WA 98663-3598; 360-992-2143, Fax 360-992-2839, lmains@clark.edu, www.clark.edu.

EDMONDS COMMUNITY COLLEGE

Lynwood/September-June

Sponsor: Community college. Program: 6-quarter ATA, 3-quarter Advanced Commercial Cooking Certificate, 2-quarter Basic Commercial Cooking Certificate, 1-quarter Professional Food Server Certificate. Established: 1988. Accredited by State. Calendar: quarter. Curriculum: core. Admit dates: Fall, winter, spring. Total enrollment: 45. 15 each admission period. 90% of applicants accepted. 25% receive financial aid. S:T ratio 20:1. 100% of graduates obtain jobs within 6 mos. Facilities: 1 kitchen, 1 classroom, 1 restaurant.

COURSES: Contemporary Northwest cuisine, fine dining service, restaurant/food service management. Other required courses: service and management. Externship provided.

FACULTY: 2 full-time, 2 part-time. Includes Walter Bronowitz, CCC, CCE; John Casey.

COSTS: Annual tuition in-state $505/quarter, out-of-state $1,987/quarter. Admission requirements: HS diploma or equivalent. Scholarships: yes. Loans: yes.

CONTACT: Nancy Lindaas, Dept. Chair, Edmonds Community College, Culinary Arts, 20000 - 68th Ave. West, Lynnwood, WA 98036; 425-640-1239, nlindaas@edcc.edu, www.edcc.edu.

LAKE WASHINGTON TECHNICAL COLLEGE

Kirkland/October-August

Sponsor: Public 2-year college. Program: Three-quarter certificate & six-quarter associate degree in Culinary Arts. Established: 1983. Accredited by State of Washington. Calendar: quarter. Curriculum: culinary, core. Admit dates: Jan, Apr, July, Oct. Total enrollment: 50. 100% of applicants accepted. S:T ratio 17:1. 95% of graduates obtain jobs within 6 mos. Facilities: Food production & teaching kitchens, demo lab, computer lab, bake shop, dining room, public restaurant.

COURSES: Food prep & purchasing, intl cuisine, garde manger, meat fabrication, menu & facilities design, nutrition, restaurant management. Optional internships available locally. The 3 courses required for ACF certification: Sanitation, Nutrition & Management.

FACULTY: 1 full-time, 2 part-time. Includes Alan H. Joynson, Rino Baglio.

COSTS: $1,750/certificate, $3,750/degree. Materials fee ~$650. Scholarships: yes. Loans: yes.

CONTACT: Alan Joynson, Chef Instructor, Culinary Arts, Lake Washington Technical College, 11605 132nd Ave. NE, Kirkland, WA 98034-8506; 425-739-8310, Fax 425-739-8298, alan.joynson@lwtc.ctc.edu, www.lwtc.ctc.edu.

NORTH SEATTLE COMMUNITY COLLEGE

Seattle/September-June

Sponsor: College. Program: 1-year certificate & 2-year AAS degree in Culinary Arts, Hospitality & Restaurant Cooking. Established: 1970. Accredited by NASC, ACF. Calendar: quarter. Curriculum: core. Admit dates: Quarterly. Total enrollment: 80. 25 each admission period. 90% of applicants accepted. 25% receive financial aid. S:T ratio 18:1. 90% of graduates obtain jobs within 6 mos. Facilities: Include 2 kitchens and classrooms, restaurant, bakery.

COURSES: Restaurant cooking and commercial cooking.

FACULTY: 4 full-time.

COSTS: Annual tuition $1,750 in-state, $6,000 out-of-state. Uniform, supplies $750. Off-campus housing cost ~$750/mo. Admission requirements: HS diploma or equivalent & admission test.

CONTACT: Darrell Mihara, Associate Dean, Culinary Arts & Hospitality, North Seattle Community College, Culinary Arts, 9600 College Way North, Seattle, WA 98103-3599; 206-528-4402, Fax 206-527-3635, dmihara@sccd.ctc.edu, www.gonorth.org.

OLYMPIC COLLEGE

Bremerton/September-May

Sponsor: College. Program: 3-quarter certificate, 2-year ATA degree. Advanced US Navy Food Service training also offered. Established: 1978. Accredited by State. Calendar: trimester. Curriculum: culinary. Admit dates: Continuous enrollment. Total enrollment: 38. 28-35 each admission period.

85% of applicants accepted. 60% receive financial aid. 15% enrolled part-time. S:T ratio 14:1. 90% of graduates obtain jobs within 6 mos. Facilities: Central kitchen, 2 classrooms, 2 restaurants.

Courses: Classical cooking, restaurant baking, dining room service, restaurant management. Other required courses: math, English, computers, business, interpersonnel communications. English composition, computers, business management.

Faculty: 2 full-time, 2 part-time.

Costs: Annual tuition: in-state $1,545, out-of-state $5,991. $50 lunch fee quarterly. Off-campus housing ~$375/mo. Admission requirements: HS diploma or equivalent. Scholarships: yes. Loans: yes.

Contact: Steve Lammers, Chef Instructor C.C.E., Olympic College, Commercial Cooking/Food Service, 16th & Chester, Bremerton, WA 98310-1688; 360-475-7570, Fax 360-475-7454, slammers@oc.ctc.edu, www.olympic.ctc.edu.

RENTON TECHNICAL COLLEGE

Renton/Year-round

Sponsor: Career college. Program: 1,620-hr certificate in Culinary Arts/Chef, AAS degree available; 1,260-hr certificate in Professional Baking. Established: 1968. Accredited by ACF, RBA. Calendar: quarter. Curriculum: culinary. Admit dates: Open. Total enrollment: 25. 10-30 each admission period. 100% of applicants accepted. 30% receive financial aid. S:T ratio 12:1. 100% of graduates obtain jobs within 6 mos. Facilities: Industry-current kitchen, full bakery, demo classroom, 3 outlet restaurants.

Courses: Hands-on skills & techniques, with emphasis on fundamentals & industry competencies. 108-hr externship provided for Culinary Arts students.

Faculty: 2 instructors & 1 assistant full-time. Includes Chef Instructor David Pisegna, CEC, CCE, & Baking Instructor Erhard Volcke, CMB.

Contact: John Fisher, Exec. Chef Instructor, Renton Technical College, Culin. Arts, 3000 N.E. Fourth St., Renton, WA 98056; 425-235-2352 x5708, Fax 425-235-7832, jfisher@rtc.ctc.edu, www.renton-tc.ctc.edu.

SEATTLE CULINARY ACADEMY

Seattle/Year-round

Sponsor: 2-yr college. Program: 6-quarter Culinary Arts certificate, 2-year Culinary AAS degree, a 5-quarter Specialty Desserts & Breads certificate. Established: 1942. Accredited by ACF. Calendar: quarter. Curriculum: culinary. Admit dates: Quarterly. Total enrollment: 100-150. 25-30 each admission period. 85% of applicants accepted. 30% receive financial aid. 2% enrolled part-time. S:T ratio 18:1. 97% of graduates obtain jobs within 6 mos. Facilities: Include 5 kitchens, 8 classrooms, bistro restaurant, gourmet restaurant, lunch buffet.

Courses: Professional cooking, restaurant cooking, specialty desserts, baking, breads, nutrition, buffet catering, costing, menu planning, management, ice carving. American regional, classical, international, & Asian cuisines, dining room operations. Last quarter internship.

Faculty: 8 full- & 2 part-time. Includes Keijiro Miyata, CEC, Linda Hierholzer, CCE, Diana Dillard, David Madayag, CEC, Cynthia Wilson, Regis Bernard, Don Reed, Tom Dillard, Greg Mowrer.

Costs: In-state tuition $579/quarter, out-of-state $2,284/quarter. Off-campus housing cost is $400-$600/mo. Total tuition costs: $5,400. Admission requirements: Admissions test or college transcripts for English & Math skills. Scholarships: yes. Loans: yes.

Contact: Joy Gulmon-Huri, Program Manager, Seattle Central Community College, Seattle Culinary Academy, 1701 Broadway, Mailstop 2BE2120, Seattle, WA 98122; 206-587-5424, Fax 206-344-4323, jgulmo@sccd.ctc.edu, http://seattleculinary.com. Greg Mowrer, Associate Deangmowrer@sccd.ctc.edu206-344-4386.

SKAGIT VALLEY COLLEGE

Mt. Vernon/September-May

Sponsor: College. Program: 1-year certificate & 2-year ATA degree in Culinary Arts/Hospitality Management. Established: 1979. Accredited by State, ACF. Calendar: quarter. Curriculum: core. Admit dates: Open. Total enrollment: 60. 6 each admission period. 100% of applicants accepted.

60% receive financial aid. S:T ratio 15:1. 100% of graduates obtain jobs within 6 mos. Facilities: Include kitchen, classrooms restaurant.

FACULTY: 3 full-time,1 part-time.

COSTS: Annual tuition in-state $1,584, out-of-state $6,234. Admission requirements: HS diploma or equivalent. Scholarships: yes. Loans: yes.

CONTACT: Lyle Hildahl, Director, Skagit Valley College, Culinary Arts/Hospitality Mgmt., 2405 College Way, Mt. Vernon, WA 98273; 360-416-7618, Fax 360-416-7890, hildahl@skagit.ctc.edu, www.skagit.edu.

SOUTH PUGET SOUND COMMUNITY COLLEGE

Olympia/September-June

Sponsor: 2-yr college. Program: 2-year ATA degree, Food Service Tech. and Food Service Management, 1-year Com. Baking Tech. Established: 1989. Accredited by State. Calendar: quarter. Curriculum: culinary. Admit dates: Sept, Jan, Apr. Total enrollment: 45. 12 each admission period. 90% of applicants accepted. 70% receive financial aid. 10% enrolled part-time. S:T ratio 12-15:1. 95% of graduates obtain jobs within 6 mos. Facilities: Bake shop, institutional foods, gourmet cooking, table-side cooking.

COURSES: Lab classes are a reflection of the industry. W.S.U.

FACULTY: 3 full-time, 5 part-time.

COSTS: Annual tuition in-state $48/credit hour, out-of-state $192/credit hour. Admission requirements: HS diploma or equivalent and admission test. Scholarships: yes. Loans: yes.

CONTACT: Debbie Van Camp, Food Service Director, South Puget Sound Community College, Food Service Technology, 2011 Mottman Rd., SW, Olympia, WA 98512; 360-754-7711 #5347, Fax 360-664-0780, admissions@spscc.ctc.edu, www.spscc.ctc.edu.

SOUTH SEATTLE COMMUNITY COLLEGE

Seattle/Year-round

Sponsor: 2-yr college. Program: 18-month certificate/AAS degrees in Culinary Arts/Food Service Production and Pastry/Specialty Baking. Established: 1975. Accredited by ACF, NASC. Calendar: quarter. Curriculum: culinary, core. Admit dates: Sept, Jan, Mar, June. Total enrollment: 130-160. 30-40 each admission period. 100% of applicants accepted. 25% receive financial aid. S:T ratio 15:1. 98% of graduates obtain jobs within 6 mos. Facilities: Include 4 kitchens, 6 classrooms & 2 waited-service dining rooms.

COURSES: Quantity, fine dining & casual food production; professional dining room service; hospitality supervision & management; pastry & specialty baking.

FACULTY: 7 full-time, 8 part-time. Qualifications: extensive industry experience.

COSTS: Annual tuition in-state $3,800. Off-campus housing $400-$500/mo. Scholarships: yes. Loans: yes.

CONTACT: Stephen Sparks, Instructor, South Seattle Community College, Hospitality & Food Science Div., 6000 16th Ave. S.W., Seattle, WA 98106-1499; 206-764-5344, Fax 206-768-6728, ssparks@sccd.ctc.edu, www.chefschool.com.

SPOKANE COMMUNITY COLLEGE

Spokane/September-June

Sponsor: 2-yr college. Program: 2-year AAS degree in Culinary Arts, 2-year AAS degree and 1-year certificate in Commercial Baking. Established: 1962. Accredited by NASC, ACF. Calendar: quarter. Curriculum: culinary, core. Admit dates: Sept, Jan, Mar. Total enrollment: 60-65 culinary, 20-30 baking. 20 culinary, 12 baking each admission period. 95% of applicants accepted. 50% receive financial aid. S:T ratio 15:1. 85% of graduates obtain jobs within 6 mos. Facilities: Include 2 kitchens, bakeshop, pastry shop, 6 classrooms, restaurant.

COURSES: Fine dining education in all areas of food preparation, including pastries & dining room service. Baking: breads, cakes, donuts, cookies, quick breads. Externship: Culinary: 250 hours required, Baking: 99 hours required.

FACULTY: Chef Douglas A. Fisher, CEC, CCE, Chef Peter Tobin, CEC, CCE, Greg Richards, Chef Robert Lombardi, CEC, CEPC, CCE, Charlie Martin, Duane Sunwold, Harryanto Wibisono.

COSTS: $627/qtr resident, $759/qtr nonresident US citizen. Knife kit $220, chef uniform set $225, miscellaneous lab fees & books. Admission requirements: HS diploma or equivalent and admission test. Scholarships: yes. Loans: yes.

CONTACT: Doug Fisher, Program Coordinator, Spokane Community College, Culinary Arts, 1810 N. Greene St., Spokane, WA 99217-5399; 509-533-7283, Fax 509-533-8108, dfisher@scc.spokane.edu, www.scc.spokane.edu/go/cularts. Commercial Baking: Marcel Kopplin, Lab Tech, 509-533-8685, SCCBakery@scc.spokane.edu.

WEST VIRGINIA

SHEPHERD COMMUNITY COLLEGE
Shepherdstown/Year-round

Sponsor: 2-yr college. Program: 2-yr AAS in Culinary Arts. Calendar: semester. Curriculum: core.

COSTS: Annual tuition is $2,228 in-state, $5,348 out-of-state. Room and board is $4,139/yr.

CONTACT: Judy Stains, Shepherd Community College, 315 West Stephen Street, Martinsburg, WV 25401; 304-754-7925, Fax 304-754-7933, jstains@shepherd.edu, www.shepherd.edu.

WEST VIRGINIA NORTHERN COMMUNITY COLLEGE
Wheeling/August-May

Sponsor: 2-yr state community college. Program: 1-yr certificate, 2-yr AAS degree in Culinary Arts. Established: 1975. Accredited by NCA, ACF. Calendar: semester. Curriculum: culinary, core. Admit dates: Open. Total enrollment: 45. 20 each admission period. 100% of applicants accepted. 75% receive financial aid. 15% enrolled part-time. S:T ratio 12:1. 95% of graduates obtain jobs within 6 mos. Facilities: Modern.

COURSES: Basics, hands-on. 1st & 2nd level; line cooking; 500 hours in industry. Sanitation, personnel mgmt, marketing, pastries.

FACULTY: 2 full-time, 3 part-time.

COSTS: Tuition in-state $1,500/yr, out-of-state $2,039/yr + books. Admission requirements: HS diploma or equivalent & admission test. Scholarships: yes. Loans: yes.

CONTACT: Marian Grubor, Program Director, West Virginia Northern Community College, 1704 Market Street, Wheeling, WV 26003; 304-233-5900, Fax 304-233-5837, mgrubor@northern.wvnet.edu, www.northern.wvnet.edu.

WISCONSIN

ACF CHEFS OF MILWAUKEE, INC.
Milwaukee/Year-round

Sponsor: ACF chapter. Program: 3-yr apprenticeship; degree program through Milwaukee Area Technical College or Waukesha County Technical College is completed by 60%. Established: 1980. Accredited by ACF. Calendar: semester. Curriculum: culinary. Total enrollment: 38. 12-15 each admission period. S:T ratio 10:1. 100% of graduates obtain jobs within 6 mos.

COURSES: ACF-approved apprenticeship accredited by Wisconsin State Apprenticeship Bureau.

FACULTY: 16 instructors.

COSTS: $2,200. Beginning salary is $6-$7/hr with 5%-10% increases every 6 mos. Admission requirements: HS or equivalent. Scholarships: yes.

LOCATION: 48 locations are restaurant, hotel, private club, country club, caterer. Most desirable settings are restaurant, hotel, country club.

CONTACT: Greg Abbate, President, ACF/Chefs of Milwaukee, PO Box 0894, Germantown, WI 53022; 414-353-8800 x16, Fax 414-353-5905, chefbrynwood@aol.com, www.acfchefs.org/chapter/wi012.html.

BLACKHAWK TECHNICAL COLLEGE
Janesville/Year-round

Sponsor: College. Program: 1-yr/34 credit-hr certificate and 2-yr/68 credit-hr AS degree in Culinary Arts. Established: 1972. Accredited by ACF. Calendar: semester. Admit dates: Aug, Jan. Total enrollment: 32. 16 each admission period. 43% receive financial aid. 25% enrolled part-time. S:T ratio 8:1. 98% of graduates obtain jobs within 6 mos. Facilities: Modern, well-equipped facility, student-run gourmet restaurant.

COURSES: Training by area professionals. Externships are provided.

FACULTY: 1 full-time, 4 part-time.

COSTS: $4,450/yr in-state plus books and uniforms. Scholarships: yes. Loans: yes.

LOCATION: South-central Wisconsin.

CONTACT: Joe Wollinger, CEC, CCE, Program Coordinator, Blackhawk Technical College, 6004 Prairie Rd., P.O. Box 5009, Janesville, WI 53547; 608-757-7696, Fax 608-743-4407, jwolling@blackhawk.tec.wi.us, www.blackhawk.edu.

FOX VALLEY TECHNICAL COLLEGE
Appleton/Year-round

Sponsor: 2-yr college. Program: 2-yr associate degree in Culinary Arts. Accredited by NACS, ACF.

COSTS: $1,300/semester, $80/credit.

CONTACT: Jeffrey Igel, Dept. Chair, Fox Valley Technical College, 1825 N. Bluemound Dr., Box 2277, Appleton, WI 54912; 920-735-5643, Fax 920-735-5655, chefjeff@foxvalleytech.com, www.fvtc.edu/tp2.asp?ID=Associate+Degrees&pix=017.

MADISON AREA TECHNICAL COLLEGE
Madison/August-May

Sponsor: Career college. Program: 2-yr AAS degree in Culinary Arts. Established: 1950. Accredited by ACF. Calendar: semester. Curriculum: core. Admit dates: Aug, Jan. Total enrollment: 60. 36 each admission period. 75% of applicants accepted. 50% receive financial aid. 20% enrolled part-time. S:T ratio 15:1. 100% of graduates obtain jobs within 6 mos. Facilities: Include 3 large labs & classrooms.

COURSES: Baking, sanitation, nutrition, gourmet foods, decorative foods, food costs and purchasing analysis, and general education. Limited courses available.

FACULTY: Qualifications: certified by state and ACF. Includes Joseph Gaglio, M. Egan, P. Short.

COSTS: Tuition in-state $59.25/credit hour. Advanced registration fee is $50. Application fee $25. Average off-campus housing cost is $400-$870. Admission requirements: HS diploma or equivalent and assessment test. Scholarships: yes. Loans: yes.

CONTACT: Mary G. Hill, Associate Dean, Madison Area Technical College, Culinary Trades Dept., 3550 Anderson St., Madison, WI 53704; 608-243-4455, Fax 608-246-6316, mhill@madison.tec.wi.us, www.madison.tec.wi.us/matc.

MILWAUKEE AREA TECHNICAL COLLEGE
Milwaukee/August-May

Sponsor: 2-yr public technical college. Program: 2-yr (67-cr, 4-sem) AAS degree; 3-yr culinary apprenticeship. Established: 1955. Accredited by ACF, NCA. Calendar: semester. Curriculum: culinary, core. Admit dates: Aug, Jan. Total enrollment: 120. 40 each admission period. S:T ratio 18:1. 98% of graduates obtain jobs within 6 mos. Facilities: 6 labs for hands-on learning, including dining room service & baking, & industry-standard demo kitchen.

COURSES: Focus is on preparing students for entry level foodservice positions. Quarterly hands-on lab course, culinary mgmt, general ed courses. 216 hrs of field experience required for graduation.

FACULTY: 9 full-time instructors with 300+ yrs of combined culinary experience.

COSTS: $73/cr in-state; $586/cr out-of-state. Admission requirements: HS diploma or equivalent, admission test. Scholarships: yes. Loans: yes.

CONTACT: Patricia Whalen, Instructional Chair, Hospitality Programs, Milwaukee Area Technical College, 700 W. State St., Milwaukee, WI 53233; 414-297-7897, Fax 414-297-7990, whalenp@matc.edu, www.matc.edu/utility/clas/prog/food/culi.htm.

MORAINE PARK TECHNICAL COLLEGE

Fond du Lac/Year-round

Sponsor: 2-yr Technical College. Program: 2-yr associate degree in Culinary Arts, 1-yr technical diploma in Food Service Production, certificates in Culinary Basics, Deli/bakery, Food Production, School Food Service. Established: 1980. Accredited by NCA, ACF. Calendar: semester. Curriculum: core. Admit dates: July-Aug, Nov-Dec, flexible. Total enrollment: 63. 24 each admission period. 90% of applicants accepted. 40% receive financial aid. 30% enrolled part-time. S:T ratio 12:1. 95% of graduates obtain jobs within 6 mos. Facilities: Include 3 kitchens, 2 classrooms.

COURSES: Food Production, Sanitation, Meat Analysis, Restaurant Mgmt & Operations, Catering, Baking, Menu Design, Nutrition, Purchasing, Ethnic Cookery, general ed courses. School food service, deli-bakery, IDDA certification.

FACULTY: 3 full-time including Ron Speich, David Weber, James Simmers.

COSTS: $5,755/yr degree, $3,004 diploma, $2,548 certificate, $684 Culinary Basics, $1,840 Food Production, $1,126 Deli/bakery, $718 School Food Service. Admission requirements: HS diploma, placement test, & interview. Scholarships: yes. Loans: yes.

CONTACT: Patricia Olson, Moraine Park Technical College, 235 N. National Ave., PO Box 1940, Fond du Lac, WI 54936-1940; 920-924-3333, polson@morainepark.edu, www.morainepark.edu.

NICOLET AREA TECHNICAL COLLEGE

Rhinelander/August-May

Sponsor: Career college. Program: 1-year diploma in Food Service Production, 2-year associate degree in Culinary Arts, certificate in Baking, Catering, Kitchen Assistant, Food Service Management, School Food Service Assistant. Accredited by NCA. Calendar: semester. Curriculum: core. Admit dates: Fall/August, Winter/January. Total enrollment: 15/program. 15 each admission period. 85% receive financial aid. 10% enrolled part-time. S:T ratio 10:1. 90% of graduates obtain jobs within 6 mos. Facilities: Fully-equipped kitchen laboratory, restaurant dining room and classrooms.

COURSES: Culinary fundamentals for restaurant and institutional cooking plus advanced courses in professional cuisine, catering, baking. Internships encouraged in summer between 1st and 2nd year. Sanitation certification and recertification for the state of Wisconsin.

FACULTY: Includes Linda Arndt, BS, MS, trained in culinary arts at La Varenne, Paris; Vicki Mendham, Whitehead, BS.

COSTS: Off-campus housing is available, cost varies. Admission requirements: HS diploma or equivalent, basic competency scores on Acuplacer. Scholarships: yes. Loans: yes..

CONTACT: Linda Arndt, Culinary Instructor, Nicolet Area Technical College, Culinary Arts, P.O. Box 518, Rhinelander, WI 54501; 715-365-4649, Fax 715-365-4596, larndt@nicolet.tec.wi.us, www.nicolet.tec.wi.us.

SOUTHWEST WISCONSIN TECHNICAL COLLEGE

Fennimore/Year-round

Sponsor: Public 2-yr college. Program: 2-yr associate degree in Culinary Mgmt. Established: 1994. Accredited by NCA, DMA. Calendar: semester. Curriculum: culinary. Admit dates: Aug. Total enrollment: 20. 20 each admission period. 100% of applicants accepted. 80% receive financial aid. 20% enrolled part-time. S:T ratio 10:1. 100% of graduates obtain jobs within 6 mos. Facilities: Food production kitchen, bake shop, computer lab, gourmet dining room, learning resource center.

COURSES: Food prep & purchasing, baking, buffet, garde manger, intl cuisine, nutrition, menu & facilities design, management of production service & staff, cost control. Management internships.

FACULTY: 2 full-time: Jeff Dombeck & Karen Bast.

COSTS: $6,100/degree, $84.60/credit part-time. Application fee $30. Admission requirements:

Application, application fee, transcripts, testing, interview, physical exam 6 wks prior to admission. Scholarships: yes. Loans: yes.

CONTACT: Kathy Kruel, Admissions Registration, Southwest Wisconsin Technical College, 1800 Bronson Blvd., Culinary Management, Fennimore, WI 53809; 608-822-3262 x2355, Fax 608-822-6019, kkreul@southwest.tec.wi.us, www.southwest.tec.wi.us.

WAUKESHA COUNTY TECHNICAL COLLEGE

Pewaukee/August-May

Sponsor: Technical college. Program: 1-yr diploma in Culinary Arts, 2-yr AAS degree in Culinary Management, Baking Certificate. Established: 1971. Accredited by NCA, ACF. Curriculum: core. Admit dates: Aug, Jan. Total enrollment: 80. 50-60 each admission period. 60% enrolled part-time. S:T ratio 12:1. 95% of graduates obtain jobs within 6 mos. Facilities: Includes 2 kitchens, 1 demo kitchen, 4 classrooms, beverage & restaurant lab, computer lab.

COURSES: Technical culinary arts training & principles of business mgmt. 1-sem internship, working under certified ACF chef. Sanitation certification & recertification, responsible beverage service, mixology, wine classes, cooking demos.

FACULTY: 4 full-time, 5 part-time, all with college degrees & industry experience. Includes James Holden, CEC, CCE, Keith Owsiany, Michael Leitzke, CEC, William Griesemer, CHA.

COSTS: Tuition in-state $70/cr-hr, cutlery $307, uniform $70 purchase + $80 rental/sem. Scholarships: yes. Loans: yes.

CONTACT: Timothy J. Graham, Associate Dean, Waukesha County Technical College, Hospitality & Culinary Arts Department, 800 Main St., Pewaukee, WI 53072; 262-691-5322, Fax 262-691-5155, tgraham@wctc.edu, www.wctc.edu.

ARGENTINA

THE BUE TRAINERS

Buenos Aires/March-December

Sponsor: Private culinary training center. Program: 2-part, 3-yr culinary training program. Degree as Commis de Cuisine after 2nd yr, degree as Chef de Partie after 3rd yr. Established: 1987. Accredited by Dept of Culture & Education of the state of Buenos Aires. Curriculum: culinary, core. Admit dates: March &/or August for semesters. Total enrollment: 300 max. 100 each admission period. 100% of applicants accepted. S:T ratio 17:1. 75% of graduates obtain jobs within 6 mos. Facilities: Auditorium for demos, 3 fully-equipped classrooms, computer classroom, 2 professional kitchens, 60-seat dining room, library.

COURSES: 3-yr chef apprenticeship: culinary skills, industrial training, Spanish, food science, cost analysis, French culinary terminology, computer science, budgeting, nutrition. Compulsory externships, employment dept. Post graduate courses with top European chefs.

FACULTY: 20 instructors including 4 fully-qualified chefs.

COSTS: $400 enrollment fee + $4,000/yr tuition including uniforms & meals on class days. Admission requirements: 16 yrs old, EGB degree (General Basic Ed), interview. Scholarships: yes. Loans: yes.

LOCATION: Buenos Aires, beside the International Airport of Ezeiza, 35 km from the city center.

CONTACT: María Cecilia García, Secretary, The BUE Trainers, Avda. Tte. Gral. Morillas s/n, Aeropuerto Intenacional de Ezeiza, Buenos Aires, B1802EZE Argentina; (54) 11 54 80 92 34, (54) 11 54 80 90 11, x250/1/2, Fax (54) 11 54 80 92 34, buetrain@gategourmet.com.ar, www.thebuetrainers.com.

COLEGIO DE COCINEROS GATO DUMAS

Buenos Aires/Year-round

Sponsor: Private professional culinary arts school. Program: 2-year degree in Cuisine & Pastry. 2-month short courses in Pastry, Wine, Bakery, Sushi, Beverages. Established: 1998. Accredited by Education Secretarie from Gouberment of Buenos Aires. Curriculum: core. Admit dates: Year-round. Total enrollment: 800. 100% of applicants accepted. S:T ratio 32:1. 100% of graduates obtain jobs within 6 mos. Facilities: 2 professional kitchens with modern equipment, conference room, 2 pastry/oenology rooms.

Courses: Cook Degree, Pastry, Barman, Sushi, Bakery, Cooking for Amateurs. Students may apply for an externship at Ritz Escoffier in Paris & Berasategui Group in Spain. Post-graduate courses with professionals.

Faculty: 20 instructors, 3 from Europe.

Costs: 2-yr course $1,750. Admission requirements: 17 yrs of age. Scholarships: yes. Loans: yes.

Location: Belgrano quarter of Capital Federal.

Contact: Student Department, Colegio de Cocineros Gato Dumas, Olazabal 2836, Boulevard Oroño 355 - Rosario, Provincia de Santa Fe, Buenos Aires, C1428DGS Argentina; (54) 11 4783-3357/1337, Fax (54) 11 4783-1197 x26, info@gatodumas.com, www.gatodumas.com.

INSTITUTO DE GASTRONOMIA PROFESIONAL MAUSI SEBESS

Buenos Aires/Year-round

Sponsor: Private professional culinary arts institute. Program: Occupational studies degree program in Cuisine & Pastry. 1-wk (45 hrs) basic, intermediate & advanced courses in cuisine & pastry for foreigners leading to a professional degree. 5-mo courses for residents. Established: 1994. Accredited by Buenos Aires Ministry of Education. Calendar: quinmester. Curriculum: culinary. Admit dates: Jan-Feb for foreigners. Mar & July for residents. Total enrollment: 780. 780 each admission period. 100% of applicants accepted. S:T ratio 10:1. 100% of graduates obtain jobs within 6 mos. Facilities: 4 professional kitchens with latest equipment; pastry lab.

Courses: 3-yr chef apprenticeship: culinary skills, sanitation, operations & events mgmt, F&B marketing, nutrition, oenology. Continuing ed: 26 courses year-round & 2 yearly 1-wk intensives with top chefs.

Faculty: 12 full-time instructors graduated in France, Spain, Italy, U.S. & Thailand.

Costs: $600-$700/course. Lodging ~$120/wk, week-end meals not included. Admission requirements: 16+ yrs old & min 8 yrs schooling.

Contact: Mariana Sebess, Executive Chef, Instituto de Gastronomia Profesional Mausi Sebess, Av. Maipù 594/6. Vicente Lopez 1638., Buenos Aires, 1638 Argentina; (54) 11-4791-4355, (54) 11-4796-5681, Fax (54) 11-4791-9132, mausisebess@hotmail.com, www.mausisebess.com. Mr. Pedro Sebess (CEO) sebess@ssdnet.com.ar.

AUSTRALIA

AUSTRALIAN SCHOOL OF TOURISM AND HOTEL MANAGEMENT

Perth/Year-round

Sponsor: Private Hotel Management & Culinary Arts School. Program: 1-yr certificate III in Hospitality (Commercial Cookery). Established: 1989. Accredited by Training Accreditation Council, Australian Hospitality Review Panel. Calendar: semester. Curriculum: culinary. Admit dates: Feb, Apr, July, Oct. Total enrollment: 240. 60 each admission period. 98% of applicants accepted. S:T ratio 16:1. 95% of graduates obtain jobs within 6 mos. Facilities: 10 lecture rooms, information technology center, 2 commercially equipped kitchens, library/reference center, student cafe.

Courses: Unit based & designed for students who wish to gain an apprenticeship or qualify for a trade cooking certificate. Compulsory industry work placement during studies. Diplomas of Hospitality Management, Bachelor of Business in Hotel and Catering Management.

Faculty: 15 full time, 18 part time.

Costs: A$8,800/1-yr program, A$200 enrollment fee, ~A$1,132 supplies & insurance. Admission requirements: Age 17 min, Australian HS or equivalent, yr 10, upper intermediate English level.

Contact: Dianne Leslie, Director of International Admissions, Australian School of Tourism and Hotel Management, 641 Wellington St., Perth, 6000 Australia; (618) 9322 3202, Fax (618) 9321 3698, info@asthm.com.au, www.asthm.com.au.

CANBERRA INSTITUTE OF TECHNOLOGY

Canberra City/Year-round

Sponsor: Career institute. Program: 6-month certificate, 3-year diploma & 3-year part-time trade certificate. Established: 1992. Calendar: semester. Curriculum: culinary, core. Admit dates: Feb, July. Total enrollment: 450. 75 each admission period. 50% of applicants accepted. 50% enrolled part-time. S:T ratio 15:1. 100% of graduates obtain jobs within 6 mos. Facilities: 6 kitchens, 4 restaurants, computer lab, butchery, bakery, bars.

FACULTY: 30 full-time, 50 part-time. Qualifications: industry and educational.

CONTACT: John Wardrop, Head, Culinary Skills, Canberra Institute of Technology, School of Tourism & Hospitality, P.O. Box 826, Canberra City, 2601 Australia; (61) 2-62073184, Fax (61) 2-62073209, john.wardrop@cit.act.edu.au, www.cit.act.edu.au. Additional contact: Gordon McDonald.

CHISHOLM INSTITUTE OF TECHNICAL & FURTHER EDUCATION

Dandenong/Year-round

Sponsor: Institute. Program: 8-wk certificate I, 20-wk certificate II, 3-yr certificate III. Established: 1986. Calendar: semester. Curriculum: culinary, core. Admit dates: Feb, July. Total enrollment: 250. 40 each admission period. 80% of applicants accepted. 75% enrolled part-time. S:T ratio 15-20:1. 100% of graduates obtain jobs within 6 mos. Facilities: 4 kitchens.

COURSES: Cookery, management & short courses.

FACULTY: 25 full-time, 15 part-time.

COSTS: A$500 in-state, A$7,000 out-of-state. Admission requirements: Apprentice cook to undertake Certificate III,Certificate I & II interview & short test.

CONTACT: Centre Manager, Chisholm Institute of Technical and Further Education, School of Hospitality & Tourism, PO Box 684, Dandenong, Victoria, 3175 Australia; (61) (0)3-9212-5410, Fax (61) (0)3-9212-5459, hospitality@chisholm.vic.edu.au, www.chisholm.vic.edu.au.

LE CORDON BLEU – AUSTRALIA

Adelaide/Year-round

Sponsor: Private school offering advanced management & business studies for culinary graduates. Program: 2.5-yr BBA degree in International Restaurant & Catering Management, MBA degree in International Hotel & Restaurant Management, MA degree in Gastronomy for 1 yr additional course work. Established: 1998. Accredited by Australian Recognition Council (ARC) and La Fondation Le Cordon Bleu. Calendar: semester. Curriculum: core. Admit dates: January & July. Total enrollment: 300/yr. 150 each admission period. 98% of applicants accepted. S:T ratio 15:1. 100% of graduates obtain jobs within 6 mos. Facilities: New facilities include 3 training restaurants, 10 commercial cookery kitchens, 10 computer suites, industry-standard wine tasting rooms, food science labs, conference rooms, auditorums.

COURSES: Include business finance, sales & marketing, information technology and human resources pertaining to the hospitality & tourism industry. Two 6-mo internships in Australia & overseas.

COSTS: Freshman: Stage 1-5 (2.5 yrs) A$54,000. Holding previous qualifications in a recognized hospitality program: Stage 3-5 (1.5 yrs) A$36,000. Admission requirements: Freshman: age 18+, HS certificate, command of English, basic math, computer knowledge. Advanced placement: graduate of recognised institutions. Scholarships: yes.

CONTACT: Elizabeth Daniels, Public Relations, Le Cordon Bleu Australia, Days Road, Regency Park, Adelaide, SA, 5010 Australia; (61) 6 8348.3022, Fax (61) 8 8346.7202, australia@cordonbleu.edu, www.lecordonbleu.com.edu. Rodger Griffiths (General Mgr.), Lindon Price (Marketing Director).

LE CORDON BLEU – SYDNEY

Sydney/Year-round

Sponsor: Private school located on the campus of Northern Sydney Institute of TAFE, Ryde Campus. Program: 9-month program consisting of 10-wk courses in Basic, Intermediate & Superior levels of Cuisine & Patisserie leading to Le Cordon Bleu Grand Diplome for completion of all six courses. Established: 1996. Calendar: quarter. Curriculum: culinary, core. Admit dates: Jan, Apr, July, Oct. Total enrollment: 110. 50 each admission period. 98% of applicants accepted. S:T ratio 12:1. 99% of graduates obtain jobs within 6 mos. Facilities: Professionally-equipped kitchens, individual workspaces, demo kitchen with video.

COURSES: Principles, theory & techniques of classical French cuisine. Le Cordon Bleu Bachelor of Business degrees in Hotel & Resort Management, Restaurant & Catering Management or Convention & Event Management, each 2.5 year degrees with 12 mos industry experience.

FACULTY: School Director Lynley Houghton. Staff consists of French & Australian Master Chefs from international restaurants & fine hotels.

COSTS: Basic Cuisine A$7,500, Intermediate Cuisine A$7,700, Superior Cuisine A$9,500. Basic Patisserie A$7,500, Intermediate Patisserie A$7,700, Superior Patisserie A$8,500. Tool Kit A$1,005-A$1,300. Admission requirements: International students must be at least age 18. Overseas students are required to have achieved a minimum level of English fluency of IELTS 5.5.

LOCATION: 25 minutes from the Central Business District, in a suburb of Ryde.

CONTACT: Lynley Houghton, Course Director, Le Cordon Bleu Sydney Culinary Arts Institute, 250 Blaxland Rd, Ryde, Sydney, 2112 Australia; (61) 2-9448-6307, Fax (61) 2-9807-6541, australia@cordonbleu.edu, www.lecordonbleu.com.au. Liz Daniels (61) (8) 8348-3022, Marketing & Public Relations.

NORTHERN SYDNEY INSTITUTE – CROWS NEST COLLEGE

Sydney/February-November

Sponsor: State government. Program: 2-yr certificate level III (part time) in Asian cookery. Established: 1989. Calendar: semester. Curriculum: culinary. Admit dates: Jan, July. Total enrollment: 150. 50 each admission period. 90% of applicants accepted. 5% receive financial aid. 100% enrolled part-time. S:T ratio 15:1. 90% of graduates obtain jobs within 6 mos. Facilities: Include 2 kitchens, classrooms & dining room, coffee shop, computer labs, library, learning resource ctr.

COURSES: Apprenticeships & traineeships in Asian cookery. Industry-specific courses, fee-for-service customized programs.

FACULTY: 3 full-time, 3 part-time; trade qualifications & education degrees.

COSTS: A$350/yr. Admission requirements: Education certificate.

LOCATION: 5 km north of Sydney CBD.

CONTACT: Geoff Tyrrell, Asian Commercial Cookery, Northern Sydney Institute - Crows Nest College, Tourism & Hospitality, 149 West St., Crows Nest, Sydney, NSW, 2065 Australia; (61) (0)2-9448 4433, Fax (61) (0)2-9448 4408, geoff.tyrrell@tafensw.edu.au, www.tafensw.edu.au. chef_47@hotmail.com.

WILLIAM ANGLISS INSTITUTE

Melbourne/Year-round

Sponsor: Career institute specializing in the hospitality, travel & food industries. Program: Certificate program in Commercial Cookery, diploma & advanced diploma in Hospitality. Students can link to degree courses at Victorian universities. Established: 1940. Calendar: semester. Curriculum: core. Admit dates: Every 1 or 2 mos (commercial cookery), 3 times a yr (cookery), February & July (advanced course). Total enrollment: 4,000. varies each admission period. S:T ratio 15:1. 91% of graduates obtain jobs within 6 mos. Facilities: $25 million teaching facility with 4 well-equipped bakeries, 6 kitchens, 3 restaurants, bars, computer rooms, butchery & confectionery centers.

FACULTY: More than 100 full-time.

COSTS: Courses vary in cost depending on length. Admission requirements: Cookery open to all applicants over 18. Advanced course open to those who have completed an apprenticeship or secondary education.

CONTACT: William Angliss Institute Information Centre, 555 La Trobe St., P.O. Box 4052, Melbourne, 3000 Australia; (61) (0)3-96062111, Fax (61) (0)3-96701330, info@angliss.vic.edu.au, www.angliss.vic.edu.au.

CANADA

ALGONQUIN COLLEGE

Ottawa, ON/Year-round

Sponsor: College. Program: 2-yr diploma in Culinary Management, 1-yr certificate in Chef Training, 40-wk certificate in Baking Techniques,2-yr diploma in Hotel & Restaurant Mgmt. Established: 1960. Calendar: semester. Curriculum: culinary, core. Admit dates: Sept, Jan. Total enrollment: 650. 380 & 270 each admission period. 50% of applicants accepted. S:T ratio 15-20:1. 98% of graduates obtain jobs within 6 mos. Facilities: Include 2 production kitchens, 3 demo labs.

COURSES: Baking, menu planning, food demo & applications, institutional cooking, food & beverage control, mgmt & computer applications. Continuing ed: cake decorating, bread baking, Italian regional cooking, 20 courses in regional & intl cuisine.

FACULTY: 7 full-time, 12 part-time. Includes Philippe Dubout, Mike Durrer, Serge Desforges, Alain Peyrun-Berron, Steve Price, Alan Fleming, Mario Ramsay.

COSTS: Annual tuition in-state C$1,600/sem, out-of-state C$5,800/sem. Books, uniforms: C$1,200. Admission requirements: Secondary school diploma or 19 yrs of age. Scholarships: yes. Loans: yes.

CONTACT: Michael Durrer, Coordinator, Cook/Culinary Programs, Algonquin College, Admissions Office, 1385 Woodroffe Ave., Ottawa, ON, K2G 1V8 Canada; 613-727-4723 Ext 5223, Fax 613-727-7670, durrerm@algonquincollege.com, www.algonquincollege.com.

CANADORE COLLEGE OF APPLIED ARTS & TECHNOLOGY

North Bay, ON/September-April

Sponsor: College. Program: 2-yr diploma in Culinary Management, 3-yr diploma in Culinary Administration, 1-yr certificate in Chef Training. Established: 1984. Calendar: semester. Curriculum: culinary. Admit dates: September. Total enrollment: 64. 64 1st yr, 25 2nd yr, 25 3rd each admission period. 100% of applicants accepted. 75% receive financial aid. 10% enrolled part-time. S:T ratio 22:1. 90-100% of graduates obtain jobs within 6 mos. Facilities: Include production & experimental kitchens with specialized equipment, 120-seat restaurant.

COURSES: Food prep, baking, sanitation, food & beverage mgmt, nutrition, intl & contemporary cuisines, wines, cost control, menu planning, quantity cooking, garde manger. Externship provided.

FACULTY: 12 full-time.

COSTS: In-state C$2,400/yr, foreign C$9,020/yr. Admission requirements: HS diploma or equivalent. Scholarships: yes. Loans: yes.

CONTACT: Daniel Esposito, Professor/Advisor, Canadore College, School of Hospitality & Tourism, 100 College Dr., P.O. Box 5001, North Bay, ON, P1B 8K9 Canada; 705-474-7600, Fax 705-494-7462, espositd@canadorec.on.ca, www.canadorec.on.ca.

COLLEGE OF THE ROCKIES

Cranbrook BC/September-June

Sponsor: 2-yr college. Program: 40-wk Professional Cook, Levels 1-2-3. Established: 1990. Admit dates: May, Sept, Jan. Facilities: Fully equipped training kitchen, classroom area, formal dining room.

COURSES: Vegetable, starch, meat, poultry, seafood cookery; stocks, soups, sauces; meat, poultry, seafood processing; cold kitchen; baking, desserts; food service, kitchen mgmt.; safety & sanitation.

CONTACT: Chris Wuthrich, Chef, College of the Rockies, 2700 College Way, Cranbrook, BC, V1C 5L7 Canada; 877-489-2687 x368, Fax 250-489-1790, info@cotr.bc.ca, www.cotr.bc.ca.

THE CULINARY ARTS SCHOOL OF ONTARIO

Mississauga, ON/Year-round

Sponsor: Private career college. Program: Cook Basic (Level I) & Cook Advance (Level II) diploma programs. Established: 2002. Curriculum: culinary. Admit dates: Continuous. 14/program each admission period. S:T ratio 14:1. Facilities: Professional learning environment with the latest equipment.

COURSES: Cook Basic: nutrition, kitchen mgmt, food theory, culinary techniques, baking, business development, sanitation. Cook Advance: Advanced kitchen mgmt, food theory, culinary & baking techniques, business development. Voluntary internship available. Red Seal Preparation certificate.

COSTS: $4,990/basic, $4,990/advance. Scholarships: yes. Loans: yes.

CONTACT: Michelle Watt, Student Services, The Culinary Arts School of Ontario, 95 Dundas St. West, 3rd Floor, Mississauga, ON, L5B 1H7 Canada; 905-273-5588, Fax 905-273-5589, info@chef-school.ca, www.chefschool.ca.

CULINARY INSTITUTE OF CANADA

Charlottetown, PEI/Year-round *(See display ad above)*

Sponsor: 2-yr career school, an institute of Holland College. Program: 80-wk diploma in Culinary Arts, 40-wk certificate in Pastry Arts. Established: 1983. Calendar: trimester. Curriculum: culinary, core. Admit dates: Sept, Mar. Total enrollment: 200. 80 Sept, 30 March each admission period. 60% of applicants accepted. 70% receive financial aid. 5% enrolled part-time. S:T ratio 16:1. 98% of graduates obtain jobs within 6 mos. Facilities: Include 7 training kitchens, 14 classrooms, 6 labs, 2 restaurants.

COURSES: 75% practical courses include Stocks, Soups & Sauces, Meat, Game & Poultry, Fish & Seafood, Baking, Cold Cuisine, International & Canadian Cuisine, Classical Cuisine, Menu Planning, Wine Appreciation. 16-week externship is included in the program. Short courses available.

FACULTY: 40 including 12 full-time chef Instructors with international experience.

COSTS: C$8,955 (US$8,500) per yr, off-campus housing ~C$500/mo. Admission requirements: HS diploma. Scholarships: yes.

CONTACT: David Harding, Culinary Programs Manager, Culinary Institute of Canada, 4 Sydney St., Charlottetown, PEI, C1A 1E9 Canada; 902-894-6805, 800-446-5265, Fax 902-894-6801, dharding@athi.pe.ca, www.hollandcollege.com/cic.

DUBRULLE INTERNATIONAL CULINARY & HOTEL INSTITUTE

Vancouver, BC/Year-round

Sponsor: Private school. Program: Full-time diploma: Bus. Mgmt. & Culinary Operations (2 yrs), Supervisory Devel & Applied Culinary/Pastry & Desserts (1 yr ea), Culinary/ Pastry & Desserts/Business Mgmt (4 mos ea), Breadmaking (13 wks). Part-time Culinary diploma (1 yr). Established: 1982. Accredited by Canadian Ed & Training Commission/Private Post-Secondary Ed Commission. Calendar: trimester. Curriculum: culinary. Admit dates: Jan, May, September. Total enrollment: 700. 225 each admission period. 90% of applicants accepted. S:T ratio 12:1. 100% of graduates obtain jobs within 6 mos. Facilities: 9,000-sq-ft facility, 5 classrooms, 6 teaching kitchens, student-operated dining facility.

COURSES: Emphasis on classic French techniques. 80% practical, 20% theory. Accreditation may be given towards the B.C. Apprenticeship program.

FACULTY: 14 credentialed full- & part-time, all with intl experience & competition awards.

COSTS: Culinary & Pastry programs C$7,650 each. Lodging assistance available. Admission requirements: Grade 10, 17 yrs of age. Scholarships: yes. Loans: yes.

CONTACT: Robert Sung, Director of Admissions, Dubrulle International Culinary & Hotel Institute of Canada, 1522 W. 8th Ave., Vancouver, BC, V6J 4R8 Canada; 604-738-3155/800-667-7288, Fax 604-738-3205, cooking@dubrulle.com, www.dubrulle.com.

GEORGE BROWN CHEF SCHOOL

Toronto, ON/Year-round

Sponsor: College. Program: 2-yr diploma in Culinary Mgmt, 1-yr certificates in Chef Training, Baking & Pastry Arts, and Advanced Pastry Arts Mgmt, 1-yr post-diploma in Italian Culinary Arts. Established: 1965. Calendar: semester. Curriculum: culinary, core. Admit dates: Sept, Jan. Total enrollment: 2,800 full-time, 3,500 part-time. 22% of applicants accepted. 50% receive financial aid. 10% enrolled part-time. S:T ratio 24:1. 95% of graduates obtain jobs within 6 mos. Facilities: 12 specialty cooking labs, mixology & wine labs, 120-seat in-house restaurant, demo labs, classrooms, bake shop, student lounge.

COURSES: Culinary Mgmt: food prep & presentation with theory, demos, preps for student-run restaurant. Baking & Pastry Arts: breads, pastries, cakes, decorating, plated desserts. 7-wks industry experience in hotels & restaurants for diploma candidates. 3,500 students in 40 different courses.

FACULTY: 40+ full-time internationally-trained chef & pastry professors, former hotel gen'l mgrs and food & beverage professionals.

COSTS: Resident (nonresident) tuition for diploma programs ~C$3,000 (C$10,000) for 2 semesters; certificates ~C$2,400-$3,000/program. Admission requirements: Min. for a diploma program is Ontario Secondary School Diploma or equivalent from within N. America. Scholarships: yes.

CONTACT: Christine Chamberlain, Chair, George Brown Chef School, George Brown College, 300 Adelaide St. E., P.O. Box 1015, Station B, Toronto, ON, M5T 2T9 Canada; 800-263-8995/416-415-5000 x2791, Fax 416-415-2834, cchamber@gbrownc.on.ca, www.gbrownc.on.ca/Marketing/FTCal/culinary-arts/index.html. www.ciaca.ca.

GEORGIAN COLLEGE OF APPLIED ARTS AND TECHNOLOGY

Barrie, ON/September-April

Sponsor: College. Program: 2-year diploma in Culinary Management. Established: 1988. Admit dates: Aug. Total enrollment: 85. 50 each admission period. 50% of applicants accepted. S:T ratio 24:1. 100% of graduates obtain jobs within 6 mos. Facilities: Include 1 large-quantity kitchen, 2 small-quantity kitchens, bake lab, classrooms, student-run restaurant.

COURSES: Bake theory/lab, menu planning, food/beverage control, creative cuisine.

FACULTY: 7 full-time, 1 to 2 part-time.

COSTS: Annual tuition in-country C$2,200, out-of-country C$10,000. Application fee C$50. On-campus housing: 252 spaces; average cost: C$405 per month. Average off-campus housing cost: C$400-C$800/mo. Admission requirements: HS diploma or equivalent.

CONTACT: Chris Cutler, Coordinator, Georgian College, Department of Hospitality & Tourism, One Georgian Dr., Barrie, ON, L4M 3X9 Canada; 705-728-1968 #1299, Fax 705-728-5123, ccutler@georgianc.on.ca, www.georcoll.on.ca.

HUMBER COLLEGE OF APPLIED ARTS & TECHNOLOGY

Etobicoke, ON/August-May

Sponsor: Career college. Program: 1-yr certificate, 2-yr diploma, 3-yr AS degree. All with integrated Industry Traineeship. Established: 1975. Calendar: semester. Curriculum: culinary. Admit dates: Sept, Jan. Total enrollment: 220. 220 each admission period. 35% of applicants accepted. 85% receive financial aid. 3% enrolled part-time. S:T ratio 20:1. 95% of graduates obtain jobs within 6 mos. Facilities: 4 culinary labs with the latest equipment, new Learning Catering Ctr with 120-seat dining room, bar/wine lab.

COURSES: Contemporary cuisine, including The Chefs Table, Charcutiere, Catering Production & Menu Management. Externship with leading industry chefs in Toronto & overseas. Canadian Fed'n of Chef de Cuisine certification. Chef Training certificate.

FACULTY: 5 full-time, 10 part-time.

COSTS: In-state C$1,530/yr, foreign C$9,600/yr + C$292 fees. Admission requirements: HS diploma or equivalent & admission test. Scholarships: yes. Loans: yes.

CONTACT: Mike Mcfadden, Coordinator-Culinary Programs Chairman, Humber College, HRT Alliance, Tourism Industries Training, T, 205 Humber College Blvd., Toronto, ON, M9W 5L7 Canada; 416-675-6622 x 4474, Fax 416-675-3062, mcfaddem@admin.humberc.on.ca, www.humberc.on.ca. http://www.hrtalliance.com or http://www.chefalliance.com.

LAMBTON COLLEGE

Sarnia, ON/August-April

Sponsor: College. Program: 2-yr cook apprenticeship program. Work in the industry and gain the theory and hands on application attending class two days per week. Established: 1967. Accredited by Ministry of Training, Colleges and Universities, Ontario. Calendar: semester. Curriculum: culinary. Admit dates: September. Total enrollment: 20. 35 each admission period. 75% of applicants accepted. 100% receive financial aid. S:T ratio 12:01. 100% of graduates obtain jobs within 6 mos. Facilities: Teaching kitchen, 35-seat restaurant, labs, classrooms, computer facilities.

COURSES: Focus on basics with emphasis on contemporary and international cuisine. Students must be working in the industry. General interest cooking and baking classes. Upgrading courses for cooks and chefs.

FACULTY: 1 full- & 5 part-time instructors, all certified chefs with both North American and European training.

COSTS: Books C$250, knives & baking tools C$250. Admission requirements: HS or mature student status (over 19 and out of school for a year). Scholarships: yes. Loans: yes.

CONTACT: Cindy Buchanan, Marketing Director, Lambton College, Culinary Programs, 1457 London Rd., Sarnia, ON, N7S 6K4 Canada; 519-542-7751 x3503, Fax 519-541-2418, info@lambton.on.ca, www.lambton.on.ca.

LE CORDON BLEU – OTTAWA

Ottawa, ON/Year-round *(See display ad page 173)*

Sponsor: Private vocational school. Program: 11-wk certificate courses in French cuisine & pastry at Basic, Intermediate, & Superior levels. 1-day to 1-mo drop-in sessions, specialized short programs, catering courses, evening classes, gourmet sessions. Established: 1988. Calendar: quarter. Curriculum: culinary. Admit dates: Jan, Mar, June, Oct. Total enrollment: 400-600. 100-150 each admission period. 95% of applicants accepted. S:T ratio 16:1 max. 85% of graduates obtain jobs within 6 mos. Facilities: Include demo room, fully equipped professional kitchens with individual workstations, specialized equipment, & observation restaurant for Superior level students.

COURSES: Basic, Intermediate, & Superior Cuisine; Basic, Intermediate, & Superior Pastry; Cuisine

Diploma; Pastry Diploma; Le Grand Diplôme de Cuisine et de Pâtisserie. Students may transfer credits to other Le Cordon Bleu schools. Specialized pastry & boulangerie courses, Art of Sugar, Intro to Catering, Vegetable/Fruit & Ice Carving, Marriage of Food & Wine.

FACULTY: Classically-trained professional master chefs, experienced in French culinary & pâtisserie techniques.

COSTS: Basic Cuisine C$6,095, Intermediate Cuisine C$6,602, Superior Cuisine C$7,125, Basic Pastry C$5,527, Intermediate Pastry C$6,095, Superior Pastry C$6,602. Admission requirements: Min 18 yrs old & HS diploma or equivalent. Scholarships: yes.

LOCATION: Embassy & University district of downtown Ottawa.

CONTACT: Andrea Smith, Registrar, Le Cordon Bleu Ottawa Culinary Arts Institute, 453 Laurier Ave. East, Ottawa, ON, K1N 6R4 Canada; 613-236-CHEF, Fax 613-236-2460, ottawa@cordonbleu.edu, www.lcbottawa.com.

LIAISON COLLEGE – CULINARY ARTS TRAINING

5 Ontario locations/Year-round

Sponsor: Private Post-secondary College. Program: 300-hr basic and/or advanced diploma in Culinary Arts. Part time recreational & baking programs. 100 hrs theory, 200 hrs practical, hands-on. Established: 1996. Accredited by Ontario's Ministry of Education & Training & Apprenticeship Board. Curriculum: culinary, core. Admit dates: Monthly. Total enrollment: 18 students/class. 15-18 each admission period. 90% of applicants accepted. 30% receive financial aid. 33% enrolled part-time. S:T ratio 18:1 max. 90% of graduates obtain jobs within 6 mos. Facilities: Latest equipment with work stations for each student.

COURSES: Include Sanitation & Safety, Basic Nutrition, Communications, Calculations, Kitchen Management, Food Theory, Bake Theory, Culinary Techniques, Techniques of Baking, Quantity Food Preparation. Voluntary co-op programs available. Graduates have option to refresh their skills at any time at no addtl cost. Professional workshops, memberships, seminars available.

FACULTY: Instructors meet the min standards that include teaching experience, 10+ yrs industry experience, professional designation.

COSTS: Cook Basic C$5,995, Cook Advanced C$5,995. Uniforms, equipment, textbook $695. Admission requirements: Grade 12 diploma, mature student, prior learning assessment. Scholarships: yes. Loans: yes.

LOCATION: 5 Ontario locations: Toronto, Hamilton, St. Catharines, Kingston & Kitchener.

CONTACT: Susanne Mikler, Admissions, Liaison College, P.O. Box 358, Campbellville, ON, L0P 1B0 Canada; 800-854-0621, 905-854-4600, Fax 905-854-4601, liaisonhq@liaisoncollege.com, www.liaisoncollege.com.

MALASPINA UNIVERSITY COLLEGE – CULINARY ARTS

Nanaimo, BC/Year-round

Sponsor: University college. Program: 12-month certificate program in Culinary Arts. Established: 1968. Calendar: semester. Curriculum: culinary. Admit dates: Jan, Mar, Aug, Oct. Total enrollment: 110. 18 each admission period. 95% of applicants accepted. 9% receive financial aid. S:T ratio 18:1. 100% of graduates obtain jobs within 6 mos. Facilities: New food lab & 2 kitchens.

COURSES: Include diet & nutrition, breakfast cookery, meat/poultry/seafood cutting & processing, vegetables/potato/starch cookery, food service & kitchen mgmt. 1 hr theory/6 hrs kitchen lab daily. 2-wk live-in practicum for B-average student at Pan Pacific Hotel, Chateau Whistler Resort. Apprenticeship training.

FACULTY: Chefs with experience in Canadian & European restaurants who have been awarded gold medals in national & international competitions.

COSTS: C$2,594 tuition, C$300 nonrefundable application fee, C$122 student fee, C$450 supplies. Admission requirements: Completion of 10th grade, age 17 minimum, interview, assessment test (most students have grade 12 or cooking experience). Scholarships: yes. Loans: yes.

LOCATION: Central Vancouver Island.

CONTACT: Alex Rennie, Coordinator, Malaspina University-College Culinary Arts Certificate Program, 900 Fifth St., Nanaimo, BC, V9R 5S5 Canada; 250-755-8777, Fax 250-741-2729, renniea@mala.bc.ca, www.mala.bc.ca.

McCALL'S SCHOOL OF CAKE DECORATION, INC.

Etobicoke, ON/September-May

Sponsor: Trade school. Program: Full-time certificate courses in baking, commercial cake decorating (10 days each), Swiss chocolate techniques (5 days), gum paste (3 days). Established: 1976. S:T ratio 10/class. Facilities: 1,000 sq ft of teaching space with overhead mirrors and two 20-seat classrooms.

FACULTY: Includes school director Nick McCall, and Kay Wong.

COSTS: Professional courses range from C$300-C$850.

LOCATION: A western subdivision of Toronto.

CONTACT: Nick McCall, President, McCall's School of Cake Decoration, Inc., 3810 Bloor St. West, Etobicoke, ON, M9B 6C2 Canada; 416-231-8040, Fax 416-231-9956, decorate@mccalls-cakes.com, www.mccalls-cakes.com.

NIAGARA CULINARY INSTITUTE

Niagara Falls, ON/September-June

Sponsor: Niagara College of Applied Arts & Technology. Program: Chef Training, Culinary Mgmt Co-op, Cook & Baker Apprenticeship, Hotel & Restaurant Mgmt Co-op. Established: 1989. Calendar: semester. Curriculum: culinary. Admit dates: Sept, Jan. Total enrollment: 96/Culinary Mgmt. 72 & 24 each admission period. 50% of applicants accepted. 60% receive financial aid. S:T ratio 24:1. 80% of graduates obtain jobs within 6 mos. Facilities: Bake shop, cafeteria, catering service, 7 classrooms, 2 computer labs, demo lab, food prod kitchen, learning resource centre, lecture theatre, public restaurant, student lounge, 3 teaching kitchens.

COURSES: Include baking, beverage mgmt, computer applications, cost control, convenience cookery, culinary French, food prep, purchasing, food service communication,intl cuisine, nutrition, patisserie, sanitation, wines & spirits. 5,000+ hrs work experience available in apprenticeship program. 400+ continuing ed courses.

FACULTY: Of 13 faculty members, 9 have received culinary certification, 7 are certified as Chef de Cuisine, 1 is an industry professional.

COSTS: C$2,600 for post-secondary, C$3,200 for post-graduate, C$8,900 for intl students. Addt'l material fees may apply. Housing ~C$400/mo. Admission requirements: Ontario Secondary School Diploma or equivalent. Scholarships: yes. Loans: yes.

CONTACT: Info Centre, Niagara College, 300 Woodlawn Rd., Welland, ON, L3C 7L3 Canada; 905-735-2211 x7559, Fax 905-736-6000, infocentre@niagarac.on.ca, www.niagarac.on.ca.

NIAGARA-ON-THE-LAKE CULINARY SCHOOL

Niagara-on-the-Lake, ON/Year-round

Sponsor: Private vocational school. Program: 2-year Chef Diploma program consisting of two 6-mo classroom training segments, & two 6-mo paid internship training modules. Curriculum: culinary. Facilities: 2,000-sq-ft purpose-built training & demo kitchen comprising a two-tiered gallery, 5 cooking stations & baking area. Facilities of 7 on-site restaurants, hotels & wineries.

COURSES: Emphasize a la carte & a la minute restaurant hot food production, garde manger, baking, pâtisserie. Selected students offered conditional paid internship with school's employer partners. 1- 3-day supervisory & mgmt training programs for chefs & hospitality professionals.

FACULTY: Executive, sous & pastry chefs in upscale food & beverage establishments.

COSTS: 1st yr program C$7,902 includes uniforms, knives; 2nd yr C$7,502. Loans: yes.

CONTACT: Geoffrey Bray-Cotton, President, Niagara-on-the-Lake Culinary School, 290 John St. East, R.R.#1, Niagara-on-the-Lake, ON, L0S 1J0 Canada;, Fax 905-684-2926, g.bc@sympatico.ca, http://notlculinaryschool.com.

NORTHERN ALBERTA INSTITUTE OF TECHNOLOGY – CULINARY ARTS

Edmonton, AB/September-April

Sponsor: Technical college. Program: 2-yr Culinary Arts diploma, Hospitality Mgmt diploma (continuing ed).5-mo Retail Meatcutting certificate, 1-yr certificate in Baking, Culinary Arts, Hospitality Supervision. Apprentice Cook, Baker. Established: 1963. Calendar: semester. Curriculum: culinary. Admit dates: September & January. Total enrollment: 168 Culin Arts, 24 Baking, 18 RMC. 42 Culin Arts each admission period. 50% of applicants accepted. 50% receive financial aid. S:T ratio 15:1. 85% of graduates obtain jobs within 6 mos. Facilities: 9 commerical kitchens, retail meat cutting lab, commercial bakery, common market, dining room.

Courses: Cold buffet, dining room & intl cuisine, patisserie, gastronomy, meat portioning, desserts, service standards, cost control, sanitation. Practicum component in all programs. Includes Hospitality Mgmt, Culinary Skills, Baking & Pastry, Mixology, Cooking Organically, Intl Sommelier Guild, Meatcutting, Food & Nutrition Mgmt.

Costs: Culinary Arts or Baking ~$3,050/yr (two 16-wk semesters), Meat Cutting ~$1,600. Books/supplies ~$700-$1,200, fees $133. Admission requirements: Transcript, resume, career investigation. Scholarships: yes. Loans: yes.

Contact: Sheila Ouellet, Administrative Support, Northern Alberta Institute of Technology Culinary Arts, 11762 106 St., Edmonton, AB, T5G 2R1 Canada; 780-471-7655, Fax 780-471-8914, webmaster@nait.ab.ca, www.nait.ab.ca/schools/hospitality/default.htm. Continuing ed: 780-471-6248.

PACIFIC INSTITUTE OF CULINARY ARTS

Vancouver/Year-round

Sponsor: Private school. Program: 2 full-time programs: Culinary Arts and Baking & Pastry Arts (each 6 mos). Established: 1996. Accredited by Private Post-Secondary Education Commission of British Columbia. Calendar: trimester. Curriculum: culinary. Admit dates: Jan, Apr, July, September. Total enrollment: 174/yr. 12 each admission period. 90% of applicants accepted. 10% receive financial aid. S:T ratio 9-12:1. 90% of graduates obtain jobs within 6 mos. Facilities: 8 commercial training kitchens, on-site white linen teaching restaurant & bakeshop.

Courses: French & intl cuisines, baking, breads, pastries. First 3 mos of 6-mo programs cover basics, last 3 mos consist of training in the Institute's restaurant & bakeshop, including participation in catering & wedding cake services. 1-wk practicum.

Faculty: 10 full-time chef instructors, all with international experience; 2 restaurant instructors.

Costs: C$11,000 for each 6-mo program.Lodging assistance provided, ranges from C$400-C$1,000/mo. Admission requirements: HS diploma or equivalent. Scholarships: yes. Loans: yes.

Location: City of Vancouver, at entrance to Granville Island Market.

Contact: Sue Singer, Director of Admissions, Pacific Institute of Culinary Arts, 1505 W. 2nd Ave., Vancouver, BC, V6H 3Y4 Canada; 604-734-4488, 800-416-4040, Fax 604-734-4408, info@picachef.com, www.picachef.com.

RED RIVER COLLEGE

Winnipeg, Manitoba/Year-round

Sponsor: 2-yr college. Program: 1-yr certificate & 2-yr diploma programs in Culinary Arts consisting of seven 3-mo terms: 5 on campus & 2 off-campus cooperative education work experience in hotels, restaurants, or private clubs. Established: 1997. Calendar: trimester. Curriculum: culinary. Admit dates: Sept, Mar. Total enrollment: 70. 35 each admission period. S:T ratio 15:1. 90% of graduates obtain jobs within 6 mos. Facilities: Prairie Lights Restaurant, a full-service open-to-the-public restaurant serving lunch & dinner + 5 other kitchen training labs.

Courses: Nutrition, food preparation, garde manger, patisserie, meat cutting, menu design, dining room service, business management, advanced cooking, communication, microcomputer productivity. Coop education: two 3-month terms. Theory courses.

Faculty: Dept. Chair David Rew & 9 instructors.

Costs: C$3,918 (C$1,070) first yr tuition (books/supplies), C$3,006 (C$850) second yr tuition (books/supplies). $35 application fee. Students have use of laptop computer during program. Admission requirements: Manitoba Senior 3 or equivalent secondary school prep or adult 11B. Scholarships: yes. Loans: yes.

LOCATION: A 160-acre site in Winnipeg near the International Airport.

CONTACT: David Rew, Chair, Hospitality Dept., Red River College, 2055 Notre Dame Ave., Rm. B185, Hospitality Dept., Winnipeg, MB, R3H 0J9 Canada; 204-632-2309/2285, Fax 204-633-3176, drew@rrc.mb.ca, www.rrc.mb.ca.

ST. CLAIR COLLEGE

Windsor, ON/September-April

Sponsor: College. Program: 4-semester diploma in Culinary Management, 2-semester certificate in Chef Training, 4-semester diploma in Hotel & Restaurant Mgmt. Established: 1993. Accredited by Province of Ontario. Calendar: semester. Curriculum: culinary, core. Admit dates: September. Total enrollment: 80. 60 each admission period. 75% of applicants accepted. 50% receive financial aid. 10% enrolled part-time. S:T ratio 18:1. 98% of graduates obtain jobs within 6 mos. Facilities: Include 2 kitchens, classrooms, student run restaurant & kiosk.

COURSES: Culinary arts, food preparation, culinary practice, hospitality marketing, nutrition & menu writing, garde manger, mgmt techniques. Externship: 16-week, 7 hrs/wk, in hotels & restaurants. Includes bartending, hotel sales mgmt, hospitality accounting, food & beverage controls.

FACULTY: 2 full-time chef instructors. All have C.C.C. designation.

COSTS: Annual tuition in-state C$2,090, out-of-state C$11,506.88. Admission requirements: HS diploma (OSSD) with grade 12 English & grade 10 math. Scholarships: yes. Loans: yes.

LOCATION: An urban setting, 2 hrs from London, Ontario. Across the river from Detroit, Michigan.

CONTACT: Rainer Schindler, St. Clair College, Hospitality & Media Dept., 2000 Talbot Rd. W., Windsor, ON, N9A 6S4 Canada; 519-972-2727 x4614, rschindler@stclaircollege.ca, www.stclaircollege.ca.

SOUTHERN ALBERTA INSTITUTE OF TECHNOLOGY

Calgary, AB/Year-round

Sponsor: Nonprofit institution. Program: 12-mo diploma in Professional Cooking, 8-mo certificate in Commercial Baking, 6-mo certificate in Retail Meat Cutting. Established: 1949. Calendar: semester. Curriculum: culinary. Admit dates: Sept, Jan, Mar, May. Total enrollment: ~500. 64 cooking/32 baking/15 meat each admission period. 50% of applicants accepted. 50% receive financial aid. 20% enrolled part-time. S:T ratio 15:1. Facilities: 1 test & 4 commercial kitchens, 2 commercial bakeries, 2 labs, 7 demo & 2 lecture classrooms, dining room, computer lab, ice plant.

COURSES: Include garde manger, patisserie, kitchen mgmt, fat & ice sculpting, breakfast & short order, technical writing, meat portioning, bar mixology, Pastry Chef, Food & Beverage Service.

FACULTY: 31 full-time, 14 part-time. Qualifications: Journeymans & Red Seal in Cooking, Chef de Cuisine certification, Master Baker.

COSTS: On-campus housing, 204 spaces, ~C$300/mo. Off-campus housing ~C$500-600/mo. Admission requirements: Transcript, resume, statement of career goals. Scholarships: yes. Loans: yes.

CONTACT: Allison Crowder, Southern Alberta Institute of Technology, Hospitality Careers, 1301 16th Ave. N.W., Calgary, AB, T2M 0L4 Canada; 403-284-8612, Fax 403-284-7034, allison.crowder@sait.ab.ca, www.sait.ab.ca.

STRATFORD CHEFS SCHOOL

Stratford/November-March

Sponsor: Nonprofit training school. Program: 2-semester full-time diploma. Established: 1983. Accredited by Province of Ontario. Calendar: semester. Curriculum: culinary. Admit dates: Nov. Total enrollment: 70. 35-40 each admission period. 25% of applicants accepted. S:T ratio 12:1. 100% of graduates obtain jobs within 6 mos.

COURSES: Gastronomy, nutrition, food styling, wine appreciation, kitchen mgmt, menu preparation, food costing. Second-year students research, prepare & serve theme menus in a restaurant setting.

FACULTY: 15 full-time. Founders/directors are restaurateurs Eleanor Kane & James Morris.

COSTS: Annual tuition C$6,550 (1st yr), C$5,850 (2nd yr) for Canadian citizens, C$12,500 out-of country. Off-campus housing ~C$300-C$400/mo.

CONTACT: Elisabeth Lorimer, Program Administrator, Stratford Chefs School, 68 Nile St., Stratford, ON, N5A 4C5 Canada; 519-271-1414, Fax 519-271-5679, elorimer@stratfordchef.on.ca, www.stratfordchefsschool.ca. Additional contact: Cindy Collins, ccollins@stratfordchef.on.ca.

UNIVERSITY COLLEGE OF THE CARIBOO
Kamloops, BC/September-May

Sponsor: 4-yr degree granting institution. Program: Certificate in Culinary Arts. 3 levels, 4 mos each. Established: 1972. Curriculum: culinary. Admit dates: Last wk of Aug, first wk of January. Total enrollment: 60. 20 each admission period. 80% of applicants accepted. 40% receive financial aid. S:T ratio 12:1. 80% of graduates obtain jobs within 6 mos. Facilities: Includes 4 kitchens (cafeteria, meatcutting lab, bakery, satellite kitchen), classrooms, public dining room.

COURSES: Include Safety, Sanitation, Vegetables & Starches, Meat & Poultry, Seafood, Stocks, Soups & Sauces, Meat, Poultry & Seafood Cutting & Processing, Cold Kitchen, Baking & Desserts. Mandatory practical work experience,160 hrs.

FACULTY: 7 full-time instructors totaling 171 yrs of experience: Ken Jakes, Kimberly Johnstone, Derrick Moffat, Peter Nielsen, Mark Perry, Franz Stieg, Kurt Zwingli.

COSTS: Canadian citizen C$690/sem, Intl students C$3,731/sem; tools & texts C$570, uniform deposit C$150. Off-campus housing ~C$400/mo. Admission requirements: HS diploma or equivalent. Scholarships: yes. Loans: yes.

CONTACT: Mark Perry, Chairperson, University College of the Cariboo, Food Training/Tourism, Box 3010, 900 McGill Rd., Kamloops, BC, V2C 5N3 Canada; 250-828-5357, Fax 250-371-5677, FTC@cariboo.bc.ca, www.cariboo.bc.ca/psd/foodtrai/foodho.htm.

CHINA

CHOPSTICKS COOKING CENTRE
Kowloon, Hong Kong/September-June

Sponsor: Private trade school. Program: 1-day to 12-wk programs, tailored for individuals & groups. Established: 1971. Calendar: quarter. Curriculum: culinary. Admit dates: Year-round. Total enrollment: 15/class max. 99% of applicants accepted. 60% enrolled part-time. S:T ratio 1-10:1. 90% of graduates obtain jobs within 6 mos. Facilities: Kitchen with full facilities for practical sessions.

COURSES: Chinese regional dishes, roasts, Asian Cuisine, dim sums, cakes & pastries, breads.

FACULTY: School principal Cecilia J. Au-Yang, domestic science graduate & author of a 40 cookbook series; Director Caroline Au-yeung, graduate of HCIMA; professional hotel & restaurant chefs.

COSTS: 1-wk course $1,500/person, 2nd-5th person less 25%; 4-wk course $3,000 basic, $4,000 intermediate; short courses & classes $50-$900. Local lodging ~$400-$600/wk.

CONTACT: Cecilia Au-Yang, Managing Director, Chopsticks Cooking Centre, 8A Soares Avenue, Ground Floor, Kowloon, Hong Kong, China; (852) 2336-8433, Fax (852) 2338-1462, cauyeung@netvigator.com.

ENGLAND

THE ASIAN AND ORIENTAL SCHOOL OF CATERING
Hackney/Year-round

Sponsor: Private school. Program: Short courses & full-time programs designed to address training & development issues within the catering industry. Aimed at the amateur, beginning entrepreneur or established business in the Asian & Oriental restaurant sector. Facilities: Modern facilities & a student-run restaurant/kitchen open to the public.

Courses: Full-time course for chef & restaurant employees; short courses in Thai, Chinese & Indian cooking; business development, food hygiene, health & safety, customer care, first aid, trainer training including coaching skills & group training.

Contact: The Asian and Oriental School of Catering, Hackney Community College, London, N1 6HQ England; (44) (0) 20 7613 9292, Fax (44) (0) 20 7613 9382, www.spice-train.com.

COOKERY AT THE GRANGE

Frome/May-March

Sponsor: Private school. Program: 4-week The Essential Cookery Course. Established: 1981. Curriculum: culinary. Admit dates: Rolling. Total enrollment: 192/yr. 14-24 each admission period. 100% of applicants accepted. S:T ratio 6:1. 90% of graduates obtain jobs within 6 mos. Facilities: 2 kitchens, cold kitchen, herb garden, game room, tennis court, satellite TV room.

Courses: Methods & principles of cookery with emphasis on classic techniques using fresh, natural ingredients & styles from around the world.

Faculty: Jane & William Averill (Grange-trained) & teaching staff.

Costs: £2,290-£2,690 includes meals & shared housing. Single room supp. £50/wk. There are both double & single bedrooms. Admission requirements: None.

Location: Converted farm buildings & gardens in rural England, 90 minutes from London by train.

Contact: Jane and William Averill, Cookery at The Grange, The Grange, Frome, Somerset, BA11 3JU England; (44) (0)1373-836579, Fax (44) (0)1373-836579, info@cookery-grange.co.uk, www.cookery-grange.co.uk.

CORDON VERT COOKERY SCHOOL

Altrincham/Year-round

Sponsor: The Vegetarian Society UK, a registered charity and membership organization. Program: Four 1-week Foundation courses leading to the Cordon Vert diploma, the 4-day Professional Certificate in Vegetarian Catering, a variety of weekend & day courses. Established: 1982. Curriculum: culinary. S:T ratio 12:1.

Courses: Basic and advanced techniques of vegetarian cookery, international cuisines, catering.

Faculty: Lyn Weller, Principal, and 10 part-time tutors.

Costs: Resident (non-resident) tuition is £450 (£350) for the 1-wk Foundation courses, £575 + VAT for the Catering course. Resident tuition includes full board & lodging in single en suite rooms.

Location: Ten miles south of Manchester.

Contact: Maureen Surgey, Cookery School Administrator, Cordon Vert Cookery School, The Vegetarian Society, Parkdale, Dunham Road, Altrincham, Cheshire, WA14 4QG England; (44) (0)161-925-2000, Fax (44) (0)161-926-9182, cordonvert@vegsoc.org, www.vegsoc.org/cordonvert.

LE CORDON BLEU – LONDON

London/Year-round

Sponsor: Private school acquired by Le Cordon Bleu Paris in 1990. Program: Standard 10 wk Classic Cycle Certificate courses in French Cuisine & Pâtisserie leading to the Grand Diplome. Intensive version also available. Established: 1933. Calendar: quarter. Curriculum: culinary. Admit dates: Jan, Feb, Mar, Apr, June, July, Aug, Sept, Oct. Total enrollment: 150/quarter. 120-150 each admission period. 100% of applicants accepted. 15% receive financial aid. 30% enrolled part-time. S:T ratio 10:1. 95% of graduates obtain jobs within 6 mos. Facilities: Professionally equipped kitchens; individual workspaces with refrigerated marble tops; demo rooms with video & tilted mirrors.

Courses: Classic Cycle consists of 3 cuisine & 3 patisserie courses, taken consecutively. Covers basic to complex technique, classic, ethnic & contemporary cuisines, planning, presentation, decoration & execution. Optional theory classes available. Students are assisted in finding an internship. Master Chef Catering Course with necessary prerequisites of Basic Cuisine & Patisserie.

Faculty: All staff full time. Chefs all professionally qualified with experience in Michelin-starred & fine quality culinary establishments. President is Andre Cointreau & School Director is Lesley Gray.

COSTS: £145-£395 for a short course. Classic Cycle Professional Diploma courses begin at £4,191 for Basic Cuisine, including uniform. Students are assisted in finding lodging. Scholarships: yes.

LOCATION: London's West End, near the underground stations of Bond & Baker Sts.

CONTACT: Natalia Whale, Enrolements Supervisor, Le Cordon Bleu, 114 Marylebone Lane, London, W1U 2HH England; 0800-980-3503(freephone within UK), (44) 20-7-935-3503, Fax (44) 20-7-935-7621, london@cordonbleu.edu, http://cordonbleu.edu. US toll-free: 800-457-CHEF.

LEITHS SCHOOL OF FOOD AND WINE

London/Year-round

Sponsor: Private school with a cooking agency. Program: 1-yr or 2-term diploma consisting of 2 or 3 consecutive 10- to 11-week Food & Wine certificate courses (Beginner, Intermediate, Advanced), foundation & beginner's cookery certification, certificate course in wine. Nonprofessional courses. Established: 1975. Admit dates: October or January (for diploma), Apr. Total enrollment: 96. 96 each admission period. 99% of applicants accepted. S:T ratio 8:1. 99% of graduates obtain jobs within 6 mos. Facilities: Include 3 kitchens, demo theatre, library, changing room.

COURSES: Basic cookery; butchery, exotic fish, catering; boned poultry, aspics, advanced patisserie, canapes, costing, menu planning, business skills.

FACULTY: 13 full-, 2 part-time. School founder & cookbook author Prue Leith is former Veuve Cliquot Business Woman of the Year. Managing Director is Caroline Waldegrave, vice-principal is Alison Cavaliero.

COSTS: From £4,800-£5,100/term; cost for all 3 is £12,600. Equipment fee £400. Prices include VAT. The school assists in obtaining lodging, which ranges from £80-£120/wk.

LOCATION: A refurbished Victorian building in Kensington, the center of London.

CONTACT: Judy Wilkinson, Registrar, Leiths School of Food and Wine, 21 St. Alban's Grove, London, W8 5BP England; (44) (0) 20-7229-0177, Fax (44) (0) 20-7937-5257, info@leiths.com, www.leiths.com.

THE MANOR SCHOOL OF FINE CUISINE

Widmerpool/Year-round

Sponsor: Proprietary institution. Program: 4-week Cordon Bleu certificate, 6-week Advanced Cordon Bleu certificate. Established: 1988. Curriculum: culinary. Admit dates: Rolling. Total enrollment: 12. 8 each admission period. 90% of applicants accepted. 5% receive financial aid. 60% enrolled part-time. S:T ratio 6:1. 100% of graduates obtain jobs within 6 mos. Facilities: Include 7 kitchens, lecture room, large dining room, cooking library, culinary video library.

COURSES: Include cuisine preparation, baking, basic nutrition, and menu planning.

FACULTY: Principal Claire Tuttey, Cordon Bleu Diploma, head chef of noted restaurants, member of Cookery & Food Association, Craft Guild of Chefs, Chefs & Cooks Circle.

COSTS: Resident (nonresident) tuition is £1,162.07 (£1,044.57). Residents are housed in The Manor. Recommendations provided for local lodging.

LOCATION: The Manor, a refurbished 17th century inn, is 9 miles from Nottingham City center and 1 hr from London's Kings Cross train station.

CONTACT: Claire Tuttey, The Manor School of Fine Cuisine, Old Melton Road, Widmerpool, Nottinghamshire, NG12 5QL England; (44) (0)1949-81371, Fax (44) (0)1949-81371.

MOSIMANN'S ACADEMY

London/Year-round

Sponsor: Private school. Program: 4-day certificate course (Anton Mosimann Food Experience) that covers all aspects of food & beverage production & the culinary arts. Established: 1996. Curriculum: culinary. S:T ratio 22-60:1. Facilities: Seminar & demo theater, library of Anton Mosimann's 6,000 cookery books.

COURSES: Anton Mosimann philosophy (Cuisine Naturelle) eschews the use of fats & alcohol. Menu planning, trends, financial mgmt, kitchen concepts, planning & technique, wine tasting,

Cuisine Naturelle, food presentation, winning strategies. Tailor-made corporate courses.

FACULTY: Academy chef & mgr Simon Boyle, assisted by 2 full- & 2 part-time staff. Anton Mosimann & guest chefs Shaun Hill, Brian Turner, Jean-Christophe Novelli & Jamie Oliver regularly appear.

COSTS: £1,200 + VAT/4-day course. Admission requirements: Background as professional chef advisable.

CONTACT: Elizabeth St. Clair George, Librarian, Mosimann's Academy, 5 William Blake House, The Lanterns, Bridge Lane, London, SW11 3AD England; (44) (0) 20 7326 8366, Fax (44) (0) 20 7326 8360, academy@mosimann.com, www.mosimann.com.

PAUL HEATHCOTE'S SCHOOL OF EXCELLENCE

Manchester/Year-round

Sponsor: Private school. Program: Apprenticeships, supervisory and management training to NVQ level 4. Established: 1997. Curriculum: culinary. Facilities: Professionally-equipped kitchen with 6 individual work spaces, demonstration auditorium with projector and screen.

FACULTY: Paul Heathcote, chef and owner of four restaurants, and his staff of instructors.

CONTACT: Administration Office, Paul Heathcote's School of Excellence, Jacksons Row, Deansgate, Manchester, M2 5WD England; (44) (0)161-839-5898, Fax (44) (0)161-839-5897, cookeryschool@heathcotes.co.uk, www.heathcotes.co.uk.

ROSIE DAVIES

Nunney/September-July

Sponsor: Culinary professional Rosie Davies. Program: 4-wk Basics Plus course for professionals, with emphasis on training for chalet or yacht chefs. Established: 1996. Curriculum: culinary. 4-5 each admission period. S:T ratio 5:1. Facilities: Farmhouse-style kitchen.

COURSES: Appetizers, soups, sauces, meat, fish, vegetables, vegetarian, ethnic foods, desserts, breads.

FACULTY: Rosie Davies trained at Oxford in Catering & Hotel Mgmt, is a freelance cookery writer/editor & has 20+ yrs teaching experience.

COSTS: £2,450/4-wk course includes meals & lodging at Penny's Mill, a 200-yr-old converted water mill.

CONTACT: Rosie Davies,, Penny's Mill, Nunney, Frome, Somerset, BA11 4NP England; (44) 1373-836210/836665, Fax (44) 1373-836018, rosiedavies@btconnect.com, www.rosiedavies.co.uk.

SQUIRES KITCHEN INTERNATIONAL SCHOOL

Farnham, Surrey/Year-round

Sponsor: Private school. Program: Part-time 1-week school certificate in sugarcraft & cake decorating. Established: 1987. Calendar: trimester. Curriculum: core. Admit dates: Rolling. 100% of applicants accepted. 100% enrolled part-time. S:T ratio 12:1/1:1. Facilities: Specialized kitchen.

COURSES: Include royal icing, sugarpaste, flowers, pastillage, chocolate, modelling.

FACULTY: 17 full- & part-time. Members of the British Sugarcraft Guild. Guest tutors include Eddie Spence, Alan Dunn, Tombi Peck.

COSTS: From £65/day.

LOCATION: Period building in a suburban area, a 2-min walk to train station, 45 min from London.

CONTACT: Course Coordinator, Squires Kitchen Intl. School of Sugarcraft & Cake Decorating, 3 Waverley Lane, Farnham, Surrey, GU9 8BB England; (44) (0)1252-731309, Fax (44) (0)1252-714714, school@squires-group.co.uk, www.squires-group.co.uk.

TANTE MARIE SCHOOL OF COOKERY

Surrey/September-July

Sponsor: Private school. Program: 36- or 24-wk Intensive Tante Marie Cordon Bleu diploma. 11-wk Certificate courses. 4-wk Essential Skills courses. 1-or 2-wk Beginners courses. Established: 1954. Accredited by British Accreditation Council. Calendar: trimester. Curriculum: culinary. Admit dates: Jan, Apr, September. Short courses throughout the year. Total enrollment: 84. 24-72 each admission period. 100% of applicants accepted. S:T ratio 12:1. 100% of graduates obtain jobs within 6 mos. Facilities: 5 modern teaching kitchens, a mirrored demo theatre, & a lecture room.

Courses: 36-wk course for beginners: three 12-wk terms of basic skills, labor-saving appliances, British cookery, French cuisine. Intensive 24-wk course for experienced cooks: practical & theoretical elements. 4-day wine seminar. Shorter courses suitable for gap year students.

Faculty: 12 full- & part-time, qualified to teach; many have held catering positions & all undergo teacher training. Well-known TV cookery demonstrators, a noted wine expert & local tradesmen.

Costs: 36-wk course £12,100, 24-wk course £9,000, 12-wk certificate course £4,250, 1-mo course £1,700. Uniform & equipment from £145. Admission requirements: English language intermediate. Scholarships: yes. Loans: yes.

Location: Turn-of-the-century country mansion, ~25 min by train from London.

Contact: Marcella O'Donovan, Principal, Tante Marie School of Cookery, Woodham House, Carlton Rd., Woking, Surrey, GU21 4HF England; (44) (0)1483-726957, Fax (44) (0)1483-724173, info@tantemarie.co.uk, www.tantemarie.co.uk.

THAMES VALLEY UNIVERSITY
Ealing-London/Year-round

Sponsor: University. Program: 3-yr NVQ Level 2 intl diploma in Culinary Arts, Level 3/4 BSC in Intl Culinary Arts. Established: 1992. Calendar: semester. Curriculum: culinary, core. Admit dates: September. Total enrollment: 400. 40 each admission period. 70% of applicants accepted. 10% receive financial aid. 70% enrolled part-time. S:T ratio 15:1. 100% of graduates obtain jobs within 6 mos. Facilities: Include 4 kitchens, demo kitchen, 2 science labs, 3 restaurants, computer lab.

Courses: International cuisine management. Key skills, management skills.

Faculty: 60 full-time.

Costs: Annual tuition £4,846 plus fees and certificate costs. Scholarships: yes.

Contact: David Foskett, Professor, Thames Valley Univ-London School of Tourism, Hospitality, Leisure, St. Mary's Rd., Ealing, London, W5 5RF England; (44) (0)1753 697603/697604, Fax (44) (0)7553 677682, david.foskett@tvu.ac.uk, www.tvu.ac.uk. Additional contact: St. Mary's Road, Ealing, London, W5 5RF England; 44 (0)82312221.

FRANCE

THE ALAIN DUCASSE TRAINING CENTER
Argenteuil/Year-round

Sponsor: School for professional chefs, seminars for non-professionals. Program: 1-wk training sessions ranging from 16-40 hrs; 5- to 10-wk seminars, 39 hrs of instruction/wk. Instruction in French, translation available for a fee. Non-professionals: 3 days/wk, 8 hrs of dedicated sessions. Established: 1999. Training sessions weekly, seminars monthly. Total enrollment: 6-12/class. 24 max each admission period. S:T ratio 8-10:1. Facilities: 3,250-sq-ft lab contains kitchens with the latest culinary technology, video equipment, computer center with Internet access.

Courses: Include micro-training, Mediterranean & multi-ethnic cuisine, new cooking techniques, fish & shellfish, Alain Ducasse's French Trilogy & wine skills, restaurant desserts. Courses can lead to an internship in one of the group's restaurant.

Faculty: Executive Chefs Bruno Caironi, Philippe Duc & Laurent Martinet for pastry; Jean-François Piège, Franck Cerutti, Didier Elena, Frédéric Robert. Gérard Margeon, wine studies.

Costs: From €688 for micro-formations to €1,548 for all other formations, €3,000 for Alain Ducasse's French Trilogy. 5 wks €5,000, 10 wks €10,000. €290/day for non-professionals. Admission requirements: Restaurant & catering professionals, members of food- & wine-related fields.

Location: 15 min from Paris by train.

Contact: Laure Frances, Client Contact, The Alain Ducasse Training Center, ADF, 41 rue de l'Abbé Ruellan, Argenteuil, 95100 France; (33) 1.34.34.19.10, Fax (33) 1.34.34.04.40, adf@ad-formation.com, www.ad-formation.com.

ÉCOLE DES ARTS CULINAIRES ET DE L'HOTELLERIE, DE LYON

Lyon/Ecully/Year-round

Sponsor: Private school. Program: 8- or 16-wk Cuisine & Culture program (taught in English), 2- or 3-yr Culinary Arts & Mgmt program (taught in French), 3-year Food Service & Hospitality Mgmt program (taught in French). Established: 1990. Calendar: semester. Admit dates: Apr, Oct. Total enrollment: 100. 50 each admission period. 55% of applicants accepted. 5% receive financial aid. S:T ratio 12:1. 100% of graduates obtain jobs within 6 mos. Facilities: 13 seminar rooms, 2 computer labs, 8 teaching kitchens, pastry/pantry facilities, video-equipped amphitheatre, sensory analysis lab, restaurants, bakery.

COURSES: Include food prep & processing, pantry, pastry & bakery, basic cooking & catering, restaurant cuisine. Seminars on cheese, wine, French ingredients, culinary culture. 5 mos externship/yr.

FACULTY: Includes 1 Meilleur Ouvrier de France, Chef Alain Le Cossec, Pastry Chef Pascal Molines (Pastry World Champion).

COSTS: 16-wk program is 46,200 FF including lunch. 2- & 3-yr programs are 59,000 FF/yr. Single lodging in student residence is 2,300 FF. Admission requirements: Students who complete the 16-wk program & pass an exam may take the longer programs. Loans: yes.

LOCATION: The restored 19th century Chateau du Vivier in a 17-acre wooded park.

CONTACT: Florence Galy, Communication Dept., Ecole des Arts Culinaires et de l'Hotellerie, de Lyon, Chateau du Vivier, B.P. 25, Ecully, Cedex, 69131 France; (33) (0)4-72-18-02-20, Fax (33) (0)4-78-43-33-51, fgaly@each-lyon.com, www.each-lyon.com.

ÉCOLE LENOTRE

Plaisir Cedex/Year-round

Sponsor: Advanced cooking school for professionals & future professionals. Program: 6-mo intensive professional culinary training diploma course & ~50 four-day certificate courses. Established: 1970. Calendar: semester. Curriculum: culinary. Admit dates: 6-mo program: January & September. Total enrollment: 3,000/yr. 50/5 classes each admission period. 95% of applicants accepted. S:T ratio 10:1. Facilities: Part of Lenotre, the school covers 170 acres with 5 specialized classrooms, a meeting room & boutique.

COURSES: Classes 90% participation. Several courses in each category: cuisine, catering, buffet decoration, breads & Viennese pastries, pastry, plated desserts, ice cream & frozen desserts, chocolate & confectionery, sugar work. Special a la carte courses for groups of 8-35 can also be arranged.

FACULTY: 4 instructors are recipients of the Meilleur Ouvrier de France in cooking, pastry & confectionery, ice cream, & bakery-Viennese pastries.

COSTS: Tuition (non-French students) including breakfasts & lunches, from ~$1,260 (€1,200)/wk-$1,485 (€1,350)/wk. School can reserve rooms in nearby hotels, which range from ~$23-$62/night. Admission requirements: Some experience in the culinary field & a knowledge of the basics of French gastronomy. Scholarships: yes.

CONTACT: Marie-Anne Dufeu, Directrice de Clientèle, Ecole Lenotre, 40, rue Pierre Curie - BP 6, Plaisir Cedex, 78375 France; (33) (0)1-30-81-46-34, Fax (33) (0)1-30-54-73-70, ecole@lenotre.fr, www.lenotre.fr. Daphné Cerisier, in charge of bookings.

ÉCOLE RITZ-ESCOFFIER

Paris/Year-round

Sponsor: Culinary school in the Ritz Paris Hotel. Program: 30-wk Superior Diploma course for future professionals. Segments: 1- to 6-wk Cesar Ritz (beginner), 10-wk Ritz-Escoffier (int-advanced), 1- to 12-wk Art of French Pastry (beginner-advanced), Master Ritz Escoffier, 2 wks (pro). Established: 1988. S:T ratio 8-10:1. Facilities: 2,000-sq-ft facility includes a main kitchen, pastry kitchen, conference room/library.

FACULTY: 4 full-time instructors.

COSTS: 6-week Cesar Ritz €5,336, 10-week Ritz-Escoffier €10,825, 12-week Art of French Pastry €10,215.75, Master 2-week Professional Course €2,140, 30-week Superior Diploma €27,100.

Admission requirements: Cesar Ritz diploma or equivalent experience; no experience required for Superior Diploma, Cesar Ritz, Pastry.

CONTACT: M. Jean-Philippe Zahm-Holbecq, Director, Ecole Ritz-Escoffier Paris, 15, Place Vendôme, Paris Cedex 01, 75041 France; 888-801-1126, (33) (0)1-43-16-30-50, Fax (33) (0)1-43-16-31-50, ecole@ritzparis.com, www.ritzparis.com.

ÉCOLE SUPERIEURE DE CUISINE FRANCAISE GROUPE FERRANDI

Paris/September-June

Sponsor: Professional restaurant and culinary school. Program: Bilingual 9-month (1,200-hr) Art and Technique of French Cuisine & 1092-hr Classic French Pastry and Bread Baking programs, each awarding a diploma issued by Paris' Chamber of Commerce & preparing qualified students for the C.A.P. certificate. Established: 1986. Accredited by French Ministry of Education. Calendar: trimester. Curriculum: culinary. Admit dates: September. Total enrollment: 200. 25 each admission period. 60-70% of applicants accepted. 50% receive financial aid. S:T ratio 12:1. 80-90% of graduates obtain jobs within 6 mos. Facilities: Include more than 12 professional kitchens, tasting laboratory, auditorium, classrooms, 2 working restaurants.

COURSES: General theoretical & practical courses, cooking, baking, pastry, butchery, delicatessen products, fish cookery. Other activities include a 3-day wine country excursion. The 9-month program includes visits to museums, markets, fine restaurant. 1- to 5-month restaurant apprenticeships in Paris and provinces arranged.

FACULTY: The curriculum is supervised by a Board of Advisors including well-known French chefs Alain Ducasse, Pierre Gagnaire and Antoine Westermann.

COSTS: Art and Technique of French Cuisine €16,700, Classic French Pastry and Bread Baking €14,300, including uniforms & equipment. Off-campus lodging $500-$800/mo. Admission requirements: Proof of full medical and accident coverage, long-term student visa, certified birth certificate, and undergraduate transcript. Loans: yes.

LOCATION: Rue Abbe Gregoire in Paris's Latin Quarter, between St. Germain de Pres and Montparnasse. Convenient to 4 major metro stations.

CONTACT: Stephanie Curtis, Coordinator, ESCF Groupe Ferrandi, Bilingual Program, 10 rue Poussin, Paris, 75016 France; (33) (0)1-45-27-09-09, Fax (33) (0)1-45-25-21-37, stecurtis@aol.com, www.egf.ccip.fr/ENGLISH/index.htm.

LE CORDON BLEU – PARIS

Paris/Year-round

Sponsor: Private school acquired by Andre J. Cointreau in 1984, at present location since 1988. Program: 9-mo Classic Cycle in Cuisine & Pastry at the basic, intermediate & superior levels leading to Le Grand Diplome; 3- & 5-wk Intensive Cuisine & Pastry Classic Cycle courses, 3-wk Intro to Catering: Buffet Techniques programs. Established: 1895. Calendar: trimester. Curriculum: culinary. Admit dates: 6 times/yr. Total enrollment: 550+. 180-200 each admission period. 100% of applicants accepted. 10% receive financial aid. S:T ratio 12:1. 90% of graduates obtain jobs within 6 mos. Facilities: Professionally equipped kitchens, demo rooms with video & overhead mirrors.

COURSES: Basic to complex techniques; classic, regional, ethnic, & contemporary cuisines; presentation, decoration, execution. Qualified students may apply for student assistantships; internships for top-ranked diploma program students.

FACULTY: 10+ full-time Master Chefs, international staff. French Master Chefs from leading restaurants & fine hotels.

COSTS: 10-wk certificate courses from €4,750 in Pastry to €6,850 in Cuisine. 9-mo Grand Diplome €29,550. Admission requirements: Personal statement, resume. Scholarships: yes.

LOCATION: Paris' 15th arrondissement in the southwestern part of the city; Metro Vaugirard.

CONTACT: Director of Admissions, Le Cordon Bleu, 8, rue Leon Delhomme, Paris, 75015 France; 800-457-CHEF (North America), (33) 1-53-68-22-50 (Paris), Fax (33) 1-48-56-03-96, info@cordonbleu.edu, http://cordonbleu.edu.

WINE MBA

Davis; Adelaide; Santiago, Chile; Bordeaux; Tokyo/Year-round

Sponsor: Bordeaux Business School. Program: 13-mo part-time program alternates travel to 5 wine-producing countries with students' work commitments. Established: 2001. 20 each admission period.

Faculty: Faculty of the Bordeaux Business School, U. of California-Davis, Universidad Catolica de Chile, Keio Business School, U. of South Australia.

Costs: $30,000 + airfare.

Contact: Isabelle Dartigues, Wine MBA Manager, Bordeaux Business School, 680, Cours de la Liberation, Talence Cedex, 33405 France; (33) (0) 5-56-84-22-29, Fax (33) (0) 5-56-84-55-00, isabelle.dartigues@bordeaux-bs.edu, www.winemba.com.

GREECE

ALPINE CENTER FOR HOTEL & TOURISM MANAGEMENT STUDIES

Glyfada, Athens/Year-round

Sponsor: Swiss-managed Associate Institute of IHTTI School of Hotel Management. Program: 2-yr certificate in Culinary Arts for Chef Training, 2 1/2-yr Swiss diploma in Culinary Arts. Graduates may transfer to Johnson & Wales U., Providence, RI, to complete BS degree in Culinary Arts. Established: 1987. Calendar: trimester. Curriculum: culinary. Admit dates: May-September.

Courses: Food & beverage, food prod, kitchen organization, menu planning, nutrition, cooking methods, baking & pastry, buffet catering, intl cuisine, professional development.

Contact: Sybil Hofmann, President, Alpine Center for Hotel & Tourism Management, PO Box 70235, 70 Possidonos Ave., Glyfada, GR-166 10 Greece; (30) 010 898 3022/3210, Fax (30) 010 898 1189, services@alpine.edu.gr, www.alpine.edu.gr.

IRELAND

BALLYMALOE COOKERY SCHOOL

Midleton, County Cork/September-July

Sponsor: Proprietary school. Program: 12-wk certificate course in Food & Wine, a variety of short courses. Established: 1983. Calendar: quarter. Curriculum: culinary. Admit dates: Sept, Jan. Total enrollment: 44. 44 each admission period. 90% of applicants accepted. S:T ratio 7:1. 100% of graduates obtain jobs within 6 mos. Facilities: Specially designed kitchen with gas & electric cookers, mirrored demo area, TV monitors, gardens that supply fresh organic produce.

Courses: Traditional Irish & contemporary classic cookery, intl cuisine, vegetarian, seafood.

Faculty: 4 full- & 4 part-time. Includes Principal Darina Allen, IACP-certified Teacher & Food Professional, her brother, Rory O'Connell, both trained in the Ballymaloe House restaurant kitchen, and her husband Tim Allen. Guest chefs are featured.

Costs: 12-wk course is IR £4,075. Students live in cottages during the course & may assist in the restaurant. Self-catering cottage lodging is IR £42/wk double, IR£55 single.

Location: A mile from the sea, outside the village of Shanagarry in southern Ireland, 4 hrs from Dublin, 45 min from Cork Airport; train station pick-up is available.

Contact: Tim Allen, Owner/Teacher, Ballymaloe Cookery School, Shanagarry, County Cork, Midleton, Ireland; (353) (0)21-4646-785, Fax (353) (0)21-4646-909, enquiries@ballymaloe-cookery-school.ie, www.ballymaloe-cookery-school.ie.

IRISH COOKERY SCHOOL OF IRELAND

Cork/June-August

Sponsor: Private School. Program: 2-week short-term certificate courses. Specializing in Irish cooking. Food service, catering, food safety, hygiene. Established: 2000. Curriculum: culinary. Admit dates: June, July, Aug. Total enrollment: 5/class. 5 each admission period. S:T ratio 5 to 2. Facilities:

Audio Visual equipment. Lecture Studio. Visits to food producers in the South of Ireland.

COURSES: Irish Menu Planning. Irish Food and Ingredients. Quality Irish Products using the best of Irish ingredients. non.*(See display ad page XX)*

COSTS: IR£400/wk, IR£800/2 week residency course. Includes single lodging & meals.

LOCATION: Ballincollig, 3 miles from the City of Cork in the South of Ireland.

CONTACT: Mary Casey O'Carroll, Director, Irish Cookery School of Ireland, Ballincollig, Cork., Kilnaglory, Ballincollig, Cork, Ireland; (353) 21 4972646, Fax (353) 21 4877655.

ITALY

APICIUS THE CULINARY INSTITUTE OF FLORENCE

Florence/Year-round *(See also page 333)(See display ad above)*

Sponsor: Private school, a member of the Federation of European Schools. Program: 1-yr diploma & 2-sem programs in Culinary Arts, Hospitality Mgmt, Wine Expertise, Italian Baking & Pastry, Food Communication & combination programs of Italian language, art history, & culinary arts. Established: 1973. Calendar: semester. Curriculum: culinary, core. Admit dates: Jan, August for semester & year-long programs. Total enrollment: 150. 40 each admission period. 80% of applicants accepted. 5% receive financial aid. 20% enrolled part-time. S:T ratio 12:1. 30% of graduates obtain jobs within 6 mos. Facilities: New facility consisting of 2 kitchens with individual workstations, wine tasting room, conference room, reading room & lounge.

COURSES: Culinary arts, hospitality & restaurant mgmt, wine, Renaissance culture, regional Italian cooking, food resources, Italian & Jewish food traditions, bakery, pastry & confectionery, creative cuisine. Internships as kitchen assistants in the school & local restaurants during diploma program. Special 10-day programs.

FACULTY: Includes professional chefs Gennaro Napolitano, Stefano Innocenti, Pierluigi Campi & Andrea Bianchini, & food historian Gabriella Ganugi, Director.

COSTS: Tuition €5,240/semester, courses from €150. Scholarships: yes.

LOCATION: Downtown Florence in the San Lorenzo district, between the Duomo & the central train station.

CONTACT: Dr. Gabriella Ganugi, Director, Apicius the Culinary Institute of Florence, Via Guelfa 85, Florence, 50129 Italy; (39) 0552658135, Fax (39) 0552656689, info@apicius.it, www.apicius.it. U.S. contact: Study Abroad Italy, 339 S. Main St., Sebastopol, CA 95472; 707-824-8965, Fax 707-824-0198, mail@tuscancooking.com, www.tuscancooking.com.

ITALIAN CULINARY INSTITUTE FOR FOREIGNERS

Piedmont region/Year-round

Sponsor: Professional culinary institute (ICIF). Program: 3-/6-month certificate programs consisting of 21 days/2 months classroom study & 70 days/4 months apprenticeship. Established: 1991. Curriculum: culinary. Admit dates: Jan, June, Sept, Oct. 20 each admission period. 70% of applicants accepted. S:T ratio 12:1. 95% of graduates obtain jobs within 6 mos. Facilities: High-tech equipment in an 18th-century castle.

Courses: Emphasis on product knowledge and developing an Italian palate.

Faculty: In-house instructors and visiting professional chefs.

Costs: $3,300 ($8,500) for the 3-month (6-month) program includes room and board and NYC-Italy roundtrip airfare. Lodging in newly-constructed student housing facility while in school.

Location: Costigliole D'Asti in the Piedmont region.

Contact: Enrico Bazzoni, Director of Programs, ICIF-USA, 126 Second Place, Brooklyn, NY 11231; 718-875-0547, Fax 718-875-5856, Eabchef@aol.com, www.icif.com.

SCUOLA DI ARTE CULINARIA 'CORDON BLEU'

Florence/Year-round

Sponsor: Private school. Program: Professional curriculum consists of 11-21 one- to nine-session hands-on courses, a total of 150-230 hrs of instruction. Established: 1985. Curriculum: culinary. Admit dates: July & November for intensive programs; yr-round for others. Total enrollment: 150. 50-70 each admission period. 90% of applicants accepted. 90% enrolled part-time. S:T ratio 8:1. 70-90% of graduates obtain jobs within 6 mos. Facilities: 40-sq-meter teaching kitchen + library & tasting room.

Courses: Include basic to advanced cooking, pastry, bread, holiday menus, regional specialties, specific subjects, history. Italian cuisine & traditions, Kosher-Italian.

Faculty: 2 full- & 2 part-time instructors. Cristina Blasi & Gabriella Mari, 18 yrs teaching experience, sommeliers & olive oil experts, authored books on ancient Roman cooking & mustard, members Commanderie des Cordon Bleus de France, IACP.

Costs: €3,820 (€4,660) for the Fall (Spring) program, €6,000 for both. Off-campus housing available in apts & hotels.

Contact: Emilia Onesti, Secretary, Scuola di Arte Culinaria 'Cordon Bleu', Via di Mezzo, 55/R, 50121 Firenze-Florence, Italy; (39) 055-2345468, Fax (39) 055-2345468, info@cordonbleu-it.com, www.cordonbleu-it.com.

JAPAN

LE CORDON BLEU – TOKYO

Tokyo & Yokohama/Year-round

Sponsor: Private school, sister school of Le Cordon Bleu Paris. Program: 9-mo diploma programs of Basic, Intermediate, Superior levels for Pastry; 12-mo diploma programs of Basic, Intermediate, Advanced, Superior levels for Cuisine. Intro courses in cuisine, pastry, catering, bread baking. Established: 1991. Calendar: quarter. Curriculum: culinary. Admit dates: Quarterly. Facilities: Professionally-equipped kitchens, individual work spaces with refrigerated marble tables, convection ovens, specialty appliances.

Courses: Diploma & Certificate core curriculum consists of 4 levels of cuisine & 3 levels of pastry, taken consecutively or together. Covers basic to complex techniques, wine & food pairing, catering, presentation. Offered at the Paris & London schools.

Faculty: 10 full-time French & Japanese Master Chefs from Michelin-star restaurants & fine hotels.

Costs: Basic Cuisine 610,050 yen, Intermediate Cuisine 630,000 yen, Advanced Cuisine 647,850 yen, Superior Cuisine 696,150 yen, Basic Pastry 573,300 yen, Intermediate Pastry 595,350 yen, Superior Pastry 599,550 yen, Basic Bakery 546,000 yen.

Location: Tokyo's Daikanyama district; Yokohama (pastry arts).

Contact: Kohyama Akiko, Student Service & Sales Manager, Le Cordon Bleu, Roob-1, 28-13 Sarugaku-cho, Daikanyama, Shibuya-ku, Tokyo, 150-0033 Japan; (81) 3 5489 0141, Fax (81) 3 5489 0145, tokyo@cordonbleu.edu, www.cordonbleu.co.jp. Toll-free in the U.S. & Canada: 800-457-CHEF. http://www.cordonbleu.edu (English).

MEXICO

MEXICAN HOME COOKING SCHOOL

Tlaxcala/Year-round

Sponsor: Private school dedicated to preserving Pre-Hispanic & traditional Mexican cuisine. Program: 1- & 2-wk certificate courses individually structured to the needs of professional chefs & their staffs. Established: 1998. Admit dates: Year-round. S:T ratio 3:1. Facilities: Fully-equipped 500-sq-ft kitchen with Talavera tile & view of volcanoes. Stove & adjacent work areas set below a 70-sq-ft skylight.

Courses: Mexican food, with emphasis on home-style gourmet cooking.

Faculty: Estela Salas Silva served a classic apprenticeship from age 7 in the traditions of the Mexican kitchen. 20 yrs experience in Mexico City & as head chef in San Francisco.

Costs: $1,000/1-wk resident course includes meals & lodging in the hacienda-style country home of Sra. Estela featuring double rms with private bath & fireplace.

Location: 90 min east of Mexico City, 30 min from Puebla, in the valley of Tlaxcala surrounded by 3 volcanos on the side of a seasonal lake.

Contact: Estela Salas-Silva, Owner, Mexican Home Cooking School, Apdo. 64, Tlaxcala, 90000 Mexico; (52) 246-46-809-78, Fax (52) 246-46-809-78, mexicanhomecooking@yahoo.com, http://mexicanhomecooking.com.

NETHERLANDS ANTILLES

KURA HULANDA EXPERIENCE

Curaçao/Year-round

Sponsor: Private culinary institute & resort for career-minded and recreational culinarians. Program: Eight different 3-month certificate programs, divided into 100 one-week modules. Established: 2003. Calendar: quarter. Curriculum: culinary. Admit dates: Monthly. 10 each admission period. 100% of applicants accepted. S:T ratio 10:1. Facilities: 6 food service outlets, teaching kitchen, lecture hall & conference center, library, internet & business centers.

Courses: Basic, Intermediate, and Advanced Culinary, Basic Intermediate, and Advanced Baking and Pastry, Food & Beverage Management. 50% of program is spent working with chefs & staff in the resort's six foodservice outlets.

Faculty: 6 chefs & 30 culinary professionals.

Costs: $1,300/mo, lab fee $140/mo. Admission requirements: Must meet passport & immigration requirements. Loans: yes.

Contact: Piroska Muller, Asst to the Director, Kura Hulanda Experience, Langestraat 8, Willemstad, Curaçao, Netherlands Antilles; 866-214-9995 (US), (599) 9 434-7700, Fax (599) 9 434-7706, info@kurahulanda.org, www.kurahulanda.org.

NEW ZEALAND

CENTRAL INSTITUTE OF TECHNOLOGY

Wellington/Year-round

Sponsor: Trade school. Program: 3-year Bachelor's degree, 2-year diploma, 1-year certificate in Hotel Reception, 6 month courses in cookery & food service including London City & Guilds qualifications. Established: 1978. Calendar: semester. Curriculum: core. Admit dates: February & July. Total enrollment: 300. 90 each admission period. 50% of applicants accepted. 40% receive financial aid. S:T ratio 14:1. 50% of graduates obtain jobs within 6 mos. Facilities: 3 kitchens, 20 classrooms, 2 restaurants.

Faculty: 18 full-time.

Costs: Tuition in-country NZ$3,725, out-of-country NZ$17,200. On-campus housing cost

NZ$160/wk. Admission requirements: HS diploma or equivalent & admission test.

CONTACT: Kay Nelson, Head of Department, Central Institute of Technology, Centre for Hospitality & Tourism Management, Private Bag 39803, Wellington, New Zealand; (64) (0)4-9202-620, Fax (64) (0)4-9202-628, kay.nelson@weltec.ac.nz, www.cit.ac.nz. School Secretary, Irene Pahina - irene.pahina@weltec.ac.nz.

THE NEW ZEALAND SCHOOL OF FOOD AND WINE
Christchurch/Year-round

Sponsor: Proprietary institution. Program: 16-week full-time certificate in Foundation Cookery Skills, which includes New Zealand certificate in wine; 22-week full-time certificate in Restaurant-Cafe Management. Established: 1994. Accredited by New Zealand Qualifications Authority. Calendar: trimester. Curriculum: culinary. Admit dates: Jan, Feb, May, July, Aug. 12 each admission period. S:T ratio 1:12. 90% of graduates obtain jobs within 6 mos. Facilities: Include 1 demonstration kitchen with overhead mirrors and 1 practical kitchen with commercial equipment, computer and seminar rooms.

COURSES: Foundation skills based on Leith's Bible, concepts of French cuisine, food presentation, menu planning, costing, catering, wine. Restaurant & cafe management, computer skills to run a restaurant business.

FACULTY: 10 full-time and part-time tutors.

COSTS: Tuition is approximately NZ$4,650 (includes tax). Registered with the New Zealand Qualifications Authority (NZQA); students eligible for student visas. Loans: yes.

LOCATION: Christchurch, a city of 300,000 in South Island.

CONTACT: Celia Hay, Director, The New Zealand School of Food and Wine, 63 Victoria St., Box 25217, Christchurch, So. Island, New Zealand; (64) (0)3-3797-501, Fax (64) (0)3-366-2302, celia@foodandwine.co.nz, www.foodandwine.co.nz.

TAI POUTINI POLYTECHNIC
Greymouth/February-November

Sponsor: Trade/technical school. Program: One-year full-time (34 weeks)London City & Guilds certificate and diplomaT.P.P. Certificate in Professional Culinary Arts. Established: 1988. Curriculum: culinary, core. Admit dates: Feb. Total enrollment: 20. 20 each admission period. 80% of applicants accepted. 90% receive financial aid. Zero% enrolled part-time. S:T ratio 10:1. 100% of graduates obtain jobs within 6 mos. Facilities: Modular training kitchen that doubles as restaurant kitchen, equipped with the latest equipment. Classrooms with overheads, TV, video. Student cafeteria & lounge. Library with computers & Internet access.

COURSES: Training geared toward entry level position in fine dining restaurants & hotels. Includes 2-week work-based training module and 5-day field trip.

COSTS: NZ$3,500 includes uniforms, knife & tool kit, field trip, qualification fees. Admission requirements: Demonstrated passion for food & cooking as a career. Good knowledge of English & mathematics. Scholarships: yes. Loans: yes.

LOCATION: South Island West Coast, 3 hrs from Nelson & Christchurch, 2-6 hrs from major ski fields, minutes from beach.

CONTACT: Jos Wellman, Chef Tutor, Tai Poutini Polytechnic, Tainui St., Greymouth, SI, 3 New Zealand; (64) 3-7680411 x747, Fax (64) 3-7684503, jos.wellman@odin.taipoutini.ac.nz, www.tpp.ac.nz/taipoutini/qualifications.asp?id=4.

PANAMA

ACADEMIA DE ARTES CULINARIAS Y ETIQUETA
Panama City/Year-round

Sponsor: Private culinary arts academy. Program: 9-month diploma in Culinary Arts. Established: 2002. Calendar: semester. Curriculum: culinary. Admit dates: Jan, July. Total enrollment: 60. 16

each admission period. 95% of applicants accepted. S:T ratio 1:16. Facilities: Fully-equipped professional kitchen, accomodating 16 students.

Courses: Intensive hands-on culinary arts program. 3-mo externships at local restaurants & hotels.

Faculty: 3 full-time chef-instructors, all educated in Europe & the U.S. 10 part-time.

Costs: $6,675. Admission requirements: HS diploma, health certificate. Scholarships: yes.

Contact: Elena Hernández, Director, Academia de Artes Culinarias y Etiqueta, Calle 51E y Federico Boyd, Casa #24, Local #3, Panama City, Panama; 507-263-6083, Fax 507-263-6083, cocina@cwpanama.net.

PHILIPPINES

CENTER FOR CULINARY ARTS, MANILA

Quezon City/Year-round

Sponsor: Private school. Program: 2-yr diploma in Culinary Arts & Technology Management, 1-yr certificate in Baking & Pastry Arts. 5 terms of 2 mos/term. Established: 1995. Accredited by TESDA (Technical Education Skills Development Authority). Calendar: quinmester. Curriculum: culinary. Admit dates: June, Aug, Oct, Jan. Total enrollment: 191. 163 each admission period. 72% of applicants accepted. 2% receive financial aid. S:T ratio 10:1. Facilities: Modern lecture & lab facilities for institutional & quantity cooking, baking lab, research center, computer facilities, restaurant outlet.

Courses: Scientific background in principles, hands-on training in strategies/procedures with emphasis on positive work attitudes, values, & ethics. Practicum training in accredited institutions. Monthly short courses for hobbyists & professional chefs.

Faculty: 20 instructors.

Costs: ~$10,000 for diploma, $6,000 for baking, includes books, supplies/materials, ingredients, certification exams. Admission requirements: HS diploma, transcript of records, recommendation letter, interview, written exam, medical exam, attendance in discovery course. Scholarships: yes.

Location: Quezon City in the university belt. Part of Cravings, a full-service restaurant.

Contact: Lotees Dell Palacios, Marketing Officer, Center for Culinary Arts, Manila, 287 Katipunan Ave., Loyola Heights, Quezon City, 1102 Philippines; (632) 426-48-41 / 40 / 35 / 37 / 25, Fax (632) 426-48-36, marketing@cca-manila.com, www.cca-manila.com.

SCOTLAND

COLLEGE RESTAURANT

Edinburgh/September-June

Sponsor: The College Restaurant is part of Edinburgh's Telford College. Program: Courses ranging from Basic Cookery to Professional Culinary Arts. Established: 1979. Calendar: trimester. Curriculum: culinary, core. Admit dates: Year-round. 16/class max each admission period. 80% of applicants accepted. 50% receive financial aid. 30% enrolled part-time. S:T ratio 16:1. 90% of graduates obtain jobs within 6 mos. Facilities: Include training restaurant, training cafe & a training bakery. 7 practical classroom/kitchens.

Contact: Colin McLaren, The College Restaurant, Edinburgh's Telford College, School of Leisure Industries, Crewe Toll, Edinburgh, EH4 2NZ Scotland; (44) (0)131 315 7373, Fax (44) (0)131 343 1218, info@collegerestaurant.com, www.collegerestaurant.com. Edinburgh's Telford College main website: http://www.ed-coll.ac.uk.

EDINBURGH SCHOOL OF FOOD AND WINE

Edinburgh/September-July

Sponsor: Private school. Program: 6-mo (2-sem) diploma in Food & Wine for career cooks, 5-wk Intensive for chalet & freelance cooks, recreational classes & courses. Established: 1987. Accredited by British Accreditation Council for Independent, Further & Higher Education. Calendar: semester. Curriculum: culinary. Admit dates: January for diploma course, year-round for other courses. Total enrollment: 20/class. 20 each admission period. 90% of applicants accepted. 10% receive financial aid. 5% enrolled part-time. 100% of graduates obtain jobs within 6 mos. Facilities: Full range of domestic & commercial equipment.

Courses: Diploma program: culinary skills courses (basic to advanced). Wine & Spirit Education Trust course, Business Start-up course, Communication Skills in Business, Health & Hygiene Certificate. Cake icing with sugarcraft & flower arranging. Work experience arranged at top restaurants.

Faculty: Certificate/Diploma.

Costs: £8500/sem for diploma course. £2,500 for certificate course. Apartment £75/wk including utilities. Admission requirements: No formal qualifications. Loans: yes.

Location: Refurbished 300-yr-old former coach house on a private country estate.

Contact: Jill Davidson, Managing Director, Edinburgh School of Food and Wine, The Coach House, Newliston, Edinburgh, EH29 9EB Scotland; (44) (0) 131 333 5001, Fax (44) (0) 131 335 3796, info@esfw.com, www.esfw.com.

SINGAPORE

AT-SUNRICE THE SINGAPORE COOKING SCHOOL & SPICE GARDEN

Singapore/Year-round

Sponsor: Center for Asian food, culinary skills & craftware. Program: 2-yr Advanced Culinary Placement Diploma, offered jointly with Johnson & Wales Univ; 2- & 4-wk pan-Asian Culinary Course + optional internship; leisure classes. Established: 2001. Admit dates: Mar, June, Oct, Nov. Facilities: Modern kitchens, spice garden.

Courses: Pan-Asian cuisine. 24-wk optional internship at partner hotels in Singapore.

Faculty: Professional chefs.

Costs: $2,500/2-wk course includes lodging, meals, 4 credits. Internship monthly allowance covers lodging, transportation, meals. Admission requirements: Internship application includes resume, 500-word essay, 3 reference letters. Scholarships: yes.

Contact: Phyllis Ong, at-sunrice, The Singapore Cooking School & Spice Garden, at-sunrice, Fort Canning Park, Fort Canning Centre, 179618 Singapore; (65) 336 3307, Fax (65) 336 9353, academy@at-sunrice.com, www.at-sunrice.com. zeke@at-sunrice.com.

SOUTH AFRICA

BARNES STREET CULINARY STUDIO

Johannesburg

Sponsor: Private school offering a professional culinary arts course. Program: Certificate and diploma in Food Preparation & Cooking Principles & Practice. ~15 each admission period.

Courses: Include safety, prep & cooking methods, kitchen maintenance & design, budgeting & cost control, nutrition, menu planning, pastry.

Faculty: Owner & principal Suzi Holzhausen, 15+ yrs as a professional chef & culinary lecturer, trained at Silwood Kitchen Cordon Bleu in Cape Town.

Costs: R12,000, fees ~R,4,000.

Contact: Suzi Holzhausen, Owner, Barnes Street Culinary Studio, PO Box 579, Auckland Park, Johannesburg, 2006 South Africa; info@barnesculinary.co.za, www.barnesculinary.co.za.

CHRISTINA MARTIN SCHOOL OF FOOD AND WINE

Durban/February-November

Sponsor: Private culinary college, culinary professional. Program: 1-yr Intensive Diploma Chef's Course. Established: 1973. Accredited by Dept. of Education South Africa. Calendar: semester. Curriculum: culinary, core. Admit dates: Feb. Total enrollment: 36. 36 each admission period. 80%

of applicants accepted. 10% receive financial aid. 36% enrolled part-time. S:T ratio 6:1. 100% of graduates obtain jobs within 6 mos. Facilities: 4 industrial kitchens with latest equipment, auditorium, delicatessen, 60-seat restaurant, 80-seat conference venue, garden restaurant.

Courses: Include food prep, food & beverage mgmt, intl cuisines, patisserie, garde manger, floral art, mgmt & labor relations. Cordon Bleu Part One & Part Two courses, short courses for the public.

Faculty: Christina Martin is a Maitre Chef de Cuisine & Commandeur Associé de la Commanderie des Cordons Bleus de France. Instructors include vice-principal Michelle Barry, Sous Chefs Warren Norton & Andrew White, Pastry Chef Eric Berullier.

Costs: R63,756 for Intensive Diploma Course, ~R955 each for Cordon Bleu 1 & 2 courses. Casual day & evening courses ~R12,500. Admission requirements: Senior School leavers certificate (matric). Scholarships: yes.

Contact: Christina Martin, Principal and Owner, Christina Martin School of Food and Wine, PO Box 4601, Durban, 4000 South Africa; (27) (0)31-3032111, Fax (27) (0)31-312-3342, chrismar@iafrica.com, www.safarichef.com.

THE SILWOOD SCHOOL OF COOKERY

Rondebosch Cape/Year-round

Sponsor: Private school. Program: Three 1-yr culinary career courses: the certificate course, the diploma course, the Grande Diplome. Established: 1964. Accredited by Hospitality Industries Training Board. Calendar: quarter. Curriculum: core. Admit dates: January. Total enrollment: 48. 48, divided into groups of 12 each admission period. 60% of applicants accepted. S:T ratio 12:1. 100% of graduates obtain jobs within 6 mos. Facilities: 200-yr-old coach-house converted into a demo & experimental kitchen, 3 additional kitchens, demo hall, library.

Courses: Cooking & baking, icing, wine, table art, mise en place, floral art.

Faculty: 11-member faculty includes school principal Alicia Wilkinson, nutrition instructor Jeanette Rietmann, menu reading instructor Alisa Smith, practical supervisors Louise Faull, Carianne Wilkinson, Lara DuToit, Gaie Gaag, Judy Sendzul, Liz Bell.

Costs: Tuition is R28,300 for the Certificate course, R12,500 for the Diploma course, R1,200 for the Grande Diplome. Housing is R1,000-R1,500/mo.

Location: Cape Town.

Contact: Mrs. Alicia Wilkinson, The Silwood School of Cookery, Silwood Rd., Rondebosch Cape, South Africa; (27) 21-686-4894/5, Fax (27) 21-686-5795, cooking@silwood.co.za, www.silwood.co.za.

SPAIN

EL TXOKO DEL GOURMET

Basque Country/Year-round

Sponsor: Specialty food shop. Program: 12-month vocational course in Basic Cuisine consisting of 160 hrs/mo. Instruction in Spanish. Curriculum: culinary. Admit dates: September. 100% of applicants accepted. S:T ratio 23:1 max. Facilities: Basement workroom.

Faculty: Chef Fernando Cendoya Ayerbe.

Costs: $300 (53.000 pesetas) subject to currency exchange.

Location: Opposite San Sebastian's covered market.

Contact: Pepa Armendáriz, Director, El Txoko del Gourmet, Aldamar, 4 Bajo, San Sebastian, 20003 Spain; (34) 943-422-218, Fax (34) 943-427-641, info@casaarmendariz.com, www.eltxokodelgourmet.com.

ESCUELA DE COCINA LUIS IRÍZAR

Basque Country/October-August

Sponsor: Private school. Program: 2-yr diploma program with instruction in Spanish. Established: 1992. Curriculum: culinary. Admit dates: Year-round, selection in May. Total enrollment: 28/yr. 28

each admission period. 80% of applicants accepted. S:T ratio 14:1. 100% of graduates obtain jobs within 6 mos. Facilities: Fully-equipped kitchen, separate classroom, TV & video.

Courses: Basque, Spanish, French & International cuisines. Apprenticeships at leading restaurants. Wine tasting, nutrition, cocktails, visits to food & wine producers.

Faculty: Founder Luis Irízar has served as chef in Spain's leading restaurants. His staff includes 3 full-time instructors plus part-time teachers for continuing ed.

Contact: V. Irízar, Escuela de Cocina Luis Irízar, c/ Mari, #5, Bajo, San Sebastian, 20003 Spain; (34) 943-431540, Fax (34) 943-423553, cocina@escuelairizar.com, www.escuelairizar.com.

ESCUELA DE HOSTELERIA ARNADI

Barcelona/Year-round

Sponsor: Private school. Program: 28-mo Cooking & Restaurant Management with optional Pastry specialization, 6-mo Intensive & 1-yr Complete Cooking course, 1-yr Basic & 6-mo Advanced Baking/Pastry course. Instruction in Spanish. Established: 1983. Curriculum: culinary. Admit dates: Mar. 98% of applicants accepted. Facilities: Classrooms, kitchen, hotel, restaurant, computer room, party room, pastry kitchen.

Courses: Cooking basics, nutrition, baking & pastry, dietetics, accounting, French & intl gastronomy. Stage, a 1-wk residency in the school kitchen; 2-day courses.

Faculty: Hands-on classes taught by chefs. Other classes taught by professionals, most are college professors with PhDs.

Contact: Mey Hoffman, Director, Escuela de Hosteleria Arnadi, C/Zaragoza 20, Barcelona, 8003 Spain; (34) 933-195-889/882, Fax (34) 95 456-3666, www.hofmann-bcn.com.

ESCUELA DE HOSTELERIA Y TURISMO DE VALENCIA

Valencia/September-July

Sponsor: Private school. Program: Vocational training courses that include cooking, bakery & confectionery, restaurant & bar services. 60-hr Spanish Cooking certificate for foreign students. Established: 1995. Accredited by Culture, Education & Science Council of Valencia. Calendar: quarter. Admit dates: July & September. 100% of graduates obtain jobs within 6 mos.

Courses: Mediterranean & Spanish cooking, rices & paella, Spanish confectionery.

Contact: Angel Campillo, President, Escuela de Hosteleria y Turismo de Valencia, Calle Correjeria,28, Valencia, 46001 Spain; (34) 96 3155250, Fax (34) 96 3155925, internacional@ehtvalencia.com, www.ehtvalencia.com. info@ehtvalencia.com.

ESC.UNIV.HOST. I TURISME SANT POL DE MAR, BARCELONA

Barcelona/Year-round

Sponsor: Hotel school offering technical, university, and post-graduate degrees in hotel administration, tourism and culinary arts. Program: Hosteleria-Cooking: 3-year technical program. Postgraduate degree in Culinary Arts: 16- or 32-week program consisting of 150 lecture hours/semester and 450 practical hours/semester. Established: 1966. Diploma accredited by the EUHT Sant Pol and EURHODIP. Curriculum: culinary, core. Total enrollment: 60. 25 each admission period. 50% of applicants accepted. 25% receive financial aid. 100% of graduates obtain jobs within 6 mos. Facilities: 3 kitchens, kitchen-auditorium, hotel used as a laboratory.

Courses: 30 courses include history of gastronomy, purchasing & restaurant management, baking & pastry, conservation & storage, decorations & garnishes, Italian cuisine, buffets, game cookery. F&B related courses concerning practice and theory.

Faculty: 35 university degrees, Ph.D., culinary school graduates. Michelin-star guest chefs.

Costs: $7,000/yr includes housing, meals, books. Scholarships: yes. Loans: yes.

Location: 30 miles north of Barcelona.

Contact: Lluis Serra, External Relations, Esc.Univ.Host. i Turisme Sant Pol de Mar, Barcelona, Hotel Gran Sol, Carrtera N-II s/n, Sant Pol de Mar, Barcelona, 8395 Spain; (34) 93-760 0051/0212, Fax (34) 93-760 0985, mail@euht-santpol.org, www.euht-santpol.org.

FUNDACIÓ ESCOLA DE RESTAURACIÓ I HOSTALARIA DE BARCELONA

Barcelona/Year-round

Sponsor: Private school. Program: 10-mo Professional Cook & 8-mo Wine Specialist programs. Instruction in Spanish. Established: 1985. Curriculum: culinary. S:T ratio 12:1. 100% of graduates obtain jobs within 6 mos. Facilities: Include 3 kitchens, cooking workshop, restaurant, students' cafeteria, wine tasting room, computer room, library, classrooms.

COSTS: $3,500/yr. Admission requirements: HS diploma. Loans: yes.

CONTACT: Antonio Muqoz, Director of Admissions, Fundació Escola de Restauració i Hostalaria de Barcelona, C/Muntaner, 70-72, Barcelona, 8011 Spain; (34) 93 451-6982/453-2903, Fax (34) 93 323-7423, direccio@ferhb.com, www.ferhb.com.

LA TAHONA DEL MAR

Barcelona

Sponsor: Bakery. Program: 1-wk (40-hr) courses in artisanal European breadmaking, Spanish & Catalan breads, pastries. Established: 1998. Curriculum: culinary. Admit dates: Spring & fall. Admission closes 2 wks before class date. Facilities: Modern culinary classroom attached to a working bakery.

COURSES: Traditional baking of Spain, in particular Catalonia, using natural starters & traditional formulas modernized for commercial production.

FACULTY: Joaquín Llarás, professional baker & owner of La Tahona del Mar, studied at LeNôtre in France & with traditional bakers in Spain & Italy. His assistants are graduates of Spanish professional culinary schools & have industry experience.

COSTS: 80,000 Spanish pesetas. Instruction is in Spanish. English interpretation is $200 additional. Admission requirements: Professional experience or training in bread or pastry making.

CONTACT: Elizabeth Duran, English Language Representative, La Tahona del Mar, 605 W. 111th St., #63, New York, NY 10025; 212-222-9062, Fax 212-222-6613, eduran@pipeline.com, www.sinix.net/paginas/tahona/ingles.htm. In Barcelona: Joaquín Llarás, (34) 93-307-1566.

SWITZERLAND

DCT SWISS HOTEL & CULINARY ARTS SCHOOL

Luzern/Year-round

Sponsor: Private school offering education only in the areas of Hotel & Tourism Management & European Culinary Arts. Program: Three 11-week courses: Foundation in European Cuisine, European Gourmet Cuisine, European Pastry & Chocolate, plus Swiss industry internship lead to Advanced Diploma in European Culinary Management. Certificate for one course. Established: 1992. Accredited by ACF, Swiss Hotel School Assn, ACBSP, HCIMA. Calendar: quarter. Curriculum: culinary, core. Admit dates: Jan, Apr, July, Oct. Total enrollment: 40. 20 each admission period. 75% of applicants accepted. S:T ratio 10:1 max. 100% of graduates obtain jobs within 6 mos.

COURSES: European regional recipes, pastries, & chocolates. Graduates who have taken at least 2 Culinary Arts courses & 2 German language courses may apply for a paid Industry Training internship in Switzerland. Those with adequate experience or training enter directly into the European Gourmet Cuisine or the European Pastry & Chocolate course, bypassing the Introduction to Classical Cuisine course.

COSTS: Sfr. 9,500 (~$7,000) for each 3-mo course includes tuition, room & board.

LOCATION: The village of Vitznau, just outside of Luzern on the shores of Lake Lucerne, 1 hr from Zurich airport.

CONTACT: Dr. Joseph Gregg, Director, Americas Office, DCT Swiss Hotel & Culinary Arts School, Seestrasse, Vitznau-Lucerne, CH6354 Switzerland; (41) 41 399 00 00, Fax (41) 41 399 01 01, j.gregg@dct.ch, http://culinaryschool.ch. Mr. Paul Haecki, Director of Admissions, admission@dct.ch.

TAIWAN

KAOHSIUNG HOSPITALITY COLLEGE (KHC)

Kaohsiung

Program: Programs in Western Culinary Arts, Chinese Culinary Arts, Baking & Pastry Arts, Food & Beverage Management, Hospitality Management. Facilities: Teaching kitchen with fully-equipped stations.

CONTACT: KHC College, 1 Sung-ho Rd. Hsiao-kang, Kaohsiung, Taiwan R.O.C.; (886) 07-8060505, Fax (886) 07-8061473, stone@mail.nkhc.edu.tw, www.nkhc.edu.tw/depart-new.htm.

THAILAND

ROYAL THAI SCHOOL OF CULINARY ARTS

Bang Saen/Year-round

Sponsor: Private cooking school specializing in professional Thai Cooking. Program: Ten 5-session courses in Royal & Regional Thai cuisine that lead to a Grand Diploma in Thai Cooking. May be taken as 5- or 10-wk intensive that includes Thai Banquet course or as 3-wk, 6-course intensive. Established: 1997. Accredited by Thai Ministry of Education. Admit dates: Year-round. Total enrollment: 160. 16 each admission period. 100% of applicants accepted. S:T ratio 4:1. 50% of graduates obtain jobs within 6 mos. Facilities: 2 professional kitchens, lounge, dining room & terrace overlooking the Gulf of Siam.

COURSES: Include Fruit & Vegetable Carving, Starters & Appetizers, Meats & Curries, Fish & Seafood, Desserts, Regional Thai, Vegetarian, Fusion. 5-wk internships available. School assists with externships.

FACULTY: 5 instructors, 2 master fruit & vegetable carvers.

COSTS: $1,200-$10,000 includes lodging & meals. Admission requirements: Basic kitchen & knife skills. Scholarships: yes.

LOCATION: Private beach in a seaside resort, 88 km from Bangkok.

CONTACT: Chris Kridakorn-Odbratt, Exec. Chef, Royal Thai School of Culinary Arts, 5 Thanon Rob Kau Sammuk; Bang Saen, T. Saen Suk; A. Muang, Chonburi, 20130 Thailand; (66) 1-867 9450, (66) 38-748 404, Fax (66) 38-748 405, info@royalthaichefs.com, www.royalthaichefs.com.

SAMUI INSTITUTE OF THAI CULINARY ARTS

Koh Samui/Year-round

Sponsor: Private institution specializing in English language instruction in the Thai culinary arts for non-Thais. Program: 3-wk Training for Professionals program that covers menu design & preparation of Thai cuisine. Established: 1999. Curriculum: culinary. Admit dates: Monthly. Total enrollment: 3. Facilities: New 12-million baht 3-story 300-sq-meter facility with 90-sq-meter instruction area, 10-burner teaching stove, gourmet restaurant with separate kitchen on 2nd floor.

COURSES: Thai cuisine, fruit & vegetable carving, menu design, napkin folding, table skirting & service.

FACULTY: 3 instructors. Director Roongfa Sringam has 12 yrs experience preparing Thai cuisine for a non-Thai clientele. She is a master food carver.

COSTS: Thai baht equivalent of ~$2440. Admission requirements: Basic kitchen experience, knowledge of food storage techniques & international hygiene standards.

LOCATION: Samui Island, a 90-min flight or 1-day train/boat/bus ride from Bangkok, Phuket or Singapore.

CONTACT: Martin Amada, Co-Director, Samui Institute of Thai Culinary Arts, 46/6 Moo 3 Chaweng Beach, Koh Samui, 84320 Thailand; (66) (77) 413-172, Fax (66) (77) 413-434, info@sitca.net, www.sitca.net/training.htm.

VIRGIN ISLANDS

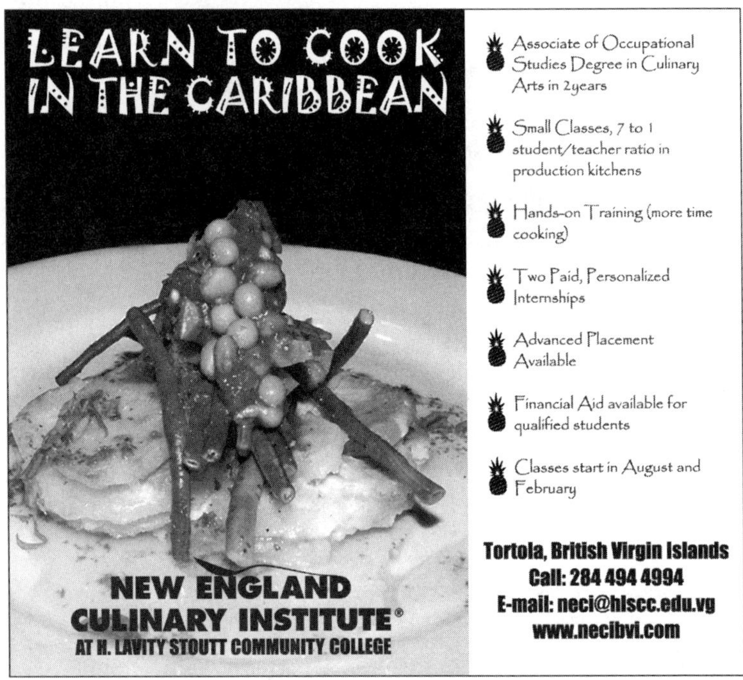

NEW ENGLAND CULINARY INSTITUTE AT H. LAVITY STOUTT CC

Road Town, Tortola, Virgin Islds (Brit)/Year-round *(See display ad above)*

Sponsor: New England Culinary Institute in partnership with H. Lavity Stoutt Community College (HLSCC). Program: 2-year AOS degree in Culinary Arts. Students spend 6 mos on campus & 6 mos on paid internships each year. Established: 2001. Accredited by ACCSCT. Calendar: semester. Curriculum: culinary. Admit dates: August & Feb. Total enrollment: 60. 21 each admission period. 40% receive financial aid. S:T ratio 7:1. Facilities: The operating kitchens at a contemporary menu restaurant, the Road Town Bakery, & the cafeteria at HLSCC. Student housing available.

COURSES: Include baking, pastry, prepared foods, a la carte, catering, meat fabrication, garde manger. 6 mos/yr.

COSTS: U.S. citizens $14,200/yr, Caribbean residents $11,360/yr, BVI residents $9,940/yr. Admission requirements: HS or college transcript, letter of reference, essay, application. Scholarships: yes. Loans: yes.

LOCATION: 60 miles east of San Juan, Puerto Rico.

CONTACT: Director of Admissions, New England Culinary Institute at H. Lavity Stoutt Community Coll, PO Box 3097, Road Town, Tortola, British Virgin Islands; 284-494-4994, Fax 284-494-4996, neci@HLSCC.edu.vg, www.hlscc.edu.vg.

National Apprenticeship Training Program for Cooks

American Culinary Federation (ACF)

The American Culinary Federation Apprenticeship is a three-year, earn while you learn, on-the-job training program reinforced by related instruction from an educational institution. The program began under the Carter Administration in 1976 with a grant from the U.S. Government and is now the seventh largest apprenticeship program in the U.S., with over 18,500 cooks being trained since its inception.

The apprenticeship program offers career-oriented cooks an alternative to private culinary institutions, community colleges, and vocational-technical schools. Apprentices, who generally range in age from 18 to 40 (average age 24), receive three years (6000 hours total) of on-the-job training while earning an income. The apprentice is registered with the Department of Labor and after a 480-hour (3-month) pr bationary period is required to become a junior member of the ACF. The apprentice attends school part-time (a minimum of 192 hours per year) and may also have the opportunity to earn an associate degree. The average cost for school is between $500 and $3,000 per year.

To qualify for the program, an applicant must be at least 17 years of age, have a high school diploma or equivalent, and have passed all entry-level academic and aptitude examinations as prescribed by the educational institution. Consideration may be given to those who have had high school food-service training or on-the-job experience. A multi-step screening process includes personal interviews, documentation of prior experience and an orientation process.

During his/her apprenticeship, an apprentice keeps a weekly Log Book in which recipes and food preparation techniques are recorded. The Log Book is reviewed periodically by the apprenticeís supervising chef, which helps the chef develop a mentor relationship with the apprentice. In addition to work skills, the apprentice completes 576 hours of classroom instruction at an approved post-secondary institution.

Upon completion of the program and successful completion of a written and practical exam, the apprentice is awarded a graduation certificate from the ACF and the Department of Labor and is granted the status of Certified Culinarian or Certified Pastry Culinarian. Apprentice graduates can confidently accept a job based on the experience received during their apprenticeship program.

CONTACT: ACF Apprenticeship Coordinator, American Culinary Federation, P.O. Box 3466, 10 San Bartola Dr., St. Augustine, FL 32085-3466; 800-624-9458, 904-824-4468, Fax 904-825-4758, E-mail educate@acfchefs.net.

ALABAMA

ACF Birmingham Chapter (p. 11)

ARKANSAS

ACF Central Arkansas Culinary School of Apprenticeship (p. 20)

CALIFORNIA

High Sierra Chefs Association (p. 28)

San Francisco Culinary/Pastry Program (p. 35)

COLORADO

ACF Culinarians of Colorado (p. 37)

FLORIDA

ACF Central Florida Chapter (p. 45)

ACF Gulf to Lakes Chefs Chapter (p.45)

ACF Palm Beach County Chefs (p. 45)

ACF Treasure Coast Chapter (p. 46)

HAWAII

Maui Chefs Association (p. 57)

INDIANA

ACF South Bend Chefs & Cooks Association (p. 66)

AMERICAN CULINARY FEDERATION ACCREDITING COMMISSION

St. Augustine, Florida

Accreditation by the ACF Accrediting Commission, the educational arm of the American Culinary Federation, evaluates the quality of an educationally accredited post-secondary institution's program in culinary arts and foodservice management Objectives, staff, facilities, policies, curriculum instructional methods, and procedures are examined to determine if they meet ACF standards for entry-level culinarians. To be eligible, a program must contain a majority of required competencies; be offered by a school that is accredited by an agency recognized by the U.S. Dept. of Education; be full-time, include at least 1,000 contact hours, and result in a certificate, diploma, or degree; have a full-time coordinator who qualifies as a Certified Culinary Educator, Executive Chef, or Executive Pastry Chef, has an appropriate master's degree or has credentials that allow for the effective direction of the program, and have existed continuously for at least two years and graduated a sufficient number of students. Accreditation application must be authorized by the department Dean and 50% of full-time faculty must have credentials equivalent to an ACF Certified Culinary Educator, Sous Chef, or Pastry Chef..

Contact: For a current list of accredited programs: ACF Accreditation, P.O. Box 3466, St. Augustine, FL 32085; 904-824-4468, www.acfchefs.org.

ACF-Accredited Schools as of June, 2003:

2

Recreational Programs

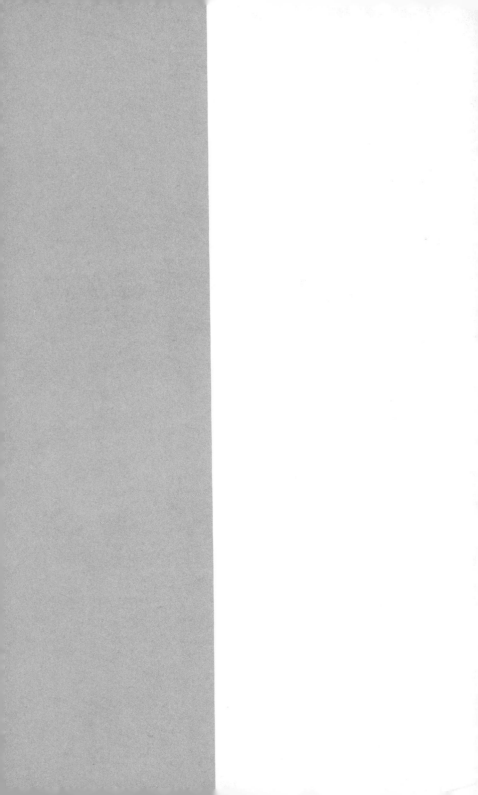

ALABAMA

COOK'S GARDEN
Mobile

Sponsor: Restaurant. Programs: Series of hands-on & demo classes that cover a variety of topics. Established: 1970. Class/group size: 25 demo, 14 hands-on. 4 programs/yr. Facilities: Restaurant kitchen. Also featured: Full-service catering, culinary tours.

EMPHASIS: Teaching the fundamental techniques & then the frills.

FACULTY: Local & guest chefs.

COSTS: $35-$85/class.

CONTACT: Priscilla Gold-Darby, CCP, Owner/Director, Cook's Garden, 306 Cottage Hill Rd., Mobile, AL 36606; 251-476-6184, Fax 251-432-2637.

CULINARD – THE CULINARY INSTITUTE OF VIRGINIA COLLEGE
Birmingham*(See also page 11) (See display ad page 13)*

Sponsor: Private, proprietary institution of higher education that offers career and recreational culinary programs. Programs: Series of programs, weekend & 1-day events on intermediate to advanced topics that include cooking, baking, wine appreciation. Established: 2000. Facilities: 7 instructional kitchens, full-service restaurant, full-service bakery, 10 lecture facilities.

EMPHASIS: Cooking, baking, wine appreciation.

FACULTY: Faculty selected for academic qualifications & real world business experience.

CONTACT: LaShondra Orum, Program Coordinator, CULINARD The Culinary Institute of Virginia College, 65 Bagby Drive, Suite 100, Birmingham, AL 35209; 205-802-1200, 877-429-CHEF (2433), Fax 205-802-7045, lorum@vc.edu, www.culinard.com.

ARIZONA

THE BISBEE COOKING SCHOOL
Bisbee

Sponsor: Culinary professional. Programs: Hands-on half-day classes in a variety of classical & regional cuisines including New Southwest, Cajun, Provincial French. Established: 2001. Class/group size: 14 demo, 6 hands-on. 100+ programs/yr. Also featured: Wine appreciation classes, garden tours.

EMPHASIS: Technique & classical foundation.

FACULTY: Helen Saul is a former restaurant owner/chef, college culinary instructor & menu advisor. She trained with Paul Prudhomme & Marcella Hazan & studied in New Orleans, Mexico & Bali.

COSTS: $35-$40/class.

LOCATION: A Victorian mining town, now an arts center, 90 min southeast of Tucson.

CONTACT: Helen Saul, Owner/chef, The Bisbee Cooking School, Box 541, Bisbee, AZ 85603; 520-432-3882, bisbeecookingschool@yahoo.com, www.geocities.com/bisbeecookingschool.

COOKING WITH CLASS, LTD.
Scottsdale

Sponsor: Private cooking school. Programs: Participation & demonstration cooking classes based on 3- or 4-course menus. Established: 1999. Class/group size: 16 hands-on, 24 demo. 250+ programs/yr. Facilities: 1,900-sq-ft teaching facility with ~900-ft kitchen & 600-sq-ft dining area. Features Dacor professional style equipment. Also featured: Custom cooking parties, cooking clubs, corporate team building, cooking camp for kids, spouse programs, gift certificates.

EMPHASIS: International cuisines, baking/pastry, cooking basics.

FACULTY: 3 full-time instructors, graduates of the Scottsdale Culinary Institute & members of the IACP.

COSTS: Average $65/participation class. Includes snack, beverages & 3- or 4-course meal.

CONTACT: Beth Cole, Director, Cooking with Class, Ltd., 14202 N. Scottsdale Rd., Ste. 100, Scottsdale, AZ 85254; 480-607-7474, Fax 480-659-6821, info@cookingwithclass.com, www.cookingwithclass.com.

CULINARY CONCEPTS
Tucson

Sponsor: Cooking school & retail kitchenware store. Programs: Participation classes include a 9-wks certificate course, series for youngsters, dinner workshops, celebrity & local chefs. Established: 1994. Class/group size: 25 hands-on/40 demo. 400+ programs/yr. Facilities: 900-sq-ft teaching kitchen with 14 gas burners, 4 ovens, 2 kitchen aids, 4 cuisinart & 9 work tables. Also featured: Wine appreciation, private classes, bridal showers, corporate parties, bimonthly Fri. luncheons, team-building programs.

FACULTY: Proprietor Judith Berger, CCP; Marilyn Davison, CCP; Marianne Bane, CCP. Each 20+ yrs culinary experience. Suzan Gross studied at Natural Gourmet Institute.

COSTS: $45-$65/class.

CONTACT: Judith B. Berger, CCP, Owner, Culinary Concepts, 2930 N. Swan, #126, Tucson, AZ 85712; 520-321-0968, Fax 520-321-0375, culinaryconcept@theriver.com, www.culinaryconcepts.net.

ELDERWOOD, THE ART OF COOKING
Scottsdale

Sponsor: Culinary professional. Programs: Personalized demo & hands-on cooking classes for individuals or small groups. Culinary tours & week-long cooking classes in Europe. Established: 1996. Class/group size: 3-15. 6 programs/yr. Facilities: European kitchens. Personalized instruction in student's home. Also featured: Group classes, private instruction.

EMPHASIS: Intl & regional cuisines, guest chef specialties, home entertaining, wine pairing menus.

FACULTY: Founder Debbie J. Elder, associated with the culinary arts since 1980, planning meal functions, catered events, & group travel. Guest chefs from around the world.

COSTS: $55+/class. Tour costs vary.

CONTACT: Ms. Debbie J. Elder, CMP, Founder, Elderwood, the Art of Cooking, 9455 E. Raintree Drive, #2030, Scottsdale, AZ 85260; 480-551-9769, Fax 480-551-9603, debbiejelder@msn.com.

GANACHE THIS
Scottsdale

Sponsor: Wholesale bakery. Programs: Hands-on chocolate & dessert classes. Established: 2001. Class/group size: 10-20. 50 programs/yr. Facilities: Wholesale industrial bake shop.

FACULTY: Pastry chef Judy Palmer, a CIA honors graduate with 27 yrs experience, is Coordinating Pastry Chef at Cannes Film Festival & formerly instructor of Advanced Pastry Arts at SCI.

COSTS: $40-$50/class. Group & series discounts available.

CONTACT: Lorin or Judy, Ganache This, 2951 N. Scottsdale Rd., Scottsdale, AZ 85251; 480-947-6503, Fax 480-941-3886, ganachethis@qwest.net, www.GanacheThis.com.

THE HOUSE OF RICE STORE
Scottsdale

Sponsor: Retail store & school. Programs: Single-session participation classes. Established: 1977. Class/group size: 13. 130 programs/yr. Facilities: Kitchen with large U-shaped counter. Also featured: Private group classes.

EMPHASIS: Chinese, Japanese, Indian & Thai.

FACULTY: Owner Kiyoko Goldhardt, Chau Liaw, Chef Santos Villarico, Salma Dutta O'Brien.

COSTS: $25-$45/class.

CONTACT: Kiyoko Goldhardt, The House of Rice Store, 3221 N. Hayden Rd., Scottsdale, AZ 85251; 480-949-9681/480-947-6698, Fax 480-947-0889, info@houserice.com, www.houserice.com.

KITCHEN CLASSICS
Phoenix

Sponsor: Kitchen retail store. Programs: Demonstration and hands-on cooking classes 4-5 times a week. Established: 1987. Class/group size: 12-32. 200+ programs/yr. Facilities: Retail store with full kitchen and dining areas. Also featured: Corporate teambuilding classes, private classes with in-house chef, private parties, etiquette lessons for groups, classes for children.

EMPHASIS: Variety of cuisines & themes.

FACULTY: Local restaurant chefs and in-store chefs.

COSTS: $28+/class.

CONTACT: Shauna Halawith, Mgr., Kitchen Classics, 4041 E. Thomas Rd., Phoenix, AZ 85018; 800-954-6828, Fax 602-954-6828, kitchenclassics@kitchen-classics.com, www.kitchen-classics.com.

LES GOURMETTES COOKING SCHOOL

Phoenix

Sponsor: Private school. Programs: Demo classes & series. Established: 1982. Class/group size: 15. 40-50 programs/yr. Facilities: Private home in central Phoenix. Also featured: Culinary travel.

EMPHASIS: French, Southwest, & other cuisines.

FACULTY: Proprietor Barbara Fenzl, CCP, studied at Le Cordon Bleu & Ecole Lenotre. Guest instructors have included Giuliano Bugialli, Hugh Carpenter, Lydie Marshall, Jacques Pepin, Anne Willan.

COSTS: $50-$125/class.

CONTACT: Barbara Fenzl, Owner, Les Gourmettes Cooking School, 6610 N. Central Ave., Phoenix, AZ 85012; 602-240-6767, Fax 602-266-2706, barbara.fenzl@cox.net.

LES PETITES GOURMETTES CHILDREN'S COOKING SCHOOL

Scottsdale

Sponsor: Culinary professional Linda Hopkins. Programs: 1-,4-, & 5-day hands-on courses for youngsters ages 6-17. Established: 1994. Class/group size: 10-12. 14-20 programs/yr. Facilities: Home kitchen.

EMPHASIS: Beginning & advanced techniques, intl holiday cuisines & specialties.

FACULTY: Linda Hopkins has assisted for 14 yrs at Les Gourmettes in Phoenix & worked with such professionals as Jacques Pepin, Emeril Lagasse, Martin Yan.

COSTS: $35/day, $135/4 days, $150/5 days.

CONTACT: Linda Hopkins, Owner/Teacher, Les Petites Gourmettes Children's Cooking School, 12007 N. 62nd Pl., Scottsdale, AZ 85254; 480-991-7648, Fax 480-991-4516, LPGourmett@aol.com, www.lespetitesgourmettes.com.

ONE MEAL AT A TIME

Phoenix, East Valley, West Valley

Sponsor: Private school. Programs: Private & group hands-on lessons, theme parties, food & wine pairing. Established: 2003. Class/group size: 1-40. Facilities: Client's home kitchen.

EMPHASIS: A variety of cuisines, menus customized to dietary & special needs.

FACULTY: Stacy Patel, graduate of Scottsdale Culinary Institute.

COSTS: $75-150/private class, $40+/group class.

CONTACT: Stacy Patel, Chef/Owner, One Meal At A Time, Chandler, AZ ; 480-664-3545, stacy@OneMealAtATime.com, www.OneMealAtATime.com.

SWEET BASIL GOURMETWARE & COOKING SCHOOL

Scottsdale

Sponsor: Cookware store. Programs: Demo classes & 1- to 3-session participation courses. Established: 1993. Class/group size: 14 hands-on/26 demo. 250 programs/yr. Facilities: 600-sq-ft kitchen with 6 workspaces, gas & electric appliances. Also featured: Field trips to herbfarms & other food related sites.

EMPHASIS: Ethnic, regional cuisines, entertaining, specific subjects.

FACULTY: 6 instructors include Amy Barnes, Chris Green, Linda Hunt-Smith, Jennifer Russo, Marcia Saldin, Ashly Young; local guest chefs.

COSTS: $20-$120/course.

CONTACT: Martha Sullivan, Owner, Sweet Basil Gourmetware & Cooking School, 10749 N. Scottsdale Rd., #101, Scottsdale, AZ 85260; 480-596-5628, Fax 480-367-1722, sweetbasil@sweetbasilgourmet.com, www.sweetbasilgourmet.com.

THAI GOURMET HOUSE COOKING SCHOOL
Scottsdale

Sponsor: Private specialty culinary school. Programs: Thai Cuisine and Basic Cooking Fundamentals and Technique. Established: 1989. Class/group size: 1-6. Facilities: Fully-equipped professional classroom kitchen with overhead mirror, individual work stations, and traditional outdoor Thai-style cooking facilities. Also featured: Specialty class: A simple and practical approach to healthy cooking for a modern lifestyle.

EMPHASIS: Selecting, preparing, and storing ingredients, meal and menu planning,cooking technique and presentation.

FACULTY: Director Praparat Sturlin, culinary professional from Thailand, has won national culinary competitions in Thailand and interned at The Oriental, The Ambassador, & The Hyatt Regency hotels in Bangkok.

COSTS: $45-$195.

CONTACT: Praparat Sturlin, Director, Thai Gourmet House Cooking School, 8313 East Monterosa St., Scottsdale, AZ 85251; 480-947-1258, thaigourmethouse@cox.net, www.thaigourmethouse.com.

ARKANSAS

COTTAGE INN RESTAURANT
Eureka Springs

Sponsor: Restaurant specializing in Mediterranean cuisine. Programs: 3-day hands-on cooking classes that cover the basics of a professional kitchen. Established: 1986. Class/group size: 8. 10 programs/yr. Facilities: Fully-equipped kitchen of a 100-seat operating restaurant. Work space for each student. Also featured: Art galleries, walking trails, antique shops, spa facilities, massage therapy.

EMPHASIS: The basics of preparing a 4-course entertaining menu paired with wine.

FACULTY: Linda Hager, restaurant owner & chef for 20 years, studied in Paris & Madrid, apprenticed in kitchens in Austria & Crete.

COSTS: $350 includes 5 meals; optional onsite lodging available.

CONTACT: Linda Hager, Chef-Owner, Cottage Inn Restaurant, 450 W. Van Buren, Eureka Springs, AR 72632; 501-253-5282, Fax 501-253-5232, lthager@ipa.net, www.cottageinneurekaspgs.com.

CALIFORNIA

ACADEMY OF COOKING – BEVERLY HILLS
Beverly Hills

Sponsor: Meredith's Marvelous Morsels catering firm. Programs: Participation classes. Established: 1990. Class/group size: 10. 12 programs/yr. Facilities: Restaurant kitchen with 10 work stations, or student's home (min 8 students). Also featured: Children's, private, corporate and group classes, culinary tours in southern California.

EMPHASIS: Afternoon tea, buffet, brunch menus; California, international, vegetarian cuisines.

FACULTY: Meredith Jo Mischen studied with chefs at New York's Plaza & Waldorf-Astoria Hotels.

COSTS: $65/class.

CONTACT: Meredith Jo Mischen, Director, Academy of Cooking - Beverly Hills, 400 S. Beverly Dr., #214, Beverly Hills, CA 90212; 310-284-4940, meredith@acbh.com.

AFFAIRS OF THE VINE
San Francisco

Sponsor: Organization. Programs: Full-day Wine Boot Camp & other wine education seminars, workshops. Established: 1999. Class/group size: 50. Also featured: Staff trainings, corporate affairs & team building events.

FACULTY: Wine educators with professional wine training.

COSTS: $50-$400.

Location: Wine workshops held at California Culinary Academy.
Contact: Barbara Drady, President, Affairs of the Vine, 696 Elliott Lane, Sebastopol, CA 95472; 707-874-1975, Fax 707-874-2553, info@AffairsoftheVine.com, www.AffairsoftheVine.com.

AMY MALONE SCHOOL OF CAKE DECORATING
La Mesa

Sponsor: Cake decorating professional Amy Malone. Programs: Morning & evening participation & demo classes. Established: 1977. Class/group size: 14 hands-on/30 demo. 150+ programs/yr.
Emphasis: Cake decorating, candy-making, creative garnishes, desserts, food presentation.
Faculty: Amy Malone is a graduate of the Wilton, Betty Newman May, John McNamara, & Frances Kuyper schools of cake decorating & was guest instructor at L'Academie de Cuisine.
Costs: $15-$75/class.
Contact: Amy Malone, Amy Malone School of Cake Decorating, 4212 Camino Alegre, La Mesa, CA 91941; 619-660-1900, amymalone@aol.com, www.amymalone.com.

THE ART OF THAI COOKING
Oakland

Sponsor: Private cooking school. Programs: 4-week, 4-session beginner, intermediate & advanced participation courses. 1-week beginner & advanced intensive classes for out-of-towners. Established: 1985. Class/group size: 12. 20 programs/yr. Facilities: Fully-equipped private kitchen. Also featured: Private instruction, classes in private homes, food & cultural tours to Thailand.
Emphasis: The major Thai ingredients & how to work with them.
Faculty: Kasma Loha-unchit, a native of Thailand, has taught Thai cooking since 1985. She is author of 2 Thai cookbooks, including It Rains Fishes, winner of IACP award for Best International Cookbook.
Costs: $145 for 4-week, 4-session series. $475 for week-long intensives. $2,850-$3,450 for 18- to 27-day tours of Thailand, including airfare, meals, and lodging.
Contact: Kasma Loha-unchit, The Art of Thai Cooking, P.O. Box 21165, Oakland, CA 94620; 510-655-8900, kasma@thaifoodandtravel.com, www.thaifoodandtravel.com.

BE GOURMET!
Los Angeles

Sponsor: Private school. Programs: Participation classes, wine & food tastings, dessert making. Established: 2000. Class/group size: 2-8. Daily programs/yr. Facilities: Fully-equipped home kitchen. Also featured: Demo & participation cooking parties, catering.
Emphasis: American & updated French cuisine; modern & practical cooking style.
Faculty: Tim Ross, CAP graduate from Paris' Ecole Superieur de Cuisine Francaise. Catering & restaurant experience in the U.S. & France.
Costs: $45-65/class.
Contact: Tim Ross, Chef, Be Gourmet!, 2419 Tesla Terrace, Los Angeles, CA 90039; 323-610-1082, begourmet@att.net, http://begourmet.home.att.net.

BERINGER MASTER SERIES ON FOOD & WINE
St. Helena

Sponsor: Beringer Vineyards. Programs: 2- to 5-day culinary & wine programs that emphasize seasonal ingredients; 11-day culinary & wine trip to Tuscany. Established: 2001. Facilities: Private kitchens, cellars, & vintner homes of Beringer & other Napa Valley wineries. Also featured: Garden tour, croquet, visit to art collection, olive oil pressing.
Emphasis: Small group food & wine programs.
Faculty: Well-known Napa Valley chefs & vintners.
Costs: 2- to 5-day programs $1,475-$3,250, $1,750-$4,850 with lodging; Tuscany trip $5,500.
Contact: David Mitchell, Director, Beringer Master Series on Food & Wine, 1000 Pratt Ave., PO Box 111, St. Helena, CA 94574; 707-967-4451, Fax 707-963-5521, david.mitchel@beringerblass.com, www.beringer.com.

BRISTOL FARMS COOKING SCHOOL

Manhattan Beach

Sponsor: Gourmet specialty foods & cookware store. Programs: 1- to 6-session demo & participation courses. Established: 1985. Class/group size: 20 hands-on/40 demo. 200+ programs/yr. Facilities: Kitchen with 6-burner stove, grill, oven. Also featured: Children's & private classes, field trips, tours.

EMPHASIS: International and regional cuisine, baking, low fat cooking, basic cooking techniques.

FACULTY: Director Grace-Marie Johnston. Guest instructors have included Graham Kerr, Paul Prudhomme, Stephen Pyles, Patricia Wells, Jacques Pepin, Tommy Tang.

COSTS: $40-$55/session.

CONTACT: Grace-Marie Johnston, Cooking School Director, Bristol Farms Cooking School, 1570 Rosecrans Ave., Manhattan Beach, CA 90266; 310-233-4752, gmjohnston@bristolfarms.com, www.bristolfarms.com/cookingschool/index.html.

CAKEBREAD CELLARS

Napa Valley

Sponsor: Winery. Programs: Demo & participation classes. Established: 1973. Class/group size: Demo 25, hands-on 16. 5 programs/yr. Facilities: Winery house & outdoor kitchens.

EMPHASIS: Seasonal specialties & local purveyors.

FACULTY: Resident chefs Brian Streeter & Richard Haake, both New England Culinary Institute graduates; guest chefs.

COSTS: $170/person.

CONTACT: George Knopp, Winery Events Coordinator, Cakebread Cellars, 8300 St. Helena Hwy., Box 216, Rutherford, CA 94573-0216; 707-963-5221 x230, Fax 707-963-1034, knopp@cakebread.com, www.cakebread.com.

CALIFORNIA CULINARY ACADEMY

San Francisco *(See also page 22) (See display ad page 23)*

Sponsor: Culinary career academy. Programs: Single topic culinary & baking & pastry classes, 5-part essentials series, food & wine pairing seminars, specialty & seasonal classes. Established: 1977. Class/group size: 20. 200+ programs/yr. Facilities: Commercial kitchens used for professional programs. Also featured: Private cooking classes.

EMPHASIS: Basic skills & advanced topics.

FACULTY: Academy chef instructors, industry professionals.

COSTS: $175/class, $625 for essentials series.

CONTACT: Weekends at the Academy, California Culinary Academy, 625 Polk St., San Francisco, CA 94102; 415-354-9198, Fax 415-292-8290, weekends@baychef.com, www.baychef.com.

CALIFORNIA SUSHI ACADEMY

Venice

Sponsor: Private school. Programs: Weekend 1-day sushi classes cover sushi rice, Nigiri sushi; California, spicy, & rainbow rolls. Class/group size: 12 max. 100+ programs/yr.

EMPHASIS: Sushi.

COSTS: $80.

CONTACT: Phil Yi, California Sushi Academy, 1611 Pacific Ave., Venice, CA 90291; 310-581-0213, Fax 310-306-2605, email@sushi-academy.com, www.sushi-academy.com.

COOKING CLASSES AT MOOSE'S

San Francisco

Sponsor: Moose's restaurant. Programs: 3-course meal prep using fresh ingredients & local produce. Established: 1993. Class/group size: 25. 3 programs/yr. Facilities: Open kitchen with overhead mirror.

EMPHASIS: Amateur-friendly recipes.

FACULTY: Chef Jeffrey Amber, formerly Executive Chef of San Francisco's W hotel, & a sous chef.

COSTS: $80/class, $220/3-class series, includes continental breakfast & lunch. TAB.

CONTACT: Barbara Carberry, Cooking Classes at Moose's, 1652 Stockton St., San Francisco, CA 94133; 415-989-7800 x11, Fax 415-989-7838, barbara@mooses.com, www.mooses.com.

COOKS AND BOOKS COOKING SCHOOL

Danville

Sponsor: Cooking school with chef's tools, chef wear, cookbooks, wine shop. Programs: Demo & participation courses, 4- & 5-part hands-on series, single topic classes, corporate team building. Established: 1991. Class/group size: 10-30 demo & hands. 100+ programs/yr. Facilities: 1,600-sq-ft teaching area & 600-sq-ft commercial kitchen. Also featured: Local shopping excursions, culinary tours.

EMPHASIS: International cuisines, seasonal & holiday menus, nutritious foods, wine & food pairing, guest chef specialties, basic series.

FACULTY: In-house instructors D.J. Rae, CCA graduate & Kent Nielsen. Other guest chef/instructors, culinary teachers & cookbook authors.

COSTS: $45-$65/class.

CONTACT: D.J. Rae, Chef/Owner, Cooks and Books and Corks, 148 E. Prospect Ave., Danville, CA 94526; 925-831-0708, Fax 925-831-0741, ckbkcrk@silcon.com, www.cooksbookscorks.com.

COPIA: THE AMERICAN CENTER FOR WINE, FOOD & THE ARTS

Napa

Sponsor: Cultural center devoted to wine, food & the arts in American culture. Programs: 60- to 90-min classes that cover wine & food pairing, ethnic & regional foods, seasonal cuisine, specific topics. Established: 2001. Class/group size: 50+. 100+ programs/yr. Facilities: 74-seat demo theatre with four 40' plasma monitors, commercial kitchen, 1,000-sq-ft vintage room for wine study. Also featured: Continuing ed & certificate courses in conjunction with the Univ of California-Davis & England's Wine & Spirit Education Trust.

EMPHASIS: Wine, food, art, culture.

FACULTY: Chefs, authors, producers. Culinary Program Mgr Brigid Callinan, a graduate of New England Culinary Inst, co-authored Mustards Grill Cookbook. Wine curator Peter Marks, MW.

CONTACT: Brigid Callinan, Culinary Program Manager, Copia: The American Center for Wine, Food & the Arts, 500 First St., Napa, CA 94559; 707-265-5929, 800-888-51-COPIA, bcallinan@copia.org, www.copia.org.

CULINARY ADVENTURES COOKING SCHOOL

San Diego

Sponsor: Culinary professional Janet Burgess. Programs: Theme classes and hands-on workshops for holidays, parties, gourmet groups, lower fat conversion, healthy cooking, and food history. Established: 1998. Class/group size: 8 hands-on, 12 demo. 40-50 programs/yr. Facilities: Private home or on-site. Also featured: Classes for youngsters, private instruction, market visits, visits to food producers and Asian, Latin, Italian and Middle Eastern specialty shops.

EMPHASIS: Cooking healthy tips & exposure to new foods in the marketplace and trends.

FACULTY: Janet Burgess, cooking teacher, lecturer, food consultant, IACP-member, has attended cooking schools in Belgium, Italy and the CIA, Greystone.

COSTS: $35-$60/class.

CONTACT: Janet Burgess, Owner/Teacher, Culinary Adventures Cooking School, PO Box 19601, San Diego, CA 92159; 619-589-6623, Fax 619-589-6623, jburgess911@msn.com.

THE CULINARY INSTITUTE OF AMERICA AT GREYSTONE

Napa Valley *(See also page 27, 107, 253) (See display ad page 108)*

Sponsor: The CIA's Greystone campus, a center for continuing education of food & wine professionals. Programs: Workshops for culinary professionals. Established: 1995. Class/group size: 18. 35 programs/yr. Facilities: 15,000-square-foot open teaching kitchens. Also featured: Travel programs & conferences.

EMPHASIS: International cuisine of Asia, Mexico, Mediterranean.

FACULTY: The CIA's chefs and instructors.

Costs: Tuition ranges from $850/30 hrs of instruction to $5,000/travel program.

Contact: Susan Cussen, Director of Marketing, CE, The Culinary Institute of America, Continuing Education Dept., 2555 Main St., St. Helena, CA 94574; 800-888-7850, Fax 845-451-1066, marketing@culinary.edu, www.ciachef.edu.

DR. ALAN YOUNG WINE PROGRAMS

San Francisco

Sponsor: Wine professional. Programs: Home study programs, 3-day seminars & study tours. Established: 1975. Class/group size: 25.

Faculty: Dr. Alan Young is an Australian wine consultant & author of 18 books, intl faculty.

Costs: Home study $197, 101 Secrets of Wine Tasting $120.

Contact: Dr. Alan Young, President, International Wine Academy, 38 Portola Dr., San Francisco, CA 94131-1518; 415-641-4767, 800-345-8466, Fax 415-641-7348, alanyoung@wineacademy.com, www.wineacademy.com.

DRAEGER'S CULINARY CENTERS

Menlo Park, San Mateo

Sponsor: Draeger's Market Place. Programs: Demonstration & hands-on classes on a variety of topics. Established: 1991. Class/group size: 35. 525/locati programs/yr. Facilities: Menlo Park: 38-seat classroom with kitchen and overhead mirror; San Mateo: 38-seat classroom with closed circuit video monitors. Also featured: Wine classes and dinners, market tours, private classes.

Emphasis: Ethnic and regional cuisines, fundamentals, baking, vegetarian and healthful foods, entertaining menus, food history.

Faculty: Guest instructors include well-known chefs, cookbook authors, & culinary professionals.

Costs: Range from $50-$95/class.

Contact: Pamela Keith, Culinary Director, Draeger's Culinary Centers, 222 E. Fourth Ave., San Mateo, CA 94401; 650-685-3795, Fax 650-685-3728, draegerscs@aol.com, www.draegers.com.

EPICUREAN SCHOOL OF CULINARY ARTS

Los Angeles

Sponsor: Private school. Programs: Participation classes in fish, chicken, and other specialties. Established: 1985. Class/group size: 15. Facilities: Teaching kitchen with 5 work stations.

Emphasis: Beginners' classes, specific cuisines.

Faculty: CIA and CCA graduates.

Costs: $65/class.

Contact: Staci Jenkins, Epicurean School of Culinary Arts, 8759 Melrose Ave., Los Angeles, CA 90069; 310-659-5990, Fax 310-659-0302, epicurean5@aol.com, www.epicureanschool.com.

ERNA'S ELDERBERRY HOUSE COOKING SCHOOL

Oakhurst

Sponsor: The Château du Sureau (Estate by the Elderberries). Programs: 3-day participation programs; 8 hrs daily cooking instruction devoted to preparing a 6-course menu. Wine pairing instruction. Established: 1985. Class/group size: 12. 7 programs/yr. Facilities: Erna's Elderberry Restaurant's full commercial kitchen, herb garden, local organic vegetable farm. Also featured: Bass fishing, golf, hiking, tennis, horseback riding, river rafting, rock climbing, visits to Yosemite Natl Park.

Emphasis: Sauces, soups, seafood & meat cookery, desserts.

Faculty: Chef-Proprietor Erna Kubin-Clanin has 30 yrs of culinary & restaurant experience together with Executive Chef James Overbaugh.

Costs: $1,200 includes lunch & dinner. Ten 2-person guest rooms at Château du Sureau range from $350-$550 including breakfast. 2-room villa $2,800/night.

Location: The chateau, a member of Relais & Chateaux, is in a mountain village near Yosemite.

Contact: Erna Kubin-Clanin, Proprietor, Elderberry House Cooking School, 48688 Victoria Ln., Box 2413, Oakhurst, CA 93644; 559-683-6800, Fax 559-683-0800, chateau@chateausureau.com, www.elderberryhouse.com.

FRED MCMILLIN WINE COURSES
San Francisco

Sponsor: Wine professional. Programs: 12, 3-session courses/yr. Established: 1965. Class/group size: 15.
EMPHASIS: Wine fundamentals for beginners & intermediates.
FACULTY: Northern California editor for American Wine on the Web, 2 degrees in chemical engineering, writes for 3 wine publications.
COSTS: $80-$100/course.
CONTACT: Fred McMillin, 2121 Broadway, #6, San Francisco, CA 94115; 415-563-5712, Fax 415-567-4468.

G.M. 'POOCH' PUCILOWSKI WINE PROGRAMS
Sacramento

Sponsor: Wine professional. Programs: 1- to 6-session wine courses. Established: 1973. Class/group size: 15-40. ~12 programs/yr.
FACULTY: G.M. 'Pooch' Pucilowski is past president of SWE; chief judge & consultant California State Fair Wine Competition.
COSTS: $50-$100.
CONTACT: G.M. 'Pooch' Pucilowski, G.M. 'Pooch' Pucilowski WIne Programs, 7784 Magnolia Avenue, Fair Oaks, CA 95628; 916-961-6150, Fax 916-961-6153, gmpooch@pacbell.net.

GOURMET RETREATS AT CASALANA
Napa Valley

Sponsor: Private school. Programs: Single sessions, week-end retreats, & 3- & 5-day courses that cover a variety of topics, including essential skills, ethnic & seasonal cuisines, desserts, food & wine pairing. Established: 1996. Class/group size: Demo 20, hands-on 8. 40-50 programs/yr. Facilities: Mediterranean style B&B with a professionally equipped kitchen, over a half acre of fruit & vegetable gardens. Also featured: Visits to specialty & farmers' markets, food producers, winemaker.
EMPHASIS: Classes for home cooks & food enthusiasts.
FACULTY: Gourmet Retreats owner Lana Richardson, an honor graduate of the California Culinary Academy with catering experience; guest chefs & authors.
COSTS: From $60/3-hr session to $725/5-day course, includes up to 36 hrs of instruction & meals.
CONTACT: Lana Richardson, Owner, Gourmet Retreats at CasaLana, 1316 S. Oak St., Calistoga, CA 94515; 877-968-2665, 707-942-0615, Fax 707-942-0204, lana@casalana.com, www.GourmetRetreats.com.

THE GREAT CHEFS AT ROBERT MONDAVI WINERY
Oakville

Sponsor: Robert Mondavi Winery. Programs: 3-day weekend programs (followed by 1-day programs) that feature cooking demos by noted chefs, wine seminars, private winery tours, theme lunches & dinners. Established: 1976. Class/group size: 26. 2 programs/yr.
EMPHASIS: International cuisines, wine seminars, table setting & flower arranging seminar.
FACULTY: Nationally- & internationally-known chefs.
COSTS: $2,000 ($150 single supplement) for 3-day program includes lodging, lunches & dinners; $225 for 1-day programs.
CONTACT: Valerie Varachi, Event Coordinator, The Great Chefs at Robert Mondavi Winery, P.O. Box 106, Oakville, CA 94562; 707-968-2100, Fax 707-968-2174, valerie.varachi@robertmondavi.com, www.robertmondavi.com.

GREAT NEWS!
San Diego

Sponsor: Cookware store. Programs: Hands-on and demo classes in basic techniques, ethnic cooking, individual subjects. Established: 1996. Class/group size: 25 hands-on, 50 demo. 375+ programs/yr. Facilities: Teaching kitchen with 5 big-screen TV monitors. Also featured: Market visits.

Emphasis: Classes for the home chef.

Faculty: Cookbook authors and local restaurant chefs.

Costs: $25-$50/class.

Contact: Megan Barnett, Cooking School Mgr, Great News!, 1788 Garnet, San Diego, CA 92109; 858-270-1582, ext. 3, Fax 858-270-6815, greatnews@great-news.com, www.great-news.com.

HUGH CARPENTER'S CAMP NAPA CULINARY

Oakville, Napa Valley

Sponsor: Chef & cookbook author Hugh Carpenter. Programs: 6-day food & wine tours that feature participation classes. Established: 1992. Class/group size: 18. 8 programs/yr. Facilities: Cakebread Cellars Winery kitchen. Also featured: Dining in fine restaurants, private winery tours, seminars on food & wine pairing, croquet tournament. Hot-air ballooning, Calistoga spa, golf, tennis.

Emphasis: California-Asian & cross-cultural cuisine; winery chef specialties.

Faculty: Hugh Carpenter is author of 13 cookbooks, including Pacific Flavors, Great Ribs, Fast Appetizers, Fast Entrees.

Costs: $1,623, includes meals & planned itinerary. A list of recommended lodging is available.

Contact: Hugh Carpenter, Camp Napa Culinary, P.O. Box 114, Oakville, CA 94562; 707-944-9112, 888-999-4844, Fax 707-944-2221, hugh@hughcarpenter.com, www.hughcarpenter.com.

INGREDIENTS COOKING/LIFESTYLE SCHOOL

Danville

Sponsor: Cooking school sponsored by grocery market group. Programs: Hands-on classes that focus on professional techniques, guest chef demos, lunch sessions, children's classes. Established: 3. Class/group size: 16 hands-on, 36 demo. 160 + programs/yr. Facilities: Commercial kitchen with granite work station, cameras & mirror. Also featured: Private classes, winemaker dinners.

Faculty: Bernhardt Chirent, executive chef of San Francisco's Fairmont Hotel, chef/instructor at Diablo Valley College; Bill Wavrin, executive chef of the Savory Inn & Cooking School in Vail, aurhor of Rancho la Puerta Cookbook.Guests chefs.

Costs: $35-$95.

Contact: Karen Alvarez, Director, Ingredients Cooking/Lifestyle School, 345 Railroad Ave., Danville, CA 94526; 925-314-4362, Fax 925-855-8934, karen.alvarez@andronicos.com, www.andronicos.com.

THE JEAN BRADY COOKING SCHOOL

Santa Monica

Sponsor: Culinary professional Jean Brady. Programs: 7-session demo series, guest chef classes, culinary tours to Europe, 1 wk summer cooking camps for kids. Established: 1973. Class/group size: 6-9 hands-on/12 demo. Facilities: Commercially-equipped home kitchen featured in Bon Appétit. Local guest chefs' restaurant kitchens. Also featured: Hands-on classes, local tours with ethnic experts, children's classes, market visits, 1-day to 1-wk seminars for private groups.

Emphasis: Low-fat/healthy savories, menus for entertaining, guest chef specialties in local restaurants.

Faculty: Jean Brady studied with Lydie Marshall, Jacques Pepin, & Paula Wolfert & attended the Cordon Bleu & La Varenne. Guest chefs & top local chefs.

Costs: Guest chef classes $60-$90. 7-session series $340.

Contact: Jean Brady, The Jean Brady Cooking School, 680 Brooktree Rd., Santa Monica, CA 90402; 310-454-4220, bradyrustic@yahoo.com.

JOHN BUECHSENSTEIN WINE PROGRAMS

Northern cities

Sponsor: Wine professional. Programs: 1- & 2-day courses, wk-long seminars, special seminars. Established: 1978. Class/group size: 50. ~10 programs/yr. Also featured: Wine tasting tours of France.

Faculty: John Buechsenstein is a winemaker & is a member of AWS, IFT, SWE, ASEV.

Costs: $150-$650/course.

Location: UC-Davis, Mendocino College, CIA at Greystone.

CONTACT: John Buechsenstein, Wine Education & Consultation, PO Box 431, Talmage, CA 95481; 707-463-0760, johnb@pacific.net.

KITCHEN ACADEMY AT THE CALIFORNIA SCHOOL OF CULINARY ARTS
South Pasadena

Sponsor: Private professional culinary school. Programs: Classes for the home chef include cooking techniques, baking series, & advanced cooking. Established: 1994. Class/group size: 20-24. Monthly programs/yr. Facilities: 6 professionally-equipped kitchen/labs. Also featured: Field trips to local farmers' markets, wineries, food events.

EMPHASIS: Cooking skills for the non-professional or home chef.

FACULTY: 4 instructors professionally trained at the California School of Culinary Arts.

COSTS: $80-$635.

CONTACT: Pamela Ramirez, Director, Kitchen Academy, 561 East Green St., Pasadena, CA 91101; 888-900-2433 x1301, pam@scsca.com, www.kitchenacademy.com.

LA BUONA FORCHETTA
Guerneville

Sponsor: Applewood Inn & Restaurant. Programs: Mini-culinary vacations offering demo & hands-on classes with field trips to Sonoma County farms, wineries & farmers markets. Dining & lodging at the inn. Established: 2003. Class/group size: 16 max. 12 programs/yr. Facilities: Kitchen & dining rooms of the inn's historic Belden House. Also featured: Hot-air balloon trips, massage, horseback riding, canoeing, kayaking.

FACULTY: Chef/instructor Brian Gerritsen, Executive Chef of the Restaurant at Applewood. Guest chefs, vintners, farmers, cheese makers.

CONTACT: Darryl Notter, Owner, La Buona Forchetta, 13555 Highway #116, Guerneville, CA 95446; 707-869-9093, Fax 707-869-9170, stay@applewoodinn.com, www.applewoodinn.com.

LA CUCINA MUGNAINI
Watsonville

Sponsor: Cooking school dedicated to the use of wood-fired ovens. Programs: Classes & demos on wood-burning oven basics. Topics range from seafood to bread-baking, Italian favorites to Asian fusion. Established: 1995. Class/group size: 32 demo, 16 hands-on. 75-100 programs/yr. Facilities: 1,000-sq-ft kitchen with 4 Italian wood-burning ovens. Also featured: Teambuilding, private parties, event planning, filming location.

EMPHASIS: Cooking techniques using a wood-fired oven.

FACULTY: In-house instructors with experience in using wood-fired ovens; visiting chef instructors.

COSTS: $50-$210, includes tasting of foods prepared in class. Nearby lodging options available.

CONTACT: La Cucina Mugnaini, Mugnaini Imports, 11 Hangar Way, Watsonville, CA 95076; 888- 887-7206 (toll free), 831-761-1767, Fax 831-728-5570, mugnaini@mugnaini.com, www.mugnaini.com.

LAGUNA CULINARY ARTS
Laguna Beach

Sponsor: Private school. Programs: Hands-on weekend, evening, full- & half-day classes for the home chef. Topics include smoking & grilling, entertaining, seafood, Italian, hors d'oeuvres, sauces, comfort food, vegetarian, sushi. Established: 2001. Class/group size: 10-12 hands-on. 350+ programs/yr. Facilities: Ocean-view teaching kitchen equipped with the latest appliances & designed for the home chef, outdoor deck & herb garden. Also featured: Team building events, wine tastings, private cooking parties, painting lessons.

EMPHASIS: The art of cooking using fresh, seasonal ingredients.

FACULTY: 6 full-time & ~6 local guest chefs.

COSTS: $65-$75/evening class, $165-$385/1- to 3-day classes, $95-$395/weekend classes.

CONTACT: Megan Rainnie, Director of Sales and Marketing, Laguna Culinary Arts, 550 South Coast Hwy., #7, Laguna Beach, CA 92651; 949-494-0745, 888-288-0745, Fax 949-494-0136, megan@lagunaculinaryarts.com, www.lagunaculinaryarts.com.

LET'S GET COOKIN'

Westlake Village

Sponsor: Private school. Programs: 1- to 6-session demo & participation classes. Class/group size: 10-35. 150+ programs/yr. Facilities: 1,500-sq-ft combination demonstration/participation facilities, cookware store. Also featured: Classes for young people, day trips, travel abroad.

EMPHASIS: Basic and advanced techniques for the home cook.

FACULTY: Includes cookbook authors and guest chefs.

COSTS: $50-$85/session ($30 for children's classes).

CONTACT: Phyllis Vaccarelli, Owner, Let's Get Cookin', 4643 Lakeview Canyon Rd., Westlake Village, CA 91361; 818-991-3940, Fax 805-495-2554, lgcookin@aol.com, www.letsgetcookin.com.

MARIAN W. BALDY WINE PROGRAMS

Chico

Sponsor: University. Programs: 45-session 3-credit university course. Established: 1972. Class/group size: 190. 1 programs/yr. Also featured: Winemaking.

FACULTY: Marian W. Baldy, Ph.D. has a doctorate degree in genetics, winemaker, CWE, author of The University Wine Course, Chair of the Education Committee & Board of Examiners of SWE.

COSTS: $500/course.

LOCATION: California State University, Chico.

CONTACT: Marian W. Baldy, Ph.D., California State University, First & Normal Sts., School of Agriculture, Chico, CA 95929-0310; 530-898-6250, Fax 530-898-5845, mbaldy@csuchico.edu, www.csuchico.edu/agr/faculty/Mbaldy.shtml.

MEADOWOOD FOOD & WINE PROGRAMS

St. Helena

Sponsor: Country resort. Programs: Cooking classes & farmer's market excursions, 2-day guest chef programs that include hands-on instruction, winery tours & tastings. Class/group size: ~10. Also featured: Special events & programs devoted to health & wellness, the arts, music, sports & nature. Tennis, golf, croquet.

EMPHASIS: Culinary programs that emphasize Napa Valley wines.

FACULTY: John Thoreen, Meadowood's Wine Center Director for 15 years. Guest chefs include Patricia Wells, cooking teacher, restaurant critic of the International Herald Tribune & author of 8 cookbooks.

COSTS: 2-day guest chef program $4,500/couple, including lodging & some meals.

LOCATION: 85 cottages, suites & lodges on a private estate in Napa Valley.

CONTACT: Ann Marie Conover, Meadowood Food & Wine Programs, 900 Meadowood Lane, St. Helena, CA 94574; 800-458-8080, 707-963-3646, Fax 707-963-3532, aconover@meadowood.com, www.meadowood.com.

MICHAEL A. AMOROSE WINE CLASSES

San Francisco

Sponsor: Wine professional. Programs: Wine tasting classes. 9 wines tasted/session. Price range $10-$40/bottle, current vintages. Established: 1974. Class/group size: 40-50. 25 programs/yr.

EMPHASIS: California & Pacific Northwest wines.

FACULTY: Michael Amorose is author of 10 books on wine.

COSTS: $25-$50/class.

LOCATION: Meetings & conventions.

CONTACT: Michael A. Amorose Wine Classes, 555 California St., #1700, San Francisco, CA 94104; 415-951-3377, Fax 415-248-2101, michael.amorose@ey.com.

MICHAEL R. BOTWIN WINE COURSES

San Luis Obispo

Sponsor: Wine professional. Programs: Three 5-session courses/yr (California wines). Two 6-session courses/yr (European wines). Established: 1973. Class/group size: 20.

Faculty: Michael Botwin is a member of AWS, chairman of AWS Luis Obispo.
Costs: $145/5-session course, $175/6-session course.
Location: California Polytechnic.
Contact: Michael R. Botwin, 2566 Santa Clara, San Luis Obispo, CA 93401; 805-543-1200.

MR. STOX RESTAURANT WINE CLASSES
Anaheim

Sponsor: Restaurant. Programs: 1- & 3-session classes. Established: 1980. Class/group size: 20. Also featured: Food classes.
Faculty: Chef Scott Raczak & wine expert Ron Marshall. Manage 22,000-bottle cellar.
Costs: $100/3-sessions.
Contact: Debbie Marshall, Mr. Stox Restaurant, 1105 E. Katella Ave., Anaheim, CA 92805; 714-634-2994, Fax 714-634-0561, mrstox@mrstox.com, www.mrstox.com.

NAPA VALLEY COOKING SCHOOL
St. Helena

(See also page 31) (See display ad page 32)

Sponsor: College. Programs: 1- to 4-session demo & participation courses. Established: 1990. Class/group size: 12-28. Facilities: New kitchen with 18 burners, 4 ovens, demonstration counter, outdoor dining area. Also featured: Wine & food classes, farmer's market visits, catering seminars.
Emphasis: Various topics, including cooking basics, bread baking, Indian, Asian, Italian, and Mediterranean cuisines, wine appreciation.
Faculty: Guest chefs have included: Bruce Aidells, Hubert Keller, Michael Chiarello, Gary Danko, Carlo Middione, John Ash, and Jeremiah Tower.
Costs: $50-$75/session.
Contact: Barbara Alexander, Executive Chef, Napa Valley College, 1088 College Ave., St. Helena, CA 94574; 707-967-2930, Fax 707-967-2909, BAlexander@campus.nvc.cc.ca.us, www.napacommunityed.org/cookingschool/wine.html.

THE NEW SCHOOL OF COOKING
Los Angeles

Sponsor: Private school. Programs: Recreational participation classes, demo classes, kid's camp, part-time professional chef & baking programs. Established: 2000. Class/group size: 16. Facilities: 1,400-sq-ft professional kitchen classroom with demo area & hands-on student work area. Also featured: Wine & food pairing classes, private parties, corporate team building.
Emphasis: Practical, classic culinary technique.
Faculty: Karen Hillenburg, Carol Thompson & Tracy Callahan, CCA graduates; May Parich, CIA graduate; Jet Tila, Le Cordon Bleu graduate; Neelam Batra, Indian chef & cookbook author.
Costs: $75/hands-on class, $325/wk kid's camp.
Contact: Anne Smith, Director, The New School of Cooking, 8690 Washington Blvd., Culver City, CA 90323; 310-842-9702, annesmith@newschoolofcooking.com, www.newschoolofcooking.com.

RAMEKINS SONOMA VALLEY CULINARY SCHOOL
Sonoma

Sponsor: Wine country cooking school, B&B, cookbook store, restaurant. Programs: Half day cooking & baking classes that include basic & general cooking instruction, ethnic & skill or ingredient specific sessions, seasonal menus; culinary team-building, cooking parties. Established: 1998. Class/group size: 36 demo, 18 hands-on. 375 programs/yr. Facilities: 2 teaching kitchens with the latest equipment: one primarily demo with TVs, mirrors & residential equipment, the other a full-service commercial kitchen. Also featured: Private team-building and dinner-party classes; culinary tours to markets, food producers, & wineries; wedding reception and meeting space.
Emphasis: Ethnic cuisines, culinary skills, specific ingredients, food & wine pairing, seasonal menus from noted restaurant chefs, e.g., Boulevard, Olives, Fleur de Lys, Gary Danko.
Faculty: 100+ instructors including celebrity chefs, cookbook authors, local restaurant chefs, and other culinary professionals.

Costs: Demos $38-$55, hands-on classes $55-$75.

Contact: Bob Nemerovski, Culinary Director, Ramekins Sonoma Valley Culinary School, 450 W. Spain St., Sonoma, CA 95476; 707-933-0450 x3, Fax 707-933-0451, info@ramekins.com, www.ramekins.com.

RUTA'S KITCHEN – REGIONAL INDIAN COOKING CLASSES

Rockridge, Oakland

Sponsor: Chef-owned cooking school. Programs: Hands-on regional Indian cooking classes followed by sit-down dinner. Established: 2000. Class/group size: 10. Weekly programs/yr.

Emphasis: Regional Indian cuisine.

Faculty: Ruta Kahate,whoo is also a culinary instrutor at Sur La Table, Draeger's & Ramekins.

Contact: Ruta Kahate, Chef, Ruta's Kitchen - Regional Indian Cooking Classes, 373 Alcatraz Ave, Oakland, CA 94618; 510-655-7882, ruta1@hotmail.com, www.rutaruta.com.

SCUOLA DI CUCINA

Mill Valley, Marin County

Sponsor: Professional chef. Programs: Hands-on classes feature restaurant-style dishes, professional tips & techniques. Specific techniques series available. Established: 2002. 6 programs/yr. Facilities: Frantoio Ristorante kitchen, serving ~200 guests/day. Also featured: On-site professional olive oil co.

Emphasis: Italian cuisine.

Faculty: Duilio Valenti, chef of Frantoio Ristorante & Olive Oil Co. Frantoio is ranked among the top 100 Bay Area restaurants by San Francisco Chronicle's food critic.

Costs: $90/class.

Contact: Liza Garfield, Manager, Scuola di Cucina, 152 Shoreline Highway, Mill Valley, CA 94941; 415-389-0755, lizagarfield@attbi.com, www.frantoio.com.

THE SEASONAL TABLE COOKING SCHOOL

Los Angeles area

Sponsor: Culinary professionals Karen Berk & Jean Brady. Programs: Private group & team-building cooking classes. Established: 1994. Class/group size: 20 max. Facilities: Private home with commercially equipped kitchen.

Emphasis: Includes seasonal & entertaining menus, healthful & vegetarian cooking, baking, restaurant specialties, ethnic cuisines.

Faculty: Co-owners Karen Berk, co-editor of Zagat LA/So. Calif. Restaurant Surveys, & Jean Brady of The Jean Brady Cooking School; restaurant chefs, cookbook authors, culinary professionals.

Costs: $75/class.

Contact: Karen Berk, Co-owner, The Seasonal Table Cooking School, 12618 Homewood Way, Los Angeles, CA 90049; 310-472-4475, Fax 310-471-3904, kjberk@linkline.com.

A STORE FOR COOKS

Laguna Niguel

Sponsor: Cookware store and school. Programs: Morning and evening demonstration classes and Lunch & Learn classes. Established: 1981. Class/group size: 25 demo. 100+ programs/yr. Also featured: Classes for private groups.

Emphasis: Ethnic and regional cuisines, holiday and seasonal foods, guest chef specialties.

Faculty: Proprietor and cookbook author Susan Vollmer, Hugh Carpenter, Phillis Carey, Kay Pastorius, George Geary, cookbook authors, and local chefs.

Costs: Lunch and Learn classes $16; demonstrations $40-$75.

Contact: Susan Vollmer, Owner, A Store for Cooks, 30100 Town Center Dr., Ste. R, Laguna Niguel, CA 92677; 714-495-0445, Fax 714-495-2139, store4cook@aol.com.

THE SUSTAINABLE KITCHEN

Berkeley

Sponsor: Culinary professional Laurel Miller. Programs: Hands-on cooking classes for adults & children. Includes sustainable agriculture/organic farming education, seasonal ingredients, organic farm & dairy tours. Established: 1997. Class/group size: 1-15. Continuous programs/yr. Facilities: Instructor's home, local restaurant, cooking schools & farmers' markets. Also featured: Culinary tours/classes at organic farms, dairies, cheesemakers, & other artisan food producers, private classes, cooking class parties, consulting for sustainable ag. education.

EMPHASIS: Food culture & cuisines of different countries.

FACULTY: Laurel Miller, a graduate of Johnson & Wales Univ, teaches classes at cooking schools & farmers' markets & conducts farm tours. She writes a food column for local newspapers.

COSTS: $45-$65 for child/adult classes.

CONTACT: Laurel Miller, Culinary Educator, The Sustainable Kitchen, 2930 Fulton St., Berkeley, CA 94705; 510-665-1446, Fax 510-665-1446, kaukau.kids@gte.net, www.sustainablekitchen.com.

TANTE MARIE'S COOKING SCHOOL
San Francisco

Sponsor: Small private school. Programs: 1-week, 3-day, weekend, 6-session evening, & single-session morning participation courses, afternoon & weekend demos, & party classes. Established: 1979. Class/group size: 12-32. 800 programs/yr. Facilities: Store front with tile floors, wooden counters, 6 ovens, 20 burners. Also featured: 1-week courses that include shopping at the Farmer's Market, visits to bread bakeries and cheese makers, winery tours, and dining in fine restaurants.

EMPHASIS: General and specific topics, including pastries and regional cuisines.

FACULTY: Founder Mary Risley studied at Le Cordon Bleu and La Varenne; guest instructors.

COSTS: 1-week course $675, 1-week vacation course $800, weekend course $50-$350, 6-session evening course $540, morning classes $95, demonstrations $50. Hotel lodging available.

CONTACT: Peggy Lynch, Admin. Director, Tante Marie's Cooking School, 271 Francisco St., San Francisco, CA 94133; 415-788-6699, Fax 415-788-8924, peggy@tantemarie.com, www.tantemarie.com.

THE TASTING SPOON
Los Gatos, Marina del Rey, Northridge, Pleasanton

Sponsor: Private school. Programs: Culinary classes & tours. 50+ programs/yr.

FACULTY: Includes Sue Young.

COSTS: Classes $40, trips $2,000-$3,200.

CONTACT: Sue Young, Owner, The Tasting Spoon, 520 Washington Blvd., #816, Marina del Rey, CA 90292; 310-306-8851, Fax 310-822-5613, sue@tastingspoon.com, www.tastingspoon.com.

UCSC EXTENSION CULINARY ARTS PROGRAM
Sunnyvale, Santa Cruz,

Sponsor: University of California, Santa Cruz Extension program. Programs: 1- to 4-session participation workshops and courses. Established: 1983. Class/group size: 18-20. 20+ programs/yr. Facilities: Historic house with modern commercial kitchen.

EMPHASIS: Stress relief cooking, and a variety of other topics.

FACULTY: Director Sharon Shipley, an IACP member who received certificates from La Varenne and Le Cordon Bleu; noted guest chefs.

COSTS: Range from $85 for a single session to $185 for four.

CONTACT: Marlene Aza, Program Representative, UCSC Extension Culinary Arts Program, UCSC Extension-Humanities Dept., Santa Cruz, CA 95060; 831-427-6695, Fax 831-427-1827, maza@ucsc-extension.edu, www.ucsc-extension.edu.

VIKING CULINARY ARTS AND HOMECHEF CENTERS
4 locations

Sponsor: Cooking school & culinary retail store. Programs: Demo classes on a variety of topics; 12-week Essential Cooking Series; 1- to 3-day Techniques of Cooking hands-on courses. Established: 1999. Class/group size: 12 hands-on; 40 demo. 800 programs/yr. Facilities: Teaching participation kitchen & demo theater equipped with Viking Range Corp. product line. Also featured: Corporate team-building programs.

EMPHASIS: Cooking techniques, guest chef specialties.

FACULTY: Chan Patterson, Corporate Cooking School Director. Local & national guest chefs.
COSTS: $35-$50 for demos, $125-$375 for techniques classes.
LOCATION: Viking HomeChef Centers: Corte Madera, San Francisco, San Jose, Walnut Creek, CA. Viking Culinary Arts Centers: GA, NY, PA, TN, TX.
CONTACT: Chan Patterson, Corporate Cooking School Director, Viking Culinary Arts Center, 1052 Highland Colony Parkway, #125, Ridgeland, MS 39157; 601-898-2778 x-6607, Fax 601-898-7947, cpatters@vikingrange.com, www.vikingrange.com.

WEIR COOKING
San Francisco & wine country

Sponsor: Culinary professional Joanne Weir. Programs: 3-7 day participation courses. Established: 1989. Class/group size: 10-15. 4-6 programs/yr. Facilities: Villas, wineries & cooking schools. Also featured: Napa & Sonoma Valley tours. Private classes & visits to restaurants, wineries & markets.
EMPHASIS: French, Italian, Mediterranean, & American regional cuisines.
FACULTY: Joanne Weir cooked at Berkeley's Chez Panisse, received the Julia Child/IACP Cooking Teacher Award of Excellence & appears on her own public TV show.
COSTS: $1,500-$3,750.
CONTACT: Joanne Weir, Weir Cooking, 2107 Pine St., San Francisco, CA 94115; 415-776-4200, Fax 415-776-0318, joanne@weircooking.com, www.weircooking.com.

WINESPEAK
Northern cities

Sponsor: Wine professional. Programs: Customized food & wine classes on demand, educational wine itineraries & tours. Established: 1986. Class/group size: 5-500.
FACULTY: Betsy Fischer, CWE, has 24 yrs experience in the food, beverage & tourism industry.
COSTS: $25-$125.
CONTACT: Betsy Fischer, Winespeak, 10 Fourth St., Santa Rosa, CA 95401; 707-577-8358, Fax 707-577-8348, gofish@sonic.net.

WOK WIZ WALKING TOURS & COOKING CENTER
San Francisco

Sponsor: Private school. Programs: Weekend Walk 'n Wok Workshop, which includes demo cooking class. Established: 1986. Class/group size: 4-7. 100+ programs/yr. Facilities: 1,100-sq-ft, 2-story building with demo area. Also featured: Walking tours of Chinatown, custom tours & classes, epicurean tours to Hong Kong & Thailand; Singapore, China, Italy.
EMPHASIS: Traditional, simple, healthy Chinese cuisine.
FACULTY: Shirley Fong-Torres, author of the Wok Wiz Chinatown Cookbook, In the Chinese Kitchen, & San Francisco Chinatown, A Walking Tour.
COSTS: Food shopping & cooking workshop $75.
CONTACT: Shirley Fong-Torres, Owner, Wok Wiz Walking Tours & Cooking Center, 654 Commercial St., San Francisco, CA 94111-2504; 415-981-8989 OR 650-355-9657, Fax 650-359-8999, wokwiz@aol.com, www.wokwiz.com.

WORLDCHEFS
San Jose, Santa Clara & Sunnyvale

Sponsor: Chefs Toussaint Potter & Suzanne Vandyck. Programs: Group & private cooking classes, team building. Established: 2000. Class/group size: 25 max. Facilities: Community centers, high schools, private locations. Also featured: Catering & personal chef services.
EMPHASIS: International cuisines.
FACULTY: Chef Toussaint is from the Caribbean, trained in France, & served as executive chef at restaurants in the Virgin Islands & northern California. Chef Suzanne is a native of Belgium.
COSTS: ~$45+ food costs.
CONTACT: Suzanne Vandyck & Toussaint Potter, Owners, Worldchefs, Santa Clara, CA 95051; 408-247-7351, info@worldchefs.net, http://worldchefs.net.

YOSEMITE CHEFS' & VINTNERS' HOLIDAYS
Yosemite National Park

Sponsor: Yosemite Concession Services Corp. Programs: A series of 2- & 3-day vacation programs that feature cooking demonstrations or wine seminars and a concluding banquet. Established: 1982. Class/group size: 180. ~15 programs/yr. Facilities: Great Lounge of The Ahwahnee Hotel.

Emphasis: Cuisines of Western chefs, California wines.

Faculty: Each program features noted chefs or wineries. Executive Chef Robert Anderson and his staff prepare the vintner's banquet, visiting chefs prepare the chefs' banquet.

Costs: Packages range from $599-$950 ($280-$450) including shared lodging at The Ahwahnee.

Contact: Yosemite Reservations, 5410 East Home Ave., Fresno, CA 93727; 559-252-4848, Fax 559-372-1362, www.yosemitepark.com.

ZOV'S BISTRO
Tustin

Sponsor: Bistro/bakery, cooking school, caterer. Programs: Demo classes on a variety of topics. Established: 1987. Class/group size: 25-40. 19 programs/yr. Facilities: Front kitchen of Zov's Bistro.

Emphasis: Chef specialties.

Faculty: Zov Karamardian, caterer & teacher for 20+ yrs; noted chefs, TV personalities, cookbook authors, including Hugh Carpenter, Joyce Goldstein, David Rosengarten, Julie Sahni, Martin Yan.

Costs: $50-$100/class.

Contact: Zov Karamardian, Chef/Owner, Zov's Bistro, 17440 E. 17th St., Tustin, CA 92780; 714-838-8855 x5, Fax 714-838-9926, zov@zovs.com, www.zovs.com.

COLORADO

COOK STREET SCHOOL OF FINE COOKING
Denver

(See also page 38) (See display ad page 39)

Sponsor: Private culinary school. Programs: Short series & one-time recreational classes. 3- & 6-mo professional Food & Wine Career Program. Established: 1999. Class/group size: 24 max. 40 programs/yr. Facilities: 3,000-sq-ft newly-remodeled teaching kitchen featuring commercial grade equipment. Also featured: Facility available for corporate & private parties, dinners & cooking parties.

Emphasis: Hands-on training in classical culinary techniques.

Faculty: Full-time staff of experienced professional chef-instructors, guest chefs.

Costs: $50-$149/single classes, $389/short series.

Contact: Cook Street School of Fine Cooking, 1937 Market St., Denver, CO 80202; 303-308-9300, Fax 303-308-9400, info@cookstreet.com, www.cookstreet.com.

COOKING SCHOOL OF ASPEN
Aspen

Sponsor: Cooking school, tour operator, retail store, cheese shop. Programs: Daily hands-on & demo classes, culinary adventures abroad, multi-day workshops. Established: 1998. Class/group size: 12-20 max. 200+ programs/yr. Facilities: 12-person hands-on design, 20-person demo design. Also featured: Customized private events, children's classes.

Faculty: Local & guest chefs.

Costs: $130-$275/class.

Contact: Rob Seideman, President, Cooking School of Aspen, 414 E. Hyman Ave., Aspen, CO 81611; 800-603-6004, 970-920-1879, Fax 970-920-2188, rob@cookingschoolofaspen.com, www.cookingschoolofaspen.com.

COOKING SCHOOL OF THE ROCKIES
Boulder

Sponsor: Private school. Programs: Individual classes, short courses, & 5-day basic techniques cooking vacations that emphasize creativity, organization, & presentation. Established: 1991.

Class/group size: 32 demos, 12-16 hand. Facilities: Modern, fully-equipped kitchen with overhead mirror. Also featured: Corporate training, private parties, bridal showers, retail cookware store, diploma/professional program.

EMPHASIS: Basic French techniques, Italian cuisine, pastry, baking, ethnic cuisines, wine appreciation.

FACULTY: Revolving visiting instructors program featuring local & national restaurant/bakery chefs, guest chefs, cookbook authors.

COSTS: Classes from $35-$75 each; intensives are $475-$525. A list of B&B & lodgings is available.

LOCATION: 25 mil northwest of Denver, at the base of the Rocky Mountain Foothills.

CONTACT: Joan Brett, Director, Cooking School of the Rockies, 637 S. Broadway, Ste. H, Boulder, CO 80303; 303-494-7988, Fax 303-494-7999, csr@cookingschoolrockies.com, www.cookingschoolrockies.com.

COOKING SCHOOL OF VAIL AT THE SAVORY INN

Vail

Sponsor: Private cooking school in a B&B inn. Programs: Hands-on day & evening courses, demos for larger groups, wine pairing by sommelier. Established: 2002. Class/group size: 6-15/day, 6-40/eve. Weekly programs/yr. Facilities: Commercial kitchen & dining room. Also featured: Corporate events, private parties.

EMPHASIS: Cooking & baking for the home chef.

FACULTY: In-house chef Deanna Scimio has restaurant experience in the US & Europe. Local & guest chefs.

COSTS: Day classes $55+, eve classes $75+.

CONTACT: Nancy Hassett, InnKeeper, Cooking School of Vail at the Savory Inn, 2405 Elliott Road, Vail, CO 81657; 970-476-1304, Fax 970-476-0433, info@savoryinn.com, www.savoryinn.com.

KATHY SMITH'S COOKING SCHOOL

Greenwood Village

Sponsor: Private school. Programs: Demo, participation & private classes. Established: 1996. Class/group size: 18 demo/10 hands-on. 40-50 programs/yr. Facilities: In-home school with seating area for demos & large viewing mirror. Kitchen equipped with Viking gas stove, double ovens & restaurant quality appliances. Also featured: Private instruction for adults & children. Instruction for elementary, middle & HS programs (Sept-May).

EMPHASIS: Developing technique, creativity & skills in the kitchen.

FACULTY: Chef Kathy Smith trained with Mary Risley, Giuliano Bugialli, Barbara Fenzl; local guest chefs.

COSTS: Demos $40-$50, participation $50.

CONTACT: Kathy Smith, Owner, Kathy Smith's Cooking School, 4280 E. Plum Ct., Greenwood Village, CO 80121; 303-437-6882, Fax 303-740-6884, kathy@kathysmithcooks.com, www.kathysmithcooks.com.

SAVORY PALETTE GOURMET RETREATS

Lyons

Sponsor: Private retreat. Programs: Classes in culinary techniques from selected menus. Established: 1997. Class/group size: 12 max hands-on. 12 programs/yr. Facilities: Full professional kitchen, dining room, lounge with fireplace, sandstone terrace with hot tub. Also featured: Hiking, biking, snowshoeing, fireside reading, hot tub.

EMPHASIS: Ethnic & regional menus.

FACULTY: Deborah DeBord, Ph.D., has taught & cooked in Latin America, Europe & Asia. She is a food writer & has published 3 cookbooks.

COSTS: Weekend retreat $190, $315/couple; $1,234/wk. Includes meals & lodging in pvt queen bedroom/bath.

LOCATION: North of Boulder at gateway to Rocky Mt National Park. Mountain forest setting.

CONTACT: Deborah DeBord, Proprietor, Savory Palette Gourmet Retreats, 81 Cree Ct., Lyons, CO 80540; 303-823-0530, Fax 303-823-0337, ddebord@indra.com, www.expressionretreats.com.

SCHOOL OF NATURAL COOKERY – THE MAIN COURSE
Boulder, Longmont & Denver

Sponsor: Vegetarian non-recipe cooking school. Programs: Intensives & weekly courses in preparing natural food, no recipes, hands-on, the language of chefs. Established: 1985. Class/group size: 4-15. Facilities: Vary from homestyle kitchen to simple apartments & elaborate commercial kitchens. Also featured: In Boulder, nearby activities incl mountain biking, hiking, skiing, music, dance, theater, festivals.

EMPHASIS: Theory & techniques for preparing whole grains, beans, vegetables, sauces, soups, natural desserts & meal composition.

FACULTY: Joanne Saltzman, founder/director, author Amazing Grains, Romancing The Bean, The Natural Cook; All Main Course teachers certified by The School of Natural Cookery.

COSTS: Tuition & materials are $395 for Parts I & II, $350 for Part III & IV. Intensives are $1,600 for the full program & $800 for the Part I weekend, ingredients & workbooks included. Text books included for intensives.

CONTACT: Joanne Saltzman, Director, School of Natural Cookery, PO Box 19466, Boulder, CO 80308; 303-444-8068, info@naturalcookery.com, www.naturalcookery.com.

THE SEASONED CHEF COOKING SCHOOL
Denver

Sponsor: Private school. Programs: Demo & participation classes. Established: 1993. Class/group size: 14 hands-on/35 demo. 100+ programs/yr. Facilities: Well-equipped home kitchen. Also featured: Classes for children, wine appreciation, ethnic & farmer's market tour.

EMPHASIS: Basic techniques, gourmet cooking, ethnic cuisines, pastry & baking, seasonal classes, low-fat/vegetarian.

FACULTY: Area cooking school instructors & restaurant chefs, guest chefs & cookbook authors.

COSTS: $40-$55/class.

CONTACT: Susan Stevens, Director, The Seasoned Chef Cooking School, 999 Jasmine St., #100, Denver, CO 80220; 303-377-3222, info@theseasonedchef.com, www.theseasonedchef.com.

THE VINEYARD WINE SEMINARS
Denver

Sponsor: Wine store. Programs: 3-session courses. Established: 1971. Class size: 40. 6 programs/yr.

FACULTY: 4-person staff has 50+ yrs cumulative wine experience.

COSTS: $75/person, $145/2 people.

LOCATION: Local restaurants.

CONTACT: Cheryl Lopez, Manager, The Vineyard, 261 Fillmore St., Denver, CO 80206; 303-355-8324, Fax 303-355-1413, email@vineyardwineshop.com, www.vineyardwineshop.com.

CONNECTICUT

ALL ABOUT WINE
Hartford

Sponsor: Wine professional. Programs: Wine courses. Established: 1988. Class/group size: 20.

FACULTY: Rick Ross is a member SWE with 20+ years of study.

CONTACT: Rick Ross, Director, All About Wine, 45 Rushford Meade, Granby, CT 06035-2325; 860-653-6057, Fax 860-653-4399, redwine5@earthlink.net.

CUCINA CASALINGA
Wilton

Sponsor: Italian cooking school. Programs: Hands-on day & evening classes, series for adults & children, 3 cooking tours to Italy/yr, Kids Cook Italian Camp in Aug. Established: 1981. Class/group size: 15 hands-on/25 demo. Facilities: Renovated home kitchen with Tuscan wood-burning pizza oven. Also featured: Private group & corporate classes, wine tastings, market tours.

EMPHASIS: Italian regional cuisine.

FACULTY: Sally Maraventano, owner/instructor, author of Festa del Giardino, studied at the U. of Florence, & learned to cook from her mother & Sicilian grandfather. Guest chefs from the US & Italy.

COSTS: Adult classes $100 (series $280), guest chef & Sat eve classes $125, children (age 11-16) $60. Kids 4-day summer camp $240. Italy tours ~3,600-$5,200 includes lodging, meals, excursions.

CONTACT: Sally Maraventano, Owner, Cucina Casalinga, 171 Drum Hill Rd., Wilton, CT 06897; 203-762-0768, Fax 203-762-0768, info@cucinacasalinga.com, www.cucinacasalinga.com.

FOURTEEN LINCOLN STREET B&B AND CULINARY STUDIO

Niantic

Sponsor: Chef-owned B&B. Programs: Weekend culinary retreats featuring cooking demos. Established: 1997. Class/group size: 12. 10 programs/yr. Facilities: Fully-equipped commercial kitchen. Also featured: Private dinners & cooking classes.

EMPHASIS: Fundamentals, new techniques, N. Italian, French, Japanese, Regional New England.

FACULTY: Cheryl M. Jean, CIA-honors graduate, named a Great New England Cook by Yankee Magazine. Costs: $650-$750/couple includes most meals, lodging w/Jacuzzi bath.

CONTACT: Cheryl Jean, Chef, Fourteen Lincoln Street, 14 Lincoln Street, Niantic, CT 06357; 860-739-8180, 860-739-6327, Fourteenlincoln@aol.com, www.14lincolnstreet.com.

LA CUCINA – INSTRUCTIONAL COOKING

Milford

Sponsor: Restaurant cooking school. Programs: Private or small hands-on classes. Established: 1992. Class/group size: 1-10. 10 programs/yr. Facilities: Restaurant or student's home kitchen.

FACULTY: Rachel Kessinger, a CIA graduate with 15+ yrs experience.

COSTS: $55-$300.

CONTACT: Rachel Kessinger, Chef-Owner, La Cucina - Instructional Cooking Restaurant, 128 Bridgeport Ave., Milford, CT 06460; 203-874-5300, MatterofThymeLLC@aol.com, http://members.aol.com/seanhaffner/lacucina.

MYSTIC COOKING SCHOOL

Old Mystic

Sponsor: Private school. Programs: Techniques, regional & ethnic cuisines, food & wine pairings, tea classes. Established: 1994. Class/group size: 16 hands-on, 25 demo. 60+ programs/yr. Facilities: Well-equipped new farmhouse-style building on 4 rural acres, near the ocean. Also featured: Occasional regional cooking tours, private classes.

EMPHASIS: Fresh local seafood & farm produce.

FACULTY: Cookbook authors, restaurant & guest chefs including George Hirsch, Micol Negrin, Jack Leonardo, Chris Prosperi, Patrick Boisjot, Daniel Rosati.

COSTS: $45-$75/class.

CONTACT: Annice Estes, Owner, Mystic Cooking School, P.O. Box 611, Mystic, CT 06355; 860-536-6005, Fax 860-536-6117, mysticcooks@yahoo.com, www.mysticcooking.com.

PRUDENCE SLOANE'S COOKING SCHOOL

Hampton

Sponsor: Culinary professional Prudence Sloane. Programs: Participation workshops, demos, dinner demo. Established: 1993. Class/group size: 8-150. 30 programs/yr. Facilities: Well-equipped teaching kitchen. Also featured: Private party classes, knife skills, food & wine pairing.

EMPHASIS: Ethnic & regional cuisines, techniques, theory, food history & flavoring, seasonal & holiday menus, wine selection.

FACULTY: Prudence Sloane was awarded the Blue Ribbon professional diploma from the Institute of Culinary Education & is a TV food show host.

COSTS: $65/session, $300-$800/intensive technique series.

CONTACT: Prudence Sloane, Prudence Sloane's Cooking School, 245 Main St., P.O. Box 41, Hampton, CT 06247; 860-455-0596, prudencesloane@aol.com, www.prudencesloane.com/htm/school.htm.

RONNIE FEIN SCHOOL OF CREATIVE COOKING
Stamford

Sponsor: Culinary professional. Programs: Hands-on classes that emphasize ingredients, techniques, & menus. Established: 1971. Class/group size: 4 hands-on. Facilities: Fully-equipped home teaching kitchen. Also featured: Children's classes, private instruction.

EMPHASIS: Regional & low-fat cuisines, seasonal & holiday menus, food gifts, ethnic foods, fresh herbs, menu structure, kitchen tools.

FACULTY: Ronnie Fein writes for food publications & attended the China Institute & Four Seasons Cooking School. She is author of The Complete Idiot's Guide to American Cooking.

COSTS: $250/session.

CONTACT: Ronnie Fein, Owner, Ronnie Fein School of Creative Cooking, 32 Heming Way, Stamford, CT 06903; 203-322-7114, Fax 203-329-3366, ronskie@aol.com.

SANDY'S BRAZILIAN & CONTINENTAL CUISINE
Waterbury

Sponsor: Private school. Programs: Culinary tours to Ireland and classes in Connecticut. Established: 1987. Class/group size: 10. 2-4 programs/yr.

EMPHASIS: Continental cooking with a Brazilian flair.

FACULTY: Sandra N. Allen Certified Member IACP, Member NYACT, CWCA, CHOC.

CONTACT: Sandra Allen, Director, Sandy's Brazilian & Continental Cuisine, 827 Oronoke Rd., # 8-3, Waterbury, CT 06708; 203-596-9685, Sandyna@juno.com.

SILO COOKING SCHOOL
New Milford

Sponsor: The Silo Store Gallery & Cooking School. Programs: Demo & participation courses. Established: 1972. Class/group size: 14 hands-on/30 demo. 70 programs/yr. Facilities: Well-equipped teaching kitchen.

EMPHASIS: Ethnic & regional cuisines, holiday menus, baking, guest chef specialties, wine selection.

FACULTY: Master chefs, authors, TV Food Network chefs. School is owned by NY Pops founder Skitch Henderson & wife Ruth.

COSTS: ~$80-$100.

CONTACT: Renee Frinder, Manager, Silo Cooking School, 44 Upland Rd., New Milford, CT 06776; 860-355-0300, Fax 860-350-5495, sales@thesilo.com, www.thesilo.com.

A WINE TUTOR
Milford

Sponsor: Wine professional. Programs: Public wine appreciation classes & private wine tasting events for corporations & social, business, & professional groups. Established: 1988. Class/group size: 20/public program.

EMPHASIS: Basic to advanced topics.

FACULTY: Len Gulino, MBA; certificate from CIA Greystone; member of SWE, journalist, retailer.

COSTS: 5-session courses $75-$150.

LOCATION: Milford Adult Ed, Sacred Heart University College, Yale Graduate Student Union.

CONTACT: Len Gulino, Owner, A Wine Tutor, 19 Derby Ave., Milford, CT 06460; 203-877-2884, len4wine@optonline.net, www.culinarymenus.com/lengulino.htm.

WINE WANDERINGS, INC.
Norwalk

Sponsor: Wine professionals. Programs: 5- to 6-session courses. Established: 1993. Class/group size: 36. 10-12 programs/yr. Facilities: Classroom or dining room style seating. Also featured: Wine education & tastings for corporations, nonprofit orgs, & private groups.

EMPHASIS: Wine education.

FACULTY: Lou Campoli & Cathi Carroll both have 15+ yrs wine education, enrolled in Master of

Wine program, Board of CT chapter AIWF, member IACP, SWE & AWS, wine column journalists, 30+ yrs. corp. career.

Costs: $30-$50/session.

Location: Norwalk Community College, business & conference ctrs, restaurants, private homes.

Contact: Lou Campoli & Cathi Carroll, Co-Owners, Wine Wanderings, Inc., 192 Gillies Lane, Norwalk, CT 06854; 203-853-9550, Fax 203-853-9550, winew@attglobal.net.

DISTRICT OF COLUMBIA

COMPANY'S COMING

Washington

Sponsor: Home-based program. Programs: Demo & participation classes that teach entertaining at home. Includes menu planning, cooking, presentation, food & wine pairing. Established: 1997. Class/group size: 8-16. 36 programs/yr. Facilities: Home-based demo kitchen. Also featured: Team building classes, customized classes for groups.

Emphasis: Entertaining menus.

Faculty: Jinny & Ed Fleischman have been entertaining together for 28+ yrs & attend cooking schools & classes. Noted in Harper's Bazaar as 'one of the best cooking schools in the US'.

Costs: $65-$80/class.

Contact: Jinny Fleischman, Company's Coming, 3313 Ross Place NW, Washington, DC 20008; 202-966-3361, Fax 202-362-8409, veflei@aol.com, www.companycoming.com.

DELIZIOSO! COOKING SCHOOL

Washington

Programs: 4-sessions or single classes by special arrangement. Established: 1985. Class/group size: 12 demo or 6 seated. 4-6 programs/yr. Facilities: Professional kitchen in Georgetown or other suitable location. Also featured: Group or private instruction.

Emphasis: Northern Italian.

Faculty: Director Eugenia Van Horn Wilkie, teacher, food writer, studied cooking in Milan for 10 yrs.

Costs: $300/4 classes, $100/group class, $250/3-hr private lesson.

Contact: Eugenia Van Horn Wilkie, Director, Delizioso! Cooking School, 3915 Ivy Terrace Ct., Washington, DC 20007; 202-338-6580, ewilkie@mindspring.com.

WHAT'S COOKING!

Washington

Sponsor: Culinary professional Phyllis Frucht. Programs: Limited participation and/or hands-on classes on a variety of topics. Series include The International Gourmet, Asian Cooking, Techniques, Vegetarian, & Contemporary Cooking. Established: 1976. Class/group size: 16. Facilities: Newly renovated townhouse kitchen.

Faculty: Phyllis Frucht has taught cooking 30+ yrs at home, in adult ed, & at the former What's Cooking! cookware store/cooking school in Rockville, MD, where she was chef/owner.

Costs: $45 for single class, $200 for a series of 5.

Contact: Phyllis Frucht, Teacher, What's Cooking!, 1917 S Street NW, Washington, DC 20009; 202-483-7282, Fax 202-483-7284, whatsckng@aol.com.

DELAWARE

CELEBRITY KITCHENS

Wilmington

Sponsor: Private school. Programs: Hands-on & demo classes. Established: 2002. Class/group size: 12 hands-on, 24 demo. 350 programs/yr. Facilities: Renovated kitchen with granite countertops. Also featured: Corporate bonding programs, kids cook, private classes, intl cooking tours.

Emphasis: International, vegetarian, & heart healthy cuisines.

Faculty: Local & regional guest chefs.

Contact: Cindy Weiner, President, Celebrity Kitchens, 1601 Concord Pike, #33, Independence Mall, Wilmington, DE 19803; 302-427-2665, Fax 302-427-9060, icook@celebritykitchensinc.com, www.celebritykitchens.com.

WHAT'S COOKING AT THE KITCHEN SINK
Hockessin

Sponsor: Kitchenware & specialty store. Programs: Demo & hands-on classes. Established: 1991. Class/group size: 18 demo/6 hands-on. 120+ programs/yr. Facilities: Well-equipped professional kitchen with overhead mirror. Also featured: Children's workshops & private classes.

Emphasis: Techniques & methods; ethnic & regional cuisines; baking & pastry; wine, seasonal/holiday menus.

Faculty: Michele DiVincenzo, director & IACP member, studied at the CIA. Local chefs, caterers & professionals such as Peter Fontaine, George Geary, Christina Pirello.

Costs: $26-$45/class. For lodging, the school recommends The Inn at Montchanin Village.

Contact: Michele DiVincenzo, Director, What's Cooking at the Kitchen Sink, 425 Hockessin Corner, Hockessin, DE 19707; 302-239-7066, Fax 302-239-7665, info@thekitchensink.com, www.thekitchensink.com.

FLORIDA

ARS MAGIRICA
Coral Gables

Sponsor: Recreational cooking school. Programs: Hands-on classes & 2- to 4-session courses. Topics include intl, regional & seasonal cuisines, techniques, entertaining, healthy cooking, wine appreciation; programs for children & teens. Established: 2001. Class/group size: 6. 120+ programs/yr. Facilities: Professional kitchen. Also featured: Private chef sevices, private & corporate catering, cookware store.

Faculty: Founder/Director Lourdes Castro, former instructor at NYU & Johnson & Wales Univ; Viviana Altesor, CIA graduate & restaurant chef; Ana Hernandez Arnholt, school teacher & tutorer.

Costs: $35-$59/class, ~$99-$165/course.

Contact: Lourdes Castro, Owner, Ars Magirica, 158 Almeria Ave., Coral Gables, FL 33134; 305-443-8303, Fax 305-443-8378, info@arsmagirica.com, www.ArsMagirica.com.

CHEF ALLEN'S
Aventura

Sponsor: Chef Allen Susser. Programs: Demo & participation classes; one-on-one sessions with student working along with restaurant staff. Established: 1986. Class/group size: 1-25. 12 programs/yr. Facilities: Chef Allen's restaurant.

Emphasis: New World cuisine, local fish, tropical fruits, Latin root vegetables.

Faculty: Chef Susser, graduate & on faculty of Fla. Int'l Univ. School of Hospitality & Rest. Mgmt. Author of Allen Susser's New World Cuisine & The Great Citrus Book, he studied at Le Cordon Bleu & was chef at Paris' Bristol Hotel & Le Cirque in NYC.

Costs: Group classes $45, individual session $195.

Contact: Chef Allen Susser, Chef/Owner, Chef Allen's, 19088 N.E. 29th Ave., Aventura, FL 33180; 305-935-2900, Fax 305-935-9062, ChefAllen@aol.com, www.chefallen.com.

CHEF ANDY'S COOKING CLASSES AT LE BISTRO RESTAURANT
Lighthouse Point

Sponsor: Culinary professional & restaurant chef/owner. Programs: Classes that include classic cooking, kitchen basics, herbs & spices, ethnic flavors, healthful cuisine. Established: 2001. Class/group size: 5-45. 100+ programs/yr. Facilities: Fully-equipped restaurant facility. Also featured: Private classes.

EMPHASIS: Professional shortcuts & tips.
FACULTY: Andy Trousdale, a culinary instructor at the Art Institute of Ft. Lauderdale, is a European-trained chef with 27 yrs experience. Guest chefs, specialty purveyors & wine specialists.
COSTS: $40, $75/couple, $175/5 classes.
CONTACT: Andy Trousdale, Chef Andy's Cooking Classes at Le Bistro Restaurant, 4626 N. Federal Highway, Lighthouse Point, FL ; 954-946-9240, andyelin@bellsouth.net, www.lebistrorestaurant.com.

CHEF JEAN-PIERRE COOKING SCHOOL
Ft. Lauderdale

Sponsor: Chef Jean-Pierre Gourmet Foods. Programs: Morning, evening & week-long demonstration classes on a variety of topics with emphasis on fundamentals. Established: 1976. Class/group size: 20. Facilities: Fully-equipped demonstration Poggen Pohl kitchen with overhead mirror. Also featured: Visits to markets & food producers.
EMPHASIS: Mediterranean cuisine with a Florida accent. Strong flavors of garlic, tomato, olive oil & fresh herbs blended with tropical fruits, fish, & seafood.
FACULTY: School director Chef Jean-Pierre Brehier is the host of the internationally distributed cooking shows Sunshine Cuisine & Incredible Cuisine.
COSTS: $45/class, $38 for 3 classes purchased at the same time.
CONTACT: Chef Jean-Pierre Brehier, Chef Jean-Pierre Cooking School, 1436 N. Federal Hwy., Ft. Lauderdale, FL 33304; 954-563-2700, Fax 954-563-9009, jp@chefjp.com, www.chefjeanpierre.com.

ITALIAN COOKING HOLIDAY
Amelia Island

Programs: Morning open for leisure activities, afternoon Italian cooking class. Dinner accompanied by songs performed by the 'The Singing Chef'. Teens welcome. Established: 2000. Class/group size: 2-6. Facilities: Hoyt House B&B. Also featured: Beach, biking, golf, tennis, horseback riding, day-spa. Private in-home chef, entertainment, business retreat services, private classes.
EMPHASIS: Trattoria style Italian Cooking.
FACULTY: Francesco Milana, 'The Singing Chef', born, raised & trained in Italy.
COSTS: 2- to 4-day packages $195-$645, includes lodging in a 10-bedroom historic home, some meals.
CONTACT: Gayl Blount, Host, Hoyt House Bed & Breakfast Inn, 804 Atlantic Ave., Amelia Island, FL 32034; 800-432-2085, Fax 904-277-9626, innkeeper@hoythouse.com, www.singingchef.net.

KITCHENIQUE COOKING SCHOOL
Destin

Sponsor: Gourmet kitchenware shop. Programs: Day & evening demo & participation classes. Established: 1999. Class/group size: 16 hands-on, 24 demo. 125+ programs/yr. Facilities: Fully-equipped kitchen with counter seating. Also featured: Private classes for individuals & groups.
EMPHASIS: Seafood, sushi, ethnic & American regional cuisines, wine pairing, menu planning.
FACULTY: Local & touring chefs, professional instructors, cookbook authors.
COSTS: $20-$100. Lodging available through Sandestin Beach Resort.
CONTACT: Vicki McCain, President, Kitchenique Cooking School, 9375 Hwy 98 West #7, The Market Shops at Sandestin, Destin, FL 32550; 800-476-2918, 850-837-0432, 850-654-2679, Fax 850-654-6996, kitchenique@gnt.net, www.kitchenique.com.

LA MAISON GOURMET
Dunedin

Sponsor: Kitchen store & cooking school for home chefs. Programs: 9-wk culinary skills course; individual classes for adults, couples & children. Established: 1998. Class/group size: 12-56. 250 programs/yr. Facilities: 750-sq-ft kitchen with 2 gas cooktops, a 13-ft center island & 2 convection ovens; 1,800-sq-ft private dining room. Also featured: Chef competitions, private & house parties, bridal showers, rehearsal dinners, personal chef services, corporate training, catering.
EMPHASIS: Culinary skills; New American, Cajun, Florribean & Italian cuisines.
FACULTY: Executive Chef Dawn Algieri, graduate of NY City Technical College's Hospitality pro-

gram. 8 other part-time professional restaurant chefs.

Costs: Individual classes $10-$50. 9-wk Culinary Skills & Techniques Course $595. B&B, hotel/motel lodging info available.

Contact: John Lewis, General Mgr., La Maison Gourmet, 471 Main St., Dunedin, FL 34698; 727-736-3070, Fax 727-733-8915, john_10245@msn.com, www.lamaisongourmet.com.

LA PALMIER

Atlantic Beach, Jacksonville\

Sponsor: Private school. Programs: Hands-on classes for groups of six or more with an emphasis on French and Italian cuisine. Established: 2000. Class/group size: 8 hands-on. 150 programs/yr. Facilities: European-style kitchen with double convection oven, gas cooktop & preparation area in private home. Also featured: Private parties, couples classes, bridal shower and birthday party classes, corporate events.

Emphasis: From basic techniques to special occasion dinner menus.

Faculty: Linda Lowman holds certificates from Cook Street School in Denver, CO, and cooking schools in France and Italy.

Contact: Linda Lowman, Owner, La Palmier, 1855 N. Sherry Dr., Atlantic Beach, FL 32233; 904-246-4839, Fax 904-246-3167, llowman@attbi.com.

THE PALM BEACH SCHOOL OF COOKING, INC.

Boca Raton

Sponsor: Private school & cafe. Programs: 1/2-day workshops & multi-session courses that include Caribbean, Pacific Rim, sushi making, vegetarian dishes; Personal Chef Certificate program; advanced training for professional chefs specializing in ethnic cuisines. Established: 1998. Class/group size: 10 hands-on, 20 demo. 200 programs/yr. Facilities: Professional cooking equipment, individual work stations. Also featured: Private parties, demos.

Emphasis: Asian gourmet low-fat & other ethnic cuisines, professional techniques for nonprofessionals.

Faculty: Professionally-trained experienced teachers.

Costs: $60/class.

Contact: Doreen N. Moore, Director/Executive Chef, The Palm Beach School of Cooking, Inc., 2950 Olivewood Terr., #108, Boca Raton, FL 33431; 561-750-9529, cybrcook@hotmail.com.

REAL.LIFE.BASIC

Miami Beach

Sponsor: Gourmet cookware store. Programs: Demonstration and participation classes on a variety of topics. 70+ programs/yr. Facilities: Demonstration kitchen with the latest equipment.

Faculty: Local chefs.

Costs: $45/class.

Contact: Simone Mayer, real.life.basic, 643 Lincoln Rd., Miami Beach, FL 33139; 305-604-1984, Fax 305-604-1994, realpeople@reallifebasic.com, www.reallifebasic.com.

THE RITZ-CARLTON, AMELIA ISLAND COOKING SCHOOL

Amelia Island

Sponsor: The Ritz-Carlton, Amelia Island. Programs: Quarterly 2-day participation courses that focus on a theme. Established: 1994. Class/group size: 15. 4 programs/yr. Facilities: The Grill kitchen. Also featured: Tour of the restaurant kitchens, pastry & butcher shop, garde manger; learn the responsibilities of the 45-chef team.

Emphasis: Seasonal & entertaining menus, regional & ethnic cuisines.

Faculty: Scott Crawford, Chef de Cuisine of The Grill; the hotel's food & beverage staff.

Costs: $798/person, $998/couple includes 2 nights lodging, lunch with chef. $260/person without lodging.

Contact: Kathleen O'Brien, Director of Marketing & Public Relations, The Ritz-Carlton, Amelia Island, 4750 Amelia Island Pkwy, Amelia Island, FL 32034; 800-241-3333, 904-277-1100, Fax 904-277-1041, diane.svela@ritzcarlton.com, www.ritzcarlton.com.

GEORGIA

THE ART INSTITUTE OF ATLANTA – SCHOOL OF CULINARY ARTS

Atlanta *(See also page 53) (See display ad page 53)*

Sponsor: Private college of creative professional studies, member of Art Institutes, with 21 locations nationwide. Programs: Hands-on programs include non-credit Saturday workshops, teen workshops & camp, certificate program in baking & pastry. Established: 1991. Class/group size: 10-15. 56 programs/yr. Facilities: Include 4 professional kitchens & 1 baking & pastry kitchen with industry-standard equipment. Also featured: Cooking & business mgmt skills; teaching-dining room, open to the community, for classical French cuisine.

EMPHASIS: Basic cooking skills & techniques.

FACULTY: 20+ professional chef instructors lead participation courses. All have bachelor's degree or higher & industry experience, many have professional credentials through the ACF.

COSTS: Sat. workshops $85, teen workshops $25-$50, teen 5-day camp $400, certificate program $850.

CONTACT: June Fischer, Director, Community Education, The Art Institute of Atlanta - School of Culinary Arts, 6600 Peachtree Dunwoody Rd., 100 Embassy Row, Atlanta, GA 30328; 800-275-4242 x2420, Fax 770-394-0008, fischerj@aii.edu, www.artinstitute.edu.

CHEF JOE RANDALL'S COOKING SCHOOL

Savannah

Sponsor: Professional chef Joe Randall. Programs: Morning & evening demo classes & series. Established: 2000. Class/group size: 20 demo. 52 programs/yr. Facilities: New well-equipped professional demo kitchen with overhead mirrors & audio system. Also featured: Catering, private classes, private dinner parties.

EMPHASIS: Southern cuisine, ethnic & heritage cooking, entertaining, holiday & seasonal menus, guest chef specialties.

FACULTY: Chef Joe Randall, proprietor, cookbook author, & food-service consultant with 30+ yrs industry experience. Guest & local chefs, cookbook authors.

COSTS: Demos $35-$110/session; 6-wk series $235.

CONTACT: Chef Joe Randall, Chef Joe Randall's Cooking School, 5409 Waters Ave., Savannah, GA 31404; 912-303-0409, Fax 912-303-0947, info@chefjoerandall.com, www.chefjoerandall.com.

COLUMBUS COOKS

Columbus

Sponsor: Private school & gourmet food store. Programs: Hands-on & demo classes. Established: 2002.

EMPHASIS: Basic cooking & techniques, ethnic cuisines, party menus, pastry & cakes.

FACULTY: Chef/caterer Mark Festa; food writer/restaurant critic Gail Greenblatt; Stacy Varner, Exec Chef at Doctors Hospital; Maurice Martin, Exec Sous Chef at the CC of Columbus; Donna Reed, 23+ yrs foodservice experience.

COSTS: $28/demo class, $45/hands-on class.

CONTACT: Becky Catrett, Owner, Columbus Cooks, 1332 13th St., Columbus, GA 31901; 706-221-8723, columbuscooks@knology.net, www.columbuscooks.com.

COOKING UP A PARTY

Atlanta & Roswell

Sponsor: Private cooking school for children. Programs: 1-wk day camps for children ages 5-12 that teach cooking basics, table settings, napkin folding & garnishing. Established: 1996. 9 programs/yr. Also featured: Advanced camps for older children, after school cooking classes, cooking parties, catering, gingerbread workshops.

EMPHASIS: Intl menus including France, Germany, England, Mexico & China.

FACULTY: Owner Margaret Konigsmark has 20 yrs experience working with children & teaching cooking classes.

Costs: $300/1 wk camp.

Contact: Margaret Konigsmark, Owner, Cooking Up A Party, 1072 Canton St., Roswell, GA 30075; 770-993-4911, Fax 678-445-3882, mkon@prodigy.net, www.cookingupaparty.com.

THE COOK'S WAREHOUSE, INC.

Atlanta & Suwanee

Sponsor: Gourmet store & cooking school. Programs: 2-4 hr demo & hands-on classes include basics, seasonal & holiday recipes, ethnic cuisines, chef specialties. Established: 1995. Class/group size: 25 demo, 16 hands-on. ~500 programs/yr. Facilities: 3 kitchens with the latest equipment. Also featured: Private classes at The Cook's Warehouse or on-location.

Faculty: ~150 restaurant chefs & other culinary professionals.

Costs: $35-$95/class.

Location: Midtown Atlanta, 10 min from downtown, 20 min from Hartsfield Intl Airport; Brookhaven, 20 min from downtown; Suwanee at HADCO, 45 min from downtown.

Contact: Mary Moore, Owner, The Cook's Warehouse, Inc., 549-1 Amsterdam Ave. NE, Atlanta, GA 30306; 404-815-4993, Fax 404-815-0543, cooley@cookswarehouse.com, www.cookswarehouse.com.

DONALD REDDICKS WINE PROGRAMS

Atlanta

Sponsor: Wine professional. Programs: 3-session courses. Established: 1979. Class/group size: 20. 3 programs/yr.

Emphasis: German wines.

Faculty: Donald Reddicks is a certified SWE instructor, member AWS & GWS.

Costs: $100/course.

Location: Goethe Institute, local hotels & restaurants.

Contact: Donald Reddicks, Wine Consultant, Harry's Farmers Market, Alpharetta, 7055 Hunters Branch Dr., Atlanta, GA 30328; 770-393-4584, 770-664-6300, Fax 770-772-9050, donredds@earthlink.net.

HERBERT F. SPASSER WINE PROGRAMS

Atlanta

Sponsor: Wine professional. Programs: 5-session courses. Established: 1976. Class/group size: 14. 2 programs/yr.

Faculty: Herbert Spasser is a wine advisor to Restaurant Society of N.Y., a member of Confrerie de la Chaine des Rotisseurs and a Certified Wine Educator from the SWE.

Costs: $220/course.

Contact: Herbert F. Spasser, D.D.S., Herbert F. Spasser Wine Programs, 2660 Peachtree Rd NW, Atlanta, GA 30305; 404-842-1651, jill-herb@2660Peachtree.com.

THE NICHOLAS LODGE SCHOOL OF CAKE DECORATING

Atlanta

Sponsor: Private school. Programs: 1- to 5-day hands-on classes on cake decorating techniques, wedding cakes, gumpaste flowers, rolled fondant & other sugar arts. Established: 1992. Class/group size: 16 max. ~30 programs/yr. Facilities: 1 work station/student. Also featured: Cake decorating tools & equipment available.

Emphasis: Cake decorating, confectionery arts.

Faculty: Nicholas Lodge, 20+ yrs cake decorating experience, has taught for 14 yrs in 26 countries. Guest teachers.

Costs: $85/day, $180/2 days, $450/5 days includes lunch. Hotel lodging available nearby.

Contact: Scott Ewing, School Director, The Nicholas Lodge School of Cake Decorating & Sugar Arts, 6060 McDonough Drive, Suite F, Norcross, GA 30093-1230; 770-453-9449, Fax 770-448-9046, nicklodge1@aol.com, http://nicholaslodge.com.

URSULA'S COOKING SCHOOL, INC.

Atlanta

Sponsor: Culinary professional Ursula Knaeusel. Programs: 4-session demo courses. Established: 1966. Class/group size: 30-40. 3 programs/yr. Facilities: 3-level classroom with 18-ft mirror over a 22-ft granite counter. Also featured: Gingerbread house, cutting & decorating classes, couples classes.

EMPHASIS: Nouvelle cuisine, time-saving methods & advance preparation.

FACULTY: Ursula Knaeusel, 50 yrs experience includes supervising kitchens, operating restaurants & teaching. She hosts PBS' Cooking With Ursula.

COSTS: $100/4-session course.

CONTACT: Ursula Knaeusel, Ursula's Cooking School, Inc., 1764 Cheshire Bridge Rd., N.E., Atlanta, GA 30324-4922; 404-876-7463, Fax 404-876-7467, Ursula@UrsulaCooks.com, http://UrsulaCooks.com.

HAWAII

ALOHA LOVING FOODS

Maui

Sponsor: Private culinary school. Programs: Mostly vegetarian with raw food preparation classes. Established: 1995. Class/group size: 20 max. 50 programs/yr. Also featured: Meditation, yoga, martial arts, gardening, mountain biking, hiking, snorkeling, kayaking with whales & dolphins.

EMPHASIS: Health & well being.

FACULTY: Includes Jeremy Safron, Annie Jubb, David Jubb, Ph.D.

COSTS: Retreats $600-$1,600, lunch classes from $25, dinner classes from $35.

CONTACT: Robert Marcus, Director, Aloha Loving Foods, 7 Laupapa Place, Maui, HI 96708-5055; 808-575-9192, Fax 808-575-7358, MauiLovesYou@aol.com, www.lovingfoods.com.

COOKING SCHOOL AT AKAKA FALLS INN

Honomu

Sponsor: Culinary teacher. Programs: Hands-on individual classes & culinary vacation programs. Includes farm tour, visits to market, winery, active volcano area. Established: 1998. Class/group size: 2-6. 12 programs/yr. Facilities: Fully-equipped home-style kitchen.

EMPHASIS: Pacific-tropical cuisine using fresh, locally-grown ingredients.

FACULTY: Sonia R. Martinez, IACP member, owned a cooking school in S. Carolina & a kitchen/gourmet shop in Florida. Guest instructors, visiting chefs.

COSTS: $45-$125/class, $625/2-days or $1,250/4 days includes meals, lodging, ground transport, planned activities.

LOCATION: On the Hamakua Coast, 13 miles north of Hilo on the Big Island of Hawaii.

CONTACT: Sonia R. Martinez, Co-owner, Cooking School at Akaka Falls Inn, PO Box 190, Honomu, HI 96728; 808-963-6860, cubans.inhawaii2@verizon.net.

ILLINOIS

BEAUTIFUL FOOD

Wilmette

Sponsor: Culinary professional. Programs: Participation classes. Established: 1973. Class/group size: 10. 20 programs/yr. Facilities: Home kitchen with professional equipment. Also featured: Culinary tours.

EMPHASIS: Fresh foods, techniques, breads, pastas, pastries, soups, low-cholesterol foods.

FACULTY: Charie MacDonald, a charter member of the IACP, studied at Le Cordon Bleu, the Ecole des Trois Gourmands & with Simone Beck.

COSTS: Classes $50. Trip $3,000, includes meals, lodging, ground transport.

CONTACT: Charie MacDonald, President, Beautiful Food, 2111 Beechwood Ave., Wilmette, IL 60091; 847-256-3979, Fax 847-853-0607, chariemacdonald@aol.com.

CALPHALON CULINARY CENTER
Chicago

Sponsor: Cookware manufacturer. Programs: Demo & hands-on classes in basic techniques, applied skills, & specifictopics such as desserts & sauces, entertaining, & ethnic cuisines. Guest chef classes & market tours. Class/group size: 12 hands-on, 60 demo. 100+ programs/yr. Facilities: 8,000-sq-ft facility includes 3 teaching areas, lecture/demo hall seating ~60 persons, 12-station hands-on classroom with separate cooktops, commercial kitchen, wine cellar & private dining area.

EMPHASIS: Basic & advanced skills, ethnic cuisines, holiday & seasonal menus.

COSTS: $50-$75/class.

CONTACT: Calphalon Culinary Center, 1000 W. Washington St., Chicago, IL 60607; 866-780-7799, 312-529-0100, Fax 866-623-2089, CCC@calphalon.com, www.calphalonculinarycenter.com.

CHEZ MADELAINE COOKING SCHOOL & TOURS TO FRANCE
Hinsdale

Sponsor: Culinary professional Madelaine Bullwinkel; Cte. & Ctesse de Sainte Croix. Programs: 1- to 3-session hands-on classes, evening menu classes, corporate team-building. Established: 1977. Class/group size: 6-12/class, 12/tour. 40-50 programs/yr. Facilities: Home: Contemporary setting. Tours: Restored 18th century Chateau de Sannat. Also featured: Three 8-day tours/yr incl hands-on classes, visits to markets, porcelain museum, cheese & foie gras artisans, meals in private homes, hunting for game & wild boar, mushroom picking; Bordeaux wine school; chateau visits.

EMPHASIS: Classes cover basics, techniques, ethnic cuisines, seasonal & holiday menus, preserving, soups, stocks, baking. Tours feature French regional cuisine.

FACULTY: Madelaine Bullwinkel received the Diplome from L'Academie de Cuisine, is author of Gourmet Preserves & Chez Madelaine, & is a member of Les Dames d'Escoffier. Occasional guest instructors & cookbook authors.

COSTS: Classes: $75. Tours: $2,500 ($2,900) incl shared (single) lodging, most meals, ground transport. Bordeaux trip: $2,000 includes hotel, 4 classroom days, 2 touring days.

LOCATION: Classes: Hinsdale, 20 mi from Chicago. Tours: Southeast of Bellac in the Haute Vienne region of the Limousin; Bordeaux.

CONTACT: Madelaine Bullwinkel, Chez Madelaine Cooking School & Tours, 425 Woodside Ave., Hinsdale, IL 60521; 630-325-4177, Fax 630-655-0355, chezmb@aol.com, www.chezm.com.

CHICAGO WINE SCHOOL
Chicago

Sponsor: Private wine school. Programs: 1-session evening seminars & 5-wk courses. Established: 1975. Class/group size: 6-42. 67 programs/yr.

COSTS: $50-$75/evening seminar, $160-$350/5-wk session.

CONTACT: Patrick W. Fegan, Director, Chicago Wine School, 2001 S. Halsted St., Chicago, IL 60608; 312-266-9463, Fax 312-266-9769, pwfegan@aol.com, www.wineschool.com.

THE CHOPPING BLOCK COOKING SCHOOL
Chicago

Programs: Daily & weekend hands-on & demo classes for the home cook; technique-oriented Building Blocks series; wine classes. Established: 1997. Class/group size: 16 demo/12 hands-on. 425 programs/yr. Facilities: Fully-equipped home-style kitchen. Classes are held around an L-shaped chopping block.

EMPHASIS: Seasonal, ethnic & healthy/vegetarian cooking, entertaining, knife skills.

FACULTY: Owner/Chef Shelley Young & staff of professional chefs, all culinary school graduates.

COSTS: Demo classes $50, hands-on classes $75, wine classes $60.

CONTACT: Shelley Young, Owner/Chef, The Chopping Block Cooking School, 1324 W Webster, Chicago, IL 60614; 773-472-6700, Fax 773-472-6779, info@thechoppingblock.net, www.thechoppingblock.net.

CORNER COOKS, INC.

Winnetka

Sponsor: Private school. Programs: Demo & hands-on classes. Established: 1999. Class/group size: 6-30. ~175 programs/yr. Facilities: Granite counter with seating for ~16, additional seating for 50; professional kitchen with home touches. Also featured: Dinner parties, private parties, corporate team building, catering, take-out.

FACULTY: Owner/teacher Betsy Simson, who studied in Italy & Chicago; Larry Smith, an executive chef; visiting chefs & lecturers.

COSTS: Classes $45-$60.

CONTACT: Betsy Simson, Owner, Corner Cooks, Inc., 507 Chestnut St., Winnetka, IL 60093; 847-441-0134, Fax 847-441-9434, cornercook@aol.com, www.cornercooks.com.

CUISINE COOKING SCHOOL

Moline

Sponsor: Private school. Programs: 4-hr classes. Established: 1985. Class/group size: 10.

EMPHASIS: Wine.

FACULTY: Mary Sue Salmon, member of SWE, IACP, & Iowa State Univ graduate in Food Science.

COSTS: $45/class.

CONTACT: Mary Sue Salmon, Owner/Instructor, Cuisine Cooking School, 1100 23rd Ave., Moline, IL 61265; 309-797-8613, Fax 309-797-8641, mscuisine@aol.com.

CULINARY CAMP AT KENDALL COLLEGE

Evanston *(See also page 63) (See display ad page 63)*

Sponsor: Private liberal arts college. Programs: 5-day camps for high school students ages 14-18 include Culinary Camp, Baking & Pastry Camp, and Advanced Culinary Camp. Camps conclude with a banquet prepared by students. Established: 1985. Class/group size: 16 max. Facilities: 7 kitchens on campus. One includes student-run cafeteria, another is an open-to-the-public fine dining room run by the students.

EMPHASIS: Basic techniques, baking & pastry.

FACULTY: Kendall College culinary faculty.

COSTS: $795 includes dormitory lodging & meals. Commuter rate $510.

LOCATION: Just north of Chicago, close to public transportation & Lake Michigan.

CONTACT: Betsy O'Brien, Coordinator, Kendall College - Culinary Arts, 2408 Orrington Ave., Evanston, IL 60201; 847-866-1300 x1317, bobrien@kendall.edu, www.kendall.edu.

GAETANO'S CUCINA ITALIANA

Forest Park

Sponsor: Private school. Programs: Hands-on classes in Italian cuisine. Established: 2001. Class/group size: 2 or more. Facilities: La Piazza restaurant kitchen. Also featured: Culinary trips & classes in Italy & France.

EMPHASIS: Innovative & classic Italian cuisine.

FACULTY: Chef Gaetano Di Benedetto, owner/chef of La Piazza Restaurant, 20 yrs culinary experience in restaurants in Italy, France, England & the US.

COSTS: $150/class. Group rates available.

CONTACT: Gaetano DiBenedetto, Executive Chef, Gaetano's Cucina Italiana, La Piazza, 410 Circle, Forest Park, IL 60302; 800-945-8606, Fax 312-803-1593, agnesevam@aol.com, www.theinternationalkitchen.com/gaetano.htm.

LA VENTURÉ

Skokie

Sponsor: Culinary professional Sandra Bisceglie. Programs: 6-session participation courses. Established: 1980. Class/group size: 8. 300+ programs/yr. Facilities: 600-sq-ft professional-style kitchen. Also featured: Private classes, classes for children.

Emphasis: French & Italian cuisines; candy making & cake decorating; baking.

Faculty: Director-owner Sandra Bisceglie attended Dumas Pere & Harrington Institute of Interior Design & has a certificate from the Natl Institute for the Foodservice Industry.

Costs: $289/6 lessons, $359/baking course.

Contact: Sandra Bisceglie, La Venturé, 5100 W. Jarlath, Skokie, IL 60077; 847-679-8845, Fax 847-679-5287, sandybisceglie@aol.com.

NORTHSHORE COOKERY
Highland Park

Sponsor: Private cooking school & cookware store. Programs: Hands-on & demo classes that include ethnic cuisines, appetizers, entertaining, breads, pastries, knife skills. Established: 2003. Class/group size: 5-25. 200 programs/yr. Facilities: Full hands-on kitchen with 20 stove tops, multiple ovens. Also featured: Catering, personal chefs.

Emphasis: Recipes & techniques for the home chef.

Faculty: Chicago-area chefs & instructors.

Costs: $50-$100.

Contact: Northshore Cookery, 600 Central Ave., #130, Highland Park, IL 60035; 847-432-2665, Fax 847-432-2606, info@northshorecookery.com, www.northshorecookery.com.

PRAIRIE KITCHENS COOKING SCHOOL
Chicago & suburbs

Sponsor: Private school. Programs: Hands-on 1- to 5-session classes that feature updated classical techniques, certification program covering basic techniques, seasonal, & ethnic foods. Established: 1989. Class/group size: 15-25. 50+ programs/yr. Facilities: Professional kitchens with work stations. Also featured: Children's classes, private instruction, visits to markets & food producers, sightseeing, dining in private homes, wine & food events for individuals & businesses.

Emphasis: Cooking for the home chef, women's foodservice apprenticeship program.

Faculty: Carolynn Friedman, chef, caterer & instructor, member of the IACP & AIWF.

Costs: ~$50/session.

Contact: Carolynn Friedman, President, Prairie Kitchens Cooking School, PO Box 372, Morton Grove, IL 60053; 847-966-7574, Fax 847-966-7589.

WHAT'S COOKING
Hinsdale

Sponsor: Cookbook author Ruth Law. Programs: Demo & participation courses & Far East tours that feature classes with professional chefs, gourmet dining, sightseeing, visits to food markets. Established: 1980. Class/group size: 15 hands-on.

Emphasis: Far East & Pacific Rim.

Faculty: Ruth Law is author of Julia Child Cookbook Award finalist Indian Light Cooking, Pacific Light Cooking, & The Southeast Asia Cookbook.

Contact: Ruth Law, What's Cooking, 7206 Chestnut Hills Dr., Burr Ridge, IL 60521; 630-986-1595, Fax 630-655-0912, lawcooks2@netscape.net.

WILTON SCHOOL OF CAKE DECORATING & CONFECTIONERY ART
Woodridge

Sponsor: Private school. Programs: 1-day to 2-week participation courses, daily workshops. Established: 1929. Class/group size: 15-20. Facilities: The 2,200-sq-ft school includes a classroom, teaching kitchen, student lounge, and retail store.

Emphasis: Cake decorating.

Faculty: Includes Sandra Folsom, Susan Matusiak, Collette Peters, Mary Gavenda, Nancy Guerine.

Costs: Range from $80 for 1 day to $725 for a 10-day course.

Contact: School Coordinator, Wilton School of Cake Decorating and Confectionery Art, 2240 W. 75th St., Woodridge, IL 60517; 630-810-2211, Fax 630-963-7299, cweeditz@wilton.com, www.wilton.com.

INDIANA

COUNTRY KITCHEN, SWEETART, INC.

Fort Wayne

Sponsor: Private school. Programs: Basic to advanced cake decorating courses, demo & participation classes on candies, desserts. Established: 1964. Class/group size: 35 hands-on/60 demo. 30-40 programs/yr. Facilities: Multipurpose classroom with cakes & desserts on display. Also featured: Classes for groups, children's parties.

EMPHASIS: Cake decorating, desserts, candies.

FACULTY: 10+ instructors.

COSTS: Cake decorating courses from $65-$70, demos from $10-$40.

CONTACT: Vi Whittington, Country Kitchen, 4621 Speedway Dr., Fort Wayne, IN 46825; 260-482-4835, Fax 260-483-4091, cntryktchn@aol.com, www.countrykitchensa.com/Index.htm.

KITCHEN AFFAIRS

Evansville

Sponsor: Cooking school, cookware & gourmet food store. Programs: Evening & weekend demo & participation classes. Established: 1987. Class/group size: 12 hands-on/20 demo. 125+ programs/yr. Facilities: 400-sq-ft kitchen with 4 work stations. Also featured: Children's classes, private classes.

EMPHASIS: Basic techniques, ethnic cuisines, menu planning & entertaining.

FACULTY: Restaurant chefs, professional instructors, cookbook authors, & school owners Shelly & Mike Sackett. Many instructors are IACP members.

COSTS: $15-$60.

LOCATION: Across from theTri-State area's largest shopping mall, ~3 hrs from Louisville, Nashville, St. Louis & Indianapolis.

CONTACT: Shelly Sackett, Director, Kitchen Affairs, 4610 Vogel Rd., Evansville, IN 47715; 800-782-6762, sales@kitchenaffairs.com, www.kitchenaffairs.com.

THE OLSON ACADEMY

Norman

Sponsor: Private school. Programs: 1- to 3-day classes for advanced nonprofessionals. Established: 1994. Class/group size: 15 demo, 6 hands-on. 10-15 programs/yr. Facilities: 6 stations, dining/demo area. Also featured: Wine seminars, programs for youngsters.

FACULTY: Joan Y. Olson, B.A.; certificate from La Varenne; practical experience in France.

COSTS: $50-$80/class.

CONTACT: Joan Y. Olson, Director of Gastronomy, The Olson Academy, 10902 N. Co. Rd., 800 W, Norman, IN 47264; 812-497-3568, Fax 812-497-3020.

IOWA

COOKING WITH LIZ CLARK

Keokuk

Sponsor: Culinary professional Liz Clark in cooperation with Southeastern Community College. Programs: Demo & participation classes. Established: 1977. Class/group size: 12 hands-on/16 demo. 80 programs/yr. Facilities: Elizabeth Clark's renovated antebellum home that houses her restaurant.

EMPHASIS: Seasonal & holiday menus, guest chef specialties.

FACULTY: Liz Clark studied in Italy & France, received a diploma from La Varenne, studied at Moulin de Mougins with Roger Verge & The Oriental in Bangkok.

COSTS: $39-$80/class. B&B is located nearby.

CONTACT: Sandy Seabold, Coordinator, Southeastern Community College, 335 Messenger Rd., Box 6007, Keokuk, IA 52632-6007; 319-752-2731 x8411, Fax 319-524-8621, sseabold@secc.cc.ia.us, www.secc.cc.ia.us.

CUISINE OF INDIA
Ames

Sponsor: Culinary professional. Programs: Indian cuisine with emphasis on healthy eating. Class/group size: 8.

FACULTY: Madhu Gadia, dietitian, author & diabetes educator, lectures on special diets & weight mgmt.

COSTS: ~$55.

CONTACT: Madhu Gadia, Piquant Enterprises, LLC. - Cuisine of India, PO Box 784, Ames, IA 50010; 515-292-7170, Fax 515-292-5234, mgadia@cuisineofindia.com, www.cuisineofindia.com.

KANSAS

COOKING AT BONNIE'S PLACE
Wichita

Sponsor: Cooking instructor Bonnie Aeschliman. Programs: Demonstrations. Established: 1990. Class/group size: 25. 40-50 programs/yr. Facilities: Demo kitchen.

FACULTY: Bonnie Aeschliman, CCP, has a master's degreee in food & nutrition; Dr. Phil Aeschliman is a member of the IACP.

COSTS: $30/class.

CONTACT: Bonnie Aeschliman, Cooking at Bonnie's Place, 5900 E. 47th St., North, Wichita, KS 67220; 316-744-1981, paeschlima@aol.com.

THE CULINARY CENTER OF KANSAS CITY
Kansas City & Overland Park

Sponsor: Culinary arts center. Programs: Cooking classes, corporate teambuilding, cooking parties. Established: 1998. Class/group size: 1-50. 350 programs/yr. Facilities: Restored turn-of-the-century buggy barn with fully-equipped teaching kitchen & dining area & herb garden. Also featured: Special event parties, food industry consulting.

EMPHASIS: Fundamentals, specialized topics, cookware usage, international & regional cuisines, grilling & smoking, nutrition & whole foods.

FACULTY: 6 full-time instructors, 15 contract maintenance staff, 35+ contract instructors.

COSTS: $30-$60/class.

CONTACT: Laura O'Rourke, Owner, The Culinary Center of Kansas City, 7917 Foster, Overland Park, KS 66204; 913-341-4455, Fax 913-341-5070, laura@kcculinary.com, www.kcculinary.com.

KITCHEN CREATIONS
Olathe

Sponsor: Private school. Programs: Demo classes. Established: 1998. Class/group size: 14. 100 programs/yr. Facilities: Home kitchen with overhead mirror & dining room. Also featured: Private classes.

EMPHASIS: Technique & presentation, expanding skills & entertaining with ease.

FACULTY: Joe Gottschall, professional chef for 15 yrs & member of ACF.

COSTS: $40/class.

CONTACT: Kathy Ales Miller, Kitchen Creations, 15032 W. 144th Terr., Olathe, KS 66062; 913-764-8790, Fax 913-768-8846, KitchenCreations@yahoo.com, www.geocities.com/kitchencreations.

KENTUCKY

CHEF NICK'S COOKING SCHOOL WEEKEND
Harrodsburg

Sponsor: Full service country inn. Programs: Weekend package that includes 3 cooking classes. Established: 1996. Class/group size: 25 demo. 1 programs/yr. Facilities: Group meeting room.

EMPHASIS: Kentucky cuisine & Southern favorites.

FACULTY: Executive Chef Nick Sundberg & regional chefs.

COSTS: $338 ($220) includes 2 nights shared (single) lodging, 2 dinners & 2 full breakfasts.

CONTACT: Chuck Dedman, Innkeeper, Chef Nick's Cooking School Weekend, 638 Beaumont Inn Dr., Harrodsburg, KY 40330; 606-734-3381, Fax 606-734-6897, micklegate@aol.com.

KREMER'S MARKET
Crescent Springs

Sponsor: Specialty market. Programs: Demo classes. Established: 1991. Class/group size: 20 max. 12+ programs/yr. Facilities: Designated area in the market. Also featured: Dinner party classes, private group classes.

EMPHASIS: Vegetarian, regional, culinary skills, desserts, single ingredients.

FACULTY: Coordinator/teacher Chef Maggie Green, RD, graduate of Sullivan Univ. Local & guest chefs.

COSTS: $40-60 for guest chefs/teachers, $30-$35 for other classes.

CONTACT: Warren or Sis Heist, Owners, Kremer's Market, 755 Buttermilk Pike, Crescent Springs, KY 41017; 859-341-1067, Fax 859-341-7008, Info@GreenApron.com, www.greenapron.com.

LOUISIANA

COOKIN' CAJUN COOKING SCHOOL
New Orleans

Sponsor: Creole Delicacies, a company specializing in Cajun & Creole gourmet items. Programs: Demo classes Monday-Sunday mornings. Established: 1988. Class/group size: 1-75. Facilities: Theater-style mirrored kitchen overlooking the Mississippi River. Also featured: Private classes, parties, fish classes for anglers.

EMPHASIS: Cajun & Creole cuisine.

FACULTY: Susan Murphy & other instructors.

COSTS: $20/class.

CONTACT: Lissette Sutton, Owner, Cookin' Cajun Cooking School, #1 Poydras, Store #116, New Orleans, LA 70130; 504-523-6425, Fax 504-523-4787, info@cookincajun.com, www.cookincajun.com.

KAY EWING'S EVERYDAY GOURMET
Baton Rouge

Sponsor: Culinary professional Kay Ewing. Programs: Full participation classes. Established: 1985. Class/group size: 8. 8-10 programs/yr. Facilities: Fully equipped kitchen in The Royal Standard, a specialized gift and antiques store. Also featured: Summer classes for youngsters, ages 9-14. Yearly culinary adventures to various cities.

EMPHASIS: International & cajun cuisines, full participation, menu classes.

FACULTY: Kay Ewing is a member of the IACP & author of Kay Ewing's Cooking School Cookbook & Kay Ewing's Cooking School Cookbook..A Second Course.

COSTS: $40 for adults, $30 for children.

CONTACT: Kay Ewing, Owner, c/o The Royal Standard, 16016 Perkins Rd., Baton Rouge, LA 70810; 225-751-0698, 225-756-2039, kaymewing@cox.net, www.kayewing.com.

LOUISIANA SCHOOL OF COOKING AND CAJUN STORE
St. Martinville

Sponsor: Private school. Programs: Classes focusing on Cajun & Creole cuisine, culinary adventures, programs for foodservice professionals, food & wine dinners. Established: 1999. Class/group size: 30-100. Facilities: Demo kitchen with overhead mirror. Also featured: Custom classes, wine tastings, children's classes, corporate & team building programs.

EMPHASIS: French Cajun & Creole cuisine.

FACULTY: Chef/owner Patrick Mould, cookbook author, TV personality, food columnist.

COSTS: $25-$75/class, cooking vacations start at $1,595.

CONTACT: Eva Hebert, Director of Guest Service, Louisiana School of Cooking, 112 South Main St., St. Martinville, LA 70587; 337-394-1710, Fax 337-394-1711, chefpat@louisianaschoolofcooking.com, www.louisianaschoolofcooking.com.

THE MARDI GRAS SCHOOL OF COOKING
New Orleans

Sponsor: Culinary professional Richard Bond. Programs: Full-day customized hands-on courses. Established: 1997. Class/group size: 2-12. Daily programs/yr. Facilities: Kitchens located in 140-yr-old home. Also featured: Private dinner parties, demo classes for up to 2,000, receptions, theme events, private group classes.

Emphasis: New Orleans specialties & other dishes selected by the student.

Faculty: Richard Bond, past owner of 2 four-star New Orleans restaurants & former instructor at The New Orleans School of Cooking and House, Gardens & Gumbo.

Costs: Full day $90. Includes wine, beer, soft drinks..

Contact: Chef Richard Bond, The Mardi Gras School of Cooking, 232 Bermuda St., Suite B, New Orleans, LA 70114; 504-362-5225, chefbond@att.net, www.gumbos.net.

THE NEW ORLEANS COOKING EXPERIENCE
New Orleans

Sponsor: Private vacation cooking school. Programs: 4- & 6-day programs featuring hands-on classes, visits to architectural sites, antiquing, dining in fine restaurants. Established: 2002. Class/group size: 10 max. 40 programs/yr. Facilities: Private kitchen, dining room & salon in a French Quarter residential setting. Also featured: Half-day classes for private groups.

Emphasis: Classic New Orleans Creole cuisine.

Costs: $2,000/4 days, $2,500/6 days.

Contact: Judy Jurisich, Director, The New Orleans Cooking Experience, 321 St. Charles Ave., 5th Flr., New Orleans, LA 70130; 504-522-4955, Fax 504-522-0538, judy@neworleanscookingexperience.com, www.neworleanscookingexperience.com.

MARYLAND

CHEFPROFESSOR IN-HOME COOKING CLASSES
Mitchellville & Upper Marlboro, Washington, DC

Sponsor: Professional executive chef & teacher. Programs: Personalized private classes & small group parties. Established: 1998. Facilities: Client's kitchen.

Emphasis: Basic skills & techniques, specific cuisines, how to prepare 1 wk of meals in a day.

Faculty: Owner Jack A. Batten, CEC, 30+ yrs culinary experience, has taught at Prince Georges CC & Anne Arundel CC.

Costs: Private classes $250-$350; group parties (6 max) from $350.

Contact: Jack Batten, Chef, ChefWorks PCS Personal Classes, 7203 Havre Turn, Upper Marlboro, MD 20772; 301-627-4496, Fax 301-574-0816, jbatten@earthlink.net, www.chefprofessor.com.

CHEZ MOI COOKING INSTRUCTION AT HOME
Annapolis & Baltimore, Washington, DC

Programs: At-home one-on-one cooking instruction. 11-session Comprehensive Cooking course covers classic French cooking. Established: 2001. Class/group size: 1-2. Facilities: Participant's home.

Emphasis: Classic French cooking.

Faculty: Culinary professionals who have worked in restaurants as chefs.

Costs: $1,150 tuition. Cooking equipment $0-$700. Food supplies ~$250.

Contact: Jordan Holtzman, Franchise Owner/Instructor, Chez Moi Cooking Instruction At Home, 618 Harborside Dr., Suite F, Joppa, MD 21085; 410-538-4600, info@chezmoicooking.com.

THE CHINESE COOKERY, INC.
Silver Spring

Sponsor: Culinary professional Joan Shih. Programs: 8 levels of participation & demo courses in Chinese cuisine. Established: 1975. Class/group size: 5. ~36-40 programs/yr. Facilities: Classroom/lab equipped for Chinese cooking, outdoor Chinese brick oven. Also featured: Japanese sushi class, classes for teenagers, private lessons for cooking professionals, market visits, restaurant kitchen tours, culinary tours to the Far East.

EMPHASIS: Chinese cuisine: basic, advanced, gourmet, Szechuan, Hunan, vegetarian.

FACULTY: Joan Shih, a retired chemist from the NIH, received a certificate in Chinese cuisine in Taiwan, has taught Chinese & Japanese cooking & is author of The Art of Chinese Cookery.

COSTS: 5-session courses are $200, vegetarian is $205, sushi class is $70.

CONTACT: Joan Shih, President & Director, The Chinese Cookery, Inc., 14209 Sturtevant Rd., Silver Spring, MD 20905; 301-236-5311, joanshih@aol.com.

A COOK'S TABLE COOKING CLASSES

Baltimore

Sponsor: Cookware store and cooking school. Programs: Participation classes on topics that include seasonal and holiday foods, guest chef specialties, American regional and international cuisines. Established: 1996. Class/group size: 20. 150 programs/yr. Facilities: Professional cooking area with close-counter seating facing the chef and cooking area. Also featured: Private cooking lessons and parties, cooking tours to Italy, market shopping tours.

EMPHASIS: A variety of topics.

FACULTY: Local and nationally known chefs, cookbook authors, TV chefs.

COSTS: $35-$75/class.

CONTACT: A Cook's Table Cooking Classes, 717 Light Street, Baltimore, MD 21230; 410-539-8600, Fax 410-539-6845, info@acookstable.com, www.acookstable.com.

THE FLAVORS IN THE GLASS & HOW THEY GET THERE

Baltimore

Sponsor: Wine professional. Programs: 8- & 10-session seminars and online study course. Established: 1997. Class/group size: 35. 3 programs/yr.

FACULTY: Lisa M. Airey is a Wine Manager of F.P. Winner (wholesaler), AWS Certified Wine Judge, Certified Wine Educator.

COSTS: $350.

CONTACT: Lisa M. Airey, Wine Manager, The Wine Educator, 1206 Corbett Rd., Monktown, MD 21111; 410-646-5500, x103, Fax 410-646-6464, lisaairey@thewinekey.com, www.thewinekey.com.

L'ACADEMIE DE CUISINE

Bethesda

Sponsor: Proprietary vocational & recreational school. Programs: 1- to 4-session demo & participation courses. Established: 1976. Class/group size: 21-30. 1,000 programs/yr. Facilities: 21-station practice kitchen, 30-seat demo classroom. Also featured: Children's classes, private dinners, guest chef demos, 1-wk culinary/culture trips to France, team building programs, wine courses.

EMPHASIS: Techniques, intl & regional cuisines, nutritional & low-fat foods, vegetarian, pastry, wine & food pairing, entertaining menus, private group classes.

FACULTY: 4 full- and 15 part-time. School President Francois Dionot, graduate of L'Ecole Hoteliere de la Societe Suisse des Hoteliers & founder of the IACP; Amy White, Patrice Dionot, Marina Ross, Nancy Novak.

COSTS: $40-$75/session.

CONTACT: Amy White, Managing Director, L'Academie de Cuisine, 5021 Wilson Lane, Bethesda, MD 20814; 301-986-9490, Fax 301-652-7970, classes@lacademie.com, www.lacademie.com.

MASSACHUSETTS

BOSTON UNIVERSITY CULINARY ARTS

Boston

Sponsor: University. Programs: 1- to 5-session demo & participation courses. Established: 1986. Class/group size: 12-130. 50 programs/yr. Facilities: Demo & wine tasting room, 8 restaurant kitchens, wine library. Also featured: Children's classes, market visits, food & wine pairing, domestic & foreign tours hosted by a culinary historian familiar with the region's food & wine.

EMPHASIS: Guest chef specialties, food & wine tours.

FACULTY: Includes Jacques Pepin, Julia Child, Jasper White, Jody Adams, Franco Romagnoli, Daniel Bruce, Sandy Block, Chris Schlesinger, Nina Simonds, Julie Sahni, Todd English.

COSTS: Seminars $10-$125, full-day classes & 3-session courses $150-$300.

CONTACT: Rebecca Alssid, Director of Special Programs, Boston University Culinary Arts, 808 Commonwealth Ave., Boston, MA 02215; 617-353-9852, Fax 617-353-4130, ralssid@bu.edu, www.bu.edu/met/programs.

THE CAMBRIDGE SCHOOL OF CULINARY ARTS

Cambridge *(See also page 82) (See display ad page 83)*

Sponsor: Proprietary school. Programs: 1- to 5-session participation courses. Established: 1974. Class/group size: 12. Facilities: 3 kitchens & demonstration classrooms with gas & electric commercial appliances. Also featured: Celebrity chef demonstrations.

EMPHASIS: Ethnic & regional cuisines, vegetarian meals, breads, pastries, appetizers, desserts.

FACULTY: Diverse faculty include CSCA graduates & instructors and other industry professionals.

COSTS: $70 for single session classes, $300 for 5-session courses.

CONTACT: The Cambridge School of Culinary Arts, 2020 Massachusetts Ave., Cambridge, MA 02140; 617-354-2020, Fax 617-576-1963, info@cambridgeculinary.com, www.cambridgeculinary.com.

THE CAPTAIN FREEMAN INN

Brewster, Cape Cod

Sponsor: Historic seaside country inn. Programs: Weekend courses that feature a hands-on Saturday class, wine tasting & dinner. Established: 1993. Class/group size: 12-18. 8-10 programs/yr. Facilities: The inn's kitchen. Also featured: Beach, theater, golf & antiquing nearby.

EMPHASIS: Mediterranean.

FACULTY: Carol Edmondson, chef & cookbook author.

COSTS: $490-$610, which includes inn lodging, breakfasts, wine tasting & dinner for 2.

CONTACT: Carol Edmondson, Innkeeper, The Captain Freeman Inn, 15 Breakwater Rd., Brewster, Cape Cod, MA 02631; 800-843-4664, 508-896-7481, Fax 508-896-5618, visitus@capecod.net, www.capecodculinary.com.

THE CHEF'S SHOP

Great Barrington

Sponsor: Cookware store. Programs: Classes, private instruction. Established: 1994. Class/group size: 30 demo, 10 hands-on. 100 programs/yr. Facilities: Cookware store's working kitchen. Also featured: Cookbook authors, food tasting, product demos.

EMPHASIS: Restaurant-quality dishes that can be created at home.

FACULTY: Local and national restaurant chefs, cookbook authors, food industry experts.

COSTS: $40/class.

CONTACT: Robert Navarino, President, The Chef's Shop, 31 Railroad St., Great Barrington, MA 01230; 413-528-0135, Fax 413-528-0139, customerservice@TheChefsShop.net, www.TheChefsShop.net.

DELPHIN'S GOURMANDISE AND SCHOOL OF PASTRY

Marblehead

Sponsor: Private school. Programs: 1- to 3-day hands-on workshops, evening demos. Established: 2000. Class/group size: 6-8 students. 5 programs/yr. Facilities: Kitchen/classroom.

EMPHASIS: Pastry making fundamentals, style & techniques.

FACULTY: Master Pastry Chef Delphin Gomes, co-owner of Delphin's Gourmandise Fine French Patisserie, received the Best of Boston award from Boston Magazine.

COSTS: $295-$840/workshop, $85/class.

CONTACT: Tone Gomes, Delphin's Gourmandise & School of Pastry, 258 Washington St., Marblehead, MA 01945; 781-639-2311, Fax 781-631-2311, DGschoolofpastry@aol.com, www.delphins.com.

GARY SANDMAN WINE PROGRAMS

Springfield

Sponsor: Wine professional. Programs: 1-night wine sessions. Established: 1988. 12 programs/yr.

Faculty: Gary Sandman has 15+ yrs as a wine retailer & educator.

Costs: $25/session.

Contact: Gary Sandman, Kappy's Liquors, 1755 Boston Rd., Springfield, MA 01129; 413-543-4495, Fax 413-543-4414, gary.sandman@kappys.com.

HOME CHEESEMAKING 101

Ashfield

Sponsor: New England Cheesemaking Supply Co., a purveyor of ingredients, supplies & education to home cheesemakers. Programs: 1-day hands-on class covers fresh mozzarella, whole milk ricotta, whey ricotta, farmhouse cheddar, queso blanco, fromage blanc, mascarpone, & creme fraiche. Established: 1978. Class/group size: 25. 6-10 programs/yr.

Emphasis: Home cheesemaking.

Faculty: Owner Ricki Carroll, teaching since 1978, is author of Home Cheese Making.

Costs: $100 includes lunch.

Contact: Ricki Carroll, Pres., Home Cheesemaking 101, PO Box 85, Main St., Ashfield, MA 01330; 413-628-3808, Fax 413-628-4061, info@cheesemaking.com, www.cheesemaking.com.

LE PETIT GOURMET COOKING SCHOOL

Wayland

Sponsor: Culinary professional Fran Rosenheim. Programs: 1- to 4-session demonstration/participation courses. Established: 1979. Class/group size: 1-2. Facilities: 330-sq-ft kitchen with two workspaces. Also featured: Private classes weekday mornings.

Emphasis: Beginning to advanced French cuisine, wild game, specific subjects. Specialty is chocolate desserts & sauces.

Faculty: Fran Rosenheim studied with local chefs & at Le Cordon Bleu and La Varenne in Paris.

Costs: $60/session.

Contact: Fran Rosenheim, Le Petit Gourmet Cooking School, 19 Charena Rd., Wayland, MA 01778; 508-358-4219, Fax 508-358-4291 (call 1st), frosenheim@aol.com.

SUMMERFARE

North Truro, Cape Cod

Sponsor: Commercial kitchen. Programs: Hands-on classes for all levels, weekend seminars, demos by visiting chefs, private classes. Established: 2000. Class/group size: 8 hands-on, 16 demo. Facilities: Full commercial kitchen, cookbook reference library, & vegetable, fruit & herb garden. Also featured: Growing & using herbs, food & wine pairing.

Emphasis: NE seafood & traditional Cape Cod dishes. Emphasis on seasonal foods, healthy preparation, & locally grown & produced foods.

Faculty: Owner/Director from Boston Culinary Arts Program, professional chef. Demos by visiting chefs, cookbook authors & culinary professionals.

Costs: Classes $75, weekend seminars $125.

Contact: Eva A. N. Hartmann, Owner/Chef, SummerFare, PO Box 502, North Truro, MA 02652; 508-487-2387, Fax 508-487-4564, summerfare@capecod.net, www.summerfare.net.

TAMING OF THE STEW

Wellesley

Sponsor: Culinary professional Sally Larhette. Programs: 3 classes/wk that feature pre- & post-cooking discussions, shopping & preparation trips, historical perspective, hands-on class of a full menu. Established: 1998. Class/group size: 15 demo, 9 hands-on. 150 programs/yr. Facilities: Fully-equipped professionally-styled home kitchen. Also featured: Private instruction, classes for youngsters, market & winery visits, dining in private homes.

Emphasis: Seasonal foods as the center of a healthy diet.
Faculty: Sally Larhette, CCP, trained in French & Italian cuisines by Madeleiine Kamman.
Costs: $35-$50/class.
Contact: Sally Larhette, School Director, Taming of the Stew, 619 C Washington St., Wellesley, MA 02181; 781-235-1792, Fax 781-235-7714, larhette@attbi.com.

TERENCE JANERICCO COOKING CLASSES
Boston

Sponsor: Cookbook author. Programs: 1- & 5-session demo & participation courses. Established: 1966. Class/group size: 6 hands-on/14 demo. 100+ programs/yr. Facilities: Home kitchen. Also featured: Private classes & special events.
Emphasis: Gourmet cooking, baking, ethnic & regional cuisines, specific subjects.
Faculty: Terence Janericco has operated a catering firm for 25+ years & teaches at education centers & schools. Author of 12 books, including The Book of Great Hors d'Oeuvres.
Costs: 5-session course $400, single session $80.
Contact: Terence Janericco, Owner, Terence Janericco Cooking Classes, 42 Fayette St., Boston, MA 02116; 617-426-7458, Fax 617-426-7458, terencej@bellatlantic.net, www.terencejanericcocookingclasses.com.

WESTPORT RIVERS LONG ACRE HOUSE
Westport

Sponsor: Vineyard. Programs: Food & wine classes. Established: 1996. Class/group size: 35. ~14 programs/yr. Also featured: Cooking demonstrations.
Faculty: Exec. Chef Kerry Downey Romaniello, a New England Culinary Institute graduate, attended Madeleine Kamman's School for American Chefs at Beringer Vineyards.
Costs: $25-$75/class.
Contact: Kerry Downey Romaniello, Executive Chef, Westport Rivers Vineyard & Winery, 417 Hixbridge Rd., Westport, MA 02790; 508-636-3423, x7, Fax 508-636-4133, kerry@westportrivers.com, www.westportrivers.com.

MICHIGAN

CULINARY SECRETS COOKING SCHOOL
Jackson

Sponsor: Gourmet kitchen shoppe and cooking school. Programs: Classes and courses ranging from vegetarian cuisine to traditional French cuisine; teens and kids programs; technical classes in pastry, knife skills, basic cooking techniques. Established: 1998. Class/group size: max 40. 150 programs/yr. Facilities: Gourmet kitchen with appliances provided by Viking. 18 burners, 5 ovens, a proofing oven, outdoor grill. Demonstration classes feature Bistro-style table and chairs. Also featured: Private parties, bridal showers, birthday parties, kids summer camp, off-site programs.
Emphasis: A variety of classes and courses to meet the needs of home chefs.
Faculty: 6 in-store instructors, guest chefs.
Costs: Classes with guest chefs and staff instructors begin at $28 (average $35). Celebrity chefs range from $45-$95. Diploma series are $300-$475.
Contact: Kathe Meade, Owner/Director, Culinary Secrets Cooking School, 1821 Horton Rd., Jackson, MI 49203; 517-788-8840, 877-788-8840, Fax 517-788-8856, www.culinarysecrets.com.

MINNESOTA

BYERLY'S SCHOOL OF CULINARY ARTS
St. Louis Park

Sponsor: School in upscale supermarket. Programs: 1-session demo & participation classes, limited series offerings. Established: 1980. Class/group size: 16 hands-on/25 demo. 200+ programs/yr.

Facilities: Large teaching kitchen with overhead mirror. Also featured: Private & couple's classes, children's birthday classes, special events, team building.

EMPHASIS: Italian, Asian, French cuisine; entertaining, seasonal, healthy cooking series.

FACULTY: Culinary Svcs Mgr Deidre Schipani has a diploma from L'Academie de Cuisine. Instructors incl CIA graduate Carol Brown, NPR host Lynne Rossetto Kasper, cookbook authors, guest chefs.

COSTS: ~$45-50/class.

CONTACT: Deidre Schipani, CCP, Manager of Culinary Services, Byerly's School of Culinary Arts, 3777 Park Center Blvd., St. Louis Park, MN 55416; 952-929-2492, Fax 952-929-7756, cooking.school@lfhi.com, www.Byerlys.com.

THE CHEFS GALLERY
Stillwater

Sponsor: Cooking school & gourmet cookware store. Programs: Demonstration & hands-on instruction on a variety of topics. Established: 1999. Class/group size: 12-30. 90+ programs/yr. Facilities: Viking-equipped teaching kitchen with participation facilities for 15 people. Also featured: Private group functions, corporate team building events.

EMPHASIS: American regional, ethnic, healthy living, baking, desserts, entertaining, local restaurant/chef specialties, wine tastings, wild game cookery.

FACULTY: 30 local chefs and instructors.

COSTS: $25-$80/class.

CONTACT: Stephanie Jameson, Cooking School Director, The Chefs Gallery, Grand Garage, 324 N. Main St., Stillwater, MN 55082; 651-351-1144, Fax 651-351-2165, steph@thechefsgallery.com, www.TheChefsGallery.com.

COOKS OF CROCUS HILL
St. Paul & Edina

Sponsor: Cooking school & gourmet retail store. Programs: 1-, 4-, & 5-session demo & participation courses. Established: 1976. Class/group size: 12 hands-on/30 demo. 450+ programs/yr. Facilities: 2 locations with modern, professional kitchens & capacity for 40 full-service dinner classes. Also featured: Private group classes, corporate team-building classes.

EMPHASIS: Basics, ethnic cuisines, holiday & seasonal menus, single subjects, guest chef specialties.

FACULTY: 60 local, national & intl chefs & cooking instructors. Guest instructors include Diana Kennedy, Giulliano Hazan, Kasma Unchit, Shirley Corriher, Deborah Madison, Hugh Carpenter.

COSTS: 4-session course $250, 5-session course $350. Classes $10-$75.

CONTACT: Kevin Wencel, Director, Cooks of Crocus Hill, 877 Grand Ave., St. Paul, MN 55105; 651-228-1333, Fax 651-228-9084, kwencel@cochmail.com, www.cooksofcrocushill.com.

KITCHEN WINDOW
Minneapolis

Sponsor: Kitchenware store & culinary arts school. Programs: Celebrated Chefs program offered in leading Twin Cities restaurants, Culinary Arts Cooking School on site. Established: 1990. Class/group size: 24 max. 180+ programs/yr. Facilities: 1,200-sq-ft space with the latest equipment & a 32-ft island. Video & sound system. Also featured: Team-building events, private parties, parent-child classes.

EMPHASIS: Cooking & baking basics, seasonal & international recipes, guest chef specialties.

FACULTY: Includes restaurant chefs & cookbook authors.

COSTS: ~$45-$85/class.

CONTACT: Ann Nelson, Cooking School Director, Kitchen Window, 3001 Hennepin Ave., Minneapolis, MN 55408; 888-824-4417, 612-824-4417, Fax 612-824-9225, info@KitchenWindow.com, www.kitchen-window.com.

SCHUMACHER'S HOTEL COOKING SCHOOL
New Prague

Class/group size: 12.

FACULTY: Chef John Schumacher.

Costs: $100/class. Cooking class packages for two $355-$455, include Friday night appetizer/dessert session, overnight lodging, breakfast, Saturday cooking class, luncheon.
Contact: Kathy Heyda, Seminar Coordinator, Schumacher's Hotel Cooking School, 212 West Main St., New Prague, MN 56071; 952-758-2133, 800-283-2049, kathy@schumachershotel.com, www.schumachershotel.com/CookingSeminar.htm.

THE WRITE COOK
Minneapolis, Paris & Provence, France

Sponsor: Culinary professional. Programs: Hands-on cooking classes in Minneapolis during fall, winter & spring; food tours to Paris & Provence. Established: 1999. Class/group size: 10. Facilities: Minneapolis: home teaching kitchen. Provence: village home.
Emphasis: French cooking, regional American cooking & baking.
Faculty: Classes in Minneapolis taught by cookbook author, food & travel writer Mary Ellen Evans with occasional guest instructors. Food tours conducted by Mary & Hallie Harron.
Costs: $55/home class, tours from ~$1,500-$2,800.
Contact: Mary Evans, Owner/Operator, The Write Cook, 4844 Colfax Ave. South, Minneapolis, MN 55409; 612-822-6114, Fax 612-822-0274, info@thewritecook.com, www.thewritecook.com.

MISSISSIPPI

THE EVERYDAY GOURMET
Jackson

Sponsor: Schools in 2 Jackson cookware stores. Programs: Demonstration and participation classes. Established: 1981. Class/group size: 12 hands-on/36 demo. 100+ programs/yr. Also featured: Guest chefs, lunch sessions, classes for children, tour groups.
Faculty: School director Chan Patterson.
Costs: $25-$60; children's classes are $20.
Contact: Director, The Everyday Gourmet, Inc., 2905 Old Canton Rd., Jackson, MS 39216; 800-898-0122, Fax 601-981-3266, info@theeverydaygourmet.com, www.theeverydaygourmet.com.

MISSOURI

CORKDORK U. – THE 'NO ATTITUDE' WINE SCHOOL
St. Louis

Sponsor: Wine store. Programs: Single- & multi-session programs. Established: 1998. Class/group size: 20. Also featured: Private wine classes & food/wine seminars available off-site for groups.
Faculty: Instructor, Ed Deutch is a member of the SWE & has taught wine classes at Univ. of Minnesota's Open U. CorkDork U. was voted Best Wine School in 1999 by The Riverfront Times.
Costs: $30-$60/session.
Contact: Ed Deutch, Instructor, Corkdork U.-The Vintage Room Wine Store, 4736 McPherson Ave., St. Louis, MO 63108; 314-FOR-WINE/367-9463, eddie@corkdork.com, www.corkdork.com.

DIERBERGS SCHOOL OF COOKING
Four locations

Sponsor: Cooking school with 4 locations in retail grocery stores. Programs: 1-session demo & participation courses. Established: 1978. Class/group size: 18. 800+ programs/yr. Facilities: Soundproof enclosures in Dierbergs Supermarkets. Also featured: Classes for couples, children's classes, parent-child sessions, corporate team classes.
Emphasis: Home cooking.
Faculty: 30+ faculty of home economists & cooking instructors; guest teachers, including industry spokespersons, restaurateurs, traveling chefs, cookbook authors.
Costs: Adult classes $25-$30, guest classes $30-$40.
Location: West Oak (Creve Coeur), Mid Rivers Center (St. Peters), Southroads (St. Louis

County), Clarkson/Clayton Center (Ellisville).

CONTACT: Barbara Ridenhour, Director of Consumer Affairs, Dierbergs School of Cooking, 16690 Swingley Ridge Rd., Chesterfield, MO 63006; 636-532-8897 x2277, Fax 636-537-2559, ridenhou@dierbergs.com, www.dierbergs.com.

JASPER'S

Kansas City

Sponsor: Restaurant. Programs: Demo & holiday luncheon classes. Established: 1954. Class/group size: 45 demo. 25 programs/yr. Also featured: Private classes for groups of 20+, children's & couples' classes, wine classes.

EMPHASIS: Northern Italian cuisine.

FACULTY: Executive Chef Jasper J. Mirabile, Jr. studied at La Varenne & the Gritti Palace. Jasper's received the Dirona, Travel/Holiday, Mobil 4-Star & the AAA 4-Diamond awards.

COSTS: $45/class.

CONTACT: Jasper J. Mirabile, Jr., Chef/owner, Jasper's, 1201 W. 103rd, Kansas City, MO 64114; 816-941-6600, Fax 816-941-4346, jasperjr@aol.com, www.jasperskc.com.

KITCHEN CONSERVATORY

St. Louis

Sponsor: Cooking school in a gourmet shop. Programs: Demonstration & participation classes. Established: 1984. Class/group size: 18. 300+ programs/yr. Facilities: Modern kitchen with front-row seats for all students. Also featured: Day trips to restaurants and shops, classes for children.

EMPHASIS: Ethnic & regional cuisines, baking, seasonal & entertaining menus, guest chef specialties.

FACULTY: Local chefs, restaurateurs, caterers, and IACP members. Guest instructors have included Hugh Carpenter, Martin Yan, Joanne Weir, Paula Wolfert.

COSTS: $34-$75/class.

CONTACT: Anne Schlafly, Owner, Kitchen Conservatory, 8021 Clayton Rd., St. Louis, MO 63117; 314-862-COOK/866-862-CHEF (toll free), Fax 314-862-2110, chef@kitchenconservatory.com, www.kitchenconservatory.com.

SUZANNE CORBETT – PANCOR PRODUCTIONS

St. Louis

Sponsor: Culinary professional Suzanne Corbett. Programs: Participation courses. Established: 1976. Class/group size: 16. 14 programs/yr. Facilities: Vocational schools, historic sites. Also featured: Wine instruction, Missouri wine country tours, summer workshops for groups.

EMPHASIS: Historic American foods, hearth-style baking, regional dishes, international cuisines.

FACULTY: Suzanne Corbett, CCP, specializes in foods from the past, is a food & wine writer with 20 yrs experience, contributing ed to Rodale Press, Victoria Magazine, Better Homes & Gardens.

COSTS: $25-$50/class.

CONTACT: Suzanne Corbett, 12150 Queen's Charter CT. Suite B, St. Louis, MO 63146-5250; 314-997-7578, Fax 314-997-7712, corbettsuzanne@aol.com.

MONTANA

APPETITES & SIGHTS

Six regions

Sponsor: Culinary tour company. Programs: 5-day culinary vacation programs that include hands-on cooking lessons, visits to wineries & food related sites, cultural tours. Established: 2003. Class/group size: 4-8. 26 programs/yr. Also featured: Customized tours.

EMPHASIS: Regional French cuisine.

FACULTY: Includes Jean-Marc Villard (Michelin-starred) in Lyon, Hubert Maetz in Alsace, & local chefs in Grenoble.

COSTS: $2,325-$2,750 includes hotel lodging.

LOCATION: Aix-en-Provence, Avignon, Bourdeaux, Grenoble, Lyon, Strasbourg.

CONTACT: Kim Wells, President, Appetites & Sights, 15037 Kelly Canyon Rd., Bozeman, MT 59715; 888-534-8300 or 406-556-8300, Fax 406-522-8665, info@appetitesandsights.com, www.appetitesandsights.com.

NEBRASKA

THE CLASSY GOURMET CULINARY ART CENTER
Omaha

Sponsor: Recreational cooking school. Programs: Demo & hands-on cooking classes, wine education programs. Topics include regional, ethnic & seasonal cuisines, guest chef specialties. Established: 2002. Class/group size: Hands-on 24, demo 35. 200+ programs/yr. Facilities: 2,000-sq-ft professional kitchen, wine bar. Also featured: Private dinner parties, personal chefs, corporate team building events.

FACULTY: Local restaurant chefs include staff chef Cory Guyer & Jeff Snow, Glenn Wheeler, Cedric Fichepain.

COSTS: $20-$75/class.

CONTACT: Colleen Cleek, Owner, The Classy Gourmet, 721 N. 98th St., Omaha, NE 68114; 402-955-COOK (2665), Fax 402-932-2634, cook@theclassygourmet.com, www.theclassygourmet.com.

NEVADA

CREATIVE COOKING SCHOOL OF LAS VEGAS
Las Vegas

Sponsor: Private culinary school with a cookware & specialty store. Programs: Hands-on & demo classes. Cooking techniques, baking, ethnic cuisines. Intl Wine Sommelier Guild classes. Established: 2001. Class/group size: 30 demo, 16 hands-on. 300 programs/yr. Facilities: 2,000 sq-ft kitchen with the latest equipment. Also featured: Celebrity chef classes, classes for kids, corporate team-building, banquet & catering, private & special events.

EMPHASIS: Techniques & a variety of cuisines. Cooking skills for the non-professional or home chef.

FACULTY: CECs, CCEs, CCPs & celebrity chefs.

COSTS: $75-$495.

CONTACT: Catherine Margles, President/Founder, Creative Cooking School of Las Vegas, 7385 W. Sahara Ave., Las Vegas, NV 89117-2757; 702-562-3900, Fax 702-562-3939, info@creativecookingschool.com, http://creativecookingschool.com.

NOTHING TO IT! CULINARY CENTER
Reno

Sponsor: Cookware store & gourmet take-out cafe. Programs: Classes that cover techniques & a variety of cuisines. Established: 1995. Class/group size: 55 demo, 16 hands-on. 200 programs/yr. Facilities: Culinary center with retail cafe. Also featured: Classes for youngsters, private instruction.

FACULTY: 2 chefs on staff; nationally-known guest chefs.

COSTS: $40-$125/class.

CONTACT: Jennifer Bushman, Owner/Culinary Instructor, Nothing To It! Culinary Center, 255 Crummer Ln., Reno, NV 89502; 775-826-2628, jennifer@nothingtoit.com, www.nothingtoit.com.

NEW HAMPSHIRE

COOKING 'INN' STYLE
Manchester

Sponsor: 3 New England country inns: Manor On Golden Pond, Rabbit Hill Inn, & Inn At Thorn Hill. Programs: 3-day theme cooking series that focus on seasonal menus, food & wine pairing, culinary tips & preparation techniques. Themes include Holiday Dinner Party, Spring Fling &

Four Diamond Picnic Party. Established: 2002. Class/group size: 12. 3 programs/yr. Facilities: Inn kitchens. Also featured: Shopping, antiquing, historic sites, & seasonal outdoor recreation.
EMPHASIS: Inn specialites.
FACULTY: Award-winning, AAA Four-Diamond Executive & Pastry Chefs.
COSTS: $150/series plus lodging at each Inn.
CONTACT: Mary Ellen Shields, Innkeeper, Cooking 'Inn' Style, Route 3, Holderness, NH 03245; 800-545-2141, Fax 603-968-2116, info@manorongoldenpond.com, www.cookinginnstyle.com.

A TASTE OF THE MOUNTAINS COOKING SCHOOL

Glen

Sponsor: Private cooking school at the Bernerhof Inn. Programs: Spring, winter, fall classes & weekend courses for novice & intermediate cooks; 3-hr Thursday guest chef classes in winter. Established: 1980. Class/group size: 10 hands-on. Facilities: Bernerhof Inn restaurant kitchen. Also featured: Custom seminars for groups of 7+.
EMPHASIS: Basic techniques including knife handling, sauces, sauteeing, breads.
FACULTY: Owner/Chef Scott Stearns of The Rare Bear at the Bernerhof Inn; northern New England area guest chefs.
COSTS: Weekend courses $479-$549, including shared lodging & meals; day rate $339 for the weekend; class rate $60.
CONTACT: Sharon Wroblewski, Owner, A Taste of the Mountains Cooking School, Box 240, Glen, NH 03838; 603-383-9132/800-548-8007, Fax 603-383-0809, stay@bernerhofinn.com, www.virtualcities.com/tastemt.htm.

NEW JERSEY

ADVENTURES IN COOKING

Wayne

Sponsor: Cooking school & cookware store. Programs: Demo & participation classes. Guest chef classes. Established: 1976. 80+ programs/yr. Also featured: Private classes.
FACULTY: Arlene Ward, a member of the IACP & NY Assn. of Cooking Teachers, has been a food stylist for professional photographers & food co's. Other instructors are IACP members. Guest instructors include Giuliano Bugialli & Rick Moonen.
COSTS: $45-$60/class.
CONTACT: Arlene Ward, Proprietor, Adventures in Cooking, 12 Legion Place, Wayne, NJ 07470-6771; 973-305-1114, Fax 973-305-4810, Arlene@adventuresincooking.com, www.adventuresincooking.com.

ATLANTIC CAPE COMMUNITY ACADEMY OF CULINARY ARTS

Mays Landing *(See also page 102) (See display ad page 103)*

Sponsor: 2-yr college. Programs: One-day themed workshops covering a variety of cooking topics. Established: 1981. Class/group size: 30 demo, 16 hands-on. 10 programs/yr. Facilities: Academy of Culinary Arts instructional kitchens. Also featured: Kids College summer cooking program for children.
EMPHASIS: Specialties of chef educators.
FACULTY: Academy of Culinary Arts faculty.
COSTS: Vary by type of instruction.
CONTACT: Mindy Hoag, Program Developer, Academy of Culinary Arts, Atlantic Cape Community College, 5100 Black Horse Pike, Mays Landing, NJ 08330; 609-343-4829, Fax 609-343-4823, mhoag@atlantic.edu, www.atlantic.edu.

CHEF AND SOMMELIER FOR A DAY

Short Hills

Sponsor: Hilton Short Hills. Programs: Thursday programs for 1-2 persons who plan & help prepare dinner + wine selection, & then dine with up to 6 guests. Established: 1997. Class/group size:

1-2. ~50 programs/yr. Facilities: Restaurant kitchen of the Hilton Hotel. Also featured: Food & wine tasting, discussion with sommelier.

Emphasis: Chef specialties & wine pairing.

Faculty: Hilton Executive Chef Walter Leffler & Sommelier Isaac Alexander.

Costs: $175 for guest chefs, $150 for dining companions.

Contact: George Staikos, Sommelier, Director of Food & Beverage, Chef and Sommelier for a Day, 41 JFK Parkway, Short Hills, NJ 07078; 973-379-0100 #7980, Fax 973-379-1153, www.hiltonshorthills.com/dinningroom.html.

CONNIE FOWLER WINE PROGRAMS
Summit

Sponsor: Wine professional. Programs: 3- to 6-session courses & custom wine tasting events. Established: 1995. Class/group size: 35. ~6 programs/yr.

Faculty: Connie Fowler, member of SWE, WSET Diploma, 14+ yrs wine industry experience.

Contact: Connie Fowler, Let's Have a Taste, 16 Sherman Ave., Summit, NJ 07901; 908-277-4330, Fax 908-277-1348, connie@letshaveataste.com, www.letshaveataste.com.

COOKTIQUE
Tenafly

Sponsor: Cooking school, gourmet & housewares shop. Programs: Day & evening demo & participation sessions. Established: 1976. Class/group size: 20 hands-on/30 demo. 150 programs/yr. Facilities: 400-sq-ft demo kitchen with overhead mirror & latest equipment. Also featured: Children's classes, birthday parties, private group events.

Emphasis: Techniques, sauces, fish, grilling, tofu, spa, bread, guest chef specialties, dessert, pasta.

Faculty: Culinary professionals & master chefs. Guest chefs have included Guiliano Bugialli, Marcella Hazan, Nicholas Malgieri, Lorenza de'Medici, Arthur Schwartz, Jaques Pepin.

Costs: From $35; guest chef classes $50-$100.

Contact: Cathy McCauley, CCP, Director, Cooktique, 9 W. Railroad Ave., Tenafly, NJ 07670; 201-568-7990, Fax 201-568-6480, cooktique@msn.com, www.cooktique.com.

GINGERCREEK COOKING SCHOOL
Stewartsville

Sponsor: Culinary professional. Programs: Regional, seasonal & holiday classes for adults. Kids Culinary College participation classes. Established: 1987. Class/group size: 12. 60 programs/yr. Facilities: English cottage, rural setting.

Faculty: Nancy L. Wyant, owner & instructor.

Costs: $45/class.

Contact: Nancy Wyant, Owner/instructor, Gingercreek Cooking School, 304 Rt. 173, Stewartsville, NJ 08886; 908-479-6062, gingercreek@hotmail.com.

GREEN GABLES RESTAURANT AND INN
Beach Haven

Sponsor: Chef-owned restaurant and inn. Programs: Culinary classes. Class/group size: Limited. Facilities: Restored Victorian-era house.

Faculty: Chef/owner Adolfo de'Martino.

Costs: $45/class.

Contact: Adolfo de'Martino, Chef/Owner, Green Gables Restaurant and Inn, 212 Centre St., Beach Haven, NJ 08008-1714; 609-492-3553, Fax 609-492-2507, greengableslbi@aol.com, www.lbinet.com/greengables.

KINGS COOKING STUDIO
Short Hills, Bedminster, Verona & Hillsdale

Sponsor: Cooking school in Kings Super Markets. Programs: Single & multi-session demo & participation classes, includes techniques, single subjects & full menus. Established: 1983. Class/group size: ~25/demo, ~15/partic. 150+ programs/yr. Facilities: Fully-equipped enclosed kitchens, overhead mirrors. Also featured: Celebrity chef demos, classes for couples & children, wine tours.

EMPHASIS: Principles of Cooking, an 8-wk diploma series, emphasizes cooking techniques. Additional series include Advanced Principles of Cooking, Mastery of Baking & Young Chefs.

FACULTY: 15+ resident faculty includes Carole Walter, Jean Yueh, Kathleen Sanderson. Guest chefs include Nick Malgieri, Julia Child, Andre Soltner, Rick Moonan.

COSTS: Principles of Cooking series $55-$65/session. Individual classes from $35-$85. Children's classes $35-$45.

CONTACT: Manager, Kings cooking studio, 700 Lanidex Plaza, Parsippany, NJ 07054; 973-463-6500, Fax 973-575-6518, cookingstudio@kingssm.com, www.kingscookingstudio.com.

L.B. BRATTSTEN WINE PROGRAMS

New Brunswick

Sponsor: Wine professional. Programs: 14-session lecture courses & wine tastings. Established: 1992. Class/group size: 60. 2 programs/yr.

FACULTY: L.B. Brattsten is an AWS Certified Judge, CWE.

CONTACT: L.B. Brattsten, Professor, L.B. Brattsten Wine Programs - Rutgers University, Dept. of Entomology, New Brunswick, NJ 08901-8536; 732-932-9774, Fax 732-932-7229, brattsten@aesop.rutgers.edu.

ON THE MARK COOKING CLASSES

Bernardsville, Martinsville, Short Hills,Westfield

Sponsor: Professional chef. Programs: In-home & on-site cooking classes. Established: 2000. Class/group size: 1-20. 24 programs/yr. Facilities: Client's home kitchen, or Kings Cooking Studios classrooms. Also featured: Corporate team building classes, personal chef services, catering.

EMPHASIS: Natural & organic cooking, special diets, vegan & vegetarian, tofu & meat alternatives, healthy cooking with wine.

FACULTY: Chef Mark Darragh, graduate of the US Personal Chef Institute, Global Wine Edcuation Program, teaches at Kings Cooking Studios & Whole Foods Markets.

COSTS: $100/hr with 2-hr hour min. Individual instruction $300 + ingredients based on 4-hr class.

CONTACT: Mark Darragh, Chef, On The Mark Cooking Classes, 727 South Avenue West, Westfield, NJ 07090; 908-789-3239, markdchef@starchefs.com, www.onthemarkpcs.com.

STAGE LEFT WINE COURSE WITH FRANCIS SCHOTT

New Brunswick

Sponsor: Stage Left restaurant. Programs: 8-session courses. Established: 1990. Class/group size: 50. 2 programs/yr.

EMPHASIS: Estate bottled wines from small producers.

FACULTY: Francis Schott, a member of SWE & American Sommelier Society, is the Owner/Wine Director of a NJ restaurant & wine catalog.

CONTACT: Francis Schott, Owner/Instructor, Stage Left Restaurant, 5 Livingston Ave., New Brunswick, NJ 08901; 722-828-4444, Fax 722-828-6228, Francis@Stageleft.com, www.stageleft.com.

NEW MEXICO

CHEFS AT WORK

Santa Fe

Sponsor: Culinary professional Vikki Nulman. Programs: 1-day hands-on classic French cooking programs, 1-wk trips. Established: 1997. Class/group size: 6-20. 20 programs/yr. Facilities: 600-sq-ft new professional kitchen with 5 ovens, Sub Zero applicances, individual work areas, mountain views. Also featured: Private instruction, market visits, culinary trips.

EMPHASIS: Classic French & Italian cooking.

FACULTY: Chef Vikki Nulman is a graduate of the French Culinary Institute & Le Cordon Bleu

Paris, a professional caterer, & studied in Venice with Marcella Hazan.

Costs: Santa Fe, $70/day. Mexico trips from $2,000, France & Italy trips from $3,200.

Contact: Vikki Nulman, Chef, Chefs at Work/MBT Traveler.Com, 4 High Ridge Rd., Santa Fe, NM 87501; 505-820-0377, Fax 505-820-0389, chefvikki@aol.com, www.MBTravelers.com.

COOKING AT VILLA FONTANA/RIO GRANDE COOKING SCHOOL

Taos

Sponsor: Restaurant Villa Fontana. Programs: 3- & 5-day classes in classical Northern Italian cuisine. Established: 2002. Class/group size: 10 max. ~20 programs/yr. Facilities: Cooking island in a marquis, overlooking the garden, with views of the Taos Mountain. Also featured: Welcome reception, farewell dinner, wine tasting.

Emphasis: Classical Italian cooking, emphasis on wild mushrooms during the season (August).

Faculty: Chef Carlo Gislimberti born in Italy, studied in Europe, & a restaurant owner since 1982. Villa Fontana is rated by Luigi Veronelli as one of the top 10 Italian restaurants in the US.

Costs: $250-$900.

Contact: Siobhan or Carlo Gislimberti, Owners, Cooking at Villa Fontana, PO Box 2872, Taos, NM 87571; 505-758-5800, Fax 505-758-0301, villafon@newmex.com, www.villafontanataos.com.

LAS COSAS KITCHEN SHOPPE AND COOKING SCHOOL

Santa Fe

Sponsor: Cookware store & gourmet food shop. Programs: Cooking classes on a variety of topics for professional & non-professional cooks. Established: 1998. Class/group size: 20 demo, 12 hands-on. 300 programs/yr. Facilities: Up-to-date home kitchen setting with the latest equipment. Also featured: Farmer's Market trips, guest chefs, private classes.

Emphasis: New Mexico & ethnic cooking, regional Italian, baking, grilling, smoking, chocolate, wine & food pairing.

Faculty: Director John Vollertsen has taught cooking in New York & Sydney, Australia, & worked with Jane Butel at her Southwestern Cooking School in Albuquerque.

Costs: $45-$75; private classes from $60/student.

Contact: John Vollertsen, Director of Cooking School, Las Cosas Kitchen Shoppe & Cooking School, 181 Paseo de Peralta, DeVargas Center, Santa Fe, NM 87501; 505-988-3394, Fax 505-983-5587, lascosas@lascosascooking.com, www.lascosascooking.com.

MUY SABROSA AT THE INN ON THE ALAMEDA

Santa Fe

Sponsor: The Inn on the Alameda, a small hotel in Old Santa Fe. Programs: 2-night package that features 1 demo cooking class. Established: 1996. Class/group size: 44. 40 programs/yr. Facilities: Demo kitchen of The Santa Fe School of Cooking.

Emphasis: Cuisine & cultural background of Santa Fe & the American Southwest.

Faculty: Cooking instructors of The Santa Fe School of Cooking.

Costs: $340-$540 includes continental breakfast, shared lodging.

Contact: Judith Moir, Marketing Director, Muy Sabrosa at Inn on the Alameda, 303 East Alameda, Santa Fe, NM 87501; 800-289-2122, Fax 505-986-8325, info@inn-alameda.com, www.innonthealameda.com.

SANTA FE SCHOOL OF COOKING

Santa Fe

Sponsor: School, food market, mail order catalog. Programs: Demonstration classes and smaller hands-on classes that include shopping at the Farmer's Market. Established: 1989. Class/group size: 15 hands-on/44 demo. Facilities: Santa Fe-style kitchen with overhead mirrors. Also featured: Private classes, shopping trips to the Farmer's Market in August & September, culinary tours of northern New Mexico.

Emphasis: New Mexican and contemporary Southwestern cuisines, vegetarian, Mexican light cooking, and cuisines of Mexico classes.

Faculty: Cookbook authors & chefs from Santa Fe's top restaurants, guest celebrities including Cheryl Alters Jamison & Deborah Madison.

Costs: Classes from $45-$90; tours are ~$800-$1,600 & include some meals, field trips, lodging.

Contact: Susan Curtis & Nicole Ammerman, Owner & Manager, Santa Fe School of Cooking, 116 W. San Francisco St., Santa Fe, NM 87501; 505-983-4511, Fax 505-983-7540, cookin@nets.com, www.santafeschoolofcooking.com.

NEW YORK

A LA CARTE CULINARY SERVICES, LTD.

Lynbrook, Long Island

Sponsor: Private culinary center. Programs: Various topics for beginners to experienced cooks, including knife skills, techniques series classes, & individual novelty classes. Established: 1999. Class/group size: 16 hands-on, 35 demo. Facilities: Full-service culinary center in a storefront facility. 4 cooking stations designed to duplicate the home cooking environment. Also featured: Private cooking parties, corporate team building & food consulting, recipe development & testing, food styling.

Emphasis: Simplicity of proper techniques, cooking & eating good food.

Faculty: Polly Talbott, CCP, owner & primary instructor; Natalie Jashyn, instructor; staff & guest chefs, culinary personalities.

Costs: $50-85; $350 for a series of 5.

Contact: Polly Talbott, CCP, Owner, A la Carte Culinary Services, Ltd., 32 Atlantic Ave., Lynbrook, NY 11563; 516-599-2922, Fax 516-599-8372, alacartecs@aol.com, http://members.aol.com/alacartecs.

THE ACADEMY OF CAKE ART

New York

Sponsor: Cake & sugar artist Scott Clark Woolley. Programs: Demos & hands-on classes in cake decorating & gum paste sugar flowers. Established: 1991. Class/group size: 7 max. 20+ programs/yr. Facilities: Woolley's studio. Also featured: Private one-on-one classes.

Emphasis: Cake designing & decorating.

Faculty: Scott Woolley is author of Cakes by Design. His cakes have appeared in Bride's mag & Martha Stewart's Weddings. Clients include President G. W. Bush, Christie Brinkley, Maria Shriver.

Costs: $120-$220 for group classes, $90/hr for private classes.

Contact: Scott Woolley, Owner, The Academy of Cake Art, 171 W. 73rd St., #9, New York, NY 10023; 212-362-5374, scw@cakesbydesign.cc, www.cakesbydesign.cc/academy_of_cake_art.html.

ALICE ROSS HEARTH STUDIOS

Smithtown

Sponsor: Culinary historian Dr. Alice Ross. Programs: Hands-on classes in culinary history & traditional methods, Native American & Civil War cookery, game butchery & prep, baking using hearth & brick ovens. Established: 1988. Class/group size: 3-15. 35 programs/yr. Facilities: Converted carriage house with open hearth & wood stove, outdoor wood-fired oven, water pump, smoke house. Also featured: Custom classes.

Emphasis: Early American cookery.

Faculty: Dr. Alice Ross is co-founder of Culinary Historians of NY, teaches at CCNY, served as consultant to Colonial Williamsburg & Lowell Natl Historic Park.

Costs: $125/day.

Contact: Dr. Alice Ross, Alice Ross Hearth Studios, 15 Prospect St., Smithtown, NY 11787; 631-265-9335, aross@binome.com, http://aliceross.com.

ALTAMONT WINE SCHOOL

Altamont

Sponsor: Wine professional. Programs: 10-12 wine sessions/yr; guided NY wine/vineyard tours by appointment, dinner tastings, winemaking class. Established: 1987. Class/group size: 20.

Faculty: Greg Giorgio is a wine educator, writer, consultant.
Costs: $20/session.
Contact: Greg Giorgio, Altamont Wine School, PO Box 74, Altamont, NY 12009; 518-861-5627.

ANNA TERESA CALLEN ITALIAN COOKING SCHOOL
New York

Sponsor: Culinary professional Anna Teresa Callen. Programs: 5-session participation and demonstration courses. Established: 1978. Class/group size: 6. 10 programs/yr. Facilities: Efficient home kitchen. Also featured: Culinary tours to Italy.
Emphasis: Italian regional cooking.
Faculty: IACP-member Anna Teresa Callen is author of Quiches and Savory Pies, Anna Teresa Callen's Menus for Pasta & Food and Memories of Abruzzo.
Costs: $675/course.
Contact: Anna Teresa Callen, Anna Teresa Callen Italian Cooking School, 59 W. 12th St., New York, NY 10011; 212-929-5640.

THE ART OF FOOD
New York

Sponsor: Culinary professional. Programs: Hands-on cooking classes, private cooking parties, culinary tours. Class/group size: 1-8. Facilities: Client's facilities. Also featured: Custom gourmet trips for groups to Provence, Southwest France and Guadeloup.
Emphasis: Health supportive cooking, international & ethnic cuisine.
Faculty: Jeri Jackson, CCP, studied at the NY Restaurant School, Natural Gourmet, La Varenne.
Costs: Private cooking class $150 + food costs & $40 for shopping. 6- to 8-person group class/party $600 + food & shopping costs.
Contact: Jeri Jackson, Certified Culinary Professional, The Art of Food, P.O.Box 250413, New York, NY 10025; 212-864-0778, Fax 212-665-5241, jericoach@aol.com.

CAKES UNIQUELY YOURS SCHOOL OF CONFECTIONERY ARTS
New York

Sponsor: Cake artist/instructor Ajike Williams. Programs: 1- to 9-session certificate courses in Wilton Method, marzipan, gumpaste, fondant, designer cookies, sugar craft, baking. Wedding cake & business development workshops. Established: 1996. Class/group size: 1-2. 18 courses programs/yr. Facilities: Modern home kitchen. Also featured: Wedding cake consultation, private lessons, customized intensives, off-site instruction for groups.
Emphasis: Wilton Method courses, wedding cakes, gumpaste flowers, techniques.
Faculty: Ajike Williams received Gold & Silvermedals from Soc. Culinaire Philanthropique, attended Peter Kump's NY Cooking School, is a Wilton Method instructor & teaches classes for the NYC Bd. of Ed.
Costs: $50-85/single session, $130-$300/4-session class.
Contact: Ajike Williams, Cakes Uniquely Yours School of Confectionery Arts, 1258 Fteley Ave., Bronx, NY 10472; 718-617-4538, 718-861-7850, Fax 718-861-7850, AjikeW@aol.com.

CAROL'S CUISINE, INC.
Staten Island

Sponsor: Culinary professional. Programs: 1- to 6-session demo & participation courses. Established: 1972. Class/group size: 18. 90 programs/yr. Facilities: Fully-equipped professional teaching kitchen with overhead mirror. Also featured: Private lessons, wine classes.
Emphasis: Techniques & theory, baking, cake decorating, intl & Italian cuisine, parent & child, teenage classes.
Faculty: Owner/Director Carol Frazzetta, IACP, advanced certificate from Le Cordon Bleu, studied at CIA, Wilton School of Cake Decorating, Marcella Hazan's School, L'Academie de Cuisine. Leonard Pickell, wine consultant.
Costs: $65-$125/session.

CONTACT: Carol Frazzetta, Owner, Chef, Cooking Teacher, Carol's Cuisine, Inc., 1571 Richmond Rd., Staten Island, NY 10304; 718-979-5600, Fax 718-987-4509, carolscuisine@aol.com, www.CarolsCafe.com.

CHINA INSTITUTE'S CHINESE COOKING SCHOOL

New York

Sponsor: Non-profit educational & cultural institution. Programs: 3-session course that focuses on a total of 12 traditional Chinese regional dishes. Class/group size: 15 max. Also featured: Chinese language & calligraphy classes, classroom teaching & seminars, art exhibitions, teacher education & curriculum development, lectures & symposia.

EMPHASIS: Chinese regional cuisine.

FACULTY: Cooking teacher & food consultant Eileen Yin-Fei Lo is author of The Chinese Kitchen, The Dim Sum Book & The Chinese Banquet Cookbook.

COSTS: $325 members, $350 non-members, $80 materials. Membership starts at $55/yr.

CONTACT: France Pepper, Associate Director, Public Programs, China Institute's Chinese Cooking School, 125 E. 65th St, New York, NY 10021; 212-744-8181, x143, Fax 212-628-4159, fpepper@chinainstitute.org, www.chinainstitute.org.

CITY ADVENTURES

New York

Sponsor: Specialty travel company. Programs: Culinary vacation programs including cooking classes. Established: 1995. Class/group size: 12. Facilities: Local culinary schools. Also featured: Art, garden travel.

FACULTY: Professional chefs.

CONTACT: Norma Greenwood, City Adventures, 32 Union Sq. E., #507, New York, NY 10003; 718-457-0672, greenwood@cityadventures.com, www.cityadventures.com.

COOKING BY THE BOOK, INC.

New York

Sponsor: Suzen & Brian O'Rourke. Programs: Full participation classes that focus on a selected cookbook or chef menu. Established: 1989. Class/group size: 10-40 max. 20 programs/yr. Facilities: Fully-equipped 600-sq-ft kitchen with 5 work stations. Separate dinning room area. Also featured: Private parties with hands-on cooking instruction, corporate events, including culinary team building classes & wine tasting events.

EMPHASIS: Hands-on approach to cooking.

FACULTY: Suzen & Brian O'Rourke; authors regularly present, 20 part-time employees.

COSTS: $100-$130/class.

CONTACT: Suzen O'Rourke, President, Cooking by the Book, Inc., 11 Worth St., New York, NY 10013; 212-966-9799, Fax 212-925-1074, Info@cookingbythebook.com, www.cookingbythebook.com.

COOKING BY HEART

New York, New Jersey, Connecticut

Sponsor: Culinary professional. Programs: Private in-home cooking classes. Established: 2003. Class/group size: 1 or more. Facilities: Client's kitchen or private culinary studio.

EMPHASIS: Cooking basics, tuning the palate, flavor literacy.

FACULTY: Dina Cheney, a graduate of the Institute of Culinary Education & Columbia Univ, is a member of the IACP & teaches at the Edgewater, NJ Whole Foods Market, JCC Manhattan.

COSTS: $195/class for 1-2 adults, parties $60/person & up.

CONTACT: Dina Cheney, Cooking Teacher, Cooking By Heart, Greenwich, CT ; 203-629-1831, dina@cookingbyheart.com, www.cookingbyheart.com.

COOKING WITH CLASS, INC.

New York

Sponsor: Culinary professional. Programs: Hands-on, semi-private cooking classes; topics include menus for dinner parties, gatherings & buffets. Established: 1975. Class/group size: 4. Facilities:

Corporate kitchen with commercial equipment. Also featured: Culinary travel programs, catering, team building, private in home instruction.

Emphasis: Seasonal foods, basics & techniques, menu planning.

Faculty: Janeen Sarlin, author of 7 cookbooks & writer of weekly cooking column.

Costs: $110/class, $305/3 classes, $630/6 classes.

Contact: Janeen Sarlin, Cooking With Class, Inc., 110 East End Ave., New York, NY 10028; 212-517-8514, Fax 212-737-5227, sarlin@sarlincookingwithclass.com, www.sarlincookingwithclass.com.

THE CULINARY INSTITUTE OF AMERICA

Hyde Park *(See also pages 27, 107, 209) (See display ad page 108)*

Sponsor: Center for continuing ed of food & wine professionals, the CIA's continuing ed department at Hyde Park, NY. Programs: Adult education demo & hands-on courses, wine instruction, classes for youngsters. Established: 1946. Class/group size: 15. ~40 programs/yr. Facilities: Includes 38 teaching kitchens, library, student recreation center & 5 public student-staffed restaurants.

Faculty: The CIA's chefs & instructors.

Costs: From $850/30 hrs of instruction; on-campus programs from $155/demo courses-$2,000/Boot Camp programs.

Contact: Susan Cussen, Director of Marketing, CE, The Culinary Institute of America, 1946 Campus Dr., Hyde Park, NY 12538-1499; 800-888-7850, Fax 845-451-1066, marketing@culinary.edu, www.ciachef.edu.

DE GUSTIBUS AT MACY'S

New York

Sponsor: Independent school in Macy's department store operated by Arlene Feltman Sailhac. Programs: Demos & on-location classes, hands-on, knife skills. Established: 1980. Class/group size: 70 demo. 120 programs/yr. Facilities: Professionally-equipped teaching kitchen. Also featured: Wine seminars, private events.

Emphasis: Regional American, French & Italian cuisines, wine selection, menus for entertaining, guest chef specialties.

Faculty: Guest chefs & cookbook authors include David Bouley, Mario Batali, Michael Romano,Tom Colicchio, Alain Sailhac.

Costs: From $85/session to $480 for a series of 6.

Contact: Arlene Feltman Sailhac, Owner/Director, De Gustibus at Macy's, 343 E. 74th Street, Apt. 14A, New York, NY 10021; 212-439-1714, Fax 212-439-1716, grtcooks@aol.com, www.degustibusinc.com.

EVENTS@DISH

New York

Sponsor: Restaurant with separate instructional kitchen. Programs: Hands-on cooking classes on a variety of topics. Established: 2002. Class/group size: 10-40. Facilities: Full professional kitchen with tree-lined deck & 2 skylights. Also featured: Catering, special events, party & corporate building cooking classes.

Faculty: 20 professional chefs & instructors.

Costs: $85-$125/class.

Contact: Nancy Evans, Event Coordinator, Events@Dish, 165 Allen St., New York, NY 10002; 212-253-8845, Fax 212-253-8872, events@dish165.com, www.dish165.com.

THE FRENCH CULINARY INSTITUTE

New York *(See also page 109) (See display ad page 110)*

Sponsor: Proprietary institution for aspiring professionals and serious amateur cooks. Programs: La Technique, a 22-session overview of classic French techniques; La Technique II, a 12-session course on menu development, seasonality, plate composition. Essentials of Pastry, a 20-session introduction to pastry & confectionary. Established: 1984. Class/group size: 22. 12 programs/yr. Facilities: 30,000-sq-ft facility with newly-equipped pastry and bread kitchens, demonstration amphitheater, L'Ecole open-to-the-public restaurant. Also featured: Cooking with Marcella, essentials of Italian cooking; Artisanal Bread Baking, 1-wk intro to European bread baking; La Technique for serious amateurs; Essentials of Pastry, intro to pastry arts; Culinary Business courses in catering, restaurant mgmt & wine.

EMPHASIS: Classic techniques, menu development, presentation, culinary business with a hands-on program.

FACULTY: 41 teachers & culinary staff, including Dean of Studies Alain Sailhac, Dean of Special Programs Jacques Pépin, Master Chef André Soltner, Dean of Pastry Arts Jacques Torres, Dean of Wine Studies Andrea Immer, Visiting Dean Alice Waters, Marcella Hazen.

COSTS: Tuition (includes knife set, tools, application, uniform): $4,900 for La Technique I, $4250 for Essentials of Pastry, $1,550 for Cooking with Marcella, $895 for Fundamentals of Wine and Great Wine & Food Made Simple.

CONTACT: David Waggoner, Dean of Enrollment, The French Culinary Institute, 462 Broadway, New York, NY 10013-2618; 888-FCI-CHEF/212-219-8890, Fax 212-431-3054, admission@frenchculinary.com, www.frenchculinary.com/seriousamateur.

GRANDMA'S SECRETS

New York

Sponsor: Custom-made desserts company. Programs: Monthly classes in basic & advanced pie making; private sessions. Established: 1995. Class/group size: 6. 9 programs/yr. Facilities: Home setting. Also featured: Specializes in occasion cakes such as wedding, birthday, baby & bridal shower; pies, dietetic desserts.

FACULTY: Classes are conducted by the founder, Regina McRae.

COSTS: $50/2-hr class, $40 for repeat students.

CONTACT: Regina McRae, Grandma's Secrets, 640 West 138th Street, New York, NY 10031; 212-862-8117, classes@grandmasecrets.com, www.grandmasecrets.com.

HARRIET LEMBECK, CWE

New York

Sponsor: Wine professional. Programs: Two 10-session courses/yr, 4-session spirits course in fall, 30+ 1- to 4-session courses/yr through New School University. Established: 1975. Class/group size: 30.

FACULTY: Harriet Lembeck is author of Grossman's Guide to Wines, Beers, & Spirits, 6th & 7th Eds; Director of New School University wine program; Charter Director SWE; Certified Wine Educator, SWE.

COSTS: $800/10-session course, $1,000 with spirits ($300 spirits along), $81-$290/course through New School University.

CONTACT: Harriet Lembeck, CWE, Wine & Spirits Program, Inc., 54 Continental Ave., Forest Hills, NY 11375; 718-263-3134, Fax 718-263-3750, hlembeck@mindspring.com.

HARVARD LYMAN WINE PROGRAM AT SUNY-STONY BROOK

Stony Brook

Sponsor: University. Programs: 14-session course. Established: 1972. Class/group size: 25-30. 1 programs/yr.

EMPHASIS: All regions, wine making & appreciation.

FACULTY: Harvard Lyman is a member of AWS & SWE.

COSTS: $270/three credits plus $40-$45 lab fee; $90/one credit option.

CONTACT: Harvard Lyman, Harvard Lyman Wine Program at SUNY-Stony Brook, Biochemistry Dept., Stony Brook, NY 11794-5215; 516-632-8534, Fax 516-632-9780, hlyman@notes.cc.sunysb.edu.

HOME COOKING NYC

Manhattan, Brooklyn, Queens

Sponsor: Culinary professional. Programs: Personalized in-home culinary instruction for individuals or groups. Established: 2001. Class/group size: 1-15.

EMPHASIS: Basic cooking techniques & ethnic-based cuisines.

Faculty: Jennifer Herman Clair, teaches at The New School, JCC of Manhattan & City Harvest. She graduated from the Institute of Culinary Education & was a food editor at Martha Stewart Living.
Costs: $175/2 people, $250/3 or more. Cost of ingredients ~$20/person.
Contact: Jennifer Herman Clair, Chef Instructor, Home Cooking NY, 13 Park Place, Brooklyn, NY 11217; 718-783-0048, jennifer@homecookingny.com, www.homecookingny.com.

THE INSTITUTE OF CULINARY EDUCATION

New York *(See also page 111) (See display ad above & page 111, 112, 113)*

Sponsor: Private school, formerly Peter Kump's New York Cooking School. Programs: Hands-on courses & workshops include the 5-session, 25-hour Techniques of Fine Cooking series, offered over 70 times a year, frequently on a Monday-Friday schedule. Established: 1975. Class/group size: 12 hands-on, 30+ dem. 1,000+ programs/yr. Facilities: 27,000-sq-ft facility opened in 1999 includes 9 kitchens, wine studies center, confectionery lab. Also featured: Other Techniques series: spa cuisine, Italian cooking, pastry & baking, cake decorating. Other courses: Japanese, Thai, Latino, Moroccan, Spanish cuisines, chocolate, vegetarian, fish & shellfish, grilling, knife skills, walking tours.
Emphasis: Hands-on cooking instruction.
Faculty: 15 staff chef-instructors & 30+ visiting guest chefs.
Costs: Hands-on classes from $85-$520.
Contact: The Institute of Culinary Education, 50 W. 23rd St., New York, NY 10010; 800-522-4610, 212-847-0770, Fax 212-847-0722, marie@iceculinary.com, www.iceculinary.com.

ITALIAN CULINARY INSTITUTE, INC.

New York

Sponsor: Italian Cooking & Living magazine. Programs: Cooking demos, dinners, wine tastings & classes. Established: 1999. Class/group size: 24. 50+ programs/yr. Facilities: Open kitchen with modern equipment & a café setting. Also featured: Olive oil tastings, seminars.
Emphasis: Italian cooking, Italian foods & wines.
Faculty: Guest chefs, the magazine's editorial & test kitchen staff.
Costs: $65 for basic courses, $75 for guest chef classes. Discounts for a package of classes. All include dinner.
Contact: Salvatore Rizzo, Center Manager, Italian Culinary Institute, Inc., 230 Fifth Avenue, Suite 1100, New York, NY 10001; 212-725-8764 x25, 212-889-9057, Fax 212-889-5057, rizzo@italiancookingandliving.com, www.italiancookingandliving.com.

KAREN LEE IMAGINATIVE COOKING CLASSES & CATERING

New York City & Amagansett

Sponsor: Culinary professional Karen Lee. Programs: 4-session participation courses, single session classes, 5-day vacation courses. Established: 1972. Class/group size: 10 hands-on.
Emphasis: Fusion & traditional Chinese cuisine, Italian cuisine, basic technique, simple & healthy dishes for entertaining.
Faculty: Owner/caterer Karen Lee apprenticed with Madame Grace Zia Chu and is author of

The Occasional Vegetarian; Nouvelle Chinese Cooking; Soup, Salad, and Pasta Innovations; and Chinese Cooking for the American Kitchen.

Costs: $520/4-session course, $140/class.

Contact: Karen Lee Imaginative Cooking Classes & Catering, 142 West End Ave., #30V, New York, NY 10023; 212-787-2227, Fax 212-496-8178, foodnow@rcn.com, www.karenleecooking.com. In July & Aug: PO Box 1998, Amagansett, NY 11930; 631-267-3653, Fax 631-267-3114.

LA CUISINE SANS PEUR

New York

Sponsor: Chef-de-Cuisine Henri-Etienne Lévy. Programs: 5- & 6-session demo courses include the 2-part 6-session basic course, 3-part 5-session intermediate, advanced, & baking courses. Specialty classes include desserts, fish, game, vegetables & seasonal. Established: 1978. Class/group size: 4. 25+ programs/yr. Facilities: Traditional French well-equipped home kitchen. Also featured: 1-wk culinary vacations in Provence & Alsace in Sept.

Emphasis: French regional cooking especially Alsace & Provence, cooking without recipes, basic to advanced courses.

Faculty: Chef & proprietor Henri-Etienne Lévy trained & worked in restaurant kitchens in France & Germany for 15 yrs.

Costs: $500/course.

Contact: Henri-Etienne Lévy, Chef/Proprietor, La Cuisine Sans Peur, 216 W. 89 St., New York, NY 10024; 212-362-0638.

LES AMOUREUX DU VIN WINE & GASTRONOMICAL TOURS

White Plains

Sponsor: Wine professional. Programs: 8-session courses, wine tours. Established: 1982. Class/group size: 24. 2 courses programs/yr.

Faculty: Tao Porchon-Lynch is editor of The Beverage Communicator, regional VP & founder of AWS, certified wine judge, member SWE. Her family owned a vineyard in France.

Costs: $280/course. $60-$75/5-course dinner & wine.

Contact: Tao Porchon-Lynch, Les Amoureux du Vin Wine & Gastronomical Tours, 5 Barker Ave., #501, White Plains, NY 10601; 914-761-7700 #2501, Fax 914-997-2617.

LOOK WHO'S COOKING, INC.

Oyster Bay

Sponsor: Culinary professional Barbara Sheridan. Programs: 1- to 4-session demo & participation courses. Established: 1994. Class/group size: 20 demo/12 hands-on. 200+ programs/yr. Facilities: 800-sq-ft well-equipped Viking kitchen with 12 workspaces. Also featured: Catering, instruction for private & nonprofit organizations, afternoon teas.

Emphasis: Gourmet, low fat, seafood & Caribbean cooking; baking, entertaining menus.

Faculty: Barbara Sheridan, graduate of N.Y. Institute of Technology Culinary Arts, attended Peter Kump's NY School & Le Cordon Bleu.

Costs: $75/session; 6-wk technique classes $450.

Contact: Barbara M. Sheridan, Executive Chef/Owner, Look Who's Cooking, 7 W. Main St., Oyster Bay, NY 11771; 516-922-2400, Fax 516-379-6067, lookwhsckn@aol.com, www.lookwhoscooking.com.

MARY BETH CLARK

New York,

Sponsor: Chef and cookbook author Mary Beth Clark. Programs: 3-hour custom-designed, full-participation private lessons in Italian cuisine. Student brings home 3-4 dishes from the class. Established: 1977. Class/group size: 1-2.

Emphasis: Italian cuisine.

Faculty: Cookbook author Mary Beth Clark operates the International Cooking School Of Italian Food And Wine.

Costs: $500/session plus ingredients, payable in advance, refundable a week prior.

CONTACT: Mary Beth Clark, 201 E. 28th St., #15B, New York, NY 10016-8538; 212-779-1921, Fax 212-779-3248, marybethclark@worldnet.att.net, www.marybethclark.com.

MIETTE CULINARY STUDIO
New York

Sponsor: Miette Culinary Studio. Programs: Hands-on classes meet Mondays & Thursdays. Established: 1995. Class/group size: 14 max. Also featured: Cooking parties, corporate team-building, cook-ins, wine tastings.

EMPHASIS: Fusion cooking and world cuisines, healthful recipes.

FACULTY: Chef Paul Vandewoude & his assistant Mariette Bermowitz.

COSTS: $65/session.

CONTACT: Mariette Bermowitz, Miette Culinary Studio, 109 MacDougal Street, Suite #2, New York, NY 10012; 212-460-9322, Fax 212-460-9579, msmiette@aol.com.

THE MIXING BOWL
New York

Sponsor: Private school. Programs: Weekly classes for children ages 2-1/2 & older that cover kitchen safety, hygiene, healthy snacks, breakfast treats, dinners & desserts. Also includes storytime or creative food projects, personalized cookbooks. Also featured: Theme kitchen parties.

FACULTY: Meredith Berman is a former nursery school teacher.

COSTS: $40/class, $140-$672/course.

CONTACT: Meredith Berman, Owner, The Mixing Bowl, 243 E. 82nd St., New York, NY 10028; 212-585-2433, Fax 212-585-2401, info@kidsinthekitchenNYC.com, www.kidsinthekitchennyc.com.

THE NATURAL GOURMET INSTITUTE FOR FOOD AND HEALTH
New York *(See also page 117) (See display ad page 117)*

Sponsor: Private trade school devoted to healthy cooking. Programs: Demo & participation programs: evening & weekend classes & series. Intensives include Basic Techniques, Pastry Arts, Food & Healing. Established: 1977. Class/group size: 8-25. 120+ programs/yr. Facilities: Include 2 kitchens, classroom, bookstore. Also featured: Classes for adults & youngsters; beginning, advanced cooking & theory.

EMPHASIS: Vegetarian, low/no fat, recipe adaptation, medicinal cooking, tofu, tempeh, seitan, fish, organic poultry, food & healing, intl cuisines, whole grain flours, natural sweeteners.

FACULTY: 10 faculty, incl founder Annemarie Colbin, MA, Certified Health Education Specialist, author of Food & Healing, The Book of Whole Meals, The Natural Gourmet; Co-Presidents/Directors Diane Carlson & Jenny Matthau, graduates of the school.

COSTS: Summer intensives $697/wk, classes & series $40-$75/session. Lodging at local hotels, B&Bs.

CONTACT: Susan Kaufman, Registration Manager, The Natural Gourmet Institute for Food and Health, 48 W. 21st St., 2nd Floor, New York, NY 10010; 212-645-5170 #106, Fax 212-989-1493, info@naturalgourmetschool.com, www.naturalgourmetschool.com.

NEW SCHOOL CULINARY ARTS
New York

Sponsor: New School University. Programs: 1- to 8-session demo & participation courses, weekend workshops. Established: 1919. Class/group size: 12-14. 300+ programs/yr. Facilities: B&B new instructional kitchen equipped with professional & high-end home equipment. Also featured: On-site restaurant chef demos, lectures on culture & cuisine, classes for youngsters, wine courses.

EMPHASIS: Culinary techniques, ethnic & regional cuisines, holiday menus, home entertaining, baking, light-style cooking.

FACULTY: 50+ faculty headed by Gary Goldberg, co-founder Martin Johner, incl Bruce Beck, Miriam Brickman, James Chew, Richard Glavin, Arlyn Hackett, Micheal Krondl, Harriet Lembeck, Lisa Montenegro, Robert Posch, Dan Rosati.

COSTS: $65-$85 (+ materials fee)/session, $40 for youngsters, $15 for lectures, $325 for weekend workshops, $45-$65 for wine classes.

Contact: Gary Goldberg, Exec Dir, New School Culinary Arts, 131 W. 23rd St., NY, NY 10011; 212-255-4141, 800-544-1978, Fax 212-229-5648, NSCulArts@aol.com, www.nsu.newschool.edu/culinary.

NEW YORK UNIVERSITY

New York *(See also page 119) (See display ad page 119)*

Sponsor: Dept. of Nutrition & Food Studies, NYU's School of Education. Programs: Lecture & demo courses for food professionals, career changers, & nutritionists. Established: 1986. Class/group size: 10-35. 60 programs/yr. Facilities: New teaching kitchen & library, computer, academic resources.

Emphasis: Food business & mgmt, food history & culture, nutrition, food writing, food marketing.

Faculty: Foodservice & industry professionals, historians, authors.

Costs: ~$50-$200/session.

Contact: Carol Guber, Director of Food Programs, NYU, 35 W. 4th St., 10th Fl., New York, NY 10012; 212-998-5588, Fax 212-995-4194, nutrition@nyu.edu, www.education.nyu.edu/nutrition.

NYC WINE CLASS

New York

Sponsor: Wine professional. Programs: Single & multiple session classes. Established: 2002. Class/group size: 16-28. Also featured: Wine dinners, cheese tastings, private dinners, corporate functions.

Faculty: Andrew Harwood was a winemaker in Hungary, France & California, masters degree from Cornell University, Asst Beverage Director for Cornell wine program.

Costs: $45-$325.

Contact: Andrew Harwood, NYC Wine Class, 67 E. 2nd St., Apt. #23, New York, NY 10003; 917-838-8591, andrew@nycwineclass.com, www.nycwineclass.com.

RONALD A. KAPON WINE PROGRAMS

New York

Sponsor: Wine professional. Programs: 1-night dinners & 6-session courses. Established: 1969. Class/group size: 20-100. 40 programs/yr. Also featured: Private wine dinners, tastings, corporate events.

Faculty: Ronald Kapon, Ph.D., grad. German Wine Acad; VP/co-dir. Tasters Guild Intl, NY; prof. FDU Hotel, Rest. & Tourism School; radio host Wonderful World of Wine & Spirits.

Costs: $100/course, $20-$130/dinners & tastings.

Contact: Ronald A. Kapon, Ronald A. Kapon Wine Programs, 230 W. 79th St., #42N, New York, NY 10024-6210; 212-799-6311, Fax 212-799-0245, vinoron@yahoo.com, www.tastersguildny.com.

RUSTICO COOKING

New York

Sponsor: Culinary professional Micol Negrin. Programs: Hands-on classes in Italian cooking. Established: 2002. Class/group size: 6-16. 90+ programs/yr. Facilities: Grace's Marketplace kitchen. Also featured: Private cooking parties, team-building events, wine tastings, theme evenings.

Emphasis: Italian cuisine, from antipasti to desserts..

Faculty: Micol Negrin, author of Rustico: Regional Italian Country Cooking, former editor of The Magazine of La Cucina Italiana.

Costs: $85-$95/class.

Contact: Rustico Cooking, 917-602-1519, micol@rusticocooking.com, www.rusticocooking.com.

SAVORY SOJOURNS, LTD.

New York

Sponsor: Culinary tour provider Addie Tomei. Programs: 1-day tours of NYC neighborhoods; customized multi-day tours combining cooking classes, fine restaurant dining, market & store visits, tastings, chef demos, food events. Established: 1997. Class/group size: 2-30+. Facilities: Institute of Culinary Education & other facilities in NYC, including private homes.

Costs: Day tours from $70-$250.

Contact: Addie Tomei, President, Savory Sojourns, Ltd., 155 W. 13th St., New York, NY 10011; 212-691-7314, 888-9-SAVORY, Fax 212-367-0984, Addie@savorysojourns.com, www.savorysojourns.com.

THE WINE SCHOOL AT WINDOWS ON THE WORLD

New York

Sponsor: Wine professional. Programs: 8-session course covering the regions of US, France, Italy, Spain, Germany. Established: 1976. Class/group size: 125. 4 programs/yr.

Faculty: Kevin Charles Zraly was Wine Director of Windows on the World until 2001; author of Windows on the World Complete Wine Course, 1993 James Beard Wine & Spirits Professional of the Year, 2002 European Wine Council Lifetime Achievement award.

Costs: $895/course.

Location: Marriott Marquis Hotel.

Contact: Kevin Charles Zraly, The Wine School at Windows on the World, 16 Woodstock Ln., New Paltz, NY 12561; 845-255-1456, Fax 845-255-2041, kevinz@netstep.net, www.wowws.com.

TO GRANDMOTHER'S HOUSE WE GO COOKING TOURS

New York

Sponsor: Culinary professional, travel company. Programs: Cooking/cultural tours that include informal classes combined with visits to folk artists in their homes, tours of cultural sites. Established: 1995. Class/group size: 10-12. 4 programs/yr. Also featured: Classes in New York City area featuring authentic recipes from grandmothers from around the world. Classes at The Natural Gourmet Cookery School and Park Slope Food Coop.

Emphasis: Home cooking using traditional recipes and preparation methods.

Faculty: Susan Baldassano studied at The Natural Gourmet Cookery School & Peter Kump's NY Cooking School & was head chef of Angelica's Kitchen, a macrobiotic organic restaurant.

Costs: $50-$60 for classes, $1,200-$2,000 for cooking tours.

Location: New York City, Long Island, New Jersey, Oaxaca, Mexico, & Sicily, Italy.

Contact: Susan Baldassano, To Grandmother's House We Go, 471-17th St., #1, Brooklyn, NY 11215; 718-768-6197, Fax 212-989-1493, info@tograndmothershousewego.com, www.tograndmothershousewego.com.

VINTAGE HUDSON VALLEY COOKING VACATIONS & SEMINARS

Hudson Valley

Sponsor: 12 country inns & Diners Club. Programs: 10-session cooking vacations at different inns on 3 consecutive days, seminars on summer dishes, special occasion recipes, heritage cookery, celebrity chef & food arts seminars. Established: 1994. Class/group size: 12. 20 programs/yr. Facilities: Kitchens of the country inns & historic homes. Also featured: Dining in country inns, visits to markets, food producers & wineries, summer theater packages, arts & crafts vacations.

Emphasis: Inn specialties.

Faculty: The inn's CIA-trained chefs.

Costs: $125-$525.

Contact: Maren Rudolph, President, Vintage Hudson Valley Cooking Vacations & Seminars, P.O. Box 288, Irvington, NY 10533; 914-591-4503, Fax 914-591-4510, vintagehudsn@earthlink.com, www.vintagehudsonvalley.com.

WINE SPECTATOR SCHOOL

Internet

Sponsor: Wine Spectator magazine. Programs: Introductory & intermediate on-line, interactive wine education courses.

Emphasis: Wine appreciation.

Faculty: Wine Spectator magazine editorial & educational staff members.

Costs: 3-class introductory course $39, 10-class intermediate course $195.

Contact: Gloria Maroti, Director of Education, Wine Spectator School, 387 Park Ave. South, New York, NY 10016; 212-481-8610, x302, winespectatorschool@mshanken.com, www.winespectatorschool.com/wineschool.

WINE WORKSHOP
New York

Sponsor: Wine store. Programs: 1-session classes. Established: 1991. Class/group size: 18-60. 100 programs/yr. Also featured: Wine tasting classes & wine dinners at top restaurants.

Faculty: Wine merchant Michael Kapon & his son John; guest winemakers & importers.

Costs: $50-$295/class.

Contact: Corrine, Director, Wine Workshop, 160 W. 72nd St., 2nd Flr., New York, NY 10023; 212-875-0222, Fax 212-799-1984, winewkshop@aol.com, www.ackerwines.com.

WINES FOR FOOD
New York

Sponsor: Wine professional. Programs: 1- & 5-session wine classes. Established: 1977. Class/group size: 40-50. 10 programs/yr. Facilities: Hotel meeting room, classroom-style seating.

Emphasis: High quality, small production, modestly priced wines.

Faculty: Willie Glückstern has written wine lists for 200 Manhattan restaurants, teaches at NYC's Institute of Culinary Education, is author of The Wine Avenger.

Costs: $65/class, $250/series of 5. Friends can attend for $50 each.

Contact: Willie Glückstern, Wines for Food, 158 W. 76th St., New York, NY 10023; 212-724-3030, Fax 212-501-0717, willie@winesforfood.com, www.winesforfood.com.

ZOË RESTAURANT
New York

Sponsor: Contemporary American restaurant. Programs: Cooking classes featuring chef demos. Established: 1992. Class/group size: 12. 10-12 programs/yr. Facilities: Counter overlooking open display kitchen with woodburning oven, grill & rotisserie.

Emphasis: Contemporary American cuisine. Themes include soups, seasonal specialties, roasting & grilling, pairing food & wine, cheeses, entertaining.

Faculty: Exec Chef Tim Kelley, Wine Director Scott Lawrence, owners Thalia & Stephen Loffredo.

Costs: $65-$95/class.

Contact: Zoë Restaurant, 90 Prince St., New York, NY 10012; 212-966-6722, Fax 212-966-6718, zoerest@aol.com, www.zoerestaurant.com.

NORTH CAROLINA

CHEZ BAY GOURMET COOKING SCHOOL
Raleigh, Durham, Chapel Hill & Burlington

Sponsor: Avocational cooking school. Programs: Beginner & intermediate techniques, baking & pastry, kid's classes, cooking camps, wine tasting, nutrition. Established: 2001. Class/group size: Hands-on: 15 max. 300+ programs/yr. Facilities: 1,500-sq-ft culinary arts center with prep area & 5 cooking stations. Also featured: Cookbook writing seminars, continuing ed, field trips, corporate team building, cooking software training.

Faculty: Chef/owner & restaurateur Joel Goldfarb, IACP & AIWF, trained at Paul Bocuse's Ecole Des Arts; Chef Vikki Lacatena trained at Academie de Cuisine.

Costs: Classes from $45; $300/4-session series.

Contact: Joel Goldfarb, Chef & Owner, Chez Bay Gourmet, 1921 North Pointe Dr., Durham, NC 27705; 919-477-7878, info@chezbaygourmet.com, www.chezbaygourmet.com.

OHIO

BUEHLER'S FOOD MARKETS
4 locations

Sponsor: Food market. Programs: Demonstration & participation classes. Established: 1983. Class/group size: 30 demo/12 hands-on. Facilities: Teaching areas with theater-type seating &

overhead mirrors. Also featured: Child, teen, & parent-child classes.
Emphasis: Seasonal menus, nutrition, children's birthday parties.
Faculty: Staff home economists & guest instructors.
Costs: $7-$20/session.
Location: Dover, Medina, Wadsworth, & Wooster, Ohio.
Contact: Mary McMillen, Director of Consumer Affairs, Buehler's Food Markets, P.O. Box 196, 1401 Old Mansfield Rd., Wooster, OH 44691; 330-264-4355 #256, Fax 330-264-0874, mmcmillen@buehlers.com, www.buehlers.com.

COLUMBUS STATE CULINARY ACADEMY
Columbus

Sponsor: Division of Columbus State Community College. Programs: Demo & participation classes for adults & children. Established: 1995. Class/group size: 18-30. 160 programs/yr. Facilities: 2 professionally-equipped kitchens.
Emphasis: Intl cuisines, theme classes, guest chefs, vegetarian & healthy cooking.
Costs: $50 for demos, $70 for hands-on classes.
Contact: Carolyn Claycomb, Program Coordinator, Columbus State Culinary Academy, 550 E. Spring St., P.O. Box 1609, Columbus, OH 43216; 614-287-5126, Fax 614-287-5973, CClaycom@cscc.edu, www.cscc.edu.

COOKING SCHOOL AT JUNGLE JIM'S
Fairfield

Sponsor: Gourmet market & cooking school. Programs: Demo & hands-on classes on a variety of topics. Class/group size: 35 demo; 15 hands-on. 100+ programs/yr. Facilities: Features the latest equipment. Also featured: Culinary travel programs.
Emphasis: Good technique & doable recipes.
Faculty: Includes school director Carol Tabone, Kathy Baker, Glenn Rinsky, Paul Teal, John Bostick, Janet Hontanosas, & Steve Lee. Visiting instructors & guest chefs.
Costs: $38-$60/class.
Contact: Carole Tabone, School Director, The Cooking School at Jungle Jim's, 5440 Dixie Hwy., Fairfield, OH 45014; 513-829-1919 x3, Fax 513-829-1512, jungle@one.net, www.junglejims.com.

COOKS'WARES CULINARY CLASSES
Cincinnati & Springboro

Sponsor: Kitchenware store. Programs: Demo & participation classes. Established: 1992. Class/group size: 24 demo/16 hands-on. 125 programs/yr. Facilities: 450-sq-ft teaching kitchen with overhead mirror. Also featured: Wine tasting, private instruction, children's & teen classes.
Emphasis: Basics, ethnic & regional cuisines, specific subjects.
Faculty: Includes Marilyn Harris, & chefs Jean-Robert de Cavel, Helen Chen, David Cooke, George Geary, Meg Galvin.
Costs: From $35-$65, $25 for youngsters.
Contact: Nancy Pigg, Director, Cooks'Wares Culinary Classes, 11344 Montgomery Rd., Cincinnati, OH 45249; 513-489-6400, Fax 513-489-1211, cookswares@aol.com.

CULINARY SOL
Cincinnati

Sponsor: Recreational cooking school. Programs: Participation workshops & demo classes on a variety of culinary topics. Established: 2001. Also featured: Children's classes. Private & corporate events.
Emphasis: Cooking techniques & fundamentals.
Faculty: ~30 instructors, chefs, & restaurateurs.
Costs: $40-$60/demo, $50-$75/participation, $25/children's.
Contact: Amy Tobin, Mgr, Culinary Sol, Rookwood Commons Mall, 2735 Edmondson Rd., Cincinnati, OH 45209; 513-841-COOK, customerservice@culinarysol.com., www.culinarysol.com.

DOROTHY LANE MARKET'S SCHOOL OF COOKING

Dayton

Sponsor: Upscale supermarket & cooking school. Programs: Demo & participation classes for the home cook. Established: 1984. Class/group size: 36 demo/12 hands-on. 80-100 programs/yr. Facilities: 1,200-sq-ft teaching kitchen with overhead mirror.

EMPHASIS: International & regional cuisines, wine & food pairing, celebrity chefs, basic skills & techniques, healthy, vegetarian, kids & teens.

FACULTY: Chefs, caterers, cookbook authors, home economists. Celebrity chefs include David Rosengarten, Hugh Carpenter, Nick Malgieri, Pam Anderson, Judith Fertig, Shirley Corriher.

COSTS: Adult classes from $50-$95, teen classes $45, kid's classes $35.

CONTACT: Deb Lackey, School of Cooking Director, Dorothy Lane Market's School of Cooking, 6161 Far Hills Avenue, Dayton, OH 45459; 937-434-1294 exr. 22269, Fax 937-434-1299, cooking@dorothylane.com, www.dorothylane.com.

GARY L. TWINING WINE PROGRAMS

Bainbridge, Oberlin, Cleveland

Sponsor: Wine professional. Programs: 1- to 4-session courses. Established: 1983. 30 programs/yr.

FACULTY: Gary L. Twining taught wine appreciation courses at Ohio State Univ. for 7+ yrs, guest lecturer at SWE's national convention, certified member of SWE, 18 yrs in wholesale wine trade.

LOCATION: Kenston Community Education, Lorain County CC, Cuyahoga CC.

CONTACT: Gary L. Twining, CWE, Gary L. Twining Wine Programs, 301 Greenwood Ct., Elyria, OH 44035; 440-458-6912, Fax 330-422-4727, winingwithtwining@hotmail.com.

HANDKE'S CUISINE COOKING CLASS

Columbus

Sponsor: Restaurant. Programs: Demonstrations and private classes year-round for groups of 20 or more. Established: 1991. Class/group size: 32.

EMPHASIS: American and European cuisine.

FACULTY: Hartmut Handke, CMC.

COSTS: $39.

CONTACT: Margot Handke, Handke's Cuisine Cooking Class, 520 S. Front St., Columbus, OH 43215; 614-621-2500, Fax 614-621-2626, finedining@chefhandke.com, www.chefhandke.com/index.html.

JAMES R. MIHALOEW WINE PROGRAMS

Cleveland & Strongsville

Sponsor: Wine professional. Programs: 5- to 12-session wine courses. Established: 1984. Class/group size: 5-15. 4 programs/yr.

EMPHASIS: Wine appreciation, tastings & sensory evaluations.

FACULTY: James R. Mihaloew is an AWS Wine Judge Training first-year course coordinator/instructor, AWS Life Member & Certified Wine Judge, & SWE Certified Wine Educator.

COSTS: $120-$260/course.

CONTACT: James R. Mihaloew, The Cleveland Wine Line, 13463 Atlantic Road, Strongsville, OH 44149-3924; 440-238-4184, cwljim@earthlink.net, http://home.earthlink.net/~awsjim.

JOHN F. KEEGAN WINE PROGRAMS

Oxford

Sponsor: Wine professional. Programs: Fall & spring sessions. Established: 1995. Class/group size: 90. 3 programs/yr.

FACULTY: John F. Keegan, CWE, masters degree in horticulture, German Wine Academy.

COSTS: $100/course. College credit additional.

LOCATION: Miami University.

CONTACT: John F. Keegan, CWE, Miami University, 316 Pearson Hall, Botany Dept., Oxford, OH 45056; 513-529-4200, Fax 513-529-4243, Keeganjf@muohio.edu.

LAUREL RUN COOKING SCHOOL
Vermilion

Sponsor: Culinary professional Marcia DePalma. Programs: Basic to advanced demo or hands-on classes on a variety of cooking topics. Established: 1996. Class/group size: 12 hands-on/24 demo. 60-75 programs/yr. Facilities: Newly remodeled 850-sq-ft school includes stainless steel work stations, 12-ft demo counter with mirrors, Viking stove top, prep kitchen with 6-burner stove. Herb garden. Also featured: Herb garden field trips, children's classes, wine appreciation.

EMPHASIS: Cooking techniques, bread making, pastry, soups, Italian cooking, herbs, entertaining.

FACULTY: Owner/instructor Marcia DePalma has 20 yrs experience growing/cooking with herbs, has been a TV guest, & was a student of Zona Spray.

COSTS: ~$25/demo, $30-$65/hands-on class. Local lodging available.

CONTACT: Marcia DePalma, Owner/Instructor, Laurel Run Cooking School, 2600 North Ridge Rd., Vermilion, OH 44089; 440-984-5727, Fax 440-984-5727, LRCS@hbr.net, http://laurelruncookingschool.com.

THE LORETTA PAGANINI SCHOOL OF COOKING
Chesterland

Sponsor: Private school affiliated with Lakeland Community College. Programs: 1- to 4-session demo & participation courses. Established: 1981. Class/group size: 28 demo/12 hands-on. 400+ programs/yr. Facilities: Large professional kitchen with overhead mirror, professional equipment. Also featured: Couples & young gourmet classes, gastronomic tours/cruises to Italy, local trips, wk-long series in Sanibel, Florida.

EMPHASIS: Professional techniques.

FACULTY: Owner/director Loretta Paganini, culinary consultant, food writer, cookbook author & guest chef on local TV. Guest faculty includes local chefs, teachers & visiting professionals.

COSTS: $25-$45/session. Tour/cruise prices $2,450-$4,850, includes airfare, lodging, meals, excursions.

CONTACT: Loretta Paganini, Owner/Director, The Loretta Paganini School of Cooking, 8613 Mayfield Rd., Chesterland, OH 44026; 440-729-1110, Fax 440-729-6459, lpsc@lpscinc.com, www.lpscinc.com.

OKLAHOMA

THE STOCK POT SCHOOL OF COOKING
Tulsa

Sponsor: Gourmet food & cooking supply store. Programs: 2-hour demo classes. Established: 2002. Class/group size: 25. 200+ programs/yr. Facilities: Modern household-style equipment, 2 video monitors, digital cameras.

EMPHASIS: Adapting professional techniques & recipes for the home chef.

FACULTY: Chef Mark Hall, a culinary professional for 20+ years, was Executive Chef for Catering by Rosemary & Hilton Hotels & taught continuing ed classes at the U. of Texas. Guest chefs.

COSTS: $35-$50/class.

CONTACT: Jill Gillen, Director of Culinary Events, The Stock Pot School of Cooking, 7227 E. 41st St., Tulsa, OK 74145; 918-627-1146, Fax 918-622-5804, chefmark@thestockpots.com, www.thestockpots.com.

OREGON

CAPRIAL & JOHN'S KITCHEN
Portland

Sponsor: Cooking school. Programs: Cooking classes. Established: 2001. Class/group size: 16-40. 280 programs/yr. Also featured: Private classes.

FACULTY: Caprial and John Pence, resident chef Spence Lack, local and national guest chefs.

Costs: $50-$135.

Contact: Caprial or John Pence, Owners, Caprial's Bistro & Wine, 7015 S.E. Milwaukie, Portland, OR 97202; 503-236-6457, Fax 503-238-8554, caprial@caprial.com, www.caprialand-johnskitchen.com.

CARL'S CUISINE, INC.

Salem

Sponsor: Culinary professional Carl Meisel. Programs: Demo classes. Established: 1978. Class/group size: 12.

Emphasis: Ethnic & regional cuisines, seasonal menus, specific subjects.

Faculty: Proprietor Carl Meisel has traveled & studied in Europe, Thailand, & the U.S. He is a consultant on menu planning, travel, & kitchen design.

Costs: $30/class.

Contact: Carl Meisel, President, Carl's Cuisine, Inc., 333 Chemeketa St. NE, Salem, OR 97301; 503-363-1612, Fax 503-363-5014.

LAYERS OF FLAVOR

Bend

Sponsor: Culinary professional. Programs: Individual & group hands-on & demo classes. Established: 1993. Class/group size: 1-15. Facilities: 450-sq-ft modern kitchen with Dacor & Bosch appliances, island with commercial cooktop. Also featured: Classes & parties for small groups.

Faculty: Chef/owner Deborah Middleton, CHE, 15 yrs experience; 2 sous chefs assist when required.

Costs: Group classes start at $50, one-on-one classes start at $75.

Contact: Deborah Middleton, Chef Owner, Bend Oregon Gourmet Gatherings, 66592 E. Cascade, Bend, OR 97701; 541-318-5042, Fax 541-318-5042, LayersofFlavor@starband.net, http://LayersofFlavor.com.

WESTERN CULINARY INSTITUTE

Portland *(See also page 133) (See display ad page 132)*

Sponsor: Accredited professional culinary institute that offers non-credit classes for food enthusiasts. Programs: 5-hr hands-on a la carte classes, 4-week series, 12-week series, Monday Night Quick Dinners, Wine and Food Pairing classes. Established: 1983. Class/group size: 10-12. 100+ programs/yr. Facilities: 12 kitchen classrooms, 2 full-service restaurants, gourmet deli. Also featured: Private classes & team building classes.

Emphasis: Skills & techniques.

Faculty: 21 chefs on the Institute staff with CEC, CEPC, CCC, CC credentials.

Costs: $130 for hands-on a la carte class, $65 for Monday Night Quick Dinners, $45 for Food and Wine Pairing classes, $550 for 4-week series, $2,500 for 12-week series.

Contact: Steve Watson, Western Culinary Institute, 1717 S.W Madison St., Portland, OR 97205; 503-219-9405, SWatson@westernculinary.com, www.westernculinary.com.

WINE TASTING & STUDY COURSE BY BOB SOGGE

Eugene

Sponsor: Wine professional. Programs: 6-wk course. Established: 1970. Class/group size: 20-100. 4 programs/yr. Also featured: Custom courses.

Faculty: Bob Sogge is a memeber SWE, Napa Valley Wine Library School, Bordeaux Wine Soc., Oregon Wine Growers Assn. 30+ yrs wine teaching, 15+ yrs in wine wholesaling & importing.

Costs: $150/6-week course.

Location: Chanterelle Restaurant.

Contact: Bob Sogge, Wine Tasting & Study Course, 3620 Donald St., Eugene, OR 97405; 541-484-9848, kaysogge@aol.com.

PENNSYLVANIA

CHADDSFORD WINERY
Chadds Ford

Sponsor: Winery. Programs: Wine classes. Established: 1983. Class/group size: 30. ~12 programs/yr.
Faculty: Eric Miller is a winemaker, viticulturist, wine educator, writer.
Costs: $25-$50.
Contact: Eric Miller, Proprietor, Chaddsford Winery, 632 Baltimore Pike, Chadds Ford, PA 19317; 610-388-6221, Fax 610-388-0360, cfwine@chaddsford.com, www.chaddsford.com.

CHARLOTTE-ANN ALBERTSON'S COOKING SCHOOL
Philadelphia

Sponsor: Culinary professional Charlotte-Ann Albertson. Programs: 1- to 4-session demo & some participation courses. Established: 1973. Class/group size: 25 demo/15 hands-on. 75 programs/yr. Also featured: Market tours, children's classes, wine seminars & dinners, European culinary vacations, winter classes in private homes in Florida.
Faculty: Charlotte-Ann Albertson, IACP member & certified teacher, studied at La Varenne & Le Cordon Bleu. CIA-trained Philadelphia chefs, caterers & experts.
Costs: $40-$80/class. Profits go to Ronald McDonald House. Trips $80-$3,500 incl bus transport or airfare from Philadelphia, hotel lodging, most meals, planned excursions.
Contact: Charlotte-Ann Albertson, Owner/Director, Charlotte-Ann Albertson's Cooking School, PO Box 27, Wynnewood, PA 19096-0027; 610-649-9290, Fax 610-649-2939, cookline99@aol.com, www.albertsoncookingschool.com.

CLASS COOKING
Bryn Mawr

Sponsor: Culinary professional Susan Winokur. Programs: Hands-on & demo classes that can be taken individually or as a series. Established: 1986. Class/group size: 5 hands-on, 13 demo. 30 programs/yr. Facilities: 14-ft counter, standard cooking appliances, overhead mirror. Also featured: Private classes, classes for special groups.
Emphasis: French, Italian, & American cuisines, menu planning, basics & advanced techniques.
Faculty: IACP-member Susan Winokur earned a BS degree from Cornell Univ, MS in Education from the Univ of Pennsylvania. Guest chefs.
Costs: $60-$75/class; $240/full-day, hands-on class. Profits go to charity.
Contact: Susan Winokur, Owner/teacher, Class Cooking, PO Box 751, Bryn Mawr, PA 19010; 610-527-1338, Fax 610-527-6069.

THE COOKING COTTAGE AT CEDAR SPRING FARM
Sellersville

Sponsor: Culinary professional Winnie McClennen. Programs: Demo classes & specialized series. Established: 1992. Class/group size: 12. 90 programs/yr. Facilities: Demonstration kitchen with overhead mirror. Also featured: Private group classes and market trips, trips to France and Italy.
Emphasis: Various types of cooking.
Faculty: Winnie McClennen and her daughter, Peggi Clauhs, guest chefs.
Costs: $35-$45.
Contact: Peggi Clauhs, Co-owner, The Cooking Cottage at Cedar Spring Farm, 1731 B Old Bethlehem Pike, Sellersville, PA 18960; 215-453-1828, Fax 215-258-5889, TheCCottag@aol.com.

COOKING AT TURTLE POND
Quakertown

Sponsor: Corporate chef Una Maderson. Programs: Demo & hands-on classes, weekend vacation courses. Private dinner classes, gift certificates. Established: 2000. Class/group size: 4-14. Facilities:

Purpose-built large country home kitchen with cookbook library at Turtle Pond, a 23-acre wildlife protected area with a 2-acre pond.

Emphasis: Professional techniques, intl, vegetarian, entertaining. Focus on flavor & healthy eating.

Faculty: Una Maderson, a professional chef with a degree in hotel & restaurant mgmt, also trained as a registered nurse.

Costs: $55/class. Weekend cooking vacations by arrangement.

Contact: Una Maderson, Turtle Pond, 210 Axehandle Rd., Quakertown, PA 18951-4904; 215-538-2564, Fax 215-538-2564, turtlepond@erols.com, www.turtlepondcooking.com.

COUNTRY WINES

Pittsburgh

Sponsor: Wine store. Programs: 3-session courses. Established: 1972. Class/group size: 5-20. 2 programs/yr. Also featured: Beermaking course.

Faculty: Alexis Hartung is an AWS-certified judge.

Costs: $30/course.

Contact: Alexis Hartung, Country Wines, 3333 Babcock Blvd., Pittsburgh, PA 15237-2421; 412-366-0151, Fax 412-366-9809, info@countrywines.com, www.countrywines.com.

CRATE

Pittsburgh

Sponsor: Retail kitchenware store. Programs: Day & evening demo & participation courses. Established: 1978. Class/group size: 40 demo/15 hands-on. 200+ programs/yr. Facilities: Demo kitchen with 10 burners, convection & microwave ovens, overhead mirror. New professional kitchen for hands-on classes. Also featured: Herbal weekends.

Emphasis: Intl cuisines, basics, vegetarian, guest specialties, techniques.

Faculty: Includes chefs & owners of top local restaurants, culinary business owners & instructors, professional caterers.

Costs: $30-$50/class.

Contact: Linda Wernikoff, Owner, Crate, 1960 Greentree Rd., Pittsburgh, PA 15220; 412-341-5700, Fax 412-341-6231, cratecook1@aol.com, www.cratecook.com.

DICK NAYLOR WINE PROGRAMS

Stewartstown

Sponsor: Vineyard. Programs: 6-session courses. Established: 1980. Class/group size: 20-30. 2 programs/yr. Also featured: Vineyard tours.

Faculty: Winemaker Dick Naylor, an AWS member, has written articles in wine-related magazines.

Costs: $65-$75.

Contact: Dick Naylor, Naylor Wine Cellars, 4069 Vineyard Rd., Stewartstown, PA 17363; 717-993-2431, 800-292-3370, Fax 717-993-9460, dick@naylorwine.com, www.naylorwine.com.

JANE CITRON COOKING CLASSES

Pittsburgh

Sponsor: Cooking teacher Jane Citron & Chef Robert Sendall. Programs: Demo & hands-on classes. Established: 1978. Class/group size: 20 demo, 9 hands-on. 12 programs/yr. Facilities: Professional kitchen. Also featured: Private classes, market visits.

Emphasis: Italian, French, Mediterranean, Middle Eastern, Bread-Baking.

Faculty: Jane Citron, freelance food writer; Robert Sendal, Chef-de-Cuisine.

Costs: $100/class.

Contact: Jane Citron, Jane Citron Cooking Classes, 1314 Squirrel Hill Ave., Pittsburgh, PA 15217; 412-621-0311, Fax 412-765-2511, janecooks@aol.com.

JULIAN KRINSKY COOKING SCHOOL

Haverford & Radnor

(See display ad above)

Programs: 2- & 3-wk summer culinary camp for teenagers ages 12-17 featuring cooking classes, celebrity chef demos, day-trips to markets & restaurants, weekend trips, camp activities. Established: 1978. Class/group size: 4-6:1. 6 programs/yr. Facilities: Air-conditioned demo kitchens. Also featured: Includes art, music, tennis, golf, fitness, business.

EMPHASIS: Herbs, oils, vinegars, fruit, vegetables, desserts, cooking at home, food presentation, table settings, ethnic & regional cuisine, healthy gourmet, fusion, celebration buffet.

FACULTY: Tina Krinsky, Culinary Director. Chef instructors & assistants.

COSTS: ~$1,100/wk residential, ~$390/wk day camp. Includes private dorm lodging, meals & trips.

LOCATION: On the campuses of Haverford College & Cabrini College, both 30 min from Philadelphia, 2 hrs from New York, 2 hrs from Washington DC.

CONTACT: Tina Krinsky, Owner, Julian Krinsky Cooking School, P.O. Box 333, Haverford, PA 19041-0333; 866-TRY-JKCP, 610-265-9401, Fax 610-265-3678, julian@JKCP.com, www.jkcp.com.

KATHY D'ADDARIO'S COOKING TECHNIQUES

Ambler

Sponsor: Culinary professional Kathy D'Addario. Programs: Hands-on technique series includes knife skills, mis en place, stocks, soups, sauces, roasting, grill, poach. Established: 1994. Class/group size: 8-25. 50 programs/yr. Facilities: Large home kitchen. Also featured: Wine instruction, market visits, private classes, small group lessons.

EMPHASIS: Traditional techniques, low-fat meals, seasonal menus, holiday entertaining. Also Italian, vegetarian, cooking on a wood burning stove.

FACULTY: Kathy D'Addario is a graduate of The Restaurant School and studied at Le Cordon Bleu, Giuliano Bugialli's in Florence, and Peter Kump's New York Cooking School.

COSTS: $50/session.

CONTACT: Kathy D'Addario, Owner/instructor, Kathy D'Addario's Cooking Techniques, 858 Tennis Ave., Ambler, PA 19002; 215-643-5883, Fax 215-257-6681, kathcook@aol.com.

KELLY THOS. SHAY: A COOKING SCHOOL IN YOUR HOME

Bethlehem

Sponsor: Culinary professional/chef Kelly Thos. Shay. Programs: Private customized cooking classes in the student's home. Established: 2001. Class/group size: 1-20. 52 programs/yr. Facilities: Client's home. Extra equipment provided. Also featured: Parties & events.

EMPHASIS: Simplicity & ease of cooking meals at home, from basic techniques to high tech methods of top restaurants, & entertaining.

FACULTY: 2-5 professional chefs.

COSTS: Based on length of class & ingredients.

CONTACT: Kelly Shay, Kelly Thos. Shay: A Cooking School In Your Home, 1536 Seidersville Rd, Bethlehem, PA 18015; 610-419-2084, Fax 520-832-8381, kshay2@hotmail.com, www.kellythosshay.50megs.com.

THE KITCHEN SHOPPE INC. AND COOKING SCHOOL

Carlisle

Sponsor: Kitchenware, gift & gourmet store. Programs: Demo & hands-on classes. Established: 1974. Class/group size: 36 demo/15 hands-on. 150 programs/yr. Facilities: Well-equipped professional kitchen with 6 work stations, overhead mirrors, audio system.

EMPHASIS: Afternoon tea, breads & pastries, grilling & smoking, ethnic & vegetarian cuisines, guest chef specialties.

FACULTY: Proprietor Suzanne Hoffman, IACP, instructors Helen Davenport, Jim Lupia, Diana Povis. Guest chefs include Hugh Carpenter, George Geary, Joanne Weir.

COSTS: $40-$60/session; children's classes $20-$40.

CONTACT: Amber Sunday, Director, The Kitchen Shoppe Inc., 101 Shady Lane, Carlisle, PA 17013; 800-391-COOK/717-243-0906, Fax 717-258-5162, kshoppe@pa.net, www.kitchenshoppe.com.

THE LEARNING STUDIO

Malvern

Sponsor: Adult education provider. Programs: 1- to 3-session hands-on courses on a variety of topics. Established: 1998. Class/group size: 16. 100+ programs/yr. Facilities: Gas-equipped cooking classroom. Also featured: Private instruction, corporate programs.

EMPHASIS: Basics of creative cooking.

FACULTY: Area restaurant chefs, most graduates of The CIA.

COSTS: $38-$130 plus $5-$20 materials fee/class.

CONTACT: Leah Stauffer, Owner/President, The Learning Studio, 412 East King St., Malvern, PA 19355; 610-578-0600, Fax 610-578-0680, leah@mail.learningstudio.net, www.LearningStudio.net.

RANIA'S COOKING SCHOOL

Pittsburgh

Sponsor: Restaurant. Programs: 20+ demonstrations each season. Established: 1984. Class/group size: 24. 48 programs/yr. Also featured: Children's classes, wine instruction, private classes.

EMPHASIS: Ethnic and regional cuisines, holiday foods, appetizers to desserts.

FACULTY: Proprietor Rania Harris and chefs Tony Pias (Baum Vivant), Joe Nolan (Cafe Allegro), Bill Fuller (Casbah), Stuart Marks (Rania's Catering); Joe Och, beer tasting.

COSTS: $40/class, children's class is $25.

CONTACT: Rania Harris, Rania's Cooking School, 100 Central Sq., Pittsburgh, PA 15228; 412-531-2222, Fax 412-531-7242, rania@rania.com, www.rania.com.

THE RESTAURANT SCHOOL AT WALNUT HILL COLLEGE

Philadelphia *(See also page 142) (See display ad page 142)*

Sponsor: 4-year private college. Programs: Hands-on & demonstration classes in a variety of culinary & pastry arts disciplines. Established: 1974. Class/group size: 24-85. 200+ programs/yr. Facilities: Include 5 classroom kitchens, two 75-seat demonstration kitchens, 3 classrooms, pastry shop, wine lab & multi-style dining complex. Also featured: The Wine Academy.

EMPHASIS: Guest chef & cookbook author series, hands-on classes.

FACULTY: The 12-member professional specialized faculty, guest chefs & cookbook authors.

COSTS: $35-$50/class.

CONTACT: GiGi Sheppard, Community Education Administrator, The Restaurant School at Walnut Hill College, 4207 Walnut Street, Philadelphia, PA 19104; 877-925-6884, 215-222-4200 #3067, Fax 215-222-4219, info@walnuthillcollege.com, www.walnuthillcollege.com.

SEWICKLEY CULINARY

Sewickley

Sponsor: Private school. Programs: 3- to 5-session hands-on courses, evening & weekend classes. Established: 1994. Also featured: Home-based classes, dinner party courses, catering, corporate team building, recipe testing.

EMPHASIS: Fine cooking series, pastry & baking, Italian cooking, healthy cuisine, theme classes.
FACULTY: School Director Gaynor Grant, former director of Peter Kump's NY Cooking School.
COSTS: Courses $250-$375; theme classes $75, $100/couple.
CONTACT: Gaynor Grant, Director, Sewickley Culinary, 443 Walnut St., Sewickley, PA 15143; 412-741-8671, Fax 412-749-1400, info@sewickleyculinary.com, www.sewickleyculinary.com.

TORTE KNOX
Hawley

(See display ad above)

Sponsor: Culinary professional & TV chef Sheelah Kaye-Stepkin. Programs: Hands-on classes & series. Established: 1993. 100+ programs/yr. Facilities: Kitchen studio & cookbook library in a turn-of-the-century bank. Baking studio with sugar artistry arena, dining room/tasting room inside the vault. Also featured: Private instruction available year-round.
EMPHASIS: Basics, ethnic & regional cuisines, special occasion dishes & menus, cake decorating & sugar artistry design, wedding cakes, guest chef specialties.
FACULTY: Founder Sheelah Kaye-Stepkin & guest chefs from New York City & surrounding area.
COSTS: $75-$150/session + food cost, weekly courses from $750 + food.
LOCATION: 3 mi from Lake Wallenpaupak, ~2 hrs from Manhattan, 3 hrs from Philadelphia.
CONTACT: Sheelah Kaye-Stepkin, Torte Knox, 301 Main Ave., Hawley, PA 18428; 570-226-8200, 866-U-CAN-COOK, Fax 570-226-8201, torteknox@hotmail.com, www.torteknox.com.

WOODEN ANGEL RESTAURANT – ALEX SEBASTIAN
Beaver

Sponsor: Restaurant. Programs: Monthly tastings, custom courses for student group or sponsor. Established: 1980. Class/group size: 12. Also featured: Wine maker dinners, food/wine dinners, wine country tours, cooking demos.

Faculty: Alex Sebastian is a California State Fair/Intervin certified judge, 30 yrs in the wine business, first California Wine Wizard.

Contact: Alex Sebastian, Wooden Angel Restaurant, 308 Leopard Lane, Bridgewater, Beaver, PA 15009-3096; 724-774-7880, Fax 724-774-7994, woodangl@ccia.com, www.wooden-angel.com.

PUERTO RICO

RUTAS GASTRONOMICAS PORTA DEL SOL – WESTERN REGION

Porta del Sol & Western Region

Sponsor: Puerto Rico Tourism Co. Programs: 1-day to wk-long culinary programs that include chef demos, hands-on classes, & tours to historical landmarks, farmers, markets. Established: 2003. Class/group size: 6 min. Facilities: Restaurants, mesones gastronomicos facilities/kitchens. Some artisanal food product factories, small farms & bakeries. Also featured: Optional extensions, custom tours, gastronomic events.

Emphasis: Puerto Rican (traditional or 'nuevo latino') Spanish-Caribbean cuisine.

Faculty: Chef Norma Llop, a bi-lingual graduate of the CIA & Univ of Puerto Rico.

Costs: Group programs $900-$1,600 (seasonal), including deluxe hotel lodging, most meals, ground transport, 2 or more cooking classes.

Contact: Norma Llop, Chef & Culinary Product Development Officer, Rutas Gastronómicas Porta del Sol- Western Region, P.O. Box 902-3960, Old San Juan Station, San Juan, PR 00902-3960; 787-722-1604, Fax 787-721-3884, nllop@prtourism.com, www.gotopuertorico.com.

RHODE ISLAND

FLOUR BUDS, LLC

Newport

Sponsor: Culinary professional. Programs: Classes on the basics, quick cuisine, kitchen tool techniques, food safety, nutrition. Established: 2002. Class/group size: 8-10. 50+ programs/yr. Also featured: Table setting, menu planning, etiquette, personal chef, theme parties, kids' classes.

Faculty: Jennifer Gower a self-taught chef, owned a gourmet luncheonette, was a chef on yachts.

Costs: $25-$60/class.

Contact: Jennifer Gower, Cooking Instuctor, Flour Buds, 59 Burnside Ave., Newport, RI 02840; 401-849-3202, jnjy5@yahoo.com.

SAKONNET MASTER CHEFS SERIES

Little Compton

Sponsor: Sakonnet Vineyards. Programs: Full-day demo & participation classes. Established: 1980. Class/group size: 12. 10 programs/yr. Facilities: Kitchen with chopping block work table & counter that can serve as individual work areas.

Emphasis: Guest chef specialties; wine selection & food pairing.

Faculty: Has included Johanne Killeen, George Germon, Jasper White, Todd English, Michael Schlow, Casey Riley, Joe Simone.

Costs: $80-$100. Lodging can be arranged.

Contact: Susan Samson, Sakonnet Vineyards, P.O. Box 197, Little Compton, RI 02837; 401-635-8486, Fax 401-635-2101, SakonnetRI@aol.com, www.sakonnetwine.com.

SOUTH CAROLINA

BOBBI COOKS II

Hilton Head Island

Sponsor: Culinary professional Bobbi Leavitt. Programs: Demo & participation classes. Established: 1993. Class/group size: 10 hands-on/15 demo. 30 programs/yr. Facilities: Large fully-equipped home kitchen. Also featured: Classes for youngsters, wine & food pairing, couples' classes.

Emphasis: Smoking & grilling, ethnic, entertaining, heart healthy, techniques, kids in the kitchen.
Faculty: Bobbi Leavitt studied at Johnson & Wales, Master Chefs Inst, Michael James French Chefs School, La Varenne, France; past president NYACT, member IACP, AIWF. Guest instructors.
Costs: $30-$40/class.
Contact: Bobbi Leavitt, Owner, Bobbi Cooks II, 9 Baynard Pk., Hilton Head Island, SC 29928; 843-671-5902, Fax 843-671-5902, BobbiCooksatHHI@juno.com.

IN GOOD TASTE
Charleston

Sponsor: Gourmet shop. Programs: 5-day hands-on MacroBalanced Series. Wine classes, generally 4 in a series. Private classes available. Established: 1982. Class/group size: 8-14. Facilities: Well-equipped teaching kitchen.
Emphasis: MacroBalanced cooking. Wines, basic & advanced.
Faculty: Owner Jacki Boyd; local guest chefs; Kushi Institute Certified Guide, Roxanne Koteles.
Costs: $30-$200/session. Reduced fee for whole series.
Contact: Jacki Boyd, In Good Taste, 1901 Ashley River Rd., Charleston, SC 29407; 843-763-5597, jackiboyd1@prodigy.net.

TENNESSEE

JOHN IACOVINO WINE PROGRAMS
Oak Ridge

Sponsor: Wine professional. Programs: 4- to 6-sessions & wine tours. Established: 1989. Class/group size: 30. 3 programs/yr.
Faculty: John Iacovino is a member of AWS, Grand Seneschal of Ducal Order of the Cross of Burgundy, Tennessee wine judge.
Costs: $80-$120/course.
Contact: John Iacovino, John Iacovino Wine Programs, 120 Westlook Circle, Oak Ridge, TN 37830; 865-483-8330, Fax 865-482-2495, JAIacovino@aol.com.

SHIELDS HOOD'S WINE CLASSES
Memphis

Sponsor: Wine professional. Programs: 1-session classes. Established: 1978. Class/group size: 40. 18 programs/yr.
Faculty: Shields T. Hood is an SWE & CWE member.
Costs: $25/session.
Contact: Shields T. Hood, Shields Hood's Wine Classes, 350 Nolley East, Collierville, TN 38107; 901-853-2693, Fax 901-854-9074, HoodWine52@aol.com.

TEXAS

AUSTIN COOKS AT THE TEXAS CULINARY ACADEMY
Austin

Sponsor: Recreational division of Texas Culinary Academy. Programs: 1-day hands-on workshops, 2- & 3-day camps, celebrity chef workshops, couples classes, KidChef classes & camps. Class/group size: 14 max. 100+ programs/yr. Facilities: Professional kitchens in the Texas Culinary Academy facility. Also featured: Private classes & corporate functions, team building.
Faculty: Professional chef instructors.
Costs: $45-$100/class.
Contact: Raleigh Gordon, Texas Culinary Academy, 11400 Burnet Rd,, #2100, Austin, TX 78758; 512-837-COOK, Fax 512-977-9753, rgordon@txca.com, http://austincooks.com.

BLAIR HOUSE COOKING SCHOOL
Wimberley

Sponsor: Country inn. Programs: 3-day hands-on cooking vacations that focus on a specific theme, such as seafood, vegetables, or intl cuisines. Established: 1992. Class/group size: 10.

Emphasis: Technique, chemistry, presentation.

Faculty: Exec Chef Christopher Stonesifer. Innkeepers/owners Mike & Vickie Schneider. Blair House was named 1 of the Top 25 B&B/Country Inns by Arrington's Bed & Breakfast Journal.

Costs: $450/2 nights includes lodging & meals.

Location: On 22 acres in Texas Hill Country.

Contact: Angel Bacon, Blair House Cooking School, 100 Spoke Hill Ln., Wimberley, TX 78676; 877-549-5450, Fax 512-847-8820, info@blairhouseinn.com, www.blairhouseinn.com.

CENTRAL MARKET COOKING SCHOOLS
Austin, Dallas, Ft. Worth, Houston, Plano

Sponsor: Specialty foods markets. Programs: Basic & advanced cooking, intl cuisines, guest chef specialties. Established: 1994. Class/group size: 20 hands-on, 36 demo. 350+ programs/yr. Facilities: Modern culinary classroom. Also featured: Shop the market classes, childrens programs.

Emphasis: Techniques & culinary expertise for the home cook.

Faculty: National & regional guest chefs & cookbook authors, Central Market culinary staff.

Costs: $25-$125/class.

Contact: Shelley Grieshaber, Central Market Cooking School, 4001 N. Lamar Blvd., Austin, TX 78756; 512-458-3068, Fax 512-206-1009, grieshaber.shelley@heb.com, www.centralmarket.com.

CREATING CULINARY OPPORTUNITIES
Houston

Sponsor: Culinary professional Ann Iverson. Programs: 1- & 2-day participation courses in a variety of cuisines. Established: 1993. Class/group size: 12. Facilities: 340-sq-ft private kitchen with 12 work areas.

Emphasis: Northern Italian & Mediterranean cuisines.

Faculty: Guest chefs & authors and Ann Iverson, who studied with Giuliano Bugialli, Mary Beth Clark, Marcella & Victor Hazan, & Lorenza di Medici.

Costs: $150-$300/session.

Contact: Ann Iverson, Owner, Creating Culinary Opportunities, 2902 West Lane Dr., Unit E, Houston, TX 77027; 713-622-6936, Fax 713-622-2924, annci@aol.com.

CUISINE CONCEPTS
Fort Worth

Sponsor: Author & food stylist Renie Steves. Programs: Private wine & cooking instruction designed to the student's requests. Established: 1979. Class/group size: 1-3:1. 10-20 programs/yr. Facilities: Kitchen in a private home. Also featured: Group classes, hands-on classes for 9 max.

Emphasis: Stocks, sauces, basic & low-fat cooking, herbs, kitchen organization, techniques.

Faculty: Owner Renie Steves, CCP, past chair of the IACP Fdn, past president Les Dames d'Escoffier Intl., studied with Madeleine Kamman, James Beard, Julia Child, Nick Malgieri, & the Hazans.

Costs: $100/hr for 1 student, $125 for 2, + $10/hr asst fee; each class is 4-hr minimum.

Contact: Renie Steves, Owner/Teacher, Cuisine Concepts, 1406 Thomas Pl., Ft. Worth, TX 76107-2432; 817-732-4758, Fax 817-732-3247, RenieSteves@msn.com.

CULINARY ACADEMY OF AUSTIN
Austin

Sponsor: Private career school. Programs: Classes that include intl & American regional cuisines, pastries & desserts, wine appreciation. Established: 1998. Class/group size: 6-10. 200+ programs/yr. Facilities: 2-story building contains commercial kitchen with demo cooking stations, classrooms, dining room, media room. Also featured: Team building programs.

Faculty: 1 pastry chef & 2 chefs.

Costs: $35-$150.

Contact: Elizabeth Falto-Mannion, Office Administrator, Culinary Academy of Austin, Inc., 2823 Hancock Dr., Austin, TX 78731; 512-451-5743, Fax 512-467-9120, emannion@culinaryacademyofaustin.com, www.culinaryacademyofaustin.com.

CULINARY INSTITUTE ALAIN & MARIE LENÔTRE

Houston *(See also page 149) (See display ad page 149)*

Sponsor: Proprietary institution with French curriculum. Programs: Chef's Club hands-on culinary & wine classes. Established: 1998. Class/group size: 8-15 hands-on. 50 programs/yr. Facilities: 14,000-sq-ft newly-equipped kitchens. Also featured: Summer camps, programs for youngsters, private instruction, travel programs, team building.

Emphasis: French cooking & baking, chocolate, desserts, intl cuisines, food & wine pairing.

Faculty: Technical Director Alain LeNôtre, French & European chefs, sommelier conseil, oenologue.

Costs: $69/cooking class, $35/wine class, $325/wk for summer camp.

Contact: Alain LeNôtre, President & CEO, Culinary Institute Alain & Marie LeNôtre, 7070 Allensby St., Houston, TX 77022-4322; 888-LeNotre, 713-692-0077, Fax 713-692-7399, lenotre@wt.net, www.lenotre-alain-marie.com.

DESIGNER EVENTS COOKING SCHOOL

Bryan

Sponsor: Culinary professional Merrill Bonarrigo. Programs: Quarterly hands-on cooking classes & food/wine pairing seminars by Messina Hof Winery. Established: 1992. Class/group size: 20-30. 4 programs/yr. Facilities: Restaurant settings. Also featured: Wine tastings, festivals, vintner dinners.

Emphasis: Menus prepared by Messina Hof resident gourmet, Merrill Bonarrigo & the Vintage House Executive Chef.

Faculty: Exec Chef Terry Howry & Maitre d' Klaus Elfeldt of the Vintage House at Messina Hof.

Costs: $29.95/class. Lodging available at The Villa B&B on the estate.

Location: The Messina Hof Winery estate in the Brazos Valley.

Contact: Merrill Bonarrigo, Owner, Designer Events Cooking School, 4545 Old Reliance Rd., Bryan, TX 77808; 979-778-9463 x34, Fax 979-778-1729, event@messinahof.com, www.messinahof.com.

DOLORES SNYDER GOURMET COOKERY SCHOOL

Irving

Sponsor: Culinary professional Dolores Snyder. Programs: Classes. Established: 1976. Class/group size: 10 hands-on/20 demo. 16 programs/yr. Facilities: Kitchen with 6 work stations. Also featured: Wine classes, private instruction, dining in fine restaurants.

Emphasis: Entertaining with English tea, French, Asian.

Faculty: Dolores Snyder, CCP.

Costs: $40-$60/class.

Contact: Dolores Snyder, Owner, Dolores Snyder Gourmet Cookery School, P.O. Box 140071, Irving, TX 75014-0071; 972-717-4189, Fax 972-717-1063, RHS629@aol.com.

HUDSON'S ON THE BEND COOKING SCHOOL

Austin

Sponsor: Restaurant. Programs: One demonstration/participation class the third Sunday of each month at the restaurant and the first Thursday of each month at the home of Chef Blank. Established: 1993. Class/group size: 20-25. 12 programs/yr. Facilities: Hudson's on the Bend restaurant kitchen, Chef Blank's home kitchen. Also featured: Sightseeing.

Emphasis: Wild game, seafood, smoking, sauces, chef specialties.

Faculty: Executive Chef Jay Moore, a CIA graduate, and Owner/Chef Jeff Blank, creators of Hudson's on the Bend Gourmet Sauces.

Costs: $90/session.

Contact: Shanny Lott, Hudson's on the Bend, 3509 Hwy 620, Austin, TX 78734; 512-266-1369/800-996-7655, Fax 512-266-3518, jeffreyblank@austin.rr.com, http://hudsons.citysearch.com/1.html.

KITCHEN FRIENDS
Duncanville (near Dallas)

Sponsor: Culinary professional. Programs: Hands-on morning & evening classes. Established: 1999. Class/group size: 12 max. 25 programs/yr.

Faculty: K.A. Tieszen taught classes in Dallas/Ft. Worth, worked with top local chefs, attended cooking school in France & completed a 1-wk program at the 3-star Troisgros restaurant in Roanne.

Costs: $40/class, children's classes are $25.

Contact: K.A. Tieszen, Chef/Owner, Kitchen Friends, Duncanville, TX 75137; 972-298-5427, Fax 972-283-8408, chefkat@kitchen-friends.com, www.kitchen-friends.com.

THE KITCHEN SHOP AT THE GREEN BEANERY
Beaumont

Sponsor: Cafe and cookware store. Programs: Demon & limited participation classes. Established: 1992. Class/group size: 30 demo/15 hands-on. 20 programs/yr. Facilities: 20-seat demo kitchen area. Also featured: Culinary tours.

Emphasis: Basics, ethnic & regional cuisines, pastries, specific subjects.

Faculty: Glenn Watz, chef/owner of the Green Beanery Cafe for 25 years; local & visiting instructors, cookbook authors.

Costs: $25-$35/class.

Contact: Carolyn Wood, Owner, The Kitchen Shop at the Green Beanery, 2121 McFaddin Ave., Beaumont, TX 77701; 409-832-9738, Fax 409-833-5134.

LAKE AUSTIN SPA RESORT
Austin

Sponsor: Lake Austin Spa Resort. Programs: 3-, 4-, & 7-night all-inclusive packages that include cooking classes, spa treatments, fitness & discovery programs. Established: 1997. Class/group size: 65. Facilities: Fully-equipped demo kitchen overlooking the Texas Hill country & Lake Austin. Also featured: Yoga, kayaking, Nia, Pilates, hiking, spinning, meditation classes.

Emphasis: International spa cuisine.

Faculty: Chef Terry Conlan has 30+ yrs restaurant experience & has appeared on TV food shows; celebrity guest chefs.

Costs: 3-day packages start at $1,350, including lodging, meals, classes, spa treatments.

Contact: Reservations, Lake Austin Spa Resort, 1705 South Quinlan Park Rd., Austin, TX 78732; 512-372-7360, 800-847-5637, Fax 512-372-7280, info@lakeaustin.com, www.lakeaustin.com.

LE PANIER
Houston

Sponsor: Private cooking school. Programs: Demo & participation classes. Established: 1980. Class/group size: 45 demo/15 hands-on. 200 programs/yr. Facilities: Well-equipped teaching area with theater seating, overhead mirror, cooking & work spaces. Also featured: Classes for youngsters, basic techniques series, catering courses.

Emphasis: Ethnic cuisines, breads, entertaining, healthful cooking, main courses, pastries, desserts.

Faculty: Owner/Director LaVerl Daily teaches basics. Other classes taught by guest chefs, teachers, & cookbook authors, including Giuliano Bugialli, Giuliano Hazan, Nicholas Malgieri.

Costs: $35-$60/session, children's classes $20.

Contact: LaVerl Daily, Director, Le Panier, 7275 Brompton Rd., Houston, TX 77025; 713-664-9848, Fax 713-666-2037, ldaily8673@aol.com.

THE MANSION ON TURTLE CREEK
Dallas

Sponsor: Mobil 5-star, AAA 5-diamond hotel & restaurant. Programs: Demo class, special dinner, or both monthly. Established: 1994. Class/group size: 10-150. 5 programs/yr. Also featured: Chef for a Day, Cooking Class & Dining Etiquette for Children.

EMPHASIS: Specific cuisines.
FACULTY: Chef Dean Fearing co-hosts the classes. Guest chefs have included Wolfgang Puck, Julia Child, Jacques Pepin, Emeril Lagasse, Norman Van Aken.
COSTS: Classes range from $100-$225, including tax. Chef for a Day is $1,600/person.
CONTACT: Rebecca Swartz, The Mansion on Turtle Creek, 2821 Turtle Creek Blvd., Dallas, TX 75219; 214-559-2100, Fax 214-871-3245, rswartz@rosewoodhotels.com, www.mansiononturtlecreek.com.

TINA WASSERMAN'S COOKING & MORE..
Dallas

Sponsor: Private school. Programs: Hands-on classes with focus on techniques & understanding the process. Established: 1982. Class/group size: 14 hands-on, 30 demo. 35-40 programs/yr. Facilities: 500-sq-ft home kitchen. Also featured: Programs for youngsters, private classes.
EMPHASIS: Science of cooking, baking, traditional Jewish, ethnic cuisines.
FACULTY: Tina Wasserman has 30+ yrs experience teaching cooking.
COSTS: $50/class.
CONTACT: Tina Wasserman, Tina Wasserman's Cooking & More, 7153 Lavendale, Dallas, TX 75230; 214-369-6269, Fax 214-369-4307, magicook@aol.com, www.cookingandmore.com.

VERMONT

CULINARY MAGIC COOKING SEMINARS
Ludlow

Sponsor: The Governor's Inn. Programs: 2-day cooking vacations featuring morning hands-on cooking classes that focus on a specific theme and include wine pairing. Established: 1992. Class/group size: 4. 9 programs/yr. Facilities: Commercial kitchen facilities of The Governor's Inn. Also featured: Afternoons free for shopping & sightseeing.
EMPHASIS: Low-fat cooking, cooking ahead for entertaining, seafood, basic cooking skills.
FACULTY: Cathy Kubec, chef, innkeeper, & graduate of the Connecticut Culinary Institute.
COSTS: $825/couple includes 2 nights shared lodging with both guests taking course, $525 single. Includes reception, afternoon tea, wine-tasting.
CONTACT: Chef Cathy Kubec, Innkeeper, Culinary Educator, Culinary Magic Cooking Seminars, The Governor's Inn, 86 Main Street, Ludlow, VT 5149; 800-468-3766, Fax 802-228-2961, thegovinn@adelphia.net, www.thegovernorsinn.com.

THE WOODSTOCK INN & RESORT
Woodstock

Sponsor: Mobil 4-star resort, AAA 4-diamond dining room. Programs: Chef for a Day program on Thursdays, Fridays, & Saturdays that includes hands-on prep of the evening's specials & a tour of the kitchen. Established: 1997. Class/group size: 2. Facilities: Kitchen of The Woodstock Inn.
EMPHASIS: Inn specialties.
FACULTY: The Resort's chefs.
COSTS: $50 + the lodging rate ($159-$325 double/night). Reservations required 48 hours prior.
LOCATION: East central Vermont, 2-1/2 hours from Boston.
CONTACT: Tom List, Inn Manager, The Woodstock Inn & Resort, 14 The Green, Woodstock, VT 05091-1298; 802-457-1100, Fax 802-457-6699, email@woodstockinn.com, www.woodstockinn.com.

VIRGINIA

BOAR'S HEAD INN
Charlottesville

Sponsor: Resort at The University of Virginia and Cuisine International. Programs: 3-day hands-on cooking vacations that include a wine seminar, winery tour, and vintner dinners. Established: 2001. Facilities: Boar's Head Inn kitchens. Also featured: Spa, 18-hole golf course, sports club.

Emphasis: New Virginia cuisine.

Faculty: Boar's Head Inn Executive Chef Alex Montiel, Mexico City native who trained under five Michelin-star chefs.

Costs: $1,400 ($300 single supplement) includes lodging, two dinner, planned excursions.

Contact: Cuisine International, P.O. Box 25228, Dallas, TX 75225; 214-373-1161, Fax 214-373-1162, CuisineInt@aol.com, www.cuisineinternational.com/us/boarshead/index.html.

CULINARY UNIVERSITY

Leesburg

Sponsor: Lansdowne Resort & Conference Center. Programs: Cooking demos featuring menus based on a seasonal theme. Food & Wine Camp weekends combine demos, garden tour, aroma class, winery tour, meals. Established: 1982. Class/group size: 75 classes, 18 camp. 16 programs/yr. Facilities: Amphitheather & ballrooms with seating. Portable kitchen equipment. Also featured: Golf, spa, tennis, racquetball, trails, indoor & outdoor swimming pool.

Emphasis: Holiday & seasonal themes.

Faculty: Konrad Meier, Executive Chef; Tony Loos, Executive Sous Chef; Mary Watson-DeLauder, Sommelier.

Costs: Demo classes $50-$75. Food & Wine Camps $925/couple, includes 2-night deluxe lodging.

Contact: Cricket Manjarrez, Executive Club Manager, Culinary University, 44050 Woodridge Parkway, Lansdowne, VA 20176; 703-858-2107, Fax 703-858- 2101, CManjarrez@benchmarkmanagement.com, www.lansdowneresort.com/events/culinaryuniversity.cfm.

THE INN AT MEANDER PLANTATION COOKING SCHOOL

Locust Dale

Sponsor: Private school in a country inn. Programs: 1- & 2-day hands-on cooking programs. Topics change monthly & include theme & holiday menus, grilling, fish, herbs & baking. Established: 1999. Class/group size: 18. 12 programs/yr. Facilities: Country B&B with professional kitchen & classrooms. Also featured: Field trip to local producers, biking, wine tasting.

Emphasis: Country inn-style cuisine & techniques.

Faculty: Chef/owner Suzie Blanchard, former food writer & columinist; Head Chef Paul Deigl & Pastry Chef Sarah Deigl.

Costs: $125/day, $225/2 days. 2-day B&B package $750 ($525) includes shared (single) lodging & meals.

Contact: Suzie Blanchard, The Inn at Meander Plantation Cooking School, 2333 N. James Madison Hwy., Locust Dale, VA 22948; 800-385-4936, 540-672-4912, Fax 540-672-0405, inn@meander.net, www.meander.net.

JOSEPH V. FORMICA WINE PROGRAM

Richmond

Sponsor: Wine professional. Programs: 15-session course. Established: 1974. Class/group size: 20. 1 programs/yr.

Emphasis: Old & New World wines.

Faculty: Dr. Joseph V. Formica is certified by Wine & Spirit Education Trust of G.B. & SWE. He is a member SWE & AWS.

Costs: $160 plus $100 lab fee.

Location: J. Sargeant Reynolds Comm. College.

Contact: Dr. Joseph V. Formica, Director, The Wine School, 8402 Gaylord Rd., Richmond, VA 23229; 804-747-8163, Fax 804-828-9946, formica@hsc.vcu.edu.

JUDY HARRIS COOKING SCHOOL

Alexandria

Sponsor: Culinary professional Judy Harris. Programs: Classes in a variety of intl cuisines including Italian, French, Spanish, American Regional, Mexican, Indian, Thai. Established: 1978. Class/group size: 12 hands-on/20 demo. 65 programs/yr. Facilities: Well-equipped kitchen, culinary herb & vegetable gardens. Also featured: Private group classes, culinary tours, restaurant trips.

Emphasis: International and American regional cuisines, basic techniques, healthy cooking.
Faculty: Judy Harris studied at La Varenne in Paris. Well-known guest chefs, teachers, and cookbook authors include Hugh Carpenter, Jacques Blanc, and Jacques Haeringer.
Costs: $42-$75/session.
Contact: Judy Harris, Judy Harris Cooking School, 2402 Nordok Place, Alexandria, VA 22306; 703-768-3767, judy@judyharris.com, http://judyharris.com.

STRATFORD UNIVERSITY
Falls Church

Sponsor: Private career institution. Programs: Demo & participation classes that cover basic techniques, special occasion menus, & international cuisines. Classes for couples, singles, & youngsters. Established: 1990. 40+ programs/yr. Facilities: Kitchens with the latest equipment.
Faculty: Stratford University culinary faculty.
Costs: $50/class.
Contact: Daniel Traster, Stratford University, 7777 Leesburg Pike, Falls Church, VA 22043; 703-734-5307, dtraster@stratford.edu, www.stratford.edu.

VIRGINIA GOURMET COOKING SCHOOL
Richmond

Sponsor: Private school. Programs: Hands-on classes & series ranging from the basics to specific subjects. Established: 2002. Class/group size: 16-30. 200+ programs/yr. Facilities: Fully equipped 900-sq-ft kitchen. Also featured: Private parties, wine classes, corporate team-building seminars.
Faculty: Local chefs, including Michelle Williams & Thomas Sears .
Costs: $35-$45/class. Series classes offered at reduced rate.
Contact: Kendra Bailey, Manager of Culinary Division, Virginia Gourmet Cooking School, 11400 West Huguenot Rd., #109, Richmond, VA 23113; 804-897-3710 x12, Fax 804-897-5311, kbailey@vagourmet.org, www.vagourmet.org.

WASHINGTON

BLUE RIBBON COOKING SCHOOL
Seattle

Sponsor: Private cooking school. Programs: Hands-on classes. Established: 1973. Class/group size: 20. Weekly programs/yr. Facilities: Teaching kitchen with the latest equipment in a 1907 Craftsman-style home. Also featured: Private & kids classes, corporate team-building, summer camps.
Faculty: Owner Virginia Johns Duppenthaler, CCP, Le Corden Bleu, Paris; Gastronomic Institute, Vienna. Owner Mike Duppenthaler, BBQ specialist. Suzanne Hunter, CCP, Iole Aguero.
Costs: ~$65/class.
Contact: Mike & Virginia Duppenthaler, Proprietors, Blue Ribbon Cooking School, 1611 McGilvra Blvd. East, Seattle, WA 98112-3119; 206-328-2442, Fax 206-328-2863, mike@blueribboncooking.com, www.blueribboncooking.com.

BON VIVANT SCHOOL OF COOKING
Seattle

Sponsor: Private school. Programs: 4- & 9-session certificate courses, demo classes. Established: 1977. Class/group size: 20 demo. 150+ programs/yr. Facilities: Select private homes. Also featured: Assistant program for graduates of the Mastering the Basics course.
Emphasis: Techniques, fine cuisine, breads, pastry, seasonal specialties, regional & intl cuisines.
Faculty: Louise Hasson, BA in Ed, 20 yrs teaching & catering, IACP member; studied at Cordon Bleu, Badia a Coltibuono, Regalaeli. Prominent Northwest chefs & teachers.
Costs: $170/5 classes, $335/12 classes, $519/20 classes.
Contact: Louise Hasson, Director, Bon Vivant School of Cooking, 4925 NE 86th, Seattle, WA 98115; 206-525-7537, Fax 206-523-2992, info@bon-vivant.com, www.bon-vivant.com.

COOKING WITH CHRISTIE

Olympia-Lacey

Sponsor: Retired caterer Christie O'Loughlin. Programs: Hands-on classes that include Northwest regional cuisine, ethnic specialties.. Established: 1990. Class/group size: 4. 6 programs/yr. Facilities: Residential restaurant-caliber gas range & grill. Outdoor BBQ. Also featured: Visits to farmers' markets, food producers, wineries; catered dinners; tailored small group classes..

EMPHASIS: Ethnic cuisines, Northwest regional cooking using fresh local ingredients.

FACULTY: Christie O'Loughlin has been a caterer & studied with local restaurant chefs for 40 yrs.

COSTS: $400/4 students, $150/person for more than 4.

CONTACT: Cooking with Christie, PO Box 232, Olympia, WA 98507-0232; 360-459-0862, coloughlin@juno.com.

COOK'S WORLD COOKING SCHOOL

Seattle

Sponsor: Cookware store. Programs: Demo & participation courses. Established: 1990. Class/group size: 20 demo/12 hands-on. 200+ programs/yr. Facilities: 400-sq-ft professionally-designed instructional kitchen with overhead mirrors, teaching classroom. Also featured: Private classes, team-building seminars.

EMPHASIS: French, Italian, Indian, Pacific Northwest, gourmet vegetarian.

FACULTY: Nancie Brecher, studied at the CIA & La Varenne; local chefs & professional food experts.

COSTS: $38-$45/3-hr class. 20% discount on merchandise.

CONTACT: Nancie Brecher, Director, Cook's World, 2900 NE Blakeley St., Seattle, WA 98105; 206-528-8192, cooksworld@aol.com, www.cooksworld.net.

SUR LA TABLE

Arizona, California, Illinois, New York, Texas, Utah, Virginia, Washington

Sponsor: Cookware store. Programs: Demo & hands-on classes covering a variety of cuisines, the basics, special subjects, chef specialties. Established: 1996. Class/group size: 16 hands-on, ~40 dem. 200-300 programs/yr. Facilities: Full demo kitchens with TV monitors & overhead mirrors above teaching islands, hands-on tables. Also featured: Professional & corporate team-building classes, culinary walking tours, market visits, programs for youngsters & spouses.

EMPHASIS: Basic cooking & baking, topics of current interest featuring popular restaurant chefs & authors.

FACULTY: Professional chefs, restaurateurs, & cookbook authors.

COSTS: $45-$100/class.

CONTACT: Martha Aitken, Culinary Program Manager, Sur La Table, 1765 Sixth Ave. South, Seattle, WA 98134; 206-682-7175, Fax 206-613-6039, maitken@surlatable.com, www.surlatable.com

THE COMPLEAT COOK

Bellevue

Sponsor: Kitchen & giftware store. Programs: Classes cover such topics as appetizers, table decorating, meal planning, quick & easy meals, roasting, Asian noodles, vegetarian gourmet, baking. Established: 1990. Class/group size: 24 max. Also featured: Corporate parties & team building.

EMPHASIS: Ethnic specialty & theme classes.

FACULTY: Local restaurant & private chefs.

COSTS: ~$45/class..

CONTACT: The Compleat Cook, Crossroads Shopping Ctr., 15600 NE 8th St., # K-10, Bellevue, WA 98008; 425-746-9201, Fax 425-746-2491, info@compleatcook.com, www.compleatcook.com.

THE KITCHEN DOOR

Langley

Sponsor: Culinary professional. Programs: 1- & 2-day hands-on programs for the home cook. Emphasis on classic techniques, healthy alternatives, fresh local ingredients, plan-ahead menus; some advanced classes. Established: 2000. Class/group size: 8-10 hands-on. 36 programs/yr. Facilities: Private home kitchens. Also featured: Private classes, corporate team building, field trips.

Emphasis: Skills for becoming comfortable & competent in the kitchen.

Faculty: Owner Shirlee Read also instructs at Sur la Table & other Seattle area cooking schools. Guest chefs, lecturers & demonstrators.

Costs: Guest chef classes $125, Shirlee Read's classes $85-$95.

Location: South Whidbey Island in Puget Sound, ~1 hr from Seattle..

Contact: Shirlee Read, Owner, The Kitchen Door, PO Box 422, Langley, WA 98260 ; 360-730-2322, shirlee@thekitchendoor.net, www.thekitchendoor.net.

WEST VIRGINIA

THE GREENBRIER CULINARY ARTS PROGRAM
White Sulphur Springs

Sponsor: The Greenbrier & La Varenne. Programs: 3- & 5-day demo programs & optional hands-on classes co-sponsored by The Greenbrier & La Varenne; 3- & 5-day demo programs, hands-on classes, & children's classes sponsored by The Greenbrier. Established: 1990. Class/group size: 60 max. 50+ programs/yr. Facilities: The Greenbrier Culinary Arts Center.. Also featured: Includes golf, tennis, spa, horseback riding, Land Rover Driving School, Falconry Academy, indoor & outdoor pools..

Emphasis: Contemporary American & international cuisine, culinary technique.

Faculty: Anne Willan, founder & director of Ecole de Cuisine La Varenne, food columnist, TV show food host, & author of 12+ cookbooks; Greenbrier chefs; guest food personalities..

Costs: La Varenne at The Greenbrier $1,900/3 days, $2,300-$3,100/5 days; The Greenbrier Signature series $1,900/3 days, $3,100/5 days includes lodging, most meals, resort amenities. Classes $125 adult, $55 child.

Location: AAA 5-Diamond resort in the Allegheny Mts, 15 min from Greenbrier Valley Airport.

Contact: Riki Senn, Cooking School Director, The Greenbrier, 300 West Main St., White Sulphur Springs, WV 24986; 800-228-5049, 304-536-7863, Fax 304-536-7754, cookingschool@greenbrier.com, www.greenbrier.com.

WISCONSIN

ECOLE DE CUISINE
Kohler & Chicago, Illinois

Sponsor: School of professional cooking for the home chef. Programs: Intensive weekend participation courses, 5-day classic cuisine courses, demo classes. Special events, customized group programs. Established: 1988. Class/group size: 10 hands-on/75+ demo. 600 programs/yr. Facilities: 2,500-sq-ft professionally-equipped facility. Also featured: Annual 8-day Food Tour of Paris.

Emphasis: Professional cooking techniques for home chefs, classic French cuisine.

Faculty: Jill Prescott, professionally trained in Paris, author of Jill Prescott's Ecole de Cuisine & host of 3 PBS cooking series. Full-time staff includes 3 chefs.

Costs: Participation courses $185-$1,200; demo classes from $60..

Contact: Jill L. Prescott, Owner, Ecole de Cuisine, 765 H Woodlake Dr., Kohler, WI 53044; 920-451-9151 (WI), 312-255-1115 (Chicago, IL), Fax 920-451-9152, jill@jillprescott.com, www.jillprescott.com.

THE COOKING SCHOOL AT KRISTOFER'S
Sister Bay

Sponsor: The Inn at Kristofer's Restaurant. Programs: 1-day demo classes for area visitors; morning participation classes.. Established: 1994. Class/group size: 22. 35 programs/yr. Facilities: A specially-designed kitchen on the 2nd floor of the restaurant, overlooking Green Bay.

Emphasis: Life-style cooking..

Faculty: Chef Terri Milligan, a graduate of the Postillion School of Culinary Arts, has been featured in Good Housekeeping & the TV Food Network..

Costs: $25-$40/demo class, $95-$125/participation class. Cooking class/dinners $35-$45.

LOCATION: Sister Bay, WI, in the Door County peninsula, a resort area 90 min from Green Bay.
CONTACT: Terri Milligan, Chef/Co-Owner, The Cooking School at Kristofer's, 734 Bay Shore Dr., Box 619, Sister Bay, WI 54234; 920-854-9419, Fax 920-854-7149, milligan@dcwis.com, www.innatkristofers.com.

ASIA

ABSOLUTE ASIA'S DELUXE CULINARY TOURS

Over 35 destinations

Sponsor: Travel company. Programs: Customized private & small group gourmet tours that emphasize the art & history of regional cuisine throughout Asia & the South Pacific. Established: 1989. Class/group size: 1-15. Daily programs/yr. Facilities: Private homes, major hotels & established cooking schools in Asia. Also featured: Market tours, gourmet meals, visits to private homes, wine certification courses, special lectures, regional sightseeing.
EMPHASIS: Local cuisine & culture.
FACULTY: Prominent culinary professionals.
COSTS: Tours start at $2,000, which includes deluxe lodging, meals, touring, & regional airfare.
LOCATION: Over 35 destinations including Asia, Australia, Bhutan, Botswana, Cambodia, Egypt, Hong Kong, India, Indonesia, Iran, Japan, Jordan, Kenya, Korea (South), Laos, Malaysia, Middle East, Mongolia, Morocco, Nepal, New Zealand, Papua New Guinea, Philippines, Singapore, Taiwan;, Thailand, Turkey, Viet Nam, Zimbabwe.
CONTACT: Absolute Asia, 180 Varick St., 16th floor, New York, NY 10014; 800-736-8187, 212-627-1950, Fax 212-627-4090, aganz@absoluteasia.com, www.absoluteasia.com.

ASIAN FOODTOURS.COM & THE GLOBETROTTING GOURMET

Asia, Australia, The Pacitic Rim

Sponsor: Food professional. Programs: Tours include demo & hands-on cooking classes & visits to markets, farmers, producers, artisanal manufacturers, Class/group size: 15 max. 4 programs/yr. Facilities: Commercial hotel kitchens & street hawker stands. Also featured: Cultural stops in craft villages..
EMPHASIS: Southeast Asian traditional cuisine & culture.
FACULTY: TV food stylist & author Robert Carmack (Thai Home Cooking, Vietnamese Home Cooking, Fondue) & film editor Morrison Polkinghorne.
COSTS: $775-$2,995 includes 4/5-star lodging, most meals, ground transport, planned activities..
CONTACT: Robert Carmack, The Globetrotting Gourmet, robert@globetrottinggourmet.com, www.asianfoodtours.com.

AUSTRALIA

AGL COOKING SCHOOL

Chatswood, NSW

Sponsor: AGL Gas & Electricity company. Programs: Evening & day courses, school holiday children's programs. Class/group size: 18-30. Facilities: Well-equipped gas & electric kitchen, class area with overhead mirror, smaller prep kitchen. Also featured: Wine & food tours, corporate team events, birthday parties, children's holiday classes.
EMPHASIS: Basic techniques, guest chef specialties, specific topics, class series.
FACULTY: Head of School Ann Cooke with 10+ yrs experience in the food industry, qualified cooking instructors, internationally known guest chefs & food writers.
COSTS: A$58-A$360.
CONTACT: Sally Muller, Head, AGL Cooking School, 31 Newland St., 1st Flr., Bondi Junction, NSW, 2022 Australia; (61) 2-(0)9389-8934, Fax (61) 2-(0)9389-2675, acooke@agl.com.au, www.agl.com.au.

AMANO
Perth

Sponsor: Cookware store. Programs: 2- to 3-session demo & participation courses. Established: 1982. Class/group size: 14 hands-on/30 demo. 60+ programs/yr. Facilities: Teaching kitchen with overhead mirror & individual work areas. Also featured: Culinary tours to France, Bali, & Italy.
Faculty: School director is IACP-member Beverly Sprague. Instructors are prominent Australian & intl culinary professionals.
Costs: A$50-A$80/session, A$90-A$180/series.
Contact: Beverly Sprague, Director, Amano, 12 Station St., Cottesloe, Perth, 6011, W. Australia; (61) 8-(0)9384-0378, Fax (61) 8-(0)9385-0379, bmsamano@echidna.id.au, www.amano.com.au.

BAN SABAI THAI COOKING SCHOOL
Brisbane

Sponsor: Thai cooking school. Programs: Culinary tours & hands-on Thai cooking classes. Annual professional course. Established: 2000. Class/group size: 6-12. Weekly programs/yr.
Emphasis: 4 Thai recipes/class. Includes curries, sweet & sour vegetables, rice noodles, cold salads.
Faculty: Owner Raymund Venzin.
Costs: $85/class, min 5 students required; complimentary for the host if held in host's home.
Location: Raymund's Brisbane bayside home or in student's home. Cooking tours to Thailand.
Contact: Ban Sabai Thai Cooking School, 27 Empire Vista Ormiston, Brisbane, Qld, 4160 Australia; (61) (0)7 3821 4460, (61) (0)409 069 161 (mobile), raymund@venzin.com.au, www.venzin.com.au/thai.

BEVERLEY SUTHERLAND SMITH COOKING SCHOOL
Mt. Waverley

Sponsor: Cookbook author Beverley Sutherland Smith. Programs: 1- to 2-session demo courses. Established: 1967. Class/group size: 20 demos 10 hands on. 15-20 programs/yr. Facilities: Mirrored teaching kitchen that overlooks garden, pool & fountain.
Emphasis: Fresh seasonal produce, guest chefs, cooking for easy entertaining.
Faculty: Beverley Sutherland Smith, Bailli Regional de Victoria magazine & newspaper food writer, authored 29 books & won the Australian Gold Book award.
Costs: From A$60, GST included.
Contact: Beverley Sutherland Smith, 29 Regent St., Mt. Waverley, Victoria, 3149 Australia; (61) 3-9802-5544, Fax (61) 39-802-7683, beverley@gu.com.au.

ELISE PASCOE COOKING SCHOOL
Elizabeth Bay, NSW

Sponsor: Private cooking school run by culinary professional Elise Pascoe. Programs: 1- to 3-day programs with overnight lodging at B&B's, guest houses or motels. Established: 1975. Class/group size: 20. 50 programs/yr. Also featured: Corporate team building, food & wine presentations, regional winery visits, rain forest walks, golf.
Emphasis: Technique & theory, Mediterranean, Italian, French, Thai, Australian country cooking.
Faculty: Elise Pascoe is a free-lance food writer, TV presenter & author of 5 cook books. She trained at Le Cordon Bleu & La Varenne in Paris, & with Roger Vergé & Angelo Paracucchi.
Costs: A$150-A$190/day.
Contact: Elise Pascoe, Managing Director, Elise Pascoe Cooking School, 2/96 Elizabeth Bay Rd., Elizabeth Bay, NSW, 2011 Australia; (61) 2-9368-7700, Fax (61) 2-9368-7733, elisep@ozemail.com.au.

FARAWAY BAY COOKING SCHOOL
Kununurra

Sponsor: Wilderness recreational lodge in the Kimberley. Programs: 4-day vacation focusing on fish cookery with Mediterranean, Asian, South American flavours. Kununurra produce and local beef is used at The Bush Camp. Established: 1999. Class/group size: 12. 1 programs/yr. Facilities: Shady open lounging kitchen/dining area overlooking the bay, commercial gas stove, bbq, camp oven, cool

room, freezer, ice machine. Also featured: Cruising, fishing, beach walks, fresh water swimming.
EMPHASIS: Freshly caught fish.
FACULTY: Andy Harris, Travel and Food Editor of Vogue Entertaining and Travel.
CONTACT: Faraway Bay Cooking School, The Kimberley, PO Box 901, Kununurra, 6743, W. Australia; (61) 891 691 214, Fax (61) 891 682 224, farawaybay@bigpond.com, www.farawaybay.com.au.

HARRY'S CHINESE COOKING CLASSES

Sydney

Sponsor: Culinary professional Harry Quay. Programs: Three 8-session demonstration courses on a rotating basis. Established: 1977. Class/group size: 20. Facilities: Rented halls and schools with kitchen facilities. Also featured: Children's classes, private classes, 4-week courses.
EMPHASIS: Basic Chinese, advanced Chinese, and Thai cuisines.
FACULTY: A third generation chef, Harry Quay has more than 30 years experience.
COSTS: A$20/session, includes full meal, payable at class.
CONTACT: Harry Quay, Harry's Chinese Cooking Classes, 47 Bruce Street, Brighton-le-Sands, NSW, 2216 Australia; (61) 2-9567-6353, Fax (61) 2-9567-3653.

HOWQUA-DALE GOURMET RETREAT

Mansfield, Victoria

Sponsor: Howqua-Dale Country House-Hotel resort. Programs: Weekend hands-on courses, 6-day gourmet cycling tours of Australia's wine regions, gastronomic tours abroad. Established: 1977. Class/group size: 12. 10 programs/yr. Facilities: Horse-shoe shaped pavilion with specialized equipment. Also featured: Fishing, skiing, swimming, horseback riding, bird-watching, bushwalking.
EMPHASIS: Modern Australian cuisine with multi-cultural influences, technique, wine appreciation.
FACULTY: Food writer & cooking demonstrator Marieke Brugman conducts classes. Her partner Sarah Stegley teaches wine selection. Noted Australian guest chefs.
COSTS: All-inclusive fee is ~$A1,100 for weekend course & A$3,750 for wine tours, excluding airfare.
CONTACT: Marieke Brugman, Director/Chef, Howqua-Dale Gourmet Retreat, P.O. Box 379, Mansfield, Victoria, 3722 Australia; (61) 35-777-3503, Fax (61) 35-777-3896, howqua@mansfield.net.au, www.gtoa.com.au.

LE CORDON BLEU – SYDNEY

Sydney

Sponsor: Private school. Programs: 10-wk Classic Cycle programs of Basic, Intermediate & Superior Cuisine & Patisserie. Established: 1996. Class/group size: ~12:1. 6 programs/yr. Facilities: Classrooms designed to resemble professional working kitchens. Individual workspaces, demo kitchen.
EMPHASIS: The principles, theory & techniques of classical French cuisine.
FACULTY: French & Australian master chefs, international staff.
COSTS: Basic Cuisine A$7,200, Intermediate Cuisine A$7,400, Superior Cuisine A$9,000. Basic Patisserie A$7,200, Intermediate Patisserie A$7,400, Superior Patisserie A$8,000.
CONTACT: Julie Ladic, Admission Manager, Le Cordon Bleu Australia, Days Road, Regency Park, Adelaide, SA, 5010 Australia; (61) 8 8346.3700, Fax (61) 8 346.3755, australia@cordonbleu.net, www.lecordonbleu.com.au. In U.S. & Canada: 800-457-CHEF.

MARCEA WEBER'S COOKING SCHOOL – HEALTHY SECRETS

Faulconbridge

Sponsor: Culinary professional Marcea Weber. Programs: Demo & hands-on classes. Sat. workshops and four terms offered. Established: 1980. Class/group size: 10-12. Facilities: Private home, large modern kitchen. Also featured: Women's workshops including hands-on Food as Medicine.
EMPHASIS: Macrobiotic and Chinese-herbal cuisine, wholefoods, Asian, Japanase.
FACULTY: Nutritionist Marcea Weber.
COSTS: A$35-A$40/class.
CONTACT: Marcea Weber, Director, Marcea Weber's Cooking School, 56 St. George's Crescent, Faulconbridge, NSW, 2776 Australia; (61) (02) 4751-1680, marceaweber@hotmail.com.

MATTERS OF TASTE
Bicton

Sponsor: Private school. Programs: Evening, lunchtime & individual classes; 3-session & seasonal courses; Christmas class. Established: 1997. Class/group size: 12. 84+ programs/yr. Facilities: Well-equipped domestic-style kitchen.

EMPHASIS: Modern Australian approach using fresh seasonal produce. Finger foods, light & main meals, desserts, baking.

FACULTY: Proprietor Tracey Cotterell has a Tech Diploma in Hotel Catering & Institutional Mgmt & is a culinary professional with 20+ yrs experience.

COSTS: A$60/class, A$175/course.

CONTACT: Tracey Cotterell, Principal, Matters of Taste, 103 Harris St., Bicton, 6157 Australia; (61)(8) 9319-1097, Fax (61)(8) 9339-0697, info@mattersoftaste.com.au, www.mattersoftaste.com.au.

THE OLIVE & THE GRAPE
Hunter Valley, Sydney

Programs: Hands-on pasta making classes at a boutique winery, includes local olive oil & wine tastings. Established: 2002. Class/group size: 12 max. Facilities: Sandalyn Estate winery.

EMPHASIS: Pasta.

FACULTY: Jane Thomson, Francesca Robinson, Helen Topp, Simon Payne.

COSTS: A$89, includes GST.

CONTACT: The Olive & The Grape, Australia; (61) 2 9590 9531, bookings@theoliveandthegrape.com, www.theoliveandthegrape.com.

PARIS INTERNATIONAL COOKING SCHOOL
Sydney (Stanmore)

Sponsor: Culinary professional. Programs: 9- & 10-session courses, 1-wk residential course, half-day workshops. Established: 1994. Class/group size: 16 demo, 10 hands-on. 240+ programs/yr. Facilities: Fully-equipped demo kitchen with mirrors & practical kitchen for 20 students. Small Application restaurant open 3 days/wk where students prepare meals for guests. Also featured: Classes for teenagers, tour of Sydney market, seasonal workshops, residential cooking tours.

EMPHASIS: Intl, French, Native Australian cuisine, pastry, cake decorating & sugar craft, food carving, wine.

FACULTY: French native Laurent Villoing trained at Ecole Lenotre, has 25 yrs experience as hotel chef, lectured at London catering colleges & in Sydney, appears on TV shows.

COSTS: A$49-A$70/half-day workshop, A$130-A$200/9-wk class, A$530/10-wk hospitality course, A$900/wk + lodging for residential course.

CONTACT: Laurent Villoing, Coordinator/Manager, Paris International Cooking School, 216 Parramatta Rd., Stanmore, NSW, 2048 Australia; (02) 9518 1066, Fax (02) 9518 1077, Laurent4@bigpond.com.au, http://au.briefcase.yahoo.com/ParisICS.

SYDNEY SEAFOOD SCHOOL
Pyrmont, Sydney

Sponsor: Sydney Fish Market Pty. Ltd. Programs: Hands-on courses in seafood cookery. Established: 1989. Class/group size: 48. 200+ programs/yr. Facilities: Practical kitchen & 66-seat demo auditorium with tiered seating & overhead mirror. Also featured: Exclusive classes for clubs, corporate groups.

EMPHASIS: Seafood cookery, guest chef specialties, advanced techniques, seafood buying & handling, sushi & sashimi.

FACULTY: Qualified home economists & seafood specialists, guest chefs from Sydney's top restaurants.

COSTS: Nonrefundable tuition, payable in advance, ranges from A$65-A$110/course.

CONTACT: Roberta Muir, Manager, Sydney Seafood School, Locked Bag 247, Pyrmont, NSW, 2009 Australia; (61) (02) 9004 1111, Fax (61) (02) 9004 1177, sss@sydneyfishmarket.com.au, www.sydneyfishmarket.com.au.

TOUR DE FORKS-AN EPICUREAN ADVENTURE DOWN UNDER
Melbourne & Sydney

Sponsor: Ex-patriot Australian & New Yorker foodies combined with tour operator Nick Piper of Destination Australia & New Zealand, Inc. Programs: Tour features Master Chef classes at restaurants, visits to artisanal producers, & the Melbourne Food & Wine Festival. Established: 2001. Class/group size: 16. 1 programs/yr.

Faculty: Master Chefs including Meera Freeman, food consultant, cooking demonstrator, writer, tour group leader; George Biron, Master Chef, writer, owner of Sunnybrae restaurant.

Costs: $7,700, includes LA/Sydney return airfare, lodging at Sydney Hyatt & Melbourne Hyatt, meals & wines, ground transport, 3 master classes, tickets to Melbourne Food & Wine Festival.

Contact: Melissa Joachim, Tour de Forks-An Epicurean Adventure Down Under, 108 East 38th St, #710, New York, NY 10016; 212-447-9640, tourdeforks@earthlink.net.

AUSTRIA

HERZERL TOURS 'A TASTE OF VIENNA'
Vienna

Programs: 1-wk trips that include 3 classes at Vienna's Am Judenplatz cooking school and one at the haute cuisine restaurant Drei Husaren. Established: 1994. Class/group size: 18. 3 programs/yr. Also featured: Market visit, winery tour & tasting, trip to tableware displays in the Imperial Palace, sightseeing on foot & per coach, dinners in gourmet restaurants, concert.

Emphasis: Traditional & nouveau Viennese cuisine & pastry making.

Costs: $2,350 includes airfare from NYC, lodging, buffet breakfast, some meals, planned activities.

Contact: Susanne Servin, Owner, Herzerl Tours, P.O. Box 217, Tuckahoe, NY 10707; 800-684-8488, 914-771-8558, Fax 914-771-5844, sms@herzerltours.com, www.herzerltours.com.

BRAZIL

BRAZILIAN ACADEMY OF COOKING & OTHER PLEASURES
Ouro Preto

Sponsor: Brazilian culinarian Yara Castro Roberts. Programs: 1-wk vacation programs that feature hands-on classes in Brazilian cuisine, including the regional dishes of Amazon, Bahia, & Minas Gerais. Established: 1996. Class/group size: 8-12. 10 programs/yr. Facilities: Professional kitchens of 5-star hotels. Also featured: Sugar cane distillery, coffee plantation, underground gold mine, market visits, cultural activities, dancing, craft workshops.

Emphasis: Brazilian culinary arts & its relationship with Brazilian culture.

Faculty: Founder Yara Castro Roberts, Emmy Award nominee host for a PBS cooking series & graduate of Boston U. Culinary Arts program; Dr. Moacyr Laterza, a Brazilian history professor; local chefs & food artisans.

Costs: $2,250 includes shared lodging, meals, planned activities.

Location: The mountains of Minas Gerais, 1 hr flight from Rio, 1 hr drive from Belo Horizonte.

Contact: Yara Castro Roberts, Director/Instructor, Academy of Cooking & Other Pleasures, Brazil, 256 Marlborough St., Boston, MA 2116; 617-262-8455, Fax 617-267-0786, yara@cookingn-pleasures.com, www.cookingnpleasures.com.

CANADA

ACCOUNTING FOR TASTE
Ottawa, ON

Sponsor: Wine professional. Programs: 4-session wine courses. Established: 1996. Class/group size: 25. 4 programs/yr. Also featured: Tastings, seminars, dinners.

Faculty: Michael Botner is Governor & co-founder of National Capital Sommelier Guild, writer, chair of the Cellars of the World International Wine Competition, member SWE.

Costs: $150/course, $275/series.

Contact: Michael Botner, Accounting for Taste, 195 Rodney Crescent, Ottawa, ON, K1H 5J8 Canada; 613-523-3389, Fax 613-523-3397, michael@accountingfortaste.ca, www.accountingfortaste.ca.

AU BON GOÛT

Montreal, QB

Sponsor: Culinary professional Sandra M. Carmichael. Programs: 1-week Italian and French cookery school holidays that feature local specialties, special occasion menus, and quick dishes. Dim sum and Szechuan classes in Montreal, 4-week, 6-level series. Established: 1996. Class/group size: 4-12. 10+ programs/yr. Facilities: Include local trattoria. Also featured: Shopping for specialties.

Emphasis: Italian, French, and Chinese cuisines.

Faculty: Trained cook & teacher.

Location: Rome & Amalfi Coast, Italy; Nice & Arles, France; Montreal, Canada.

Contact: Sandra M Carmichael, President, Au Bon Goût, 369 52nd Ave., Lachine, QB, H8T 2X3 Canada; 514-637-0740, Fax 514-637-1642, abg@aubongout.com, www.aubongout.com.

BONNIE STERN SCHOOL OF COOKING

Toronto, ON

Sponsor: Private school. Programs: Demo & participation classes for corporate & private group functions. Established: 1973. Class/group size: 30 demo/15 hands-on. 50 programs/yr. Facilities: Interchangeable demo/participation area with overhead mirror & closed circuit TV.

Emphasis: Basic techniques, ethnic & regional cuisines, low fat cookery, holiday menus with mixology session & wine tasting option.

Faculty: Bonnie Stern, a George Brown College graduate, studied with Simone Beck & Marcella Hazan & authored 9 cookbooks, including Simply Heartsmart Cooking; TV cooking show host, newspaper columnist.

Contact: Bonnie Stern, Bonnie Stern School of Cooking, 6 Erskine Ave., Toronto, ON, M4P 1Y2 Canada; 416-484-4810, Fax 416-484-4820, bonnie@bonniestern.com, www.bonniestern.com.

BUTTERNUT INN GOURMET GETAWAY WEEKEND

Port Hope, ON

Sponsor: Butternut Inn B&B. Programs: Gourmet hands-on cooking classes for guests that include 2-night stay in the Butternut Inn, breakfasts & 4-5 course dinners. Established: 1996. Class/group size: 8 hands-on. 16-20 programs/yr. Facilities: A large kitchen with an island, or BBQ cooking in the garden. Also featured: Hiking, shopping, golfing, fishing.

Emphasis: Traditional Mediterranean (French, Spanish, Greek, Italian) & Asian (Thai, Japanese, Chinese). BBQ techniques in summer mos.

Faculty: Chef/instructor Linda Stephen, trained at Ryerson, worked with Bonnie Stern & other established chefs, & has led cooking tours to Thailand.

Costs: C$499/couple, all inclusive.

Contact: Bonnie Harrison, Innkeeper, Butternut Inn Bed & Breakfast's Gourmet Getaway Weekend, 36 North St., Port Hope, ON, L1A 1T8 Canada; 800-218-6670, 905-885-4318, Fax 905-885-5464, info@butternutinn.com, www.butternutinn.com.

CAREN'S COOKING SCHOOL

Vancouver, BC

Sponsor: Private school. Programs: 3- to 4-session evening demonstration courses. Established: 1978. Class/group size: 28. 60 programs/yr. Facilities: Overhead mirror, butcher block demonstration table, 8 gas burners. Also featured: Wine classes.

Emphasis: Italian, French, and Continental Asian cuisine.

Faculty: Owner Caren McSherry-Valagao, CCP, trained at the Cordon Bleu, the CIA, and The Oriental in Bangkok.

Costs: Range from C$60-C$80 per class. Cancellations with 1 week notice receive credit.

CONTACT: Caren McSherry-Valagao, Owner, Caren's Cooking School, 1856 Pandora St., Vancouver, BC, V5L 1M5 Canada; 604-253-3022, Fax 604-253-1331, caren@gourmetwarehouse.ca, www.gourmetwarehouse.ca.

CHEZ SOLEIL
Stratford, ON

Sponsor: Cooking school with bed & breakfast facilities. Programs: Hands-on cooking weekends & classes based on participants' choice of menus. Harvest to Table Cooking Week. Established: 1996. Class/group size: 6. Facilities: Commercial kitchen in a residential setting. Also featured: Wine instruction, classes for youngsters, day trips, market visits, private instruction, cooking library, discussions on cooking resources.

EMPHASIS: Custom-designed menus to reflect students' interests. Organics & fair trade emphasized.

FACULTY: Liz Mountain, 20 yrs professional experience, graduate of George Brown College; Janet Sinclair, valedictorian class of '95 & instructor of restaurant design at Stratford Chefs School.

COSTS: C$400/weekend includes 2 nights lodging at an English Tudor cottage B&B. C$2,000/cooking wk.

CONTACT: Janet Sinclair, Chez Soleil Cooking School, 120 Brunswick St., Stratford, ON, N5A 3M1 Canada; 519-271-7404, Fax 519-271-7404, cooking@chezsoleil.com, www.chezsoleil.com.

CINNABAR CULINARY DELIGHTS
Toronto, ON

Sponsor: Culinary professional. Programs: In-home cooking classes for individuals or small groups; corporate team-building cooking events. Established: 1998. Class/group size: 35 max.

EMPHASIS: Cooking by method with less reliance on recipes.

FACULTY: Chef Paul Mesbur, an honors graduate of the Stratford Chefs School, has 10 yrs. experience in the restaurant, hotel & catering trade.

COSTS: $75/person.

CONTACT: Paul Mesbur, Chef-Owner, Cinnabar Culinary Delights, 400 Walmer Rd., #1012, Toronto, ON, M5P2X7 Canada; 416-963-9675, cinnabarculinarydelights@rogers.com, http://cinnabar10.tripod.com.

COOKING AT THE HARVEST KITCHEN
Oakville, ON

Sponsor: Recreational cooking school. Programs: Demo classes with hands-on components for public, corporate entertaining & team-building. Established: 1979. Class/group size: 18. 25+ programs/yr. Facilities: Demo country kitchen in a 160 year-old home with herb garden. Also featured: Private chef's tables, birthday cooking parties, gourmet trips to local food & wine festivals & to Italy & France.

EMPHASIS: Regional Canadian cuisine.

FACULTY: Gurth Pretty, past Canadian culinary consultant for Emeril Live! & a graduate of George Brown College's Culinary Mgmt program, writes food columns & has worked professionally.

COSTS: C$80-C$95/class.

CONTACT: Gurth M. Pretty, Culinary Director, Harvest Kitchen Cookery School, 134 Thomas St., Oakville, ON, L6J 3B1 Canada; 416-760-9504, Fax 416-760-0150, info@epicureanexpeditions.com, www.epicureanexpeditions.com.

COOKING WITH LARKELL
Creemore, ON

Sponsor: Private school & caterer. Programs: Evening & weekend classes in meal preparation & baking skills. Established: 2002. Class/group size: 6-8. 10-15 programs/yr. Facilities: Studio kitchen, professional equipment. Also featured: Personal chef.

EMPHASIS: Baking & pastry.

FACULTY: Larkell Bradley, Le Cordon Bleu-trained catering chef.

COSTS: C$85/class.

Contact: Larkell Bradley, Co-owner, Larkell's Sweet Sensations & Fine Cuisine, 15 Elizabeth St W, PO Box 272, Creemore, ON, L0M 1G0 Canada; 705-466-6315, toona@infinity.net.

THE COOKING STUDIO
Winnipeg, MB

Sponsor: Private school. Programs: Hands-on and demonstration classes. Established: 1994. Class/group size: 14-24. 100 programs/yr. Facilities: 1,200-sq-ft professional kitchen with Miele, Garland & Dacor equipment. Also featured: Private dinning room & catering.

Faculty: Owner Marisa Curatolo, BS, Dubrulle French Culinary School, Ecole LeNotre.

Costs: Hands-on classes C$75, demos C$45, children's classes C$25.

Contact: Marisa Curatolo, Owner, The Cooking Studio, 3200 Roblin Blvd., Winnipeg, MB, R3R OC3 Canada; 204-896-5174, Fax 204-888-0628, cookingstudio@mts.net, www.thecookingstudio.ca.

COOKING WORKSHOP
Toronto, ON

Sponsor: Private school. Programs: Weekend hands-on workshops, evening workshops/demos. Established: 1985. Class/group size: 8-12. Facilities: Industrial kitchen of Dufflet Pastries, a cafe/bakery equipped with skylights & double ovens; a private home kitchen, & large cooking labs. Also featured: Wine-tastings, private group classes, culinary tours to Italy & Toronto.

Emphasis: Italian cuisine, breads, pastry, foundations.

Faculty: Maria Pace, author of The Little Italy Cookbook, studied at La Varenne with Marcella Hazan. Baker Paula Bambrick trained at George Brown College. Doris Eisen creates bread & pastry recipes. Chef Steve Jukic, European trained, leads culinary events.

Costs: C$75-C$90. Group rates available.

Contact: Maria Pace, Owner, The Cooking Workshop, 10 Beaconsfield Ave., Ste. 2, Toronto, ON, M6J 3H9 Canada; 416-588-1954, Fax 416-588-1954, marypace@enoreo.on.ca.

COOKSCHOOL AT THE COOKSHOP
Vancouver, BC

Sponsor: Cookware store. Programs: Demo & participation classes, 2 classes/day, 6 days/wk. Established: 1992. Class/group size: 8-20. Facilities: 1,000-square-foot area with overhead mirror. Also featured: Private lessons/functions, wine pairing, nutrition counseling, cookbook author signings, guided tours of wineries & other facilities.

Emphasis: Fresh & healthy.

Faculty: School director, restaurateur, & teacher Nathan Hyam; 60 guest chefs from local hotels & restaurants.

Costs: From C$19-C$199/class. Payment in advance. Good hotels within 5 min walk.

Contact: Peter Haseltine, COOKSCHOOL at the COOKSHOP, 3-555 W. 12th Ave., Vancouver, BC, V5Z 3X7 Canada; 604-873-5683, Fax 604-876-4391, info@cookshoponline.com, www.cookshoponline.com.

THE COOKWORKS
Toronto, ON

Sponsor: Privately owned cooking school operated in conjunction with Mildred Pierce Restaurant. Programs: Evening & weekend classes on such topics as fish & seafood, pasta, grilling, breads, kitchen basics, sushi, chocolate & pastry. Established: 1997. Class/group size: 14 hands-on. 100 programs/yr. Facilities: The studio kitchen next to Mildred Pierce Restaurant is equipped with professional cooking equipment & individual work stations. Also featured: Corporate hands-on cooking classes for groups.

Faculty: 3 full-time chef-instructors, Mildred Pierce Restaurant chefs, & chefs from top Toronto restaurants.

Costs: ~$135/class..

Contact: Donna Dooher, Director, The Cookworks, 99 Sudbury St., Ste. 8, Toronto, ON, M6J 3S7 Canada; 416-537-6464, Fax 416-537-2653, cook@thecookworks.com, www.thecookworks.com.

DISH COOKING STUDIO

Toronto, ON

Sponsor: Chef-owned school. Programs: Hands-on & demo classes. Established: 2000. Class/group size: 12-24. 150 programs/yr. Facilities: Modern, casual kitchen with counter seating 16. Also featured: Private, children's, corporate, & team-building classes.

EMPHASIS: Entertaining, make ahead & easy work-week meals, dinner menus, ethnic cuisines.

FACULTY: 8 professional resident teachers/chefs, visiting & celebrity guest chefs including Ted Reader, Greg Couillard.

COSTS: $65-$135/class, lunch & learn $65, evening core class $110, guest chef demo $125.

CONTACT: Trish Magwood, Owner, Dish Cooking Studio, 390 Dupont St, Toronto, ON, M5R 1V9 Canada; 416-920-5559, Fax 416-920-6469, trish@dishcookingstudio.com, www.dishcookingstudio.com.

DUBRULLE INTERNATIONAL CULINARY & HOTEL INSTITUTE

Vancouver, BC

Sponsor: Private accredited culinary training institute. Programs: Hands-on day, evening, & weekend classes & series for the serious amateur chef. Established: 1982. Facilities: 9,000-sq-ft facility has 5 classrooms, 6 teaching kitchens, the Chef's Table student-operated dining facility. Also featured: Wine instruction, classes for youngsters, custom classes, corporate team building programs.

EMPHASIS: Basic & advanced techniques, international and special occasion menus, guest chef specialties, food & wine pairing.

FACULTY: The school's full-time professional faculty chefs, notable local and visiting guest chefs.

COSTS: C$68/class-C$700/series.

CONTACT: Serious Amateur Reservations Coordinator, Dubrulle International Culinary & Hotel Institute of Canada, 1522 W. 8th Ave., Vancouver, BC, V6J 4R8 Canada; 604-738-3155, 800-667-7288, Fax 604-738-3205, party@dubrulle.com, www.dubrulle.com.

THE GOOD EARTH COOKING SCHOOL

Beamsville, ON

Sponsor: Private school. Programs: Hands-on and demo classes focusing on techniques & seasonal products, wine education dinners. Class/group size: 12 max. ~ 50 programs/yr. Also featured: Corporate events, private functions, catering.

EMPHASIS: Niagara regional cuisine.

FACULTY: Resident chefs Lenny Karmiol & Lisa Rollo, associate chef Raymond Poitras, wine lecturer Ben Simmons, guest chefs.

COSTS: Demos C$125, hands-on C$175.

CONTACT: Nicolette Novak, Proprietor, The Good Earth, 4556 Lincoln Ave., Beamsville, ON, L0R 1B3 Canada; 800-308-5124, 905-563-7856, Fax 905-563-9143, info@goodearthcooking.com, www.goodearthcooking.com.

GREAT COOKS AND THE TEA SPOT

Toronto, ON

Sponsor: Cooking school. Programs: Afternoon & evening demo & hands-on classes. Established: 1989. Class/group size: 24. 60+ programs/yr. Facilities: 600-sq-ft modern kitchen, similar to a chef's table. Also featured: Wine tastings, group classes, culinary trips, tours of Toronto markets, dining in top restaurants.

EMPHASIS: International & regional cuisines, menus for entertaining, vegetarian meals, guest chef specialties, wine appreciation.

FACULTY: 30+ Toronto chefs, including Massimo Capra, Jean Pierre Challet, Marc Picone, Jason Barato, Albino Silva, Amthony Walsh.

COSTS: C$80-C$110/class.

LOCATION: Toronto's largest department store, The Bay.

CONTACT: Esther Benaim, Proprietor/Director, Great Cooks, 176 Yonge St, Lower Level, Toronto, ON, M5C 2L7 Canada; 416-861-4727, Fax 416-861-9762, cook@greatcooks.ca, www.greatcooks.ca.

HEALTHY GOURMET INDIAN COOKING

Oakville, ON

Sponsor: Private school. Programs: Hands-on Indian, Thai, Malaysian & Mexican cooking classes. Established: 1993. Class/group size: 8. 80+ programs/yr. Facilities: Kitchen & dining area. Also featured: Culinary trips, field trips, tours.

EMPHASIS: Healthful vegetarian, Ayurvedic & non-vegetarian Indian & Thai cuisine.

FACULTY: Arvinda Chauhan, owner, instructor, recipe developer, cookbook author.

COSTS: $50-$60/class. $150/6-wk Indian beginners class, includes visit to Toronto's Indian bazaar.

CONTACT: Arvinda Chauhan, Cooking Instructor, Healthy Gourmet Indian Cooking, 1334 Creekside Dr., Oakville, ON, L6H 4Y2 Canada; 905-842-3215, info@hgic.ca, www.hgic.ca.

HOLLYHOCK RETREAT CENTRE

Cortes Island, BC

Sponsor: Seasonal retreat center. Programs: Include well-being, wisdom practices, arts, culture, business, leadership, cooking. Established: 1982. 80 programs/yr. Also featured: Yoga, meditation, birdwalks, star talks, body work, garden tours, beach combing, kayaking, sailing, guided hikes.

EMPHASIS: Seasonal meals using primarily organic ingredients.

FACULTY: The Natural Gourmet Institute's Diane Carlson & Peter Berley.

COSTS: ~$1,400, includes double occupancy with shared bath, meals & some activities.

LOCATION: Island wilderness setting ~100 mi north of Vancouver.

CONTACT: Information, Hollyhock Retreat Centre, Box 127, Manson's Landing, Cortes Island, BC, V0P 1K0 Canada; 800-933-6339, Fax 604-935-6424, registration@hollyhock.ca, www.hollyhock.ca.

LE CORDON BLEU – OTTAWA

Ottawa, ON

Sponsor: Private school. Programs: 1-day to 1-month drop-ins, specialized short courses, evening demos. Established: 1988. Class/group size: 16:1 max. Facilities: Include demonstration room, fully-equipped Pastry and Cuisine kitchens with individual work spaces, specialized equipment.

FACULTY: Classically-trained professional master French chefs.

COSTS: C$25 (C$15 students/seniors)/demo, C$561-C$696/short courses. Intensives: C$525/one wk, C$975/two wks, C$175/one-day demo/practical, C$1,950/one-month demo/practical. C$187/Gourmet Sessions.

CONTACT: Niki Swain, Registrar, Le Cordon Bleu Ottawa Culinary Arts Institute, 453 Laurier Ave. East, Ottawa, ON, K1N 6R4 Canada; 613-236-CHEF, Fax 613-236-2460, ottawa@cordonbleu.edu, http://lcbottawa.com.

MAMMA WANDA COOKING SCHOOL

Kirkland, QB

Sponsor: Culinary professional Wanda Calcagni. Programs: Weekend seminars & 3- & 5-session courses featuring demo & hands-on classes. Class/group size: 8.

EMPHASIS: N. Italian cuisine, Italian vegetarian cuisine, homemade Italian baby & children's dishes.

FACULTY: Wanda Calcagni, author of The Mamma Wanda Cookbook, free-lance consultant.

COSTS: Weekend course $300, 3-session baby & children meals course $180, 5-session course $250.

CONTACT: Wanda Calcagni, Mamma Wanda Cooking School, 1 Viger St., Kirkland, QB, H9J 2E4 Canada; 514-695-0864.

MARGARET SWAINE WINE PROGRAMS

Toronto, ON

Sponsor: Wine professional. Programs: The Toronto Life Wine Experience dinners. Established: 1996. Class/group size: 90. 8 programs/yr.

EMPHASIS: Wine & food pairings themed to different regions.

FACULTY: Margaret Swaine, a wine columnist since 1979 for Toronto Life & other magazines.

COSTS: $125/session includes dinner.

CONTACT: Margaret Swaine Wine Programs, 744 Duplex Ave., Toronto, ON, M4R 1W3 Canada; 416-961-5328, Fax 416-961-4251, m.swaine@rogers.com, www.margaretswaine.com.

McCALL'S SCHOOL OF CAKE DECORATION, INC.

Etobicoke, ON

Sponsor: Private school. Programs: Half- or all-day hands-on workshops and 1- to 4-session cake decorating, baking, chocolate, and specialty courses. Established: 1976. Class/group size: 10. Facilities: 1,000 sq ft of teaching space with overhead mirrors and two 20-seat classrooms.

FACULTY: Includes school director Nick McCall, and Kay Wong.

COSTS: C$55-C$190/session. Lodging available at area hotels.

CONTACT: Nick McCall, President, McCall's School of Cake Decoration, Inc., 3810 Bloor St. West, Etobicoke, ON, M9B 6C2 Canada; 416-231-8040, Fax 416-231-9956, decorate@mccalls-cakes.com, www.mccalls-cakes.com.

MY PLACE FOR DINNER

Toronto, ON

Sponsor: Culinary professional. Programs: Hands-on cooking classes: scheduled, private group, corporate entertaining & team-building. Established: 1996. Class/group size: 8-24. Facilities: Kitchen & dining room. Classes can be held in student's home if within 2 hrs of central Toronto.

EMPHASIS: Ethnic cuisines, low-fat, entertaining & holiday menus.

FACULTY: Debbie Diament, cookbook writer, recipe tester & developer.

COSTS: $85/workshop.

CONTACT: Debbie Diament, My Place for Dinner, 56 Arundel Avenue, Toronto, ON, M4K 3A4 Canada; 416-465-7112, Fax 416-465-7112, mpfd@idirect.com, www.myplacefordinner.com.

SILVER SPRINGS CULINARY RETREAT

Flesherton, ON

Sponsor: Private & corporate conference & retreat center. Programs: Culinary weekend retreats feature hands-on & demo classes, wine education, Asian ingredients seminar. Established: 1999. Class/group size: 8-10. Also featured: Include guided hiking, fly-fishing, swimming, cycling, skiing, snowshoeing, yoga, Thai Chi, meditation, spa, area tours.

EMPHASIS: East-West fusion, techniques, wine.

FACULTY: Chef Greg Couillard & hosts Sue & Derek Tennant.

COSTS: C$650 (C$799) includes shared (single) lodging, some meals.

CONTACT: Sue Tennant, Owner/Director, Silver Springs Culinary Retreats, R.R. #4, Flesherton, ON, N0C 1E0 Canada; 800-546-5601, Fax 519-922-1136, stennant@georgian.net, www.silver-springsretreat.com.

SIMPLY INDONESIAN

Toronto, ON

Sponsor: Private cooking school & caterer. Programs: Afternoon, evening & weekend classes on Indonesian cuisine, workshops for youngsters. Established: 2002. Class/group size: 6 hands-on. 80+ programs/yr. Facilities: Kitchen with home professional cooking equipment. Also featured: Catering, cooking at clients' homes, culinary adventure tour.

EMPHASIS: Indonesian cuisine, vegetarian, Rijsttafel.

FACULTY: Owner/teacher Linda Clarke, an Indonesian, is also a recipe developer.

COSTS: $45-$85/class.

CONTACT: Linda Clarke, Owner, Simply Indonesian, 33 Triller Ave., Toronto, ON, M6K 3B7 Canada; 416-523-6875, info@simplyindonesian.com, www.simplyindonesian.com.

WEDGE RITCHER WINE PROGRAMS

Winnipeg, MB

Sponsor: Wine professional. Programs: 1- & 5-session courses. Established: 1990. Class/group size: 20.

FACULTY: Wedge Ritcher, member SWE, teacher certificate, Wine & Spirit Education Trust.

Costs: $80/5-wk course, $25/single course.
Location: Manitoba Liquor Control Commission.
Contact: Wedge Ritcher, M.L.C.C., PO Box 1023, Winnipeg, MB, R3C 2X1 Canada; 204-474-5553, Fax 204-474-7686, writcher@mlcc.mb.ca.

WINE COUNTRY COOKING SCHOOL
Niagara-on-the-Lake, ON

Sponsor: Strewn estate winery. Programs: Hands-on 1- & 2-day culinary weekends, week-long culinary vacations focusing on food, wine & seasonal ingredients. Established: 1997. Class/group size: 16 hands-on. 30 programs/yr. Facilities: An estate winery, includes a teaching kitchen, demo classroom, private dining room & patio. Also featured: Field trips to producers, tutored wine tastings, meals at top Niagara restaurants, corporate team-building events.
Emphasis: Regional cuisine using fresh, seasonal ingredients, cooking with wine, wine pairing.
Faculty: Jane Langdon, proprietor/chief instructor, food writer, charter member of Cuisine Canada, & IACP member. Her husband is winemaker/president of Strewn estate winery. Other instructors incl food writers & cookbook authors.
Costs: Weekend hands-on classes: 2-day C$350; 1-day C$195; couples 1-day classes C$300. 5-day Culinary Vacations C$1,450.
Contact: Jane Langdon, Owner, Wine Country Cooking School, General Delivery, 1339 Lakeshore Rd., Niagara-on-the-Lake, ON, L0S 1J0 Canada; 905-468-8304, Fax 905-468-8305, info@winecountrycooking.com, www.winecountrycooking.com.

CHINA

CHOPSTICKS COOKING CENTRE
Kowloon, Hong Kong

Sponsor: Private trade school. Programs: 1-day to 4-wk individual & group programs, including 2-hr demo classes, half-day tourist classes, 1-day courses, 1- & 12-wk intensive courses. Established: 1971. Class/group size: 15 max. Ongoing programs/yr. Facilities: Fully-equipped kitchen. Also featured: Kitchen & market visits.
Emphasis: Understanding Chinese culinary culture & regional cooking techniques.
Faculty: Cecilia J. Au-Yang, proprietor, with 40+ yrs experience; Caroline Au-Yeung, graduate of hotel mgmt school, with 15+ yrs experience; other culinary professionals.
Costs: Group classes (up to 6 students) begin at $400 for 2-hr demo session; $500+ for a customized 1- to 2-day course. Local lodging starts from $400/wk.
Contact: Cecilia Au-Yang, Managing Director, Chopsticks Cooking Centre, 8A Soares Ave., Ground Floor, Kowloon, Hong Kong, China; (852) 2336-8433, Fax (852) 2338-1462, cauyeung@netvigator.com.

INSPIRASIANS COOKING SCHOOL VACATION
Zhongshan

Sponsor: Professional chef. Programs: 4-day recreational program focusing on the fundamentals of Chinese cooking. Includes hands-on classes, restaurant visits, & sightseeing. Established: 2001. Class/group size: 4-10:1. Facilities: Large cookery demonstration classroom with fully-equipped kitchen area.
Emphasis: Fundamentals of Chinese cooking. Includes soups, meat, vegetable dishes & desserts.
Faculty: Maria Lee, culinary professional, published cookbook author, visiting professor at Chinese univeristies; has appeared on Chinese TV & radio.
Costs: $1,400-$1,600, includes lodging & meals at a lake-side country villa, ground transport.
Location: Zhongshan, in the Province of Guangdong, China.
Contact: May Lee, Owner, InspirAsians Cooking School Vacation, Rm 210, Bank of East Asia Central Tower, 31-37 Des Voeux Road Central, Hong Kong, China; (852) 2522-0361, Fax (852) 2813-6251, info@inspirasians.com, www.inspirasians.com.

PENINSULA ACADEMY CULINARY EXPERIENCE

Hong Kong

Sponsor: The Peninsula Hotel, Hong Kong. Programs: The Culinary Experience features a chef's welcome dinner, tour of hotel kitchens, & 4 days of morning cooking classes & class luncheons. Established: 1997. Class/group size: 10-15. 10 programs/yr. Facilities: Hotel kitchens, restaurants & function rooms. Also featured: The 4-day Chinese Cultural Experience includes Tai Chi, dim-sum prep, market tour, Chinese meals.

EMPHASIS: The Peninsula Hotel restaurant specialities, with chefs presenting themed cuisine.

FACULTY: Chefs of the hotel's restaurants.

COSTS: 4 classes from HK$16,600 (~$2,107)/1 guest or HK$20,600 (~$2,614)/2 guests; includes 4 nights lodging in a Jr Suite, welcome dinner, daily breakfast & lunch, Rolls-Royce transfers.

CONTACT: Director, Peninsula Academy, Peninsula Hotel, Salisbury Rd., Tsim Sha Tsui, Kowloon, Hong Kong, China; (852) 2315 3142, Fax (852) 2311 7107, academy.pen@peninsula.com, www.peninsula.com.

ENGLAND

ACORN ACTIVITIES

Herefordshire

Sponsor: Activity holiday provider. Programs: 2-day gourmet cooking course. Established: 1989. Class/group size: 12. Facilities: Well-equipped kitchen with individual work areas & cookers. Also featured: Study tours, courses, & recreational programs including air, water & motor sports, horseback riding, hunting, shooting, falconry, fishing, arts & crafts, music, languages.

EMPHASIS: Low-fat gourmet cooking.

FACULTY: A professional chef who has appeared on the BBC2 Food & Drink program.

COSTS: Tuition is £100. Lodging, including breakfast, ranges from farmhouses & cottages at £20/night to luxury hotels at £95/night.

CONTACT: Derren Hotchkiss, Accounts Manager, Acorn Activities, P.O. Box 120, Hereford, HR4 8YB England; (44) (0)8707 40 50 55, Fax (44) (0)1432-830110, info@acornactivities.co.uk, www.acornactivities.co.uk.

AGA WORKSHOP

Buckinghamshire

Sponsor: Culinary professional Mary Berry. Programs: 1- & 2-day Aga demo workshops. Established: 1990. Class/group size: 20. 50 programs/yr. Facilities: Watercroft, Mary Berry's home. Also featured: Half Aga cooking, half gardening days.

EMPHASIS: The Aga cooker for grilling & frying, saving fuel, fresh herbs & vegetables, entertaining & holiday cookery.

FACULTY: Mary Berry studied at the Paris Cordon Bleu & Bath College of Home Ec & has a City & Guilds teaching qualification. She is author of 30+ cookbooks & presenter for TV series.

COSTS: 1-day (2-day) workshop £115 (£223) incl VAT. Group bookings, 4 or more, £109/person/day.

CONTACT: Lucy Young, Assistant to Mary Berry, Aga Workshop, Watercroft, Church Rd., Penn, Buckinghamshire, HP10 8NX England; (44) 1494-816535, Fax (44) 1494-816535, agawshop@maryberry.co.uk, www.maryberry.co.uk.

THE ALDEBURGH COOKERY SCHOOL

Aldeburgh, Suffolk

Sponsor: Private school. Programs: Day & weekend hands-on courses on a variety of topics, single-subject master classes. Established: 1999. Class/group size: 10 max. ~100 programs/yr. Facilities: 2 demo rooms, sitting & dining room. Also featured: Corporate programs.

EMPHASIS: Seasonal ingredients.

FACULTY: Co-owners Thane Prince, journalist, TV cook, author of 7 books; Sara Fox, chef/proprietor of the Lighthouse Restaurant in Aldeburgh.

Costs: £110/day or masterclass, £125/fish, shellfish class, £425/weekend includes lunch & dinner.
Contact: Thane Prince & Sara Fox, The Aldeburgh Cookery School, 84 High St., Aldeburgh, Suffolk, IP15 5AB England; (44) 01728-454039, Fax (44) 01728-454039, info@aldeburghcookeryschool.fsnet.co.uk, www.aldeburghcookeryschool.com.

ANNETTE GIBBONS COOKERY
Mawbray, Cumbria

Sponsor: Private school. Programs: Cooking demos. Established: 1996. Class/group size: 8-10. 50-100 programs/yr. Facilities: Converted stable kitchen, dining room, organic kitchen garden.
Emphasis: Skills, local food, traditional recipes.
Faculty: Anette Gibbons, Certificate in Education, 'A' level Domestic Science, City & Guilds Advanced Cooking.
Costs: ~£20, includes lunch.
Contact: Annette Gibbons Cookery, Ostle House, Mawbray, Maryport, Cumbria, CA15 6QS England; (44) 1900 881356, Fax (44) 1900 881356, annette@ostlehouse.fsnet.co.uk.

AUTHENTIC ETHNIC COOKING SCHOOL
London

Sponsor: Private school. Programs: Full-day professional workshops, non-professional classes. Established: 1995. Class/group size: 12 max. 150 programs/yr. Facilities: Chefs' homes & restaurants.
Emphasis: Ethnic world cuisines.
Faculty: 20-30 chefs who teach their own home cuisine.
Costs: £160/day session, £65/evening class.
Contact: Tertia Goodwin, Director, Authentic Ethnic Cooking School, 14 Redcliffe Sq., London, SW10 9JZ England; (44) 020 7373 3651, Fax (44) 0207 854 1271, tertiagoodwin@aol.com.

BOOKS FOR COOKS COOKING SCHOOL
London

Sponsor: Specialty cookbook store. Programs: 3-day hands-on courses, demos, hands-on children's classes. Established: 1988. Class/group size: 8-22. 150+ programs/yr. Facilities: Purpose-built demo kitchen with overhead mirror. Also featured: Gourmet evenings, food & wine evenings, Italian days.
Emphasis: Techniques, Italian & other intl cuisines, Basic Skills Classes.
Faculty: Includes cookbook authors Eric Treuillé, Ursula Ferrigno, Kimiko Barber, Jennifer Joyce, Celia Brooks Brown, Nada Saleh, Sophie Braimbridge.
Costs: £25 for demos to £170 for 3-day courses.
Contact: Eric Treuillé, Workshops, Books for Cooks Cooking School, 4 Blenheim Crescent, London, W11 1NN England; (44) (0)20-7221-1992, Fax (44) (0)20-7221-1517, info@booksforcooks.com, www.booksforcooks.com.

BREAD MATTERS
Melmerby, Penrith

Sponsor: Organic artisan baker Andrew Whitley. Programs: Bread basics, including mixing, fermenting, shaping, proving & baking. Each student makes a variety of products. Specialist options include sourdoughs, yeasted pastries & gluten-free baking. Established: 1976. Class/group size: 12. 20 programs/yr. Facilities: The Village Bakery, which has a separate workstation for each person and a seminar room/library. Also featured: Meals in the Village Bakery Organic Restaurant, which include a dinner and discussion, visits to the adjacent Lake District and Pennine hills.
Emphasis: The why & how of baking, especially sourdoughs.
Faculty: Andrew Whitley, founder of The Village Bakery, assisted by a fellow master baker.
Costs: £295 (£495) for 2-day (5-day) course includes meals in the organic restaurant and materials. Lodging available at extra cost in local bed & breakfasts.
Contact: Andrew Whitley, Breadmatters Ltd, The Tower House, Melmerby, Penrith, Cumbria, CA10 1HE England; (44) (0) 1768 881899, Fax (44) (0) 1768 889146, andrew@breadmatters.com, www.village-bakery.com.

CONFIDENT COOKING

Wiltshire

Sponsor: Private school. Programs: Monthly demos & residential weekend hands-on courses that include market visits, visits to food producers, mushroom forays, sightseeing, & dining in a country home. Established: 1996. Class/group size: 8 hands-on, 25 demo. 36 programs/yr. Facilities: High-tech professional kitchen with overhead mirror. Also featured: Children's classes, private instruction, men-only classes.

EMPHASIS: Vegetarian cuisine, breads.

FACULTY: Cook, author, & food consultant Caroline Yates & guest chefs.

COSTS: £30-£35/class, £315 for weekend courses; includes meals, lodging, & planned activities.

CONTACT: Caroline Yates, Confident Cooking, PO Box 841, Devizes, Wiltshire, SN10 4UX England; (44) (0)1380-812846, cyates@confidentcooking.com, www.confidentcooking.com.

COOKERY AT THE GRANGE

Frome

Sponsor: Private school. Programs: 5-day hands-on course in addition to its certificate program. Established: 1981. Class/group size: 16-24. 8 programs/yr. Facilities: Main kitchen, cold kitchen, herb garden. Also featured: Wine instruction, basic food hygiene certificate.

EMPHASIS: European & intl cuisines, herbs, wine tasting.

FACULTY: Jane & William Averill (Grange-trained) & teaching staff.

COSTS: All-inclusive rates from £790 for 5-day program to £2,390-£2,790 for certificate program.

CONTACT: Jane & William Averill, Cookery at The Grange, Whatley, Frome, Somerset, BA11 3JU England; (44) (0)1373-836579, Fax (44) (0)1373-836579, info@cookery-grange.co.uk, www.cookery-grange.co.uk.

COOKERY SCHOOL AT LITTLE PORTLAND STREET

London

Sponsor: Private school. Programs: Courses for adults & children, lunchtime classes, evening demos. Class/group size: 15 max. Facilities: Custom-designed premises.

EMPHASIS: Techniques, quick & simple food preparation.

FACULTY: Principal Rosalind Rathouse, a professional cook & culinary teacher; demos by visting cooks.

COSTS: £40/session, £210/6-session adult course, £150/4-session childrens' course, lunch classes £150/4 or £210/6.

CONTACT: Rosalind Rathouse, Cookery School at Little Portland Street, 15B Little Portland St., London, W1W 8BW England; (44) (0) 20 7631 4590, information@cookeryschool.co.uk, www.cookeryschool.co.uk.

COOKING WITH CLASS

Herefordshire

Sponsor: Professional chef. Programs: Demos & hands-on classes. Established: 1981. Class/group size: 22 demo/10 hands-on. Facilities: Modernized home kitchen.

EMPHASIS: Techniques, seasonal ingredients, specific topics.

FACULTY: Victoria O'Neill, professional chef 25 yrs, trained at Le Cordon Bleu London. Guest chefs.

COSTS: £35-£55/class, £25/children's class. B&B lodging £65/night, £175-£350/wk.

CONTACT: Victoria O'Neill, Cooking with Class, Ltd., Pyon House, Canon Pyon, Herefordshire, HR4 8PH England; (44) (0)1432 830122/830185, Fax (44) (0)1432 830499, sales@cookingwithclass.co.uk, www.cookingwithclass.co.uk.

THE COOKING EXPERIENCE LTD

Hadleigh, Suffolk

Sponsor: Private school. Programs: 1-day, 2-day & weekend residential hands-on courses for any skill level. Established: 2001. Class/group size: 8. 100+ programs/yr. Facilities: Includes 2 range cookers & cooking utensils. Also featured: Weekends include visits to food producers & vineyards.

EMPHASIS: Theme-based, includes Fruits of The Sea, Quick & Easy Entertaining, Budget Supper Dishes, Aga Masterclass, Tastes of Italy, Christmas Without Tears.
FACULTY: Mark David, chef, caterer, restaurant mgr, hotel/restaurant inspector, radio guest.
COSTS: Day course £99 incl lunch. Evening class £55 incl supper. Residential course from £399 incl meals, 2 nights lodging.
LOCATION: Small town 15 mi from Colchester, 1 hr by train from London.
CONTACT: Mark David, The Mark David Cooking Experience, 9 High Street, Hadleigh, Ipswich, Suffolk, IP7 5AH England; (44) (0) 1473 827568, Fax (44) (0) 1473 828523, info@mdcookeryschool.co.uk, http://cookingexperience.co.uk.

CORDON VERT COOKERY SCHOOL
Altrincham, Cheshire

Sponsor: The Vegetarian Society UK, a registered charity & membership organization. Programs: Weekend & day courses on vegetarian topics in addition to the 4-week diploma course & 1-week Cordon Vert certificate course. Established: 1982. Class/group size: 12 maximum. 40 programs/yr.
FACULTY: Lyn Weller, Principal, & 10 part-time tutors.
COSTS: Weekend residential (non-residential) courses range from £250 (£200); day courses are £65, which includes lunch. Local hotel/motel lodging.
CONTACT: Mureen Surgey, Cooking School Administrator, Cordon Vert Cookery School, Parkdale, Dunham Road, Altrincham, Cheshire, WA14 4QG England; (44) (0) 161-925-2000, Fax (44) (0) 161-926-9182, cordonvert@vegsoc.org, www.vegsoc.org/cordonvert.

DENISE'S KITCHEN
London

Sponsor: Private cookery school. Programs: Jewish cooking demonstrations. Established: 1998. Class/group size: 22-100. Facilities: Mirrors & equipment designed for demonstrations.
EMPHASIS: Presentation skills & new cooking techniques. Modern Jewish kosher cuisine.
FACULTY: Denise Phillips, caterer, author of Modern Jewish Cooking with Style & The Book of Jewish Cooking, writer of cookery columns for London & USA weekly.
COSTS: £55 includes a book.
CONTACT: Denise's Kitchen, PO Box 83, Northwood, Middlesex, HA6 2HD England; (44) (0) 1923 836 456, Fax (44) (0) 1923 826 180, deniseskitchen@easynet.co.uk, www.jewishcookery.com.

FOOD OF COURSE
Sutton, Somerset

Sponsor: Professional cook. Programs: 4-wk residential foundation cookery course; 5-day course emphasizing new foods, recipes & tips; 1-day refresher course on advanced prep & easy entertaining. Established: 2000. Facilities: Farmhouse kitchen with modern appliances. Also featured: Visits to local markets & suppliers.
FACULTY: Lou Hutton, professional cook with 14+ yrs teaching experience, was principal instructor at The Grange for 4 yrs; guest chefs, wine experts &suppliers.
COSTS: Foundation Course £2,450; 5-day New Food Course £720; 1-day Refresher Course £85; 1-day Young Chefs Course £55.
CONTACT: Louise Hutton, Food of Course, Middle Farm House, Sutton, Somerset, BA4 6QF England; (44) (0)1749 860116, Fax (44) (0)1749 860765, louise.hutton@foodofcourse.co.uk, www.foodofcourse.co.uk.

GREEN CUISINE LTD
Kington, Herefordshire

Sponsor: Private school. Programs: 2- to 5-day residential courses include Food & Health, Women's Health, Seeds of Change (weight control), Pregnancy & Babycare. Established: 1995. Class/group size: 6-12. 20 programs/yr. Facilities: Penrhos, a 700-yr-old manor farm. Also featured: Yoga, aromatherapy, walking.
EMPHASIS: Healthful foods, ingredients & preparation methods to improve the diet.

FACULTY: Proprietor Daphne Lambert, nutritionist, chef, author, organic gardener; practitioners.
COSTS: £240-£265/2 days, £295/3 days, includes lodging & meals.
CONTACT: Daphne Lambert, Head of Studies, Green Cuisine Ltd, Penrhos Court, Kington, Herefordshire, HR5 3LH England; (44) 01544 230720, Fax (44) 01544 230754, daphne@greencuisine.org, www.greencuisine.org.

HAVE YOUR CAKE AND EAT IT

New Longton

Sponsor: Cake decorator. Programs: 1-day classes & 6-session cake decorating courses.
EMPHASIS: Cake decoration.
FACULTY: Carol has decorated cakes for 20+ yrs & creates custom wedding cakes.
COSTS: £16/workshop, £45/course.
CONTACT: Carol , Have Your Cake and Eat It, Preston, Lancashire, England; (44) 01772 628 798, haveyourcakeandeatit@lineone.net, www.haveyourcakeandeatit.org.

HAZLEWOOD CASTLE

North Yorkshire

Sponsor: Hotel. Programs: Cookery demos & hands-on Masterclasses. Class/group size: 20/cookery. Facilities: Fully-equipped demo kitchen.
EMPHASIS: Seasonal dishes, individual topics.
FACULTY: Professional chefs.
COSTS: £45/cookery demo, £55/Masterclass.
CONTACT: Hazlewood Castle, Paradise Lane, Hazlewood, Tadcaster, Near York & Leeds, North Yorkshire, LS24 9NJ England; (44) (0)1937-535353, Fax (44) (0)1937 530630, info@hazlewood-castle.co.uk, www.hazlewood-castle.co.uk.

HINTLESHAM HALL

Suffolk

Sponsor: Country hotel. Programs: Demo classes. Class/group size: 12. 20 programs/yr. Also featured: Interior design day, flower arranging, golf, snooker, pigeon shooting, horseback riding, pool, spa.
EMPHASIS: Vegetarian & fish dishes, seasonal menus, herb cookery, sugarcraft, specific topics.
FACULTY: Hintlesham's Chef Alan Ford.
COSTS: £47.50/class. Special rate lodging £98/night includes continental breakfast & VAT.
CONTACT: Claire Hills, Hintlesham Hall, Hintlesham, Ipswich, IP8 3NS England; (44) (0)1473-652268, Fax (44) (0)1473-652463, reservations@hintleshamhall.com, www.hintleshamhall.com.

INSPIRED TO LOVE COOKING

Rutland

Sponsor: Cooking school. Programs: Inspired to Love Cooking course for young people. Chalet Cooks course preparatory to ski season. Established: 1978. Class/group size: 6. Facilities: Country house kitchen in a converted old school. Also featured: Sailboarding, bird watching, cycling, golf.
EMPHASIS: Traditional skills with modern shortcuts.
FACULTY: Miranda Hall, a former teacher/examiner at London's Cordon Bleu Cooking School, studied at the Cordon Bleu in Paris & has a teaching diploma in Home Economics.
COSTS: Inspired to Love Cooking course, non-residential, £285. Chalet Cooks course, residential, £495.
CONTACT: Miranda Hall, Inspired to Love Cooking, Old School House Hambleton, Rutland, LE158TJ England; 44-01572723576, miranda@hall.vispa.com.

ITALIAN SECRETS

Beaconsfield, Bucks

Sponsor: Private school. Programs: UK: Demo & hands-on 1- to 5-day programs in Italian cuisine. Sicily: 1-wk gastronomic holidays that include cooking lessons, trips to wineries, cheese farms, citrus & oil mills, sightseeing. Established: 1995. Class/group size: 18 demo, 12 hands-on. 40 programs/yr. Facilities: High tech kitchens accommodating 12 students. Also featured: Private instruction.

Emphasis: Classic Italian & Sicilian cuisine.
Faculty: Anna Venturi, raised in Milan, learned to cook from grandmother & family cook.
Costs: UK: £80-£250. Sicily: £1280 includes lodging, meals, ground transport, excursions.
Location: UK: Small town 25 mi NW of London. Sicily: Anna Venturi's Italian villa in the northern coastal village of Capo d'Orlando, ~2 hrs from Catania airport.
Contact: Anna Venturi, Owner, Italian Secrets, 13 The Broadway, Penn Rd., Beaconsfield, Bucks, HP9 2PD England; (44) 1494 676136, Fax (44) 1494 681704, enquiries@italiansecrets.co.uk, www.italiansecrets.co.uk.

KILBURY MANOR COOKERY COURSES
Devon

Sponsor: Private school in a 350-year-old farmhouse-guesthouse on six acres. Programs: Short hands-on courses for beginners to professionals. Established: 1995. Class/group size: 1-4. Facilities: Refurbished farmhouse kitchen.
Emphasis: Customized to students' interests.
Faculty: Suzanne Lewis is a home economist with Advanced City and Guilds training, Qualified Teacher and Trainer, former restaurateur, caterer with experience in the food industry.
Costs: £150-£195 for 1-day course and lodging with meals; £295 [one-on-one] for 2 night's lodging and 3 half-day classes; 2 pers: £225; 3 pers: £200; 4 pers: £185 [2002].
Location: Devon, 20 miles from Plymouth/Exeter, 10 minutes from the Moors, ~20 minutes from Dartmouth and the coast.
Contact: Suzanne Lewis, Kilbury Manor Cookery Courses, Kilbury Manor Farm, Colston Road, Buckfastleigh, Devon, TQ11 OLN England; (44) (0) 1364 644079, Fax (44) (0) 1364 644059, suzanne@kilbury.co.uk, www.kilbury.co.uk.

LA PETITE CUISINE
London

Sponsor: Culinary professional Lyn Hall. Programs: 3-session evening classes - Bachelor Cooks. Established: 1977. Class/group size: 1 or 6, 15 for demos. ~30 programs/yr. Facilities: Bulthaup's kitchen studio; private venue in South Kensington. Also featured: Hands-on 1-day workshops, demonstrations, private & corporate classes.
Emphasis: Modern gourmet cuisine, mainly French, Italian, Chinese, Italian, English.
Faculty: Owner Lyn Hall, BA, MFCA, former chef & restaurateur, accredited teacher 24 yrs, certificates in wine, bread, cake decorating, & butchery, & is an Olympic Culinary Gold Medalist.
Costs: 3-day course £230, workshops £89/one day, demos £38, private classes & tutorials start at £190 + VAT.
Contact: Lyn Hall, La Petite Cuisine, 21 Queen's Gate Terrace, London, SW7 5PR England; (44) 207-584-6841, Fax (44) 207-225-0169, lynhall@lapetitecuisine.co.uk.

LE CORDON BLEU – LONDON
London

Sponsor: Private school, sister school of Le Cordon Bleu-Paris. Programs: Daily half-day demonstrations, 1- to 5-day gourmet hands-on sessions, evening classes, 1-month courses. Established: 1933. Class/group size: 10. 50 programs/yr. Facilities: Professionally equipped kitchens; individual workspaces with refrigerated marble tops; demonstration rooms with video & tilted mirror. Also featured: Children's workshops, guest chef demonstrations, First Certificate in Food Safety.
Emphasis: Intensive and comprehensive cuisine and pastry courses.
Faculty: All staff full time. Chefs all professionally qualified with experience in Michelin-starred and fine quality culinary establishments.
Costs: Range from £15-£395.
Contact: Richard O'Leary, Sales & Promotions Executive, Le Cordon Bleu, 114 Marylebone Lane, London, W1U 2HH England; (44) 20-7-935-3503, Fax (44) 20-7-935-7621, london@cordonbleu.edu, http://cordonbleu.edu. Toll free in U.S. & Canada: 800-457-CHEF.

LEITHS SCHOOL OF FOOD AND WINE

London

Sponsor: Private school with cooking agency. Programs: 1- & 4-wk holiday courses, 1-wk fish, healthy eating, Oriental cooking, dinner party, & holiday cooking courses; 10-session beginner to advanced courses, Sat. demos, 5-session Certificate in Wine. Established: 1975. Class/group size: 48 demo, 16 hands-on. Facilities: Demo theatre, 3 kitchens, prep kitchen, library, changing room.

EMPHASIS: Easy entertaining & cookery skills.

FACULTY: 13 full-, 2 part-time. School founder & cookbook author Prue Leith is former Veuve Cliquot Business Woman of the Year. Principal is Caroline Waldegrave.

COSTS: 10-session evening courses £500, Wine Certificate course £265. Housing list provided.

CONTACT: Judy Wilkinson, Registrar, Leiths School of Food & Wine, 21 St. Alban's Grove, London, W8 5BP England; (44) 020 72290177, Fax (44) 020 79375257, info@leiths.com, www.leiths.com.

THE MANOR SCHOOL OF FINE CUISINE

Widmerpool

Sponsor: Private school. Programs: 5-day Foundation course, 4-day Entertaining course, theme weekends, and day and evening courses. Established: 1988. Class/group size: 12. 40 programs/yr. Facilities: Residential school in Georgian manor house with purpose-built kitchens & demonstration theatre. Also featured: Water sports, clay pigeon shooting, horseback riding, golf.

EMPHASIS: Vegetarian, Thai, and Indian cooking and wine courses. Focus on healthy eating, holiday cookery, seasonal menus, Aga cookery, game cookery, specific topics.

FACULTY: Cordon Bleu diploma, head chef of noted restaurants. Member of Cookery & Food Assoc., Craft Guild of Chefs, Chef & Cooks Circle.

COSTS: Inclusive of VAT, tuition is £390 resident (£295 nonresident) for Foundation course, £330 (£285) for Entertaining course, £130 for weekend courses. Lodging at the Manor.

CONTACT: Claire Tuttey, The Manor School of Fine Cuisine, Old Melton Road, Widmerpool, Nottinghamshire, NG12 5QL England; (44) (0)1949-81371.

THE MISTLEY KITCHEN

Mistley, Essex

Sponsor: Small private school. Programs: Hands-on single session & 5-session day, evening & weekend workshops. Lunchtime & evening demonstrations. Established: 2001. Class/group size: 14 hands-on, 22 demo. 90 programs/yr. Facilities: Kitchen in a Georgian townhouse with the latest equipment including Viking ranges & an Earthstone wood-fired oven. Also featured: Culinary field trips, bespoke workshops & tours, private party classes.

EMPHASIS: Seasonal ingredients. The kitchen & the table as centres of creativity & pleasure.

FACULTY: Sherri Singleton, proprietor/chief instructor, restaurateur & executive chef, food writer, & IACP member. Other instructors include wine experts, food writers & guest chefs.

COSTS: Single session hands-on classes £45, 5-session classes $200, lunch & evening demos £25.

CONTACT: Sherri Singleton, Owner/Director, The Mistley Kitchen, Acacia House, High St., Mistley, Essex, CO11 1HD England; (44) 1206 391545, Fax (44) 1206 390122, sherrisingleton@aol.com, www.mistleykitchen.com.

MOSIMANN'S ACADEMY

London

Sponsor: Private school. Programs: Half- & one-day demos & courses that focus on intl cuisine, fine dining & wines, chocolate & pastry arts, specialized food presentation, food & flowers. Established: 1996. Class/group size: 60. 50 programs/yr. Facilities: New seminar & demo theater, library of Anton Mosimann's 6,000 cookery books. Also featured: Tailor-made corporate courses.

EMPHASIS: The Anton Mosimann philosophy (Cuisine Naturelle), which eschews fats & alcohol.

FACULTY: Academy chef & mgr Simon Boyle, assisted by 2 full- & 2 part-time staff. Anton Mosimann & guest chefs Shaun Hill, Brian Turner, Jean-Christophe Novelli & Jamie Oliver.

COSTS: £125 for demo & lunch at Mosimann's Dining Club in Belgravia, £65 demo only.

CONTACT: Simon Boyle, Academy Chef & Manager, Mosimann's Academy, 5 William Blake House, The Lanterns, Bridge Lane, London, SW11 3AD England; (44) (0) 20 7326 8366, Fax (44) (0) 20 7326 8360, academy@mosimann.com, www.mosimann.com.

MY WAY COOKING

London & Somerset

Sponsor: Culinary professional Victoria Blashford-Snell. Programs: Cookery demonstrations. Established: 1996. Class/group size: 12-16. Facilities: Professional, full-equipped kitchen. Also featured: Hands-on classes for small groups.

EMPHASIS: Methods of advance preparation, party cooking, building confidence.

FACULTY: Victoria Blashford-Snell, caterer and author of Hors D'Oeuvres.

COSTS: From £35.

CONTACT: Victoria Blashford-Snell, My Way Cooking, Glyn House, West Hill, Wincanton, Somerset, BA9 9BY England; (44) (0) 1963 31937, Fax (44) (0) 1963 824517, victoria-matthews@lineone.net.

PADSTOW SEAFOOD SCHOOL

Padstow

Sponsor: Established by the BBC TV chef Rick Stein. Programs: Residential & non-residential 1-, 2-, & 4-day hands-on/demo seafood courses designed around a daily lunch menu; 1-day fish filleting courses. Established: 2000. Class/group size: 16. 142 programs/yr. Facilities: Purpose-built facility features with the latest equipment & dining area overlooking the Camel Estuary. Also featured: Cliff walks, beaches, water sports, golf courses, fishing trips, local visits, trips to Newlyn Fish Market.

EMPHASIS: Sauces for seafood; Thai, Chinese, French, Italian, S. Indian & Australian fish cookery.

FACULTY: Paul Sellars, 25+ yrs restaurant experience including sous chef at Rick Stein's Seafood Restaurant & running his own fish restaurant.

COSTS: £155-£615/1- to 4-day non-residential courses include lunch; £615-£1,395/2- to 4-day residential courses includes meals, lodging, VAT. Participants' guests stay on B&B basis.

CONTACT: Debbie Hill, Cookery School Mgr, Padstow Seafood School, Riverside, Padstow, PL28 8BY England; (44) (0) 1841 532700, Fax (44) (0) 1841 532942, seafoodschool@rickstein.com, www.rickstein.com.

PATRICIA STEFANOWICZ WINE PROGRAMS

London

Sponsor: Wine professional. Programs: 1- to 6-session courses. Established: 1988. Class/group size: 5-15. 2 programs/yr.

EMPHASIS: Grape varieties around the world, winemaking, wine faults, Wine & Art and Wine & Music tasting events.

FACULTY: Patricia Stefanowicz, Masters in Architecture/Fine Arts, Higher Nat'l Diploma in Horticulture (Oenology), Wine & Spirit Ed Trust Diploma with Honors, & is a member of SWE.

COSTS: £15-£100/course.

CONTACT: Patricia Stefanowicz, Patricia Stefanowicz Wine Programs - Vino Vino, 31 Randolph Crescent, Little Venice, London, W9 1DP England; (44) 207 286 4505, Fax (44) 207 266 3166, vinovino@nildram.co.uk.

PAUL HEATHCOTE'S SCHOOL OF EXCELLENCE

Manchester

Sponsor: Private school. Programs: Demonstrations and hands-on classes on a variety of topics. Established: 1997. Class/group size: 12 hands-on, 40 demo. Facilities: Professionally-equipped kitchen with 6 individual work spaces, demonstration auditorium with projector and screen.

FACULTY: Paul Heathcote, chef and owner of four restaurants, and his staff of instructors.

CONTACT: Marketing Director, Paul Heathcote's School of Excellence, Jackson Row, Deansgate, Manchester, M2 5WD England; (44) (0)161-839-5898, Fax (44) (0)161-839-5897, cookeryschool@heathcotes.co.uk, www.heathcotes.co.uk.

RAYMOND BLANC'S ECOLE DE CUISINE

Oxford

Sponsor: Le Manoir, 12th century manor house. Programs: 5-day cooking vacations that feature hands-on stage 1, 2, & 3 classes; 1-2 day courses including fusion, nutrition, & la cuisine moderne. Established: 1991. Class/group size: 10. Year-round programs/yr. Facilities: Individual work areas in the restaurant kitchen. Also featured: Themed courses include vegetarian, fish & shellfish, Christmas, 1-day dinner parties, nutrition.

EMPHASIS: Contemporary French cuisine, including appetizers, fish, meat, vegetables, pastries.

FACULTY: Chef Raymond Blanc owns & operates Le Manoir. Stephen Bulmer, director of L'Ecole.

COSTS: From £550 for 1-day courses to £1,775. Includes all meals & luxury lodging at Le Manoir aux Quat' Saisons, which has the highest classification of Relais & Chateaux. Lodging free for non-cooking guests.

CONTACT: Raymond Blanc, Chef Patron, Le Manoir aux Quat' Saisons, Great Milton, Oxford, OX9 7PD England; (44) (0)1-844-278-881, Fax (44) (0)1-844-278-847, lemanoir@blanc.co.uk, www.manoir.com. In the U.S.: Judy Ebrey, Cuisine International Inc., P.O. Box 25228, Dallas, TX 75225; 214-373-1161, Fax 214-373-1162, Email CuisineInt@aol.com, www.cuisineinternational.com.

REAL ENGLAND – WORCESTERSHIRE COOKERY

Worcestershire

Sponsor: Specialty tour company. Programs: Dining in private homes, excursions including cookery schools, gardens. Established: 1989. Class/group size: 8-16. 2-5 programs/yr. Facilities: Modern purpose-built kitchen with work stations & overhead mirror. Also featured: Individual visits to food related venues.

EMPHASIS: British cuisine.

FACULTY: Professional cooks & teachers. Tour leaders Tina Boughey & Jenny Mills trained in college for 5 yrs.

COSTS: £895/week includes bed & breakfast lodging, most meals, excursions.

CONTACT: Tina Boughey & Jenny Mills, Real England, Pudding Bag, Elm Hill, Sinton Green, Worcestershire, WR2 6NU England; (44) 01905-640126, (44) 01905-26529, Fax (44) 01905-640126, (44) 01905-26529.

RED EPICURUS

London

Sponsor: Gourmet & culinary organization. Programs: Demo & participation classes that focus on a selected cookbook or chef menu. Established: 2002. Class/group size: 8-15. 24+ programs/yr. Also featured: Wine & spirits tastings, culinary tours, food & wine pairing.

EMPHASIS: Food & wine education.

FACULTY: 15+ rotating faculty, all experienced in their fields.

COSTS: £25+/class.

CONTACT: Karey Butterworth, Director, Red Epicurus, PO Box 31601, London, W11 2XF England; (44) (0) 7900691632, karey@redepicurus.com, www.redepicurus.com/calendar.html.

ROBERT REES AND THE COUNTRY ELEPHANT

Bisley, Gloucestershire

Sponsor: Country Elephant restaurant. Programs: Customized courses using local produce from Stroud Farmers Market & other sources. Established: 1994. Also featured: Private dining, lectures, food advice.

EMPHASIS: Whole school approach to food & nutrition.

FACULTY: Robert Rees, chef for the Country Elephant restaurant & Stroud Farmers' Market, nominated for BBC Radio 4 Best Food Educator.

CONTACT: Robert Rees, Director/Chef, Robert Rees and The Country Elephant, Norwich House, High St., Bisley, Gloucestershire, GL6 7AA England; (44) (0)1452770872, Fax (44) (0)1452770872, robertrees@btopenworld.com.

ROSEMARY SHRAGER'S COOKERY COURSES AT SWINTON PARK

Masham, Ripon, North Yorkshire

Sponsor: Castle hotel. Programs: 1- to 5-day demo & hands-on cooking courses. Local excursions. Established: 2003. Class/group size: 14 max. 10 programs/yr. Facilities: 2 professional kitchens.

EMPHASIS: Techniques in classic cooking using local produce.

FACULTY: Rosemary Shrager has been a professional chef for 20+ yrs. She has a TV series & has worked for Pierre Koffman at Tante Claire in London and for Jean-Christophe Novelli.

COSTS: £75/day, £1,275/5-days includes shared lodging in Swinton Park, a 30-bedroom luxury castle hotel on 200 acres bordering the Yorkshire Dales Natl Park. £200 additional for single lodging.

CONTACT: Bridget Miller Mundy, Rosemary Shrager's Cookery Courses at Swinton Park, Swinton Park, Masham, Ripon, North Yorkshire, HG4 4JH England; (44) (0) 1765 680 947, Fax (44) (0) 1765 680 947, bridgetflodabay@yahoo.com, www.rosemaryshrager.co.uk.

SONIA M. STEVENSON

Lot Valley, France; Various locations, Great Britain

Sponsor: Culinary professional Sonia Stevenson. Programs: 2-day hands-on courses in Sauce Making & Fish Cookery, Entertaining with Ease, one-on-one courses. Established: 1992. Class/group size: 6. 20 programs/yr. Facilities: Private kitchens. Also featured: One-week residential hands-on course in France studying the food of the Lot Valley.

FACULTY: Sonia Stevenson, a Master Chef of Great Britain for 25 years & the first woman in Great Britain to be awarded a Michelin star for cuisine.

COSTS: £230 for 2 days, £400 for private day course. Residential course in France £1350. Non-participating partner £300.

CONTACT: Sonia Stevenson, The Old Chapel, Bethany, Trerulefoot, Saltash, Cornwall, PL12 5DA England; (44) 01752 851 813, Fax (44) 01752 851 911, sonia@soniastevenson.com, www.soniastevenson.com.

SQUIRES KITCHEN INTERNATIONAL SCHOOL OF SUGARCRAFT

Farnham, Surrey

Sponsor: Private school. Programs: 1-hour to 3-day demo and participation courses. Established: 1987. Class/group size: 12 hands-on/35 demo. 74+ programs/yr. Facilities: A kitchen with specialized equipment and materials. Also featured: Classes for youngsters, private instruction.

FACULTY: 17 full- and part-time. Members of the British Sugarcraft Guild. Guest tutors include Eddie Spence, Alan Dunn, Toribi Peck.

CONTACT: Course Coordinator, Squires Kitchen, Int'l School of Sugarcraft & Cake Decorating, 3 Waverley Lane, Farnham, Surrey, GU9 8BB England; (44) (0)1252-734309, Fax (44) (0)1252-714714, school@squires-group.co.uk, www.squires-group.co.uk.

SRI'S KITCHEN

London

Sponsor: Culinary professional. Programs: Half- & full-day Southeast Asian cooking classes; demos & workshops. Established: 2002. Class/group size: ~12. ~40 programs/yr. Facilities: Newly-equipped kitchen. Also featured: Private lunches & dinner parties.

EMPHASIS: Indonesian, Thai & Malaysian cuisines.

FACULTY: Culinary professional Sri Owen. 20 yrs experience writing & teaching SE Asian cooking.

COSTS: £48 half-day, £100 full-day. Payment in $ & Euros accepted.

CONTACT: Sri Owen, Sri's Kitchen, 96 High St. Mews, Wimbledon Village, London, SW19 7RG England; (44) 20 8946 7649, Fax (44) 20 8946 2180, sriowen@compuserve.com, www.sriowen.com.

A TABLE

Richmond, Surrey

Programs: Hands-on cooking courses. 4 evening or morning classes weekly. 1-day theme classes. Established: 2000. Class/group size: 7-9. Facilities: Martina's kitchen, purpose-built for instructing.

EMPHASIS: International modern cuisine that can be prepared in advance.

Faculty: Martina Lessing.
Costs: ~£95 for 4-class course, £25-£30 for single class.
Contact: Martina Lessing, A Table Cooking Classes & Catering, 7 Arlington Road, Richmond, Surrey, TW10 7BZ England; (44) 0208 940 9910, martina@lessing.freeserve.co.uk.

TANTE MARIE SCHOOL OF COOKERY
Surrey

Sponsor: Private school. Programs: Certificate courses thrice yearly, 3- to 5-day hands-on courses, 1-day theme demonstrations. Established: 1954. Class/group size: 12/group max. 3 programs/yr. Facilities: Include 5 modern teaching kitchens, a mirrored demonstration theatre, and a lecture room. Also featured: Wine instruction, private group demonstrations.
Emphasis: Basic and advanced skills, wine appreciation, specific subjects.
Faculty: 12 full- & part-time. Qualified to teach adult ed. Many have held catering positions. Well-known TV cookery demonstrators, a noted wine expert, & local tradesmen also present.
Costs: From £3,650 including all food.
Location: Turn-of-the-century country mansion near Woking, ~25 min by train from London.
Contact: Marcella O'Donovan, Principal, Tante Marie School of Cookery, Woodham House, Carlton Rd., Woking, Surrey, GU21 4HF England; (44) (0)1483-726957, Fax (44) (0)1483-724173, info@tantemarie.co.uk, www.tantemarie.co.uk.

TWO BABES FROM BRITAIN
Essex

Sponsor: Caterers Alyson Cook & Maxine Martens. Programs: 1-wk culinary tour based in an English country mansion that combines cooking classes, visits to local markets, cheesemakers & food producers, sightseeing & dining in fine restaurants. Established: 1996. Class/group size: 16. 2 programs/yr.
Faculty: Alyson Cook & Maxine Martens are from London & have 30 yrs combined catering experience. Cook graduated from Le Cordon Bleu & cooked for the royal family. Martens has been a Hollywood caterer for 10+ yrs.
Costs: $4,999 includes airfare from NYC, lodging, meals, planned activities.
Contact: Alyson Cook, Partner, Two Babes From Britain, P.O. Box 40281, Pasadena, CA 91114; 626-791-9757, 818-784-8274, Fax 626-791-9698, 818-784-8463, alysoncook@earthlink.net.

THE VEGETARIAN COOKERY SCHOOL
Bath

Sponsor: Private but allied to Demuths Vegetarian Restaurant in Bath. Programs: Hands-on 1- to 3-day vegetarian cooking courses including international, breadmaking, spices & herbs, gluten-free, entertaining menus. Established: 1999. Class/group size: 8 max. ~75 programs/yr.
Emphasis: Vegetarian cuisine.
Faculty: Rachel Demuth, Jan Berridge, Nick Troup.
Costs: £45-£225.
Contact: The Vegetarian Cookery School, 30 Belgrave Crescent, Bath, BA1 5JU England; (44) (0)1225 789682, us@vegetariancookeryschool.com, www.vegetariancookeryschool.com.

WOODEND COOKERY
Woodend, Egremont, Cumbria

Sponsor: Culinary professional. Programs: Informal cookery demos that cover traditional & modern techniques with emphasis on the use of seasonal & local produce. Facilities: Home kitchen.
Faculty: Grainne Jakobson.
Contact: Grainne Jakobson, Woodend Cookery, Woodend House, Woodend, Egremont, Cumbria, CA22 2TA England; , gmjakobson@aol.com, www.woodendcookery.50megs.com.

EUROPE

AMELIA CULINARY ADVENTURES

Cyprus, Italy, Malta, Tunisia

Sponsor: Culinary & cultural travel company. Programs: 2-day to 2-week culinary & cultural vacations featuring cooking classes, winery tours, tastings, visits to cheese farms, pastry shops, & markets. Established: 1983. Class/group size: 6-15. Facilities: 4- & 5-star hotels. Travel by mini-coach or chauffeured cars. Also featured: Chauffeur-driven holidays, 3-night independent vacations with 3 half-day cooking lessons.

EMPHASIS: Mediterranean cuisine.

FACULTY: Owner Dawn Bosco, ASTA; Cindy Hill, IACP. Contributing faculty: cookbook authors Eleonora Consuolo & Anna Tasca Lanza; food writer Claudia Caruana, journalist Eleonora Consoli.

COSTS: $2,300-$3,500,land only. $175+ for single supplements.

LOCATION: Mediterranean locations including Sicily, Sardinia, Malta, Cyprus & Tunisia.

CONTACT: Cindy B. Hill, Amelia Culinary Adventures, 176 Woodbury Rd., Hicksville, NY 11801; 800-742-4591, Fax 516-822-6220, culinary@ameliainternational.com, www.ameliainternational.com.

ART OF LIVING– CULINARY & LIFE STYLE TOURS WITH SARA MONICK

France, Italy, Morocco, Spain

Sponsor: Culinary & travel professional Sara Monick. Programs: 5- to 11-day culinary tours that include hands-on & demo classes. Established: 1986. Class/group size: 8-14. Also featured: Visits to markets, food producers, wineries, private homes & gardens; dining at fine restaurants; sightseeing; language classes; custom tours for private groups.

EMPHASIS: French, Italian, Spanish & Moroccan cuisines.

FACULTY: Tour escort Sara Monick, a cooking instructor since 1977 & Certified Member of the IACP, owns The Cookery in Minneapolis. She studied with Madeleine Kamman, Jacques Pepin, Nicholas Malgieri & Giuliano Bugialli. Local chefs.

COSTS: $2,300-$4,000, which includes double occupancy lodging, most meals & planned excursions. Lodging in first-class hotels or private homes.

CONTACT: Sara Monick, Hilliard & Olander Ltd., 226 East Myrtle, Stillwater, MN 55082; 651-275 8960, 800-229-8407, Fax 651-275-8962, Diane@hilliardolander.com, www.hilliardolander.com.

BEV GRUBER'S EVERYDAY GOURMET TRAVELER

France, Italy, United States

Sponsor: Culinary professional Beverly Gruber. Programs: Small group culinary tours that feature visits with local artisan food producers. Established: 1988. Class/group size: 4-12. 6-8 programs/yr. Also featured: Trip planning services in Italy for individuals desiring independent travel.

EMPHASIS: Italian, French & regional US cuisines.

FACULTY: Beverly Gruber, professional chef and culinary guide, has lead international tours since 1988, working with professional colleagues in Italy, France & US.

COSTS: $1,500-$2,900 includes shared lodging.10% discount on select trips.

LOCATION: Tuscany, Venice, Liguria/Cinque Terre, Rome, Sicily, Umbria, Puglia, Provence;U.S.A.

CONTACT: Beverly Gruber, Everyday GOURMET TRAVELER, 5053 NE 178th St., Seattle, WA 98155; 206-363-1602, 888-636-1602, Fax 206-363-1602, gourmetravel@aol.com, www.gourmetravel.com.

BIKE RIDERS

France & Italy

Sponsor: Travel company. Programs: 1-week tours to Italy & France that combine hands-on cooking classes & 15-40 miles biking/day with guest chefs. Established: 1990. Class/group size: 16 max. 14 programs/yr. Facilities: Inn & restaurant kitchens. Also featured: Market visits, wine classes, winery tours, olive oil tastings.

EMPHASIS: Regional Italian & French cuisine.

Faculty: Chefs of well-known restaurants.

Costs: $2,820/Umbria & Sicily; $2,920/Burgundy, Tuscany, Provence. Includes support van, lodging, most meals, planned activities. Bike rental $150. Single supplement $420-$480.

Contact: Eileen E. Holland, Director, Bike Riders, P.O. Box 130254, Boston, MA 2113; 800-473-7040, 617-723-2354, Fax 617-723-2355, info@bikeriderstours.com, www.bikeriderstours.com.

COOKEURO

France & Italy

Sponsor: Travel company. Programs: 1-wk hands-on culinary vacations: l'Amore di Cucina Italiana in Italy, La Cuisine de Provence in France. Include visits to wineries, markets, food producers, dining in fine restaurants, cultural evenings. Established: 1992. Class/group size: 12. 9 programs/yr. Facilities: Italy: kitchens of Locanda di Praticino (Tuscany), Il Rotolone (Umbria) & Locanda dei Cinque Cerri (Emilia Romagna). France: kitchen of Domaine de la Fontaine.

Emphasis: Tuscan, Umbrian, Bolognese & regional Italian cuisines; Provencale & regional French.

Faculty: Cristina Blasi, Gabriella Mari, own Scuola di Arte Culinaria Cordon Bleu; Silvia Maccari, author; Eros Patrizi, chef, Trattoria del Festival; Marcello Dall'Aglio, chef, Locanda del Castello. Jean-Claude Aubertin, member Academie Culinaire de France.

Costs: $2,495 includes meals, shared lodging, planned activities. Single supplement $400, non-cook/guest $2,295.

Location: Pomino (Tuscany), Gualdo Cattaneo (Umbria), Sasso Marconi (Emilia Romagna), Italy; L'Isle sur la Sorgue (Provence).

Contact: Ralph P. Slone, Inland Services, Inc., 708 Third Ave., 13th flr., New York, NY 10017; 212-687-9898, incook@earthlink.net, www.cookeuro.com.

A COOK'S TOUR

France, Italy, South Africa

Sponsor: Culinary tour operator. Programs: Guided culinary tours that feature hands-on cooking lessons taught by local chefs. Established: 2000. Class/group size: ~12. ~15 programs/yr. Also featured: Visits to local wineries & food production facilities, cultural excursions, restaurant dining.

Emphasis: Regional cuisines of France & Italy.

Faculty: Provence: Marie-Claude Ricard; Northern Italy & the Veneto: Rinaldo Biraldi; Tuscany: Gianluca Pardini; Mediterranean: Paolo Monti; Tuscany: Marcello Crimini.

Costs: From $2,160 includes meals, lodging, planned activities.

Contact: Patty LeDonne, Partner, A Cook's Tour, 221 214th NE, Sammamish, WA 98053; 800-726-6388, Fax 425-557-9906, patty@acookstour.com, www.acookstour.com.

CUISINE INTERNATIONAL INC.

Brazil, England, France, Greece, Italy, Portugal, United States

Sponsor: Tour operator specializing in culinary vacations. Programs: Cooking schools & culinary tours. Established: 1987. Class/group size: 8-20. Facilities: Hotel & restaurant kitchens, private homes, castles. Also featured: Excursions to food-related & historical sites; winery visits, tastings, shopping.

Emphasis: Regional cuisines & cultures.

Faculty: Owner Judy Ebrey, CCP.

Costs: $2,250-$4,700/week including lodging, meals, planned activities, ground transport.

Location: Italy: Tuscany, Amalfi, Puglia, Sicily, Venice, Bologna, Rome. France: Provence, Paris, Gascony. Brazil: Ouro Preto. England: Oxford. Portugal: Portel. Greece: Ikaria. US: Charlottesville, VA.

Contact: Judy Ebrey, Owner, Cuisine International, P.O. Box 25228, Dallas, TX 75225; 214-373-1161, Fax 214-373-1162, info@cuisineinternational.com, www.cuisineinternational.com.

CULINARY TOURS

France, Italy, New Zealand, Spain, Thailand, United States

Sponsor: Culinary professional Glenn Watz, travel company & cookware store. Programs: Intl food-focused tours featuring demo classes, market tours, wine tastings, restaurant meals. Established: 1994. Class/group size: 12-25. 12 programs/yr. Facilities: Hotels, restaurants, chateaux, villas.

Emphasis: International food culture.
Faculty: Glenn Watz, professional chef for 23 yrs, and other chefs in destination cities.
Costs: $1,195-$2,295 includes shared lodging, most meals, tours.
Contact: Glenn Watz, Owner, Culinary Tours, 2450 Gladys Ave., Beaumont, TX 77702; 409-832-4929, Fax 409-833-5134, grwatz@earthlink.net, www.culinarytours.net.

EPICULINARY INC.

Italy, France, Spain, Mexico, United States *(See display ad above)*

Sponsor: Tour company specializing in cooking vacations to Italy, France, Spain, Mexico & the U.S. Programs: 2- to 14-night cooking vacations featuring cooking lessons, excursions, & wine tastings. Established: 1999. Class/group size: 2-8. 100+ programs/yr. Facilities: Cooking schools, restaurant kitchens, country villa kitchens. Also featured: Customized group travel, individual itineraries, specialized tours.
Emphasis: Regional cuisine of Italy, France, Spain, Southwestern U.S., N. California, & Mexico.
Faculty: Michelin-star chefs such as Helene de Stoquelet of Italy & Luis Irizar of Spain, 4-star chef Martin Rios of Santa Fe, Master Chef Rene Berard of France.
Costs: $575-$3,000 includes lodging (from 5-star hotels like Villa d'Este to a country farmhouse), meals, wine tastings, & excursions.
Location: Rome, Lake Como, Florence, San Gimignano, Spoleto, Venice, Italy; Provence, Bordeaux, Paris, Burgundy, France; San Sebastian, Costa del Sol, Andalusia Spain; Oaxaca & Cuernavaca, Mexico; Santa Fe, NM, Napa & Calistoga, CA.
Contact: Catherine Merrill, Owner/President, Epiculinary Inc., 321 E. Washington Ave., Lake Bluff, IL 60044; 888-380-9010, 847-295-5363, Fax 847-295-5371, info@epiculinary.com, www.epiculinary.com.

FOOD & WINE TRAILS

France, Italy, New Zealand, Spain

Sponsor: HMS Travel Group, which produces travel programs for Cooking Light Magazine, Fine Cooking Magazine, the American Wine Society, & the Culinary Institute of America. Programs: 5- to 12-day cooking vacation programs that feature hands-on classes, winery tours, visits to food-related sites, & cultural activities. Established: 1983. Class/group size: 20-25. 10+ programs/yr.
Emphasis: Regional cuisine & wines.
Faculty: Culinary & wine experts including chefs, cookbook authors, wine judges.
Costs: $2,200-$3,300 includes lodging, most meals, planned activities.
Contact: Diane Hudson, Marketing Manager, Food & Wine Trails, 707-A Fourth St., Santa Rosa, CA 95404; 800-367-5348, 707-526-2922, Fax 707-526-6949, diane@hmstravel.com, www.foodandwinetrails.com.

CLASSIC JOURNEYS

France & Italy

Sponsor: Tour provider. Programs: Week-long tours featuring hands-on cooking instruction, walks, & visits to cultural sites, wineries, olive oil mills, local markets. Established: 1995.

Class/group size: ~10 (max 18). 25 programs/yr. Facilities: Cooking instruction in chateaux, local homes & restaurants. Also featured: Walking, cultural & natural history tours available.

FACULTY: Local chefs & guides knowledgeable about the regional history & culture.

COSTS: ~$2,500/wk includes shared lodging, ground transport, most meals.

CONTACT: Hilary Achauer, Communications Director, Classic Journeys, 5580 La Jolla Blvd., #104, La Jolla, CA 92037; 800-200-3887, Fax 858-454-5770, moreinfo@classicjourneys.com, www.classicjourneys.com.

GOURMET ON TOUR

Europe, Asia, Australia, United States

Sponsor: Travel company specializing in gourmet,cooking, & wine tours. Programs: 1-day to 1-week culinary experiences with hands-on cooking courses & wine appreciation. Established: 2000. Class/group size: 1-18. 70 programs/yr. Facilities: Professionally-equipped hotel & restaurant kitchens, private villas, chateaus, farmhouses. Also featured: Truffle & mushroom hunts, spa treatments, cycling tours, corporate events, master classes.

EMPHASIS: Regional cuisines & wine appreciation.

FACULTY: Restaurant chefs, cookbook authors, wine experts.

COSTS: $100-$3,900 ranging from day classes to packages that include deluxe or private lodging, meals & excursions.

CONTACT: Judith von Prockl-Palmer, Managing Director, Gourmet On Tour, Berkeley Square House, 2 Fl, Berkeley Square, Mayfair, London, W1J 6BD England; UK: (44) 20-7396-5550, US: 800-504-9842, Fax (44) 20-7900-1527, info@gourmetontour.com, www.gourmetontour.com.

THE INTERNATIONAL KITCHEN

France, Italy, United States

Sponsor: Travel company specializing in culinary tours. Programs: 1-day classes, & week-long & shorter vacations that include hands-on instruction in the regional cuisine, market visits, winery tours, visits to food producers, dining in private homes & fine restaurants, sightseeing, cultural activities. Established: 1995. Class/group size: 2-12. 50 programs/yr. Facilities: Varies from restaurant kitchens to home kitchens. Also featured: Some programs include spa treatments, walking, bicycling, or truffle hunting.

EMPHASIS: French & Italian cuisine.

FACULTY: Restaurant chefs, regional experts.

COSTS: France: $2,250-$3,290, which includes B&B to deluxe lodging, meals, planned activities. Italy: $1,660-$3,950, which includes farmhouse to deluxe lodging, meals, planned activities.

LOCATION: France: Provence, Burgundy, Bordeaux, Paris. Italy: Tuscany, Umbria, Amalfi Coast, Sicily, Veneto, Lake Como, Emilia-Romagna. USA: Chicago.

CONTACT: Karen Herbst, The International Kitchen, Inc., One IBM Plaza, 330 N. Wabash, Ste. 3005, Chicago, IL 60611; 800-945-8606, Fax 312-803-1593, info@intl-kitchen.com, www.theinternationalkitchen.com.

JC FOOD & WINE TOURS

England, France, Italy, Spain

Sponsor: Special interest tour operator. Programs: Customized itineraries to Italy, France, Napa Valley. Occasional trips to other countries in the UK, Europe, southeast Asia. Established: 1992. Class/group size: 6-18. Also featured: Small group tours to visit wineries, private villas, agritourismos, markets, food/wine producers; dining at fine & local restaurants, truffle hunts, sightseeing, meeting locals. Private tours offered.

EMPHASIS: Food & wine travel focusing on specialties of the regions.

FACULTY: Winemakers, food producers, chefs, restaurateurs, culinary consultants. Joyce Capece, a 30-yr travel professional, specializes in food & wine tours & special interest travel.

CONTACT: Joyce Capece, CTC, DS, JC Food & Wine Tours, 2101 Golden Rain Rd., #7, Walnut Creek, CA 94595; 925-938-9635, Fax 925-938-5692.

L'ECOLE DES CHEFS RELAIS & CHATEAUX

Europe, United States, Canada, Japan, South Africa, Spain *(See display ad above)*

Sponsor: Relais & Chateaux. Programs: 2 & 5-day internship programs at Michelin- & Mobil-starred Relais Gourmands restaurants. Open to amateur cooks. Certificate upon completion. Established: 1998. Class/group size: 1:1. Facilities: The kitchens of participating Relais Gourmands restaurants. Also featured: Group classes & internships for two people available at some locations.

EMPHASIS: One-on-one instruction with exec chef, garde-manger, saucier, sauté cook, pastry chef.

FACULTY: Michelin- & Mobil-starred chefs, including Patrick O'Connell, Thomas Keller, Charlie Trotter, Gary Danko, Rick Tramonto, Michel Troisgros, Alain Passard, Michel Rostang.

COSTS: 2-day (5-day) programs $1,100-$1,400 ($1,900-$2,950). Does not include travel or lodging. Must submit application with non-refundable $25 fee. ~80% of applicants accepted.

LOCATION: Los Angeles, San Francisco, & Napa Valley, California; Washington, DC; Atlanta, GA; Chicago, IL; New Jersey; New York; Charleston, SC; Belgium; Montreal & Vancouver, Canada; Denmark; Paris & other locales, France; Germany; Great Britain; Japan; Luxembourg; Netherlands; Norway; South Africa; Spain; Switzerland

CONTACT: Jennifer L. Iannolo, Director, L'Ecole des Chefs Relais & Chateaux, 11 E. 44th St.,, #707, New York, NY 10017; 877-334-6464, Fax 212-856-0193, info@ecoledeschefs.com, www.ecoledeschefs.com.

PROVENCE ON YOUR PLATE

France & Italy

Sponsor: Culinary professional Connie Barney. Programs: 7- to 10-day culinary vacation programs that include classes in contemporary & traditional dishes, winery tours, dining in fine restaurants & private homes, visits to markets & food producers, sightseeing. Established: 1993. Class/group size: 6-16. 10-12 programs/yr. Facilities: Fully-equipped kitchens in venues ranging from farmhouses to luxury hotels. Also featured: Food artisan visits, hand-made crafts.

EMPHASIS: Regional French & Italian cookery using fresh herbs, fish, olive oil, fruit, vegetables.

FACULTY: Connie Barney, CCP, holder of Grand Diplome from La Varenne, former director of Roger Vergé's cooking school in Mougins, recipe consultant for Markets of Provence.

COSTS: From $2,250/8 days in a country inn to $5,250/10 days in a luxury hotel. Includes shared lodging, most meals, ground transport, planned activities.

CONTACT: Connie Barney Wilson & Andrew Wilson, Owners/Directors, Provence on Your Plate, 915 E. Blithedale, #10, Mill Valley, CA 94941; 800-449-2111, 415-389-0736, Fax 415-389-0736, info@provenceonyourplate.com, www.provenceonyourplate.com.

RHODE SCHOOL OF CUISINE

Theoule sur Mer, France; Vorno, Tuscany, Italy; Marrakech, Morocco

Sponsor: Private school. Programs: 7-day hands-on cooking vacation programs. Established: 1996. Class/group size: 10-14. ~45 programs/yr. Facilities: Luxury villas with full demo kitchen. Large dining facilities. Also featured: Cultural excursions, dining at Michelin-star restaurants, market visits, mushroom hunting in season, activities for non-cooking guests.

EMPHASIS: Italian, French & Moroccan cuisines, sauces, pastry, wine & cheese.
FACULTY: Chefs of the regions:Frederick Riviere (France/Morocco),Giancarlo Talericco (Italy).Guest chef: Anissa Helou (Morocco).
COSTS: $1,995-$2,895 includes shared lodging, ground transport, meals, planned excursions. Non-cook rate $1,795-$2,395.
CONTACT: Beverley Ellis, Client Services Director, Rhode School of Cuisine c/o Luxury Destinations Ltd., The Courtyard Suite, Hambledon House, Vann Lane, Hambledon, Surrey, GU8 4HW England; 888-254-1070, (44) 1428-68-51-40, Fax (44) 1428-68-34-24, info@rhodeschoolofcuisine.com, www.rhodeschoolofcuisine.com.

TASTE OF EUROPE
France & Italy

Sponsor: Teachers' Travel, a travel agency focusing on special interest vacations that include cooking & walking holidays. Programs: Five- to seven-day hands-on cooking holidays in Provence and Tuscany that focus on preparing food the old-fashioned way. Established: 1994. Class/group size: 8 max. 40 programs/yr. Facilities: Teaching kitchens with specialized cooking and baking equipment (wood-fired baking oven). Also featured: Market visits, sightseeing excursions, wine-tasting.
EMPHASIS: Regional cuisine of Tuscany and Provence.
FACULTY: Signora Rener of La Chiusa, René Bérard of Hostellerie Bérard, Sylvie Lallemand of Les Mégalithes. All are English-speaking chefs.
COSTS: $769-$950 includes lodging, breakfast and dinner plus cooking classes.
LOCATION: One location in Italy: La Chiusa in Umbria. Two locations In Provence: Hostellerie Bérard in the Bandol region near Marseilles and Les Mégalithes in the Luberon.
CONTACT: Cathy Kinloch, Tour specialist, Taste of Europe, 21 St. Clair Ave. East #1003, Toronto, ON, M4T 1L9 Canada; 800-268-7229, 416-922-2232, Fax 416-922-8410, teacherstravel@cs.com, www.taste-of-europe.com.

THREE PEAR CULINARY & CULTURAL RETREATS
France, Italy, Morocco, Portugal, Spain

Sponsor: Culinary tour provider. Programs: 3- to 8-day cooking & cultural programs in Europe that include regional cooking courses, artisan culinary tours, wine tastings, olive picking & pressing, truffle hunting, local excursions. Established: 2002. Class/group size: ~8-12. 50+ programs/yr. Facilities: Fully-equipped professional & home kitchens in European villas & chateaux. Also featured: Spa, golf, hiking, swimming, tennis, yoga & meditation, horseback riding, language classes.
EMPHASIS: Authentic regional cooking, easy-to-prepare healthful recipes, vegetarian cuisine.
FACULTY: Founder Mareya Burton, 10+ yrs experience in the food industry; native cooks & experienced chefs, private chateau & villa owners.
COSTS: $1,300-$2,900 includes meals, lodging, excursions, ground transportation.
CONTACT: Mareya Burton, Founder, Three Pear Culinary & Cultural Retreats, Five Night Heron, Aliso Viejo, CA 92656; 949-374-3984, Fax 949-215-3827, information@cookineurope.com, www.cookineurope.com.

VANTAGGIO TOURS
France, Italy, Morocco

Sponsor: Travel company. Programs: 1-week travel programs that feature cooking classes, visits to markets, wineries, farms, churches, cultural sites. Established: 1998. Class/group size: 12 max. Facilities: Restaurant kitchens & Il Faè Cooking Center. Also featured: Hands-on classes.
EMPHASIS: Tuscan & foods of Veneto Region withgluten-free classes.
FACULTY: Marco Fatorell, chef for Il Faè.
COSTS: $1400-$2,850/wk, includes shared first-class lodging or bed/breakfast inn.
CONTACT: Margot Cushing, CTC, Principal, Vantaggio Tours c/o Linden Travel Bureau, 41 E. 57th St., New York, NY 10022; 800-808-6237 x259, 212-784-0259, Fax 212-421-2790, mcushing@lindentravel.com, www.vantaggio.com.

WINE-KNOWS TRAVEL
France & Italy

Sponsor: Travel company specializing in wine & gourmet food tours. Programs: 1-2 week vacations that feature private tastings at wineries, cooking classes, visits to artisanal food producers, dining at Michelin-star restaurants, winemaker dinners. Established: 1978. Class/group size: 14. 1 programs/yr. Facilities: Michelin-star restaurants, professional kitchens, artisanal bakeries, wineries. Also featured: Visits to historical & cultural sites, outdoor antique & food markets.

FACULTY: June Forkner-Dunn & Toby Dunn, members of the SWE & AIWF. June has guided groups to Europe since 1978, taught wine classes at the Univ of London & American Embassy in Paris. Toby is a wine collector.

COSTS: $2,739-$4,179 includes lodging in chateaux, villas & castle hotels, meals, planned activities.

LOCATION: France: Burgundy, Provence, Rhone Valley. Italy: Venice-Friuli, Portofino Peninsula.

CONTACT: June Forkner-Dunn, Wine-Knows Travel, 4382 Bridgeview Dr., Oakland, CA 94602; 510-336-0303, Fax 510-336-0303, dunn@wineknowstravel.com, www.wineknowstravel.com.

FINLAND

HELSINKI CULINARY INSTITUTE
Helsinki & Mustio Manor

Sponsor: Owner/Chef Gero Hottinger. Programs: Individualized 1-day, hands-on theme workshops. Instruction in Finnish, Swedish, German, English. Established: 1994. Class/group size: 10-18. Facilities: Teaching kitchen, conference & dining room.

EMPHASIS: New & special flavors of Finland, Scandinavian cookery.

FACULTY: Chef de Cuisine Gero Hottinger, Pia Wahlberg, visiting chefs from Finland & Europe.

COSTS: $80-$220.

CONTACT: Pia Wahlberg, Sales Manager, Helsinki Culinary Institute, Uudenmaankatu 7 B, Helsinki, 120 Finland; (358) 9-68117212, Fax (358) 9-68117213, toimisto@kulinaarineninstituutti.com, http://kulinaarineninstituutti.com.

FRANCE

ABM FRENCH COOKING COURSES
Montpellier

Sponsor: Private education institution & vocational training company. Programs: 7-day cooking vacation program featuring 4 cooking classes & culinary excursions; 7-day wine program with 12 hrs of wine courses & wine excursions. Established: 1996. Class/group size: 6-8. 6 programs/yr. Facilities: Professional kitchen in an inn close to Montpellier. Professional wine tasting equipment. Also featured: French language courses may be combined with cooking or wine classes.

EMPHASIS: Classical French & regional cuisine & wines.

FACULTY: Chefs, restaurateurs, oenologists, wine growers.

COSTS: Cooking course €810, wine course €700.Lodging available in a 3- or 2-star hotel or residential hotel (one-room flat or apartment).

CONTACT: Anaïs Baurens, Director, ABM, 23 avenue Saint Lazare, Parc des Roses D, Montpellier, 34000 France; (33) 4 67 02 75 00, Fax (33) 4 67 02 76 00, info@abm-france.com, www.abm-france.com.

THE ASSOCIATION CUISINE AND TRADITION (ACT)
Arles

Sponsor: Private school. Programs: Evening, full-day, weekend, half- and full-week hands-on programs that feature seasonal ingredients. Established: 1996. Class/group size: 4-8. Facilities: Traditional Provencal kitchen outfitted with professional equipment for teaching. Also featured: Half- & full-wk programs include excursions such as market visits, winery tours, herb collecting, visits to an olive oil mill, cheese maker, honey collector & bakery.

Emphasis: Provencal & Mediterranean cuisine, dishes from the instructor's 1,000+ recipes.
Faculty: Author of l'Archeologie de la Cuisine, business member IACP.
Costs: €100/eve class, €180/full-day, €750/4 days, €1200/full wk. Lodging at school available, hotels within walking distance.
Contact: Madeleine Vedel, Course Coordinator, The Association Cuisine and Tradition (ACT), 30, rue Pierre Euzeby, Arles, 13200 France; (33) (0)4-90-49-69-20, Fax (33) (0)4-90-49-69-20, actvedel@wanadoo.fr, www.cuisineprovencale.com.

AT HOME WITH PATRICIA WELLS
Provence & Paris

Sponsor: Journalist & author Patricia Wells. Programs: 5-day cooking vacations that include 4 hrs of daily hands-on instruction. 4-day truffle workshops. Established: 1995. Class/group size: 6-10. 13 programs/yr. Facilities: 18th-century Provençal farmhouse kitchen with a wood-fired bread oven. Cooking studio in Paris with the latest equipment. Also featured: Includes visits to local markets, cheese & wine shops & bakers, wine & oil tastings, restaurant dining.
Emphasis: Regional foods & wines.
Faculty: Patricia Wells has lived in France since 1980, is restaurant critic of The International Herald Tribune, & author of 8 books, including Bistro Cooking & The Paris Cookbook.
Costs: $3,500 includes meals & planned activities. Recommended lodging list supplied.
Location: Provence: Ms. Wells' hilltop home outside Vaison-la-Romaine, ~30 mi from Avignon. Paris: central Saint-Germain-des-Pres on the Left Bank.
Contact: Judith Jones, Program Coordinator, At Home with Patricia Wells, 708 Sandown Place, Raleigh, NC 27615; , Fax 919-845-9031, JJ708@bellsouth.net, www.patriciawells.com.

AUFRAGERE COOKERY SCHOOL
Fourmetot, Normandy

Sponsor: Private cookery school in French manor house. Programs: 4-day cookery courses, mostly demo with some hands-on. Includes wine tastings & trips to local market, cheese merchant, boulangerie. Established: 1996. Class/group size: 4-8. 20-25 programs/yr. Facilities: Domestic kitchen & dining room, sitting-room with fire-place, garden terrace. Also featured: Customized cookery tours of Normandy, Versailles & the Loire.
Emphasis: New ideas in French cuisine, easy-to-do dinner parties & entertaining.
Faculty: Nicky Dussartre, Cordon Bleu Chef. Regis Dussartre, vintner & cheese specialist, who oversees the organic farming & makes the Calvados, cider & pommeau.
Costs: €550/4-day course includes meals & lodging.
Location: Restored 18th-century Normandy manor on 8 acres of farmland in Fourmetot, 6 km from Pont Audemer, ~90 min from Paris.
Contact: Regis & Nicky Dussartre, Le Manoir de L'Aufragere, PO Box: La Croisee, Fourmetot, Normandy, 27500 France; (33) 2 32 56 91 92, Fax (33) 2 32 57 75 34, regis@laufragere.com, http://laufragere.com.

BASQUE CUISINE
Biarritz

Sponsor: Private school. Programs: 3- to 6-day cooking vacations that feature hands-on cookery sessions, trips to local markets, vineyards, cheese producers and culinary landmarks. Established: 2001. Class/group size: 2-8. 38 programs/yr. Facilities: Well-equipped new kitchen. Also featured: Golf, surfing, walks in the Pyrenees, horseback riding, white water rafting, fishing, sightseeing, tennis.
Emphasis: Basque, Spanish, & French cuisine.
Faculty: Two instructors: one Cordon Bleu-trained with 20+ years experience, one an international chef with 30+ years experience.
Costs: €900/3 days, €1,800/6 days includes meals & planned activities.
Location: Ahetze, a 15-minute drive from Biarritz airport.

Contact: Stephen & Carolyn Harrington, Basque Cuisine, 551 Chemin D'Aguerria, Ahetze, 64210 France; (33) 559 418187, info@basquecuisine.com, www.basquecuisine.com.

BOUDREAUX'S – COOKING ON THE FRENCH RIVIERA

French Riviera

Sponsor: Master Chef Allan Boudreaux. Programs: Tailor-made cooking classes in the student's villa. Established: 2000. Class/group size: 1-5 or 6. Also featured: Holiday villas for rent. Chef Boudreaux available as a private chef.

Emphasis: Personalized cooking courses for individuals or small groups.

Contact: Hanne Boudreaux, Boudreaux's - Cooking on the French Riviera, 462 rte des Vallettes Sud, Tourrettes s/Loup, 6140 France; (33) 493592610, Fax (33) 493592736, allan@stratege.net.

CHATEAU COOKING IN THE LOIRE VALLEY

Beaumont-en Veron & Chinon

Sponsor: Culinary professional. Programs: 6 days of cooking & exploring the Loire Valley with a professional chef, including 1 day of cooking with a Michelin-star chef. Established: 2001. Class/group size: 8-16. 4 programs/yr. Facilities: The chateau kitchen, which is outfitted with a La Cornue range & prep tables. Also featured: Swimming, sightseeing, winetasting, visits to vineyards & artisanal cheesemakers.

Emphasis: New recipes & techniques.

Faculty: Chef Mondiale Marc Vogel, an instructor at the California Culinary Academy for the last 6 years. He cooked the inaugural dinner for the president of Peru.

Costs: $3,200/wk, includes shared chateau lodging, meals, & local transport.

Contact: Holly Le Du, Asst., Chateau Cooking in the Loire Valley, 100 Varennes #3, San Francisco, CA 94133; 415-576-9007, Fax 925-979-1196, chefmarc@hotmail.com, www.chateaudetilly.com.

CHATEAU COUNTRY COOKING COURSE

Montbazon-en-Touraine

Sponsor: Denise Olivereau-Capron and her children, Xavier & Anne. Programs: 6-day participation courses. Established: 1986. Class/group size: 8-12. 3-6 programs/yr. Facilities: The chateau's renovated kitchen, lounges, dining rooms, 15-hectare park, swimming pool, tennis court, rowboat on river. Also featured: Dining at fine restaurants and visits to the Tours flower market, the chateaux of the region, a goat cheese farm, the Chinon market, and the caves of Vouvray with wine tasting.

Emphasis: French regional cuisine.

Faculty: Chef Freddy LeFebvre.

Costs: Course fee of 12,500 FF single, 11,500 FF double, includes chateau lodging, meals, wine tastings, planned excursions. Complimentary stay for 8 paying guests.

Location: Le Domaine de la Tortiniere, a 19th century manor-house chateau in the Loire Valley.

Contact: Denise, Anne & Xavier Olivereau-Capron, Owners, Chateau Country Cooking Course, Montbazon en Touraine, 37250 France; (33) (0)247-34-35-00, Fax (33) (0)247-65-95-70, domaine.tortiniere@wanadoo.fr, www.tortiniere.com.

CHATEAU MEYRE COOKING SCHOOL

Bordeaux

Programs: 5-day Masterchef Adventures featuring French cooking classes, food & wine pairing, vineyard tours & tastings, fine dining, Arcachon Bay boat tour to explore the oyster beds. Class/group size: 10 max. Also featured: Wine tour programs also offered.

Emphasis: French cuisine including fish & seafood, poultry & meat, desserts.

Faculty: Well-known local chef.

Costs: $2,500. Includes 5 days lodging at Chateau Meyre. Single supplement $200.

Location: 18th-century estate in central Medoc, 30 km from Bordeaux.

Contact: Sophie Viterale, Chateau Meyre Cooking School, 908B, Lippo Centre, Tower 2, 89 Queensway, Hong Kong; (852) 2918 9492, Fax (852) 2521 2626, michael@winebond.com, www.winebond.com.

CHATEAU DE QUARANTE

Quarante

Sponsor: B&B. Programs: French hands-on cooking classes & gourmet tours. Market & producer visits. Also featured: Wine tours, guided sightseeing.

EMPHASIS: Mediterranean cuisine.

COSTS: €1100/4 nights includes shared lodging at the Chateau de Quarante, meals, excursions.

LOCATION: 18th-century château in Languedoc, southern France, near Beziers, Montpellier & Carcassonne. 30 minutes from beaches, 20 minutes from the Cévennes Mountains.

CONTACT: Nicole & Klaus Neukirch, Chateau de Quarante, Quarante, France; (33) 4 67 89 40 41, Fax (33) 4 67 89 40 41, chateau.quarante@wanadoo.fr, www.chateaudequarante.com/cooking.htm.

CHOCOLATE WALKS PARIS

Paris

Sponsor: Culinary professional. Programs: Full-day custom tours concentrating on chocolate, confectionery, & pastry shops in Paris. Can also include visits to wine emporiums, cheese caves, & restaurant equipment supply shops. Established: 2001. Class/group size: 1-12. Also featured: Week-long culinary tours with Anne Block of Take My Mother Please, as well as other groups.

EMPHASIS: Confectionery & pastry.

FACULTY: David Lebovitz, author of Room for Dessert, attended Callebaut College in Belgium & Ecole Lenôtre in Paris. He was a pastry chef at Chez Panisse & Monsoon restaurants.

COSTS: €500/day.

CONTACT: David Lebovitz, Chocolate Walks Paris, Paris, France; , david@davidlebovitz.com, www.davidlebovitz.com.

COOK IN FRANCE WITH LES LIAISONS DELICIEUSES

Several locations, France; Morocco

Sponsor: Culinary tour company. Programs: 1-wk vacations in different provinces that include 12 hrs of hands-on cooking instruction. Established: 1994. Class/group size: 8-10. 10-12 programs/yr. Facilities: Hotel & restaurant kitchens with individual workspaces. Also featured: Visits to wineries, food producers, markets, & restaurants, sightseeing, hiking & biking. Custom trips to various regions of France.

EMPHASIS: French regional cuisine.

FACULTY: Founder Patricia Ravenscroft is tour director & translator. Classes are taught by Michelin-star restaurant chefs & proprietors.

COSTS: $1,990-$3,990, includes lodging, meals. Lodging: Hotel Les Pyrenees (Basque), L'Auberge de la Truffe (Dordogne), Auberge La Feniere (Provence), Chateau d-Amondans (Jura), Chateau St. Paterne (Normandy), Bastide St. Antoine (Côte d'Azur).

LOCATION: France: includes Alsace, Bordeaux, Brittany, Normandy, Dordogne, Jura, Provence, the Pays-Basque, the Côte d'Azur.

CONTACT: Patricia R. Ravenscroft, Program Founder & Director, Cook in France with Les Liaisons Delicieuses, 4710 - 30th St. N.W., Washington, DC 20008; 877-966-1810, 202-966-1810, Fax 202-966-4091, info@cookfrance.com, www.cookfrance.com.

COOKERY LESSONS IN THE SOUTH-WEST OF FRANCE

Bordeaux & Saint Emilion

Sponsor: French chef Stéphane Brieff. Programs: French cooking lessons of a few hours to gastronomic holidays up to one week. Holidays feature wine-tasting, market visits & excursions. Customized classes also offered. Class/group size: 2-12. Facilities: The Châteaux's traditional family kitchens. Also featured: Swimming, fishing, forest walks. Vineyards, wineries, golf course & horseback riding nearby.

EMPHASIS: Traditional regional cuisine of southwest France, local history & culture.

FACULTY: Stéphane Brieff, French chef with 10 yrs gastronomic experience. Classes available in English & French.

Costs: €700-€2,000 includes lodging, meals, planned activities.
Location: Château de Courtebotte in Saint Emilion in southwest France, 10 minutes from Saint Emilion, 20 minutes from Bordeaux. Château Meyre in Medoc.
Contact: Stéphane Brieff, Cookery Lessons in the South West of France, 1 Chemin des Bouvreuils, Saint Médard d'Eyrans, 33650 France; (33) 05 56 72 68 09, stephane.brieff@wanadoo.fr, www.classicfrenchcookinginbordeaux.com.

COOKERY LESSONS AND TOURAINE VISIT

Brehemont

Sponsor: Maxime & Eliane Rochereau in the 18th-century Le Castel de Bray et Monts. Programs: 1-wk hands-on vacation programs that include morning instruction & afternoon tours of chateaux, visits to wineries, shopping excursions. Established: 1983. Class/group size: 2-8. 32 programs/yr. Facilities: The manor's restaurant kitchen.
Emphasis: Gastronomic French cuisine.
Faculty: Chef Maxime Rochereau, former executive chef at the Ritz Carlton in Chicago.
Costs: $1,660 includes lodging at the manor, meals, wine, planned activities.
Location: A vineyard village on the Loire River in the chateau region, 16 mi from Tours.
Contact: Maxime Rochereau, Cookery Lessons and Touraine Visit, Brehemont, Langeais, 37130 France; (33) (0)247-96-70-47, Fax (33) (0)247-96-57-36, cooking-class-infrance@wanadoo.fr, www.cooking-class-infrance.com.

COOKING AT THE ABBEY

Salon-de-Provence

Sponsor: The Hostellerie Abbaye de Sainte Croix resort. Programs: 3-, 4-, & 7-day vacation participation courses; afternoon classes (min 6 students) on request. Established: 1987. Class/group size: 6-12. Facilities: Restaurant kitchen with 4 ovens & 12 work stations. Also featured: Local sightseeing & vineyard visits.
Emphasis: Provençal cuisine.
Faculty: Chef P. Morel of the Abbey's Michelin 1-star restaurant.
Costs: €1,042/4 days, €2,020/7 days, includes most meals, lodging in the 12th-century Abbey's Roman-style rooms, planned activities. Additional afternoon class €116.
Location: The Abbey, a member of Relais & Chateaux, 20 mi west of Aix-en-Provence.
Contact: Catherine Bossard, Director, Cooking at the Abbey, Abbaye de Sainte Croix, Route Val-de Cuech, Salon-de-Provence, 13300 France; (33) (0)490-56-24-55, Fax (33) (0)490-56-31-12, saintecroix@relaischateaux.fr, www.relaischateaux.fr/saintecroix. US Contact: Michael Giammarella, EMI Int., Box 640713, Oakland Gardens, NY 11364-0713; 800-484-1235, #0096; 718-631-0096; Fax 718-631-0316.

COOKING COURSES IN BURGUNDY

Grancey le Chateau

Sponsor: Private cookery school & tour organizer. Programs: Hands-on short cooking courses & 1-wk gastronomic holidays featuring visits to the vineyards of Burgundy & Champagne, cultural & culinary excursions. Established: 1994. Class/group size: 10 max. 12 programs/yr. Facilities: 200-yr-old converted farmhouse with modern facilities. Also featured: Gourmet weekends in Burgundy for private groups; 1- & 2-day short courses near Canterbury, England.
Emphasis: Cuisine of France using fresh seasonal ingredients.
Faculty: Michel Robolin, an English-speaking French chef who has run restaurants in France, taught in the UK, France, & USA, & consults for restaurants. Penny Easton trained in England.
Costs: From £395/4-day course including lodging, meals & planned activities, to £975/1-wk gastronomic holiday including lodging, meals, & tours to Burgundy, Champagne, Chablis, Alsace, Jura.
Contact: Penny Easton, Burgundy Encounters, Ltd., Garden House, Chillenden, Canterbury, Kent, CT3 1YA England; (44) 1304-841136, cell (44) 077-88414927, Fax (44) 1304-841136, info@cookingcourses.co.uk, www.cookingcourses.co.uk.

COOKING WITH FRIENDS IN FRANCE

Chateauneuf de Grasse *(See display ad above)*

Sponsor: Vacation school on the property once shared by Julia Child & Simone Beck. Programs: 6-day participation courses. Established: 1993. Class/group size: 8. 28-30 programs/yr. Also featured: Visits to the Forville Market, a butcher shop, cheese ripener, cutlery shop, & Michelin 2-star restaurant kitchens; demo by a French chef.

EMPHASIS: French cuisine, including techniques, tricks, menu-planning, lighter dishes.

FACULTY: Proprietor/instructor Kathie Alex apprenticed at Roger Vergé's Le Moulin de Mougins, assisted well-known chefs at the Robert Mondavi Winery, studied catering at Ecole Lenotre, & studied with & assisted Simone Beck at her school.

COSTS: ~$2,350 includes shared lodging (most with pvt baths), breakfasts, lunches, cheese tastings, planned excursions (car required). Lodging at La Pitchoune or La Campanette, private homes formerly owned by Julia Child & Simone Bec.

LOCATION: The Cote d'Azur, ~9 mi from Cannes, 4 mi from Grasse, 20 mi from Nice Intl Airport.

CONTACT: Kathie Alex, Owner, Cooking with Friends in France, 696 San Ramon Valley Blvd., #102, Danville, CA 94526-4022; 800-236-9067 (US), (33) 493-60-10-56 (France), Fax (33) 493-60-05-56, info@cookingwithfriends.com, www.cookingwithfriends.com.

COOKING IN PROVENCE

Crillon le Brave

Sponsor: Hostellerie de Crillon le Brave, member of Relais & Chateaux. Programs: 5-day/6 night hands-on cooking vacation courses. Established: 1992. Class/group size: 8. 4 programs/yr. Facilities: The hotel's restaurant kitchen. Also featured: Market visits, winery tour, truffle hunting, visits to Avignon & other Provence sites, dining at the hotel & fine restaurants, golf, tennis, cycling, hiking.

EMPHASIS: Provencal & Mediterranean cuisine.

FACULTY: Chef de Cuisine Philippe Monti, a native of Provence, trained at Pic, l'Esperance, Auberge de l'Ill, & Taillevent, plus 2 other members of his brigade. Classes taught in English.

COSTS: $2,800 ($3,200) includes meals, shared (single) lodging at Hostellerie de Crillon le Brave, planned excursions; supplement for non-cooking partners is $1,300.

CONTACT: Valérie Mansis, Cooking in Provence, Place de l'Eglise, Crillon le Brave, 84410 France; (33) (0)490-65-61-61, Fax (33) (0)490-65-62-86, crillonbrave@relaischateaux.fr, www.crillonlebrave.com.

COOKING IN PROVENCE

Dieulefit, Provence

Sponsor: Hans Meijer & Candee Christoforides, hosts of cooking, painting & photography workshops from their home in Provence. Programs: Hands-on instruction plus daily excursions including open air market, wine tastings, wild herbs & edibles hunt, goat farm visit, picnics, on-site lunch with painters. Established: 1999. Class/group size: 5-8. 12-15 programs/yr. Facilities: The original kitchen of the Chateau with individual workstations. Also featured: Strolls through villages, shops & galleries.

EMPHASIS: Creative Provençal cuisine & the chefs' personal techniques.

FACULTY: Jacqulyn van Beugen, Maggie Zimmerman, NY food stylist Rori Trovato.

Costs: $2,650 includes 6 nights at the Chateau, guided excursions, ground transportation, most meals.
Location: The Chateau de Mazenc, a mansion with swimming pool & walled garden in Dieufelt, a village in the Drome Provençal region.
Contact: Hans Meijer, Director, Cooking in Provence, P.O. Box 155, Woodstock, VT 5091; 802-457-5169, Fax 802-457-1806, info@artinprovence.com, www.cookinginprovence.com.

DISCOVER FRANCE

France

Sponsor: Tour operator specializing in activity tours in France. Programs: 5- to 8-day cooking programs that feature regional cooking classes, restaurant dining, market visits. Some offer optional truffle hunt. 7-day Bordeaux wine tour. Established: 1994. Class/group size: 6-10. 5-10 programs/yr. Facilities: French manors with teaching kitchens.
Faculty: Master Chefs & Certified Wine Experts.
Costs: $750-$2,000 includes lodging & breakfast; some may include lunch or dinner.
Location: Alsace, Brittany, Loire Valley, Normandy, Provence.
Contact: K Moore, Sales, Discover France, 8690 E. Via de Ventura, S-220, Scottsdale, AZ 85258; 480-905-1235, 800-960-2221, Fax 480-905-1307, sales@discoverfrance.com, www.discoverfrance.com.

ECOLE DES TROIS PONTS

Roanne *(See display ad above)*

Sponsor: French cooking & language institute in a château. 1-wk courses include: French Country Cooking courses in English, French Pastry, French & Cooking, Wine & Gastronomy. Features 4 afternoon hands-on cooking or pastry classes, 3 morning market visits with guided excursion, optional wine course. Established: 1991. Class/group size: 10. 14 programs/yr. Facilities: Classes, meals & lodging are in the Château. Also featured: Cooking-only option (instruction in English), French & Cooking option. Also General, Intensive & Private French instruction.
Emphasis: French Country Cooking, Pastry, Wine.
Faculty: Chef Jean-Marc Villard for French Country Cooking, Meilleur Ouvrier de France Chef Alain Berne for Pastry. Wine grower Simon Hawkins for Wine.
Costs: €1,190-€1,340 for Cooking or Pastry course, €1,390-€1,540 for Cooking or Pastry & French course. Includes single or twin room with private facilities & meals. Pool, tennis, equestrian center nearby.
Location: The 18th-century Château de Mâtel is on 32 acres of park & forest, 5 min from central Roanne in the Burgundy/Beaujolais/Auvergne area, 1 hr from Lyons, 3 hrs from Paris.
Contact: Mr. René Dorel, Ms. Valérie Perez, Ecole des Trois Ponts, Château de Mâtel, Roanne, 42300 France; (33) 4-77-71-53-00, Fax (33) 4-77-70-80-01, info@3ponts.edu, www.3ponts.edu.

ECOLE LENÔTRE

Plaisir Cedex

Sponsor: French gastronomy school. Programs: 2- to 4-day participation courses for amateur cooks. Established: 1970. Class/group size: 12.

EMPHASIS: Basics, regional specialties, pastries, wine & food pairing, theme menus.

FACULTY: 4 instructors are recipients of the Meilleur Ouvrier de France. Founded by Gaston Lenôtre & managed by Marcel Derrien, Meilleur Ouvrier de France in pastry-confectionery.

LOCATION: ~30 mi from Paris, 6 mi from Versailles.

CONTACT: Marie-Anne Dufeu, École Lenôtre, 40, rue Pierre Curie-BP 6, Plaisir Cedex, 787373 France; (33) (0)1-30-81-46-34, Fax (33) (0)1-30-54-73-70, ecole@lenotre.fr, www.lenotre.fr.

ECOLE RITZ-ESCOFFIER

Paris

Sponsor: Private school in the Ritz Paris. Programs: 1-week hands-on theme and pastry courses, half-day workshops, demonstrations Monday & Thursday afternoons. Established: 1988. Class/group size: 10 hands-on/40 demo. Facilities: 2,000-sq-ft custom-designed facility includes a main kitchen, pastry kitchen, conference room/library, changing rooms. Also featured: Wine tastings, children's courses, custom-designed programs for groups.

EMPHASIS: Themes include brasserie & bistro cooking, Provencal specialties, sauces, chocolate.

FACULTY: 4 full-time. School Director Jean-Philippe Zahm.

COSTS: Demos 45.75€, themed courses start at 488€/3 days, Art of French Pastry course 885€/wk, César Ritz course 915€/wk, César Ritz Escoffier course 5336€/6 wks. Lodging packages available.

CONTACT: M. Jean-Philippe Zahm, Director, Ecole Ritz-Escoffier, 15, Place Vendôme, Paris Cedex 01, 75041 France; (33) (0)143-16-30-50, Fax (33) (0)1-43-16-31-50, ecole@ritzparis.com, www.ritzparis.com.

EVE'S FEAST

Paris

Sponsor: Professional chef. Programs: Hands-on classes, ethnic food tours to Paris markets. Courses taught in French or English. Established: 1998. Class/group size: 5 max (10 for tours). Facilities: Home-size professional kitchen in a private townhouse. Also featured: Private tutoring.

EMPHASIS: Includes party buffets & canapes, jams & preserves, sherbets, granita & ice-cream, Jewish holiday food, medieval recipes, floral foods, personal creations.

FACULTY: Eve Tribouillet-Rozencweig, professional home chef, food consultant, food writer.

COSTS: Group classes $150/half-day, $250/day. 10% discount for groups of 3+. Private tutoring 40% addtl.

LOCATION: Newly redecorated 1930's townhouse in La Butte aux Cailles.

CONTACT: Eve Tribouillet-Rozencweig, Eve's Feast, 9 rue des Iris, Paris, 75013 France; (33) 145892040, (33) 6826855556, Fax (33) 145892060, evetribouillet@idea4u.com.

FAMOUS PROVENCE

Goult, Luberon

Sponsor: Chef Patrick Payet. Programs: One-week cooking vacations that include daily hands-on classes preparing 3-course menus, guided tours, visits to markets & food producers. Established: 1998. Class/group size: 4-6. ~15 programs/yr. Facilities: Restaurant kitchen.

EMPHASIS: Provencal cuisine.

FACULTY: Patrick Payet, owner-chef of Restaurant 'Le Tonneau'.

COSTS: $1,900 includes continental breakfasts & 6-course dinners, lodging in an 18th-century house restored by Patrick Payet, & daily guided tours.

CONTACT: Patrick Payet, Owner, Famous Provence, Place de l'Ancienne Mairie, Goult, 84220 France; (33) (0)4-90-72-22-35, Fax (33) (0)4-90-72-22-35, famous.provence@wanadoo.fr, www.leluberon.net/famous-provence.

FRANÇOISE MEUNIER'S KITCHEN
Paris

Sponsor: Culinary professional. Programs: Hands-on classes featuring preparation of French meal; diploma after 20 classes. Established: 1997. Class/group size: 8-10. Facilities: Modern, purpose-designed kitchen. Also featured: Demos for groups of 12-15, visits to food markets, young people's workshops, private lessons.

Emphasis: French cooking emphasizing shortcuts.

Faculty: Françoise Meunier worked in luxury hotel kitchens. She teaches in French & English.

Costs: €90/class, €360/5 classes.

Contact: Françoise Meunier's Kitchen, 7, rue Paul-Lelong, Paris, 75002 France; 33 (0) 1 40 26 14 00, Fax 33 (0) 1 40 26 14 08, fmeunier@easynet.fr, www.fmeunier.com.

FRENCH COOKING CLASSES – A WEEK IN PROVENCE
Nyons, Provence

Sponsor: Private owners. Programs: 5-day cooking vacations featuring hands-on classes, cultural excursions, meal with French family, wine tour/tasting, visits to artisans/craftsmen & open air market. Established: 1999. Class/group size: 10 max. 4 programs/yr. Facilities: Restored & fully-equipped Provencal farm kitchen with 6 burner gas stove, work tables with bar stools. Also featured: Hiking, cycling, swimming, horseback riding.

Emphasis: French cuisine basics, specializing in Provencal foods & techniques, cultural immersion.

Faculty: Chef Daniel Bonnot, trained in France. Experience includes London's Savoy Hotel, Chef Saucier at La Caravelleat in Guadeloupe. His Bizou was named one of the 10 Best New Restaurants in the U.S. by Esquire magazine.

Costs: $2,200 includes shared lodging at the farmhouse, most meals. $200 for optional pick-up/return to Montelimar.

Location: 18th-century Provencal farmhouse in the foothills of the pre-Alps.

Contact: Anne Reinauer, Owner, French Cooking Classes - A Week in Provence, 813 Shell Beach Dr., Lake Charles, LA 70601; 337-436-4422, Fax 337-310-3726, david@lakecharlescommercial.com, http://FrenchCookingClasses.com.

THE FRENCH KITCHEN IN GASCONY
Southwest France

Sponsor: Kate Hill, cookbook author, chef & artist. Programs: Culinary programs including hands-on classes on Gascon cuisine & cultural visits. Established: 1987. Class/group size: 8 max. 12+ programs/yr. Facilities: 18th-century stone farmhouse kitchen of Camont featuring original brick fireplace & potager garden on the Canal de Deux Mers. Traditional French cooking equipment & techniques suited to home chefs. Also featured: Farmer's markets, antique hunting in medieval villages, armagnac cellars, foie gras farms, fine restaurants, bakeries, wineries, escorted sightseeing. Custom classes for larger groups.

Emphasis: Culinary culture & traditions of Gascony; seasonal Gascon cuisine.

Faculty: Kate Hill, owner/chef & author of the cookbook/travelogue A Culinary Journey in Gascony, has lived in France since 1988. Local chefs including Madame Vetou Pompele of Chez Vetou.

Costs: $1,950-$2,650 includes lodging, meals, local transportation & planned activities.

Location: Gascony, near Agen, 4 hrs by train from Paris.

Contact: Kate Hill, The French Kitchen Cooking School at Camont, 5 Ledgewood Way, #6, Peabody, MA 1960; 800-852-2625, 978-535-5738, Fax 978-535-5738, Thefrenchkitchen@cs.com.

FRENCH WINE EXPLORERS
Avignon

Sponsor: A wine & culinary tour company. Programs: Week-long program that includes hands-on Provençal cooking classes, wine tasting instruction & winery visits, wine & food pairing, visit to cheese farm, olive oil tasting. Established: 1998. Class/group size: 10 max. 2 programs/yr. Facilities: Professional kitchen/classroom. Also featured: Antiquing, sightseeing, dinners at fine local restaurants.

Emphasis: Escorted wine & culinary vacation programs in France.
Faculty: Chef Tamara Milstein, cooking teacher & author of 5 cookbooks; chef & restaurant-owner Jean-Marc Larrue; sommeliers Jean-Pierre Sollin & Lauriann Greene.
Costs: $2,995 includes 6 nights shared lodging, most meals, local transport, sightseeing.
Location: The Mas d'Alleyrac, a restored 16th century home in Provence.
Contact: Lauriann Greene, Sommelier-Conseil, Company President, French Wine Explorers, Coconut Creek, FL 33063; 877-261-1500, Fax 253-423-5316, info@cooking-wine-provence.com, www.cooking-wine-provence.com.

GEORGEANNE BRENNAN'S HAUTE PROVENCE
Aups

Sponsor: Culinary professional Georgeanne Brennan. Programs: 1-wk culinary vacations that include daily hands-on instruction, visits to local markets, artisan cheese makers, honey makers, wineries & market gardens. Established: 2000. Class/group size: 7. 8 programs/yr. Facilities: The farm kitchen of a restored 17th-century convent. Also featured: Herb & vegetable gathering, private Provencal music concerts, visit to eco-museum of Haute Provence & the Museum of Prehistory of the Gorge du Verdon, sightseeing, visit to potter's studio.
Emphasis: Home-style Provencal cuisine, including seasonal vegetables & fruits & charcuterie.
Faculty: Teacher & cookbook author Georgeanne Brennan is recipient of a James Beard, Julia Child, & International Versailles Cookbook Award and has had a home in Provence for 30 yrs. She is a jury member of Slow Food & a member of the IACP.
Costs: $2,750 includes lodging in the convent, all meals, accompanied trips, pick-up & return to Nice, ground transport.
Location: Aups, in the Dept. of the Var, 90 min from the Nice airport.
Contact: Georgeanne Brennan, Georgeanne Brennan's Haute Provence - Culinary Vacations in the H, PO Box 502, Winters, CA 95694; 530-795-3043, Fax 530-795-4190, gbrennan@mother.com, www.georgeannebrennan.com.

A GOURMET CONNECTION
Morance

Sponsor: Cookery school. Programs: 6-day program in France featuring hands-on cookery classes, wine tasting, visits near Lyon/Beaujolais. Established: 2001. Class/group size: 4-12. 10 programs/yr. Facilities: Chateau kitchen facilities.
Emphasis: Preparation & presentation of traditional French recipes.
Faculty: Guy Chanudet has worked in Michelin-starred restaurants & as Executive Chef in a major hotel.
Costs: $2,570 ($2,870) includes shared (single) lodging, meals, ground transport, visits. $1,950 for non-student guest. Price without lodging available.
Location: The 13th-century Château du Pin in Morance, ~20 min from Lyon.
Contact: Guy Chanudet, Chef/Owner, A Gourmet Connection, L'etang, St Etienne Sur Chalaronne, France; (33) (0)4 74 24 04 76, Fax (33) (0)4 74 24 05 31, contact@agourmetconnection.com, www.agourmetconnection.com.

HOLIDAYS IN THE SUN IN THE SOUTH OF FRANCE
Gordes

Sponsor: Les Megalithes school in a private country home. Programs: 1-wk participation courses with instruction in English, French, & German. Feb: truffle specialties; Jul: summercooking. Established: 1980. Class/group size: 6. 17 programs/yr. Facilities: Indoor & outdoor home kitchen. Also featured: Horseback & bicycle riding, handicraft shopping, visits to museums & historic sites.
Emphasis: Provence cuisine.
Faculty: Sylvie Lallemand, president/founder of Assn des amis de la cuisine, learned to cook from her mother & studied with Roger Vergé; author of Enchanted Provence.
Costs: €670 includes lodging & most meals.

Location: Near Avignon, a 3+ hour drive from Nice.

Contact: Sylvie Lallemand, Les Megalithes, Gordes, 84220 France; (33) (0)490-72-23-41.

INTERNATIONAL AGA COOKERY SCHOOL
Varaignes, Dordogne

Sponsor: Culinary professional Nelleke Launspach. Programs: Two-day hands-on courses in AGA cookery using mostly organic ingredients. 25 recipes/session. Established: 1996. Class/group size: 12-24. Facilities: 2- and 4-oven AGA cookers. Also featured: Visits to French markets, wine tasting.

Emphasis: Stress-free cooking & entertaining for large groups.

Faculty: Nelleke Launspach, author of the International Cookbook for the AGA.

Costs: 2,500 FF includes 2 lunches & one dinner.

Contact: Nelleke Launspach, International AGA Cookery School, Le Moulin de Varaignes, Varaignes, 24360 France; (33) 553-56-31-46, Fax (33) 553-56-30-43, nelleke.launspach@planet.nl.

LA COMBE EN PÉRIGORD
Dordogne

Sponsor: Private cooking school at La Combe, an 18th-century French manor house. Programs: 8-day cooking programs include hands-on classes, visits to farmers' markets, vineyards, & food artisans including walnut oil, truffle & foie gras producers; dining in restaurants ranging from farmhouse cuisine to Michelin 2-star. Established: 1998. Class/group size: 8. 18 programs/yr. Facilities: 400 sq-ft French country kitchen with imported American & European appliances. Seating & work spaces for 12. Also featured: Antiqueing, canoeing, cycling, horseback riding, shopping for housewares, visiting historic caves & castles.

Emphasis: Traditional & modern French cuisine using fresh ingredients.

Faculty: Noted culinary professionals including Stephanie Alexander, Catherine Bell, Lora Brody, Marieke Brugman, Barbara Pool Fenzl, Diane Holuigue, Cheryl Jamison, Paula Lambert, Louise Lamensdorf, Sara Monick, Betty Rosbottom, Marie Simmons, Beverley Sprague.

Costs: $3,000-$3,500 includes shared lodging at La Combe, meals, scheduled activities, ground transport.

Contact: La Combe en Périgord, 3450 Sacramento St., #436, San Francisco, CA 94118; 888-LACOMBE (415-673-0429), Fax 888-522-6623, 415-673-0429, info@lacombe-perigord.com, www.lacombe-perigord.com. In France: Wendely Harvey, La Combe, 24620 Les Eyzies, France; (33) 5-53-35-17-61, Fax (33) 5-53-35-25-64, wendelyh@ctanet.fr.

LA CUISINE DE MARIE-BLANCHE
Paris

Sponsor: Culinary professional Marie-Blanche de Broglie (formerly Princess Ere 2001). Programs: 1- to 4-week participation courses with instruction in French, English, or Spanish. Diplomas: Grand Diplome Princesse Marie-Blanche de Broglie, Le Diplome de La Cuisine de Marie-Blanche. Established: 1975. Class/group size: 6-8. 10 programs/yr. Facilities: 50-sq-meter kitchen, 40 sq-meter lecture room for slides. Also featured: Discovering French Style for groups; French Cheeses, French Pastry & Tasting. A Gastronomic Tour of France: French wines, table setting, candlelight dinner, visit to a Parisian market.

Emphasis: The art of entertaining at home.

Faculty: Marie-Blanche de Broglie, founder & director, is author of The Cuisine of Normandy & A La Table des Rois.

Costs: 1 class 760FF, 5 classes 3,010FF, 10 classes 5,510FF, 3 pastry classes 1,760FF, The Little Pastry Chef 150FF, 1-wk course in (Cooking) l'Art de Vivre (5,500FF) 4,500FF, 1 class 1,500FF, Grand Diplome 19,500FF, Le Diplome 45,000FF.

Contact: Marie-Blanche de Broglie, Mgr, La Cuisine de Marie-Blanche, 18 Ave. de la Motte-Picquet, Paris, 75007 France; (33) (0)145-51-36-34, Fax (33) (0)145-51-90-19, infocmb@CuisineMB.com, www.CuisineMB.com/index.htm.

LA CUISINE DE SAVOIE

Albertville

Sponsor: Hotel Restaurant Million. Programs: 6-day participation courses featuring cooking lessons, visits to market, escargot farm, foie gras & cheese producers, vineyards; wine tastings, dinners in homes & restaurants, local trips. Established: 1999. Class/group size: 8. 4-8 programs/yr. Facilities: Professional restaurant kitchen. Also featured: Custom-designed programs including cycling tours, wine tours, artists' & photography groups.

EMPHASIS: Savoie cuisine, local products, cheese & wine.

FACULTY: Chef Jose DeAnacleto, Betsy Jane Clary, Ph.D., professional staff of Restaurant Million.

COSTS: $2,295 ($2,495) includes shared (single) lodging at Hotel Million, meals, planned excursions. Supplement for non-cooking partner is $1,295 & includes lodging & meals.

LOCATION: In the French Alps, ~1-1/2 hrs from Geneva airport.

CONTACT: La Cuisine de Savoie, P.O. Box 21570, Charleston, SC 29413; , Fax 843-577-2720, cuisinesavoie@att.net, www.lacuisinedesavoie.com.

LA VARENNE

Burgundy *(See display ad above)*

Sponsor: Private school. Programs: Master Class program with 5-day sessions (hands-on classes, demo, wine tasting). Class/group size: 10. Facilities: The school is in the 17th-century Château du Feÿ, a registered historic monument owned by founder Anne Willan. Also featured: Visits to Joigny & Chablis, market place & vineyard tours, dinner at a fine country restaurant.

EMPHASIS: Classic, contemporary, and regional French cuisine, bistro cooking, pastry, wine appreciation, guest chef specialties.

FACULTY: Visitor Series features different chef-instructors each week.

COSTS: $3,245, which includes transport from Paris, full board, shared twin lodging at Château du Feÿ, & planned activities. Single supplement $400.

LOCATION: 90 min south of Paris. Amenities include tennis court & outdoor swimming pool.

CONTACT: La Varenne, P.O. Box 25574, Washington, DC 20007; 800-537-6486, Fax 703-823-5438, mail@lavarenne.com, www.lavarenne.com.

LATITUDE CULTURAL CENTER

La Toulzanie

Sponsor: Non-profit association, organized under the Loi de 1901 in France. Programs: Week-long summer culinary adventures, in French & English. Course also offered in The Art of Patisserie. Established: 1998. Class/group size: 18 max. 6-9 programs/yr. Facilities: A 14th century mill, a converted tobacco hangar, pool, gardens, motor boat. Also featured: Free evening conferences on such diverse topics as local Quercy history, world affairs, Freud's theories. Swimming, fishing.

EMPHASIS: Wide range of intellectual adventures plus appreciation of tranquil setting in which to commune & converse with new acquaintances.

FACULTY: U.S. & French college professors & experts, including CNRS researcher Paul Verdier & pastis-maker Yvette Andissac.

COSTS: $950-$1,050/week includes 15 hrs instruction, lodging, most meals. Special rate for full-time students.

CONTACT: E. Barbara Phillips, Director, Latitude Cultural Center, 1043 Oxford St., Berkeley, CA 94707; 510-525-8436, barbara@latitude.org, www.latitude.org.

LE BAOU D'INFER COOKERY SCHOOL

La Mole

Programs: Five-day cookery courses with daily themes that include pasta, bread & Provençal classics. Established: 1999. Class/group size: 6 max. 10 programs/yr. Facilities: Air-conditioned studio with demonstration area & 3 fully-equipped work stations. Also featured: Wine tasting at nearby producers, country walks, swimming.

EMPHASIS: Techniques & tricks for cooking at home. Seasonal Provençal ingredients.

FACULTY: Alex Mackay, 5 yrs sous chef & director of the cookery school at Raymond Blancs Le Manoir aux Quat Saisons; chef in Michelin-starred kitchens in France, Italy, Germany; TV series, cookery writer.

COSTS: £1,185-£1,860 includes lodging, meals, visit to a local restaurant.

LOCATION: 20 min from St Tropez, 90 min from Nice airport.

CONTACT: Peter & Diana Knab, Le Baou D'Infer Cookery School, 63 Campden Street, London, W8 7EL England; (44) 2077270997, Fax (44) 2077270997, alex@lebaou.com, www.lebaou.com.

LE CORDON BLEU – PARIS

Paris

Sponsor: Private school. Programs: 1/2-day to 4-day courses in French cuisine, pastry & bread-baking, daily demos, market tours, wine seminars. (Basic, Intermediate, & Superior levels). Established: 1895. Class/group size: 8-14 hands-on. 60+ programs/yr. Facilities: Professionally equipped kitchens, demo rooms with video & overhead mirrors.

EMPHASIS: Cuisine, pastry & bread-baking courses focusing on French culinary techniques.

FACULTY: 10 full-time French Master Chefs from Michelin-starred restaurants & fine hotels. International staff. Wine lecturers Patricia Gastaud-Gallagher & Jean-Michel Deluc.

COSTS: €29 for a half-day class, €39 for daily demos), € €849-1 200 (Food & Wine Pairing).

LOCATION: Southwest Paris near the Eiffel Tower & Montparnasse. Metro Vaugirard.

CONTACT: Director of Admissions, Le Cordon Bleu, 8, rue Leon Delhomme, Paris, 75015 France; 800-457-CHEF (USA & Canada), (33) (0)1-53-68-22-50, Fax (33) (0)1-48-56-03-96, paris@cordonbleu.edu, http://cordonbleu.edu.

LE MARMITON – COOKING IN PROVENCE

Avignon

Sponsor: Hotel-restaurant. Programs: 1- & 5-day participation courses. Established: 1994. Class/group size: 12. Facilities: Restored 19th century kitchen with its original wood-fired cast-iron stove & restored counters. Also featured: Visit to wineries, markets, sightseeing, special itineraries can be arranged through concierge.

EMPHASIS: Provencal cuisine.

FACULTY: Christian Etienne, Robert Brunel, Jean-Claude Aubertin, Daniel Hébet, Frédérique Féraud.

COSTS: 95€ (70€, 115€) for an AM (PM, evening) class, 2,510€ for 6 days double occupancy.

CONTACT: Martin Stein, Artist Director, Le Marmiton-Cooking in Provence, 4, place de La Mirande, Avignon, 84000 France; (33) (0)490-85-93-93, Fax (33) (0)490-86-26-85, mirande@la-mirande.fr, www.la-mirande.fr.

L'ECOLE DE CUISINE DU DOMAINE D'ESPERANCE

La Bastide d'Armagnac

Sponsor: 18th-century country house. Programs: 1-wk hands-on vacations that include theoretical instruction in the mornings & preparation of the evening meal in the afternoons. Established: 1993. Class/group size: 9. 6 programs/yr. Facilities: Country kitchen with 8 work areas. Also featured: Market trip, visits to nearby wine cellars.

Emphasis: French cuisine based on the season.

Faculty: Natalia Arizmendi, recipient of the Cordon Bleu Grand Diplome, has taught cooking & pastry for 15+ yrs.She is tri-lingual in French, English, & Spanish.

Costs: $2,000 double, $2,200 single includes meals & lodging at the Domaine. Amenities include outdoor swimming pool & tennis court.

Contact: Claire de Montesquiou, L'Ecole de Cuisine du Domaine d'Esperance, Mauvezin d'Armagnac, La Bastide d'Armagnac, 40240 France; (33) (0) 558-44-85-33, Fax (33) (0) 558-44-85-33, info@esperance.com.fr, www.esperance.com.fr. In the U.S.: Judy Ebrey, Cuisine International, P.O. Box 25228, Dallas, TX 75225; 214-373-1161, Fax 214-373-1162, Email CuisineInt@aol.com, www.cuisineinternational.com.

LES MIMOSAS COOK SCHOOL

Roquebrun

Sponsor: Sarah & Denis La Touche. Programs: 3-, & 5-day cooking vacations. Established: 1998. Class/group size: 6-8. 12 programs/yr. Facilities: Professional kitchen in the guest house. Also featured: Visits to local produce markets & olive oil mill, wine tasting, dinner at a fine restaurant, herb gathering.

Emphasis: French Mediterranean country cooking, food & wine matching.

Faculty: Sarah La Touche has lived in France since 1992 & runs Les Mimosas Guesthouse with her photographer husband Denis. They have written 3 books on food, wine & travel, including The Les Mimosas Cookbook.

Costs: €1,595/5-days, €1,110/3-days includes lodging, meals, visits.

Contact: Sarah and Denis La Touche, Les Mimosas Cook School, Les Mimosas, Avenue des Orangers, Roquebrun, 34460 France; (33) (0)4-67-89-61-36, Fax (33) (0)4-67-89-61-36, welcome@foodiesinfrance.com, www.foodiesinfrance.com.

LES SAVEURS DE PROVENCE

Merindol-les-Oliviers

Sponsor: Gastronomic association. Programs: 4- to 6-day hands-on programs, including grape harvest weeks in autumn. Established: 1995. Class/group size: 4-8. 12 max programs/yr. Facilities: Custom-built fully-equipped kitchen, library of wine & cook books. Also featured: Winery tours & instruction, dining in private homes & local restaurants, visits to markets & food producers, sightseeing.

Emphasis: French Mediterranean cooking, wine & food pairing.

Faculty: Elizabeth Miller, graduate City & Guilds & L'Academie du Vin, 3 time winner of French Natl competitions. Isabelle Bachelard, Paris wine journalist, graduate L'Academie du Vin.

Costs: 11,700FF/6 days or 7,800FF/4 days, including B&B lodging in private country houses, dinners, ground transport, planned activities. Optional wine tutorial 1,100FF/half-day.

Location: Near Vaison-la-Romaine, 40 mi from Avignon.

Contact: Elizabeth Miller, President, L'Association Les Saveurs de Provence, 26170 Merindol-les-Oliviers, Drome Provencale, France; (33) (0)475-28-78-12, Fax (33) (0)475-28-90-11, miller@club-internet.fr, www.ifrance.com/saveurs. US Contact: Epiculinary Distinctive Cooking Journeys, 888-380-9010 (toll-free in US), http://www.epiculinary.com.

LES VOLETS BLEUS

Truinas, Provence

Sponsor: Bed & Breakfast. Programs: 2-day baking weekends & 7-day Mediterranean cooking lessons; cooking alternates with wine-tasting. Meeting locals, visits to cheese-farms, oil-mills, walks in the country side. French, English, Italian & Spanish spoken. Class/group size: 5-10. Facilities: B&B with kitchen facilities that include an old baking oven, 5 rooms (each w/private bath), separate living room & dining room. Also featured: French language courses; countryside outings on foot, horseback, donkey or by car; music, theater, storytelling festivals; village fairs, local celebrations.

Emphasis: Baking (including kneading, baking pizzas & bread, pastas) & Mediterranean (recipes of Provence, Italy & Spain).

FACULTY: Carlo & Pillar Fortunato.

COSTS: 2-day Baking Weekend: 1,170-1,230 FF shared lodging. 7-day Mediterranean Cooking Lessons: 6,000 FF shared lodging. Includes meals & wine. 1,000 FF drive from/to airport or station & excursions.

CONTACT: Pilar & Carlo Fortunato, Les Volets Bleus, Truinas, 26460 France; (33) 4 75 53 38 48, Fax (33) 4 75 53 49 02, lesvolets@aol.com, www.guideweb.com/provence/gastronomie/volets-bleus/indexa.html.

MAS DE CORNUD
St. Remy-de-Provence

Sponsor: David & Nitockrees Carpita's cooking school in their private 18th-century Provençal farmhouse/country inn. Programs: Home Cooking in Provence, offers 5 days of participation classes, market shopping & visits to regional artisans. Established: 1993. Class/group size: 10. 2 programs/yr. Facilities: Indoor & outdoor professional teaching kitchens, wood-burning oven & grill, herb & vegetable garden, boules court, swimming pool, private property. Also featured: Wine tastings, open air village market trips, walks & shopping.

EMPHASIS: Provençal & Mediterranean cuisine.

FACULTY: Nitockrees Tadros Carpita, CCP, member IACP, trained in France. She teaches in the US at Draegers, Viking & private homes.

COSTS: $2,700 includes shared lodging ($2,500 non-participant) at the 4-star Mas de Cornud, most meals, ground transport, outings. Single sessions from $130-$150.

CONTACT: David Carpita, School Administrator, Mas de Cornud, Route de Mas Blanc, St. Remy-de-Provence, 13210 France; (33) 490-92-39-32, Fax (33) 490-92-55-99, mascornud@compuserve.com, www.mascornud.com.

NEW HEALTH GASTRONOMY
Minervois County

Sponsor: Private school. Programs: 7-day hands-on vacations focusing on modern interpretation of traditional Mediterranean diet. Established: 2000. Class/group size: 10. 4 programs/yr. Facilities: Well-equipped home kitchen in a 13th century newly restored farmhouse. Also featured: Wine tastings, visits to markets, olive oil mill, wineries, bakeries, medieval city, Roman museum.

EMPHASIS: Healthy home cooking includes cereal grains, legumes, fresh vegetables, fruits, olive oil.

FACULTY: Hélène Magariños-Rey is a cookbook author, cooking teacher & nutritional counselor; Didier Chabrol, a food & wine specialist, chairs Languedoc Slow Food Convivium & organizes culinary travels.

COSTS: $1,500 includes meals, suite-lodging, ground transport.

CONTACT: Didier Chabrol, New Health Gastronomy through Traditional Mediterranean Diet, 210 rue de Sicile, Montpellier, 34080 France; , Fax (33) 4 67 54 78 32, didchabrol@wanadoo.fr.

ON RUE TATIN, COOKING IN FRANCE WITH SUSAN HERRMANN LOOMIS
Louviers, Normandy

Sponsor: Susan Herrmann Loomis, journalist, cooking teacher, culinary professional. Programs: Week-long program featuring hands-on cooking classes, visits to farmers markets, artisanal food producers & nearby villages. Established: 2000. Class/group size: 8 max. 8 programs/yr. Facilities: Fully-equipped modern kitchen in a restored 15th-century convent. Also featured: Links with regional tour guides, French country lunches for groups of 6+. Special interest classes available.

EMPHASIS: French culinary tradition in an English-speaking environment.

FACULTY: Susan Herrmann Loomis, owner/chief instructor who has lived in France for 10 yrs, & 2 assistants, each with 7+ yrs experience in professional kitchens.

COSTS: $2,000/5-day course includes most meals.

CONTACT: Margaret Fox-Kump, U.S. Director, On Rue Tatin, 10701 Gurley Lane, Mendocino, CA 95460; 707-937-0618, Fax 707-937-0618, cookingclasses@onruetatin.com, www.onruetatin.com.

PROVENCAL COOKING AT LES TUILLIÈRES

Pont de Barret, Drôme Provençale *(See display ad above)*

Sponsor: Guest house in 17th-century mas provençal. Programs: 5-day cooking classes (M-F), advanced course in spring & fall. Established: 1995. Class/group size: 3-6. 16 programs/yr. Facilities: Newly refurbished farmhouse kitchen with up-to-date equipment, cookbook library, vegetable & herb gardens, heated pool, 40 acres of woodland & fields with stream & nature path. Also featured: Excursions to markets, wineries, goat cheese farm, potteries, medieval villages.

EMPHASIS: Provençal style cuisine, intro to Côte du Rhône wines.

FACULTY: Owner Hermann Jenny, trained chef with Swiss diploma in classical French cooking, career in managing luxury hotels.

COSTS: $1,300 ($1,450, $1,150) includes double (single, triple) occupancy lodging, meals, excursions; $1,800 for couple with only one partner cooking.

LOCATION: Near Montélimar, 100 miles S of Lyon, ~50 miles NE of Avignon.

CONTACT: Hermann & Susan Jenny, Provencal Cooking at Les Tuillieres, Les Tuillières, Pont de Barret, 26160 France; (33) 475 90 43 91, Fax (33) 475 90 43 91, h.jen@infonie.fr, www.guideweb.com/provence/gastronomie/tuillieres/indexa.html.

PROVENCAL GETAWAY VACATIONS

Provence, France; Tuscany, Italy

Sponsor: Cooking instructor Eileen Dwillies. Programs: Open-ended participation vacations in a restored 17th century house - cooking, hiking, painting. B&B format. Established: 1994. Class/group size: 4-5. 7 programs/yr. Facilities: Home-style kitchen. Also featured: Daily tours of outdoor markets, vintners caves, artists' workshops, and olive mills. Walking, reading, free time.

EMPHASIS: Provençal and Mediterranean cuisine.

FACULTY: Eileen Dwillies, author of 9 cookbooks, has taught cooking for 20 years and is a former food editor and TV show host.

COSTS: $250/pp/per day for cooking and touring, all inclusive. $50/pp/per day for B&B with optional cooking classes of $60 each.

CONTACT: Eileen Dwillies, Provencal Getaway Vacations, 11373 Kingcome Avenue, Richmond, BC, V7A 4W1 Canada; 604-271-8722, Fax 604-271-1497, eileen@telus.net.

PROVENCE BONJOUR!

Grasse

Sponsor: Private family villa. Programs: 5- to 7-day theme programs, some of which include cooking lessons. Established: 2002. Class/group size: 8. 12 programs/yr. Also featured: Concerts, tastings, restaurant dining, local excursions, market visits.

EMPHASIS: Provençal cuisine & culture.

FACULTY: Josette Andre, a Provence native.

COSTS: $2,800-$3,200 includes meals & lodging in a Provençal villa.

CONTACT: Josette Andre, Provence Bonjour!, 402 Washington St., Wellesley, MA 2481; 781-239-1101 or 866-PROVENCE, info@provencebonjour.com, www.provencebonjour.com.

RESTAURANT HOTEL LA COTE SAINT JACQUES
Joigny, Burgundy

Sponsor: Michelin 2-star restaurant. Programs: 3-day demo programs that feature French cuisine, market visit, wine tasting, dining in the restaurant. Some programs taught in English, others in French. Established: 1948. Class/group size: 8-15. 10 programs/yr. Also featured: Boat rides, indoor swimming pool, sauna, tennis, golf, vineyard visits.

EMPHASIS: Chef's French cuisine.

FACULTY: Jean Michel Lorain, Chef of La Cote Saint Jacques.

COSTS: €705/wk (€865) or €765/wk-end (€940) incl standard (superior) lodging & half-board at Hotel La Cote Saint Jacques, a member of Relais & Chateaux. €165 for non-participant guest.

CONTACT: Jean-Michel Lorain, Hotel Restaurant La Côte Saint Jacques, 14, Faubourg de Paris, Joigny, 89300 France; (33) (0)3-86-62-09-70, Fax (33) (0)3-86-91-49-70, lorain@relaischateaux.fr, www.cotesaintjacques.com.

ROGER VERGÉ COOKING SCHOOL
Mougins

Sponsor: Restaurant l'Amandier. Programs: 2-hour demos from Tuesday through Saturday. Established: 1984. Class/group size: 20. 12 programs/yr. Facilities: Restaurant kitchen specially designed for classes.

EMPHASIS: Seasonal menus, Provencal cuisine.

FACULTY: Serge Chollet & other chefs from the Moulin de Mougins restaurant.

COSTS: €51/class, €230/5 classes.

CONTACT: Sylvie Charbit, Manager, Roger Vergé Cooking School, Restaurant l'Amandier, Mougins Village, 6250 France; (33) (0)493-75-35-70, Fax (33) (0)493-90-18-55, info@moulin-mougins.com, www.moulin-mougins.com.

ROUTAS EN PROVENCE
Chateauvert, Provence

Sponsor: Chateau in a working vineyard. Programs: One-week cooking vacation programs that include trips to local markets & villages & French language instruction. Established: 1993. Class/group size: 12 max. 2 programs/yr. Facilities: The chateau kitchen. Also featured: Visits to local markets, hiking on the property, swimming.

EMPHASIS: Provencale cuisine.

FACULTY: Frances Wilson, Routas Culinary Director & cooking teacher in the San Francisco Bay Area. Anne Le Masson, native French speaker & teacher at the Alliance Francais in Berkeley, CA.

COSTS: $2,500-$3,000 includes chateau lodging, meals, & planned activities.

CONTACT: Frances Wilson, Culinary Director, Routas en Provence, 1814 Addison St., Berkeley, CA 94703; 510-848-2654, ferw@onebox.com, www.franceswilson.net.

SAVOUR OF FRANCE
Burgundy, Provence, Alsace, Champagne, Bordeaux, France; Tuscany, Italy

Sponsor: Specialty travel company. Programs: 6-day cooking & wine-tasting tours that include chateau lodging, private winery tours, dining at Michelin 3-star restaurants, visits to local producers. Established: 1995. Class/group size: 12. 15 programs/yr. Facilities: Professional chateau kitchen in Burgundy, home-style kitchen in Provence. Also featured: Mediterranean day cruise, Rhine cruise, Burgundy Canal barging, ballooning.

EMPHASIS: Classic regional French cuisine paired with fine wines.

FACULTY: Local French chefs including Chef Vignaud of the Michelin-star Hostellerie des Clos, Burgundy; Collette Aron in Provence.

COSTS: $2,495-$3,495 includes lodging, meals, wines, ground transport, & planned activities except ballooning.

CONTACT: David Geen, Director, Villas and Voyages, 2450 Iroquois Ave., Detroit, MI 48214; 800-827-4635, Fax 313-331-1915, dgeen1@aol.com, www.savourfrance.com.

A TASTE OF FRANCE

Loire Valley, Paris, Provence, France; Tuscany, Italy

Programs: 1-wk programs that include hands-on cooking classes, Michelin-star restaurant dining, market visits & excursions. Established: 1998. Class/group size: 12. Also featured: Tennis, golf, bicycling, excursions to St. Tropez, Cannes, Nice.

EMPHASIS: Regional cuisine & wine.

FACULTY: Guest Chefs include Jacques Pepin, Reine Sammut, Jean-Andre Charial, Christian Etienne, Daniel Hébet, Jean-Michael Minguella, Nito Carpita.

COSTS: $2,900-$4,900 includes lodging, meals, ground transport, excursions.

CONTACT: Kathryn Copeland, A Taste of France, Norfolk, VA 23510; 415-331-1226 (California), 757-216-2662(Virginia), Fax 757-216-2663, kathryn@thetasteoffrance.com, www.thetasteoffrance.com.

A TASTE OF PROVENCE

Le Bar sur Loup

Sponsor: Private cooking program. Programs: Hands-on culinary vacations in a private farmhouse in Provence. Includes a class at Roger Vergé cooking school, market visits, winery tours, sightseeing, visits to food producers & private homes. Established: 1994. Class/group size: 8. 12 programs/yr. Facilities: Provençal kitchen, swimming pool, grounds with orchards & olive groves. Also featured: Special programs on olives & olive oil, wine & food pairings; 1 day gourmet tours of Nice; 1 day market/cooking class/lunch.

EMPHASIS: Provençal cooking, Niçoise cuisine, Mediterranean diet, wine appreciation & pairings.

FACULTY: Tricia Robinson, IACP, owner; Jeanette Locker, M.S., CFCS, professor in nutrition dept at CSU, San Luis Obispo; Jonathan Waters, sommelier of Chez Panisse restaurant in Berkeley; Nella Opperman, decorative artist.

COSTS: $2,400 includes lodging, most meals, planned activities; $350 single supplement. Special programs & guest chef weeks are higher. 1 day courses from $150.

LOCATION: Between Grasse & Vence, 40 min by car from Nice.

CONTACT: Tricia Robinson, Owner, A Taste of Provence, 925 Vernal Ave., Mill Valley, CA 94941; 415-383-9439, Fax 415-383-6186, info@tasteofprovence.com, www.tasteofprovence.com.

TWO BORDELAIS

Basque country, Bordeaux & Normandy

Sponsor: Culinary professionals. Programs: 4- to 7-day culinary participation vacations. Established: 1988. Class/group size: 8-12. 6 programs/yr. Facilities: Professional kitchen of Chateau La Louviere & a small farmhouse kitchen with grilling fireplace. Also featured: Visits to chateaux, wine estates, markets, cheese shops, medieval villages, oyster beds, regional inns, local artisans.

EMPHASIS: French classic & regional cuisine, wine appreciation.

FACULTY: Jean-Pierre Moulle, graduate of Ecole Hoteliere in Toulouse, was head chef at Chez Panisse, restaurant consultant. Bordeaux native Denise Moulle markets her family's French chateau wines in the US. Ken Hom, authority on Oriental cooking.

COSTS: $1,800 includes meals, excursions, ground transportation; $3,240 with hotel lodging.

LOCATION: Includes Bordeaux, Normandy & Pyrenees, Armagnac & Cathar country.

CONTACT: Denise Lurton-Moulle, Owner, A Week in Bordeaux, P.O. Box 8191, Berkeley, CA 94707-8191; 510-848-8741, Fax (33) 5 57 74 98 59, jdmoulle@pacbell.net, www.twobordelais.com.

VINEYARDS AND KITCHENS IN FRANCE

Provence, Burgundy, Rhone Valley, Cote d'Azur

Sponsor: Travel company specializing in culinary & vineyard programs in France. Programs: One-week culinary & wine programs that include cooking classes, vineyard visits, dining in fine restaurants. Established: 2002. Class/group size: 8-12 min. 10 programs/yr.

EMPHASIS: French regional cuisine & wine.

FACULTY: Owner/director Chuck Hornsby is a food & wine writer/educator & creator of vineyard & culinary theme programs in France.

Costs: $2,680-$2,780 land only, all-inclusive except for two meals.
Contact: Chuck Hornsby, Owner/Director, Vineyards and Kitchens in France, PO Box 1151, Brattleboro, VT 5302; 866-200-8394, 802-251-6044, Fax 802-254-4436, info@vineyardsandkitchensinfrance.com, www.vineyardsandkitchensinfrance.com.

WALNUT GROVE COOKERY

Mayenne region

Sponsor: Chefs Maynard Harvey & Benedict Haines. Programs: 5-day hands-on gourmet cookery holidays that feature daily cooking instruction & afternoon cultural activities. Established: 2002. Class/group size: 8. 30 programs/yr. Facilities: Professionally-equipped kitchen across the courtyard from the farmhouse; stainless steel work surfaces & oven. Also featured: 4-day stays for up to 8 people that include 6-course dinners & the services of a personal butler.
Emphasis: Modern gourmet cuisine.
Faculty: Maynard Harvey worked with the personal chef to Princess Diana, was chef/owner of Seland Newydd restaurant, & has won gold medals in national competitions; Benedict Haines was head chef at the country house hotel Tyddyn Llan in Snowdonia National Park.
Costs: £825 includes shared lodging, meals, planned excursions. Single room supplement available. Non-participant guest £425.
Contact: Freya Harvey, Proprieter, Walnut Grove Cookery, Le Hunaudiere, Livre la Touche, Mayenne, 53400 France; (33) 2 43 98 50 02, Fax (33) 2 43 98 50 02, walnutgrovecook@aol.com, www.walnutgrovecookery.com.

A WEEK IN PROVENCE WITH SARAH AND MICHAEL BROWN

Gordes

Sponsor: Cultural & culinary specialists Sarah & Michael Brown. Programs: Week-long vacation programs, scheduled every other week in spring & fall, that include daily hands-on cooking demos, art & architectural tours, visits to markets in Provence, lectures. Established: 1996. Class/group size: 6. 16 programs/yr. Facilities: 6-bedroom family home with library, sitting rooms, dining room, & kitchen overlooking the Luberon Valley. Also featured: Swimming, tennis, golf, hiking, biking, riding.
Emphasis: Provençal cuisine, history & culture.
Faculty: Sarah Ferguson Brown, a Ph.D. in Medieval Art History, has been cooking since she was 8, & has lived in the region on & off for 40+ years. Michael Brown represented food interests in Washington, DC, & exports wines to the U.S.
Costs: $2,000 includes lodging in the Brown's converted farmhouse, 7 breakfasts & dinners, lectures.
Location: Near Gordes, 25 mi east of Avignon, 45 min from the Marseille airport.
Contact: Sarah & Michael Brown, A Week in Provence, Les Martins, Gordes, 84220 France; (33) (0)490-72-26-56, Fax (33) (0)490-72-23-83, lesmartins@compuserve.com, www.week-in-provence.com. In the US: Sheppard Ferguson, 4700 Connecticut Ave. NW, #304, Washington, DC 20008; 202-537-7202, shepferg@ix.netcom.com.

A WEEK IN THE HEART OF THE BORDEAUX WINE COUNTRY

Gauriac

Sponsor: Winemaker Pascal Méli & food & wine expert Michèle Rousseau. Programs: One-week cooking & wine appreciation vacations that include visits to wineries of the Bordeaux region. Established: 1999. Class/group size: 6. 20 programs/yr. Facilities: Chateau Bujan, a 42-acre vineyard. Lodging at La Maison des Vignes, a restored 17th century home in the estate. Also featured: Swimming, hiking, biking.
Emphasis: Wine & food of the Bordeaux wine country.
Faculty: Pascal Méli, agricultural engineer, winemaker & owner of Château Bujan; Michèle Rousseau, admin director of a Bordeaux wine Controlled Appellation for the last 9 yrs.
Costs: $2,100 ($250 single supplement) includes lodging, most meals, daily excursions, wine tastings.
Location: Gauriac, ~30 miles northwest of Bordeaux.

Contact: Michèle Rousseau & Pascal Méli, Château Bujan, Gauriac, 33710 France; (33) 557 64 86 56, Fax (33) 557 64 93 96, pmeli@maison-des-vignes.fr, www.maison-des-vignes.fr.

GREECE

AEGEAN HARVEST
Athens, Peloponnese, Santorini

Sponsor: Culinary tour operator Aegean Harvest in conjunction with National Travel. Programs: 10-day organized Mediterranean food, wine & cultural programs. Custom group & independent travel culinary programs. Established: 1999. Class/group size: 20. 4+ programs/yr. Facilities: Private villa near the ancient Venetian port of Nafplio. Also featured: Visits to wineries, markets & artisanal food producers, food demos, tours of ancient ruins & historic sites.

Emphasis: Greek & Mediterrenean cuisine.

Faculty: Author of books on Greek wines.

Contact: Lisa Meyer, Aegean Harvest, 251 Livingston Ave., Livingston, NJ 7052; 877-330-3648, 888-888-9969, aegeanharvest@hotmail.com.

COOKING WITH STAVROS
Symi

Sponsor: Specialty travel company. Programs: 5 half-day Mediterranean-style cooking classes featuring such chef specialties as feta mousse, squid in basil sauce & sea food filo. Established: 2001. Class/group size: 10. 4 programs/yr. Facilities: Restaurant kitchen. Also featured: Gardening courses, painting & walking holidays.

Emphasis: Local & traditional Greek cuisine.

Faculty: Stavros Gogios, owner/chef of the harborside Mythos restaurant.

Costs: £220 includes lunch.

Contact: Laskarina Holidays, St. Marys Gate, Wirksworth, Derbyshire, DE4 4DQ England; (44) 01629 822203, Fax (44) 01629 822205, info@laskarina.co.uk, www.laskarina.co.uk/cooking.html.

CULINARY JOURNEYS IN GREECE
Heraklio, Crete & surrounding area

Sponsor: Culinary professional Nikki Rose. Programs: Culinary classes & cultural tours covering ingredients, cooking techniques, menu planning & nutrition, organic farming, wine. Established: 1994. Class/group size: 4-10. 15 programs/yr. Facilities: Hotels, tavernas, vineyards, archeological & production sites. Also featured: Cultural-culinary research, sustainable agriculture.

Emphasis: Traditional lifestyle & foodways, seafood, wild edible plants, organic farming.

Faculty: Professional chef-guides from 4-star hotels & village tavernas, home cooks, farmers & fishermen. Nikki Rose is a CIA graduate & food historian/writer.

Costs: $150-$2,500 for 1- to 5-day classes, includes lodging in seaside resort bungalows, some meals & tours.

Contact: Nikki Rose, Director, Culinary Journeys in Greece, T.K. 72053, Elounda, Crete, TK 72053 Greece; (30) 28410-42797, rosenikki@hotmail.com.

GLORIOUS GREEK KITCHEN
Athens & the Greek Islands

Sponsor: Chef & cooking teacher Diane Kochilas. Programs: 1-wk cooking vacation courses in Ikaria that include meetings with culinary artisans, village home cooks & farmers; regional cheese, wine, honey & olive oil tastings. Culinary walking tours in Athens. Established: 2002. Class/group size: 5-20. Year-round programs/yr. Facilities: Ikaria: Diane's restaurant, The Glorious Greek Kitchen, at Villa Thanassi, an island home with working garden & outdoor/indoor kitchens. Also featured: Custom trips to other parts of Greece including Crete, Peloponessos, Epirus.

Emphasis: Regional & healthful Greek cuisine, fish & vegetarian cookery.

Faculty: Diane Kochilas, food writer & IACP-award-winning author of The Glorious Foods of

Greece, The Greek Vegetarian, & The Food and Wine of Greece.

Costs: Ikaria: $1,700/1-wk course includes lodging, meals, & excursions. Athens: culinary walking tour & lunch $85.

Contact: Diane Kochilas, Owner, Glorious Greek Kitchen, Kehagia 29 Filothei, Athens, 152 37 Greece; (30) 210-653-6800, info@cuisineinternational.com.In the U.S.: Judy Ebrey, Cuisine International, P.O. Box 25228, Dallas, TX 75225; 214-373-1161, Fax 214-373-1162, Email CuisineInt@aol.com, www.cuisineinternational.com.

NUTRITION & CULTURE AT THE MOUTH OF SANTORINI VOLCANO

Santorini

Sponsor: Magma, a division of Heliotopos Inc., a destination management company in Santorini, Greece. Programs: 4-day program focusing on nutrition and culture. Established: 1985. Class/group size: 6-14. 4 programs/yr. Facilities: Hotel Heliotopos, overlooking the volcano, the sea, & the neighboring islands. Also featured: Geological tours.

Emphasis: Traditional Greek Mediterranean diet.

Faculty: Dr Connie Phillipson, prehistoric archeologist, nutritionist, Greek food columnist of Athens News, president of the Institute of Paleonutrition.

Costs: €1,090 (€290) includes shared (single) lodging.

Contact: Yiota Aidoni, Manager, Santorini Cultural and Culinary Holidays, Magma, Imerovigli, Santorini, 84700 Greece; (30) 2286 024758, Fax (30) 2286 023867, magma@heliotopos.net, http://e-magma.santorini.net/index.php?brink.

INDIA

JULIE SAHNI'S SCHOOL OF INDIAN COOKING

India & Brooklyn Heights, New York

Sponsor: Cooking school owner and cookbook author Julie Sahni. Programs: NY: two 3-day hands-on courses (3 students max) are Indian Cooking and Understanding Spices & Herbs. Include shopping in an Indian/spice market. India: 16-day cultural & culinary tours that include visits to farm kitchens & cooking demos. Established: 1973. 2 trips to India programs/yr. Facilities: Specially-designed teaching kitchen in Ms. Sahni's studio. Also featured: 3-day courses can be taught anywhere in USA as a 1-day intro for 6 students. India trips (Feb & Oct) also include visits to spice and tea plantations, markets and bazaars, private receptions.

Emphasis: Classic Indian cuisine and spices & herbs seminar covers techniques, ingredients, healthful meal planning, historical background, social ideology.

Faculty: Julie Sahni is author of Classic Indian Cooking, Indian Vegetarian Cooking, & Savoring Spices and Herbs. She is a member of the IACP and Les Dames D'Escoffier and has degrees in Architecture and Classical Dance.

Costs: 3-day course: $985/person. Trip: $4,975, includes shared lodging (single supplement $1,475), most meals, ground transport, planned activities. Lodging in deluxe hotels or best available.

Location: Western, southern & northern India. NY: near Brooklyn entrance to the Brooklyn Bridge.

Contact: Julie Sahni, Director, Julie Sahni's School of Indian Cooking, 101 Clark St., #13A, Brooklyn Heights, NY 11201; 718-625-3958, Fax 718-625-3456, jsicooking@aol.com.

INDONESIA

THE COOKING SCHOOL, FOUR SEASONS RESORT BALI

Bali

Sponsor: Four Seasons Hotels. Programs: Cooking classes that focus on Asian cuisines & include tours of local markets, visits to the resort's vegetable gardens, meetings with local food & wine experts. Established: 2001. Class/group size: 12 max. ~300 programs/yr. Facilities: Purpose-built full-service kitchen with the latest equipment.

Emphasis: Indonesian/Balinese, Asian, Spa and Balinese Entertaining.

Faculty: Four Seasons & celebrity chefs.
Costs: $90/person per module + tax & service.
Contact: Putu Indrawati, Director of Public Relations, Four Seasons Resorts Bali, Jimbaran, Bali, 80361 Indonesia; (62) 361-701010, Fax (62) 361-701020, Putu.Indrawati@fourseasons.com, www.baliparadise.net/four-seasons/index.cfm/hotel/cooking-school.

RICE AND SPICE ADVENTURES
Pemuteran, North Bali

Sponsor: Puri Ganesha Villas resort. Programs: Weekend and week-long courses that focus on Balinese spices and local specialties. Established: 1998. Class/group size: 8-10. Facilities: Restaurant kitchen of Puri Ganesha. Also featured: Visits to markets, a silk weaving factory, a spice farm; snorkeling trip; dining in restaurants & private homes.
Emphasis: Balinese cuisine, spices, culture.
Faculty: Diana von Cranach, former Cordon Bleu cook at Winkfield Place, UK.
Contact: Diana von Cranach, Puri Ganesha Villas, Pantai Pemuteran, Gerokgak, Singaraja, Bali, 81155 Indonesia; (62) 362-93433, Fax (62) 362-93433, pganesha@indosat.net.id, www.puriganeshabali.com.

THE SERAI COOKING SCHOOL
Bali

Sponsor: Resort. Programs: Half-, 2-, & 5-day programs that feature a half day of hands-on cooking classes, & the other half exploring Bali's culinary & cultural aspects. Established: 1997. Class/group size: 10. 20-25 programs/yr. Also featured: Market tours, visits to food producers, sightseeing, dinners, cultural events, concluding Balinese feast.
Emphasis: Indonesian cuisine with emphasis on Balinese food.
Faculty: Matthew Coates, The Serai's exec chef, has experience in leading Sydney restaurants.
Costs: $75 ($220, $550) for the 1/2- (2-, 5-) day course, includes most meals. Nonparticipant guest fee is $35 for dinner & tour. Lodging starts at $155/night + 21% tax & service.
Contact: Matthew Coates, Executive Chef, The Serai Cooking School, P.O. Box 13, Manggis, Karangasem, Bali, 80871 Indonesia; (62) 363-41011, Fax (62) 363-41015, serai-1@ghmhotels.com, www.balilife.com/serai/cookingschool.htm.

IRELAND

BALLYMALOE COOKERY SCHOOL
Midleton, County Cork

Sponsor: Proprietary school. Programs: 1- to 5-day hands-on vacation programs that include a 1-day Christmas cooking demo & a weekend Entertaining course. Established: 1983. Class/group size: 46 hands-on/60 demo. 30 programs/yr. Facilities: Include a specially-designed kitchen with gas & electric cookers, mirrored demo area with TV monitors, gardens that supply fresh produce. Also featured: Fishing & golf.
Emphasis: Entertaining menus, seafood, vegetarian dishes.
Faculty: 4 full- and 4 part-time. Includes Principal Darina Allen, IACP-certified teacher & food professional, her brother, Rory O'Connell, both trained in the Ballymaloe House restaurant kitchen, & her husband Tim Allen. Featured guest chefs.
Costs: 1-day courses IR£125, weekend courses IR£275, 5-day courses IR£495. Lodging in self-catering cottages at school during short courses is IR£15.50/night shared, IR£19.50/night single.
Contact: Tim Allen, Ballymaloe Cookery School, Kinoith, Shanagarry, County Cork, Midleton, Ireland; (353) 21-646785, Fax (353) 21-646909, enquiries@ballymaloe-cookery-school.ie, www.ballymaloe-cookery-school.ie. In the U.S.: Judy Ebrey, Cuisine International, P.O. Box 25228, Dallas, TX 75225; 214-373-1161, Fax 214-373-1162, Email CuisineInt@aol.com, www.cuisineinternational.com.

BERRY LODGE COOKERY SCHOOL
County Clare

Sponsor: Cooking school in a country guest house. Programs: 2- & 3-day residential & 1-day non-residential cooking programs. Themes include seafood, vegetarian, desserts, breakfast & brunch, easy entertaining. Class/group size: 10. Facilities: Modernized 18th-century Victorian family home & restaurant. Also featured: Walking, fishing, swimming.

EMPHASIS: Traditional local Irish cuisine.

FACULTY: Rita Meade, IACP-member, chef, home economist, teacher of food programs for 25+ yrs.

COSTS: 2-day program (non-participant) €152 (€102), 3-day program €290 (€140), 1-day non-residential €50-€70 includes most meals.

CONTACT: Rita Meade, Berry Lodge, Annagh, Miltown Malbay, Co. Clare, Ireland; (353) 65 708 7022, Fax (353) 65 708 7011, info@berrylodge.com, www.berrylodge.com.

THE GOURMET SOLUTION
Ennis, Co. Clare

Sponsor: Private school. Programs: Demo & hands-on 6-session courses, Irish & contemporary cuisine.

FACULTY: Proprietor James Hunt has worked in 4- & 5-star establishments in Ireland & fine restaurants in London, Paris, Munich & Sydney, incl 7 yrs in 1- & 2-star Michelin restaurants.

COSTS: €110-€180/course.

CONTACT: James Hunt, Owner, The Gourmet Solution, 31 Maiville, Ennis, Co. Clare, Ireland; (353) (0)65 6864743, jahunt@eircom.net.

ITALY

A TAVOLA CON LO CHEF
Rome

Sponsor: Private school. Programs: Amateur & professional training courses include basic & advanced cooking, confectionery, pizza, fish, monographic lessons on specific themes, hands-on or demonstration courses. Established: 1992. Class/group size: 15 hands-on, 25 demo. Facilities: 3 well-equipped professional kitchens. Also featured: Children's programs, private instruction for groups, market visits.

EMPHASIS: Traditional & modern Italian & regional cuisine.

FACULTY: Antonio Sciullo, Alberto Ciarla, Leonardo Di Carlo, Nazzareno Lavini, Salvo Leanza, Gianni Alicino, Agata Parisella Caraccio, Salvatore Tassa.

COSTS: $90/$120 for each 3/4-hour lesson.

LOCATION: Rome's historic center, next to St. Peter Cathedral.

CONTACT: Maria Teresa Meloni, Fiorella D'Agnano, A Tavola con lo Chef, Via dei Gracchi 60, Rome, 192 Italy; (39) 06-32 22 096, Fax (39) 06-320 34 02, atavola@pronet.it, www.atavolaconlochef.it.

ADVENTURES IN CULTURE
Abruzzo & Tuscany

Sponsor: Special interest travel company. Programs: 4-day vacations at La Cucina di Viviana, 7-day vacations at Pettirosso Gourmet Cooking School that include daily cooking lessons, winery tours, market shopping, visits to nearby towns. Class/group size: 4-16. Facilities: Pettirosso restaurant kitchen, Viviana's & Barbara's villa kitchen.

EMPHASIS: Cuisine of the Abruzzo & Tuscan regions.

FACULTY: Master Chef Angelo Chiavaroli, owner of the 4-star Hotel Montinope & chef of its restaurant, Pettirosso. Chefs Viviana & Barbara.

COSTS: $2,650 ($1,295) for Pettirosso (Viviana) includes round-trip airfare from the US (no airfare), ground transport, shared lodging at Hotel Montinope (La Cucina di Viviana) for 6 (4) nights, most meals, planned excursions.

CONTACT: Adventures in Culture c/o The Parker Company, 152 Lynnway, Lynn, MA 1902; 800-280-2811, 781-596-8282, italy@theparkercompany.com, www.adventures-in-culture.com.

ADVENTURES IN TUSCANY

Siena, Italy

Sponsor: Azienda Agrituristica, Vittorio Cambria. Programs: 5 different Sunday-Saturday programs that focus on Tuscan cuisine. Includes daily classes & culinary & cultural excursions. Established: 1997. Class/group size: 6-16. 22 programs/yr. Facilities: Professional kitchen, wood-burning oven, herb & vegetable garden, outdoor dining with view. Also featured: Private tours for groups. Walking, cultural & cooking holidays for 8 or more.

Emphasis: Tuscan culture experienced through the exploration of its culinary traditions.

Faculty: Chef Giancarlo Giannelli, chef-owner of L'oste Poeta Restaurant in Tocchi, cookbook author; anthropologist Vittorio Cambria, an expert on the culture of the region; Sergio Villani, Ph.D. in Art History.

Costs: $2,100-$2,950 all-inclusive for land portion. Lodging in a restored 1,000-year-old castello.

Location: 25 min south of Siena in the 1,000-yr-old Castello di Tocchi.

Contact: Ann Dunne, Program Director, Adventures in Tuscany, P.O. Box 644, Solana Beach, CA 92075; 619-989-9416, Fax 858-258-1474, ann_dunne@attglobal.net, www.tuscany-adventures.com.

AGRITURISMO MALAGRONDA

Perugia, Umbria

Sponsor: Countryside vacation resort. Programs: 1-week tours of Umbria & Tuscany that include 4 cooking lessons. Established: 2002. Class/group size: 8-16. 4 programs/yr. Facilities: Guest facilities include 7 apartments on a 120,000 sq-meter estate & a nearby house. Also featured: Regional excursions, wine tasting, restaurant dining, swimming pool, mountain biking.

Emphasis: Traditional regional cuisine.

Costs: €2,550 includes shared lodging, most meals, local tours, transfers; single supplement €200.

Location: Pausillo Regional Natural Park, ~30 mi from Perugia.

Contact: Carla Graziani, Sales Mgr, Agriturismo Malagronda, Loc. Schiacciato 17, Moiano, 6060 Italy; (39) 0578 294100, cell (39) 338 3910476, Fax (39) 0578 293700, info@malagronda.it, www.malagronda.it.

ALFREDO'S CUCINA E CULTURA AT ALIMANDI IN ROME

Rome; Milltown, New Jersey

Sponsor: Chef Alfredo de Bonis & Hotel Alimandi. Programs: Rome: 5-day hands-on cooking vacation programs that include market visits, sightseeing, dinner at a different restaurant each night. Established: 1990. Class/group size: 10. 12 programs/yr. Facilities: Italy: remodeled kitchen at Hotel Alimandi. New Jersey: Alfredo's home kitchen, high school facilities. Also featured: New Jersey: 4-session courses, adult school classes featuring 8 Italian regions, classes at Alfredo's home.

Emphasis: Italian regional, gourmet cooking, Roman cuisine.

Faculty: Alfredo de Bonis, a chef in his own restaurant for 25+ yrs, now owns & operates Bravo Alfredo Catering, teaches at North Brunswick High School.

Costs: Italy: $1,995 incl shared lodging at Hotel Alimandi, meals, planned activities.New Jersey: $150 for 4-session course.

Location: Italy: next to the Vatican Museum. New Jersey: Milltown, 35 mi from NYC.

Contact: Alfredo de Bonis, Chef Instructor, Alfredo's Cucina & Cultura at Alimandi Rome, 375 Tremont Ave., Milltown, NJ 08850-2013; 732-828-8460, adbonis@aol.com, www.alfredotours.com.

AOLMAIA TUSCANY SOCIETY

San Miniato, Tuscany

Sponsor: Italian language & culture school. Programs: Hands-on 1-day cooking classes & 1-wk courses. Established: 1997. Class/group size: 9 max. 24 programs/yr. Facilities: Restaurant & private home kitchens. Also featured: Guided wine tours & tastings by sommelier, cultural & walking excursions.

Emphasis: Traditional Tuscan, Italian & Mediterranean cuisine.

Faculty: Restaurant chefs & home cooks.

Costs: $230/day includes meals, lodging, tours, local transportation.

LOCATION: San Miniato, between Florence & Pisa; other Tuscan towns & producing areas.
CONTACT: Pierpaolo Chiartosini, Coordinator, Aolmaia Tuscany Service Sas, Via Cafaggio 12, San Miniato - Pisa, 56027 Italy; (39) 571-408038, Fax (39) 571-466941, countrypost@aolmaia.com, www.aolmaia.com.

APICIUS THE CULINARY INSTITUTE OF FLORENCE

Florence *(See also page 186) (See display ad page 186)*

Sponsor: Private school, a member of the Federation of European Schools. Programs: 10-day food/wine/culture programs, 1-mo language/cooking/wine courses, wine & cooking classes, 1-yr diploma programs. Established: 1973. Class/group size: 15 max. 15 programs/yr. Facilities: New facility with 2 kitchens & individual workstations, wine tasting room, conference room, reading room & lounge. Also featured: Market tour, wine tastings, gastronomic walking tours, culinary lectures.
EMPHASIS: Culinary arts, Italian & historic Renaissance cuisine, regional Italian & Tuscan cuisine, wine appreciation.
FACULTY: Chefs, restaurateurs, culinary professionals, incl founder/director Gabriella Ganugi, author of The Four Seasons of the Tuscan Table.
COSTS: Programs that combine private & group cooking classes, wine tasting, Italian language, & gastronomic walking tours from €790.
LOCATION: The San Lorenzo district of Florence, between the Duomo & the central train station.
CONTACT: Dr. Gabriella Ganugi, Director, Apicius the culinary institute of Florence, Via Guelfa 85, Florence, 50129 Italy; (39) 0552658135, Fax (39) 0552656689, info@apicius.it, www.apicius.it. U.S. contact: Study Abroad Italy, 339 S. Main St., Sebastopol, CA 95472; 707-824-8965, Fax 707-824-0198, mail@tuscancooking.com, http://www.tuscancooking.com.

ARTE E MESTIERI

Montopoli in Val d'Arno

Sponsor: Cultural association. Programs: 1-day, weekly & week-end programs that include 4 cooking classes, wine tasting, & the use of plants in phytoterapy. Established: 2000. Class/group size: 6:1. 4 programs/yr. Facilities: Restored kitchen in Villa Belvedere country house with garden & swimming pool. Also featured: Workshops in stained glass, mosaic art, ceramics, decoupage, fresco, & paintings; archeological excursion, mountain biking, swimming.
EMPHASIS: Tuscan, Roman & Mediterranean cuisine & wines.
FACULTY: Anna Ciampolini & Cesare Ciurli (cooking), Cesare Ciurli (wine), Gianna (art tours), Marcella Cuccu (art teacher).
COSTS: $900-$2,000 includes meals, shared lodging in Villa Belvedere & restored apts; planned activities.
LOCATION: Near San Miniato, Pisa, Florence, Lucca.
CONTACT: Anna Maria Ciampolini, Artist, Arte e Mestieri, Via Guicciardini 50, Montopoli in Val d'Arno, Pisa, 56020 Italy; (39) 0571 466937, Fax (39) 0571 466937, info@arteemestieri.com, www.arteemestieri.com.

ARTISANAL COOKING

Montelama, Tuscany

Programs: Weekend hands-on classes in Viennese pastry, Moroccan cooking or Lunigiana specialties that cover basic recipes & techniques, special ingredients. Established: 1997. Class/group size: 1-3 preferred. Facilities: Indoor & outdoor kitchen facilities including grill, stove, oven & tables. Also featured: Visits to local farmers' market & traditional trattorias.
EMPHASIS: Food prepared by hand with an artisanal & traditional approach.
FACULTY: Christine Berl, pastry chef & author of The Classic Art of Viennese Pastry, & her husband, Chef Hamid, specialist in Moroccan Berber cuisine.
COSTS: $300/weekend class. Lodging available with bedrooms for up to 4 people.
LOCATION: A 17th-century stone house surrounded by forests in the Rossano Valley of the Lunigiana mountain region near the Cinque Terre.
CONTACT: Christine Berl, Pastry Chef, Artisanal Cooking, Montelama, 54020 Italy; (39) 335 649 5827, cinqueterreetc@yahoo.com.

BADIA A COLTIBUONO

Tuscany

Sponsor: Badia a Coltibuono, a medieval abbey, Tuscan wine estate & villa. Programs: Residential 3- or 5-day vacation courses (usually Mon-Sat) that include participation cooking classes, wine & olive oil tastings, gastronomic & cultural visits. Established: 1985. Class/group size: 16. 8 programs/yr. Facilities: Large teaching kitchen in an 11th-century abbey. Also featured: Visits to food producers, wineries & castles; trip to the Palio horse race (July).

EMPHASIS: Regional Italian cooking & wines.

FACULTY: Chef Paolo Pancotti & Guide John Meis.

COSTS: Land cost is $1,300 double, $1,500 single for 3 day program; $3,300 double, $3,900 single, for 5 day program; includes lodging at Badia a Coltibuono; $500 supplement for Palio week.

LOCATION: A Tuscan estate in Chianti that produces wine, extra virgin olive oil, vinegar & other products. Amenities include large swimming pool. 20 mi north of Siena, 40 mi south of Florence.

CONTACT: Louise Owens, Badia a Coltibuono, 3128 Purdue, Dallas, TX 75225; 214-739-2846, Fax 214-691-7996, coltibuono@charter.net, www.coltibuono.com.

BEI RICORDI – A ROAD THROUGH TUSCANY & UMBRIA

Orvieto, Tuscany & Umbria

Sponsor: Private culinary company. Programs: Seasonal programs that include cooking classes, cultural tours, & visits to markets, winemakers, cheese makers & bakers. Established: 1997. Class/group size: 3-7. 12 programs/yr. Also featured: Truffle searches, pheasant & wild boar hunts, olive & grape harvests, baking classes, language lessons.

EMPHASIS: Culinary & historical culture of Tuscany & Umbria.

FACULTY: Marlena DeBlasi, a chef & cooking teacher, has authored 3 books on the regional foods of Italy, including 1000 Days in Venice.

COSTS: $3,500 includes 5 nights lodging & meals.

LOCATION: Orvieto is the central location. Locations in Umbria & Tuscany vary with the season.

CONTACT: Marlena & Fernando de Blasi, Owners, Bei Ricordi, 34 via del Duomo, Orvieto, 5018 Italy; 011-39-0763-393-549, Fax 011-39-0763-341-718, join-us@beiricordi.com, www.beiricordi.com.

BOOKS FOR COOKS IN TUSCANY, THE ITALIAN COOKING SCHOOL

Tuscany

Sponsor: Heidi Lascelles, founder of Books for Cooks in London. Programs: Customized 1- & 2-day cooking courses & weekend & week-long culinary vacations that include daily hands-on classes. Established: 1998. Class/group size: 8 max. ~6 programs/yr. Facilities: Kitchens include open fireplaces & wood-burning ovens. Also featured: Grape picking in Sept & Oct, olive picking in Nov, well-being weeks with healthy cooking classes & therapies that include shiatsu massage & tai chi.

EMPHASIS: Tuscan & Italian cuisine.

FACULTY: Principal tutor Olivia Greco.

COSTS: €100-€120/day, €500/weekend, €2,000/week includes lodging & meals.

LOCATION: Casa Colonica, a 500-year-old restored farmhouse surrounded by vineyards & olive groves, situated between Florence & Siena.

CONTACT: Heidi Lascelles, Books for Cooks in Tuscany, The Italian Cooking School, Strada della Paneretta 11, Barberino V.E. (Fi.), 50021 Italy; (39) 055-8072231/(39) 348 773 0009, Fax (39) 055-8072231, heidi.lascelles@libero.it, www.booksforcooks.com.

CAMILLA IN CUCINA

Tuscany

Sponsor: Private school. Programs: 1-week vacations that include 5 hands-on cooking lessons with lunches, excursions to Modena, a city-tour with optional visits to markets, food producers & wineries, & restaurant dining. Established: 1998. Class/group size: 12. 8 programs/yr. Facilities: Fully-equipped kitchens in restored villas. Also featured: Swimming pools & nearby golf courses.

EMPHASIS: Italian regional cuisine.

Faculty: Mrs. S. Maccari, a cooking teacher, gastronome & cook book author, writes articles for Italian Cooking & Living.
Costs: $2,400 includes lodging, all lunches, some dinners, planned activities, airport transfers in Italy.
Location: An estate in Lucca, 5 km from downtown.
Contact: Silvia Maccari, Owner, Camilla in Cucina, Via Atto Vannucci 3, Florence, 50134 Italy; (39) 055-461-381, Fax (39) 055-461-381, smaccari@iol.it.

CAPEZZANA WINE & CULINARY SCHOOL

Carmignano, Florence, Italy

Sponsor: Private school & winery. Programs: 5-day hands-on vacation programs designed for food professionals & others interested in Tuscan cuisine. Covers basic and advanced concepts & includes market visits, winery tours, visits to food producers, dining in private homes. Established: 1994. Class/group size: 14. 10 programs/yr. Facilities: The family kitchen at Tenuta di Capezzana and restaurant kitchens. Also featured: One day is devoted to Tuscan wines; sessions for tour groups. Special classes by arrangement.
Emphasis: Food & wine of Tuscany.
Faculty: The Capezzana Wine & Culinary Center family chef, directors, family members, visiting chefs. Wine program is taught by a Master of Wine.
Costs: $2,300-$3,000, includes lodging, meals, all activities.
Location: Via di Capezzana 100 in Carmignano, Florence.
Contact: Nikki & Richard Walters, Booking Agent, Bacioni Inc., 235 E. 22nd St., #9T, New York, NY 10010; 212-679-3660, Nikki@bacioni2000.com, www.capezzana.it.

CAPRI DOLCE VITA

Capri

Sponsor: Culinary vacation company. Programs: 3-, 4- & 8-day Capri vacation programs that include hands-on cooking lessons, wine, grappa & cheese tastings. Programs offered in English & Italian, other languages on request. Established: 2002. Class/group size: 10 max. 15 programs/yr. Facilities: Agriturismo equipped with both modern & traditional kitchen facilities. Also featured: Include guided walks, excursions, boat trips, nightlife.
Emphasis: Traditional Caprese & Neopolitan cuisine.
Faculty: Exec Chef Renato De Gregorio, Maitre Cuisinier, Chaine des Rotisseurs, Assn. mondiale de la gastronomie.Activities are led by Capri Dolce Vita's owners Massimo & Elisabeth.
Costs: From €1,500 includes meals, activities, shared 4-star hotel lodging, transfers from Naples.
Location: Anacapri on the Isle of Capri, 40 min by ferry from Naples, 20 min from Sorrento.
Contact: Massimo & Elisabeth , Owners, Capri Dolce Vita, via Tito Minitti 9, Anacapri, 80071 Italy; (39) 334 367 2794, info@capridolcevita.com, www.capridolcevita.com.

CHIANTI IN TUSCANY – TOSCANA MIA

Gaiole in Chianti & Florence

Sponsor: Private school. Programs: 1- to 5-day hands-on cooking & wine programs that focus on Tuscan & Italian recipes. Established: 1986. Class/group size: 6-10 hands-on. 24 programs/yr. Facilities: Chianti: Podere Le Rose, a 13th-century restored Tuscan farmhouse, which is also Marquis de' Mari's private home. Florence: private homes. Also featured: Food, olives & wine intinerary, 1-day market visit, Italian language & art history programs, customized programs for groups.
Emphasis: Traditional home-style Italian & Tuscan cuisine using fresh seasonal ingredients.
Faculty: Sisters Paola & Simonetta de' Mari, assisted by a Tuscan chef.
Costs: $750/5-day cooking course.
Location: Chianti: 30-min from Siena, 1 hr from Florence. Florence: Italian family apartment in a residential area 5 min from the historic center.
Contact: Simonetta de'Mari di Altamura, Toscana Mia, Poggio S. Polo 2, Gaiole in Chianti (SI), 53013 Italy; (39) 0577-746152, Fax (39) 0577-746132, info@welcometuscany.com, www.welcometuscany.com.

COOK ITALY

Tuscany, Umbria, Sicily, Bologna, Emilia-Romagna

Sponsor: Private cooking school. Programs: Classes in authentic Italian food that is quick & simple to prepare. Established: 1999. Class/group size: 4-8. 25 programs/yr. Facilities: Italian family homes. Lucca: converted stable block with pool; Florence: villa with pool; Cortona: country villa; Arezzo: country house with pool; Siracusa: small hotel. Also featured: Market shopping, wine tastings, food producer vists, dining at fine restaurants, demos by chefs & in private homes.

EMPHASIS: Italian food as cooked in Italian homes, using seasonal produce, simple culinary techniques.

FACULTY: Culinary expert, cook & gastronome Carmelita Caruana; local bread & pizza chefs & expert pasta makers. Restaurant chef demos on request.

COSTS: $790-$850/3-day classes, $1,400- $2,000/week includes shared lodging, meals, food trip. 1-day custom lessons from $200, weekend custom tour from $750.

CONTACT: Carmelita Caruana, Cook Italy, Via Bellombra 10, Bologna, 40136 Italy; (39) 051-644-86-12, Fax (39) 051-644-8612, carmelita@cookitaly.com, www.cookitaly.com.

COOK AT SELIANO

Paestum, Naples & Salerno

Sponsor: Cookbook author Arthur Schwartz. Programs: 5-day program that includes 3 half-day Neapolitan cooking classes, visits to a mozzarella di bufala producer, intro to regional wines, dining in local restaurants, visits to private homes.. Established: 2002. Class/group size: 16 max for hands-on. 4 programs/yr. Facilities: New kitchen classroom. Tenuta Seliano, a vegetable farm, & Masseria Eliseo, a water buffalo farm, have modern rooms with private baths.. Also featured: Tours to Naples & Salerno, a visit to the Greek temples of Paestum with an archaeologist, pottery shopping, swimming pool, horseback riding.

EMPHASIS: Traditional seasonal Neapolitan cuisine.

FACULTY: Arthur Schwartz, New York radio program host, cookbook author & experienced cooking teacher, & Baronessa Cecilia Bellelli Baratta; assistants include Iris Carulli, an American who lives in Italy, & local women.

COSTS: $3,350 includes shared lodging, meals, local transportation; $450 single supplement.

CONTACT: Arthur Schwartz, Cook At Seliano; 718-783-2626, Fax 718-783-4242, CookAtSeliano@aol.com, www.arthurschwartz.com.

COOKING WITH GIULIANO HAZAN AT VILLA GIONA

Verona

Sponsor: Giuliano Hazan, cookbook author & Italian cooking teacher, & the Allegrini Winery. Programs: Hands-on classes & field trips that include the Allegrini winery (producer of Amarone), a risotto mill, an olive oil frantoio, a maker of Parmigiano-Reggiano, food markets, the Lake of Garda, fine restaurants. Established: 2000. Class/group size: 12. 4-6 programs/yr. Facilities: Modern teaching kitchen in the newly restored Villa Giona.

EMPHASIS: Easy to make, genuine Italian food for the home cook, including homemade pasta. Basic Italian ingredients & techniques.

FACULTY: Giuliano Hazan, author of The Classic Pasta Cookbook & Every Night Italian.

COSTS: $3,500-$3,800 includes deluxe lodging at the Villa Giona, most meals, planned excursiont.

LOCATION: Veneto. Villa Giona is in 12 acres of private park & vineyards, 5 mi from Verona.

CONTACT: Giuliano Hazan, Cooking With Giuliano Hazan at Villa Giona, 4471 S. Shade Ave., Sarasota, FL 34231; 941 923-1333, Fax 941 923-1335, giuliano@giulianohazan.com, www.giulianohazan.com/school.

COOKING AT THE VILLA

Verona

Sponsor: Culinary professional Luisa Zecchinato. Programs: 6-day cooking vacations that feature daily classes, a wine tour, & sightseeing. Established: 1996. Class/group size: 8-14. ~2 programs/yr. Facilities: The Contatti Studio overlooking the main artery of historic Verona.

EMPHASIS: Regional cuisine of northeast Italy.
FACULTY: Luisa Zecchinato, who was born & raised in Verona, Italy; & French-trained chefs.
COSTS: $1,625 includes shared 4-star hotel lodging, most meals, ground transport, planned activities.
CONTACT: M. Luisa Zecchinato, Chef &Teacher, Cooking At The Villa, P.O. Box 1135, W. Falmouth, MA 2574; (39) 457971312, zecchinato@cooking-at-the-villa.com, www.cooking-at-the-villa.com.

COOKING & WINE TASTING IN ETRUSCANS LAND

Monti della Tolfa (near Rome)

Sponsor: Private school in a family villa. Programs: 5-8 day cooking vacations featuring hands-on & demo classes using home-grown products, visits to food producers, tutored wine & grappa tastings, restaurant dining. Established: 1998. Class/group size: 2-8. 100 programs/yr. Facilities: Large furnished kitchen & a wood fired oven on the terrace. Also featured: Horse riding, Italian language classes, pottery, archaeology, mountain biking, trekking, sightseeing, free climbing, painting.
EMPHASIS: Light cooking based on organic, self-produced olive oil. Local Italian specialties.
FACULTY: Owners Claudio & Assuntina; local experts & professional cooks.
COSTS: $1,680-$1,950/wk, $992/5 days includes lodging, meals, excursions; $150/1 day cooking class with lunch.
LOCATION: Fontana del papa, a 16th century restored estate villa overlooking the Monti della Tolfa, 50 min north of Rome.
CONTACT: Assuntina Antonacci, Owner, Cookery in Etruscans Land, Fontana del papa, Tolfa, 59 Italy; (39) 766 92196, (39) 328 9463763, Fax (39) 766 92196, info@fontanadelpapa.it, www.cookitaly.it.

COSELLI SCHOOL OF TUSCAN CUISINE

Coselli, Lucca, Tuscany

Sponsor: Private school affiliated with La Famiglia Tuscan restaurant in London & Italian cheese producer Alival/Mandara. Programs: 4- & 6-day Tuscan hands-on cooking vacations with cultural program. Established: 1966. Class/group size: 10-16. Facilities: Purpose-built cooking school kitchen. Also featured: Visits to Lucca, Pisa, Chianti vineyards, wineries, a distillery, markets; pizza, chocolate & truffle making; olive oil & balsamic vinegar tastings.
EMPHASIS: Tuscan cuisine with an emphasis on selecting & understanding produce & inspiring hands-on experience in the kitchen.
FACULTY: Professional Italian chef Valter Roman, guest chef Alvaro Maccioni, owner of La Famiglia restaurant & author of Mamma Toscana cookbook, sommelier/master of wine Raoul Ferrari.
COSTS: 4-day (6-day) course €2,200-€2,500 (€2,900-€3,200) includes lodging, meals, ground transport, planned excursions. Lodging at Borgo Bernardini, a restored historic property.
LOCATION: In the Lucca hills, 10 min from the walled city, 30 min from Pisa, 1 hr from Florence.
CONTACT: Valter & Julia Roman, Borgo Bernardini, Via di Coselli 77/79, Lucca, Tuscany, 55060 Italy; (39) 0583 94404, Fax (39) 0583 947681, info@coselli.com, www.coselli.com. In the U.S.: Judy Ebrey, Cuisine International, P.O. Box 25228, Dallas, TX 75225; 214-373-1161, Fax 214-373-1162, Email CuisineInt@aol.com, www.cuisineinternational.com.

CUCINA MEDIEVAL IN ITALY

Viterbo

Sponsor: Special interest tour company. Programs: Hands-on programs that focus on nutrition and Mediterranean diet, with emphasis on kitchen-tested recipes of the 12th-14th centuries. Established: 1993. Class/group size: 10-12. 24 programs/yr. Facilities: Professional kitchen in the Villa Ex convente of Cistercian (Villa Citerno). Also featured: Winery tours, visits to markets & food producers, dinner in private homes, spa, 1-day sightseeing trips to Rome & Florence.
EMPHASIS: Medieval Age & Alto Lazio cuisines.
FACULTY: Giovanna Scapucci, owner of Il Richiastro restaurant.
COSTS: $1,400 ($2,200) includes all meals and 5 (7) days shared lodging at Villa Citerno. $200 single supplement, $1,800 non-cook friend.
LOCATION: Viterbo (Alto Lazio), 80 km from Rome, 200 km from Florence.

Contact: Iolanda Alexander Davidov, President, Aquilanti Viaggi S.R.L., Via Marzio 46, Vitorchiano (Viterbo), 1030 Italy; (39) 0761-370210, Fax (39) 0761-371240, aquilantiviaggi@libero.it, www.aquilantiviaggi.com.

CUCINA CON MIA

Coldigioco

Sponsor: Culinary professional. Programs: Week-long hands-on cooking vacations that include visits to artisan food producers, markets & wineries, & dining in private homes & fine restaurants. Established: 2000. Class/group size: 4-10. 3-4 programs/yr. Facilities: Professional kitchen, woodburning oven, organic vegetable garden.

Emphasis: Regional farmhouse cooking.

Faculty: Mia Chambers, program director & California Culinary Academy graduate; local Italian artisans, chefs, & home-cooks.

Costs: $1,850-$2,000/wk includes lodging in restored farmhouses, meals, planned excursions, ground & airport transport.

Location: Small 16th century village of Coldigioco, in the Marche region, 45-min from Ancon.

Contact: Chef Mia Chambers, Cucina con Mia, 4096 Piedmont Avenue #263, Oakland, CA 94611-5221; 510-814-0758, Chefmiachambers@aol.com, www.cucinaconmia.com.

CUCINA MONDIALE

Florence countryside

Sponsor: Private cooking school. Programs: 1-wk regional culinary tours that include hands-on cooking, wine tasting, cheese making, visits to kitchens, markets, & ceramic producers, restaurant dining. Established: 1999. Class/group size: 8. 4 programs/yr. Facilities: The kitchens of a 650-acre working farm/estate that produces cheese & wine. Features woodburning ovens & fireplace. Also featured: Guided walking tours, art tours.

Emphasis: Regional cooking with emphasis on local & organic food producers, wines, & culture.

Faculty: Timothy Bartling trained at the California Culinary Acad, was a chef at Zuni Cafe & works privately in NY & Italy. 4 local chefs present demos. Hostess Andrea Blum has lived in Italy for 10+ yrs.

Costs: $2,500 includes 6 nights shared lodging in restored 500-yr-old villa (single supplement available), meals, planned activities.

Location: The Fattoria Corzano/Paterno in San Casciano Val in Pesa, 45 min from Florence.

Contact: Andrea Blum, Owner, Cucina Mondiale, 166 Carl Street, San Francisco, CA 94117; 415-731-2429, Fax 415-731-2429, cucinamondiale@earthlink.net.

CUCINA TOSCANA

Florence

Sponsor: Culinary travel service, culinary professional. Programs: Customized 1-day to 1-mo gastronomic excursions in Italy & cooking classes. Established: 1983. Facilities: Gourmet kitchen in private home. Also featured: Wine tastings, regional food producers, walking tours of Florence, shopping, special interest tours.

Emphasis: Regional Italian cuisine.

Faculty: Owner Faith H. Willinger, author of Red, White & Greens: The Italian Way with Vegetables and Eating in Italy. She is afeatured chef on PBS-TV & columnist for Epicurious.com.

Costs: Itinerary planning from $75/day/person; exclusive cooking lessons $450/day/person (6 max).

Contact: Faith Heller Willinger, Cucina Toscana, via della Chiesa, 7, Florence, 50125 Italy; (39) 055-2337014, Fax (39) 055-2337014, fwillinger@dinonet.it.

CUCINA CON VISTA IN FLORENCE

Florence

Sponsor: Private cooking school. Programs: 1- to 4-day cooking courses based on traditional Tuscan & Florentine cooking. Established: 2001. Class/group size: 1-16. 20 programs/yr. Facilities: Modern farmhouse kitchen & dining room. Also featured: Guided tour of the Sant'Ambrogio market, wine tour through the Chianti Hills, promenades in Florence.

EMPHASIS: Tuscan home-style cookery.

FACULTY: Elena Mattei, owner/chef of La Baraonda Restaurant in Florence.

COSTS: Cooking classes: ~€200/day. Cooking packages (cooking classes + activities): €350-€600. Farmhouse lodging available.

LOCATION: An ancient Villa at the gates of Florence, 4 miles from downtown. Transportation to the school is available.

CONTACT: Elena Mattei, Owner, Cucina con Vista, via delle Cinque Vie 4, Florence, 50125 Italy; (39) 347-210-1677, Fax (39) 06-233-237-227, jacopo@cucinaconvista.it, www.cucinaconvista.it.

CULINARY ARTS, INTL: ITALIAN FOOD ARTISANS

Tuscany, Emilia-Romagna, Campania & Piemonte

Sponsor: Pamela Sheldon Johns, culinary professional & cookbook author. Programs: Week-long excursions with emphasis on regional artisan products. 1-day workshops for small groups. Established: 1994. Class/group size: 8 max. 15 programs/yr. Facilities: Restaurants, cooking schools, & farms. Also featured: Hands-on cooking classes, wine tastings, visits to markets & artisan food producers, dining in fine restaurants & private homes.

EMPHASIS: Regional cuisines of Tuscany, Emilia-Romagna, Campania, or Piemonte with a focus on artisanal foods.

FACULTY: Program Director Pamela Sheldon Johns is author of 12 cookbooks including Italian Food Artisans, Parmigiano!, Balsamico!, Risotto, Gelato!, Pasta!, & Pizza Napoletana!. She oversees the local Italian chef/instructors.

COSTS: $2,650/wk for Tuscany, Campania, & Emilia-Romagna, & $2,850 for Piemonte includes all land costs: shared lodging in a villa or 4-star hotel, meals, ground transport, planned excursions.

LOCATION: Tuscany: Montepulciano, Pienza, Cortona, & Chiusi. Emilia-Romagna: Modena, Parma, & Bologna. Piemonte: Alba & Torino. Campania: Naples, Amalfi, & Sorrento.

CONTACT: Pamela Sheldon Johns, Director, Culinary Arts, Intl., 1324 State St., J-157, Santa Barbara, CA 93101; 805-963-7289, Fax 805-499-6714, Pamela@FoodArtisans.com, www.FoodArtisans.com.

CULINARY TOUR OF TUSCANY

Tuscany

Sponsor: The Clown, wine cellar, art gallery, & retail shop. Programs: Week-long culinary vacation in Tuscany featuring cooking classes, wine tastings, cultural & shopping trips. Established: 1999. Class/group size: 8-10. 10-15 programs/yr. Facilities: 2 well-equipped kitchens. Also featured: Visits to restaurants, vineyards and historic sights.

EMPHASIS: Focus on regional cuisine and wines.

FACULTY: Tom Gutow, chef at Trattoria Delia in Burlington, VT.

COSTS: $2,500 includes shared lodging ($600 single supplement).

LOCATION: Tramonti, a Tuscan estate, winery & olive oil producer on 200 acres 10 mi north of Siena, 20 mi south of Florence.

CONTACT: THE CLOWN, 123 Middle St., Portland, ME 4101; 207-756-7399, Fax 207-828-1549, workshops@the-clown.com, www.the-clown.com/tc-lists/mod.php?mod=userpage&menu=23&page_id=12.

DIANE SEED'S ROMAN KITCHEN AND CULINARY ADVENTURES

Rome, Amalfi Coast & Naples, Puglia

Sponsor: Culinary professional Diane Seed. Programs: 6-day cooking vacations that include hands-on classes & excursions. Established: 1996. Class/group size: 12. 12 programs/yr. Facilities: Rome: Purpose-designed kitchen in 17th-century Doria Pamphili palace. Amalfi coast: kitchens in local trattorias. Puglia: historic fortified farmhouse, now a Rerlais Chateaux hotel. Also featured: Market visits, fine dining, wine, olive oil & balsamic vinegar tastings, pizza making.

EMPHASIS: Italian regional cuisine with seasonal ingredients.

FACULTY: Diane Seed, British cooking teacher & author, who has lived in Rome for 30 years.

Costs: Rome: $1,000 includes some meals. List of small hotels supplied. Amalfi coast: $2,000 includes lodging, meals, ground transport, day Naples trip. Puglia $2,500 all-inclusive from Brindisi airport.
Location: Central Rome at Piazza Venezia in historic palace. Amalfi coast: Sant'Agata sui Due Golfi, a small town between Sorrento & Positano. Puglia: Hotel Melograno, Monopoli.
Contact: Diane Seed, Diane Seed's Roman Kitchen, Via del Plebiscito 112, Rome, 186 Italy; (39) 06-6797-103, Fax (39) 06-6797-109, dianeseed@compuserve.com, www.italiangourmet.com.

DIVINA CUCINA
Florence

Sponsor: Judy Witts Francini, IACP member & Certified Culinary Professional. Programs: Shopping in the Central Market and hands-on cooking classes (offered Tues-Thurs); food-lover's walking tours of Florence (offered Mon-Fri); tours of the Chianti wine region (offered daily). Established: 1984. Class/group size: 4-8 hands-on courses. 100+ programs/yr. Facilities: Fully-equipped apartment kitchen overlooking Florence's Mercato Centrale. Also featured: Winery tours, day trips, private instruction, visits to markets & food producers, dining in fine restaurants & private homes, sightseeing, visits to Italian artisans.
Emphasis: Tuscan cuisine prepared with market-fresh produce & ingredients.
Faculty: Judy Witts Francini, CCP.
Costs: 3-day cooking session $750; 1-day cooking class $250; half-day walking tour of Florence with lunch $125; 1-day Chianti tour $250.
Location: Central Florence near San Lorenzo Market (Mercato Centrale).
Contact: Judy Witts Francini, Owner, Divina Cucina, Via Taddea, 31, Florence, 50123 Italy; (39) 055-29-25-78, Fax (39) 055-29-25-78, info@divinacucina.com, www.divinacucina.com.

ESPERIENZE ITALIANE
Tuscany, Veneto, Umbria, Piedmont, Sicily

Sponsor: Lidia Bastianich, co-owner of Felidia Ristorante. Programs: 7- to 10-day trips that feature cooking demos, dining in fine restaurants, art tours, meetings with wine producers, chefs, & Italian artists, visits to wine estates. Established: 1997. Class/group size: 15-20. 4 programs/yr. Also featured: Custom-designed group trips.
Emphasis: Regional Italian cuisine & wines, Renaissance art.
Faculty: Lidia Bastianich, author of Lidia's Italian Table & star of PBS series; Burton Anderson, author of The Wine Atlas of Italy; art historians Tanya Bastianich & Shelly Burgess.
Costs: $3,800-$4,100, includes 4- & 5-star shared hotel lodging, most meals, planned excursions, ground transport.
Contact: Shelly Burgess Nicotra, Program Director, Esperienze Italiane Travel c/o Felidia Ristorante, 243 E 58th St., New York, NY 10022; 212-758-1488, 800-480-2426, Fax 212-935-7687, shelly@lidiasitaly.com, www.lidiasitaly.com.

FLAVOURS COOKERY HOLIDAYS
Bologna, Puglia & Rome

Sponsor: Cookery holiday operator. Programs: Hands-on cookery holidays in Italy. Weekly courses & short breaks. Established: 1998. Class/group size: 8 max. 26 programs/yr. Facilities: Private luxury villas with fully-equipped kitchen. Also featured: Excursions to local food producers (wine, olive oil, cheese, honey) & other places of interest.
Emphasis: Equal balance between cooking & holiday.
Faculty: Professional local cooks.
Costs: £1,049/8 days, £599/5 days includes lodging, meals, excursions, airport transfers.
Location: 1 hr from Rome in N. Lazio; 40 min outside Bologna; rural location in Puglia.
Contact: Lorne Blyth, Flavours of Italy Ltd., PO Box 525, Broxburn, West Lothian, EH52 5WB Scotland; (44) (0)1506 854621, Fax (44) (0)1526 854102, info@flavoursholidays.com, www.flavours-foodiehols.co.uk.

FOOD LOVERS' ADVENTURES IN EMILIA ROMAGNA

Emilia-Romagna

Sponsor: Travel company specializing in Italian culinary vacations, tourism experience since 1978. Programs: 7-day programs that include hands-on classes in restaurants & private homes, visits & tastings with producers of parmesan cheese, balsamic vinegar, prosciutto, olive oil, wines. Established: 1996. Class/group size: 2-8+. Monthly programs/yr. Facilities: Restaurant & private home kitchens. Also featured: Excursions to markets, herb garden, ceramic studio, castle, mosaics in Ravenna, Bologna shops, truffle hunting, spa, golf. Customized tours on request.

EMPHASIS: Cuisine of Italy's Emilia-Romagna region.

FACULTY: Restaurant & family chefs.

COSTS: $2,750 includes shared lodging, meals, planned excursions.

LOCATION: Bologna, Modena, Imola, Faenza, Ravenna, Dozza, Riolo Terme, Castrocaro, Brisighella, Casola Valsenio.

CONTACT: Marcello and Raffaella Tori, Owners, Bluone Tour Operator, Via Parigi, 11, Bologna, 40121 Italy; (39) 051-263546, Fax (39) 051-267774, info@bluone.com, www.bluone.com. In North America: Margaret Cowan, 101-1184 Denman St., #310, Vancouver, BC, Canada V6G 2M9; 800-557-0370 or 604-681-4074, Fax 604-681-4909, www.italycookingtours.com.

FROM MARKET TO TABLE IN A ROMAN KITCHEN

Rome

Sponsor: Culinary professional Carla Lionello. Programs: 1/2-day private custom-designed hands-on workshops include an olive oil tasting and discussion of local food culture. Established: 1995. Class/group size: 1-5. Facilities: Professional kitchen.

EMPHASIS: Regional Italian cuisine.

FACULTY: Carla Lionello, pastry chef, food researcher & travel writer, author of Fodor's Guide to Venice and Insight Guide to Southern Italy.

COSTS: $275 for one participant, $25 for each additional participant.

LOCATION: Historic center of Rome, near the Trevi Fountain.

CONTACT: Carla Lionello, From Market to Table in a Roman Kitchen, Via Due Macelli, 106, Rome, 187 Italy; (39) 06-699-20435, Fax (39) 06-699-22189, md2063@mclink.it.

GOURMET GETAWAYS

Sorrento & Perugia

Sponsor: Travel company specializing in culinary tours. Programs: Four different 5- to 6-night cooking programs combined with sightseeing trips to nearby towns. Established: 1998. Class/group size: 4-9. 10 programs/yr. Facilities: Hotel kitchens.

EMPHASIS: Regional cooking.

FACULTY: Chef Giancarlo with the Excelsior Vittorio hotel in Sorrento. Chef Massimo Infarati at Castello Dell'Oscano in Perugia.

COSTS: $1,795-$2,400 includes shared lodging for 5-6 nights. Single supplement extra.

CONTACT: Marlene Iaciofano, Pres., Gourmet Getaways, 45 Eagle Nest Rd., Morristown, NJ 7960; 973-644-0906, 888-95-Italy, Fax 973-644-0907, getaways@optonline.net, www.gourmetget.com.

GIULIANO BUGIALLI'S COOKING IN FLORENCE

Florence *(See display ad page 342)*

Sponsor: Cookbook author Giuliano Bugialli. Programs: 1-wk hands-on vacation programs. Established: 1973. Class/group size: 18. 4 programs/yr. Facilities: Large newly-equipped kitchens in a Chianti villa, wood-burning brick oven & hearth. Also featured: Dining in fine restaurants & trattorias, gastronomic & oenologic trips, tastings.

EMPHASIS: Italian authentic cooking of all regions.

FACULTY: Giuliano Bugialli is author of The Fine Art of Italian Cooking, Tastemaker Award winners Giuliano Bugialli's Classic Techniques of Italian Cooking, Giuliano Bugialli's Foods of Italy, Julia Child Award winner Foods of Sicily & Sardinia.

Costs: $3,800 includes most meals, planned excursions, & first class or superior hotel lodging in central Florence.

Location: In Florence with classes in a Chianti country villa.

Contact: Giuliano Bugialli's Cooking in Florence, 252 Seventh Ave., #7R, New York, NY 10001; 646-638-0883, 646-638-1099, Fax 646-638-0381, bugialli@aol.com, www.bugialli.com.

IL CHIOSTRO

Vagliagli, Siena

Sponsor: Private school. Programs: Hands-on one-wk or 10-day (June & October) traditional Tuscan country cooking courses in Italy, featuring visits to olive oil, vinegar, grappa, & honey producers, butchers, bakers. Established: 1995. Class/group size: 8-12. 2 programs/yr. Facilities: Authentic Tuscan country villa or inn at 900-year-old Chianti winery, with pool. Also featured: Excursions to Tuscan hilltowns, day trips to Florence, walking tour of Siena, winery & sommelier tours, private entree to castle & gardens, local artisans.

Emphasis: Tuscan cuisine.

Faculty: Chef Michael Vignapiano from New York Restaurant School, Chef Linda Mironti.

Costs: $1,400-$2,000 including meals, lodging, planned activities, transfers from Siena.

Location: Vagliagli, a hamlet in the Chianti Classico (Gallo Nero) wine region of Tuscany, on the Chiantigiana, 15 min from Siena, 45 min from Florence.

Contact: Michael Mele, Director, Il Chiostro Inc., 241 W. 97th St., #13N, New York, NY 10025; 800-990-3506, Fax 212-666-3506, ilchiostro@hotmail.com, www.ilchiostro.com.

IL FAÈ COOKING COURSES
San Pietro di Feletto, Veneto

Sponsor: Il Faè B&B. Programs: 5-day cooking classes on traditional Italian cuisine. Courses for professionals on blast chiller application & vacuum system. Class/group size: 5 min. Facilities: Kitchen of Il Faè. Also featured: Gluten-free & private cooking classes on request.

EMPHASIS: Traditional Italian cuisine.

FACULTY: Chef Marco Fattorel, member of Fed'n of Italian Cooks; Chef Nicola Michieletto, specialist in Mediterranean & natural cuisine.

LOCATION: 30-min drive from Venice airport.

CONTACT: Salvatore Valerio, Il Faè Cooking Courses, via faè 1, San Pietro di Feletto, Veneto, 31020 Italy; (39) 0438 787117, Fax (39) 0438 787818, mail@ilfae.com, www.ilfae.com.

INTERNATIONAL COOKING SCHOOL OF ITALIAN FOOD AND WINE
Bologna, Piedmont, Tuscany

Sponsor: Private school established by chef & author Mary Beth Clark. Programs: Hands-on courses include: 4-day Taste of Emilia-Romagna, 6-day Basics of Great Italian Cooking, 7-day Savoring Emilia-Romagna & Tuscany and October Truffle Festival. Established: 1987. Class/group size: 12. 11 programs/yr. Facilities: Modern professional kitchen with individual work stations in a Renaissance palazzo. Also featured: Visits to food producers & outdoor food markets, regional olive oiltastings, private winery tours, truffle hunt, dining in Michelin-star restaurants with private demos.

EMPHASIS: Classic & contemporary light-style dishes of Bologna, Emilia-Romagna, Tuscany, Rome, Piedmont, Naples.

FACULTY: Chef Mary Beth Clark, cooking teacher & cookbook author; a pasta chef; a Neapolitan pizza chef; Michelin-star Italian chef.

COSTS: $1,895-$3,725 includes most meals, first-class to deluxe lodging, ground transport, excursions, Michelin-star dining.

LOCATION: Bologna's Historic Center, close to the outdoor food market; Tuscan estates & Piedmont.

CONTACT: Mary Beth Clark, Owner, International Cooking School Of Italian Food And Wine, 201 E. 28th St., #15B, New York, NY 10016-8538; 212-779-1921, Fax 212-779-3248, contact@marybethclark.com, www.internationalcookingschool.com.

ISTITUTO VENEZIA
Venice

Sponsor: Private school offering courses in Italian language, culture & cooking. Established: 1995. Class/group size: 8. Facilities: Private apartments or residences. Also featured: Custom programs for groups.

EMPHASIS: Italian cuisine.

CONTACT: Matteo Savini, Director, Istituto Venezia, Dorsoduro 3116/A (Camp S. Margherita), Venice, 30123 Italy; (39) 041-5224331, Fax (39) 041-5285628, info@istitutovenezia.com, www.istitutovenezia.com.

ITALIAN ART & COOKING
Siena, Tuscany *(See display ad page 344)*

Sponsor: Private Italian cooking & language school. Programs: 1- to 4-wk intensive seasonal Italian cooking courses for groups & individuals. Established: 1979. Class/group size: 5-12. 10 programs/yr. Facilities: New fully-equipped professional kitchen & frescoed dining room. Established language school. Also featured: Italian language & cultural courses, excursions to vineyards & sites of interest.

EMPHASIS: Italian cuisine: traditional Tuscan, Mediterranean, seasonal, medieval & regional.

FACULTY: Professional cooking school instructors Mario Neri, Serena Massari; sommeliers & specialized chefs.

COSTS: Amateur: $465/1 wk, $715/2 wks.Professional: $800/2 wks, $1,350/4 wks.

LOCATION: Just outside the medieval city walls of Siena.

CONTACT: Sonia Di Centa, Executive Director, Soc. Dante Alighieri - Siena, Via Tommaso Pendola, 37, Siena, 53100 Italy; (39) 0577 49533, Fax (39) 0577 270646, marketing@dantealighieri.com, www.dantealighieri.com.

ITALIAN COOKERY COURSE

Colere

Sponsor: Private school. Programs: 6-day hands-on Italian cookery course featuring antipasti, primi, secondi, contorni e dolce. Established: 2001. Class/group size: 8-10. 2 programs/yr. Facilities: Hotel kitchen. Also featured: Seasonal hunting for & cooking wild mushrooms. Mountain walks for trekkers, with guides available.

EMPHASIS: Traditional Italian.

FACULTY: 3 professional chef/teachers. Head chef Elena Vecchio.

COSTS: €750 includes 5 nights 3-star hotel lodging & meals.

LOCATION: The Hotel Alpino & Ristorante La Vecchia Cantoniera, a family-owned & managed hotel at the summit of the Presolana pass, 30 mins from Bergamo & 90 mins from Milan.

CONTACT: Gary Vincent, Chef/Teacher, Italian Cookery Course, Albergo Alpino, Via Cantoniera 7, Colere, (Bg), 24020 Italy; (39) 34631103, Fax (39) 34638770, albalp@tin.it.

ITALIAN COOKERY IN TUSCANY WITH URSULA FERRIGNO

Lucca, Tuscany

Sponsor: Private school. Programs: 4- & 7-day residential cookery programs featuring hands-on classes, & excursions to Lucca & Florence, & to wineries of the Lucchese Hills. Wines of Tuscany programs also offered. Established: 1996. Class/group size: 10-14. 5-6 programs/yr. Facilities: Tuscan farmhouse kitchen. Traditional wood-burning oven for pizza & bread-making. Also featured: Art & architectural visits. Swimming, horseback riding, tennis.

EMPHASIS: History & regional variety of Italian food & wine.

FACULTY: Ursula Ferrigno, cookbook author, TV/radio guest; plus her assistant.

COSTS: 4-day program: £585/£625. 7-day program: £985. Includes shared lodging, meals with wine, ground transport, wine tastings, excursions.

LOCATION: Vallicorte, a restored farmhouse in Lucca.

CONTACT: Berenice Bonallack, Italian Cookery in Tuscany with Ursula Ferrigno, Box 15, London, E1W 2NB England; (44) 20 7680 1377, Fax (44) 20 7680 1377, tours@vallicorte.com, www.vallicorte.com.

ITALIAN COOKERY WEEKS LTD

Amalfi Coast, & Umbrian/Tuscan border

Sponsor: Culinary professional Susanna Gelmetti. Programs: 7-day gastronomic holidays that include regional cookery instruction & excursions to local sites of cultural & historical interest. Established: 1990. Class/group size: 20. 10 programs/yr.

EMPHASIS: Modern, traditional & regional Italian cuisine.

FACULTY: Professional Italian chefs.

COSTS: £1,399 includes 7 nights shared lodging, meals, excursions.

LOCATION: Marina del Cantone, Amalfi & Grotte di Castro, Umbria.

Contact: Susanna Gelmetti, Italian Cookery Weeks Ltd, PO Box 2482, London, NW10 1HW England; (44) (020) 8208-0112, Fax (44) (020) 7627 8467, info@italian-cookery-weeks.co.uk, www.italian-cookery-weeks.co.uk.

ITALIAN COOKING VACATION AT CASA OMBUTO

Tuscany *(See display ad above)*

Sponsor: Casa Ombuto. Programs: 1-week hands-on culinary vacation that includes visits to wineries, olive oil & cheese producers, mushroom hunting in season, shopping in Arezzo. Established: 2000. Class/group size: 8-12. 10-15 programs/yr. Facilities: Professional kitchen designed for cooking lessons in an old Tuscan cantina. Also featured: Shopping in Arezzo & dining at local restaurant. Golf course nearby, hiking, day trip to Florence.

Emphasis: Traditional & modern Italian, Tuscan & regional Italian cuisine.

Faculty: Paola Baccetti was chef in her own restaurant in Bibbiena for 10 yrs. She speaks English.

Costs: $1,950 ($2,400)/wk includes shared (single) lodging at the luxury villa Casa Ombuto, most meals, use of facilities including heated pool. Non-cooking guest $1,200/wk.

Location: Poppi Arrezo, Tuscany, 35 mi from Florence, 55 mi from Siena, 40 mi from Cortona.

Contact: Pippa Ward-Smith, Casa Ombuto, Larniano 21, Poppi, AR, 52014 Italy; (39) 3487363864, Fax (31) 33 2863455, info@italiancookerycourse.com, www.italiancookingvacation.com.

ITALIAN CUISINE IN FLORENCE

Florence

Sponsor: Culinary professional Masha Innocenti. Programs: 3- to 5-day hands-on courses. Special 1- or 2-day demo classes for larger groups with travel agencies. Established: 1983. Class/group size: 8 hands-on/18 demo. 11 programs/yr. Facilities: 300-sq-ft kitchen with modern equipment. Also featured: Private instruction, food lectures.

Emphasis: Regional & nouvelle Italian cuisine, Italian desserts.

Faculty: Masha Innocenti, CCP, IACP, diploma from Scuola di Arte Culinaria Cordon Bleu, a member of the Assoc Italiana Sommeliers & Commanderie des Cordons Bleus de France.

Costs: $780/5-day gourmet cuisine courses, $470/3-day intensive course, includes meals. Private classes $165/day.

Contact: Masha Innocenti, Italian Cuisine in Florence, Via Trieste 1, Florence, 50139 Italy; (39) 055-499503, Fax (39) 055-480041.US Contact: William Grossi, 182 Four Corners Rd., Ancramdale, NY 12503, 518-329-1141.

ITALIAN CULINARY COURSE

Sorrento

Sponsor: Private cooking school. Programs: 3- to 7-session courses that focus on the food, techniques, culinary traditions & artisans of the south of Italy; individual classes. Established: 2002. Class/group size: 8 max. Facilities: Country-style home with kitchen & classroom. Also featured: Visits to cheese factories (Mozzarella di Bufala production), Antica Gelateria Sorrentina, guided tours.

Emphasis: Traditional southern Italy cuisineemphasizing naturally-grown products.

Faculty: Biagio, the lead native Italian chef, has 30 yrs of international culinary experience.
Costs: €35-€2,500.
Contact: Italian Culinary Course, Via Cocumella 4, 80065 S. Agnello di Sorrento, Naples, Italy; (39) 081 878 20 67, Fax (39) 081 878 20 67, dedello@hotmail.com, www.mamicamilla.com.

ITALIAN CULINARY INSTITUTE FOR FOREIGNERS
Costigliole d'Asti, Torino

Sponsor: Professional cooking school in Italy that offers theory & practice courses to intl students. Programs: 3-, 4-, & 7-day hands-on culinary & enology courses. Established: 1991. Class/group size: 10. 8 programs/yr. Facilities: New high-tech facilities include Modulari stainless steel equipment. Wine cellar & olive oil tasting room.
Emphasis: Italian regional/classic cooking & wines, with emphasis on Piedmontese.
Faculty: Chef Pietro Baldi has 30+ yrs experience in Italian cuisine & wine making. Sergio Zanetti has worked in major European hotels.
Costs: $799-$1,799 includes meals, lodging in mini-apartments, airport transportation.
Contact: Enrico Bazzoni, Director, ICIF-USA, 126 2nd Place, Brooklyn, NY 11231; 718-875-0547, Fax 718-875-5856, Eabchef@aol.com, www.icif.com.

ITALIAN GOURMET COOKING CLASSES IN PORTOVENERE
Portovenere, Sicily, Venice & Tuscany

Sponsor: Grand Hotel Portovenere - Chef Paolo Monti's Culinary Program. Programs: 7-day courses covering fish, vegetables, antipasti, sauces, soups, salads, pasta, main dishes, desserts. Established: 1994. Class/group size: 6-12. 8-10 programs/yr. Facilities: Cooking class kitchen with overhead mirror & audio system. Also featured: Visit to vineyards, olive oil mill, Parma, Cinque Terre. Shorter courses & 1-day classes available. Instruction in English, French, German. Wine tasting & wine tours.
Emphasis: Gourmet Italian (Mediterranean) cuisine using fresh herbs & ingredients, short cooking times, fish.
Faculty: Grand Hotel Portovenere's Chef Paolo Monti.
Costs: €2,090 includes shared lodging at the 4-star Grand Hotel Portovenere (single room supplement €400), meals, trips.
Location: Italian Riviera near the Cinque Terre & Portofino. Culinary tours to Sicily & Venice. Tuscan food & wine tour to the Palio di Siena.
Contact: Paolo Monti, Chef, Grand Hotel Portovenere Chef Paolo Monti's Culinary Program, Via Garibaldi, 5, Portovenere, 19025 Italy; (39) 0187-79-26-10, Fax (39) 0187-79-06-61, paolomonti@cucina-italiana.com, www.cucina-italiana.com.

LA NOSTRA TOSCANA
Pisa, Lucca, Florence, Greve in Chianti, Siena

Sponsor: Sommelier Fabrizio Ferruzzi & his wife Cathy. Programs: 4-day food & wine tour with hands-on cooking classes preparing lunch. Afternoons devoted to escorted Tuscan city tours & fine dining. Established: 1999. Class/group size: 5-8. 5 programs/yr. Facilities: Corte di Valle, a renovated villa with modern kitchen. Also featured: Wine & olive oil tastings.
Emphasis: Food, wine & culture of Tuscany.
Faculty: Tuscan gourmet/sommelier Fabrizio Ferruzzi, founder of Arte degli Oliandoli; Cathy Fabrizio, 20+ yrs experience with Tuscan cooking; Tuscan chef Beppe Ceserali.
Costs: $2,900/4-days includes meals, lodging, ground transport, activities.
Location: Corte di Valle near Greve in Chianti.
Contact: Mary Frances Sheffield, General Manager, La Nostra Toscana, 3045 West Ardmore, Chicago, IL 60659; 773-275-6903, Fax 773-275-6985, Theshefs@aol.com.

LA PENTOLA DELLE MERAVIGLIE
Florence

Sponsor: Culinary professional. Programs: 1- to 10-session courses on a variety of topics.
EMPHASIS: International cuisines, holiday & special occasion menus.
FACULTY: Barbara Desderi.
COSTS: €45/session.
CONTACT: Barbara Desderi, Owner, La Pentola delle Meraviglie, Via Aretina, 118 r, Florence, 50136 Italy; (39) 055670205, Fax (39) 055670205, info@lapentoladellemeraviglie.it, www.lapentoladellemeraviglie.it.

LA VILLA CUCINA
Umbria

Sponsor: Culinary travel provider. Programs: 1-wk vacations that combine a villa holiday & cooking school vacation, including hands-on classes, visits to markets, wineries, olive oil & artisan food producers, sightseeing, restaurant dining. Established: 1998. Class/group size: 12. 3+ programs/yr. Facilities: Professional kitchen. Also featured: Private instruction.
EMPHASIS: Regional Italian cooking.
FACULTY: Daniel Rosati has been a cooking instructor at The New School in NYC 12+ yrs, was teaching assistant to Giuliano Bugialli, & received the Auguste Escoffier gold medal.
COSTS: $3,450 includes shared lodging at Il Poggio degli Olivi, a restored 17th-century villa & working agricultural complex, meals, ground transport, planned activities.
LOCATION: Minutes from Perugia.
CONTACT: Daniel Rosati, Owner, La Villa Cucina, 14 Wilson Ave., 3rd Floor, Newark, NJ 7103; 973-344-7577, info@lavillacucina.com, www.lavillacucina.com.

LAURA NICCOLAI COOKING SCHOOL
Naples, Siena

Sponsor: Culinary professional Laura Niccolai. Programs: 1-week demonstration courses (4 classes) in S'Agata sui Due Golfi, Naples, and Locanda Dell'Amorosa in Sinalunga, Siena. Established: 1987. Class/group size: 20. Facilities: Well-equipped, professional kitchens. Also featured: Naples: dinners in selected restaurants, visits to Limoncello liqueur & mozzarella factories, guided tours to Capri and Positano. Siena: wine & olive oil tastings, cultural & gastronomic tours. 1-day.
EMPHASIS: Traditional and modern Italian, Tuscan, and Neapolitan cuisine with emphasis on light and healthy recipes.
FACULTY: IACP-member Laura Niccolai studied with Michelin 3-star chef Gualtiero Marchesi and French pastry chef Jain Bellouet.
COSTS: $3,000 ($3,500) for the Naples (Siena) program, which includes double occupancy lodging, meals, planned activities. Lodging at luxury hotels in Sorrento (Naples) and the Locanda dell'Amorosa in Siena.
LOCATION: S. Agata sui Due Golfi is 30 miles south of Naples; Locanda dell'Amorosa is 50 miles south of Florence.
CONTACT: Laura Niccolai, Laura Niccolai Cooking School, Via Termine 9, S. Agata sui Due Golfi-NA, 80064 Italy; (39) 081-8780152, Fax (39) 081-8780152.In the U.S.: The International Kitchen, Inc., 1209 N. Astor St., #11N, Chicago, IL 60610; 800-945-8606, Fax:312-654-8446, info@intl-kitchen.com, http://www.intl-kitchen.com.

L'OLMO
Catania, Sicily

Sponsor: Private estate. Programs: 7-day vacation programs that include cooking classes, dining in fine restaurants, visits to wineries & private estates. Established: 2003. Class/group size: 12-14. Facilities: The kitchen of l'Olmo. Also featured: Cultural activities, excursions to Mt. Etna, archaeological sites, & nearby cities, boat & fishing trips, water-skiing, sailing.
EMPHASIS: Sicilian cuisine.

Faculty: Giuliana Spadaro di Passanitello, author of Notebook of Joy, a collection of Sicilian recipes, & articles on Sicilian history & culinary art.

Costs: $3,150 includes lodging, meals & planned excursions.

Location: 30 min from the Catania airport, 15 min from Taormina.

Contact: Alexis Magarò, l'Olmo, 11, rue Chapon, Paris, 75003 France; (33) (0) 1 48 04 54 29, Fax (33) (0) 1 48 04 54 29, alexis.magaro@mageos.com, www.lolmo.it.

LUNA CONVENTO COOKING CLASSES WITH ENRICO FRANZESE

Amalfi

Sponsor: Luna Convento Hotel. Programs: 1-wk culinary vacations that include 4 morning demo & participation classes. Established: 1991. Class/group size: 12-18. 8 programs/yr. Facilities: Luna Convento Hotel's Saracen Tower, overlooking the sea. Also featured: Guided excursions to Sorrento, Ravello, Pompeii, & Amalfi; dinner at Don Alfonso, a Michelin 3-star restaurant owned by Alfonso & Livio Iccharino.

Emphasis: Regional Neapolitan cuisine.

Faculty: Enrico Franzese trained at the Cipriani in Venice & the Hassler in Rome, won the 1990 Parma Ham Chef's Competition in Bologna, & appears on Italian TV; interpreter Rosemary Anastasio.

Costs: $2,700 ($3,000) includes meals, planned excursions, transportation from Salerno, & first class double (single) occupancy lodging & private bath at the 4-star Luna Convento Hotel, a restored 13th-century convent.

Location: A resort area on Italy's west coast, ~150 mi south of Rome & 40 mi south of Naples.

Contact: Rosemary Anastasio, School Director, Luna Convento, Amalfi, SA, 84011 Italy; (39) 089-830-130, info@cuisineinternational.com, www.cuisineinternational.com. In the U.S.: Judy Ebrey, Cuisine International, Inc. P.O. Box 25228, Dallas, TX 75225; 214-373-1161, Fax 214-373-1162.

MAMMA AGATA COOKING CLASSES

Ravello

Sponsor: Travel company owned by Chiara Lima, daughter of Mamma Agata. Programs: 1-wk courses, daily lessons, & private dinners by Mamma Agata also available. Established: 1997. Class/group size: 8 max. Facilities: Mamma Agata's simple, well-equipped kitchen in her cliff-top home with terraces & gardens. Also featured: Visits to cheese & lemon factories, boat excursion, sightseeing in Pompeii, Capri, Ischia, Sorrento & Amalfi coasts.

Emphasis: Traditional Mediterranean & Italian cuisine.

Faculty: Mama Agata has cooked for Humphrey Bogart, Audrey Hepburn, Jacqueline Kennedy, & Gore Vidal.

Costs: €200/day includes AM class & lunch.

Location: Ravello, 5 km from Amalfi, 20 km from Positano.

Contact: Chiara Lima, Proprietor, Mamma Agata Cooking Classes, Via San Cosma, 9, Ravello, Salerno, 84010 Italy; (39) 089-857019, (39) 089 858432, Fax (39) 089-858432, chiaralima@yahoo.it.

MAMA MARGARET AND FRIENDS' COOKING ADVENTURES IN ITALY

Piedmont, Tuscany, Umbria, Emilia-Romagna, Amalfi

Sponsor: Margaret Cowan Direct Ltd. & specialty tour operators in Italy. Programs: 3- to 8-day cooking holidays with cooking classes in fine restaurants, winery visits & tastings, winemakers' dinners, food producer visits, walks with local hosts. Established: 1995. Class/group size: 2-7. 60 programs/yr. Facilities: Restaurant kitchens. Also featured: Custom designed tours.

Emphasis: Regional specialties. Barolo, Vino Nobile, Brunello wines.

Faculty: Restaurant chefs. A farm family in Tuscany.

Costs: $1,200-$3,095, all-inclusive.

Contact: Margaret Cowan, Mama Margaret and Friends' Cooking Adventures in Italy, 310 101-1184 Denman St., Vancouver, BC, V6G 2M9 Canada; 800-557-0370/604-681-4074, Fax 604-681-4909, margaret@italycookingschools.com, www.italycookingtours.com.

MARIA BATTAGLIA – LA CUCINA ITALIANA, INC.
Regions of Italy

Sponsor: Culinary professional. Programs: 9-day demo cooking vacation courses. Established: 15. 5 programs/yr. Also featured: Sightseeing, fine restaurant dining, shopping, visits to nearby towns.
Emphasis: Regional Italian food, wine, culture.
Faculty: Maria Battaglia has conducted seminars on food, wine & culture of Italy for 15+ yrs. She was national spokesperson for Contadina Foods.
Costs: $3,250-$4,260 includes air-fare, lodging, meals, planned activities.
Location: Sicily, Campania, Tuscany/Rome, Emilia-Romagna/Venice, Sorrento, Naples, Pompeii, Amalfi, Ravello, Capri.
Contact: Maria Battaglia, President, Maria Battaglia - La Cucina Italiana, P.O. Box 6528, Evanston, IL 60204; 847-933-0077, Fax 847-933-0088, mbcucina@aol.com, www.la-cucina-italiana.com.

MEDITERRANEAN LIFE
Bari, Brindisi, Lecce, Taranto

Sponsor: Tour operator specializing in Apulia & Southern Italy. Programs: Culinary tours featuring lessons on traditional Apulian recipes, wine, olive oil, architecture, history, heritage. Includes excursions to orchards, citrus groves, oil-mill, olive tree farm. Established: 1992. Class/group size: 4-12. 12 programs/yr. Facilities: Farmhouse or hotel kitchens.
Emphasis: Traditional Apulian cuisine.
Faculty: Local chefs or experts in Mediterranean cooking.
Contact: Rossana Muolo, Owner, Itinerant Course of Mediterranean Cooking, SS.379 Savelletri - Torre Canne Loc. Forcatella Piccola, Savelletri di Fasano , BR, 72010 Italy; (39) 080 48 29 421, Fax (39) 080 48 28 036, info@mediterraneanlife.com, www.mediterraneanlife.com.

PALAZZO TERRANOVA
Umbria

Sponsor: Bed & breakfast hotel. Programs: Cooking weekends in November during the Porcini & Truffle festival. Truffle hunting, Umbrian cooking classes; visits to markets, farms, food producers & vineyards; olive oil, balsamic vinegar & wine tastings; local excursions. Class/group size: 6 min. 5 programs/yr. Facilities: Hotel kitchen including wood fired oven. Also featured: Courses on wine, art, art history. Swimming pool, boules, horseback, trekking, golf, hot air ballooning, tennis, archery, cultural tours.
Emphasis: Umbrian cooking with seasonal ingredients.
Faculty: Hotel owner Sarah Townsend.
Costs: From €200/day including lunch. Lodging €685/night including breakfast.
Contact: Sarah Townsend, Palazzo Terranova Srl, Loc. Ronti Morra, Perugia, 6010 Italy; (39) 075 8570083, Fax (39) 075 8570014, bookings@palazzoterranova.com, www.palazzoterranova.com.

PANE, VINO E LINGUA
Florence

Sponsor: Enoteca de'Giraldi wine bar & restaurant. Programs: 1- & 2-wk hands-on programs that combine exposure to the Italian language with cooking classes & Tuscan food & wine activities, incl excursions to the Chianti region. Established: 1994. Class/group size: 10 max. 12 programs/yr. Facilities: Facilities of the Enoteca de'Giraldi. Also featured: Visits to markets, food producers, & farms, winery tours.
Emphasis: Tuscan food, wine & language.
Faculty: Andrea Moradei, Ph.D., owner & Tuscan food & wine expert.
Costs: €1,000 (€560) with language instruction, €700 (€390) without language instruction for 2 (1) wks.
Location: Central Florence near the Bargello museum.
Contact: Andrea Moradei, Owner, Vinaio.com Travel Agency, Via de' Pepi 56 red, Florence, 50122 Italy; (39) (0)55-213881, Fax (39) (0)55-216949, info@vinaio.com, www.vinaio.com.

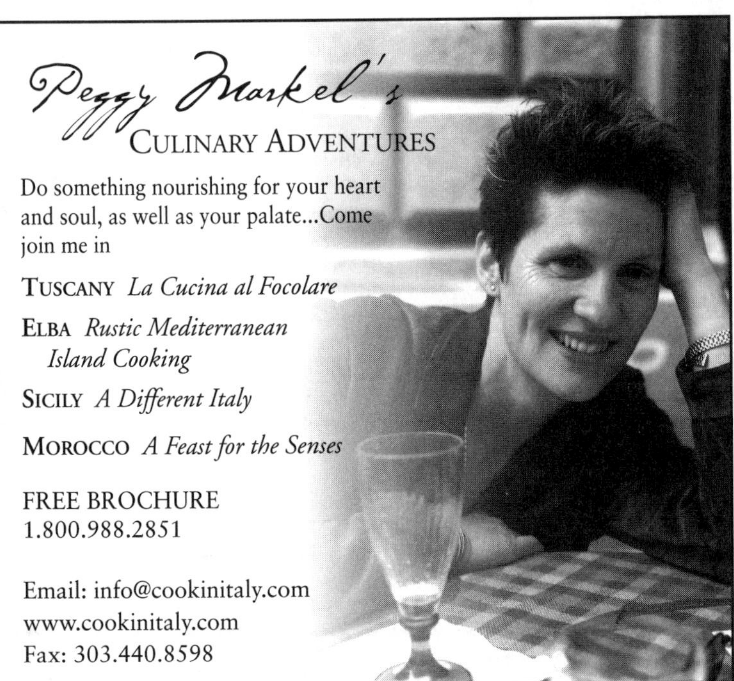

Peggy Markel's
CULINARY ADVENTURES
Do something nourishing for your heart and soul, as well as your palate...Come join me in
TUSCANY La Cucina al Focolare
ELBA Rustic Mediterranean Island Cooking
SICILY A Different Italy
MOROCCO A Feast for the Senses
FREE BROCHURE
1.800.988.2851
Email: info@cookinitaly.com
www.cookinitaly.com
Fax: 303.440.8598

PEGGY MARKEL'S CULINARY ADVENTURES

Tuscany, Elba & Sicily, Italy; Laos; Morocco *(See display ad above)*

Sponsor: Culinary tour provider Peggy Markel. Programs: 5-, 7- & 10-day hands-on culinary vacations: La Cucina al Focolare, Rustic Mediterranean Island Cooking, A Different Italy, A Feast for the Senses, Southeast Asian Artistry. Weekend summer & winter intensives in the US. Established: 1991. Class/group size: 16 max. 15+ programs/yr. Facilities: Professional kitchens with the latest equipment, including wood-burning oven, individual work stations. Also featured: Visits to bakery, artisan cheese maker & herb farm, market tour, winery tour, dining in fine restaurants, cultural excursions.

EMPHASIS: Tuscan, Mediterranean & Sicilian regional specialties, Moroccan cuisine of Marrakech, Thai & Laotian Southeast Asian.fare.

FACULTY: Program founder Peggy Markel; Piero Ferrini, chef-professor; Luciano Casini, chef/owner of Il Chiasso, Elba; author/cook Anna Tasca Lanza, women chefs of Morocco. Mr. Pat, Thailand. Chefs of Laos.

COSTS: $2,500-$4,195 includes lodging, meals, excursions, ground transport.

LOCATION: Fattoria Degli Usignoli, 45 min from Florence. Jnane Tamsna, 15 min from Marrakech.Laem Set Inn, 20 min from Koh Samui Airport. Duang Champa Hotel, 15 min from Laos airport.

CONTACT: Peggy Markel, Director, Peggy Markel's Culinary Adventures, P.O. Box 54, Boulder, CO 80306-0646; 800-988-2851, 303-413-1289, Fax 303-440-8598, info@cookinitaly.com, www.cookinitaly.com.

ROBERTO'S ITALIAN TABLE
Venice

Sponsor: Culinary professional Robert Wilk. Programs: 1-wk culinary & cultural holiday that includes cooking lessons at the Hotel Cipriani, cultural activities, visits to private palaces. 1-day customized program that includes a Rialto Market tour, cooking lesson in Roberto's kitchen, & cultural event. Established: 1995. Class/group size: 1-20. Daily programs/yr. Facilities: Kitchens of Hotel Cipriani, Roberto's home kitchen in the 15th-century Palazzo Michiel Berlendis. Also featured: Tours of countryside, wineries & vineyards, dining in fine restaurants & private homes, sightseeing.

EMPHASIS: Italian cuisine & culture.

FACULTY: Chefs Renato Piccoloto & Roberto Gatto (Hotel Cipriani), Cultural Director Dr. Joseph A. Precker, Host/Cooking Teacher Roberto Wilk.

COSTS: $4,950/1-wk program includes 5-star hotel lodging, most meals, planned activities. $550/1-day program ($450 for each additional person).

CONTACT: Robert Wilk, Roberto's Italian Table, Dorsoduro 3441, Venice, 30123 Italy; , Fax (39) 041-714-571, roberto@italiantable.com, www.italiantable.com.

ROMANTICA COOKING TOURS
Regions of Italy

Sponsor: Tour operator specializing in vacations in Italy. Offices in USA & Italy. Programs: Vacations that include cooking classes, wine, cheese & olive oil tastings, vinery tours, sightseeing & excursions. Established: 1985. Class/group size: 1-50. 150+ programs/yr. Facilities: Cooking schools, restaurant kitchens, country villa kitchens & home kitchens. Also featured: Customized group & individual travel. Itineraries & tours with overnight in small boutique hotels. Private boat rental.

EMPHASIS: Regional cuisine of Italy.

FACULTY: Restaurant chefs, regional experts.

COSTS: $200-$3,460 including hotel lodging, most meals, tastings, excursions & sightseeing.

LOCATION: Rome, Florence, Venice, Amalfi Coast, Spoleto, Perugia, Parma, Tuscany & Umbria.

CONTACT: Aldo Caronia, V.P. - Director of USA Operations, Romantica Tours, 2101 Waukegan Road, Bannockburn, IL 60015; 800-227-1908, x5931, Fax 847-948-8473, acaronia@romantica-tours.com, www.romanticatours.com.

SAY ITALY!
Messina, Sicily

Sponsor: Specialty travel company. Programs: One-week culinary & cultural tours that include hands-on cooking classes and visits to markets, winemakers, museums, & nearby towns. Established: 2002. Class/group size: 10-16. ~5 programs/yr. Also featured: Horseback riding, tennis, swimming, boat excursions.

EMPHASIS: Sicilian cuisine.

FACULTY: Elena Feminò & other native Italian cooks.

COSTS: $1,400 includes shared apartment lodging, meals, excursions.

LOCATION: Torre di Marmora, a farm/estate near Messina.

CONTACT: Jackie Hendrix, Owner, Say Italy!, P. O. Box 1600, Houston, TX 77251-1600; 866-621-6676 or 713-621-6676, Fax 713-552-9512, info@sayitaly.com, www.sayitaly.com.

SCUOLA DI ARTE CULINARIA 'CORDON BLEU'
Florence, Tuscany

Sponsor: Private school. Programs: 4-session courses & 7-day cooking, wine, art, culture programs. Established: 1985. Class/group size: 15 max. 12 programs/yr. Facilities: 40-sq-meter teaching kitchen. Also featured: Wine tasting, guided excursions & tours, market visit.

EMPHASIS: Basic, advanced, Tuscan, & new Italian cuisine; bread, history, nutrition, wines, olive oil.

FACULTY: 2 full- & 2 part-time instructors. Cristina Blasi & Gabriella Mari, 18 yrs teaching experience, sommeliers & olive oil experts, authored books on ancient Roman cooking, members Commanderie des Cordon Bleus de France, IACP.

COSTS: Classes from €60; 4-session course €360 including VAT & insurance; 7-day program €750 including one 5-session course, 3 dinners, planned activities.

LOCATION: Near the Duomo Cathedral, 15 min from Florence airport.

CONTACT: Emilia Onesti, Secretary, Scuola di Arte Culinaria 'Cordon Bleu', Via di Mezzo, 55/R, Florence, 50121 Italy; (39) 055-2345468, Fax (39) 055-2345468, info@cordonbleu-it.com, www.cordonbleu-it.com.

SCUOLA DI ARTE CULINARIA CORDON BLEU, PERUGIA

Ponte Valleceppi, Umbria

Sponsor: Private school. Programs: 1- to 9-session courses on basic to advanced cooking plus specific topics from appetizers to desserts. 3- to 5-day programs in collaboration with wineries, restaurants & food producers. Established: 1997. Class/group size: 8-12. 25+ programs/yr. Facilities: 16th century estate with a home kitchen.

EMPHASIS: Italian cuisine.

FACULTY: Andrea Sposini & Roberto Menichetti, who both studied at the Cordon Bleu School of Culinary Arts in Rome.

COSTS: €60/session, $600-$1,000 for multi-day programs.

LOCATION: ~10 km from Perugia, 2 hrs north of Rome, 2 hrs east of Florence.

CONTACT: Sheila Santolamazza, Scuola di Arte Culinaria Cordon Bleu Perugia, viale Ponte Nestore, 23, Marsciano, 6055 Italy; (39) 333 9813695, Fax (39) 075 874 1690, Sheila@gestionecupido.com, www.gestionecupido.com/ENG/corsi/default.htm.

SCUOLA LEONARDO DA VINCI

Rome, Florence & Siena

Sponsor: Private school. Programs: Hands-on Italian cooking & Italian wine courses held 1 evening weekly for a 2-wk or 4-wk session. Established: 1977. Class/group size: 10-15. ~40 programs/yr. Facilities: Fully-equipped professional kitchen. Also featured: Italian language & culture courses, excursions to vineyards & other places of interest.

EMPHASIS: Cooking course: typical Italian meals & recipes from different regions of Italy. Wine course: introduction to grape cultivation, processing & storing, tastings, wine-cellar visit.

FACULTY: Professional cooking school instructors & sommeliers.

COSTS: Italian cooking or wine course 2 evenings over 2 wks €95; 4 evenings over 4 wks €150.

LOCATION: Each school in Rome, Florence and Siena is located in the historical center of the city.

CONTACT: Niccolò Villiger, Co-webmaster, Italian Cuisine & Wine Courses in Florence, Rome, Siena, Via Brunelleschi 4, Florence, 50123 Italy; (39) 055-290305, Fax (39) 055-290396, info@scuolaleonardo.com, www.scuolaleonardo.com.

SICILIAN AND APULIAN CUISINE

Apulia, Sicily

Sponsor: Tour operator. Programs: Week-long vacations that include Mediterranean cooking demonstrations & excursions that focus on art history, architecture & visits to local craftsmen. Established: 2000. Class/group size: 4-12. 5-10 programs/yr. Also featured: Include Italian or Latin for foreigners, drawing lessons, reed basket weaving.

EMPHASIS: Typical regional food & wine.

FACULTY: Includes Ms. Lanera of Masseria Serragambetta, who is also a TV cook.

LOCATION: Southern Italy.

CONTACT: Natalie Hoerner, Capeland Tours, Via B. D'Acquisto 17, Monreale (PA), I-90046 Italy; , sales@capeland.it, www.capeland.it/english/Tours/frameMain.html.

SICILIAN ODYSSEY

Catania

Sponsor: Culinary travel company. Programs: 7 night culinary & sightseeing program that features cooking with 2 well-known Sicilian chefs. Established: 1998. Class/group size: 4-10. 2 programs/yr.

Also featured: Visits to the major tourist sites on Sicily, wine tasting, visits to food artisans, dinners in private homes.

EMPHASIS: Sicilian cuisine.

FACULTY: Jack Bruno, president of the Sicilian Chef's Org & owner/chef of the restaurant Villa Albanese Rubicon. Signora Giuliana Condorelli & her husband are experts in ancient cuisine of the Sicilian nobility.

COSTS: $2,500 includes 4-star hotel lodging, most meals, transfers, planned excursions.

LOCATION: Palermo, Marsala, Agrigento, Syracusa, Taormina.

CONTACT: Roberta Barbagallo, Sicilian Odyssey, Via Cesare Vivante, 28, Catania, Italy; (39) (0)95-552725, Fax (39) (0)95-446628, info@intl-kitchen.com, www.theinternationalkitchen.com/sicily.htm. Local Contact: The International Kitchen, Email: info@intl-kitchen.com; Toll-free: 800-945-8606; Local: 312-726-4525, Fax: 312-803-1593.

SIENA CULTURE COOKING

Siena

Sponsor: Private school. Programs: 3-hr Italian cooking classes offered daily or weekly. Established: 1990. Class/group size: 6 max. Facilities: Kitchen with Tuscan furniture restored by Marco. Also featured: Italian language classes, wine instruction, visits to local farms.

EMPHASIS: Traditional Tuscan cooking, holiday menus, preparing the table, selecting olive oil.

FACULTY: Elisabetta, her husband Marco, & staff. Elisabetta has 10+ yrs teaching foreign students, & holds a degree in English Lit. Marco works in the wine & olive oil industry.

CONTACT: Elisabetta Ungaro, Siena Culture Cooking, Via Pian D'ovile - 21, Siena, 53100 Italy; (39) 0577 920451, cell 3337526246, sienaculturacucina@libero.it, www.sienaculturecooking.it.

SPA AND COOKING IN THE VENETO

Sponsor: Culinary tour company. Programs: Six-night program that combines an Italian spa with hands-on cooking lessons and excursions. Established: 1998. Class/group size: 2-8. 4 programs/yr. Facilities: Villa kitchen. Also featured: Spa treatments, market visit, excursion to Lake Garda and Verona, grappa tasting, dinner cruise on the Venetian lagoon.

EMPHASIS: Italian cuisine.

FACULTY: Sergio Torresini has taught cooking at Abano's hotel management school for ten years.

COSTS: $2,550 includes six nights lodging in a 4-star spa hotel, meals, excursions, spa treatments.

LOCATION: Abano Terme.

CONTACT: Lino Barillari, Spa and Cooking in the Veneto, Via Monteortone, 19, Abano Terme, Italy; (39) (0)49-8669990, Fax (39) (0)49-667549, info@intl-kitchen.com, www.theinternationalkitchen.com/abano.htm. The International Kitchen, Email: info@intl-kitchen.com, Toll-free: 800-945-8606,Local: 312-726-4525,Fax: 312-803-1593.

SPOLETO COOKING SCHOOL

Spoleto

Sponsor: The Spoleto Arts Symposia: Cooking School, Writers' Workshop, Vocal Arts Symposium, Improvisation Workshop. Programs: 1-wk hands-on courses that include dining and demos at fine restaurants, excursions, truffle hunting & visits to a truffle factory, olive oil production, & Lungharotti wine makers, shopping at local food market. Established: 1997. Class/group size: 10 max. 2 programs/yr. Facilities: Professional kitchens at La Scuola Alberghiero, featuring individual professional-level work stations. Also featured: Italian language class with culinary focus, interaction with opera master class, writers' workshop, improv workshop.

EMPHASIS: Regional cooking of Umbria including the black truffle, farro, cicerchie, lentils, oils.

FACULTY: Master chef from La Scuola Alberghiero di Spoleto, a national chef's training school; restaurant owners & chefs.

COSTS: $2,200, includes most meals, lodging at a 4-star hotel, planned activities.

LOCATION: The Umbrian hills, 75 mi north of Rome, 12 mi south of Assisi.

CONTACT: Clinton J. Everett III, Executive Director, Spoleto Cooking School, 760 West End Ave. #3A, New York, NY 10025; 212-663-4440, Fax 212-663-4440, clintoneve@aol.com, www.spoletoarts.com.

SUSAN SCHIAVON'S VENETIAN EXPERIENCE

Venice

Sponsor: Culinary professional Susan Schiavon. Programs: 5-day hands-on Italian/Venetian cookery vacations that include 3 classes, shopping at Rialto market, boat trip, visit to Murano & Veneto countryside. Established: 1996. Class/group size: 7. 5-6 programs/yr.

EMPHASIS: Basics of Italian/Venetian cooking.

COSTS: $1,350/5 days includes full board & lodging in a luxury home in central Venice, ground transport, planned activities.

LOCATION: A gondola ferry ride from the Rialto market, & a 10-15 min walk from St. Mark's.

CONTACT: Susan Schiavon, Susan Schiavon's Venetian Experience, Calle Zanardi 4133, Cannaregio, Venice, 30121 Italy; (39) 0415237194, Fax (39) 0415212705, susan.venice@iol.it.

A TASTE OF VENICE

Venice, Italy

Sponsor: Specialty travel company. Programs: 8-day travel programs that include two cooking classes. Established: 2002. Class/group size: 6 maximum. 13 programs/yr. Facilities: Palazzo Fuseri. Also featured: Craft class, visit to glass factory, concerts, museums, market visits, city tours, dining at fine restaurants.

FACULTY: Chef Daniella Penso of Lido, Venezia.

COSTS: $1,950 includes some meals, lodging in 4-star apartment, planned activities.

LOCATION: St. Marks district.

CONTACT: Denise Marie Corsile, Owner, A Taste of Venice, Via Lepanto 10, Lido, Venice, 30126 Italy; (39) 041-276-9798, Fax (39) 041-276-9798, info@atasteofvenice.com, www.atasteofvenice.com.

TASTES OF ITALY LTD

Venice, Verona, Bologna, Florence

Sponsor: Specialist Italian gourmet travel company, based in London. Programs: Scheduled and customized programs that feature fine dining, visits to food-related sites, cooking demonstrations, cultural activities. Established: 2000. Class/group size: 8-16. 15 programs/yr. Facilities: Restaurant kitchens or country villas.

EMPHASIS: Italian food & culture.

FACULTY: Includes restaurateurs Giancarlo Gianelli (Tuscany), Giancarlo Gioco (Verona), Bonifacio Brass, grandson of Giuseppe Cipriani (Venice), Nico Costa (Bologna).

COSTS: From £300-£750 for a 3- to 5-day program, which includes deluxe lodging, meals, planned activities.

CONTACT: William Goodacre, Director, Tastes of Italy Ltd, 15 Greswell St., London, SW6 6PR England; (44) 20 87882337, Fax (44) 870 169 5324, info@tastesofitaly.co.uk, www.tastesofitaly.co.uk.

TASTING PLACES

Italy, Greece, Thailand, England

Sponsor: Culinary travel company. Programs: Master classes at notable London restaurants. One-week hands-on cookery courses & holidays focusing on regional cuisine. Food & wine tours. Corporate food & wine events. Established: 1992. Class/group size: 12-16. 30+ programs/yr. Facilities: Houses with well-equipped kitchens, including pizza ovens, grills, & open fire cooking. Restaurant kitchens in London. Also featured: Wine tastings, visits to markets, vineyards, & fine restaurants, customized gourmet trips.

EMPHASIS: Regional cooking, hands-on classes, food & wine matching, wine & olive oil tastings.

FACULTY: Restaurateurs, chefs & cookery writers Alastair Little, Carla Tomasi, Maxine Clark, Thane Prince, Hugo Arnold, Franco Taruschio, Peter Gordon. Notable London restaurant chefs.

COSTS: Trips from £1,200 ($1,650), which includes lodging, meals, wine, excursions. London master classes £120-£200.

LOCATION: UK: London. Italy: Tuscany, Umbria, Sicily, Veneto, Piedmont. Greece: Santorini. Thailand: Koh Samui Island.

CONTACT: Sara Schwartz or Sarah Robson, Tasting Places, Unit 108, Buspace Studios, Conlan St., London, W10 5AP England; (44) (0) 207-460-0077, Fax (44) (0) 207-460-0029, ss@tastingplaces.com, www.tastingplaces.com.

TASTY TUSCANY
Agliati (Pisa) & Tuscany

Sponsor: Private school. Programs: Weekly 1- & 2-wk hands-on vacation programs that include 4 cooking classes/wk, wine tastings, tour of chianti producers, dining with local families, truffle hunting, cultural events. Established: 1995. Class/group size: 2-10. 5 programs/yr. Facilities: Kitchen of a restored 16th-century country house with marble working stations, garden & patio facing the Tuscan hills. Also featured: Art excursions, archaeological hiking, horseback riding, mountain biking, swimming, ceramic making, basket weaving, painting, yoga & massage workshops.

EMPHASIS: Traditional family Mediterranean & vegetarian cooking using organic products.

FACULTY: Includes Patrizia d'Intino & Paolo Vecchia (cooking), Steve Armstrong (wine), Giovanni Corrieri (archaeological excursions), Grazia Bodino & Luciano Dallapè (art tours). Staff speaks English, French, Spanish.

COSTS: $1,980-$2,200/wk ($1,540 for non-cooking guest) includes shared villa lodging, meals, planned activities. 2- to 3-day courses also available.

LOCATION: Near Montopoli Valdarno & Palaia, between Pisa (30 min) & Florence (45 min).

CONTACT: Patrizia d'Intino, Culinary Artist, Tasty Tuscany, Via Agliati, 123, Località Agliati - Palaia (Pisa), 56036 Italy; (39) 0587 622531/622186, cell phone (39) 335 569 5678, Fax (39) 0587 622186, patrizia@tastytuscany.com, www.tastytuscany.com.

TOSCANA SAPORITA TUSCAN COOKING SCHOOL
Massarosa, Lucca, Tuscany

Sponsor: Culinary professional Sandra Lotti. Programs: include 6-day traditional Tuscan cuisine. Each features 17-20 hrs of hands-on instruction & afternoon tours. Established: 1995. Class/group size: 8-12. 24 programs/yr. Facilities: Professional, modern kitchen housed in a 15th-century villa with a wood-beamed dining room, antique furniture, modern plumbing & electricity. Also featured: Market shopping, fine dining, tours of Lucca, Portovenere, Pietrasanta, Viareggio, Pisa.

EMPHASIS: Tuscan cuisine.

FACULTY: Sandra Lotti (author of Sapore di Maremma, L'Anno Toscano, & Zuppe Toscane), cousin of the late Anne Bianchi (author of From The Tables of Tuscan Women, Zuppa!, Solo Verdura, Italian Festival Food). Both co-authored Dolci Toscani. 2-3 assistants.

COSTS: $2,050-$2,450 incl meals, ground transport, tours, & lodging at Toscana Saporita.

LOCATION: Camporomano, an olive oil producing 70-acre estate with swimming pool, hiking trails, & three 15th century villas. 20 mi from Pisa Intl Airport, 50 mi from Florence, 3 mi from the seaside resort of Viareggio.

CONTACT: Toscana Saporita, P.O. Box 686, Prince Street Station, New York, NY 10012; 212-219-8791, Fax 212-219-8791, toscana@compuserve.com, www.toscanasaporita.com.

TOSCANAINBOCCA
Florence

Sponsor: Private school. Programs: 1- to 5-day courses in Tuscan cuisine. Established: 1998. Class/group size: 2-12. Also featured: Visits to specialty shops & craftsmen, sightseeing.

EMPHASIS: The art, history, culture & traditions of food in Tuscany. The art of entertaining.

FACULTY: Anna has a degree in literature & manages a school for children. Gloria is an art historian & lived in the US.

COSTS: 5-day course €750, 3-day course € 460, 1-day course € 300/couple, €160/person.

LOCATION: Country house in Sesto Fiorentino, 30 min from downtown, & the pedestrian-only area of Florence, overlooking the cathedral.

CONTACT: Gloria Marinelli, Toscana in Bocca, Via Cimatori, 5, Florence, 50122 Italy; (39) 055 2678149, Fax (39) 055 2678149, toscanainbocca@yahoo.it, www.toscanainbocca.it.

TUSCAN WAY – LA VIA DEI SENSI

Tuscany

Sponsor: Casa Innocenti, a medieval home; Villa Gaia, a country estate; Villa Castelletti, an estate west of Florence. Programs: 1-week and 1/2-week hands-on Tuscan cuisine culinary vacations that feature daily classes & excursions. Established: 1999. Class/group size: 4-8. 30+ programs/yr. Facilities: Historic kitchens equipped with stoves & a wood-burning oven. Also featured: Wine tastings, grape harvest tours, excursions to small villages of Tuscany. Lunches at local restaurants.

EMPHASIS: Tuscan cuisine & rustic Tuscan dishes.

FACULTY: Carlo Innocenti, chef-owner of Casa Innocenti; Isabel Innocenti, program founder/director. Linda Sorgiovanni, hostess of Villa Castelletti.

COSTS: $2,790 ($1,690) for 7 days (4 days) includes shared lodging in Casa Innocenti, meals, excursions. Single $3,190 ($1,890).

LOCATION: Casa Innocenti & Villa Gaia are southwest of Siena, Villa Castelletti is 9 miles from the historical center of Florence.

CONTACT: Isabel Innocenti, Director, Tuscan Way - La Via dei Sensi, 2829 Bird Ave., Suite 5, PMB 242, Coconut Grove, FL 33133; 800-766-2390, 305-598-8368, Fax 305-598-8369, Isabel@tuscanway.com, www.tuscanway.com.

TUSCAN WOMEN COOK

Montefollonico, Tuscany

Sponsor: Specialty travel company. Programs: 1-day, 3-day & week-long culinary & cultural vacation programs that feature morning hands-on cooking classes & afternoon visits to food artisans, olive oil producers, local food markets, & food festivals. Established: 1998. Class/group size: 12. 9 programs/yr. Facilities: Kitchens in Tuscan country homes & restaurants. Also featured: Fine dining, trekking, cycling, hot air ballooning, outlet shopping, excursions to historic Tuscan cities.

EMPHASIS: Tuscan cuisine.

FACULTY: Local Tuscan women who use fresh local ingredients and prepare family recipes.

COSTS: $2,350 includes 7 nights shared first class lodging at Hotel La Costa, a 14th-century restored farmhouse, most meals, planned activities. $350 single supplement.

LOCATION: Montefollonico (Siena), 1 hr south of Florence, 2 hrs north of Rome. Near Siena, Cortona, & Arezzo.

CONTACT: Bill & Patty Sutherland, Owners, Tuscan Women Cook, Podere Poggio Castagni, Montefollonico (SI), 53040 Italy; (39) 0577 669 444, Fax (39) 0577 668 707, info@tuscanwomencook.com, www.tuscanwomencook.com. Philip Cecchettinipolenta@pacbell.net.

VENETIAN COOKING IN A VENETIAN PALACE

Venice

Sponsor: Culinary professional Fulvia Sesani. Programs: Cooking classes in her 13th-century Venetian palace. Established: 1984. Class/group size: 10. Facilities: Modern, fully-equipped kitchen. Also featured: Shopping in the Rialto market, visits to the Ducal palace, museums, and private homes, dinner at Harry's Bar, and the Palazzo Morosini. Also available: day classes, private lessons.

EMPHASIS: Traditional Venetian cooking, edible works of art.

FACULTY: Fulvia Sesani.

LOCATION: The Palazzo Morosini is in the Santa Maria Formosa area of Venice.

CONTACT: Fulvia Sesani, Venetian Cooking in a Venetian Palace, Castello 6140, Venezia, 30122 Italy; (39) 041-522-8923.In the U.S.: Judy Ebrey, Cuisine International Inc., P.O. Box 25228, Dallas, TX 75225; 214-373-1161, Fax 214-373-1162, Email CuisineInt@aol.com, www.cuisineinternational.com.

VERBENA BLU VIAGGI – COOKING CLASSES IN SIENA

Siena & Florence, Tuscany

Sponsor: Cultural & culinary specialists. Programs: Cooking classes & gourmet tours. Visits to Tuscany countryside, Chianti wine & olive oil tastings. Established: 1999. Class/group size: 8. 24 programs/yr. Facilities: Kitchen-classroom. Also featured: Walking, biking, wine & customized tours.

Emphasis: Italian cuisine.
Faculty: Culinary professionals.
Costs: From $2,000 including lodging, most meals, escorted tours, ground transport.
Contact: Franco Battista, Verbena Blu Viaggi - Cooking Classes in Siena, V.le Toselli, 35, Siena, 53100 Italy; (39) 0577 226691, Fax (39) 0577 221051, info@verbenabluviaggi.com, www.verbenabluviaggi.com.

VILLA CROCIALONI COOKING SCHOOL
Fucecchio, Tuscany

Sponsor: Private villa on 35 acres. Programs: 5-day programs every other week include hands-on classes daily & an excursion to Viareggio (seashore) fish market and Central Market in Florence. Established: 1996. Class/group size: ~4-8. 25 programs/yr. Facilities: Family kitchen with large oven & 6 burners, wood burning oven. The villa produces olive oil, vegetables, herbs, & raises farm animals. Also featured: Pool, jogging, visits to Santa Croce leather factories, and to Lucca, on request. B&B stays available between cooking courses.
Emphasis: Tuscan-American cuisine.
Faculty: Buncky Pezzini, who trained in New York City, has 47 yrs experience in Italian cuisine.
Costs: $2,800 includes lodging at the villa, meals, excursions, ground transport; single supplement $350. Airport transfers additional.
Location: 50 min from Florence, 40 min from Pisa, 20 min from Lucca, ~2 hrs from Siena.
Contact: Patricia (Buncky) Pezzini, Cook/Owner, Villa Crocialoni Cooking School, Via Delle Cerbaie #60, Fucecchio, Florence, 50054 Italy; (39) 0571-296237, Fax (39) 0571-296237, villacrocialoni@leonet.it.In the U.S.: Judy Ebrey, Cuisine International Inc., P.O. Box 25228, Dallas, TX 75225; 214-373-1161, Fax 214-373-1162, Email CuisineInt@aol.com, www.cuisineinternational.com.

VILLA DELIA HOTEL & TUSCANY COOKING SCHOOL
Ripoli di Lari

Sponsor: Tuscan villa hotel & cooking school. Programs: 10-day vacation packages that include 7 hands-on cooking classes. Established: 1995. Class/group size: 22. 18 programs/yr. Facilities: 16th century restored Tuscan villa on 54 acres of olive groves & vineyards; swimming pool & tennis courts. Also featured: Wine & private instruction, day trips, market visits, wine & olive oil tastings, dining in fine restaurants, cultural sightseeing.
Emphasis: Tuscan cooking.
Faculty: Resident chef Marietta. Umberto Menghi teaches some spring & fall classes.
Costs: €4,700 double, €5,200 single occupancy. Includes meals, excursions, Pisa airport transfers & deluxe lodging with private bath.
Location: 20 min from Pisa.
Contact: Kim Lloyd, Sales Director, Umberto Management Ltd., 1376 Hornby St., Vancouver, BC, V6Z 1W5 Canada; 604-669-3732, Fax 604-669-9723, inquire@umberto.com, www.umberto.com.

VILLA UBALDINI
Florence

Sponsor: Villa originally built in the 13th century. Programs: 1-wk hands-on programs devoted to kitchen-tested recipes of Italian cuisine, nutrition & the Mediterranean diet. Instruction can be in English, Italian, Spanish, French, or German. Established: 1995. Class/group size: 16. 10 programs/yr. Facilities: Large teaching kitchen. Also featured: Visits to food producers, winery & guided tours of lesser known Tuscany, dining in private homes & Villa Ubaldini, cultural activities.
Emphasis: Medieval, Renaissance & Italian cuisine; cooking with flowers; table decoration; food culture through the centuries.
Faculty: Margherita Vitali, mgr of the courses & a founder of the Italian Assn. of Cooking Teachers, and Chef Janet Hansen, author of Medieval Fires..Renaissance Stoves.
Costs: $2,900-$3,500, includes shared lodging at Villa Ubaldini, private bath, most meals, planned excursions. Amenities: pool, billiards. Golf, horses, gliders at additional cost.

Location: 20 min north of Florence in an environmentally protected area.
Contact: Margherita Vitale, Villa Ubaldini, via Genova 10, Grosseto, 58100 Italy; (39) 335 6543530, Fax (39) 055 8428998.

VILLA & VACATION COOKING SCHOOLS – TUSCANY & AMALFI COAST
Tuscany & Amalfi Coast

Sponsor: Tour operator in Italy specialising in cookery schools & villa rentals. Programs: 1-day to 1-week cooking vacations that include hands-on lessons, visits to wineries, dining in fine restaurants, sightseeing. Established: 2003. Class/group size: 2-10. 10 programs/yr. Also featured: Custom wine & food tours, villa rentals.
Emphasis: Regional Italian cuisine.
Faculty: Chef Lory has 10 yrs teaching experience & owned a restaurant in Arezzo; Chef Tonino has a one Michelin star Restaurant in Marina del Cantone.
Costs: €150/day including meals to €2,600/wk including lodging, some meals, planned excursions.
Location: Tuscany: Villa Fonte del Leccio, 40 km south of Siena; Casa Bellavista near Cortona; La Badia & Villa Pomaio near Arezzo. Amalfi Coast: Ristorante Quattro Passi, Marina del Cantone near Positano.
Contact: Elisa Biagini, Villa & Vacation Srl, Sede Operativa, Via Giotto 7, Arezzo (AR), 52100 Italy; (39) 0575 40 32 63, (39) 0575 30 29 33, Fax (39) 0575 40 79 86, info@villa-and-vacation.com, www.villa-and-vacation.com.

VILLA VALENTINA
Tuscany

Programs: 1-wk Italian cookery holidays featuring hands-on cooking lessons, visits to local markets, trip to Parma for local ham & Parmesan cheese making; wine, olive oil, grappa, & cheese tastings. Class/group size: 15. Facilities: Professional kitchen with traditional & modern kitchen implements, sitting room, terrace, coffee bar, private dining room. Also featured: Gardening course may run concurrently with a cookery course.
Emphasis: Antipasti, stocks, soups, risotto, gnocchi, polenta, pasta, bread, pizza, game, poultry.
Faculty: Valentina Harris, author of 19 Italian cookery books, Italian food writer for magazines/newspapers, TV/radio guest. Dan DeGustibus teaches bread & baking course.
Costs: £1,220 (£1,185) includes lodging with private (shared) bath; £650 non-participant sharing bedroom with a participant.
Location: Villa Valentina in Tavernelle, a 13th century village in the Lunigiana mountains.
Contact: Villa Valentina, Ltd., PO Box 3038, CR2 0XS England; 44 (0)20 8651 2997, Fax 44 (0)20 8651 2997, pronto@villavalentina.com, www.villavalentina.com.

WINE HARVEST & TUSCAN COOKERY COURSE
Florence

Sponsor: Pagnana Country Cottages. Programs: 3-day Tuscan cooking course includes hands-on classes, wine harvest & tastings, agricultural museum visit. 1-day theme classes & 5-day advanced course also offered. Established: 2000. Class/group size: 5-10. 6 programs/yr. Facilities: Fully-equipped professional kitchen. Also featured: Golf, tennis, swimming.
Emphasis: Theory & practical aspects of traditional Tuscan cooking & agriculture.
Faculty: 1 chef registered with the Italian F.I.C. & F.C.T.
Costs: $200 (guest), $300 (non-guest) for 3-day course includes meals. Cottage lodging available.
Location: 10 miles SE of Florence, in the Valdarno Valley.
Contact: Letizia Breschi, Manager, Fattoria Pagnana, Via Pagnana 42, Rignano sull'Arno, Florence, 50067 Italy; (39) 055.8305336, Fax (39) 055.8305315, info@fattoria-pagnana.com, www.fattoria-pagnana.com.

JAPAN

FACES OF FOOD, THE COOKING SCHOOL
Tokyo

Sponsor: Private cooking school. Programs: Beginner to advanced cooking classes. Established: 1999. Class/group size: 5-10. Facilities: Cooking room set-up for hands-on & demonstration classes. Also featured: Food tours, recipe writing.

EMPHASIS: Western European/Asian influence, Thai, seafood, Japanese food with Western taste, Japanese cooking, wine & food matching.

FACULTY: Angela Nahas, chef, cooking teacher, food consultant; writer & contributor to 30+ cookbooks; has worked in Australia, Paris, London & Japan. Other guest chefs & teachers.

COSTS: Demonstration classes JPY5,000. Hands-on classes JPY6,000. Wine Meets Food classes JPY7,500. Includes food, recipes, wine.

CONTACT: Angela Nahas, Faces of Food, The Cooking School, office: 18 Shinanomachi, Shinjuku-ku Tokyo, 160-0016 Japan; (81) 3 3356 8090, Fax (81) 3 3356 8090, cook@facesoffood.com, www.facesoffood.com.

HAYATO KOJIMA WINE PROGRAMS
Tokyo

Sponsor: Wine professional. Programs: 12- to 14-sessions. Established: 1991. Class/group size: 80-100.

FACULTY: Hayato Kojima, is Pres./Dir. Assoc. de Sommelier-Volant Japonais, president Japan Chapter CWE, Sr. Sommelier of Japan & a wine judge.

COSTS: 177.240 yen (~$1,430)/12 sessions.

LOCATION: Headquarters of Mercian Wine Corp in Kyobashi.

CONTACT: Hayato Kojima, CWE, Wine & New Life Ltd. (WINNEL), 1-2-1 Oyamadai, Setagaya, Tokyo, 158-0086 Japan; (81) 3-3704-0722, Fax (81) 3-3704-0722, fwkc8479@mb.infoweb.ne.jp.

KONISHI JAPANESE COOKING CLASS
Tokyo

Sponsor: Culinary professional Kiyoko Konishi. Programs: Hands-on classes with flexible schedule. Home-style Japanese dishes/decorative cutting also included. Established: 1969. Class/group size: 4-7. 42 programs/yr. Facilities: 300-sq-ft kitchen with Japanese & Chinese utensils & Japanese tableware. Also featured: Classes for youngsters, fish market & supermarket visits, private lessons.

EMPHASIS: Japanese cooking basics, healthy, seasonal & traditional menus with artistic presentation, sushi/one-pot table cooking.

FACULTY: Kiyoko Konishi has taught foreigners in English for 32 yrs & is author of Japanese Cooking for Health & Fitness, Entertaining with a Japanese Flavor, & 3 bilingual cooking videos.

COSTS: 4,000 yen/class includes tax. List of nearby hotels is available.

CONTACT: Kiyoko Konishi, Principal, Konishi Japanese Cooking Class, 3-1-7-1405, Meguro, Meguro-ku, Tokyo, 153-0063 Japan; (81) 3-3714-8859, Fax (81) 3-3714-8859, kikonishi@aol.com, www.seiko-osp.com/kjcc.

LE CORDON BLEU – TOKYO
Tokyo & Yokohama

Sponsor: Private school, sister school of Le Cordon Bleu Paris. Programs: Half-day to 1-yr courses, daily demos, gourmet sessions, cuisine & pastry courses, Introduction to Cuisine, Pastry, & Bread Baking. Established: 1991. Class/group size: 8-16. 10-20 programs/yr. Facilities: Professionally-equipped kitchens; individual work spaces with refrigerated marble tables, convection ovens; specialty appliances. Also featured: Guest chef demos.

EMPHASIS: Diploma & certificate program.

FACULTY: 10 full-time French & Japanese Master Chefs from Michelin-star restaurants & fine hotels.

COSTS: From 5,250 yen (2-hr demo) to 696,150 yen (12-wk Cuisine Superior course).

Contact: Akiko Kohyama, Students Services & Sales Mgr, Le Cordon Bleu Tokyo, ROOB-1, 28-13 Sarugaku-cho, Daikanyama, Shibuya-ku, Tokyo, 150-0033 Japan; (81) 3 5489 0141, Fax (81) 3 5489 0145, tokyo@cordonbleu.edu, www.cordonbleu.co.jp. Toll free in U.S. & Canada: 800-457-CHEF.

A TASTE OF CULTURE
Tokyo

Sponsor: Culinary professional Elizabeth Andoh. Programs: Theme participation classes, programs devoted to traditional Japanese ingredients, Tokyo neighborhood market tours. Established: 1970. Class/group size: 6. 25-30 programs/yr. Facilities: Home kitchen fully equipped for teaching Japanese cooking. Also featured: Customized market tours & workshops.

Emphasis: Japanese food preparation & information about Japan's ancient & modern foodways.

Faculty: Elizabeth Andoh trained at Yanagihara Kinsaryu School of Traditional Japanese Cuisine, Tokyo. She contributes to The NY Times & is Gourmet magazine's Japan correspondent.

Costs: $75/tour, $85/thematic workshop, $95/tasting session.

Contact: Elizabeth Andoh, Director & Instructor, A Taste of Culture, 1-22-18-401 Seta, Setagaya-ku, Tokyo, 158-0095 Japan; (81) 3-5716-5751, Fax (81) 3-5716-5751, andoh@tasteofculture.com, www.tasteofculture.com.

MEXICO

ARCOS MEXICAN COOKING VACATION IN SAN MIGUEL ALLENDE
San Miguel de Allende

Sponsor: Culinary professional. Programs: 1-wk culinary vacation featuring daily cooking classes, market excursion, visits to a restaurant kitchen & Queretaro Culinary Institute. Established: 2002. Class/group size: 7 max. 8 programs/yr. Facilities: Traditional cooking utensils.

Emphasis: Classic & nouvelle Mexican cuisine.

Faculty: Patricia Merrill Marquez, 35 yrs experience Mexican cooking. Guest Instructor Maria Marquez, taught Mexican cooking in León. Other native guest instructors.

Costs: $1,500-$1,700 includes lodging at Arcos Del Atascadero B&B, meals, airport & ground transport, planned activities.

Contact: Patricia Merrill Marquez, Lead Instructor, Mexican Cooking Vacation in San Miguel Allende, Callejon Atascadero # 5B, San Miguel de Allende, GT, 37700 Mexico; (52) 415 152 5299 or 2276, Fax (52) 415 152 5299, congusto@cybermatsa.com.mx, www.mexicancookingvacation.com.

BILLY CROSS CULINARY ADVENTURE TOURS OF MEXICO
Oaxaca, Puebla & Veracruz

Sponsor: Culinary professional Billy Cross. Programs: Culinary adventure tours of Mexico featuring cooking classes, wine tasting, town & city tours, visits to markets, restaurants, private homes. Established: 1972. Class/group size: 6 min. 24 programs/yr. Facilities: Private residence.

Emphasis: Mexican, French, Italian, American.

Faculty: Billy Cross co-founded the Great Chefs of France Cooking School at the Robert Mondavi Winery & has provided tours & cooking classes in Mexico since 1972.

Costs: Cooking classes $150. 1-, 2-, & 3-day tours $125, $250, $375.

Contact: Billy Cross, Owner/Tour Guide, Billy Cross Culinary Adventure Tours, Oaxaca, Mexico; mexicochef@yahoo.com, www.billycross.com.

CABO CASA COOKING
Los Cabos

Sponsor: Travel consultant/agency. Programs: 3- to 5-day seafood cooking programs with opportunities to catch & cook fish. Class/group size: 10 max. 10 programs/yr. Facilities: 13,500-s-ft villa with new kitchen & home-style equipment. Also featured: fishing, golf, scuba, shopping, night life.

Emphasis: Fresh local seafood.

Faculty: Top local Mexican chefs.

Costs: From $150/day including airport pickup, shared lodging, transportation to/from classes.
Location: Villa Los Cabos on Pedregal overlooking the Pacific.
Contact: Marion Snyder, Owner, Cabo Casa Cooking, Plaza Nautica, Los Cabos, 23140 Mexico; (52) 1435872, Fax (52) 1435872, cabocasa@juno.com.

CHEF'S TOUR

Oaxaca, Huatulco, Puebla, Merida

Sponsor: Chef & cooking instructor. Programs: 4-day to 3-week culinary adventure tours with cooking classes and cultural activities. Established: 2000. Class/group size: 8-24. 12 programs/yr.
Faculty: Chef with 25 yrs experience teamed with local guides and experts.
Costs: $2,300 for 10 days, all inclusive.
Contact: Daniel Hoyer, Chef/tour leader, Chef's Tour, Box 2-d, Pilar Route, Embudo, NM 87531; 505-751-4611, hoyer@laplaza.org, www.freeyellow.com/members8/cooks-tour/index.html.

COCINAR MEXICANO

Tepoztlán

Sponsor: Private cultural organization. Programs: 1-wk classical Mexican cuisine courses that include daily hands-on classes & shopping for ingredients in local markets. Established: 2003. Class/group size: 12. 2-4 programs/yr. Facilities: The kitchen of the Posada del Tepozteco, kitchens of local restaurants & homes. Also featured: Excursions to archaeological ruins & museums, massage, traditional adobe sweatbath, hiking, swimming, horseback riding, optional Spanish classes.
Emphasis: Classical Mexican cuisine & variations.
Faculty: Marta García, chef of El Ciruelo in Tepoztlán; guest chefs recruited from noted Mexican restaurants; lecturers in art history & archeology.
Costs: $2,295 includes shared lodging at the 4-star Posada del Tepozteco (single option available), ground transport, most meals, planned activities.
Location: Historic village 35 miles southeast of Mexico City, 15 miles from Cuernavaca.
Contact: Cocinar Mexicano, Mexico; , info@cocinarmexicano.com, www.cocinarmexicano.com.

CULINARY ADVENTURES OF MEXICO

San Miguel de Allende

Sponsor: Culinary travel company. Programs: 1-wk culinary tours that include hands-on classes, market visits, sightseeing, 2-day trips, optional language classes. Established: 1996. Class/group size: 4-10. 5 programs/yr. Also featured: Spa treatments, yoga, salsa dance classes.
Emphasis: Traditional Mexican cuisine & Mexican fusion.
Faculty: Local prominent chefs.
Costs: $1,650 includes luxury lodging, meals, ground transport, planned activities. $400 single suppl.
Contact: Kristen Rudolph, Director, Culinary Adventures of Mexico, Jesus 23, San Miguel de Allende, 37700 Mexico; 0-11-52-(4)-154-4825, Fax 0-11-52-(4)-154-4825, culadv@unisono.net.mx.

FLAVORS OF MEXICO-CULINARY ADVENTURES, INC.

Mexico City, Merida, Veracruz & Yucatan

Sponsor: Marilyn Tausend's Culinary Adventures. Programs: 7- to 10-day cooking vacations to different regions of Mexico. Established: 1988. Class/group size: 6-16. 2-3 programs/yr. Facilities: Home & restaurant kitchens. Also featured: Visits to food markets and cottage industries, meals in homes of local cooks, tours of historical and archaeological sites & artisans' workshops.
Emphasis: Regional Mexican cuisine & cultural background.
Faculty: Marilyn Tausend, author of Cocina de la Familia; Mexican cooking authority Diana Kennedy; culinary consultant Maria Dolores Torres Yzabál; Executive Chef Ricardo Munoz Zurita; Rick Bayless, chef/owner Frontera Grill.
Costs: ~$2,550 includes meals, shared lodging, planned excursions, local transport.
Contact: Marilyn Tausend, Culinary Adventures, Inc., 6023 Reid Dr. N.W., Gig Harbor, WA 98335 ; 253-851-7676, Fax 253-851-9532, E-mail cul_adv_inc@attglobal.net, URL http://www.marilyntausend.com.

LA VILLA BONITA SCHOOL OF MEXICAN CUISINE

Cuernavaca

Sponsor: Chef Ana Garcia, co-owner of La Villa Bonita. Programs: 4- & 7-night hands-on culinary vacation programs that cover traditional & nouvelle Mexican dishes, salsas & condiments, & beverages. Vegan & vegetarian programs available. Established: 2000. Class/group size: 6. 40-44 programs/yr. Facilities: The historic kitchen of a 16th-century mansion, one of the first Spanish colonial structures in the Americas. Also featured: Shopping at local markets, visits to villages in the state of Morelos.

EMPHASIS: Traditional Mexican cuisine.

FACULTY: Chef Ana Garcia, owner of La Villa Bonita and her restaurante Reposado in Cuernavaca. Native cooks assist.

COSTS: $1,495 ($1,795)/7 nights or $950 ($1,195)/4 nights plus tax includes meals & shared (single) lodging at La Villa Bonita. Non-participant guest $500/7 nights, $350/4 nights.

CONTACT: Robb Anderson, La Villa Bonita School of Mexican Cuisine, Netzahualcoyotl #33, Colonia Centro, Cuernavaca, 62000 Mexico; 800-474-3975, Fax 800-474-3975, reservations@lavillabonita.com, www.lavillabonita.com.

MEXICAN COOKING COURSE/LEARNING HOLIDAYS

Cancun

Sponsor: Hotel Cancun Suites 'El Patio'. Programs: 1-week cooking course featuring 5 Mexican cooking lessons & an archaeological site tour. For organized groups of 6 minimum. Established: 1995. Class/group size: 6-10. Varies programs/yr. Facilities: Fully-equipped kitchen & restaurant. Also featured: Spanish lessons, Mayan culture excursions.Healing holidays, osteopathy treatments, chelation therapy, diabetes mellitus treatments.

FACULTY: Mexican chefs.

COSTS: $470 includes 7 nights shared lodging at the Mexican colonial Cancun Inn Suites 'El Patio', breakfast & lunch, archaeological site tour, airport transportation.

CONTACT: El Patio-Reservations, Mexican Cooking Course, Learning Holidays, Bonampak 51 SM 2A, corner of Cereza, Cancun, Q. Roo, 77500 Mexico; (52) (9) 8 84 35 00, Fax (52) (9) 8 84 35 40, lia2001@mail.com, www.cancun-links.com/cooking.htm.

MEXICAN HOME COOKING

Tlaxcala

Sponsor: Culinary professional Estela Salas Silva. Programs: 7-day & customized hands-on cooking vacations. Periodic special menus, cultural events or holiday weeks. Established: 1996. Class/group size: 4 max. Facilities: Fully-equipped 500-sq-ft kitchen with stove & adjacent work areas set below a 70-sq-ft skylight. Also featured: Visits to market, pulquerias, sightseeing.Optional trips to Puebla, archaeological sites at Cacaxtla, Xochitécatl, Cholula; pool & tennis at 4-star hotel in Tlaxcala.

EMPHASIS: The cuisine developed in pre-Hispanic times, influenced by the French and Spanish.

FACULTY: Estela Salas Silva, chef in Mexico City & San Francisco since 1974; local guest cooks.

COSTS: $1,000 includes meals, single occupancy lodging in the Silva family home.

LOCATION: 15 min. from Tlaxcala, a colonial city in central Mexico & 2 hrs from Mexico City airport. Farmland on the side of a seasonal lake surrounded by 3 volcanoes.

CONTACT: Estela Salas Silva, Owner, Mexican Home Cooking, Apartado 64, Tlaxcala, Tlaxcala, 90000 Mexico; (52) 246-46-809-78, Fax (52) 246-46-809-78, mexicanhomecooking@yahoo.com, http://mexicanhomecooking.com.

SEASONS OF MY HEART COOKING SCHOOL

Oaxaca

Sponsor: Private school. Programs: 1-wk courses, 7- to 10-day regional culinary tours, 4- & 5-day weekend courses, day classes, all hands-on. Established: 1993. Class/group size: 4-28. Facilities: Rancho Aurora, a working farm, with a spacious Mexican kitchen & 12 stations, outdoor kitchen with parilla, wood-fire, adobe oven, & pre-Hispanic cooking utensils. Also featured: Visits to corn

& chocolate mills, mezcal factory, markets, archaeological sites, farms, weavers, pottery makers, private homes. Private group tours and lectures.

EMPHASIS: Native & pre-Hispanic foods, chiles, wild plants & herbs, chocolate, contemporary.

FACULTY: Susana Trilling, teacher, writer, TV host, lecturer, chef, caterer, IACP member; part-time teachers, registered tour guides, cheese & chocolate makers, bread bakers, chefs, farmers, herbal healers.

COSTS: Day classes from $75; 4-day/5-day weekend course $950/$1,200; 1-wk course $1,695 includes meals, lodging, planned activities.

CONTACT: Cheryl Camp, Adminstrative Manager, Seasons of My Heart Cooking School, Apdo. 42, Admon 3, Oaxaca, Oaxaca, CP, 68101 Mexico; (52) 951-518-7726/(52)951-508-0044, Fax (52)951-518-7726, seasons@spersaoaxaca.com.mx, www.seasonsofmyheart.com.

TRAVELS WITH CHEF MANUEL

Mexico City & San Miguel de Allende

Sponsor: Culinary professional. Programs: Cooking classes; culinary & cultural tours to Mexico that include cooking classes, meals prepared by executive chefs, visits to restaurants & fresh produce, fish, & game suppliers. Established: 1998. Class/group size: 14. 4 tours programs/yr.

FACULTY: Manuel Otero, a graduate of the Pacific Institute of Culinary Arts, teaches Mexican cooking at Dubrulle.

COSTS: $1,890 includes lodging & most meals.

CONTACT: Manuel Otero, Chef, Travels with Chef Manuel to Mexico, # 205-525 Wheelhuose Sq., Vancouver, BC, V5Z 4L8 Canada; 604-876-2099, Fax 604-876-9040, contact@chefmanuel.com, http://chefmanuel.com.

MOROCCO

COOKING AT THE KASBAH

Morocco

Sponsor: Cookbook author Kitty Morse. Programs: 2-wk tour emphasizing local cuisine & culture, including cooking demo with Kitty Morse & local experts. Established: 1983. Class/group size: 24 max. 1 programs/yr. Facilities: Morse's home, a restored pasha's residence; private & hotel kitchens. Also featured: Visits with friends, excursions to historic locales, marketplaces, working farms; special events; golf & tennis available.

EMPHASIS: Moroccan cuisine & culture.

FACULTY: Native of Casablanca, Kitty Morse is author of Cooking at the Kasbah, Couscous, & The Scent of Orange Blossoms: Sephardic Cooking from Morocco.

COSTS: ~$5,300 includes airfare, land transport, most meals, planned activities, shared lodging in first class or deluxe hotels.

LOCATION: Coastal cities of Casablanca, El Jadida, Azemmour, Essaouira; Imperial cities of Fez, Marrakech, Meknes, Rabat.

CONTACT: Kitty Morse, P.O. Box 433, Vista, CA 92085; , kmorse@adnc.com, www.kittymorse.com.

THE NETHERLANDS

LA CUISINE FRANCAISE

Amsterdam

Sponsor: Culinary professional Patricia I. van den Wall Bake-Thompson. Programs: 1- & 4-session demo & participation courses. Established: 1980. Class/group size: 25 demo/16 hands-on. 60 programs/yr. Facilities: 90-sq-meter kitchen rebuilt in 1994, private dining room in 1647 canal house. Also featured: Sessions in English for groups, private classes, market visits.

EMPHASIS: French, Italian, & English/Dutch cuisines.

FACULTY: School owner & instructor Patricia I. van den Wall Bake-Thompson was born in Great Britain & studied home ec at Harrow Technical College. She is a consultant to food companies.

COSTS: Cooking session from €55. Lodging by arrangement in nearby hotels.

CONTACT: Pat van den Wall Bake-Thompson, La Cuisine Francaise, Herengracht 314, Amsterdam CD, 1016 Netherlands; (31) 20-627-8725, Fax (31) 20-620-3491, info@lacuisinefrancaise.nl, www.lacuisinefrancaise.nl.

NEW ZEALAND

EPICUREAN WORKSHOP
Auckland

Sponsor: Cookware store & cooking school/espresso bar. Programs: Demo & participation classes, 1-hr Gourmet on the Run classes 3 times/wk. Established: 1989. Class/group size: 10-40. 200-250+ programs/yr. Facilities: Teaching kitchen with overhead mirrors. Also featured: Tailor-made Taste of New Zealand classes for visitors, private classes, corporate events, team-building.

EMPHASIS: Seasonal themes, classics, technique & method, ethnic cuisines, local & overseas guest chef specialties.

FACULTY: Director Catherine Bell, CCP, a graduate of Leith's School in London & an IACP member. Local chefs & cookbook authors include Ray McVinnie, Greg Heffernan, Julie le Clerc, Peta Mathias.

COSTS: Demos NZ$22-NZ$85, hands-on classes from NZ$200.

CONTACT: Catherine Bell, Epicurean Workshop, 6 Morrow St., P.O. Box 9255, Newmarket, Auckland, New Zealand; (64) 9 524-0906, Fax (64) 9-524-2017, info@epicurean.co.nz, www.epicurean.co.nz.

LONGHOUSE ISLAND RETREAT NEW ZEALAND
Auckland

Sponsor: Private culinary school. Programs: 5 to 7-day cooking & wine-matching vacations. Demonstration classes, visits to vineyards, olive groves, local village and restaurants. Established: 2001. Class/group size: 8-10. 12 programs/yr. Facilities: Purpose-built teaching facility with commercial demonstration kitchen, outdoor wood-fired bread oven and the latest stainless steel appliances. Dining area with ocean views. Also featured: Visits to art studios, charter fishing, sailing and sea kyaking, swimming, coastal and beach walks and horse trekking. Excursions to Auckland city.

EMPHASIS: Cooking simple, attractive meals using fresh produce, organic where available.

FACULTY: Local and international guest chefs offering modern cuisine.

COSTS: NZ$2,750 to NZ$3,500 includes twin lodging, island transfers, tours and specified meals.

LOCATION: Waiheke Island, 35 mins by ferry from Auckland City.

CONTACT: Longhouse Island Retreat, 155 Nick Johnstone Dr., RD1 Waiheke, Auckland, New Zealand; (64) 09 3729619, Fax (64) 09 3722537, molly@longhousenz.com, http://longhousenz.com.

RUTH PRETTY COOKING SCHOOL
Te Horo, Kapiti Coast

Sponsor: Ruth Pretty Catering. Programs: Full-day weekend classes. Established: 1994. Class/group size: 32 demo, 10 hands-on. 40 programs/yr. Facilities: Commercial catering kitchen. Also featured: Group classes that include a talk & focus on such topics as gardening or wine (no cooking), wine tastings, company dinners.

EMPHASIS: Each class offers a menu with a topic heading.

FACULTY: Caterer Ruth Pretty & a variety of New Zealand & overseas instructors.

COSTS: NZ$155/class.

CONTACT: Ruth Pretty, Ruth Pretty Cooking School, P.O. Box 41, Te Horo, Kapiti Coast, 5560 New Zealand; (64) (0)6-3643161, Fax (64) (0)6-3643262, ruth@ruthpretty.co.nz, www.ruthpretty.co.nz.

PANAMA

ACADEMIA DE ARTES CULINARIAS Y ETIQUETA
Panama

Sponsor: Private cooking school & retail store. Programs: 1-, 2- & 3-day hands-on cooking classes. Established: 2002. Class/group size: 12. 100 programs/yr. Facilities: 12-person professionally-equipped kitchen. Also featured: Etiquette, restaurant service & bartending classes; foodservice industry consulting.

Faculty: Local & guests chefs.

Costs: $30-$50/class.

Contact: Elena Hernández, Owner/Director, Academia de Artes Culinarias y Etiqueta, Calle 51 E y Federico Boyd, Casa #24, Local #3, Panama, Panama; 507-263-6083, Fax 507-263-6083, cocina@cwpanama.net.

PHILIPPINES

HENY SISON CULINARY SCHOOL
Quezon City

Sponsor: Private culinary school. Programs: 20-day Essential Cooking Series;10-day Master Course in Cake Decorating; 5-day Advanced Gumpaste/Foreign Methods Cake Decorating. Short term & specialty courses. Established: 1985. Class/group size: 40 demo, 25 hands-on. 300 programs/yr. Facilities: Air-conditioned lecture room with the latest baking & cake decorating equipment. Also featured: Design & production of cakes for special occasions.

Faculty: Heny Sison & experienced guest chef-lecturers.

Costs: $40-$1,200.

Contact: Heny Sison, Proprietress, Heny Sison Culinary School, 33 Bonnie Serrano Avenue, corner Sunrise Drive, Crame, Quezon City, Metro Manila, Philippines; 632-726-5316, 632-412-7792, Fax 632-412-7792, henysison@pacific.net.ph, www.henysison.com.

PORTUGAL

REFUGIO DA VILA HOTEL & COOKING SCHOOL
Portel, Alentejo

Sponsor: Resort hotel. Programs: 7-day hands-on cooking vacations. Established: 1997. ~30 programs/yr. Facilities: Specially-designed teaching kitchen with a fireplace for baking Portuguese breads and curing sausages. Also featured: Wine, art, & cultural excursions.

Emphasis: The cuisine of Portugal.

Faculty: Chef António Miguel Amaral.

Costs: $2,195 includes lodging, meals, planned activities.

Location: One hour from the Spanish border and 90 minutes from Lisbon.

Contact: Refugio da Vila Rural Hotel, Largo Dr. Miguel Bombarda, 8, Portel, Alentejo, 7720-369 Portugal; (351) 266 619010, Fax (351) 266 619011, refugiodavila@iname.com, www.refugiodavila.com. In the U.S.: Judy Ebrey, Cuisine International, P.O. Box 25228, Dallas, TX 75225; 214-373-1161, Fax 214-373-1162, Email CuisineInt@aol.com, www.cuisineinternational.com.

SCOTLAND

EDINBURGH SCHOOL OF FOOD AND WINE
Edinburgh

Sponsor: Private school. Programs: 1- to 5-days, include demo & hands-on classes, short courses & master classes. 1- & 5-wk intensive certficate courses & 6-mo Diploma in Food & Wine. Established: 1987. Class/group size: 20 max. Facilities: Full range of domestic & commercial equipment.

Emphasis: Practical, hands on course with modern presentation using Scottish produce.

Costs: From £25-£8,500.

Location: Private country estate 5 min from airport, 20 min from city center.

Contact: Jill Davidson, School Director, Edinburgh School of Food and Wine, The Coach House, Newliston, Edinburgh, EH29 9EB Scotland; (44) (0) 131 333 5001, Fax (44) (0) 131 335 3796, info@esfw.com, www.esfw.com.

SINGAPORE

AT-SUNRICE THE SINGAPORE COOKING SCHOOL & SPICE GARDEN

Singapore

Sponsor: at-sunrice, a center for Asian food, culinary skills & craftware. Programs: Demo & hands-on classes, chef courses, baking classes for children, teens culinary camp, course with internship, culinary adventure. Established: 2001. Class/group size: 20. Also featured: Corporate team building, spice garden walks, farmers market.

EMPHASIS: Culinary skills & pan-Asian cuisine.

FACULTY: Professional chefs.

COSTS: S$60-S$80/evening class, S$30-S$40/children's, S$450/week teen camp. $2,500/2-wk course + internship includes lodging & meals. Singapore/Bali adventure $2,800 includes shared lodging, meals, spa treatment, excursions, ground transport.

CONTACT: Angie Lim, Marketing & Communications, at-sunrice The Singapore Cooking School & Spice Garden, at-sunrice, Fort Canning Park, Fort Canning Centre, Singapore, 179618 Singapore; (65) 336 3307, Fax (65) 336 9353, angie@at-sunrice.com, www.at-sunrice.com.

COOKERY MAGIC

Katong

Sponsor: Culinary professional Ruqxana Vasanwala. Programs: Classes that cover asian & intl cuisines, chocolates, cakes, desserts, pastries. Established: 2002. Class/group size: 1-10. 50-100 programs/yr. Facilities: Well-equipped home kitchen. Also featured: Harvesting, cooking & dining at an eco-farm, Kids Kan Kook classes for children, market tours.

EMPHASIS: Cultural aspects of cooking & ingredients.

FACULTY: Ruqxana was an engineer & has been cooking for 33 yrs. Her specialty is 3D children's birthday cakes.

COSTS: S$50-S$150/class.

CONTACT: Ruqxana Vasanwala, Cooking Teacher, Cookery Magic, Haig Rd., Katong, East Coast, 438779 Singapore; (65) 63489667, Fax (65) 63489667, classes@cookerymagic.com, www.cookerymagic.com.

CORIANDER LEAF – THE NEW ASIAN FOOD HUB

Singapore

Sponsor: Asian Food Hub - bistro, shop, cooking school. Programs: Courses featuring traditional & interpreted dishes from the cuisines of the Middle East, South Asia, South East Asia & the Orient. Established: 2001. Class/group size: 6-10. 50 programs/yr. Facilities: Domestic home appliances. Also featured: Corporate team building, wine tastings & wine pairings, private dining.

EMPHASIS: Home cooking & dishes that can be replicated easily at home. Insights & techniques including food & table presentation, & how to fuse Asian & Western presentation styles.

FACULTY: Culinary professionals.

COSTS: S$75-S$125.

CONTACT: Samia Ahad, Director, Coriander Leaf - The New Asian Food Hub, 76 Robertson Quay #02-01, The Gallery Evason, Singapore, 238254 Singapore; (65) 732-3354, Fax (65) 732-3374, info@corianderleaf.com, www.corianderleaf.com.

EPICUREAN WORLD

Singapore

Sponsor: Culinary professional Devagi Sanmugam. Programs: Demo & hands-on cooking classes. Established: 1990. Class/group size: 10-24. 20 programs/yr. Facilities: Home-based well-equipped air-conditioned cooking studio. Also featured: Workshops, market & spice tours, kids' cooking classes.

EMPHASIS: Local & regional Thai, Indonesian, Chinese Indian, & Singaporean cuisines.

FACULTY: Director Devagi Sanmugam, a food columnist, consultant, & cooking teacher with 21+

yrs experience; author of 8 cookbooks, including Great Bakes No Eggs & South Indian Cookbook.
Costs: $50/class or $350/hr.
Contact: Devagi Sanmugam, Culinary Consultant, Epicurean World, 52 Jalan Leban, 577589 Singapore; (65) 458 0572, Fax (65) 458 7364, sandegi@pacific.net.sg, www.epicureanworld.com.sg.

RAFFLES CULINARY ACADEMY
Singapore

Sponsor: Raffles Hotel, Singapore. Programs: 1-2 classes daily, both demo & hands-on. Established: 1995. Class/group size: 24. Facilities: Well-equipped residential-type kitchen with demo area. Also featured: Wine instruction, classes for youngsters, dessert & pastry classes.
Emphasis: Singapore, Asian, Mediterranean, French cuisines & Raffles Hotel signature dishes.
Faculty: Raffles Hotel chefs, including Executive Chef Jean Paul Naquin & Executive Deputy Chef Gregoire Simonin.
Costs: $60-$100/class. Suites range from $650/night at the 103-suite Raffles Hotel, which has 18 restaurants & bars, a Victorian-style playhouse, & a 40-shop arcade.
Contact: Raffles Culinary Academy Executives, 1 Beach Rd., 189673 Singapore; (65) 6412-1256, Fax (65) 6339-7013, rca@raffles.com, www.raffleshotel.com/facilities/culinary/culinary.htm.

SOUTH AFRICA

CAPE WINELAND TOURS
Capetown

Sponsor: Tour operator. Programs: Educational food & wine tours of South Africa, featuring introductory lecture by industry professional & winemaker-hosted tastings at 10-15 wine estates. Established: 1996. Class/group size: 6-15 max. 8 programs/yr. Facilities: Hotels, inns, restaurants. Also featured: Visit to Hermanus (whale-watching), Cape Town, safari extensions.
Emphasis: South African wines, food & wine pairings, cultural experience.
Faculty: South African winemakers, wine guides, chefs, other food & wine experts.
Costs: $3,200-$3,900 includes luxury lodging, most meals, ground transport.
Location: Winelands of the Cape, Hermanus, Kruger Natl Park, Cape Town.
Contact: Lisa Hough, President, Cape Wineland Tours, 3263 Juniper Lane, Falls Church, VA 22044; 888-868-7706, 703-532-8817, Fax 703-532-8820, info@capewinetours.com, www.capewinetours.com.

CHRISTINA MARTIN SCHOOL OF FOOD AND WINE
Durban

Sponsor: Private school. Programs: Cordon Bleu 6-session courses, theme classes, 2-wk culinary tours of South Africa. Established: 1988. 30+ programs/yr. Facilities: Auditorium, delicatessen, 60-seat restaurant, 80-seat conference venue, garden restaurant.
Emphasis: Cordon Bleu cookery, a variety of topics.
Faculty: Christina Martin is a Maitre Chef de Cuisine & Commandeur Associé de la Commanderie des Cordons Bleus de France. Instructors include vice-principal Michelle Barry, Chef de Cuisine Gerhard Van Rensburg, Andrew White.
Costs: R995/Cordon Bleu course, R110/class, $6,200 for 2-wk trip includes round trip airfare from NYC & lodging.
Contact: Christina Martin, Principal and Owner, Christina Martin School of Food and Wine, PO Box 4601, Durban, 4000 South Africa; (27) (0)31-3032111, Fax (27) (0)31-312-3342, chrismar@iafrica.com, www.safarichef.com.

SILVER PLATE COOKERY ACADEMY OF SOUTH AFRICA
Pretoria

Sponsor: Private school. Programs: 1-day intro to South African cooking, weekly hobbyist workshops, 1- or 2-day themed hostess workshops, 10-session intro to fine cooking. Classes incorporate theory & application. Established: 1999. Class/group size: 10-15. ~ 8 programs/yr. Facilities: Fully-

equipped demo kitchen. Also featured: Sampling of South African food & wine.
EMPHASIS: Cooking as a therapeutic group activity.
FACULTY: Ilze van der Merwe trained at the Cordon Bleu Cookery School, South Africa; Marita Pieterse, trained at the Prue Leith Cookery School, London.
CONTACT: Ilze van der Merwe, Silver Plate Cookery Academy of South Africa, 93 Gardenia St., Lynnwood Ridge, Pretoria, 81 South Africa; (27) (0)83-656-7830, Fax (27) (0)12-361-7267, ilzev@btinternet.com, www.angelfire.com/il/silverplate.

THE SILWOOD SCHOOL OF COOKERY
Rondebosch Cape

Sponsor: Career school. Programs: Guest chef demos, part-time cooking courses. Established: 1964. Class/group size: 4 groups of 10 stude. 6 programs/yr. Facilities: A 200-yr-old coach-house converted into a demo & experimental kitchen, 3 additional kitchens, demo hall & library. Also featured: 1-wk hands-on classes for children twice yearly, weekly participation classes.
FACULTY: 11-member faculty, includes principal Alicia Wilkinson, Rene Larsen, Alisa Smith, Louise Faull, Carianne Wilkinson, Lara DuToit, Gaie Gaag, Toinet Brink, Liz Bell.
COSTS: R225/part-time lesson.
CONTACT: Mrs. Alicia Wilkinson, The Silwood Kitchen School of Cookery, Silwood Rd., Rondebosch Cape, South Africa; (27) 21-686-4894/5, Fax (27) 21-686-5795, cooking@silwood.co.za, www.silwood.co.za.

SPAIN

CASA CANELA COOKING SCHOOL HOLIDAYS
Facinas, Cadiz

Sponsor: Private cooking school. Programs: 7-day demo & hands-on classes, visits to local markets & sherry vineyards. Established: 1978. Class/group size: 12. 12+ programs/yr. Facilities: Country kitchen, outside barbeque, modern facilities. Lodging available for 6 couples or 12 sharing. Also featured: Include golf at Valderrama & a local course, whale watching, windsurfing at Tarifa, paragliding, mountainbiking, tennis, riding, beach mudbaths.
EMPHASIS: North African, Italian & Spanish Mediterranean cuisines.
FACULTY: Susanna Redman, has catered to embassies in Lisbon & cooked for heads of state & members of the European royal families.
COSTS: 485.000 pesetas-515.000 pesetas/7 nights, all inclusive, shared lodging.
CONTACT: Susanna Redman, Casa Canela Cooking School Holidays, Rua do Serrado, Sintra, 2710-413 Portugal; (351) 21 924 2438, cell (351) 91 409 6464, Fax (351) 21 924 4891 Attn SMR, redman_pt@yahoo.com.

CATACURIAN
El Masroig *(See display ad page 369)*

Sponsor: Privately owned 4th-generation family home. Programs: 6-day (9-day) cooking vacation programs that include classes in Catalan cuisine, Priorat wines, & olive oils. 9-day programs include grape or olive-picking sessions. Established: 2002. Class/group size: 6. 40 programs/yr. Facilities: Restored village house with fully-equipped kitchen, prep area, fireplace; wine cellar & wine tasting room; outdoor barbecue. Also featured: Visits to Priorat villages, wine producers & museum, olive oil presses, historical sites.
EMPHASIS: Regional Catalan cuisine of Spain, wines of the Priorat region.
FACULTY: Alicia Juanpere Artigas studied at the Terra d'Éscudella & Bell-Art chef schools in Barcelona & has worked in the kitchens of the Restaurante Julian Tomas. An oenologist teaches Priorat wines.
COSTS: 6 days/9 days $1,950/$2,900 ($2,300/$3,425) includes shared (single) lodging, meals, ground transport, planned activities. 10-day Christmas program shared $3,300, single $3,880.
LOCATION: Priorat region of Catalonia, 30 mi from Tarragona, 100 mi southwest of Barcelona.

CONTACT: Vicki Austin, US Manager, Catacurian, PO Box 245, Palmetto, FL 34220-0245; 800-601 5008, 941-723 7588, Fax 941-723 7876, info@catacurian.com, www.catacurian.com.

COCINA CASTELLANA
Madrid & Segovia

Sponsor: Educational travel specialists for Spain. Programs: One-wk culinary tours featuring 4 days of hands-on lessons, wine tastings, meals at noted restaurants, visits with artists & artisans, cultural excursions. Established: 1970. Class/group size: 4-8. 4-6 programs/yr. Facilities: The kitchen of La Matita, originally a country mansion & now a restaurant in the Castilian pueblo of Collado Hermos. Also featured: Add-on weekend in Madrid emphasizing cuisine & culture. Custom-designed group tours focusing on such special interests as cuisine, art history, crafts, religion.

EMPHASIS: Cuisine, wine, & culture of Castilla, Spain.

FACULTY: Professional Spanish chefs & wine aficionados. Guides/translators are Suzy & Mark Markowitt, who have worked as intl educators specializing in Spain.

COSTS: $2,270 ($175 single supplement) includes first class hotel, ground transport, planned activities.

CONTACT: Suzy & Mark Markowitt, Co-Directors, Travel as a Second Language Co., LLC, RR1 Box 42, Warren, VT 5674; 888-266-1922, 802-583-1922, Fax 802-583-1923, TSL@spaincooks.com, www.spaincooks.com.

COOKING HOLIDAYS AT CASA ALMENDRA
Granada

Sponsor: Private guest house. Programs: 1-wk Spanish regional cookery course, trips to market, olive oil refinery, bodega wine tasting. Established: 2000. Class/group size: 1-8. 4-8 programs/yr. Facilities: Purpose-built kitchen specifically for teaching small groups. Also featured: Walking, hiking, painting, shopping in Granada & Malaga, visit to trout hatcheries, Oct/Nov almond-picking from orchard on the property.

EMPHASIS: Regional Spanish dishes, tapas, local specialities.

FACULTY: Paul Bruce, owner, trained in the UK & was head chef at Mount Hotel Leeds, England, before taking over the kitchens of the Domino Resturant group.

COSTS: £400 (€635) includes lodging, meals, ground transport.

CONTACT: Paul Bruce, Cooking Holidays at Casa Almendra, Casa Almendra, Las Pilas 51, Fuente Camacho, Loja, Granada, 18314 Spain; (34) 958 313 877, Fax (34) 958 313 877, pbruce@terra.es, www.takeabreakinspain.com.

ESCUELA DE COCINA LUIS IRIZAR
Basque Country

Sponsor: Private school. Programs: 1-wk courses for professionals & amateurs (4 hrs/day). Instruction in Spanish, English-speaking courses available. Optional visits to markets & food producers, winery tours, sightseeing, dining in Michelin-star restaurants. Established: 1992. Class/group size: 10-15. 8 programs/yr. Facilities: Fully-equipped kitchen, separate classroom, TV & video.

EMPHASIS: Basque, Spanish & French cooking.

FACULTY: Founder Luis Irizar has served as chef in Spain's leading restaurants. Staff includes 3

full-time instructors & part-time teachers for continuing ed.
Location: Old part of San Sebastian, facing the port & beach.
Contact: V. Irizar, Escuela de Cocina Luis Irizar, c/ Mari, #5, Bajo, San Sebastian, 20003 Spain; (34) 943-431540, Fax (34) 943-423553, cocina@escuelairizar.com, www.escuelairizar.com.

LA SERRANIA RETREATS
Pollensa, Mallorca

Sponsor: Private retreat center offering workshops in cooking, creative writing, art, bodywork & yoga. Programs: Hands-on morning sessions & pre-dinner sessions including demonstrations, talks & some hands-on involvement. Established: 1999. Class/group size: 6-12. 3 programs/yr. Facilities: All teaching takes place in the large kitchen with ample working space. Also featured: Walks in the country or visits to local market towns, massages.
Emphasis: Healthy traditional Mediterranean cuisine, including Spanish & Mallorcan specialities such as paella, tortilla español, sopas Mallorquinas.
Faculty: Margalida Colomar & Martina Singer, experienced chefs, have been with La Serranía cooking since opening in 1999.
Costs: €700 (+ €180 single) includes lodging w/pvt bath & meals. La Serrania features a swimming pool, terrace, living/room library.
Location: In the foothills of Mallorca, Spain, 10 min from a village & 20 min from the beach.
Contact: La Serrania Retreats, Apartado 211, Pollensa, Mallorca, 7460 Spain; (34) 639 306 432, Fax (34) 971 182 144, retreats@laserrania.com, www.laserrania.com.

A QUESTION OF TASTE
Seville

Sponsor: Tour provider emphasizing Spanish food & wine. Programs: 3- & 6-night gastronomic breaks. Includes cooking classes, visits to markets, wineries, olive oil mill, & ham factory, wine & olive oil tastings, tapas tour & meals in local restaurants. Established: 2002. Class/group size: 4-8. 12 programs/yr. Facilities: Fully-equipped kitchen with prep area for 8 students. Meals served on a balcony overlooking Seville´s cathedral & Giralda. Also featured: 1-day food & wine excursions, group tapas tours & wine-tastings, customized regional gastronomic tours of Spain.
Emphasis: Andalusian cuisine, wines & culture.
Faculty: Tour guide Roger Davies has lived in Spain since 1987 & worked in Spanish wine industry. Cooking instructor Ruth Roberts has 20+ yrs professional experience in Spain. Local professionals.
Costs: €700/3-night break, €1800/6-night break, shared lodging.
Contact: Roger Davies, A Question of Taste, Calle Alcazar, 12, Espartinas, Seville, 41807 Spain; (34) 954713710, enquiries@aqot.com, www.aqot.com.

QUIXOTE'S KITCHEN
Six regions

Sponsor: Private school. Programs: Week-long hands-on cooking vacations. Established: 2001. Class/group size: 6-12. 10 programs/yr. Facilities: Modern professional kitchens with individual work stations. Also featured: Visit to the fish market, dinners at Michelin-star restaurants, field trips to producers of wine, olive oil, marzipan, jamon serrano, & cheese.
Emphasis: Spanish Mediterranean cuisine.
Faculty: Food consultant & teacher Isabel Sanchez, a native of Spain; noted regional chefs.
Costs: \$3,000-\$3,500 includes shared luxury lodging, most meals, ground transport, planned activities.
Location: Madrid; Toledo, Castilla La Mancha; Jerez, Andalucia; Santiago de Compostela, Galicia (north coast) Extremadura.
Contact: Clara Garcia, Marketing Mgr, Quixote's Kitchen, Oakridge Centre, North Tower, 650 W 41st Ave., #567, Vancouver, BC, V5Z 2M9 Canada; Fax 604-267-0291, clara.garcia@quixoteskitchen.com, www.quixoteskitchen.com.

SPANISH & MEDITERRANEAN COOKING WITH JEANNIE AT BUENVINO
Aracena Nature Park

Sponsor: Buenvino, a family-run B&B inn & cookery school. Programs: 1-wk hands-on cookery courses focusing on Andalucian & Mediterranean/North African cooking. Sherry tasting. Established: 1985. Class/group size: 6-8. 16 programs/yr. Facilities: Well-equipped family kitchen with marble-topped work table & outside kitchen courtyard. Also featured: Walking in the nature reserve, visit to a goat farm & Jerez winery, sightseeing trip to Sevilla.

EMPHASIS: Andalucian cooking with roots in N. Africa & Mediterranean Italian & Greek influences.

FACULTY: Jeannie Chesterton trained at the Cordon Bleu School, cooked in Hong Kong, London & Scotland & has lived in Spain for 18 yrs. runningBuenvino with her husband.

COSTS: €900 includes 6 nights shared lodging, most meals, transport from Seville, excursion to Jerez. Single supplement €25/night. Non-cooking partners €95/night.

CONTACT: Jeannie Chesterton, Cooking with Jeannie at Buenvino, Finca Buenvino, Los Marines, Huelva, 21293 Spain; (34) 959 12 40 34 (10am-9pm central European time), Fax (34) 959 50 10 29, buenvino@facilnet.es, www.buenvino.com.

THAILAND

BLUE ELEPHANT
Bangkok

Sponsor: Private school associated with the Blue Elephant restaurant. Programs: Morning market visit followed by demo & hands-on instruction; 5-day private course available for professional chefs. Established: 2002. Class/group size: 14. 300 programs/yr. Facilities: Practice room with 14 individual cooking stations, 28-seat teaching classroom.

EMPHASIS: Royal Thai cuisine.

FACULTY: Khun Chang, corporate chef of the Blue Elephant Group; Khun Chumpol, executive chef of the Blue Elephant restaurant.

COSTS: 2,800 Baht/class, 5,000 Baht/2 classes, 10,000 Baht/5 classes; 68,000 Baht/5-day professional private course.

LOCATION: Century-old mansion opposite Bangkok's Surasak Sky train station.

CONTACT: Frederic Meyer, GM, Blue Elephant, 233 South Sathorn Rd., Kwaeng Yannawa, Khet Sathorn, Bangkok, 10120 Thailand; (66) 2 673 93 53, Fax (66) 2 673 93 55, cooking.school@blueelphant.com, www.blueelephant.com/cookingschool.html.

CREATIVE PHUKET
Phuket

Sponsor: Holiday workshop organizer. Programs: One-week Thai cooking workshops including hands-on classes & market visits. Class/group size: 6 max. Facilities: Open walled Thai style kitchen set in tropical gardens of fruits & herbs.

FACULTY: Executive Chef Khun Sirikarn.

COSTS: $380 ($420) includes shared (single) lodging, daily breakfast & dinner.

LOCATION: Kata Thai Cooking School in Kata Beach.

CONTACT: Creative Phuket, PO Box 103, Patong Beach, Phuket, 83150 Thailand; (66) 189 224 19, Fax (66) 76 385 168, kirjon@samart.co.th, www.phuket.net.

SAFFRON 59
Myanmar

Sponsor: Caterer/event planner. Programs: Culinary tours to Asia featuring regional cooking classes, market visits, tastings of local delicacies, & sightseeing. Class/group size: 15. 1 programs/yr. Facilities: Classes held in restaurants & local homes.

EMPHASIS: Regional Asian cuisine.

FACULTY: Chef Irene Khin Wong, director of Saffron 59, is on the faculty of the New School for Culinary Arts, is a board member of the Asian Culinary Soc & has appeared on the TV Food Network.

Costs: 14-day Burma/Cambodia tour $4,500, includes shared hotel lodging ($899 single supplement), some meals, domestic travel within Indochina.

Contact: Saffron 59, 59 Fourth Ave., New York, NY 10003; 212-253-1343, Fax 212-253-0477, saffron59@juno.com, www.saffron59.com.

SAMUI INSTITUTE OF THAI CULINARY ARTS

Koh Samui

Sponsor: Private institute. Programs: Twice daily Thai cooking classes, 3-day courses in decorative fruit & vegetable carving. Established: 1998. Class/group size: 5-10. 52 programs/yr. Facilities: Modern, fully-equipped 90-sq-meter teaching facility with individual cooking stations. Fine dining restaurant. Also featured: 3-4 wk professional training programs.

Emphasis: Authentic home-style Thai cuisine using traditional ingredients & techniques.

Faculty: Director Roongfa Sringam has 10+ yrs experience in the kitchens of 5-star hotels & is a master fruit & vegetable carver. 2 addtitional instructors.

Costs: $25-$35/class, $75/3-day carving course.

Contact: Roongfa Sringam, Director, Samui Institute of Thai Culinary Arts, 46/26 Moo 3, Chaweng Beach, Koh Samui, 84320 Thailand; (66) 77-413172, Fax (66) 77-413172, info@sitca.net, www.sitca.net.

THAI COOKING SCHOOL AT THE ORIENTAL, BANGKOK

Bangkok

Sponsor: The Oriental resort hotel. Programs: Weekly 4-day demonstration courses (Monday-Thursday). Established: 1986. Class/group size: 15. Facilities: Classroom, participation/demonstration room, kitchen, eating area.

Emphasis: Introduction, ingredients, snacks, salads/soups, desserts, fruit & vegetable, carving/curries, condiments, side/dishes, steam, stir fry, fry & grill menu prep & how to order.

Costs: $1,788 ($2,500), includes double (single) occupancy lodging at The Oriental, most meals, planned activities. Amenities include swimming pools, sports center, tennis, squash, spa & health center.

Contact: Chanida Srimanoj, Administrator, Thai Cooking School at the Oriental, 48 Oriental Ave., Bangkok, 10500 Thailand; (662) 437-6211, (662) 437-3080, Fax (662) 439-7587, bscorbkk@loxinfo.co.th.In the U.S.: Mandarin Hotel Group 800-526-6566.

THAI FOOD COOKING SCHOOL

Chiangmai

Sponsor: Private school. Programs: One-day hands-on courses that include a market visit & overnight stay.

Emphasis: Thai cuisine.

Faculty: Chef Teng Trairat.

Contact: Teng Trairat, Chef, Thai Food Cooking School, Thapae Gate, 2-6 Ratchadumnern Rd., Chiangmai, 50200 Thailand; (66) 53 357 456 (day), (66) 53 431 344, (66) 53 431 344 (cell), mrthaifood2002@yahoo.com, http://thai-food-cooking-school.infothai.com.

THE THAI HOUSE COOKING SCHOOL

Nontaburi

Sponsor: Private school. Programs: 1-, 2- & 3-day courses that include lectures, preparation of ingredients, hands-on cooking. Established: 1991. Class/group size: 2-10. Facilities: Open-air kitchen, farm & orchard. Also featured: 2- & 3-day courses include an excursion to an open-air market.

Emphasis: Thai cuisine.

Faculty: Pip Fargrajang.

Costs: $100 for 1-day course. 2- (3-) day courses $255 ($475) including lodging at Thai House. Price includes transport from/to Bangkok.

Location: 22 km from Bangkok.

Contact: Pip Fargrajang, The Thai House Cooking School, 3 2/4 Moo 8 Tambol Bangmuang, Ampur Bangyai, Nonthaburi, 11140 Thailand; (662) 9039611, 9475161, Fax (662) 9039354, pip_thaihouse@hotmail.com, http://newsroom.tat.or.th/article/thai_cuisine.html.

TIME FOR LIME CREATIVE THAI COOKING WORKSHOPS
Saladan, Koh Lanta, Krabi

Sponsor: Thai cooking school. Programs: 1-, 2- & 3-day hands-on workshops that concentrate on seafood & vegetables. Established: 2003. Class/group size: 10-16. Year-round programs/yr. Facilities: Specially designed Thai-temple buildingwith 8 woks, chopping & eating tables. Also featured: Group workshops can be arranged.

EMPHASIS: Thai & fusion cooking, creative presentation.

FACULTY: Junie Kovacs, a graphic, conceptual & food designer; Naum, an experienced Thai chef who has worked in resorts & restaurants.

COSTS: 1,500-1,600 Baht/day; 4,400-4,500 Baht/3 day course.

LOCATION: 70 km from Phuket off the coast of southern Thailand.

CONTACT: Junie Kovacs, Instructor, 20 moo 3, Klong Dao Beach, Saladan, Koh Lanta, Krabi, 81150 Thailand; (66) 75 697 069/(66) 99 675 017, timeforlime@kolanta.net, www.timeforlime.net.

WAYFARERS TRAVEL THAILAND
Chiang Mai

Sponsor: Travel company specializing in tours, trekking and Thai cookery courses in Chiang Mai, Northern Thailand. Programs: One-day group courses in Thai cuisine; specialized private courses also offered. Established: 1988. Also featured: Market visit, vegetable carving, curry paste making. Northern Thailand trek that includes farm visit and cookery lesson.

EMPHASIS: General Thai cuisine & specialized private courses. Treks with homestay, farm visit & cookery lesson.

COSTS: $20/day for group course.Private course cost varies with group size; group of 2 people:$80/person/day.3 day trek, including farm visit & cookery lesson: $210/person, for a 2-person group.

CONTACT: Sarah Leelaphat, Manager, Wayfarers Travel, 20 Tapae Rd., Soi 4, Chiang Mai, 50100 Thailand; (66) 53208271, Fax (66) 53279423, info@wayfarersthailand.com, www.wayfarersthailand.com/thaicook.htm.

ZOLOTRIPS
Bangkok & Chiang Mai

Sponsor: Travel company specializing in adventure, holistic & cultural trips to Asia & the Pacific. Programs: 1- to 2-wk trips that include hands-on cooking classes & market visits. Established: 1996. Class/group size: 5-12. 30 programs/yr. Facilities: Hotels & private homes or kitchens.

EMPHASIS: Regional Thai cooking.

FACULTY: Local expert chefs.

COSTS: $150-$200/day.

CONTACT: Adam Zolot, Co-Founder, ZOLOtrips, 101 Baker St., San Francisco, CA 94117; 415-255-9520, Fax 415-680-1522, info@zolotrips.com, www.zolotrips.com.

TURKEY

CULINARY ADVENTURE IN TURKEY
Istanbul

Sponsor: Culinary travel company. Programs: 10-day program includes 5 cooking classes in different regions of Turkey, cooking & dining with locals. Final dinner on a Bosphorus cruise. Established: 1990. Class/group size: 6-12. 4 programs/yr. Facilities: Fully-equipped cooking school in Istanbul, hotel kitchens in some regions, facilities of a ranch in the country. Also featured: Private culinary tours in Turkey.

EMPHASIS: Turkish cuisine.

FACULTY: Turkish wine/dine magazine, cooks of 5-star hotels.

COSTS: $1,800-$2,400 includes shared lodging.

CONTACT: Asli Mutlu, Owner, Culinary Adventure in Turkey, 7319 Croy Lane, Dublin, CA 94568; 800-434-1989, 925-556-1278, Fax 925-556-0371, info@tourag.com.

CULINARY EXPEDITIONS IN TURKEY

Turkey

Sponsor: Kathleen O'Neill, culinary historian, foodresearcher & resident of Turkey. Programs: Culinary & cultural cruises & land tours focusing on Turkish cuisine; culinary walking tours of Istanbul. Established: 1996. Class/group size: 6-12. Year-round programs/yr. Also featured: Custom itineraries.Regional & historical aspects of Turkish & Ottoman cuisine.

FACULTY: Kathleen O'Neill; local chefs & home cooks.

COSTS: $2,200-$2,850, includes meals, lodging, planned activities, internal transport.

LOCATION: Istanbul & southeast Turkey; Aegean & Mediterranean coasts.

CONTACT: Kathleen O'Neill, Culinary Expeditions in Turkey, P.O. Box 1913, Sausalito, CA 94966; 415-437-5700, Fax 925-210-1337, info@turkishfoodandtravel.com, www.turkishfoodandtravel.com.

3

Food & Wine Organizations

AMERICAN CULINARY FEDERATION (ACF)

St. Augustine, Florida

Founded in 1929. Membership 25,000+. Largest nationwide professional cooks' & chefs' membership organization recognized by other leading food service organizations. Objectives: to make a positive difference for culinarians internationally through education, apprenticeship, and certification, while creating a fraternal bond of respect & integrity. Over 300 local chapters in the U.S. & abroad. ACF sponsors educational seminars at national convention & regional meetings; produces a monthly magazine, The National Culinary Review, offers opportunities to earn gold, silver, & bronze medals in ACF-approved culinary competitions. ACF also sponsors the ACF Culinary Team USA, which represents the American culinary profession in the largest & oldest international cooking competition, the International Culinary "Olympics", held every 4 years in Germany. The ACF accredits secondary & post-secondary culinary programs through its Accreditation Commission, awards scholarships to students, & provides a U.S. Department of Labor recognized 2- & 3-year National Apprenticeship Training Program for Cooks & Pastry Cooks. The ACF Certification Department certifies chefs on the basis of experience & testing of skills & knowledge. Certification categories include Certified Culinarian (CC), Pastry Culinarian (CPC), Sous Chef (CSC), Chef de Cuisine (CCC), Working Pastry Chef (CWPC), Executive Chef (CEC), Executive Pastry Chef (CEPC), Culinary Educator (CCE), Certified Secondary Culinary Educator (CSCE), & the highest levels of Certified Master Chef (CMC) & Master Pastry Chef (CMPC). The American Academy of Chefs is the honor society of the American Culinary Federation.

CONTACT: ACF, P.O. Box 3466, St. Augustine, FL 32085; 800-624-9458, 904-824-4468, Fax 904-825-4758, E-mail acf@acfchefs.net, URL http://www.acfchefs.org.

AMERICAN DIETETIC ASSOCIATION (ADA)

Chicago, Illinois

Founded in 1917. Membership 70,000, of which 75% are registered dietitians in diverse areas of practice, including clinical dietetics, hospital, college or university, school and foodservice administration, community and public health, organizations, extended care facilities. Promotes optimal nutrition, health, and well-being through various activities, publications, educational meetings, media and marketing programs. Establishes and enforces quality standards for more than 600 educational programs and internships in dietetics and nutrition. Maintains a legislative affairs office in Washington, DC, and has a nonprofit foundation established for charitable, educational, and scientific research and scholarship purposes.

CONTACT: ADA, 216 W. Jackson Blvd., Chicago, IL 60606-6995; 800-877-1600, Fax 312-899-4845, E-mail webmaster@eatright.org, URL http://www.eatright.org.

AMERICAN INSTITUTE OF BAKING (AIB)

Manhattan, Kansas

Founded in 1919. This non-profit educational organization's objective is to promote the cause of education in nutrition and in the science and art of baking and bakery management. The AIB employs about 135 full-time personnel and is supported by the contributions of more than 600 member companies. Programs include the 14- and 20-week Baking Science and Technology course, the 10-week Bakery Maintenance Engineering program, and short courses and seminars. Correspondence courses include Science of Baking, Bakery Maintenance Engineering, and Maintenance Engineering. Scholarships and financial aid are available. The AIB's Certified Baker Program provides companies with training that does not require lengthy stays away from the job; the research department develops new techniques and evaluates new ingredients; the Technical Assistance group provides information on scientific, technical, and regulatory subjects; the Department of Food Product Safety offers training and in-plant inspection; the Department of Safety Education offers training and in-plant audits; and the Library responds to information requests. The Food Labeling Program provides information for FDA-required food labels.

CONTACT: AIB, 1213 Bakers Way, Manhattan, KS 66502; 800-633-5137, 785-537-4750, Fax 785-537-1493, URL http://www.aibonline.org.

THE AMERICAN INSTITUTE OF WINE & FOOD (AIWF)

Lousville, Kentucky

Founded in 1981. Membership 10,000+. This non-profit educational organization's objectives are to advance the appreciation of wine and food and stimulate greater scholarly education in gastronomy. Membership is open to all and benefits include special prices and invitations to national and chapter programs, savings on wine and food publications, and the AIWF's American Wine & Food newsletter. There are more than 30 AIWF chapters in the U.S. and abroad. Annual membership contributions range from $40 for students to $2,500 for corporations.

CONTACT: AIWF, 304 West Liberty St., Suite 201, Lousville, KY 40202; 502-992-1022, 800-274-AIWF(2493), Fax 502-589-3602, E-mail aiwf@hqtrs.com, URL http://www.aiwf.org.

AMERICAN VEGAN SOCIETY (AVS)

Malaga, New Jersey

Founded in 1960. Nonprofit educational organization dedicated to teaching a compassionate way of living and abstinence from animal products. Lectures, discussions, and live-in weekend classes in vegan cooking are available. Member services: books & videos available by mail order including cookbooks on nutrition and health. An educational convention is held annually. Members receive a subscription to the American Vegan quarterly newsletter. Annual dues are $20, students & low income $10.

CONTACT: AVS, 56 Dinshah Ln., P.O. Box 369, Malaga, NJ 08328-0908; 856-694-2887, Fax 856-694-2288, URL http://www.americanvegan.org.

AMERICAN WINE SOCIETY (AWS)

Rochester, New York

Founded in 1967. Membership 5,800. Non-profit consumer organization dedicated to bringing together wine lovers and educating people about wine production and use. The national conference, held in November, features tastings, contests, tours of wineries and vineyards, and well-known speakers. Publications include a quarterly journal newsletter, specialized technical manuals, and lists of related books and publications. The organization assists in publicizing regional events and helps organize local chapters (currently 110), which sponsor tastings, tours, wine making and other social and educational events. Members with at least 2 years of chapter comparative tastings or equivalent are eligible for the AWS Wine Judge Certification Program. Membership is open to all and annual dues are $45 per individual or couple. Professional Memberships are $70 per year and Lifetime Memberships, for ages 60 and over, are $355.

CONTACT: AWS, 3006 Latta Rd., Rochester, NY 14612-3298; 716-225-7613, Fax 716-225-7613, E-mail Angel910@aol.com, URL http://www.americanwinesociety.com.

THE BREAD BAKERS GUILD OF AMERICA

Pittsburgh, Pennsylvania

Founded in 1993. Membership 1,300. Objectives are to bring together individuals involved in the production of high quality bread products, to raise professional standards, and to encourage the education and training of people interested in careers as bread baking professionals. It also seeks to promote the exchange of information between artisan bakers, their suppliers, and specialists in the science of baking and baking ingredients. The Guild publishes a newsletter and sponsors seminars and workshops in the U.S. and abroad, as well as regional and national baking competitions. Membership is open to anyone but the focus of the Guild is professional bread bakers. Business membership yearly dues are based upon annual company sales, starting at $120; non-business yearly dues: $45 students, $60 educators, $75 all others.

CONTACT: The Bread Bakers Guild of America, 3203 Maryland Ave., North Versailles, PA 15137; 412-823-2080, Fax 412-823-2495, E-mail info@bbga.org, URL http://www.bbga.org.

CAREERS THROUGH CULINARY ARTS PROGRAM, INC. (C-CAP)
New York, New York

Founded in 1990 by cookbook author/educator Richard Grausman. Membership 10,000 students in 190 schools in Arizona, California, Illinois, New York, Pennsylvania, Washington, DC, Virginia. Nonprofit corporation whose mission is to promote and provide career opportunities in the foodservice industry for inner-city youth through culinary arts education and apprenticeship. Supports public high school home economics classes through professional development opportunities for teachers, donations of product and equipment from sponsors, industry mentors, jobs and internships for students. Conducts annual culinary competitions and awards scholarships.

Contact: C-CAP, 155 W. 68th St., New York, NY 10023; 212-873-2434, Fax 212-873-1514, E-mail info@ccapinc.org, URL http://www.ccapinc.org.

CONFRERIE DE LA CHAINE DES ROTISSEURS
New York, New York

Founded in 1950. Membership 7,650 (152 U.S. chapters). International gastronomic organization, purpose is to encourage educational functions and promote fellowship among individuals with a serious interest in wine and cuisine. The nonprofit, tax-exempt Chaine Foundation supports culinary educational programs. Membership benefits at the local level include gastronomic functions, usually 4-6 formal dinners per year supplemented by 2-4 smaller events. On a regional and national level, members can join in Chaine-sponsored excursions, attend the national convention, and share, by invitation, activities of other chapters. Professionals make up approximately 30% of the membership and include authors, critics, and food service professionals. Membership is normally by invitation only. Interested individuals who do not know a member should contact the National Office for information.

Contact: Confrerie de la Chaine des Rotisseurs, 444 Park Ave. So., New York, NY 10016; 212-683-3770, Fax 212-683-3882.

COOKING CLUB OF AMERICA
Minnetonka, Minnesota

Founded in 1998. Membership 350,000. Membership organization for people who enjoy cooking. Benefits include free cooking products to test, contests, product giveaways, free reprints of published recipes on recipe cards and Cooking Pleasures magazine.

Contact: Cooking Club of America, Box 3438, Minnetonka, MN 55343; 888-850-8202, E-mail mail@cookingclub.com, URL http://www.visitors.cookingclub.com.

COPIA: THE AMERICAN CENTER FOR WINE, FOOD & THE ARTS
Napa, California

Founded in 2001. Not-for-profit organization that is a cultural museum and educational center dedicated to exploring the American contribution to the character of wine and food in association with the arts and humanities. Membership benefits include participation in events and programs at a discounted rate, free admission for one year, complimentary subscription to the quarterly newsletter, gift shop discounts and exhibition previews. Membership levels range from $72-$1,000. Seniors, students & AIWF members receive 20% discount on any membership level.

Contact: COPIA: The American Center for Wine, Food & the Arts, 500 First Street, Napa, CA 94559; 707-259-1600, 888-51-COPIA, Fax 707-257-8601, E-mail info@copia.org, URL http://www.copia.org.

COUNCIL ON HOTEL, RESTAURANT, & INSTITUTIONAL EDUCATION – (CHRIE)
Washington, DC

Founded in 1946. Membership 2,000 members from 52 countries. This trade and professional organization's mission is to foster the international advancement of teaching and training in the field of hospitality and tourism management and facilitate the professional development of its members, who include administrators, educators, industry professionals, and government executives. Membership benefits include an annual conference and several publications: The CHRIE Communique monthly newsletter, the Hospitality & Tourism Educator interdisciplinary quarterly, the 4 times yearly Hospitality Research Journal, HOSTEUR magazine for students at member schools, and the Annual Directory of CHRIE Members. CHRIE also publishes A Guide to College Programs in Hospitality & Tourism, which describes curricula, admission requirements, scholarships, and internships.

CONTACT: CHRIE, 1200-17th St., NW, Washington, DC 20036-3097; 202-331-5990, Fax 202-785-2511, E-mail rtolson@chrie.org, URL http://www.chrie.org.

FOODSERVICE EDUCATORS NETWORK INTERNATIONAL (FENI)

Chicago, Illinois

Founded in 1998. Nonprofit network of foodservice educators whose mission is to advance professional growth through seminars and workshops, an annual Educators' Summit, summer institutes, consulting services, resource guides, a continuing education scholarship program, and a quarterly magazine, *Chef Educator Today.*

CONTACT: Morgan Holzman, FENI, 20 W. Kinzie St., #1200, Chicago, IL 60610; 312-334-8081, Fax 312-849-2174, E-mail mholzman@talcott.com, URL http://www.feni.org.

INSTITUTE OF FOOD TECHNOLOGISTS

Chicago, Illinois

Founded in 1939. Membership 28,000. Nonprofit scientific society dedicated to advancing the science and technology of food. 50+ regional sections nationwide and four outside the U.S., specialized divisions of expertise, a student association, awards, scholarships and fellowships for outstanding food scientist, technologist and students. IFT offers scientific publications (e.g. Food Technology and Journal of Food Science), continuing education, career guidance, employment service, networking opportunities, regional meetings, Annual Meeting & Food Expo®, and an International Food Safety & Quality Conference & Expo.

CONTACT: Institute of Food Technologists, World Headquarters: 525 West Van Buren Street., #300, Chicago, IL 60607-3814; 312-782-8424, Fax 312-782-8348, E-mail info@ift.org, URL http://www.ift.org.

INTERNATIONAL ASSOCIATION OF CULINARY PROFESSIONALS (IACP)

Louisville, Kentucky

Founded in 1978. Membership 4,000+ representing over 35 countries. This not-for-profit professional association's objectives include: providing continuing education and professional development, sponsoring of the annual IACP Cookbook Awards, promoting the exchange of culinary information among members of the professional food community, establishing professional and ethical standards, and funding scholarships. Membership benefits include the annual spring and regional conferences, newsletters and research reports, the annual IACP Membership Directory, the Certified Culinary Professional (CCP) certification program. Annual dues are $245 (plus $50 one-time fee) for Professional Members, $380 (plus $50) for Cooking School Members, $435 (plus $50) for Business Members; $1,050 (plus $100) for Corporate Members, and $50 for Student Members.

CONTACT: IACP, 304 W. Liberty St., #201, Louisville, KY 40202; 502-581-9786, 800-928-4227, Fax 502-589-3602, E-mail iacp@hqtrs.com, URL http://www.iacp.com.

INTERNATIONAL ASSOCOCIATION OF CULINARY PROFESSIONALS (IACP) FOUNDATION

Louisville, Kentucky

Founded in 1984. Solicits, manages, and distributes funds for educational and charitable programs related to the culinary profession. Areas of interest include research grants for food writers, culinary scholarships, cookbook preservation, hunger alleviation and children's cooking workshops.

CONTACT: IACP Foundation, 304 W. Liberty St., #201, Louisville, KY 40202; 502-581-9786, Fax 502-589-3602, E-mail tgribbins@hqtrs.com, URL http://www.iacp.com.

INTERNATIONAL FOOD SERVICE EXECUTIVES ASSOCIATION
Las Vegas, Nevada

Founded in 1901. Membership 2,000. Nonprofit educational and community service organization. Services include student scholarships, monthly gatherings, military awards, savings on health insurance, debt collection, and Hotline Magazine. Also has certification program for executives, chefs, managers, bar managers, and others. Memberships are Active (management, ownership, purchasing) and Member-at-Large (reside more than 50 miles from an IFSEA branch). Annual dues are $130 for active members, $95 for members-at-large.

CONTACT: International Food Service Executives Association, 2609 Surfwood Dr., Las Vegas, NV 89128; 702-838-8821, Fax 702-838-8853, E-mail hq@ifsea.org, URL http://www.ifsea.org.

INTERNATIONAL FOODSERVICE EDITORIAL COUNCIL (IFEC)
Hyde Park, New York

Founded in 1956. Membership 275. This nonprofit association is dedicated to improving the quality of media communications in the foodservice industry. Membership benefits include an annual directory & conference, newsletter, & networking. 4 to 6 scholarships ranging from $1,000 to $2,500 are awarded annually to students whose career aspirations combine foodservice & communications. Membership is open to individuals employed in editorial functions within the industry.

CONTACT: IFEC, P.O. Box 491, Hyde Park, NY 12538; 845-229-6973, Fax 845-229-6993, E-mail ifec@aol.com, URL http://www.ifec-is-us.com.

THE JAMES BEARD FOUNDATION, INC.
New York, New York

Founded in 1986. Membership 5,000. Nonprofit organization whose mission is to keep alive the ideals and activities that made James Beard the "Father of American Cooking" and to maintain his home as the first historical culinary center in North America. Membership benefits include discounts on the more than 200 events (workshops and dinners featuring well-known American chefs) each year; a subscription to Beard House magazine; the Foundation directory, which lists professional members; and the annual James Beard Awards (first weekend in May), which includes cookbook, journalism, chef, and restaurant categories. A scholarship and apprenticeship program and library have been developed. Tax-deductible annual dues begin at $125 ($275 for professional members within 75 miles of Manhattan).

CONTACT: James Beard Foundation, Inc., 167 W. 12th St., New York, NY 10011; 212-675-4984, (800)-36-BEARD, Fax 212-645-1438, E-mail jbeard@pipeline.com, URL http://www.jamesbeard.org.

NAPA VALLEY WINE LIBRARY ASSOCIATION (NVWLA)
St. Helena, California

Founded in 1963. Dedicated to preserving and sharing information regarding viticulture, enology, and wine lore, particularly as it pertains to the Napa Valley. Acquires books and other publications for the Napa Valley Wine Library, a more than 4,000-title collection including oral history transcripts and historic photographs, which is housed at the St. Helena Public Library. Membership benefits include the seasonal Wine Library Report, first notice of wine appreciation weekends and one-day seminars, and admission to the annual wine tasting, an August event that presents the wines of more than 100 Napa Valley wineries. Membership is open to anyone and dues are $25 per year.

CONTACT: NVWLA, P.O. Box 328, St. Helena, CA 94574; 707-963-5145, E-mail info@napawinelibrary.org, URL http://www.napawinelibrary.org

NATIONAL RESTAURANT ASSOCIATION (NRA)
Washington, DC

Founded in 1919. Membership 40,000+. This organization is the leading business association for the restaurant industry. Along with the National Restaurant Association Educational Foundation, the Association works to represent, educate, and promote the restaurant industry.

CONTACT: NRA, 1200-17th St., NW, Washington, DC 20036-3097; 202-331-5900, Fax 202-331-2429, E-mail info@dineout.org, URL http://www.restaurant.org.

NATIONAL ASSOCIATION FOR THE SPECIALTY FOOD TRADE, INC.

New York, New York

Founded in 1952. Membership 2,500 companies in the U.S. and overseas. Nonprofit business trade association that fosters trade, commerce, and interest in the specialty food industry. Sponsors the semi-annual International Fancy Food and Confection Show every winter (West Coast), spring (Mid-West), and summer (East Coast), attracting 25,000-35,000 attendees. Other services include the Annual Product Awards held every summer, the Scholarship and Research Fund, and the bimonthly NASFT Specialty Food magazine. Membership requires that a company be in business for a minimum of one year. The Admissions Committee reviews applications and makes recommendations to the Board of Directors for a final decision. Annual dues are $200 (for annual sales under $1 million), $400 ($1-$5 million), and $600 (over $5 million).

CONTACT: National Association for the Specialty Food Trade, Inc., 120 Wall St., 27th Floor, New York, NY 10005-4001; 212-482-6440, Fax 212-482-6459, E-mail amotayne@nasft.org, URL http://www.fancyfoodshows.com.

NEW YORK ASSOCIATION OF COOKING TEACHERS (NYACT)

Ridgewood, New Jersey

Founded in 1980. Membership 125 + in NY, NJ, CT, PA. Professional organization of teachers, caterers, food writers, stylists, chefs, restaurateurs, retailers, and other culinary professionals. Purpose is promote the interests and professional standards of those in the culinary field, provide educational opportunities and scholarships, honor those who have made lasting contributions. Member benefits include workshops and seminars, membership directory, quarterly newsletter, meetings, and review workshops for the CCP exam. Annual dues are $75 for individuals, $150 for corporations (up to 3 members), and $37.50 for full-time students (1 year limit).

CONTACT: NYACT, 282 Richards Rd., Ridgewood, NJ 07450; 201-445-0295, E-mail Sarappo@worldnet.att.net, URL http://www.nyact-online.org.

NORTH AMERICAN VEGETARIAN SOCIETY (NAVS)

Dolgeville, New York

Founded in 1974. Nonprofit educational organization dedicated to promoting the vegetarian way of life. Sponsors an annual Vegetarian Summerfest conference that features cooking demonstrationss & the World Vegetarian Day (Oct. 1). Provides information to members, the public, and the media. Members receive the quarterly magazine, Vegetarian Voice. Membership begins as $22 annually.

CONTACT: NAVS, P.O. Box 72, Dolgeville, NY 13329; 518-568-7970, Fax 518-568-7979, E-mail navs@telenet.net , URL http://www.navs-online.org .

OLDWAYS PRESERVATION AND EXCHANGE TRUST

Boston, Massachusetts

Founded in 1990. Non-profit food issues think tank that promotes healthy eating, sustainable agriculture, and preservation of traditional foodways. A primary focus is the series of Oldways healthy eating pyramids and eating guides that are based on traditional diets. Programs include international symposiums, scientific conferences, grade school curriculums on food, culture, and sustainable agriculture, aquaculture; and ongoing education for health professionals and their patients.

CONTACT: Oldways Preservation and Exchange Trust, 266 Beacon Street, Boston, MA 02116; 617-421-5500, Fax 617-421-5511, E-mail oldwayspt@oldways.org, URL http://www.oldwayspt.org.

THE RETAILER'S BAKERY ASSOCIATION (RBA)

Laurel, Maryland

Founded in 1918. Trade association representing 3,500 member companies who bring consumers bakery foods from bakery departments, independent bakeries, and foodservice facilities. Objective is to create industry-specific training programs, develop profit tools, and connect retailers with suppliers and experts to help build profitable bakeries. Grants certification as Certified Master Baker (CMB), Certified Baker (CB), Certified Bread Baker (CBB), Certified Decorator (CD), and Certified Journey Baker (CJB). Provides a baking curriculum for 30+ post-secondary schools, hosts an annual trade show and a baking competition for high school and post-secondary school students, publishes career guides and videos and a newsletter.

CONTACT: RBA, 14239 Park Center Dr., Laurel, MD 20707-5261; 800-638-0924, 301-725-2149, Fax 301-725-2187, E-mail bhelsing@rbanet.com, URL http://www.rbanet.com.

SLOW FOOD
Italy

Founded in 1986. Membership 40,000+ in 35 countries and 400 convivia (branches) that promote eating enjoyment, local traditions, and products of superior quality. Activities include a taste education program, wine conventions, consumer information, a project aimed at safeguarding and benefiting small-scale agricultural and food production, and the annual Salone del Gusto, which features hundreds of food and wine events. Publishes the quarterly magazine Slow, the international herald of tastes. Membership is $60 per year in the U.S., C$90 in Canada.

CONTACT: 212-988-5146 (in the US & Canada), (39) (0)172 419611, Fax (39) (0)172 421293, E-mail international@slowfood.com, URL http://www.slowfood.com.

SOCIETY OF WINE EDUCATORS (SWE)
Washington, DC

Founded in 1977. Membership 1,500. International nonprofit organization dedicated to furthering knowledge of wine, including wine service, wine and food pairing, and wine and health, among wine educators, consumers, and all levels of the wine trade. Membership services include the annual conference, professional development programs, and educational trips to wine regions worldwide. The Society provides an annual test of wine knowledge and awards a Certified Specialist of Wine and the Certified Wine Educator credential. Publications include the quarterly SWE Chronicle and various teaching materials. Annual dues are $40 (student), $55 (associate), $100 (professional), $400 (industry).

CONTACT: SWE, 1200 G Street, NW, #360, Washington, DC 20005; 202-347-5677, Fax 202-347-5667, E-mail conference@societyofwineeducators.org. URL http://www.wine.gurus.com.

SOMMELIER SOCIETY OF AMERICA
New York, New York

Founded in 1954. Membership: 1,000+. Not-for-profit organization for industry professionals dedicated to the ongoing education and growth of wine knowledge and service from basic to internationally competitive levels. Represented internationally through the Association de le Sommellerie Internationale. Offers 20-week Sommelier Certificate Diploma course, wine education classes, tasting programs (including wine & other spirits), and consulting services for events. Chapters in New York City, Chicago, Atlanta, Los Angeles. Membership benefits include events discounts, magazine subscription, job-networking, referrals. Annual dues are $125. Sponsorships and corporate memberships begin at $600.

CONTACT: Sommelier Society of America, P.O. Box 20080, West Village Station, New York, NY 10014; 212-679-4190, Fax 212-255-8959, E-mail info@sommeliersocietyofamerica.org, URL http://www.sommeliersocietyofamerica.org.

TASTERS GUILD INTERNATIONAL
Ft. Lauderdale, Florida

Founded in 1985. Membership 78 chapters in the U.S. Objective is to promote the appreciation, understanding, and moderate use of wine and food through education, dinner seminars, tastings, consumer/member benefits, and travel opportunities. Conducts an annual international wine judging each spring and a wine competition in the fall for members. Publishes Tasters Guild

Journal, and sponsors an annual Food and Wine Cruise and other excursions. Local chapters sponsor wine and food events and discounts are offered to members by affiliated wine and gourmet establishments. Annual membership dues are $40 per family.

CONTACT: Tasters Guild International, 1451 W. Cypress Creek Rd., #300-78, Ft. Lauderdale, FL 33309; 954-928-2823, Fax 954-928-2824, E-mail jjschagrin@aol.com, URL http://www.tasters-guild.com.

UNITED STATES PERSONAL CHEF ASSOCIATION (USPCA)

Rio Rancho, New Mexico

Founded in 1991. Membership 3,000+. Association that supports and certifies Personal Chefs. Member services: continuing education, business support, regional training, referral database, monthly magazine.

CONTACT: USPCA, 481 Rio Rancho Blvd. NE, Suite A, Rio Rancho, NM 87124; 800-995-2138, Fax 505-994-6399, E-mail uspcainc@uspca.com, URL http://www.uspca.com.

WINE BRATS

Santa Rosa, California

Founded in 1993. Membership 30,000+, 25 chapters in the U.S. Organization of (mostly young) wine enthusiasts dedicated to providing education, encouraging responsible drinking, and organizing social events. Membership is free.

CONTACT: Wine Brats, PO Box 5432, Santa Rosa, CA 95402; 877-545-4699, 707-545-3539, E-mail info@winebrats.org, URL http://www.winebrats.org.

WOMEN CHEFS AND RESTAURATEURS (WCR)

Louisville, Kentucky

Founded in 1993. Membership 2,000+. Promotes the education and advancement of women in the restaurant industry and the betterment of the industry as a whole. The WCR publishes the quarterly newsletter Entrez! Educational and networking opportunities are offered through the annual conference, regional programs and local events. Provides nationwide job networking, offers national mentoring program, publishes membership and service directory, and awards grants and scholarships. Membership categories/annual dues include Professional (employed in the restaurant industry)/$85, Student/$50, Small Business/$250, Corporate/$1,500.

CONTACT: WCR, 304 W. Liberty St., #201, Louisville, KY 40202; 502-581-0300, Fax 502-589-3602, E-mail wcr@hqtrs.com, URL http://chefnet.com/wcr.

4

Index

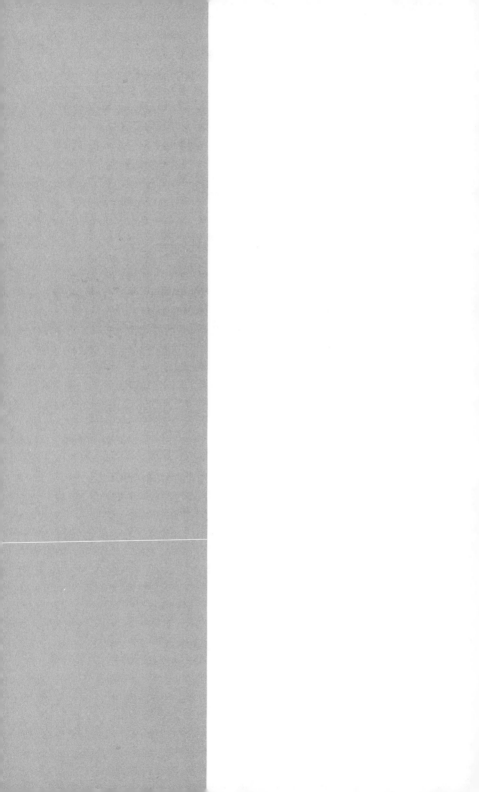

INDEX OF ADVERTISERS

Cooking School Index

A

B

C

D

E

F

G

H

I

J

K

L

M

N

O

P

Q

R

S

T

U

V

W

Y

Z